SOCIOLOGY
Concepts and Characteristics

Fifth Edition

SOCIOLOGY
Concepts
and
Characteristics

JUDSON R. LANDIS

California State University, Sacramento

WADSWORTH PUBLISHING COMPANY
Belmont, California
A Division of Wadsworth, Inc.

Sociology Editor: Bill Oliver
Production: Greg Hubit Bookworks
Text design: Marvin Warshaw
Cover Design: Steve Renick

Printed in the United States of America

2 3 4 5 6 7 8 9 10—87 86 85 84 83

Photo Credits

Chapter 1	©Arthur Grace / Stock, Boston
Chapter 2	Abigail Heyman / Archive Pictures Inc.
Chapter 3	Richard Kalvar / Magnum Photos, Inc.
Chapter 4	Carey Wolinsky / Stock, Boston
Chapter 5	©George W. Gardner / Stock, Boston
Chapter 6	Richard Kalvar / ©Magnum Photos, Inc.
Chapter 8	©Michael O'Brien / Archive Pictures Inc.
Chapter 9	Charles Harbutt / ©Archive Pictures Inc.
Chapter 10	Burk Uzzle / ©Magnum Photos, Inc.
Chapter 11	Peter Southwick / Stock, Boston
Chapter 12	Elliott Erwitt / ©Magnum Photos, Inc.
Chapter 13	Gilles Peress / ©Magnum Photos, Inc.
Chapter 14	©Charles Gatewood / Magnum Photos, Inc.

Library of Congress Cataloging in Publication Data
Landis, Judson R
Sociology: concepts and characteristics.

Bibliography: p.
Includes index.
1. Sociology.   I. Title.
HM51.L255   1983   301   82-23733
ISBN: 0-534-01381-3

ISBN 0-534-01381-3

Contents

3   Norms, Roles, Culture   62

Part II   SOCIAL ORGANIZATION   91

4   Groups   93

5   Social Differentiation: Social Class   133

14 Sociology: Another Perspective   418

Preface

The purposes of a first course in a discipline usually are several—to introduce an area of study, to communicate its unique perspective or way of looking at the world, and to offer the promise of secrets yet to be discovered—all in the hope that interested students will come back for more (maybe even thirty units more). That there are many different views of the best way to achieve these ambitions is apparent in sociology from some of the introductory textbooks available.

Many books provide an encyclopedic analysis of what a discipline is and does—all its tools, techniques, and substantive areas. I have decided not to try to do that in this book. It seems to me that a feeling for an area of study and its unique perspective may be gained by sampling the concepts of that field. Concepts are the building blocks—the language—of most disciplines. Once one has this language, the rest comes more easily and makes more sense. This book approaches the task of helping students develop a general understanding of the sociological perspective by focusing on the basic concepts of sociology. Through examining several substantive areas and the research connected with them, students can begin to see how the concepts contribute to sociological analysis.

At the end of most of the chapters I have included readings to further illustrate the chapter's concepts. These readings are drawn from a variety of sources. Included are descriptions of research and excerpts from novels, autobiographies, and nonfiction works. Some of the selections were written by professional social scientists; some were not. For example, writings of both Helen Keller and Malcolm X are used to illustrate socialization and development of self. In addition, there are selections by William Domhoff on where the powerful play, Studs Terkel on social class differences, Christopher Edwards on joining the "moonies," Stanley Milgram on the conditions of obedience to authority, Dee Brown on the history of the American Indian, and Jerzy Kosinski on reactions to deviants. The readings, I think, illustrate the concepts and ideas in an interesting and unusual way.

A number of changes have been made in this edition. Two new chapters on social institutions have been added. All the chapters have been revised, some (social change, population, family) extensively. All statistical information has been updated to the most recent available. Several illustrative boxes and introductions to topics and fourteen of the thirty-six readings are new to this edition.

Many people have helped me on this and earlier editions with ideas and criticism (although they may now refuse to admit it): colleagues Louise Kanter, Carole Barnes, Pat McGillivray, Dean Dorn, David Lee, Worth Summers, Ivy Lee, Andres Rendon, Ayad Al-Qazzaz, Robi Chakravorti, Frank Darknell, Linda Fritschner, and Rodney Kingsnorth. Reviewers Letitia Alston, Mary Frances Antolini, Robert Frenier, Doug Kachel, and Jane Snell were also most helpful. I'd also like to thank secretary Lois Hill; the people at Wadsworth—Curt Peoples, Bill Oliver, and Peggy Meehan—and Greg Hubit and helpers at his bookworks.

This is dedicated to Sheron, who criticized and encouraged, and to Jeffrey, Brian, and Kevin, who hindered constantly (but were patient with me).

Judson R. Landis

1
Introduction: Knowledge, Science, and Sociology

The purpose of this book is to acquaint you with a field of study called *sociology*. Generally speaking, sociology is the study of human society; it is the study of social behavior and the interaction of people in groups. Sociologists study various aspects of social life, including behavior in large organizations and small groups, deviant behavior, the characteristics of political and religious institutions and social movements, and social psychological explanations for behavior.

Why do we want to study sociology? For ages people have been fascinated about their own existence, and they have persistently tried to find out more about themselves and the world in which they live. Their attempts have occasionally been bumbling and crude, but this has not discouraged them. Slowly but surely a body of knowledge has accumulated. This knowledge has come through several means, one of which is science. Science has developed to the extent that we must break it down into categories: the physical sciences, the biological sciences, and the social sciences. The common denominator of these various areas of study is their commitment to the scientific method as the appropriate way to gain knowledge. Sociology, as one of the social sciences, has its own particular perspectives, techniques, and theories that it uses to examine human behavior. In this chapter, I want to expand on the relationship among these three concepts: knowledge, science, and sociology.

KNOWLEDGE

Early attempts at gaining knowledge were sometimes very primitive, sometimes amazingly sophisticated. In the late Neolithic period (around 1900 B.C.) the Beaker people began building Stonehenge, a structure of posts, mounds, holes, and stones on the Salisbury plain southwest of London. Some of the stones they used were huge, up to thirty feet long and weighing fifty tons. The stones were placed in holes on end in an intricate pattern of circles and alleys. It took the Beaker people and the Wessex people who continued the work some 300 years to complete what amounted to a giant calendar, a sort of Stone Age computer. The stones were set up so that sighting through cracks between stones would show sunrise, sunset, moonrise, and moonset on certain important days (for example, midsummer day, midwinter day, first day of summer, first day of winter). Other sightings allowed the Wessex people to predict eclipses of the moon.

Why was this elaborate structure built? As a calendar it was useful to tell the proper time for planting and harvesting of crops. It probably also proved helpful to the priest, who could amaze and impress with his apparent power to make the sun and moon rise and set wherever he wanted. And possibly it was built just because the Beaker and Wessex people were curious and wanted to see if it could be done.

Aside from the enormous physical work involved, the builders of Stonehenge had to collect and correlate a great deal of information—harvest and planting times, times of sunrise and sunset, phases of the moon. They had to pass this information on from generation to generation. Archeologists who have studied Stonehenge tell us that what looks like a single monument is actually several. The first structure didn't work as well as the builders wanted, and a second model was built over the first. It likewise needed improvement, and a third was constructed.

Unlike most primitive structures, Stonehenge has lasted to modern times. Some stones weathered and fell from their positions. Others were taken by farmers for stone fences. But much of the structure remains intact. Its presence and purpose have confounded people for years, although some who have studied it are convinced that its purpose had something to do with positions of the sun and moon. Ironically, the true complexity of Stonehenge did not come to light until 1961 when astronomy professor Gerald Hawkins fed the positions and relationships of the stones, posts, and holes into a computer for analysis.

Then modern people learned what it was that the Beaker and Wessex people learned 3,500 years earlier.[1]

In the late 1600s some chemists, faced with perplexing problems in explaining what happens when substances are heated or burned, came up with the theory of *phlogiston*. The theory stated that phlogiston is an invisible substance that exists in all combustible bodies and is released during combustion (burning). Substances rich in phlogiston burned easily. Perhaps fire was a manifestation of phlogiston. The theory was immediately accepted. It helped explain things, and the famous scientists of the day were guided by the new theory. The problem, of course, was that it was totally wrong. It is interesting that even when confronted with evidence that discredited the phlogiston theory, scientists in the 1780s were very slow to give up on it. Joseph Priestley, a famous scientist of the time, died in 1804 still believing in phlogiston.[2]

These are just two of countless examples of people's attempts to describe and understand their world, to gain knowledge about their existence. Regardless of how it is collected and sometimes even regardless of its accuracy, knowledge tends to accumulate. Explanations seem to last if they are convincing. That is, they are believed as long as they seem to explain a part of human experience. If the explanations leave elements out or don't explain something they should, then they tend to be modified or abandoned to be replaced by something better.

Exchanging an inaccurate for a better explanation, however, isn't always easy. Some explanations are very dearly held. Their backers (even fans) may believe in them so fiercely that the ideas remain in vogue even when other theories work better. Scientists have been known to compete with and conceal findings from each other in order to arrive at a discovery first and to make certain the discovery stands. This situation, unfortunately, can hinder the growth of knowledge.

But one way or another, knowledge accumulates, and it usually does so in one of three general ways—mysticism, rationalism, or empiricism. **Mysticism** refers to knowledge gained by intuition, revelation, inspiration, magic, visions, or spells. Societies often hold special places for those among them who know in special ways—the magician, the spiritualist, the priest, the witch doctor. The ceremonial use of drugs to produce vision is also highly valued among some peoples. In the seventeenth century, the Puritans of Massachusetts Bay Colony were heartily convinced of the presence of witchcraft in their midst. Their evidence came from several young girls, who, between dramatic seizures, were able to point out fellow villagers who were aiding the devil in his work. The girls became so energetic in their attempts to cast out evil that 350 people were taken into custody or accused of witchcraft.[3]

---

[1]For more detail on the fascinating story of Stonehenge, see Gerald Hawkins, *Stonehenge Decoded* (New York: Dell, 1965).

[2]There is a short discussion of phlogiston in *On Understanding Science*, by James Conant (New York: New American Library-Mentor, 1951), Chapter 3.

[3]For a more detailed discussion of the Puritans and their problems, see Kai Erikson, *Wayward Puritans* (New York: Wiley, 1966).

Knowledge arrived at through mysticism tends to be private. Only the person experiencing the revelation or vision has it, and others must take the mystic's word for it. While this may enhance the appeal of the mystic, it tends to compromise the quality of the product. If no one else sees or feels it, can it really be true?

Rationalism refers to knowledge gained through common sense, logic, and reason. The writings of Aristotle and the dialogues of Plato in ancient times, and the ideas of Descartes, Spinoza, Voltaire, and Thomas Paine in the seventeenth and eighteenth centuries provide examples of knowledge emerging through the careful use of logic and reason. In the twentieth century many continue to find the use of common sense, logic, and reason the most appropriate way to arrive at knowledge. As with mysticism, however, there are limitations. For example, at one time knowledge emerging from a common-sense analysis told us that the earth is flat ("Couldn't be round, people on the other side would fall off . . . ."), and that if two metal objects—a heavy one and a light one—were dropped from a height, the heavy object would fall much faster. We see that the intellectual approach alone can be as inaccurate as the mystical.

⟶ **Empiricism**, on the other hand, refers to knowledge that is gained by sense observation—by observing or experiencing phenomena with the senses of touch, sight, hearing, smell, or taste. This is the basis of science. Instead of simply thinking about the heavy and light objects, we actually drop them from a tall building and observe whether the heavy one falls faster. Public knowledge then grows as we invite a crowd of observers to help us watch the fall of the objects, or we suggest that the experiment be tried by others in other places.

SCIENCE

We have said that empiricism is the basis of science. A one-sentence definition of what scientists are up to could go something like this: *Science* is *understanding* through *description* by means of *measurement* making possible *prediction* and thus *adjustment* to or *control* of the environment. The essential points of this definition are *description, prediction,* and *control.*

For example: violent windstorms occasionally spring out of the Caribbean and the western North Atlantic. Huge waves caused by the storms are hazardous to shipping, and tremendous damage often results if a storm crosses land. Scientists, in trying to understand these storms, begin by collecting information on numerous storms. They list the traits common to most such storms until a fairly consistent description emerges: Certain conditions of wind and atmospheric pressure lead to a situation in which a low-pressure cell is surrounded by circular moving winds traveling counterclockwise at speeds in excess of seventy miles per hour. Then predictions about these storms (called hurricanes) become possible. The conditions that produce them, the time of year when they are most likely to occur (June to November, most frequent in September), their direction (west, then north, finally east), speed (ten to thirty miles per hour), and destructive power can all be predicted, allowing societies to control their impact. Seeding clouds with chemicals can reduce the force of the hurricane, and advance knowledge of the hurricane's arrival means that measures can be taken to move people and material out of its way.

In a similar way, medical researchers observe a disease. Careful description of its characteristics allows predictions about its future occurrence and suggestions for control—antibiotics, isolation, rest, and so on.

Science (or empiricism) as a way of gaining knowledge involves certain characteristics and assumptions. One such assumption is that the best way to know about the world is through the senses, aided when possible by mechanical means—microscopes, scales, telescopes, and other such extensions of the senses. Scientists assume that knowledge obtained in this way is better than that of the rationalists and mystics before them. If we pressed the scientists on what they meant by *better*, they would probably admit that science doesn't remove all doubt and that absolute truth is impossible, but they would add that the knowledge gained through science seems to explain and predict phenomena more adequately than does that obtained by other methods.

Another basic assumption of most scientific endeavors is that phenomena are related causally. Science maintains that a *cause-effect relationship* exists in that each event has a prior cause or causes that theoretically can be discovered. Gravity (cause) makes an object fall (effect) from a building. If the heavy one falls faster or if they fall at the same speed, these effects are also caused by something that we can try to discover.

However, there are usually many causes of an event rather than a single cause. This is referred to as *multiple causation*. A person dies. Why? His heart stopped. Why? He had lung cancer that had spread to the sac enclosing his heart and affected the heart's function. Shallow, rapid breathing resulting from inefficient lungs changed his blood chemistry and worsened his condition. Hardening of the arteries related to advanced age (he was seventy-five years old) reduced the circulation of his blood. Finally, since he was in much pain, he decided he had lived long enough—he had no more will to live. Again, what caused his death?

Because isolating a single cause or even several causes becomes enormously difficult when working on a complex problem, scientists search for relationships and correlations. One such complex problem is that of juvenile delinquency. Why does a young person commit crime? The factors involved are very complicated. Instead of searching for a single cause, therefore, criminologists try to isolate factors associated or correlated with becoming delinquent. Family background, living conditions, social class, number of delinquent friends, and criminal opportunities are among the factors that seem to be related to becoming delinquent. The point is that by itself a certain family background doesn't cause delinquent behavior. Some young people from unhappy families become delinquent, but some do not. Obviously other factors affect the situation. The best explanation is that delinquent behavior is the outcome of a complex relationship of factors. Some of these factors we know about—others we don't.

The idea of *control* is essential to science. Control has several meanings. I used it above to describe a *product* of knowledge. If we know certain things (when a hurricane will hit), then we can regulate or control events to a certain extent (get people out of the way). As we learn about disease we can often control its effects with antibiotics. The second meaning of control refers to its use as an aid in the process of gaining knowledge. Scientists attempt to control those factors in the environment that they are not studying but that might have an effect on what they are studying. Our friends who are dropping objects from tall buildings may decide to perform their experiment only on calm, clear days. They are not studying wind and rain, but these might affect how the objects drop, and so they would want to control for them. (Ideally, they would probably want to perform the experiment in a vacuum if that were possible.)

As problems or experiments become more complicated, controlling for all the relevant variables becomes more difficult. Important control variables may be left out, either because they are overlooked or because they are too difficult to control. Two psychologists decided to test the idea that hospitalization for serious mental illness (psychosis) had increased over the century between 1845 and 1945. They found that it *had* increased substantially, and they had many good reasons to offer in explanation—increased stress, shift from farm to city, breakdown of family and religion, more complex life, and so on. The information and conclusion make sense. But they are *wrong*. The results and interpretation changed completely when the psychologists controlled for *age*. When they looked at hospitalization for each age group, instead of an increase in hospitalization they found virtually no change over the century-long period. People lived longer in 1945 than in 1845. That fact meant that the population contained more old people, who are more susceptible to the senility psychoses related to physiological degeneration of the brain and central nervous system. Conclusion: (1) same percentage of hospitalization by age; (2) more total hospitalization only because of more older people (over fifty years old) in the population; (3) variations have nothing or very little to do with societal stress.[4]

Careful *definitions of terms* is part of science. These are often called operational or working definitions. They allow others to know precisely what the scientists studied and how they carried out their experiments. The object-dropping experiment would include at least the following information: the size and weight of the objects being dropped, how far they are to be dropped, method of observation of the drop, and pressure and temperature of the air at the time of the drop.

Scientists are assumed to be *objective*. They are expected to record what they actually see, not what they hope to see or wish they had seen. They don't select or choose only those data that will fit or prove the hypothesis on which they are working while ignoring contrary evidence. (One doesn't test the idea that sociology professors are absent-minded by looking for a sociology professor who is so afflicted and then saying, "I told you so.") If the light object falls faster, or if both objects *rise* when dropped, then that is what the scientist reports.

Of course absolute objectivity is impossible, and the scientists who suggest that they are totally objective are misleading themselves and everyone else. Scientists are humans, with beliefs and values that are bound to affect their work.

---

[4]This and other examples of control failures are discussed in *The Logic of Survey Analysis*, by Morris Rosenberg (New York: Basic Books, 1968), pp. 29-33.

The suggestion that when scientists put on their white coats they leave behind all nonscientific human emotions and biases is unreasonable. It's just not that way. Objectivity asks rather that scientists try to be aware of their biases and make them public so that they may be considered when their work is evaluated.

Finally, *replication* is an essential characteristic of science. Studies are repeated by others in similar and in unique circumstances to see if the results are consistent. The objects would be dropped numerous times from the same height. Then the experimenters might change the height from thirty feet to sixty feet, then to ninety feet. Then the weight of the objects might be varied, and so on. It is through replication that one develops confidence in the results.

TYPES OF SCIENCE

The range of matters in which scientists are involved is probably far wider than most people think. There are numerous types or categories of science, and they involve widely differing methods. *Pure* and *applied* science represent two complementary approaches. Pure science attempts to discover facts and principles about the universe without regard for possible uses the knowledge may have. Applied science concerns itself with making knowledge useful to people. The applied scientist devises practical and utilitarian uses of knowledge obtained through pure scientific endeavors. Splitting the atom was for the most part a product of pure science. Harnessing the atom to make bombs, power submarines, and fuel power plants is a product of applied science. The two—pure and applied—are closely linked, and the distinction between them is sometimes more artificial than real.

Science is also categorized by subject matter. The *physical* sciences—astronomy, chemistry, physics, geology—are concerned with the nature of the physical universe. The *biological* sciences—botany, zoology, biology, paleontology—are concerned with the study of living organisms, plants, and animals. The *social* sciences—anthropology, economics, history, political science, geography, psychology, sociology—are concerned with the study of people, groups, and societies. The physical and biological (or natural) sciences are older and more exact, and hence, possibly more respected than the social sciences. Whether the scientific method and the controlled experiment can work as well in the study of human behavior as they have in the natural sciences remains to be seen.

SOCIAL SCIENCE

Social science in general and sociology in particular have developed as a result of studying certain characteristics observed in human beings. For example, humans tend to group together and cooperate. People discovered long ago that they could accomplish much more working together than they could separately. Cooperation had obvious rewards. But we also know that not all human behavior is cooperative. Conflict is also an important part of the human condition. One of those first cooperative group efforts probably involved a battle or conflict with another group. Conflict arises when people compete for the same resources—such as wealth or power. Very often when one party or group benefits, another party or group is deprived; this conflict is a major focal point of social science.

Another observable characteristic of human beings is that they tend in similar situations to behave in the same ways time after time. We all know this. When a car comes toward us, we have a pretty good idea of which side of the road it will be on. Students can correctly predict the behavior of their instructor on the first day of class, just as the instructor can usually anticipate the questions and concerns that the students will have about the class. I can tell you how the people on almost any elevator will behave. Generally they will get in, push the button for their floor, stand as far as possible from others, face the front, stare at the numbers flashing, and be quiet and subdued. Amazing? Not really, for human behavior in its simpler aspects is not difficult to predict.

The more complex aspects of behavior, however, are more difficult to predict. As people get together in groups, organizations, and societies, factors multiply, and behavior becomes more complicated. Consider these questions. Many young people in high-crime areas of the city are involved in crime, but some aren't. What insulates these few from delinquency? Do large organizations—General Motors, the CIA, your school—have similar characteristics? If so, what are they and why do they occur? Are these beneficial or detrimental to the organization's performance? How do people behave in a disaster—a flood, earthquake, or bombing? Is their behavior consistent, or is it different in every disaster situation? Do they panic? Do they become immobilized?

To be sure, these questions are far more difficult than guessing which side of the road that car approaching us will be on. But the answers to these complex questions can be found. Social scientists, guided by the general principles of science, study these and similar questions about human behavior. They describe regularities and attempt to find consistent patterns in human activities. As regularities are described, prediction of future events becomes possible. If description and prediction are achieved, control may become possible. Let's say that we're worried about airplane hijacking. We first try to describe the condition. What sort of people are involved—first offenders or people with prior criminal histories? What motivates them—psychological problems, financial needs, a political viewpoint? Adequate description of the event may allow us to predict its occurrence. Careful screening of passengers in order to select out the hijacker type may, if we're very good at it, allow us to control the occurrence of the event. The experts aren't that good at it yet, as you know. There are fewer airplane hijackings than there used to be, but they still occur. Maybe we'll get better at controlling them. But the point is that knowledge can be gained about human behavior using the general principles of science. This is the work of the social scientist.

Different social sciences approach the task of studying and recording human behavior in a variety of ways. *Anthropologists* traditionally have gone about the task by examining artifacts and remains of long-extinct communities, or by living with and studying preliterate tribes and societies. The study of culture is of central importance in anthropological analysis. *Historians* record an accurate chronology of past events. As events are placed in perspective, analysis of emerging trends may lead historians to make predictions about the future. *Political scientists* study the characteristics and patterns of political systems, the principles and conduct of government. Their topics include political parties, elections, systems of government, foreign policy, and the comparative structure of governments. *Economists* are interested in patterns of production, distribution, and consumption of goods and services. They study such topics as price and market theories; consumer behavior; merchandising and selling practices; money, banking, and credit; economic growth and development. *Psychologists* deal with individuals, their adjustment and personalities, their patterns of learning, motivation, and perception. *Sociologists* focus on groups, on patterns of interaction, on descriptions of the institutions and social organization of society.

The techniques used by social scientists are as varied as their subject matter. Historians study documents, archives, and other records for evidence about the past. Psychologists gain knowledge by using projective tests such as the Rorschach inkblot test, by using sensitive laboratory equipment to conduct experiments on perception, by running rats through mazes, and by using interview rooms with one-way mirrors. Anthropologists use the technique of participant observation to study primitive societies, delinquent gangs, and community, ethnic, and class stratification. Sociologists spend time with survey research using large numbers of questionnaires and interviews analyzed by computers.

And yet distinguishing between the social sciences can be difficult. In some areas, anthropologists and sociologists approach their tasks in the same way. Sociologists frequently make use of cross-cultural analysis and participant observation, the techniques anthropologists use. Likewise, many anthropologists are studying aspects of contemporary industrialized societies, which are usually the province of sociologists. In other areas, it is difficult to distinguish between sociological and psychological approaches. A relatively new social science—social psychology—has developed, formally combining aspects of sociology and psychology. Many sociologists use historical analysis, and many historians conduct their research in ways that we are convinced are sociological. In his book *Wayward Puritans*, sociologist Kai Erikson applied current theories of deviant behavior to the seventeenth-century Puritans of Massachusetts Bay Colony (see footnote 3). His study involved extensive analysis of historical documents and represented a coordination of historical and sociological analyses. In summary, we find some slight differences among respective social sciences in matters of emphasis and perspective rather than marked differences in approach.

SOCIOLOGY

A sociologist is a person who goes to a football game and watches the crowd.

This book is about a particular social science called sociology. The dictionary tells us that sociology is the "science or study of the origin, development, organization, and functioning of human society." Sociologists study human so-

ciety and social behavior, and they focus on groups, institutions, and social organization. There are several areas of study within the discipline of sociology.
For example, sociologists specialize in such areas as small groups, large-scale
organizations, race relations, religion, marriage and the family, social problems, collective behavior, criminology and delinquency, social class, urban and
rural sociology, population and demography, age and sex roles, political sociology, and the sociology of medicine and law.

In sociology as in other disciplines, the process of discovery centers
around the interplay of two elements: *theory* and *research methods*. A theory
provides a framework for understanding phenomena. The theory suggests certain hypotheses or predictions that one might make. Then by employing appropriate research methods, one can test the hypotheses empirically through
controlled sense observation. The research findings often suggest modifications
of the theory that in turn will make it more complete. This is the interplay of
research and theory. For example, Einstein's theory of relativity provides a
framework for making predictions about the speed of light under various conditions. Physicists and astronomers test these predictions using sophisticated
research methods involving laser beams, high-speed aircraft, and complicated
mathematics.

In the next few pages we will examine more closely these two elements—
theory and research methods—that sociologists use in their search for understanding of the human condition. First, let's look at sociological theories.

Sociological Theories

A theory is a coherent set of propositions used to explain a class of phenomena. Scientists develop theories to explain that aspect of the world that they
are studying. They then attempt to test the theories with information or data
that they collect. Theories are crucially important, for scientific research is
organized around them. If the theory is reasonably accurate, it will explain
many of the phenomena with which it is concerned. If it does not, then it is not
much good, and eventually a better theory, one that explains more, will replace
it.

In the second century A.D., the Greek scholar Ptolemy theorized that the
earth was the center of the universe and the other planets rotated in complicated ways around it. This was *the* theory and it had strong support in the scientific and religious communities. But it did not explain the movements of the
planets as well as it should have. Some 1,300 years later the Polish astronomer
Copernicus began publishing papers that outlined a new theory—that the sun
was the center of the universe and the earth and other planets rotated around
the sun. It was a revolutionary idea. In the years after Copernicus died in 1543,
Kepler, Galileo, and others made continued observations enabling them to re-
fine the theory that Copernicus had suggested. There was substantial opposition
to the new theory because it challenged some beliefs that were very important
to the Catholic Church. In fact, Galileo was imprisoned for a time because of his
support of the theory. It slowly became accepted, however, because it was a
better explanation for phenomena than the Ptolemaic theory before it had been.

All disciplines have competing theories that attempt to explain the phenomena that are important to that discipline, and sociology is no exception. In

the following paragraphs I will briefly outline some of the major theories in sociology. The theories we will examine are functional analysis, conflict theory, and symbolic interaction. Remember that this is a brief summary of fairly complex theories. Keep in mind also that there are variations in how each theory is defined and that there is some overlap between them.

Functional Analysis   The key terms in **functional analysis** are *structure* and *function*. A good way of understanding functional analysis is to start with a biological analogy. If one looks at the human body, one sees that numerous functions must be performed—breathing and eating, for example—in order for the organism to survive. To perform these functions, structures have developed—nose, lungs, digestive tract, and so on. Functional analysis holds that society can be analyzed in the same manner. Societies (and groups) need to perform certain functions to maintain their existence. They must populate themselves, they must care for the sick, the young must be socialized, there must be distribution of goods and services. Structures develop to perform these functions—a family system to control reproduction, an educational system to train the young, economic and medical institutions to carry out other functions. This theory holds that structure and function are closely linked, and that they are the crucial factors in understanding and explaining society. Again, functional analysis explains a given pattern of activity by defining its contribution (function) to the group or society of which it is a part. Functional analysis tends to emphasize social equilibrium, stability, and the integration of the elements of society. One of the criticisms of this theory is that it has a conservative bias; in its emphasis on social order, functional analysis tends to ignore conflict and social change.

Several terms commonly connected with functional analysis should be clarified. Function refers to an act that contributes to the existence of a unit (breathing and eating for the life of the organism). *Dysfunction* is the opposite—an act that leads to change or destruction of a unit (cancer in an organism). *Manifest* function is an intended and recognized function. *Latent* functions are those that are unintended and unrecognized. According to Robert Merton, the Hopi Indians continue their ceremonial rain dancing even though the dances do not produce much rain. The latent function—reinforcing group identity by providing a periodic reason for getting together and engaging in a common activity—has become more important than the manifest function of producing rain.[5]

Try a functional analysis of a sociology class. Why *is* there such a class? It functions to pass on knowledge, viewpoints, and information. A structure has developed consisting of an instructor, forty-eight students, and a set of rules in order to facilitate this passing of knowledge. It also functions to provide the teacher with a job. Some feel a need for the function of finding out how well the knowledge is getting across, and the structure of tests and a grading system develops. Attending class is functional if the student wants to get a good grade; cutting class often is dysfunctional. Giving a test is functional in enabling the

---

[5]Robert Merton, *Social Theory and Social Structure*, 2d ed. (New York: Free Press, 1957), pp. 64-65.

teacher to evaluate how the material is getting across. The first big test given in a class may be dysfunctional if it changes the mood of the class. The rapport and mutual understanding that develop between teacher and students over six weeks is suddenly compromised, and an adversary relationship develops. A manifest function of the typical classroom procedure—teacher makes assignments, students listen and read, obey, memorize, and give back on tests what the instructor has said—is that it facilitates the learning process, it works better if it is done that way. A latent function of this procedure may be to train students to take orders and become good bureaucrats in the large organizations they will join in the future.

Now that you have some idea how it works, try a functional analysis of some events or behaviors—for example, prostitution, professional football, a funeral ceremony, or punishment for a crime. The discussion of family and religious institutions in Chapters 7 and 8 are the clearest examples in this book of functional analysis.[6]

Conflict Theory   In contrast to the social order and stability stressed in functional analysis, another group of theorists focus on conflict and discord. In examining social interaction, conflict theorists ask who benefits and who is deprived. As we have said, conflict arises as people compete for scarce resources such as wealth, status, power, or territory. Conflict also arises over differences in values and interests—for example, between superiors and subordinates, management and labor, in-groups and out-groups. **Conflict theory** suggests that

[6]From among the numerous sources available on functional analysis, the following have been especially helpful: Neil Smelser, ed., *Sociology* (New York; Wiley, 1967), pp. 706-708; and Robert Merton, *Social Theory and Social Structure*, 2d ed. (New York; Free Press, 1957). See the section on functional analysis in the *International Encyclopedia of the Social Sciences* for a summary and an excellent bibliography.

competition and conflict are common in social interaction and the study of these processes is the most appropriate way to understand society. Some conflicts are minor and of little consequence. Others are deeply felt and may result in the division of whole societies into hostile classes. For example, Karl Marx felt that the capitalists' or industrialists' exploitation of workers inevitably led to conflict which could only be resolved by a workers' revolution resulting in a classless society.

Getting back to our sociology class, what would a conflict theorist see? The testing and grading system necessary to facilitate the passage of information creates a system of domination (instructor) and subordination (students) and sets up conflicting interests. Consequently, the conflict theorist would not be at all surprised with the sudden change in mood as the first test is given. Competition for scarce resources (A's) leads to predictable types of behavior: cheating to get grades, memorization of masses of soon-to-be-forgotten material, and rivalries with other students. The conflict theorist might also call attention to the tendency of the educational system to reinforce the current stratification system. Students from lower-class backgrounds, who often have less adequate educational preparation, may do less well in college classes, receive lower grades or perhaps flunk out, and because of this obtain lower-level jobs, and as a consequence, stay near the bottom of the social-class ladder.

Try using conflict theory on some events or behaviors—prostitution, professional football, or punishment for a crime. Ask who benefits and who is deprived. Conflict theory will come up several times in this book, probably most clearly in Chapters 5, 6, and 9 in the discussion of stratification, power, prejudice, and discrimination.[7]

Symbolic Interaction   **Symbolic interaction** theory focuses on interaction between people, on the processes by which individuals come to develop viewpoints about themselves and relate to their associates. In comparison with functional analysis and conflict theory (which examine social structure in groups, institutions, and societies), symbolic interaction theory narrows the focus to person-to-person interaction. People interpret and define the symbols, gestures, and words of people around them, and they modify their own behavior accordingly. It is this activity that the symbolic interactionist is interested in. Symbolic interactionists see social life as *process*. They are interested in describing patterns of interaction, how parties to the interaction interpret what is going on, the use of signs, symbols, and other forms of communication, the meanings actions have for others, and the processes of socialization and development of the self.

Let's return once more to the sociology class, this time as symbolic interactionists. We would be interested in the type of interaction between instructor and students and would look at the signals (verbal and nonverbal bits of com-

---

[7]For a background on conflict theory see the works of Karl Marx; Lewis Coser, *The Functions of Social Conflict* (Glencoe, Ill.: Free Press, 1956); Ralf Dahrendorf, *Class and Class Conflict in Industrial Society* (Stanford, Calif.: Stanford University Press, 1959); and see the section on conflict in the *International Encyclopedia of the Social Sciences* for an overview and bibliography.

munication) that pass back and forth. Suppose a difficult point is being made. The instructor attempts to evaluate how well the class is getting the point and adjusts the lecture according to his or her interpretations of the students' responses. Back in the corner is a student totally disgusted with this instructor, and yet class participation is required. Notice the way the student balances competing values—hostility, deference, and desire for an A—in his gestures, tone of voice, body language, asides to other students, and so on.

The instructor has a particular self-concept—how is it expressed in his or her behavior? One instructor is informal and innovative; another is vastly self-confident, secure in the knowledge that he is the best instructor in the Western world. A student in the classroom who has always seen herself as an A student gets a C on a test. What responses does she make that help her maintain her original self-concept? If a change in mood appears after the first test, the symbolic interactionist would be interested in how it is expressed by students and how the instructor reacts to it. The symbolic interactionist, knowing that interaction is a two-way process, would be interested not only in changes in the students, but also in how the instructor changes as a consequence of his or her interaction with the class.

I tend to favor the symbolic interactionist approach more than functional analysis or conflict theory, so it should be no surprise to you that it will come up frequently in this book. The following examples come to mind: the discussion of nonreactive techniques coming later in this chapter, all of Chapter 2 on socialization and self, parts of the discussion of groups in Chapter 4, self-fulfilling prophecy throughout, much of the chapter on deviation (labeling theory is based on the symbolic interactionist approach), and many other places as well.[8]

These theories represent contrasting approaches used to explain or organize the material of sociology. Each theory emphasizes certain aspects and ignores others, and each has particular strengths and weaknesses. It is a good idea when reading sociology to be aware of the author's theoretical perspective, for it will suggest to you why certain factors are stressed and others are not.

RESEARCH METHODS IN SOCIOLOGY

Like other social sciences, sociology attempts to understand human behavior from the scientific point of view. This means that the sociologist is guided by the principles and assumptions of science that were outlined earlier in this chapter. To get some idea of what this means, let's consider some of the ways in which sociological research has been done. First, we must distinguish between two categories of research, reactive and nonreactive.[9] **Reactive re-**

---

[8]See the works of Charles Cooley or George H. Mead (see index) or a social psychology text such as *Social Psychology*, 4th ed., by Alfred Lindesmith, Anselm Strauss, and Norman Denzin (Hinsdale, Ill.: Dryden Press, 1975) for more on symbolic interaction.

[9]This distinction is best made in *Unobtrusive Measures: Nonreactive Research in the Social Sciences*, by Eugene Webb, Donald Campbell, Richard Schwartz, and Lee Sechrest (Chicago: Rand McNally, 1966). Also see a good summary in *The Research Act*, by Norman Denzin (Chicago: Aldine, 1970), Chapter 11.

search refers to situations in which the observer or researcher is a part of the research situation. Much of social science research is based on questionnaires and interviews. The researcher creates a questionnaire or interview, administers it to a group of people—the subjects—and measures the attitudes or behaviors of the subjects responding to the questionnaire or interview. These reactive measures are widely used because they are relatively inexpensive, easy to administer, can be done on a group basis, and are less complicated than other methods. Also, in some cases they require less time to develop and administer than other methods.

The problem is that this type of research tends to influence attitudes and behavior. Something new (a questionnaire or interview) is injected into the situation, and the subjects react—they react to the researcher and to the study. Here's a simple illustration: If you *know* you're being observed and your behavior is being recorded, what happens? Well, you behave *differently*—you are uneasy, on guard, tentative. The situation is not normal, and you don't behave the way you usually would. The researcher may be liked or disliked, the subjects may cooperate or not, they may be ignorant of the subject matter of the questionnaire or knowledgeable—any of a number of things may happen. This is the issue with reactive research—by introducing a foreign element into a situation we create attitudes as well as measure them.

Nonreactive research has no intruding observer and doesn't use questionnaires or interviews. Instead, nonreactive research focuses on physical traces and signs left behind by people, on records and archives (hospital records, census data, government records), and on simple observation in which the researcher observes but does not intrude. Some simple comparisons between reactive and nonreactive studies may help at this point.

1. Suppose you want to know which radio station is most listened to in your city.
   Reactive study: Go door to door and ask the people who answer what their favorite radio station is.
   Nonreactive study (using physical traces): Go to a busy gas station and as each car comes in, look in and note the spot on the dial the car radio is tuned to.

2. Suppose you want to determine who are the most liberal and most conservative members of Congress in your state.
   Reactive study: Devise an in-depth interview or questionnaire measuring liberalism/conservatism, and give it to each member of Congress.
   Nonreactive study (using records): Choose several issues that came up during the last legislative session that divided people along liberal and conservative lines, and see how the members of Congress actually voted on these issues.

3. Suppose you want to find out who uses more profanity in everyday conversation, males or females.
   Reactive study: Design a questionnaire or interview that asks people about their language patterns (including how often they swear), and administer it to a group of males and a group of females.
   Nonreactive study (using simple observation): Gather several observers and have each of them listen in on several casual conversations of people in all-male or all-female groups. The observers could jot notes, though tape recording the conversations would be better. It is important that the observers *not* affect the group's behavior (the observers could appear to be part of the groups, or totally removed from them—sitting across the room apparently reading).

The value of the nonreactive study is that it is unobtrusive. Traces or records of behavior are examined after the people have left them, or the observation is hidden in that the people don't know they are being observed. If people don't know they are being studied, it seems that we should get a more accurate measurement of whatever it is that we are studying. On the other hand, nonreactive studies tend to lack depth and flexibility. We may know about *what* but be curious about *why*, and nonreactive studies won't provide us with motives. The reactive study—the interview—is more flexible and can probe at some of the answers that escape the nonreactive study. In summary, these contrasting approaches—reactive and nonreactive—each have strengths and weaknesses. Probably the most effective study is one that combines elements of each approach. Keep these two categories in mind as we look further at sociological research.

In the previous paragraphs we have mentioned several sources of research information: questionnaires, interviews, census data, hospital records, government records, and so on. To get a better idea of how sociologists gain knowledge, let's look at three typical research techniques in more detail: participant observation, survey research, and the experiment.

Participant observation (often now called field research) is a study in which the researcher is or appears to be a participant in the activity or group that is being studied. *Street Corner Society* by William F. Whyte is a classic participant observation study. While a student at Harvard some years ago, Whyte decided he wanted to study a slum district of a large city. He walked around Boston until he came upon "Cornerville," an area that looked interesting to him. How should he study the area? He first tried a door-to-door questionnaire but was totally dissatisfied with this approach. After several other false starts, Whyte sought help from settlement house social workers in Cornerville, and they introduced him to "Doc." Doc was a native of Cornerville and knew everybody in the area. He took Whyte around as "my friend," and Whyte became involved in the community in ways that he never could have as an outsider. Shortly after, he rented a room in Cornerville, further establishing himself in the community. He found that as he got to know key members of groups, he could get what he wanted from other members of the group. He learned how to join in streetcorner conversations, and it wasn't long before Doc told him that he was as much a fixture on the street corner as the lamppost.

Everything did not go smoothly, however. On one occasion Whyte was talkign about police payoffs to a gambling operator. When he became too inquisitive, the gambler became suspicious. On another occasion while talking with some Cornerville people, he decided to swear and use obscenities like they did. The conversation immediately stopped, and he was gently reminded that although they talked that way, they knew that he did not.

Whyte's relationship with Doc changed as his research continued. At first Doc was a friend and entrée into situations and groups. Later Doc became more of a collaborator as he helped Whyte interpret what he was seeing. In Whyte's case, many of the citizens in Cornerville knew he was something more than just another fellow on the street. It was reasonably well known that he was "working on a book." However, he was well enough integrated into the community that the knowledge that he was observer as well as a participant didn't seem to change the way people behaved around him. By using participant observation Whyte learned things about Cornerville that he probably never could have otherwise. Through participant observation he was able to analyze "the structure and functioning of the community through intensive examination of some of its parts—*in action.*"[10]

We touched on **survey research,** a very common social science research technique, in discussing reactive studies. The survey involves the systematic collection of information from or about people through the use of self-administered questionnaires or interviews.[11] The researcher is interested in the general characteristics of a sample or in some experience or event in which they have been involved. Surveys generally fall into one of two categories: descriptive surveys and causal-explanatory surveys.

A *descriptive* survey is like a photograph in that it provides a picture—in this case a numerical description—of certain characteristics of a group of people. A descriptive survey might investigate voting behavior or attitudes and opinions. Or a descriptive survey may tell us how often certain traits or conditions occur in a particular group. A recent descriptive survey of my college sociology class provides the following profile:

Size of class:	247		
Year in school:		**Sex:**	
Freshman	2%	Male	62%
Sophomore	4%	Female	38%
Junior	56%	**Age:**	
Senior	36%		
Graduate student	2%	Range of 19 to 58	
		Average 23	
Hometown:			
		Marital status:	
Sacramento area	58%		
Elsewhere in the state or country	42%	Single	66%
		Married	26%
Employment status:		Divorced/separated	8%
Not working	32%		
Working part-time	43%		
Working full-time	25%		

---

[10]William Foote Whyte, *Street Corner Society* (Chicago: University of Chicago Press, 1943; 2d ed., 1955). Also see a good summary of Whyte's work in *The Origins of Scientific Sociology*, by John Madge (New York: Free Press, 1962), Chapter 7.

[11]I found the following research methods texts especially helpful: Julian Simon, *Basic Research Methods in the Social Sciences* (New York: Random House, 1969), Chapter 6; Denzin, *The Research Act*, Chapter 8 (see footnote 9); Herbert Hyman, *Survey Design and Analysis* (New York: Free Press, 1955); and Earl Babbie, *The Practice of Social Research*, 2d ed. (Belmont, Calif.: Wadsworth, 1979).

I asked the class in this survey to rank the following behaviors from 1 (most deviant) to 9 (least deviant):

forgery
armed robbery
prostitution
homicide
arson
homosexual act
rape
suicide
shoplifting

I took the students' ranks for each behavior, added them up, and divided the total by the number of students (247). This gave me a set of average ranks:

Behavior	Rank
Homicide	1.7
Rape	2.6
Armed robbery	3.7
Arson	4.2
Suicide	4.9
Homosexual act	6.3
Forgery	6.6
Prostitution	7.5
Shoplifting	7.8

The responses were analyzed one step further by controlling for sex. That is, the group was divided into males and females, and the attitudes of each group about the nine behaviors were examined.

Males			Females	
Behavior	Rank		Behavior	Rank
Homicide	1.7		Homicide	1.6
Rape	2.7		Rape	2.3
Armed robbery	3.7		Armed robbery	3.7
Arson	4.3		Arson	4.0
Suicide	4.7		Suicide	5.1
Homosexual act	5.8		Forgery	6.1
Forgery	6.9		Homosexual act	7.2
Prostitution	7.7		Prostitution	7.2
Shoplifting	7.8		Shoplifting	7.7

As you can see, the lists are similar, but there are a few differences. Armed robbery has identical scores in each group, for example, and several others are very close. The two groups differ most on the homosexual act. The males see it as more deviant than the females do. The males also see suicide as more deviant than the females do. On the other hand, the females see rape, forgery, and prostitution as more deviant than the males do.

If we wanted to analyze this information further, controls for age, marital status, and year in school could be introduced to see how each subgroup scored.

A descriptive survey, then, provides us with a numerical description of a group or category of people.

The *causal-explanatory* survey studies the relationships between sets of relevant variables. (A variable is a condition that changes or has different values, such as I.Q., weight, temperature, number of arrests, and so on.) The idea is to see whether change in one variable is linked with change in another variable. The next step is to see whether change in one variable *explains* change in another variable. Consistent explanations may then lead to inferences about cause. In its attempt to manipulate and link appropriate factors, the causal-explanatory survey is a more ambitious undertaking than the descriptive survey.

To take a simple example, suppose we want to measure the idea that religiosity is related to delinquent behavior. That is, if a person is religious, that person is less likely to become a juvenile delinquent; a person who isn't religious is more likely to become a delinquent. This is a reasonably straightforward idea that we could try to test. A causal-explanatory survey to examine this question might look like this: As an operational definition of religiosity we will use church attendance. Then we select two groups of people. One is a group of one hundred fifteen-year-old males who are heavy church attenders—they go to church two or three times a week. Assuming that church attendance is a good measure, they are obviously very religious. Group two is a group of one hundred fifteen-year-old males who have never attended church. So we have two groups: one apparently very religious, the other not religious. The next step is to look into the backgrounds of these boys for evidence of delinquent behavior. We try to find out whether they have been hard to handle at school, have been arrested, or have been in correctional institutions. We would predict that if religiosity is related to delinquency, then group one will turn out to be disgustingly good kids, and members of group two will be in all sorts of trouble. But several outcomes are possible. Consider these categories:

1. Those males who are very religious are not delinquent
2. Those males who are not religious are delinquent
3. Those males who are very religious are delinquent
4. Those males who are not religious are not delinquent

If our idea is correct that if one is religious he is less likely to become a delinquent, then we would expect our subjects generally to fall into categories 1 and 2. But what if we are wrong? In that case our subjects might fall generally into categories 3 and 4. This would mean that there seems to be a relationship between religiosity and delinquency but it is the reverse of the one we predicted (delinquents are religious, nondelinquents are not). Or our subjects might be scattered rather equally across all four categories. This would mean that there is apparently *no* relationship between religiosity and delinquency as we tried to measure them.

There's more to a causal-explanatory survey, but this example illustrates some of the essentials of this type of study. The important point is that attempts are made to link or find relationships between variables in order to get to explanation and cause.

Several times in this chapter we have mentioned "cause" and this brings to mind the story (perhaps true) of the student who was comparing auto traffic over a bridge with water level of the bay under that bridge. After many careful measurements the student discovered that there was a relationship or correlation between the two—specifically, the more cars on the bridge, the higher the water under the bridge. Amazing! A cause and effect relationship: The heavy traffic on the bridge must be compacting the land somehow and forcing the water higher. A wise instructor intervened at this point and suggested that contrary to the apparent cause-effect relationship, perhaps some other variables were involved. Further study indicated that traffic was heaviest during morning and evening rush hours and that high tides often occurred at about those same times. The lesson is that correlation doesn't necessarily mean cause, and relationship may come from sources other than those first assumed.

The **experiment** represents a third kind of research technique. In an experiment, the researcher manipulates one variable (the causal or **independent variable**) and watches for changes in the other variable (the effect or **dependent variable**). For example, find two groups of people in good health. Then have one group run several miles a day while the other group does no physical exercise. Finally, watch the two groups for incidence of heart disease. The independent variable, exercise, is manipulated for two groups, and one watches for changes in the dependent variable, heart disease.

As you can see, the experiment searches for explanatory or causal relationships. In this it is like the causal-explanatory survey discussed earlier. The basic difference between the survey and the experiment is that the survey takes the world as it comes—surveys it without altering it. The experiment, on the other hand, systematically alters or manipulates aspects of the world in order to see what changes follow.[12] Suppose you are interested in the relationship between studying and academic performance—that is, you want to improve your grades. You could keep a record of how much you study for each test and the grades you get. This would be a type of survey. Or you could systematically vary your studying—ten hours for one test, twenty hours for another, forty hours for a third—and check the effect on your grades. This would be an experiment.

In the last few pages we have described three research techniques: participant observation, survey research, and the experiment. You might find it interesting and challenging to try out one or more of these techniques. For example, take one of the groups you belong to (athletic team, dorm group, social club, political organization, or whatever) and study it. A short questionnaire could give you a descriptive survey of attitudes on the death penalty, political conservatism, types of deviant behavior, or presidential candidates. Or, more informally, as participant observer, watch the group in action. Who interacts with whom? Who are the leaders of the group and why? Is disruption caused by the same people, or is it spread throughout the group? Are some people left out by the rest of the group? See whether, by using controlled observation, you can discover something new about your group.

---

[12]This comes from Simon's discussion in *Basic Research Methods in the Social Sciences*, Chapter 16, p. 229 (see footnote 11).

A Study In Response Bias

Several students and I performed an experiment that centered upon two ideas. First, the women's liberation movement was receiving wide attention in our area, and we were interested in the viewpoints college women held on some of the issues of the movement. Second, we were interested in response bias. For example, will your responses to a questionnaire or interview be the same if you are questioned by a white as compared to a black? By a young person as compared to an older person? By a man as compared to a woman? Probably not. Your responses on the questionnaire vary, not so much because of the questions asked (although that is important, too), but because of *who* is asking them. This, of course, greatly affects the accuracy of the study.

As we discussed earlier (p. 10), theories (in this case, theories about response bias) provide a framework for understanding phenomena. From this general framework we derive more specific testable statements or propositions which are used to guide the study. These statements are called **hypotheses.** The hypothesis for our study stated: "Response to statements concerning women's roles will be affected by the sex of the interviewer." A series of items dealing with these attitudes were collected, and ninety married college women were interviewed. They were asked whether they agreed or disagreed with statements such as "A woman's place is in the home," "Motherhood and a career should not be mixed," "Males have higher I.Q.'s and better abilities than females." The subjects were selected randomly and were divided into two groups. Half of the subjects were contacted by a male interviewer; the other half were asked the same questions by a female interviewer. When we analyzed their answers, we found that the response to the male interviewer was much different from the response to the female interviewer. I'll return to this later, but for now consider this question: Would you anticipate a pro–women's liberation response to the male interviewer ("the enemy") or to the female interviewer ("one of us"), and why?

Let's review some of the factors in this study. We were trying to test a cause-effect relationship. The sex of the interviewer was the independent variable, or cause; the women's response on the items was the dependent variable, or effect. By having a man interview one group and a woman interview the other group, we manipulated or altered the independent variable. By selecting the sample randomly we hoped to control for factors we weren't interested in but that might affect the results.

The term **random sample** has been used several times and perhaps should be explained further. The subjects of our study were women, but to interview all the women in the United States was impossible. So we really narrowed it down to a group of 900 women living in a campus housing project. It can be seen that this represents substantial compromises. In return for specifying a group we could manage, we lost other geographical areas as well as age, education, and marital status differences. Almost any attempts at reducing down from a large group will involve a compromise of sorts, although not necessarily as severe as ours. Nine hundred was still too large for us. We wanted a small sample of ninety, but at the same time we wanted it to be representative of the total group. How to do this? If all people in the sample were alike we could pick anybody—

the first ninety we found—and it wouldn't matter. But people aren't alike—they vary tremendously. To be valid, our sample of ninety had to show the same variations and peculiarities as the original 900. A random sample in which each element has an equal chance of being selected should, we decided, give us what we want. This could be done in a practical way by placing 900 names in a barrel, scrambling them, and then picking out ninety. The way we did it was to start with an address (apartment 7) and go to every tenth apartment after that (17, 27, 37, 47, etc.). This gave us a one-in-ten sample, or ninety out of 900. Careful sampling, while it can only approximate the entire population, is a vital step toward an accurate and manageable experiment.

In describing our project to others, we included details of the characteristics of the subjects and interviewers and the questions that were asked, as well as the errors or weaknesses of the study. The major weakness, by the way, lies in the area of controls. For example, it was assumed that the interviewer's sex was the cause of the differing responses, but the cause could have been a difference in the personalities of the two interviewers or in the clothes they were wearing or something else that had not been controlled. We should have used more interviewers of both sexes and of varying types. It may be that *another* cause produced the apparent effect we noted; or perhaps *several* causes (of which the interviewer's sex was only one) were operating. The study should be repeated by others to verify the results, and when it is, controlling for the additional factors we missed would be appropriate.[13]

Problems in Social Science Investigation

We have been describing sociological research efforts—how sociologists come to know what they know. We have found that working within the general guidelines of science, they develop special techniques to study human behavior. All sciences do the same thing. And for the natural sciences these procedures have worked beautifully. The explosion of knowledge in the natural sciences in the last several decades attests to the value of the scientific mode of inquiry. But do these techniques work as well in the social sciences? So far, they don't seem to.

In February 1979, we had a total eclipse of the sun. Astronomers handled it beautifully—they told us when it would happen, how long it would last, and what we should expect to see depending on where we were watching from. They compounded that achievement by telling us when the *next* eclipse of the same type would happen—February 16, 2017! Then they asked a social scientist to tell them about social conditions in the United States in 2017—family size, migration patterns, form of government, crime patterns, economic conditions, types of social movements, popular social problems, and so on. The social scientist told them he would check out his data and get back to them in 2018 . . . .

---

[13]For more detail on this study, see Judson R. Landis, Daryl Sullivan, and Joseph Sheley, "Feminist Attitudes as Related to Sex of the Interviewer," *Pacific Sociological Review*, vol. 16, no. 3 (July 1973), pp. 305-314.

There are numerous explanations offered for the different levels of results in the natural and social sciences. One explanation has it that because the natural sciences historically got a head start on the social sciences, they are further ahead at this point. If this explanation is accurate, then as the social sciences gather more maturity and sophistication in their techniques and theories, they may reach a higher level of performance.

There are other issues as well. A more basic explanation has to do with the nature of the subject matter—in the case of the social sciences, the subject is *people.* Variations in humans and their behavior are vast. Multiple causation is the rule, not the exception, and digging out all the related factors is always difficult and often impossible. Social scientists are convinced that their subject matter is more complex than that of natural scientists. Whether social scientists are right about this can be argued, but there are certainly complicating factors introduced when the subject matter of the study is people. For one thing, the study of people is an *interactive* process. When oxygen, force fields, a laser beam, or light rays are studied, they probably do what they always do. The fact of their being studied is unlikely to change their behavior. But when people are studied, they usually know it, and the process of being studied may change their behavior. (We commented on this earlier in discussing reactive and nonreactive studies.) For example, look at a study done some years ago at the Hawthorne Works of the Western Electric Company. Some researchers were interested in increasing production among women who wired electrical relays. They experimented with two groups. For one group, lighting was improved so they could see their work better. For the other group nothing was done. Output improved equally in *both* groups. Next, lighting was reduced to the point where the workers had difficulty seeing what they were doing. But there was no decrease in efficiency or speed of production! What was going on? It became apparent that there was much more to working efficiency than just physical working conditions. In fact, the workers were responding to *being studied* by the researchers, and this had more effect on their output than changing supposedly important physical factors. This finding, sometimes called the *Hawthorne effect,* was the impetus for a series of studies dealing with psychological and social aspects of the work situation.[14]

The problem begins with multiple causation of human behavior, and now we find that one of these causes is one *we* introduce by trying to study it. It is difficult enough as it is, and we make it worse (more complicated) by looking at it.

Another problem when people are the subject matter is that of introducing *controls.* People vary across so many factors that it becomes difficult to take all of them into account. Look again at the survey of delinquency and religiosity suggested a few pages back. Ideally, the two groups should be of the same social class, same age, same sex, and so on. In fact, they should be the same on *everything* except the two variables being studied—delinquency involvement and religiosity (church attendance). And that's not possible.

Social scientists are involved in the unique situation of *humans studying*

---

[14]The Hawthorne-Western Electric studies are summarized by Madge in *The Origins of Scientific Sociology,* Chapter 6 (see footnote 10).

humans, and this leads to problems. It is hard to be objective under the best of circumstances, and here scientists are studying people like themselves. If it were oxygen or laser beams, one would be less likely to identify with the subject. But in social science the subject is people, and scientists may identify with their feelings, their reactions, their beliefs. I suppose we are asking, Can people possibly be objective and unbiased when, in effect, they are studying *themselves?* This question has bothered social scientists for decades, and their responses to it vary. Some believe that one can put aside biases and beliefs and become a dispassionate observer. Others say no—humans can't study other humans and be objective. If this last group is right, there isn't much future for social science, or at least we will always have to bear in mind its limitations. Who's right? Well, certainly there are problems with objectivity when studying humans. Most social scientists probably see this as another variable present in their studies that needs to be taken into account but one that by itself doesn't compromise the scientific effort. Valuable knowledge about human behavior has been achieved and will continue to be achieved in spite of the various problems we have just outlined.

We have described how sociologists use the techniques of science to gain knowledge and some of the problems they encounter along the way. You may have an impression of sociologists as superscientists bustling about in white coats guided by the strict principles of empiricism. Well, it's not necessarily so. There has always been a strong humanistic theme in sociology. Rather than just describing human activity, humanists attempt to interpret and focus on the meaning, value, and richness of life. At the center of the humanistic approach is the conviction that all people have dignity and worth. The sociologist as humanist is concerned about human welfare and conduct and wants to improve the lot of people in general. Humanism and science may be cooperative, but there are certain sharp contrasts between them. The scientist encourages value-free observation; the humanist believes that values are an essential part of the study of humans. The scientist studies what is; the humanist is concerned about what could be. These differences have led some philosophers to the view that if there is too great an emphasis in a society on science and technology, humanistic values and the well-being of the society are seriously challenged. At this point suffice it to say that sociology contains both of these sometimes conflicting viewpoints—the scientific and humanistic. We will return to this issue in Chapter 14.

Is It Common Sense?

Students of introductory sociology, and many others as well, frequently describe and consequently dismiss sociology as mere common sense. Or, worse, they say, "Sociologists describe what we all knew anyway in language that none of us can understand."

Unfortunately, there may be some truth to this statement, especially the indictment for obscure and complicated language. Sociologists might benefit if they learned to use more four-letter words and fewer twenty-four-letter ones. The belief, however, that sociology deals only with common sense is, I think, inaccurate. One reason people say that is because sociologists deal with contemporary human behavior, or patterns of interaction between people. Since most of us are humans, we feel quite familiar with the topic. We think that atoms and rockets and the theory of relativity are one thing, but when it comes to understanding people, we're all experts.

In some aspects of human behavior our experiences and our intuition may serve us well. None of us, however, has experienced all situations. Because we live in a particular society, area, social class, and community, at a particular time in history, our experiences are necessarily limited. We in fact know much less about human behavior than we think. For example, let's return to the study of women's attitudes, described earlier. The women were more pro–women's liberation to the male interviewer. To the female interviewer asking the same questions, they were much less pro–women's liberation. Did you guess right? Perhaps you did and had a logical explanation as well, but a peculiarity of common sense is that it can provide a rationale for almost *any* response. It takes a more sophisticated analysis to predict human behavior accurately and to answer the complex questions of why people do what they do. To further put what we know by means of common sense in perspective, try this adaptation of Gerald Maxwell's social awareness test. How well does your common sense serve you?[15] (The answers are at the bottom of this page.)

    "Social Awareness" Test   Are the following true or false?

1. There are about *twice* as many arrests of fifteen to nineteen year olds as there are of twenty-five to twenty-nine year olds.
2. Because of discrimination and depressed living conditions, more blacks commit suicide proportionately than whites.
3. With the exception of movie stars, people who divorce are slow to remarry.
4. Land is generally less expensive in the suburbs than in other parts of the city.
5. Women, being somewhat more emotional, are more likely to commit suicide than men.
6. There are more Hindus in the world than Protestants.
7. Cities are where the jobs are; consequently, there are generally more men than women in cities.

---

[15]Gerald Maxwell describes a social awareness test that he has devised (*The American Sociologist*, November 1966, pp. 253-254). I have used his title as well as one or two of his questions.
    Answers to "Social Awareness" test:
    1. True. (See *Uniform Crime Reports—1980*.)
    2. False. See pp. 172 and 393.
    3. False. Divorced persons are generally more likely to marry than single persons of the same age.
    4. True. See p. 298.
    5. False. See p. 393.
    6. True. See p. 240.
    7. False. See p. 293.
    8. False. Couples whose parents had unhappy marriages have a greater proneness to divorce.
    9. False. See p. 361.
   10. True. See p. 247.

8. Children from divorced or unhappy homes are usually more careful in selecting a mate and make better marriages.
9. Panic is a common response for people confronted by disaster.
10. People with some college education are more likely to attend church than are people with only a high school education.

THIS BOOK

This book focuses on the *concepts* of sociology. Concepts provide a way of generalizing about phenomena. Sociologists use concepts—role, motivation, anticipatory socialization, culture, in-group, cult, institution, mob—to help them organize and understand the events they are studying. In fact, one could say that the major task of sociology (and probably other disciplines as well) is to build concepts—that is, to isolate certain unifying, abstract qualities that underlie and thus "explain" behavior. This book attempts to gather together some of the major concepts of sociology and define and illustrate them. Not all concepts are included, but the important ones are.

The discussion of concepts that follows is divided into three major sections. These discuss (1) the individual in society, (2) the organization of society, and (3) society in flux, under the headings Socialization and Culture, Social Organization, and Social Change and Social Deviation.

Terms for Study

applied science (7)	manifest function (11)
causal-explanatory study (19)	multiple causation (5)
cause-effect relationship (5)	mysticism (3)
conflict theory (12–13)	nonreactive research (15)
dependent variable (20)	participant observation (16)
descriptive survey (17)	pure science (7)
dysfunction (11)	random sample (21)
empiricism (4)	rationalism (4)
experiment (20)	reactive research (14–15)
functional analysis (11)	science (4)
hypotheses (21)	sociology (9)
independent variable (20)	survey research (17)
latent function (11)	symbolic interaction (13)

I
SOCIALIZATION AND CULTURE

In this section, we discuss how the infant develops into a social being. The socialization process is of major importance. Through this process values are transmitted from one generation to the next, and infants grow and learn to adapt to their environments. The *self,* the person's conception of what and who he or she is, slowly emerges from interaction with others. Through this interaction, individuals are introduced to norms as well as roles, those behaviors that are expected of them in specific situations and positions. This personal and social development takes place within the context of a specific culture. The culture provides a set of behaviors, traditions, customs, habits, and skills that also become a part of the individual. These processes—socialization, development of the self, internalization of norms, roles, and other aspects of the culture—are particularly evident in young children, although they continue to be important throughout life.

2

Socialization and Self

Few people spend much time thinking about the transformation they went through in the process of becoming mature human beings. Not only are we not concerned with the steps required to carry us from an early blob of protoplasm to a complicated, interacting individual, but it is even hard for us to believe that we were ever at the stage of egg and sperm. Beyond a certain idle curiosity as we watch a baby grow up, we take these changes in the developing human for granted. They are like the phases of the moon or the coming of summer—they seem to just happen.

However, if one decides to analyze the development of the individual in some detail, several approaches are available. A biological approach would emphasize physiological maturation. As a man's hair changes from brown to gray to gone, so does the person grow and mature in other ways. This approach might suggest that maturity is merely a matter of changes in cells, and that given enough time, these changes produce a mature social being.

But there is much more to human development than just biological and physiological changes. Interaction with other humans is of critical importance. Isolation from (or inadequate) human interaction can affect our normal growth in a number of ways. Examples of extreme isolation are unusual, but occasionally such cases are described. Some years ago, Kingsley Davis described the cases of Anna and Isabelle, who, because they were illegitimate children, were kept in nearly total isolation the first years of their lives.[1] Anna's mother was mentally retarded and left Anna alone in an attic room most of the time. Isabelle's mother was a deaf mute who stayed in a dark room with Isabelle, shut off from the rest of the family. When Anna was discovered, she was about six years old and could not walk, talk, or do anything that showed intelligence. She was in bad physical condition as well. After about two years in a county home she had learned to walk, understand simple commands, feed herself, and achieve some neatness, but she still did not speak. She spent the next three years of her life (she died at the age of ten and a half) in a private home for retarded children, and here she made some further progress. Her hearing and vision were normal, and she walked and ran fairly well. She could bounce and catch a ball, string beads, identify a few colors, and build with blocks. And she finally began to develop speech. She attempted conversations with others, although she spoke in phrases rather than in sentences. In summary, when Anna was found at the age of six, she had the mental capacity of a newborn infant. Four and a half years later she had progressed to a mental level of two and a half or three years.

Isabelle was six and a half years old when she was found. Like Anna, Isabelle was in bad shape both physically and mentally when she was discovered. For speech she made a strange croaking sound. She reacted to strangers, especially men, with much fear and hostility. In many ways she behaved like a deaf child, and her mental capacity was no more than that of a six-month-old baby. Specialists working with her at first believed her to be feebleminded and uneducable. An intensive training program was started. At first it seemed hopeless, but gradually Isabelle began to respond. Then suddenly she began to learn rapidly. Two months after starting to speak, she was putting sentences together. Sixteen months later she had a vocabulary of 1,500–2,000 words and was asking complicated questions. She covered in two years the stages of learning that ordinarily require six. Her I.Q. tripled in a year and a half. Davis concluded his description of Isabelle by noting that she was over fourteen years old and had passed the sixth grade. She was bright, cheerful, and energetic, and her teachers reported that she participated in school activities as normally as other children.

What do these cases tell us? It seems apparent that inadequate social interaction (near isolation in these cases) inhibits the development of the individual. Although they were six years old, neither Anna nor Isabelle had developed beyond the infant level, and both were believed to be feebleminded. Yet when effective interaction with others began, both girls progressed. In Isabelle's case the development was remarkable. This is probably because she had concentrated and expert training from the beginning and because she learned lan-

---

[1]This section is summarized from "Final Note on a Case of Extreme Isolation," by Kingsley Davis, *American Journal of Sociology* 52 (1947), pp. 432–437. Also see Bruno Bettelheim, "Feral Children and Autistic Children," *American Journal of Sociology* 64 (March 1959), pp. 455–467.

guage quickly. Perhaps this is the key. Or perhaps Anna was more isolated—Isabelle's mother stayed with her while Anna was often by herself. Or perhaps Isabelle's mental capacity was superior to Anna's to begin with. This we don't know. But in each case the effect of inadequate social interaction on human development is clearly demonstrated. Sociologists are convinced that the development of the individual is, at least in part, a *social* process.

SOCIALIZATION: A SOCIAL PROCESS

The process by which the organism becomes a social being is called socialization. **Socialization** refers to the learning of expectations, habits, skills, values, beliefs, and other requirements necessary for effective participation in social groups. Biological maturity is necessary, hereditary factors may set limits, and the process takes place in a physical environment, but the crucial aspect of socialization is that it is a social process. The individual develops through interaction in the social environment; the social environment determines the result. This is not to imply that if baby Reggie Jackson and baby Leonard Bernstein had been switched in the nursery shortly after birth, Bernstein would have played right field for the California Angels and Jackson would have directed the New York Philharmonic. We would have to look at other factors as well, and biology and heredity certainly play an important part. The exact extent of the role of biological factors is hard to determine. In fact, there is a heated and interesting debate going on now on this very issue—biology versus social environment. Edward Wilson, an entomologist from Harvard, proposed in a book published in 1975 that a new science called sociobiology be established. **Sociobiology** is defined as "the systematic study of the biological basis of all forms of social behavior, including sexual and parental behavior, in all kinds of organisms, including man." Sociobiologists are convinced that the behavior of lower organisms is biologically determined, and they believe that the same may be true of much of human behavior. In their writings they cite apparent genetic constraints on human social behavior in such areas as choice of sexual partners (the incest taboo and homosexuality), sex roles, aggression, kinship rules, and infant development.[2] The ideas of the sociobiologists are controversial (some say inflammatory); they have delighted some social scientists and threatened and angered others. Probably most social scientists recognize that biology places certain limits or conditions on human development. Beyond this, however, social scientists and especially sociologists believe that the crucial elements for understanding human behavior are the social environment

---

[2]Edward C. Wilson's books include *Sociobiology: The New Synthesis* (Cambridge, Mass.: Harvard University Press, 1975), and *On Human Nature* (Cambridge, Mass.: Harvard University Press, 1978). His newer book devotes much more attention to human behavior than his earlier book did. Also see *Society* 15 (September/October 1978). The whole issue is on sociobiology. The quote above comes from p. 10 of the *Society* issue. Also see numerous reviews in the popular press (for example, *Time* and *Newsweek* during September and October 1978) and in *Contemporary Sociology* 5 (November 1976).

and social interaction. By and large (according to sociologists) these are the primary determinants of who we are.

By **social interaction** we mean the process of being aware of others when we act, of modifying our behavior in accordance with others' responses. Social interaction occurs in a variety of ways, and its patterns are complex. When a student asks a teacher a question, he speaks differently than he does when he talks to the student next to him in class. The teacher evaluates the question as fairly sophisticated, and this affects his response to the student. If the interaction continues, each response is modified and determined by the response of the other immediately preceding it. The pattern of interaction may be affected by manner, body language, deference, relative status, degree of acquaintance, eye contact, and numerous other factors in addition to the spoken words. Social interaction occurs between two people—husband and wife, strangers on the street—and in groups and even large organizations. Try watching some examples of social interaction, and see whether you can identify the more subtle aspects of communication. How do the parties show agreement and disagreement, interest and boredom, and happiness and unhappiness through the use of body language, spatial distance, and facial expressions?

Socialization is continuous—it takes place throughout life, starting as soon as the infant leaves the womb and continuing until death. It occurs through interaction with other humans. We could call these other humans *agents of socialization*. Who they will be depends on one's place in the life span. For the baby, the socialization agents are the parents, who begin very early to communicate accepted and expected modes of behavior to the infant. Brothers and sisters also become socialization agents. An aspect of the socialization process can be observed in children as they pretend to be mothers, fathers, airplane pilots, or truck drivers. They are already anticipating and playing future roles. Later, peers become socialization agents, and, regardless of whether they are school friends or members of a delinquent gang or teammates on the football team, their influence becomes very important. Still later, one's colleagues on the job, one's spouse, and even one's own children become agents of socialization. Also, indirect influences such as vicarious participation or involvement in what we are reading or watching on TV continually play a part in the socialization process. In fact, in our interaction with others, we all become agents of socialization.

As you can see, socialization is extremely important. Through this lifelong process we gradually take specific points of view. Our views of religion, politics, and sports, style of family life, how to commit certain crimes, and how to raise children are all learned through the socialization process. I throw a volleyball to my seven-year-old son. He catches it in his hands and throws it back. Very easy, he doesn't even think about it. But suppose I throw the ball to a French or English boy—what happens? If the throw is above his shoulders, he will probably "head" it back to me. If it's lower he will control the ball with his legs and feet and kick it back to me. Each child has been socialized—has learned—to respond in a certain way. They respond differently because different things are emphasized where each child lives. But again, the socialization process "tracks" them into a certain response.

Research with parents and their newborn babies tells us that from the moment of birth female and male infants are treated differently. They are described differently (girl babies are seen as softer, smaller, more beautiful and delicate than boy babies), dressed differently, given different types of toys, and expected to behave in different ways, all because of their sex. Sex-role socialization begins at birth and continues through childhood. One effect of this socialization is illustrated in a study by Philip Goldberg.[3] Goldberg chose written articles from six fields—law, city planning, elementary education, dietetics, linguistics, art history—and asked a group of college women to evaluate each article. The catch was that Goldberg manipulated the names of the authors of the articles. For half the women, the author of an article was a man ("John McKay"); for the other half of the women, the *same* article was by a woman ("Joan McKay"). In other words, the women were reading the same six articles, but in half the cases the authors were listed as men, and in the other half the authors were women. What happened? In nearly all cases, the women rated the article supposedly written by the man *higher* than the same article supposedly written by a woman! Several fields were selected by Goldberg because they were traditionally viewed as women's areas (elementary education, dietetics), but even here, articles supposedly written by men were ranked higher than those supposedly written by women. The explanation is inescapable: Women have been socialized to see themselves as inferior to men. A major goal of the women's liberation and equal rights movements is to counteract this "inferior woman" socialization, in women as well as in men.

Socialization may be better understood as occurring at two levels—primary and secondary. According to Berger and Luckmann, **primary socialization** refers to the first socialization an individual undergoes in childhood, through which he becomes a member of society. **Secondary socialization** refers to any subsequent process that inducts an already socialized individual into new sectors of his or her society.[4] Primary socialization usually takes place in the family. Here, the individual has no choice about the important or significant socializing agents—the child almost automatically and inevitably accepts and internalizes the family's view of the world. As primary socialization proceeds, the child's referents move from specific to general. A progressive abstraction occurs whereby at one stage the child understands that her parent specifically wants her to do certain things (for example, not play with food), and at a later stage she understands that people in general expect her to behave in certain ways (to use correct manners and not play with food). It is through primary socialization that the individual's first world is constructed. Consequently, according to Berger and Luckmann, it is the most important, for the basic structure of all secondary socialization must resemble that of primary socialization. Primary socialization ends when the "generalized other" has been established.[5]

---

[3]This study is described in "Are Women Prejudiced Against Women?" by Philip Goldberg, *Trans-Action* 5 (April 1968), pp. 28–30.

[4]This discussion follows that contained in *The Social Construction of Reality*, by Peter Berger and Thomas Luckmann (Garden City, N.Y.: Doubleday, 1966), especially pp. 129–147.

[5]See Mead's ideas about the "generalized other" on p. 39.

Secondary socialization takes over where primary socialization leaves off and involves the individual's moving into and internalizing knowledge of new areas or sectors of life. Secondary socialization takes place when the individual decides to learn to read or to type, to take up skydiving, to become a police officer, or to raise a family. Secondary socialization does not need an emotionally charged atmosphere to succeed, nor does it presuppose a high degree of identification, and its contents do not possess the quality of inevitability. In secondary socialization, the individual can be more objective than in primary socialization.

A person entering a new profession illustrates adult secondary socialization; an example is the steps in the socialization of the new police officer, outlined by Arthur Niederhoffer. The rookie patrolman proudly accepts the symbols of his new job—uniform, revolver, and badge. At police academy he learns about law, police procedures, human relations, rules and regulations, first aid, and how to fire weapons. He graduates, becomes a patrolman, faces a hostile and unappreciative public, and reality shock occurs. The more experienced officers tell him that in order to become a real policeman, he will have to forget everything he learned at the academy. The patrolman learns a new language, he learns to treat people differently in different areas of the city, and he learns to react to people's language, attitudes, and dress as well as to their criminal behavior. He learns when to enforce the law and when to look the other way. He learns how to make an arrest effectively, and he learns about graft. According to Niederhoffer, his attitudes change the longer he is on the force; if the officer has a college education but is slow to get promoted, he becomes more and more cynical. And generally as officers near retirement they become less cynical.[6]

RESOCIALIZATION AND ANTICIPATORY SOCIALIZATION

Socialization at the adult level (secondary socialization) is usually of a gradual nature; that is, the changes in the individual are more minor than those which occurred during primary socialization. Occasionally, however, major modifications or reconstructions of people are attempted. This could be called **resocialization.** It usually represents a concentrated effort by a group or organization. For example, look at prisons. Individuals commit crime, are caught, convicted, and sent to reformatories if they are young or to prisons if they are older. The idea is that the discomfort of their confinement will help them see the error of their ways, counseling and training programs there will help them change their behavior, and criminals will be resocialized into good citizens.

What actually happens? Resocialization certainly does take place, but it is far more diversified than one might imagine. Prisons are very effective crime schools for some prisoners. Regardless of the inmates' expertise upon entering, they can improve their crafts while inside. Through association with other in-

---

[6]See Arthur Niederhoffer, *Behind the Shield: The Police in Urban Society* (Garden City, N.Y.: Doubleday, 1967).

mates, they can learn new skills and techniques of crime. They can set up networks of important criminal friends and contacts for when they are released. Inmates learn a new language in prison. For example, "gleaning," "low riders," "bonaroos," "shots," "politicians," "merchants," "hoods," and "toughs" are prison slang for types of convicts.[7] The inmates learn new sexual practices, sometimes against their will, and they must learn how to get what they want in a society that is not at all like the one they are used to. Some inmates even *like* prison—they have found a new home. These inmates find it easier to get along inside than outside, and they take steps to make sure they can return quickly once they are released. These people, too, have been resocialized. Draft resisters and others convicted of minor offenses may also be resocialized into a criminal role while in prison.

When marines or soldiers go through basic training, they are being resocialized. Recruits are taught to get up at times when they would ordinarily be going to bed, to cut their hair in peculiar ways, and to spend enormous amounts of time on the maintenance and appearance of their shoes, clothing, and equipment. They are told that a patch of dirt, rock, and sand outside the barracks is in fact a plot of grass that must be raked and cleaned every morning. They are taught to obey authority unquestioningly, that the individual is unimportant, and to act as a unit with their fellow recruits at all times.

There are other examples of major changes in people. The Patty Hearst the world learned about in the months after her kidnapping by the SLA was not the Patty Hearst known to her family and friends. Somehow she had been quickly and effectively resocialized. Brainwashing of war prisoners through isolation and sensory deprivation is another type of resocialization. One technique used by the Chinese in Korea to lower morale was to allow only collection notices, divorce subpoenas, "Dear John" letters, and other demoralizing mail to get to the prisoners. They held back positive letters and let the negative ones through.[8] Organizations such as Alcoholics Anonymous, dedicated to helping people recover from dependence on alcohol, are also involved in attempts at resocialization.

When a person adopts the values, behavior, or viewpoints of a group he or she would like to belong to, but does not yet, this is called **anticipatory socialization.** This is a common occurrence and explains the behavior of the lower-class person who develops middle-class values, or the behavior of the "gung-ho" military recruit who wants to become an officer, or the new behaviors and viewpoints of law or medical students who anticipate becoming doctors or lawyers. Anticipatory socialization has the interesting function of easing the transi-

---

[7]There are numerous books and articles on prison life that describe the language or argot of inmates. For example, see Gresham Sykes, *Society of Captives* (New York: Atheneum, 1958). The example I have used here comes from *The Felon*, by John Irwin (Englewood Cliffs, N.J.: Prentice-Hall, 1970), pp. 66–85. Also Peter Letkemann, *Crime as Work* (Englewood Cliffs, N.J.: Prentice-Hall, 1973).

[8]*The Brain Benders*, by Charles Brownfield (New York: Exposition Press, 1972), has an interesting description and analysis of brainwashing. Brownfield deals with the actual occurrence in wartime and with scientific experiments. The example cited here comes from p. 55.

tion from one stage in life to another. When individuals practice for a new role ahead of time, their assumption of the new role is probably much less difficult. On the other hand, if the new stage in life is never reached, the trauma may be even greater than a sudden, unprepared-for change would have been.

Virginia Military Institute (VMI) is a state-run military college. In Virginia it is called the West Point of the South.

At the very bottom of the VMI pyramid are those cadets known as rats. Rats are incoming freshmen. The first thing they're told is that they're the lowest form of life imaginable. Then they're given a week-long experience that bears this out. This week—VMI's version of freshman orientation—is known as cadre. Cadre begins the evening after matriculation, after mom and dad have left for home. The rats have all had their heads sheared and have been given baggy fatigues and shirts and baseball caps to wear. They look stupid and feel stupider. The only upperclassmen present are the officers and noncoms who run cadre. They are immaculately uniformed, polished to a glistening shine, and in total command. The rats quickly learn to fear them.

"You get a bunch of guys out of high school," explained one first classman, "they're all going every which way. You get 'em all in here together, you get 'em all looking alike, and they may feel miserable, but it serves a purpose. It gets everybody moving in the same direction—doing the same thing at the same time. And you can't be nice and do it, because some of them are going to tell you where you can get off. So you have to be hard. You've got to put the fear of God into 'em."

From cadre until sometime after Christmas, "ratline" prevails. During ratline, rats are not permitted to drink liquor, to walk to the bathroom or the showers except in full uniform, or to say the name of their class—the class of '82, for instance. They are given a rat bible with assorted facts to memorize, such as the names of the cadets who were killed at New Market, and they are forced to strain in barracks—to hold chest and face perfectly rigid, with chin tucked into throat. Hazing is no longer permitted; sweat parties—late-night workouts that turn the fourth-class stoop slippery with sweat—are the rule now. Only regulation Army exercises are allowed, but that's little consolation to the rat who has just been ordered to do 250 pushups.

The honor system, one hears from every quarter, is the foundation on which VMI is built. It governs all academic work, all official statements, all theft, no matter how petty. It's administered by a cadet honor court, elected by the corps, which conducts all its proceedings (investigations, pretrial hearings, and trials) in absolute secrecy. The accused has the right to civilian counsel. If nine of the court's eleven voting members find him guilty, he is immediately dismissed. Once he has gone—in the very early hours of the morning, as it usually happens—his departure is announced by a low drum roll that grows steadily in intensity until it is broken by a boom on the bass drum. As the drum rolls and the intermittent booms continue, the members of the honor court march through the arch and up to the topmost stoop. From there, they work their way around and down, their president pronouncing as they go the name of the disgraced cadet, the charge on which he was convicted, and the admonition never to utter his name again. By this time he is far from Lexington, on his way alone toward whatever home he might have.

SELF AND PERSONALITY

Psychology and sociology are most closely linked when they attempt to define the individual and explain developmental processes. A separate discipline, social psychology, has developed and deals with theories of socialization and individual development. Self and personality are the major concepts in this analysis. The words are similar in meaning, but **personality** is a somewhat more general term and may be defined as the sum total of the physical, mental, emotional, social, and behavioral characteristics of an individual. **Self** refers to one's awareness of and ideas and attitudes about one's own personal and social identity. Psychologists are perhaps more inclined to use the term *personality;* sociologists generally prefer to use *self.*

Generally, psychologists have placed more emphasis on hereditary and biological factors in personality development, whereas sociologists focus on social interaction and the social environment. Psychologists place more emphasis on early childhood than do sociologists. Although there are numerous psychological theories, the most famous ideas are those of Sigmund Freud. Freud was a Viennese physician and founder of psychoanalysis. According to Freud, the personality is made up of three major components: the id, the ego, and the superego.[9] The **id** is the most primitive aspect of the personality and represents the basic instinctual drives with which the person is born. Sexual and aggressive desires in the id constantly seek expression. The **ego** is the acting self; it is the mediator between the id and the outside world. Whereas the id operates by a pleasure principle—maximizing pleasure for the organism—the ego operates by a reality principle—balancing the instinctual needs of the organism against the conditions in the surrounding environment. The **superego** is an internalized set of rules and regulations that represent the values and ideas of society initially interpreted for individuals by their parents. The superego, commonly referred to as the conscience, is the aspect of personality that controls behavior. We can think of id, ego, and superego as three sets of processes whose sometimes conflicting purposes combine to function as personality. Freud believed that the individual passed through a series of psychosexual stages and that personality was fixed very early in life, around the age of six. Unlike Freud, sociologists believe that although the early years are extremely important, socialization and development of self are lifelong processes. Since Freud was a psychoanalyst and was working with people who were mentally ill, he emphasized the restricting nature of parents and society, and the conflict aspects of group life. Sociologists have focused more on the positive roles played by parents and groups in socialization and development of self.

With this brief view of Freud as introduction, let's turn to sociological theories of the self. Sociologists believe that self-development is rooted in social behavior, and not in biological, hereditary, or instinctual factors. The self is developed during the socialization process. Through interaction and association with others, you as an individual develop an image of *what you are.* This in-

---

[9]For more detail, see Calvin Hall and Gardner Lindzey, *Theories of Personality* (New York: Wiley, 1957).

volves a perception of your role requirements and your position and behavioral expectations in the various social groupings with which you identify. As sociologist Charles H. Cooley put it, the word *self* means simply that which is designated in common speech by the pronouns of the first person singular, *I, me, mine,* and *myself.*[10] Aspects of one's self might include: I am male, I am a college student, I am of medium height, I am athletic, I am usually happy, I am intelligent. The self might include as well: I can never do anything right, I am not worth much, nobody listens to me, I am inadequate, I am unloved, I am not as capable as my older brother.

Individuals develop these images or viewpoints about themselves from the way others respond to them. More specifically, they develop them from the way *they think* others are responding to them. Development of the self is a two-way interactive process that takes place throughout the period of socialization, the entire life span. Development of the self is an extremely subjective process involving interpretations of others' evaluations. Current evaluations are based on past evaluations, so that earlier mistakes become additive. A father may continually tell his daughter that she is extremely intelligent. This becomes part of her self, one of the ways she views herself, and she behaves and has certain expectations because of it. If she flunks bonehead English as a college freshman, contradictory information comes in. What happened? She makes excuses and rationalizes her failure in order to support the view of self that she had held. She will probably seek reinforcement from other sources (father, girl friend, I.Q. test scores) to support her self-view. If evidence is lacking or rein-

---

[10]Charles Horton Cooley's books are *Human Nature and the Social Order* (New York: Charles Scribner's, 1902) and *Social Organization* (New York: Charles Scibner's, 1909).

forcement becomes harder to find (other bad grades, low I.Q. test scores), this part of her self-conception will probably begin to change.

Aspects of self constantly undergo change. Often these changes occur slowly. Occasionally changes may be more rapid, sudden, and dramatic as we mentioned earlier in cases of resocialization of inmates of prisons and concentration camps and recruits in military basic training. All of these changes are a result of our evaluations of others' evaluations of us.

Cooley also described the development of the self in his concept, the **looking-glass self.** The looking-glass self contains three elements: the imagination of our appearance to the other person, the imagination of his judgment of that appearance, and some sort of self-feeling, such as pride or mortification. Suppose, for example, a person eating in a crowded restaurant accidentally knocks his plate off the table. It makes a huge crash, and the food spills all over him. According to Cooley, he first "steps outside himself" and observes himself from the viewpoint of others in the room (". . . a well-dressed fellow with spaghetti all over him . . ."). Next, still examining himself as object, he imagines that others are evaluating his behavior (". . . must be a rather clumsy and awkward person . . ."). Finally, the individual as subject develops feelings and reactions to these imaginary evaluations of himself as object. He gets embarrassed, his face reddens, and he tries unsuccessfully to pretend it didn't happen. The process is made more interesting when we note that probably the same things would have happened if the person had been the only one in the restaurant. We are carrying our judges around with us in our head, and they are constantly evaluating our behavior.

George Herbert Mead[11] described the development of the self this way: Individuals will conceive of themselves as they believe significant others conceive of them. They will then tend to act in accordance with expectations they impute to these significant others concerning the way "people like them" should act. As children develop the ability to examine and control their behavior in accordance with others' views and attitudes about their behavior, they are learning to "take the role of the other." At this first stage of development (called *primary socialization* by Berger and Luckmann), children do not cooperate with others and relate only to specific individuals such as parents and perhaps an older brother or sister or a teacher—persons whom Mead described as **significant others.** Later, as individuals develop, they are less likely to continue to react to individual others and learn instead to react more to a less personalized grouping of others. This grouping of others, which Mead called the **generalized other,** represents the sum of the viewpoints of the social group or community of people to which one belongs. The second stage of development (secondary socialization) begins, then, when children are mature enough to cooperate with others in joint activities and to be able to react to the idea of people in general rather than to specific others.

Although our internalized attitudes of others are crucial, they do not de-

[11]George Herbert Mead's writings include *Mind, Self, and Society* (Chicago: University of Chicago Press, 1934) and "The Genesis of the Self and Social Control," from *International Journal of Ethics* 35 (April 1925), pp. 251–273.

George Orwell tells the story of the English police officer on duty in a Burmese town who is told one day that an elephant has run amok, is ravaging the bazaar, and has killed a native—"caught him with its trunk, put its foot on his back and ground him into the earth." The officer gets a rifle and seeks out the elephant. When he finds the elephant, he realizes immediately that he ought not to shoot him—the elephant is eating peacefully and is not dangerous. "But at that moment I glanced round at the crowd that had followed me. It was an immense crowd, two thousand at the least and growing every minute. I looked at the sea of yellow faces all happy and excited over this bit of fun, all certain that the elephant was going to be shot. They did not like me, but with the magical rifle in my hands I was momentarily worth watching. And suddenly I realized that I should have to shoot the elephant after all. The people expected it of me and I had got to do it; I could feel their two thousand wills pressing me forward, irresistibly. Here was I, the white man with his gun, standing in front of the unarmed native crowd—seemingly the leading actor of the piece; but in reality I was only an absurd puppet pushed to and fro by the will of those yellow faces behind."

The officer did not want to shoot the elephant, but he did, many times, and the elephant finally died. Later there was much discussion about whether he had done the right thing. "The older men said I was right, the younger men said it was a damn shame to shoot an elephant for killing a coolie. And afterwards I was very glad that the coolie had been killed; it put me legally in the right and it gave me a sufficient pretext for shooting the elephant. I often wondered whether any of the others grasped that I had done it solely to avoid looking a fool."

Excerpts from "Shooting an Elephant" in *Shooting an Elephant and Other Essays* by George Orwell are reprinted by permission of Harcourt Brace Jovanovich, Inc.

termine all behavior. Mead made a distinction between two aspects of the self, the "I" and the "me." The "I" represents the subjective, acting self, which may initiate spontaneous and original behavior. The "me" sees self as object and represents a conception of others' attitudes and viewpoints toward self. The "I" is freer, more innovative; the "me" is more conventional. "I" behaves, "me" judges and evaluates. "I" is in part governed by "me" but not completely. The abstract scrawling on the wall or in the dirt by the young child might represent "I" behavior; the same child's in-school drawing of the houses or trees that seem to please the teacher so much would be closer to "me" behavior. The driver involved in an auto accident who leaps out of the car and punches the other driver, swears at the passenger, and kicks a passing dog is probably showing us the "I" aspect of self, while another passenger who goes to the nearest phone to call the highway patrol illustrates the "me." Or imagine the football player about to catch a punt as a group of monstrous players from the other team race down the field to smash him. The player's "I" says, "I don't want to catch that thing. It's coming down hard and is going to hurt my hands; look at all those guys going to tackle me—I think I'll let the ball bounce off my helmet." The "me," however, says, "Oh no you don't—lot of people watching. You're supposed to *catch* that ball and *run* with it. The team and the coach are depending on you. *Do* it!"

THE IMPORTANCE OF LANGUAGE

It was also Mead who first emphasized that socialization and development of the self could not occur without *language.* Indeed, it is argued that it is largely language that distinguishes humans from other animals. The essential factor in language and symbolic communication is that a symbol arouses in one's self the same meaning it arouses in another. Primitive communication begins with a conversation of gestures, such as the mating dance of birds, the snarl of dogs, the roar of lions, or the cry of an infant. At this level, meanings of gestures are not shared. To be sure, the gestures may bring forth a response in some observer (another dog or lion, the infant's parent), but the important fact, according to Mead, is that the gesture does not arouse in the actor the same response it arouses in the observer. For example, a very young baby feels discomfort and cries. The parent interprets this as hunger and feeds the baby. If the parent is right, this is communication of a sort, but for the baby, the act of crying had no communicative intent; it was merely a biological response. This represents primitive communication because the meanings were not shared by both parties.

As children mature they learn to use symbols and words. The words are poorly formed at first, and probably only a parent could understand them, but they are the beginnings of language—something beyond primitive communication. As their use of language improves, children learn that what they say and do elicits responses from others. Language allows them to replace behavior with ideas—they can now say they are hungry rather than acting it out by crying or pointing at food. Language allows them to think, makes possible the internalization of attitudes of others, and allows individuals to control their responses to others. We can imagine an internal conversation in the child: "I would really like to have ice cream and cake, but my parents seem to like me better if I eat that other stuff they put out. . . ." Mead suggests that the use of symbolic communication continues to develop, and through language individuals are able to think, to develop shared social meanings, to take themselves as objects and evaluate their own behavior as they think others do. In sum, then, language makes possible the development of mind and self.

Language is important in another way. The language and symbols we use influence us to "see" the world and to "think" in particular ways. Imagine trying to balance your checkbook or do your algebra or geometry homework using *Roman numerals* instead of the number system we are used to. Much modern math probably could not have developed using the Roman system. The Eskimo has many ways of expressing the experience we describe by the single term "snow." Navaho language is more literal, concrete and specific than English. Spanish has two verbs for "to be" whose different uses reflect a type of thinking unique to Spanish culture. French makes distinctions between a familiar and a formal "you." Even color is "seen" differently in different societies depending on the words or symbols available—some societies only recognize two or three colors. There are numerous examples to make this same interesting point: The language and symbols we use act as a "filter" through which we experience the world. It is a filter *we* construct which nevertheless leads us to see what we see in particular ways, to focus on certain elements, and to miss others entirely.[12]

DEFINITION OF THE SITUATION

An important principle of socialization and self-concept is that our understanding of reality is subjective and socially structured. We respond to what we *think* is so, rather than what really is so. When we peer into Cooley's looking glass the view may be quite distorted, but we believe what we see. Two ideas, *definition of the situation* and *self-fulfilling prophecy*, help illustrate this point.

Sociologist W. I. Thomas introduced **definition of the situation** by saying, "If men define situations as real, they are real in their consequences." The point he was making is that reality is socially structured and that people respond as much or more to the meaning a situation has for them as to the objective features of a situation. If a student defines passing a certain exam as the most important thing in the world, then for her it is, and she goes to great extremes to ensure that she does. People define certain races as inferior and certain cultural beliefs or practices (cannibalism, polygamy) as peculiar, regardless of the objective reality of the situation. Or recall the old club initiation stunt. The victim is blindfolded and fed cold cooked spaghetti. Halfway through the meal he is told he is eating worms. What happens? He gags and is sick to his stomach. Why? He responds to what he thinks is true. That response has been socially defined and includes what his feeders tell him, how important initiation is to him, and what his background has taught him regarding the relative merits of angleworms and spaghetti. Even worse and horrible to consider, suppose we feed our friend angleworms and tell him it's spaghetti. That, I'm afraid, would work too.

The **self-fulfilling prophecy** is an extension of the idea of definition of the situation. A self-fulfilling prophecy occurs when a *false* definition of a situation evokes a new behavior that makes the originally false conception come *true*.[13] A student is worried that he will flunk an exam. This makes him so nervous and anxious that he is unable to study effectively, and he flunks the exam. Or police believe Gorples to be very criminal types. Consequently, more police patrols and surveillance are concentrated in those sections of the city where the Gorples live. Increased police surveillance leads to greater visibility and reporting of crime, so the crime rate of Gorples increases. As Merton explains, "Confident error generates its own spurious confirmation."[14] If we look carefully, we can see this phenomenon frequently in everyday situations.

---

[12]This discussion on the importance of language and the Sapir-Whorf school of thought draws in part from *Social Psychology*, rev. ed., by Alfred Lindesmith and Anselm Strauss (New York: Holt, 1956), Chapter 8.

[13]This discussion of definition of the situation and self-fulfilling prophecy follows that of Robert Merton in *Social Theory and Social Structure*, 2d ed. (New York: Free Press, 1957), pp. 421–436.

[14]Merton, *Social Theory and Social Structure*, p. 128 (see footnote 13).

Robert Rosenthal performed several interesting experiments that illustrate what we are discussing here.[15] In one experiment six students were given five rats each. They were told that their rats were very bright ones bred especially for running a maze. Six other students were given five rats each and were told that their rats were genetically inferior and probably would be poor at running through mazes. Then both groups of students attempted to train their rats to run the maze. What the students didn't know was that there were no "bright" rats and no "dull" rats—they were all the same with equal capacities for learning. What happened? Well, right from the beginning of the training the "bright" rats performed better. The "dull" rats made little progress and sometimes would not even budge from the starting position in the maze. And there were differences on more than just performance. The students found the "bright" rats to be brighter, more pleasant, and more likeable than the "dull" rats. The self-fulfilling prophecy explains what happened this way: The students with "bright" rats helped, coaxed, and encouraged their animals to do what they expected them to, and the "dull" rats got little encouragement. Or perhaps the students so expected "brights" to do well and "dulls" to do poorly that that is what they saw—regardless of what was actually happening.

In another experiment, Rosenthal and Lenore Jacobson tested the intelligence of some elementary school children in San Francisco.[16] They told the children's teachers that based on tests, twenty percent of the children were identified as "academic spurters." They told the teachers the children's names and that they could be expected to do well in school. As with the rats in the earlier study, the children were all alike. The "spurters" were *not* of higher intelligence, and in fact Rosenthal and Jacobson had chosen them at random. The children were tested again later in the year, and the teachers evaluated the students. You can guess what happened. The students labeled "academic spurters" were described as happier than other students, more curious, more interesting, more appealing, and better adjusted. They also showed greater gains in intelligence than the other children. The teachers acted in terms of what they thought to be true (definition of the situation) and behaved so that what was expected to occur did occur (self-fulfilling prophecy).[17] Again, the point is that our reality is subjective and is socially structured.

---

[15]The study is first reported in "The Effect of Experimenter Bias on the Performance of the Albino Rat," by Robert Rosenthal and Kermit Fode, *Behavioral Science* 8 (July 1963), pp. 183–189. The discussion here is summarized from another report, "Teacher Expectations for the Disadvantaged," by Rosenthal and Lenore Jacobson, *Scientific American* 218 (April 1968), pp. 19–23.

[16]This is summarized from "Teacher Expectations for the Disadvantaged," mentioned in footnote 15. Also see Rosenthal and Jacobson's book *Pygmalion in the Classroom: Teacher Expectation and Pupils' Intellectual Development* (New York: Holt, Rinehart and Winston, 1968).

[17]We mentioned in Chapter 1 the importance of verification in science, and the Rosenthal study provides an interesting sidelight in this regard. When the study appeared in 1968 it drew wide interest. Then, a series of critical reviews appeared taking Rosenthal to task for the research methods he used in his study. Next, numerous attempts were made to repeat Rosenthal's study on other samples. Some researchers have been able to repeat his findings and conclusions, many have not been able to do so, and the debate goes on about the original study. If you would like to get involved in the discussion, see Glen Mendels and James Flan-

In the paragraph above we introduced the process of **labeling**, which is an important one in sociology. Labeling refers to the tendency of people to stamp or type or categorize others. Often these categories are negative, and understanding the concept of labeling is important for precisely the reasons we have just been discussing. If one is labeled bright, dull, academic spurter, stupid, ex-con, deviant, lesbian, mentally ill, or sex offender, it is bound to have an effect on that individual. The label may be accurate or it may be false. But as we have just discovered, accuracy is of little consequence because reality is subjective and people believe what they are told. Labeling leads to different treatment by others (who respond to the label rather than to the individual), to effects on the individual's self-concept, and perhaps to a self-fulfilling prophecy. We will return to labeling in more detail in a later chapter on deviant behavior.

SUMMARY

Our study of sociology starts with the assumption that humans are social animals. The obvious question is, how do they become that way? In this chapter we have discussed some of the processes that sociologists feel are important and essential if we are to understand how one changes from a blob of matter into a complex, interacting social being.

The process through which this transformation occurs is called socialization. During socialization, the self is developed. The self is the individual's set of images about what he or she is. Its development is a social process; it arises out of our interpretations of others' reactions to us. Several theories were examined that describe in detail how the self is developed. Cooley's explanation involves the looking-glass self; Mead describes self-growth through significant others, the generalized other, and taking the role of the other. In Mead's view, language is a complex method of symbolic communication that is essential in socialization and in development of the self.

Although the individual is a combination of biological, hereditary, and social factors, sociologists focus their studies on interaction in the social environment. The social environment is the stage or setting in which socialization and self-development take place. The emphasis throughout this chapter has been on interaction and on interpretation and internalization of others' reactions to us. The effect of the social environment on the individual is also a very subjective process. There are substantial variations in how individuals perceive, interpret, and react to their social environment. Suppose twenty people observe an accident at a busy intersection, and then each person writes a description of what happened. How many different descriptions might we get? Probably at least ten or fifteen, maybe even twenty (or more, if we have a few schizophrenics in the group). Or observe how different students react to a good or bad grade on an

ders, "Teachers' Expectations and Pupil Performance," *American Educational Research Journal* 10 (Summer 1973), pp. 203–212, which describes a replication and cites most of the other attempts and critiques up to 1973.

exam—again, there is a great variation. The effect of the social environment, then, is a very subjective and interpretive phenomenon; no two people react in exactly the same way. Differences multiply because future perceptions and interpretations are based on past perceptions and interpretations. In like manner, socialization and development of the self are building processes that take place throughout the life span.

Four readings follow that will help illustrate some of the concepts we have discussed in this chapter. In an excerpt from her book *The Story of My Life*, Helen Keller, who was deaf and blind from early childhood, recalls meeting her new teacher and beginning her education. This reading illustrates how important language and symbolic communication are in the processes of socialization and self-development. The second reading is an excerpt from Malcolm X's autobiography in which he describes how some events that occurred during his early teens seemed to have a great and lasting impact on him. In the third reading, a sad story about the death of a boy, Jean Mizer illustrates socialization, agents of socialization, and the self-fulfilling prophecy. An interview with Jerome Kagan provides some cross-cultural viewpoints on child development and continues the debate on the importance of the early years of life.

Terms for Study

anticipatory socialization (35)	primary socialization (33, 39)
definition of the situation (42)	resocialization (34)
ego (37)	secondary socialization (33–34, 39)
generalized other (33, 39)	self (37–38)
I (40)	self-fulfilling prophecy (42)
id (37)	significant other (39)
labeling (44)	social interaction (32)
looking-glass self (39)	socialization (31)
me (40)	sociobiology (31)
personality (37)	superego (37)

Reading 2.1

THE STORY OF MY LIFE

HELEN KELLER

Socialization is defined as the process by which the organism becomes a social being—the learning of habits, skills, and other requirements for effective participation in social groups. Socialization is a continuing process and occurs through interaction with other humans—parents, teachers, friends.

Helen Keller was deaf and blind from early childhood. In this excerpt from one of her books, she describes the period when her new teacher first arrived and a new form of learning began to take place.

The most important day I remember in all my life is the one on which my teacher, Anne Mansfield Sullivan, came to me. I am filled with wonder when I consider the immeasurable contrasts between the two lives which it connects. It was the third of March, 1887, three months before I was seven years old.

Have you ever been at sea in a dense fog, when it seemed as if a tangible white darkness shut you in, and the great ship, tense and anxious, groped her way toward the shore with plummet and sounding-line, and you waited with beating heart for something to happen? I was like that ship before my education began, only I was without compass or sounding-line, and had no way of knowing how near the harbour was. "Light! give me light!" was the wordless cry of my soul, and the light of love shone on me in that very hour.

I felt approaching footsteps. I stretched out my hand, as I supposed to my mother. Someone took it, and I was caught up and held close in the arms of her who had come to reveal all things to me, and, more than all things else, to love me.

The morning after my teacher came she led me into her room and gave me a doll. The little blind children at the Perkins Institution had sent it and Laura Bridgman had dressed it; but I did not know this until afterward. When I had played with it a little while, Miss Sullivan slowly spelled into my hand the word "d-o-l-l." I was at once interested in this finger play and tried to imitate it. When I finally succeeded in making the letters correctly I was flushed with childish pleasure and pride. Running downstairs to my mother I held up my hand and made the letters for doll. I did not know that I was spelling a word or even that words existed; I was simply making my fingers go in monkey-like imitation. In the days that followed I learned to spell in this uncomprehending way a great many words, among them pin, hat, cup and a few verbs like sit, stand and walk. But my teacher had been with me several weeks before I understood that everything has a name.

One day, while I was playing with my new doll, Miss Sullivan put my big rag doll into my lap also, spelled "d-o-l-l" and tried to make me understand that "d-o-l-l" applied to both. Earlier in the day we had had a tussle over the words "m-u-g" and "w-a-t-e-r." Miss Sullivan had tried to impress it upon me that

From *The Story of My Life* by Helen Keller. Reprinted by permission of Doubleday & Company, Inc.

"m-u-g" is mug and that "w-a-t-e-r" is water, but I persisted in confounding the two. In despair she had dropped the subject for the time, only to renew it at the first opportunity. I became impatient at her repeated attempts and, seizing the new doll, I dashed it upon the floor. I was keenly delighted when I felt the fragments of the broken doll at my feet. Neither sorrow nor regret followed my passionate outburst. I had not loved the doll. In the still, dark world in which I lived there was no strong sentiment of tenderness. I felt my teacher sweep the fragments to one side of the hearth, and I had a sense of satisfaction that the cause of my discomfort was removed. She brought me my hat, and I knew I was going out into the warm sunshine. This thought, if a wordless sensation may be called a thought, made me hop and skip with pleasure.

We walked down the path to the well-house, attracted by the fragrance of the honeysuckle with which it was covered. Some one was drawing water and my teacher placed my hand under the spout. As the cool stream gushed over one hand she spelled into the other the word water, first slowly, then rapidly. I stood still, my whole attention fixed upon the motions of her fingers. Suddenly I felt a misty consciousness as of something forgotten—a thrill of returning thought; and somehow the mystery of language was revealed to me. I knew then that "w-a-t-e-r" meant the wonderful cool something that was flowing over my hand. That living word awakened my soul, gave it light, hope, joy, set it free! There were barriers still, it is true, but barriers that could in time be swept away.

I left the well-house eager to learn. Everything had a name, and each name gave birth to a new thought. As we returned to the house every object which I touched seemed to quiver with life. That was because I saw everything with the strange, new sight that had come to me. On entering the door I remembered the doll I had broken. I felt my way to the hearth and picked up the pieces. I tried vainly to put them together. Then my eyes filled with tears; for I realized what I had done, and for the first time I felt repentance and sorrow.

I learned a great many new words that day. I do not remember what they all were; but I do know that mother, father, sister, teacher were among them—words that were to make the world blossom for me, "like Aaron's rod, with flowers." It would have been difficult to find a happier child than I was as I lay in my crib at the close of that eventful day and lived over the joys it had brought me, and for the first time longed for a new day to come.

I recall many incidents of the summer of 1887 that followed my soul's sudden awakening. I did nothing but explore with my hands and learn the name of every object that I touched; and the more I handled things and learned their names and uses, the more joyous and confident grew my sense of kinship with the rest of the world.

When the time of daisies and buttercups came Miss Sullivan took me by the hand across the fields, where men were preparing the earth for the seed, to the banks of the Tennessee River, and there, sitting on the warm grass, I had my first lessons in the beneficence of nature. I learned how the sun and the rain make to grow out of the ground every tree that is pleasant to the sight and good for food, how birds build their nests and live and thrive from land to land, how the squirrel, the deer, the lion and every other creature finds food and shelter.

As my knowledge of things grew I felt more and more the delight of the world I was in. Long before I learned to do a sum in arithmetic or describe the shape of the earth, Miss Sullivan had taught me to find beauty in the fragrant woods, in every blade of grass, and in the curves and dimples of my baby sister's hand. She linked my earliest thoughts with nature, and made me feel that "birds and flowers and I were happy peers."

I had now the key to all language, and I was eager to learn to use it. Children who hear acquire language without any particular effort; the words that fall from others' lips they catch on the wing, as it were, delightedly, while the little deaf child must trap them by a slow and often painful process. But whatever the process, the result is wonderful. Gradually from naming an object we advance step by step until we have traversed the vast distance between our first stammered syllable and the sweep of thought in a line of Shakespeare.

At first, when my teacher told me about a new thing I asked very few questions. My ideas were vague, and my vocabulary was inadequate; but as my knowledge of things grew, and I learned more and more words, my field of inquiry broadened, and I would return again and again to the same subject, eager for further information. Sometimes a new word revived an image that some earlier experience had engraved on my brain.

I remember the morning that I first asked the meaning of the word, "love." This was before I knew many words. I had found a few early violets in the garden and brought them to my teacher. She tried to kiss me; but at that time I did not like to have any one kiss me except my mother. Miss Sullivan put her arm gently round me and spelled into my hand, "I love Helen."

"What is love?" I asked.

She drew me closer to her and said, "It is here," pointing to my heart, whose beats I was conscious of for the first time. Her words puzzled me very much because I did not then understand anything unless I touched it.

I smelt the violets in her hand and asked, half in words, half in signs, a question which meant, "Is love the sweetness of flowers?"

"No," said my teacher.

Again I thought. The warm sun was shining on us.

"Is this not love?" I asked, pointing in the direction from which the heat came. "Is this not love?"

It seemed to me that there could be nothing more beautiful than the sun, whose warmth makes all things grow. But Miss Sullivan shook her head, and I was greatly puzzled and disappointed. I thought it strange that my teacher could not show me love.

A day or two afterward I was stringing beads of different sizes in symmetrical groups—two large beads, three small ones, and so on. I had made many mistakes, and Miss Sullivan had pointed them out again and again with gentle patience. Finally I noticed a very obvious error in the sequence and for an instant I concentrated my attention on the lesson and tried to think how I should have arranged the beads. Miss Sullivan touched my forehead and spelled with decided emphasis, "Think."

In a flash I knew that the word was the name of the process that was going on in my head. This was my first conscious perception of an abstract idea.

For a long time I was still—I was not thinking of the beads in my lap, but trying to find a meaning for "love" in the light of this new idea. The sun had been under a cloud all day, and there had been brief showers; but suddenly the sun broke forth in all its southern splendour.

Again I asked my teacher, "Is this not love?"

"Love is something like the clouds that were in the sky before the sun came out," she replied. Then in simpler words than these, which at that time I could not have understood, she explained: "You cannot touch the clouds, you know; but you feel the rain and know how glad the flowers and the thirsty earth are to have it after a hot day. You cannot touch love either; but you feel the sweetness that it pours into everything. Without love you would not be happy or want to play."

The beautiful truth burst upon my mind—I felt that there were invisible lines stretched between my spirit and the spirits of others.

Questions 2.1

1. Without language and communication, socialization cannot take place. Discuss.
2. What skills were developed by Helen Keller during the period discussed in this article? Could she have learned these skills without the help of others? Is the same true for a person who doesn't have the handicaps that Helen Keller had?

Reading 2.2

MASCOT

MALCOLM X

Socialization involves many things. Part of it is learning that you are male or female, short or tall, black or white; a major part is learning how people react to you *because* you are male or female, short or tall, black or white. These reactions and interpretations become an important part of the self. Many people probably do not recall the stage in the socialization process when they became aware of their sex or race. In order to remember, one must be very perceptive, and the new learning must be so unique or unexpected that it creates a lasting impression. In this excerpt from his autobiography, Malcolm X recalls learning what it means to be black in America.

. . . They told me I was going to go to a reform school. I was still thirteen years old.

But first I was going to the detention home. It was in Mason, Michigan, about twelve miles from Lansing. The detention home was where all the "bad"

boys and girls from Ingham County were held, on their way to reform school—
waiting for their hearings.

The white state man was a Mr. Maynard Allen. He was nicer to me than
most of the state Welfare people had been. He even had consoling words for the
Gohannas and Mrs. Adcock and Big Boy; all of them were crying. But I wasn't.
With the few clothes I owned stuffed into a box, we rode in his car to Mason. He
talked as he drove along, saying that my school marks showed that if I would
just straighten up, I could make something of myself. He said that reform
school had the wrong reputation; he talked about what the word "reform"
meant—to change and become better. He said the school was really a place
where boys like me could have time to see their mistakes and start a new life
and become somebody everyone would be proud of. And he told me that the
lady in charge of the detention home, a Mrs. Swerlin, and her husband were
very good people.

They were good people. Mrs. Swerlin was bigger than her husband, I remember, a big, buxom, robust, laughing woman, and Mr. Swerlin was thin, with
black hair, and a black mustache and a red face, quiet and polite, even to me.

They liked me right away, too. Mrs. Swerlin showed me to my room, my
own room—the first in my life. It was in one of those huge dormitory-like buildings where kids in detention were kept in those days—and still are in most
places. I discovered next, with surprise, that I was allowed to eat with the
Swerlins. It was the first time I'd eaten with white people—at least with grown
white people—since the Seventh Day Adventist country meetings. It wasn't my
own exclusive privilege, of course. Except for the very troublesome boys and
girls at the detention home, who were kept locked up—those who had run away
and been caught and brought back, or something like that—all of us ate with
the Swerlins sitting at the head of the long tables.

They had a white cook-helper, I recall—Lucille Lathrop. (It amazes me
how these names come back, from a time I haven't thought about for more than
twenty years.) Lucille treated me well, too. Her husband's name was Duane
Lathrop. He worked somewhere else, but he stayed there at the detention home
on the weekends with Lucille.

I noticed again how white people smelled different from us, and how their
food tasted different, not seasoned like Negro cooking. I began to sweep and
mop and dust around in the Swerlins' house, as I had done with Big Boy at the
Gohannas'.

They all liked my attitude, and it was out of their liking for me that I soon
became accepted by them—as a mascot, I know now. They would talk about
anything and everything with me standing right there hearing them, the same
way people would talk freely in front of a pet canary. They would even talk
about me, or about "niggers," as though I wasn't there, as if I wouldn't understand what the word meant. A hundred times a day, they used the word "nigger." I suppose that in their own minds, they meant no harm; in fact they
probably meant well. It was the same with the cook, Lucille, and her husband,
Duane. I remember one day when Mr. Swerlin, as nice as he was, came in from
Lansing, where he had been through the Negro section, and said to Mrs.
Swerlin right in front of me, "I just can't see how those niggers can be so happy

and be so poor." He talked about how they lived in shacks, but had those big, shining cars out front.

And Mrs. Swerlin said, me standing right there, "Niggers are just that way. . . ." That scene always stayed with me.

It was the same with the other white people, most of them local politicians, when they would come visiting the Swerlins. One of their favorite parlor topics was "niggers." One of them was the judge who was in charge of me in Lansing. He was a close friend of the Swerlins. He would ask about me when he came, and they would call me in, and he would look me up and down, his expression approving, like he was examining a fine colt, or a pedigreed pup. I knew they must have told him how I acted and how I worked.

What I am trying to say is that it just never dawned upon them that I could understand, that I wasn't a pet, but a human being. They didn't give me credit for having the same sensitivity, intellect, and understanding that they would have been ready and willing to recognize in a white boy in my position. But it has historically been the case with white people, in their regard for black people, that even though we might be <u>with</u> them, we weren't considered <u>of</u> them. Even though they appeared to have opened the door, it was still closed. Thus they never did really see <u>me</u>.

This is the sort of <u>kindly</u> condescension which I try to clarify today, to these integration-hungry Negroes, about their "liberal" white friends, these so-called "good white people"—most of them anyway. I don't care how nice one is to you; the thing you must always remember is that almost never does he really see you as he sees himself, as he sees his own kind. He may stand with you through thin, but not thick; when the chips are down, you'll find that as fixed in him as his bone structure is his sometimes subconscious conviction that he's better than anybody black.

But I was no more than vaguely aware of anything like that in my detention-home years. I did my little chores around the house, and everything was fine. And each week-end, they didn't mind my catching a ride over to Lansing for the afternoon or evening. If I wasn't old enough, I sure was big enough by then, and nobody ever questioned my hanging out, even at night, in the streets of the Negro section.

I was growing up to be even bigger than Wilfred and Philbert, who had begun to meet girls at the school dances, and other places, and introduced me to a few. But the ones who seemed to like me, I didn't go for—and vice versa. I couldn't dance a lick, anyway, and I couldn't see squandering my few dimes on girls. So mostly I pleasured myself these Saturday nights by gawking around the Negro bars and restaurants. The jukeboxes were wailing Erskine Hawkins' "Tuxedo Junction," Slim and Slam's "Flatfoot Floogie," things like that. Sometimes, big bands from New York, out touring the one-night stands in the sticks, would play for big dances in Lansing. Everybody with legs would come out to see any performer who bore the magic name "New York." Which is how I first heard Lucky Thompson and Milt Jackson, both of whom I later got to know well in Harlem.

Many youngsters from the detention home, when their dates came up, went off to the reform school. But when mine came up—two or three times—it was always ignored. I saw new youngsters arrive and leave. I was glad and grateful. I knew it was Mrs. Swerlin's doing. I didn't want to leave.

She finally told me one day that I was going to be entered in Mason Junior High School. It was the only school in town. No ward of the detention home had ever gone to school there, at least while still a ward. So I entered their seventh grade. The only other Negroes there were some of the Lyons children, younger than I was, in the lower grades. The Lyons and I, as it happened, were the town's only Negroes. They were, as Negroes, very much respected. Mr. Lyons was a smart, hardworking man, and Mrs. Lyons was a very good woman. She and my mother, I had heard my mother say, were two of the four West Indians in that whole section of Michigan.

Some of the white kids at school, I found, were even friendlier than some of those in Lansing had been. Though some, including the teachers, called me "nigger," it was easy to see that they didn't mean any more harm by it than the Swerlins. As the "nigger" of my class, I was in fact extremely popular—I suppose partly because I was kind of a novelty. I was in demand, I had top priority. But I also benefited from the special prestige of having the seal of approval from that Very Important Woman about the town of Mason, Mrs. Swerlin. Nobody in Mason would have dreamed of getting on the wrong side of her. It became hard for me to get through a school day without someone after me to join this or head up that—the debating society, the Junior High basketball team, or some other extracurricular activity. I never turned them down.

And I hadn't been in the school long when Mrs. Swerlin, knowing I could use spending money of my own, got me a job after school washing the dishes in a local restaurant. My boss there was the father of a white classmate whom I spent a lot of time with. His family lived over the restaurant. It was fine working there. Every Friday night when I got paid, I'd feel at least ten feet tall. I forget how much I made, but it seemed like a lot. It was the first time I'd ever had any money to speak of, all my own, in my whole life. As soon as I could afford it, I bought a green suit and some shoes, and at school I'd buy treats for the others in my class—at least as much as any of them did for me.

English and history were the subjects I liked most. My English teacher, I recall—a Mr. Ostrowski—was always giving advice about how to become something in life. The one thing I didn't like about history class was that the teacher, Mr. Williams, was a great one for "nigger" jokes. One day during my first week at school, I walked into the room and he started singing to the class, as a joke, " 'Way down yonder in the cotton field, some folks say that a nigger won't steal." Very funny. I liked history, but I never thereafter had much liking for Mr. Williams. Later, I remember, we came to the textbook section on Negro history. It was exactly one paragraph long. Mr. Williams laughed through it practically in a single breath, reading aloud how the Negroes had been slaves and then were freed, and how they were usually lazy and dumb and shiftless. He added, I remember, an anthropological footnote on his own, telling us between laughs how Negroes' feet were "so big that when they walk, they don't leave tracks, they leave a hole in the ground."

. . . Then, in the second semester of the seventh grade, I was elected class president. It surprised me even more than other people. But I can see now why the class might have done it. My grades were among the highest in the school. I

was unique in my class, like a pink poodle. And I was proud; I'm not going to say I wasn't. In fact, by then, I didn't really have much feeling about being a Negro, because I was trying so hard, in every way I could, to be white. Which is why I am spending much of my life today telling the American black man that he's wasting his time straining to "integrate." I know from personal experience. I tried hard enough. . . .

That summer of 1940, in Lansing, I caught the Greyhound bus for Boston with my cardboard suitcase, and wearing my green suit. If someone had hung a sign, "hick," around my neck, I couldn't have looked much more obvious. They didn't have the turnpikes then; the bus stopped at what seemed every corner and cowpatch. From my seat in—you guessed it—the back of the bus, I gawked out of the window at white man's America rolling past for what seemed a month, but must have been only a day and a half.

When we finally arrived, Ella met me at the terminal and took me home. The house was on Waumbeck Street in the Sugar Hill section of Roxbury, the Harlem of Boston. I met Ella's second husband, Frank, who was now a soldier; and her brother Earl, the singer who called himself Jimmy Carleton; and Mary, who was very different from her older sister. It's funny how I seemed to think of Mary as Ella's sister, instead of her being, just as Ella is, my own half-sister. It's probably because Ella and I always were much closer as basic types; we're dominant people, and Mary has always been mild and quiet, almost shy.

Ella was busily involved in dozens of things. She belonged to I don't know how many different clubs; she was a leading light of local so-called "black society." I saw and met a hundred black people there whose big-city talk and ways left my mouth hanging open.

I couldn't have feigned indifference if I had tried to. People talked casually about Chicago, Detroit, New York. I didn't know the world contained as many Negroes as I saw thronging downtown Roxbury at night, especially on Saturdays. Neon lights, nightclubs, poolhalls, bars, the cars they drove! Restaurants made the streets smell—rich, greasy, down-home black cooking! Jukeboxes blared Erskine Hawkins, Duke Ellington, Cootie Williams, dozens of others. If somebody had told me then that some day I'd know them all personally, I'd have found it hard to believe. The biggest bands, like these, played at the Roseland State Ballroom, on Boston's Massachusetts Avenue—one night for Negroes, the next night for whites.

I saw for the first time occasional black-white couples strolling around arm in arm. And on Sundays, when Ella, Mary, or somebody took me to church, I saw churches for black people such as I had never seen. They were many times finer than the white church I had attended back in Mason, Michigan. There, the white people just sat and worshiped with words; but the Boston Negroes, like all other Negroes I had ever seen at church, threw their souls and bodies wholly into worship.

Two or three times, I wrote letters to Wilfred intended for everybody back in Lansing. I said I'd try to describe it when I got back.

But I found I couldn't.

My restlessness with Mason—and for the first time in my life a restlessness with being around white people—began as soon as I got back home and entered eighth grade.

I continued to think constantly about all that I had seen in Boston, and about the way I had felt there. I know now that it was the sense of being a real part of a mass of my own kind for the first time.

The white people—classmates, the Swerlins, the people at the restaurant where I worked—noticed the change. They said, "You're acting so strange. You don't seem like yourself, Malcolm. What's the matter?"

I kept close to the top of the class, though. The top-most scholastic standing, I remember, kept shifting between me, a girl named Audrey Slaugh, and a boy named Jimmy Cotton.

It went on that way, as I became increasingly restless and disturbed through the first semester. And then one day, just about when those of us who had passed were about to move up to 8-A, from which we would enter high school the next year something happened which was to become the first major turning point of my life.

Somehow, I happened to be alone in the classroom with Mr. Ostrowski, my English teacher. He was a tall, rather reddish white man and he had a thick mustache. I had gotten some of my best marks under him, and he had always made me feel that he liked me. He was, as I have mentioned, a natural-born "advisor," about what you ought to read, to do, or think—about any and everything. We used to make unkind jokes about him: why was he teaching in Mason instead of somewhere else, getting for himself some of the "success in life" that he kept telling us how to get?

I know that he probably meant well in what he happened to advise me that day. I doubt that he meant any harm. It was just in his nature as an American white man. I was one of his top students, one of the school's top students— but all he could see for me was the kind of future "in your place" that almost all white people see for black people.

He told me, "Malcolm, you ought to be thinking about a career. Have you been giving it thought?"

The truth is, I hadn't. I never had figured out why I told him, "Well, yes, sir, I've been thinking I'd like to be a lawyer." Lansing certainly had no Negro lawyers—or doctors either—in those days, to hold up an image I might have aspired to. All I really knew for certain was that a lawyer didn't wash dishes, as I was doing.

Mr. Ostrowski looked surprised, I remember, and leaned back in his chair and clasped his hands behind his head. He kind of half-smiled and said, "Malcolm, one of life's first needs is for us to be realistic. Don't misunderstand me, now. We all here like you, you know that. But you've got to be realistic about being a nigger. A lawyer—that's no realistic goal for a nigger. You need to think about something you can be. You're good with your hands—making things. Everybody admires your carpentry shop work. Why don't you plan on carpentry? People like you as a person—you'd get all kinds of work."

The more I thought afterwards about what he said, the more uneasy it made me. It just kept treading around in my mind.

What made it really begin to disturb me was Mr. Ostrowski's advice to others in my class—all of them white. Most of them told him they were planning to become farmers. But those who wanted to strike out on their own, to try something new, he had encouraged. Some, mostly girls, wanted to be teachers.

A few wanted other professions, such as one boy who wanted to become a county agent; another, a veterinarian; and one girl wanted to be a nurse. They all reported that Mr. Ostrowski had encouraged what they had wanted. Yet nearly none of them had earned marks equal to mine.

It was a surprising thing that I had never thought of it that way before, but I realized that whatever I wasn't, I was smarter than nearly all of those white kids. But apparently I was still not intelligent enough, in their eyes, to become whatever I wanted to be.

It was then that I began to change—inside.

I drew away from white people. I came to class, and I answered when called upon. It became a physical strain simply to sit in Mr. Ostrowski's class.

Where "nigger" had slipped off my back before, whenever I heard it now, I stopped and looked at whoever said it. And they looked surprised that I did.

I quit hearing so much "nigger" and "What's wrong?"—which was the way I wanted it. Nobody, including the teachers, could decide what had come over me. I knew I was being discussed.

In a few more weeks, it was that way, too, at the restaurant where I worked washing dishes, and at the Swerlins'....

Questions 2.2

1. Malcolm X believes he was treated as a "mascot." What does he mean by this? Why was he treated this way? Discuss.
2. Outline the important aspects of socialization that occurred during the period described by Malcolm X. Who were the socialization agents in this section?
3. Review Chapter 2, and using examples from Malcolm X, illustrate development of the self using Cooley's and Mead's theories.

Reading 2.3

CIPHER IN THE SNOW

JEAN E. MIZER

Socialization and development of self are interactive processes that are critically important in the growth and future of every individual. Seldom, however, are these processes so graphically and dramatically displayed as they are in this reading. Jean Mizer was a school teacher in Idaho when she wrote this memoir of a personal experience.

It started with tragedy on a biting cold February morning. I was driving behind the Milford Corners bus as I did most snowy mornings on my way to school. It veered and stopped short at the hotel, which it had no business doing,

Reprinted from the November 1964 issue of *NEA Journal* by permission of the National Education Association and the author.

and I was annoyed as I had to come to an unexpected stop. A boy lurched out of the bus, reeled, stumbled, and collapsed on the snowbank at the curb. The bus driver and I reached him at the same moment. His thin, hollow face was white even against the snow.

"He's dead," the driver whispered.

I didn't register for a minute. I glanced quickly at the scared young faces staring down at us from the school bus. "A doctor! Quick! I'll phone from the hotel. . . ."

"No use. I tell you he's dead." The driver looked down at the boy's still form. "He never even said he felt bad," he muttered, "just tapped me on the shoulder and said, real quiet, 'I'm sorry. I have to get off at the hotel.' That's all. Polite and apologizing like."

At school, the giggling, shuffling morning noise quieted as the news went down the halls. I passed a huddle of girls. "Who was it? Who dropped dead on the way to school?" I heard one of them half-whisper.

"Don't know his name; some kid from Milford Corners," was the reply.

It was like that in the faculty room and the principal's office. "I'd appreci-ate your going out to tell the parents," the principal told me. "They haven't a phone and, anyway, somebody from school should go there in person. I'll cover your classes."

"Why me?" I asked. "Wouldn't it be better if you did it?"

"I didn't know the boy," the principal admitted levelly. "And in last year's sophomore personalities column I note that you were listed as his favorite teacher."

I drove through the snow and cold down the bad canyon road to the Evans place and thought about the boy, Cliff Evans. His favorite teacher! I thought. He hasn't spoken two words to me in two years! I could see him in my mind's eye all right, sitting back there in the last seat in my afternoon literature class. He came in the room by himself and left by himself. "Cliff Evans," I muttered to myself, "a boy who never talked." I thought a minute. "A boy who never smiled. I never saw him smile once."

The big ranch kitchen was clean and warm. I blurted out my news some-how. Mrs. Evans reached blindly toward a chair. "He never said anything about bein' ailing."

His step-father snorted. "He ain't said nothin' about anything since I moved in here."

Mrs. Evans pushed a pan to the back of the stove and began to untie her apron. "Now hold on," her husband snapped. "I got to have breakfast before I go to town. Nothin' we can do now anyway. If Cliff hadn't been so dumb, he'd have told us he didn't feel good."

After school I sat in the office and stared bleakly at the records spread out before me. I was to close the file and write the obituary for the school paper. The almost bare sheets mocked the effort. Cliff Evans, white, never legally adopted by step-father, five young half-brothers and sisters. These meager strands of information and the list of D grades were all the records had to offer.

Cliff Evans had silently come in the school door in the mornings and gone out the school door in the evenings, and that was all. He had never belonged to *a club. He had never played on a team. He had never held an office. As far as I could tell he had never done one happy, noisy kid thing. He had never been anybody at all.*

How do you go about making a boy into a zero? The grade school records showed me. The first and second grade teachers' annotations read "sweet, shy child"; "timid but eager." Then the third grade note had opened the attack. Some teacher had written in a good, firm hand, "Cliff won't talk. Uncooperative. Slow learner." The other academic sheep had followed with "dull"; "slow-witted"; "low I.Q." They became correct. The boy's I.Q. score in the ninth grade was listed at 83. But his I.Q. in the third grade had been 106. The score didn't go under 100 until the seventh grade. Even shy, timid, sweet children have resilience. It takes time to break them.

I stomped to the typewriter and wrote a savage report pointing out what education had done to Cliff Evans. I slapped a copy on the principal's desk and another in the sad, dog-eared file. I banged the typewriter and slammed the file and crashed the door shut, but I didn't feel much better. A little boy kept walking after me, a little boy with a peaked, pale face; a skinny body in faded jeans; and big eyes that had looked and searched for a long time and then had become veiled.

I could guess how many times he'd been chosen last to play sides in a game, how many whispered child conversations had excluded him, how many times he hadn't been asked. I could see and hear the faces and voices that said over and over, "You're dumb. You're dumb. You're nothing, Cliff Evans."

A child is a believing creature. Cliff undoubtedly believed them. Suddenly it seemed clear to me: When finally there was nothing left at all for Cliff Evans, he collapsed on a snowbank and went away. The doctor might list "heart failure" as the cause of death, but that wouldn't change my mind.

We couldn't find ten students in the school who had known Cliff well enough to attend the funeral as his friends. So the student body officers and a committee from the junior class went as a group to the church, being politely sad. I attended the services with them, and sat through it with a lump of cold lead in my chest and a big resolve growing through me.

I've never forgotten Cliff Evans nor that resolve. He has been my challenge year after year, class after class. I look up and down the rows carefully each September at the unfamiliar faces. I look for veiled eyes or bodies scrouged into a seat in an alien world. "Look, kids," I say silently, "I may not do anything else for you this year, but not one of you is going to come out of here a nobody. I'll work or fight to the bitter end doing battle with society and the school board, but I won't have one of you coming out of here thinking himself into a zero."

Most of the time—not always, but most of the time—I've succeeded.

Questions 2.3

1. How does the self-fulfilling prophecy apply in this situation?
2. Who were the agents of socialization in this story? Why did they define Cliff Evans as they did?

Reading 2.4

A CONVERSATION WITH JEROME KAGAN

SATURDAY REVIEW

The importance of the first year or two of life in determining intelligence and learning capacity is emphasized by numerous experts, including Freud, Piaget, and many learning theorists. Jerome Kagan believed it, too, until he discovered a village in Guatemala in which the children broke all the rules of development. What follows is an interview with Kagan by the editors of *Saturday Review* on his research. Jerome Kagan is a professor of human development at Harvard University.

SR   *What happened in Guatemala to make you reverse your thinking?*
Kagan   *I found myself in a thirteenth-century, pre-Columbian village, located on the shores of Lake Atitlan. I saw 850 Indians, poor, exploited, alienated, bitter, sick. I saw infants in the first years of their lives completely isolated in their homes, because parents believe that sun and dust and air or the gazes of either pregnant women or men fresh with perspiration from the field will cause illness. It's the evil-eye belief. So the infants are kept in the hut. Now these are bamboo huts, and there are no windows, so the light level in this hut at high noon in a perfectly azure sky is what it should be at dusk. Very dark. Although parents love their children—mothers nurse on demand and hold their infants close to their bodies—they don't talk or interact with them. And there are no toys. So at one and one-half years of age, you have a very retarded child.*
SR   *What are the children like?*
Kagan   *Not only are they quiet, somber, motorically passive, and extremely fearful, but on tests of maturational and intellectual development, they are four or five months behind American children.*
SR   *What kinds of tests do you use?*
Kagan   *Here's an example of a maturational test. Take a child nine months of age, cover an object with a cloth, and then, through sleight of hand, remove the object. We know from Piaget's work that if he pulls off the cloth and the object's not there, he shows surprise, indicating that he knows the object should be there. That ability should occur somewhere in the last third of the first year. None of the Guatemalan babies showed this until 18 months of age. We also know that babies in the Western world become frightened of strangers at about eight months. It's called "stranger anxiety." You won't get that [in Guatemala] until the middle of the second year. In the Western world children begin to talk about 12 and 18 months. The Guatemalan kids don't talk until about two and a half to three years. If I had seen infants like the Guatemalans in America prior to my experience, I would have gotten very upset, called the police, had the children removed, and begun to make gloomy statements about the fact that it was all over for these children.*
SR   *But they do recover.*

Kagan   *That's the paradox. The 11-year-olds in this Guatemalan village are beautiful. They're gay, alert, active, affective, just like 11-year-olds in the United States. They're* more *impressive than Americans in a set of "culture-fair" tests—where the words and the materials are familiar. For example, we asked them, "What is brown, hard, and found near the shore of the lake?" And they'd say, "a wharf." They have no problem with this. In reasoning, memory, inference, deduction, and perception, these children at 11—who, we must assume, were "ghosts" as infants—had recovered. Therefore, one must conclude that the first two years of life do not inexorably doom you to retardation and that there's much more potential for recovery than Western psychologists have surmised, including me. I didn't go to Guatemala to prove this; I found it a complete surprise.*

SR   *Don't the experiments that Harry Harlow [a psychologist at the University of Wisconsin] conducted with monkeys contradict that conclusion?*

Kagan   *They did until last year, when Harlow published a very important report. He took monkeys and put them in isolation for six months, and they emerged with the expected bizarre, abnormal, crazy behavior. But this time he placed them with normal infant female monkeys three months younger than themselves for 26 weeks (seven months). He reports that after seven months they could not be distinguished from normal monkeys. If we can do this in seven months with a creature less complex than we, then certainly it does not require an enormous stretch of imagination to believe that in nine years a human infant, treated less bizarrely, can recover.*

SR   *Any human studies to support your findings?*

Kagan   *Freda Rebelsky spent several years in eastern Holland, where there is a middle-class, stable, nuclear family arrangement. In this small part of this very small country, it's local custom to isolate a child for the first ten months. He's put in a room outside the house; he's tightly bound—no mobiles, no toys, and minimal interaction. Like our Guatemalan children. He emerges at one year absolutely retarded, but at five years of age he's fully recovered.*

SR   *But what about René Spitz's [a professor of psychiatry at the University of Colorado] observations?*

Kagan   *Spitz made his observations on South American children in an orphanage. He saw ghostlike (what he called "marasmic") children much like the ones I saw. They lacked both stimulation and affection, so he made the same mistake many analysts have made and concluded their retardation was due to lack of affection. It's not affection, because my infants in San Marcos are on their mothers' bodies three-quarters of the day, and they get lots of physical holding, lots of skin contact. So it's not the love, but the input, that's important.*

SR   *If you kept the infant or the monkey deprived for a longer period of time, would there be permanent effects?*

Kagan   *We don't know. I am not saying that there is no treatment you can give a child from which he cannot recover. That is obviously too strong. We do have extreme case-history reports: for instance, a mother locked her kid up in a closet for six years. He emerged mute but still managed to learn language later. But I'm trying to be a reasonably cautious person. What I can say with confidence—and had I not had this experience, I would have resisted it—is that an*

abnormal experience in the first two years of life in no way affects basic intellectual functions or the ability to be affectively normal—to experience gaiety
and sadness, guilt and shame.

SR   *What implications do you see for American schools?*

Kagan   I think my work suggests we've got to stop the very early, and I think,
premature rank-ordering of children in grades one, two, and three. We decide
too soon. Poor children enter the school system (a) with less motivation, because they see less value in intellectual activity, and (b) one or two years behind
in the emergence of what I call executive-cognitive functions (what Piaget
would call concrete operational thinking). They are going to get there, but they
are a year or two behind. We arbitrarily decide that age seven is when the race
starts, so you have a larger proportion of poor than of privileged children who
are not yet ready for school instruction. And then we classify them, pre-
maturely. Let's use the example of puberty. Suppose we decided that fertility
was important in our society and that fertility should occur at age 13. Then if
you're not fertile at 13, we conclude that you are never going to be fertile, and
we give you a different kind of life. It's illogical, because that 13-year-old who is
not fertile now will be next year.

SR   *In other words, learning does not follow the same pattern in every child.*

Kagan   Yes. We used to think that all learning was continuous—like a "freight
train." There is a series of closely connected cars: you start at car one and do
certain things; then you jump to car two, and you carry your baggage with you.
But now let me substitute an analogy that makes more sense: development as a
series of lily pads. I choose that because lily pads are farther apart, because
each child dumps a lot of baggage in traversing the lily pads (he doesn't have to
carry everything with him), and because he can skip some of the lily pads.
American psychologists have surmised that you could never walk unless you
crawled. Now we know that is false. I could prevent a child from crawling—
bind him up until he was two and then unbind him—and we know he would
walk. He wouldn't have to crawl. Now maybe that analogy holds for a lot more
in mental development than we have surmised.

SR   *How has the public reacted to your rather optimistic conclusions?*

Kagan   What I say is often misunderstood. When I say kids can catch up, people say that can't be right, because they know that a poor child always remains
retarded relative to a middle-class child in the school system. But these people—most Americans—are confusing relative and absolute standards. Absolute
retardation refers to a lack of certain fundamental motor, affective, and intellectual skills that are basic to our species. They include crawling, walking,
standing, speaking, inference, and reasoning. Now if a child isn't walking by
three, he is absolutely retarded. If a child cannot remember four numbers
when he is ten years old, he is absolutely retarded.

SR   *Then what is "relative retardation"?*

Kagan   If kids don't have certain culturally arbitrary skills—like being able to
read—they are retarded relative to some other reference group. When we say a
Mexican-American child from a ghetto is retarded, we mean relative to that
arbitrary reference which is the middle-class child. The analogy of physical
development should make that distinction clearer. There are natural skills like

walking or running which you get better at each year; if a child of ten cannot run as fast as a three-year-old, we worry about it. So it makes sense to say that this ten-year-old is physically retarded. But would we ever say that a ten-year-old who can't play hockey is retarded? Well, when it comes to intellectual skills, that's exactly what we do; we say if this child can't multiply, he is retarded. But multiplication is like hockey; no child's going to know how to multiply unless you teach him how to multiply. See the mistake we make? In the physical area we never confuse relative with absolute retardation. But in the mental area we do.

SR *Given the vast implications of your study, where do you plan to go from here?*

Kagan *I want to see schools begin to serve the needs of society. Ancient Sparta needed warriors, Athens needed a sense of the hero, the ancient Hebrews needed knowledge of the Testament, nineteenth-century Americans needed managers and technicians—and the schools responded beautifully in each case by providing the kind of people the society needed. What do we need now? I believe that we need to restore faith, honesty, humanity. And I am suggesting in deep seriousness that we must, in the school, begin to reward these traits as the Spartans rewarded physical fitness. I want children rank-ordered on the basis of humanism as we rank-order on the basis of reading and mathematics. I'm dead serious. When I was a kid, deportment was always a grade. In a funny way, I want that, but instead of deportment, I want him graded on humanism: How kind is he? How nurturant is he?*

SR *But aren't we getting back then to the same problem of sorting?*

Kagan *Every society must sort its children according to the traits it values. We will never get away from that. A society needs a set of people whom it can trust in and give responsibility to for the management of its capital and resources, for the health of its people, the legal prerogatives of its people, the wars of its people. The function of the school system is in fact to prepare this class.*

Questions 2.4

1. Isolation in the early years of life leads to retardation. Discuss.
2. Can socialization occur without interaction, or is some kind of social interaction actually occurring between the Guatemalan infants and their parents?
3. Different socialization patterns in different societies still result in normal, nonretarded children. Discuss.
4. If it is true that learning does not follow the same pattern in every child, what implications does this have for our school systems?

3

Norms, Roles, Culture

A sociology instructor is lecturing to a class of college freshmen and sophomores. At one point in her lecture, she asks a student to help her illustrate a point by standing up. The student is belligerent and upset at being interrupted in his reading of the school newspaper. The student replies that he would rather not help and that the teacher should ask someone else. The teacher asks the student once more to please help her with the experiment and to stand up. The student replies in a louder voice that he doesn't think much of this stupid class or the teacher, and he is not about to participate in some silly experiment. The now-angry teacher responds, "Either stand up or get out of this classroom!" The student replies, "I'm not standing up—and if you want me out of here you'll have to throw me out!" The two then glare at each other for what seems like a year.

If we were watching the scene and could take our eyes off the principal characters, we would notice that the rest of the class is behaving strangely. Nearly all appear to be very uncomfortable, many are obviously embarrassed. They are twisting and squirming and are avoiding meeting the eyes of the instructor. At the beginning of the confrontation some may have laughed nervously; now all are quiet. They act as if they are trying to deny that what is happening is actually happening. . . . Why?

SOCIETY AND SOCIAL STRUCTURE

We learned in Chapter 1 that sociology studies the origin, development, organization and functioning of human society. At its most general, the term *society* refers to human association and the existence of social relationships. This is too general for our use, however, because it suggests that any set of people interacting could be called a society. A more precise definition states that a **society** is a continuing number of people living in a specific area who are relatively organized, self-sufficient and independent, and share a common culture. Continuing means that there is some permanence to the society. The number of people can vary greatly—American society numbers more than 220 million people while there are other societies that number less than 1,000 people. By *organized* we mean that there is some systematization and structure to the patterns of social interaction. A society occupies an area; it has boundaries that separate it from other societies. In part these boundaries are what we usually think of—an ocean, a river, a mountain, or a line drawn on a map. The essential point, however, is that these are *social* boundaries—the vast majority of the social interactions of a society take place within a particular area. Finally, each society, because of its particular cultural beliefs, habits, and traditions, has certain unique characteristics that distinguish it or make it different from other societies.

As you can see, several of the terms in our definition involve matters of degree. There is often much interaction between societies, and probably no society is totally independent of others. Although interpretation will always be necessary, I think this definition should give us a reasonably good idea of what is meant by society. There are other uses of the term that don't fit our definition. Special interest groups such as professional organizations (Society for the Study of Social Problems), political groups (John Birch Society), social clubs

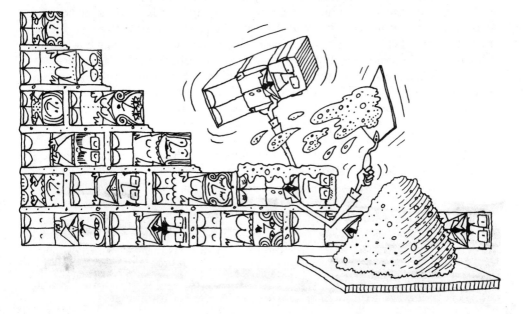

(Second Street Skateboard Society), and other groups are *not* societies in the sociological sense. And whatever it is that those people have whose pictures appear in the "society" pages of the newspapers, it isn't society. None of these groups alone constitutes a society; all of them are part of a society.

How do sociologists study human society? Let's suggest for a moment that any given society has a form, a composition, a structure. Imagine society to be like a building with many parts—wood, steel, bricks, and concrete—all somehow attached together into a coherent structure. Look at the end product and you see a five-story building, but there are actually thousands of elements that make up the whole. It is not a group of random parts, but a network, a structure. Now take society as a building. The many parts are people, and they are held together by the ways they relate to each other, their relationships to each other. The people of society, just like the steel and concrete of the building, are held together in very specific ways.

We can take the five-story building apart to examine its elements, and we can do the same with a society. As we look at the ways people relate to each other we find that these ways fit consistent patterns. The same important elements seem to appear again and again. **Social structure** refers to the network of ways people relate to each other in society. Sociologists study human society by concentrating on social structure. The important elements of social structure appear to be norm, status, role, group, and institution. Norm, status, and role will be discussed in this chapter, group and institution in later chapters.

NORMS

All societies have rules that specify what people should do in specific situations. Sociologists call these shared standards for behavior **norms**. Norms describe the accepted or required behavior for a person in a particular situation. When a person gets into a car, that person unconsciously begins to behave according to a whole set of norms relating to driving procedure. In America the driver knows that he or she should drive on the right side of the road, pass on the left, signal before turning, and so on. The norms vary from place to place, but they always exist. These shared standards for behavior allow us to predict what other people will do. Without even thinking about it or knowing him or her, I know how the driver of the car approaching me will behave. The system of norms allows us to predict what other people will do in specific situations and to pattern our own behavior accordingly.

Where do norms come from? Like much of what we discuss in this book, norms emerge through the process of social interaction. As people interact, they come to understand that certain ways of behaving are proper and acceptable, and that other ways are improper and unacceptable. These general opinions and beliefs are called **values.** Values represent broad perspectives that people carry regarding usually intangible concepts such as patriotism, progress, equality and democracy, the importance of telling the truth, and so on. Norms are based on values, but the difference is important: values are broader based, representing general perspectives, whereas norms represent specific rules for particular situations. Norms as well as values can be longstanding, born of custom and tradition, or they can be of shorter duration.

Norms take many forms, from written laws to informal agreements among group members as they try to complete a task or manage emotion and interaction between members. Superstitions, customs, and myths may act as norms. Many buildings don't have a thirteenth floor; people take care not to walk under ladders or on cracks in the sidewalk; alcohol consumption is much higher around certain holidays; and June is the month to get married (which in turn probably influences the sale of rice). Koya Azumi reports that the birth rate in Japan suddenly dropped in 1966 by half a million births from the year before, and in 1967 went back up sharply. There was no war or substantial change in the standard of living. What explained the sudden decline? Apparently a superstition related to the lunar-solar calendar which, although abandoned by the Japanese in 1872, still had a great effect on Japanese behavior. Every sixtieth year is a year of Hinoeuma, and superstition held that a girl born in that year would be of harsh temperament and prone to misfortune—she may even have difficulty finding a husband. 1966 was a year of Hinoeuma and the Japanese took no chances—they practiced careful birth control (abortion rates were also higher) rather than risk having a girl. In 1906, the previous year of Hinoeuma, modern birth control techniques were not available but the Japanese solved the problem of potentially unpleasant girl babies by falsifying the statistics. The head of household, who was responsible for registering births, likely registered late and recorded girl children born in 1906 as born in either 1905 or 1907 (according to the statistics, fewer girl babies were born in 1906 and more than would be expected in 1905 and 1907). In 1966, a more modern society with birth control didn't need to falsify statistics, but even in this modern society the power of an ancient superstition still had its effect.[1]

It is disturbing when the normative system breaks down and predictability of behavior vanishes. Norm breakdown occurs when there are conflicting sets of norms and when groups and societies change. We see norm breakdown most vividly during periods of rapid social change, such as wars or disasters. When norms cease to be effective at controlling people's behavior, we say that a state of normlessness is present. One tends to lose all sense of stability, security, and orderliness when norms break down. Imagine the consternation if we did not know what to expect of that oncoming driver—if we had *no* idea what he or she was going to do.

This may explain the strange behavior of the students in the classroom. There are norms that govern the student-teacher relationship. These norms are so obvious and ingrained that we do not even think about them. Characteristically, norms do not become apparent until they are violated. According to norms dealing with student-teacher relationships, the student will show respect for the teacher, will laugh at his or her jokes, and will generally obey the authority that the teacher represents. That is, students will respect any reasonable demands made by the teacher without resorting to mutiny. When, as in our example above, behavior is contrary to the norms, the situation becomes uncomfortable for others. Instructors who have tried this "stand up" experiment on classes (with the aid of a willing villain) report that the experience is almost as

---

[1]This study is described in "The Mysterious Drop in Japan's Birth Rate," by Koya Azumi, *Transaction* 5 (May 1968), pp. 46–48.

hard on the two of them (instructor and villain), who know it's a fake, as it is for the rest of the class, who don't know that it has been set up. Thus even planned and legitimate norm violation may be hard on individuals when done in the context of a group that is unaware of the new definitions.

Other experiments in norm violation have been devised.[2] For example, get somebody you don't know very well in a game of ticktacktoe. Invite the other person to make the first move. After he or she makes a mark, you erase it, move it to another square, and make your own mark. Act as if nothing unusual has happened. Or select a person (not a family member or very close friend) and during the course of an ordinary conversation, and without indicating that anything unusual is happening, bring your face closer to the person's until your noses are almost touching. The first experiment deals with norms concerning game playing, and the second with norms concerning spatial invasion or the appropriate distance between people. In each case, the subject will react noticeably (and possibly unpredictably) because common norms that ordinarily one doesn't even think about are suddenly being violated.

Types of Norms

Norm strength varies greatly. One way of determining the relative strength of norms is by the sanctions that the norms carry. A **sanction** is the punishment one receives for violation of a norm or the reward one receives for correct norm performance. Sanctions take a variety of forms: a look on someone's face, an "A" on an exam, a sharp word from a spouse or boss, a kind word from a parent, a traffic ticket from a police officer, a life sentence in a penitentiary. Norms that are most important to a society, that tend to be obeyed without question, and that have harsh sanctions if they are violated are called **mores.** In our society, norms dealing with taking another's life, eating human flesh, and sexual activity with one's parents are examples of mores. Mores are often traditional norms that are a part of the customs of a society—"things have always been that way." When a society feels it necessary (perhaps because increasing violations mean that the informal sanctions aren't working), mores may be translated into written law. Whether written or unwritten, the emotional force of mores is strong—they still represent the "musts" of behavior.

There are also norms dealing with what we *should* do rather than what we *must* do. These norms are less obligatory than mores, and the sanctions for violation are milder in degree. People may look at us rather strangely if we violate these norms, but they probably will not lock us up or banish us. These norms are called **folkways.**[3] Practices such as shaking hands when meeting someone or norms regulating the type of clothes one wears would be considered folkways. A student coming to class in a bathing suit and golf shoes would probably be allowed to stay in spite of the obvious violation of the folkways. At the same

---

[2]These and other examples are contained in *Studies in Ethnomethodology*, by Harold Garfinkel (Englewood Cliffs, N.J.: Prentice-Hall, 1967).

[3]The terms "folkways" and "mores" were introduced by William Graham Sumner in *Folkways* (Boston: Ginn, 1907).

time there would likely be ample private discussion of the student's character and intelligence.

A further distinction should be made between ideal norms and statistical norms. **Ideal norms** refer to what people agree *should* be done. **Statistical norms** refer to what they *actually* do. Ideal norms indicate that cheating on tests, premarital sexual intercourse, and falsifying one's income tax are wrong. However, statistical norms—what people are actually doing—would indicate that a substantial number of people are performing these activities. Often, amazingly enough, these are the same people who previously told us these things were wrong. It shouldn't surprise us that there may be quite a discrepancy between talk and action—or, "Do as I say, not as I do. . . ."

Norm Conflict

As we said earlier, norms develop out of a set of beliefs and values that people have about the way things should happen. Norms probably develop first at the group level when specific friendship groups, clubs, work groups, clans, organizations, or communities of people establish rules. Often these rules are informal and unwritten. Sometimes, if the people have sufficient power, their rules may become written in the form of laws.

Norms vary in how widely they are supported. For example, norms dealing with taking a human life, stealing property, or eating human flesh are probably looked at the same way by most people in United States society. On the other hand, since norms emerge from groups and since each group has its own interests and viewpoints, we shouldn't be at all surprised to see norm conflict— the norms of one group conflicting with the norms of another. People who have been taught the norm of not killing other people may find themselves as soldiers being trained to kill. The norms of the consumer often conflict with the norms of the manufacturer. Car owners want a vehicle that runs cheaply, looks beautiful, is safe, and won't fall apart in the first six months. The manufacturer is interested more in reducing costs per unit and cutting corners where possible. One would hope that the producers of the food you eat are as concerned about its purity and wholesomeness as you are when you eat it. Perhaps they're not, however; consider that laws and agencies (Food and Drug Administration, for example) are necessary to *force* food producers to maintain standards. So, because different groups have conflicting viewpoints and motivations, norm conflict is bound to occur.

Examples of conflict over norms are not hard to find. There seems to be almost constant conflict over norms dealing with sexual conduct. Prostitution is not unknown in our society, although it is against the law nearly everywhere. Groups upset by the existence of prostitution get together to stamp it out. Other groups get together to defend prostitution. Police agencies often don't know whether to attempt to enforce laws prohibiting prostitution or to ignore its existence. For a time, narcotics laws defined possession and use of marijuana as a serious crime. In parts of society a different set of norms existed that didn't view marijuana as dangerous and encouraged its use. The energy crisis and the related effort to conserve fuel led in 1973 and 1974 to a law lowering the speed limit to fifty-five miles per hour. Highways and cars are designed for high

speeds, and drivers are used to going faster than fifty-five, so there are problems with the law. In some areas, even with a continuing energy crisis so many
drivers ignore the speed law that enforcement has become almost impossible.

Society's laws usually reflect its mores, but sometimes they don't. As we
have said, it is natural for different segments of society to disagree on norms.
Occasionally, however, a special interest group gains enough power to manipulate laws. Also, sometimes the change in norms is rapid, and the change in laws
does not keep pace. When either of these situations occurs, laws may not reflect
the mores of society. Usually, when laws and mores are in conflict, mores will
win in the long run. The prohibition laws in the 1920s and 1930s apparently did
not reflect the mores of the country, and the laws were flagrantly violated until
they were changed. Recently, as a result of the norm conflict over marijuana
use, marijuana laws have been modified. A 1976 California law states that a
person found to be carrying less than an ounce of marijuana will be issued a
citation (similar to a traffic ticket) and will have to pay a small fine. People
carrying more than an ounce may be arrested, but penalties have been reduced
considerably. Another approach is for police to give enforcement of existing
laws low priority. This won't resolve all norm conflict, but it represents an attempt to achieve a compromise between conflicting viewpoints. It will be interesting to see what happens on highway speed limits. Will the law be changed,
will it remain, with drivers and enforcement agencies alike ignoring it, or will
driving habits (norms) gradually change to conform to the slower speeds?

STATUS AND ROLE

When students and an instructor walk into class the first day of the semester, they know without thinking what to expect of each other and how each will
behave. They know these things even though they have not seen each other before. The students know that the instructor will stand in front of the class behind a lectern, probably call roll, assign reading, and dismiss them early the
first day. The instructor knows that, unless the class is required, students will be
shopping around. They will be trying to decide whether to take this class, and
their decision will be based on course content, the viewpoint and personality of
the instructor, the amount and type of work required, or how the instructor is
known to grade.

We know these things about each other partly because of the system of
norms discussed previously. The concepts of status and role are closely related
to norms, and they play a major part in the situation described above. By **status**
we mean a position in society or in a group. There are innumerable positions
that one may occupy—teacher, student, police officer, president, football player,
father, wife, convict. Furthermore, each of us may occupy several positions at
once—teacher, handball player, father, husband, and so on. By **role** we mean
the behavior of one who occupies a particular status. As Robert Bierstedt puts
it, a role is what an individual *does* in the status he or she occupies; statuses are
occupied, roles are played.[4]

---

[4]Robert Bierstedt, *The Social Order*, 4th ed. (New York: McGraw-Hill, 1974), Chapter 9.

A set of norms surrounds each status and role. These norms, called **role requirements,** describe the behavior expected of persons holding a particular position in society. Recalling our earlier example, the behavior of the student who refused to stand up was disturbing because it was unpredictable. He was occupying the status or position of student, but the role he played—his behavior—was contrary to the expected behavior of a person in that status. His behavior was outside the limits set by the norms or role requirements.

Within the boundaries set by the role requirements, there is often extensive variation in how a role is played. On a football team, status would refer to the positions, role to the behavior of the incumbent of the position. One status would be quarterback. Role requirements of quarterbacks are generally that they call the plays, direct the team, and try to move the ball down the field. But now look at the actual performance of several quarterbacks. One passes frequently, another seldom passes but runs with the ball often, and a third does neither but usually blocks. Compare four or five of your instructors in their role behavior. Although all occupy the status of college professor, no doubt their behavior varies markedly. One paces the floor, another stays behind the podium while lecturing. One demands class discussion, the next dislikes having lectures interrupted. One has beautifully organized and prepared lectures, and another has a disorganized, stream-of-consciousness presentation put together on the way to class. Or compare the behavior of the last three Presidents of the United States. Again we see marked differences in role within a given status. These differences in behavior obviously occur because people holding the same status define the role differently. This should sound familiar because it's essentially the idea we had in mind in discussing definition of the situation in the last chapter. As a result of a particular pattern of socialization, each individual defines status and role in a particular way. Each individual brings to the situation a specific personality and a set of skills, interests, and abilities. Therefore, although each status carries with it certain role requirements, there is still variation and flexibility in actual behavior.

Role—behavior that is suited to a particular status—varies not only because of the style of a particular quarterback, college professor, or President. Roles must be seen in an *interaction* setting. While behaving, people are always socially interacting with others, and consequently their behavior adjusts to and is modified by the responses of others. This continues the viewpoint introduced in the previous chapter in which we pointed out that socialization and self-development occur through the process of social interaction. Roles we play are shaped by others' reactions to us: After comments and complaints from an unhappy class, the unprepared, stream-of-consciousness professor mentioned above may modify his or her performance. It is a common occurrence to go into a situation prepared for one sort of role only to find that in the process of the interaction, another sort of behavior is necessary.

Achieved and Ascribed Status

How do we happen to occupy the statuses that we do? Some, probably most, statuses are earned or achieved in some way, and hence these are called **achieved statuses.** Astronaut, policeman, college professor, and truck driver represent achieved statuses. Some statuses are automatically conferred on us with no effort or choice on our part. These are **ascribed statuses.** One's sex, race, and nationality are ascribed (although occasionally some changes can be made). Sometimes it is difficult to tell whether a status is ascribed or achieved. Take the student who feels forced to go to college because of the wishes of his or her parents—is the status of student ascribed or achieved? Or how about the statuses that a child inherits from his or her parents, such as political and religious affiliations—are they ascribed or achieved?

Statuses are stratified or ranked at a number of levels. Some statuses are of high rank and bring much prestige to the occupant. Doctor, board director of a large corporation, college president, author, artist, scientist, and movie star are statuses that have high value and prestige in our society. Evaluation of positions is usually determined by the requirements that one must have to fill that status—extensive education, wealth, beauty, skill, or some other extraordinary characteristic. Sometimes this ranking is based on a societal tradition that automatically ranks certain characteristics above others, such as being of a particular sex, race, or religion, or born in a particular aristocratic family. Sometimes having high ascribed status makes it easier to obtain desired achieved statuses. For example, a child born in a middle-class family (ascribed status) will have a better chance of becoming a doctor or scientist (achieved status) than will a lower-class child. Sometimes having high ascribed status is limiting, however. People who are members of royalty may find that their freedom is severely restricted. Living up to their ascribed status may mean declining to pursue a perhaps more attractive achieved status.

Role Strain and Role Conflict

Problems may occur when a person must play several roles simultaneously, or when one role requires a person to perform in several different ways. These situations are called role conflict and role strain, and they may lead to personal stress and discomfort. **Role strain** refers to the situation in which there are differing and conflicting expectations regarding one's status or position. A student may experience role strain when he compares the expectations of his parents (to study, get A's, prepare for a vocation) with the expectations of his fraternity brothers (be social, be active in fraternity affairs, be athletic). Police officers who are trained to arrest people who have committed crimes probably feel role strain when they are ordered by superiors who do not want to make a bad situation worse to stand by and watch looting take place during a riot. A typical situation on college campuses leads to role strain for young professors. Their students expect them to be good teachers, but the school tells them that keeping their jobs and getting promoted will depend on how many articles and books they publish. Doing one takes valuable time from the other— what to do?

Role conflict occurs when a person occupies several statuses or positions that have contradictory role requirements. Here there is not the confusion or disagreement about the requirements of a single role that we saw in the first case. The requirements of the roles are clearly understood—the problem is that the requirements of two or more roles are contradictory. Imagine the dilemma of a police officer invited by friends to a party where marijuana is being smoked. Police officers are trained to respond to violations of the law with the authority of their position, both on and off duty. But the officer is a normal citizen who is expected by friends—and who wants—to behave like everyone else at the party and have fun. The requirements of the two roles are clearly contradictory. Doctors seldom treat members of their own families because of the role conflict that may occur. Similarly, the football coach whose son is trying out for the team experiences conflict between the contradictory requirements of two different roles—coach and father. And finally, if we have ever marvelled at the phenomenon of the champion tennis player beating everyone in the world except her future husband, we should have recognized and sympathized with her attempt to resolve her role conflict.

OTHER CULTURES, OTHER NORMS

Normative behavior varies from one place to another. Actions that are correct and expected in one part of the world are wrong and peculiar in another part of the world. Appropriate behavior in one country is inappropriate in another. Social scientists use the concept of *culture* to understand and explain these phenomena. Before defining culture, it might be well to illustrate some aspects of culturally related behavior. There are many examples, but the following come to mind.

Every four years, writers from England and Europe flock to the United States to observe a very peculiar ritual the like of which is unknown throughout the rest of the civilized world. These strange ceremonies are written up and read about by disbelieving audiences everywhere. The tribal celebrations being enacted are called locally the "American political conventions." Strange indeed.

Imagine that you are dropped onto a small South Sea island, and your only possession is a golf club—a number 2 iron. To avoid being eaten alive you have to explain the function and purpose of the golf club to the natives. Where do you start?

As recently as 1978 two British men on a picnic with an Egyptian airline hostess in Saudi Arabia had car trouble and flagged down a police car for assistance. The two men were immediately arrested and later deported to England. The problem? Under Islamic law it is illegal for a man to be alone with a woman to whom he is not married.

Anthropologists specialize in the study of cultural patterns in different societies, especially in primitive or preliterate societies, and in their studies they have made many discoveries that seem strange to Americans. They describe a society in which very fat women are highly regarded. Women in this society spend weeks in fattening sheds where they eat starchy, fatty foods and have their bodies greased to make them more attractive. On festival day they are paraded before the king, who chooses the fattest and heaviest as his mate. Very peculiar people. But imagine for a moment that you have to explain to a member of that society the popularity in America of the various dieting and health spas where men and women spend great sums of money to lose weight.

Some Indian tribes living along the Amazon have an interesting reaction to childbirth. The woman breaks off from work in the fields and returns home for only two or three hours to give birth to the child. Meanwhile, her husband has been lying at home in a hammock, tossing about and groaning as if in great pain. Even after the birth when the woman has returned to the fields, the husband remains in bed with the baby to recuperate from his ordeal. It appears that pain is determined by something more than the nature of the wound.

Anthropologist Margaret Mead visited three primitive tribes in New Guinea and wrote about them in her book *Sex and Temperament*. First, Mead describes the mountain-dwelling Arapesh, among whom both the men and women behave in a way that Americans would describe as maternal or feminine. Both parents devote their lives to raising the children. The men are gentle, and there is complete cooperation between both sexes at all times. Next, Mead describes a cannibalistic tribe, the Mundugumor, living on a river. Here both the men and women behave in a way that Americans would describe as masculine. Men and women work in the fields together and are aggressive individualists. Finally, Mead describes the lake-dwelling Tchambuli. In this society the men behave in a manner that Americans define as feminine or maternal, and the women are masculine by our standards. The women spend the days fishing and weaving, and they have all the power. The men spend their time dancing in ceremonies, dressing and making themselves up, and in artistic endeavors. The men gossip, quarrel, and get very jealous of each other over the affections of a woman. The women's attitude toward the men is one of kindly tolerance and appreciation—they watch the shows that the men put on.

We tend to believe that certain patterns of behavior and temperament are automatically, necessarily related to sex. We may believe that to be male is to naturally behave a certain way, and that female behavior is innate as well. The point of Mead's research is that the relationship between sex and the corresponding behavior and temperament is not necessarily biological but is determined by the society in which one lives—as are body shape and size preference, taste in food or art, belief in a supreme being, nature of recreational activity, and many other characteristics.

Culture

By **culture** we mean that complex set of learned and shared beliefs, customs, skills, habits, traditions, and knowledge common to the members of a society. Culture is viewed as the social heritage of a society. According to anthropologist Clyde Kluckhohn, culture represents the distinctive way of life of a group of people, their complete design for living.[5] So, society (as we learned at the beginning of this chapter) refers to an organized, independent, continuing number of people living in a specific area, and culture refers to the learned, shared patterns of beliefs and behaviors common to that people.

---

[5]Clyde Kluckhohn, "The Study of Culture," in *The Policy Sciences*, edited by Daniel Lerner and Harold D. Lasswell (Stanford, Calif.: Stanford University Press, 1951), p. 86.

For social scientists, the concept of culture is very important. The culture is shared by the members of a society and is learned through the socialization process. In fact, the socialization process is the process whereby one learns and internalizes the norms and roles of the culture in which one lives. The culture determines for us what we will want to eat, whom we will like or hate, what we will fear (snakes and mice, but not evil spirits), how we will express our emotions, how we will dress (blue jeans and bikinis, but not turbans or saris), our manners, and how we will celebrate New Year's Eve. In a previous chapter, I mentioned that when I throw a volleyball to my son, he catches it with his hands and throws it back, but a ball thrown to a French or English child is likely to be headed or kicked back. We can now see that these are *cultural* differences. In American culture, ball sports emphasize the use of hands—catching and throwing in basketball, baseball, volleyball, and handball, for example. In France and England and many other cultures, the major sport is soccer, which emphasizes controlling the ball with one's feet and head.

All cultures differ to some extent, and yet because we are so used to our own we often forget that basic fact. The tourist is reminded of this even in countries similar to our own when he or she encounters the English driving on the wrong side of the road, the German driver approaching at a very high speed with lights flashing, Volkswagens and Porsches used as police cars, Spanish restaurants not opening for dinner until after 9:30 in the evening, French children drinking wine, or English police officers not carrying guns. The failure to anticipate and plan for cultural differences is common. Professor David Ricks has found that companies doing business in foreign countries make the same mistake. Chevrolet had trouble selling Novas in Latin American markets—*"no va"* in Spanish means "does not go." Pepsodent's promise of white teeth did not go over well in part of Southeast Asia where black, discolored teeth are a sign of prestige. "Body by Fisher" became "Corpse by Fisher" in a Belgian ad. "Come alive with Pepsi" in a German translation became "Come alive out of the grave." Some firms forgot when labeling their products that green is the color of disease in Africa and white the color of death in Japan. And a firm had difficulty selling a refrigerator to the mostly Moslem Middle East using an ad picturing the refrigerator full of food including a giant ham on the middle shelf.

The distinction is frequently made between the material and nonmaterial aspects of a culture. **Material culture** refers to the concrete things that a society creates and uses—screwdriver, house, classroom, desk, car, plane, telephone. **Nonmaterial culture** refers to the more abstract creations of a society, such as customs, laws, ideas, values, and beliefs. The nonmaterial culture would include beliefs about religion and courtship, ideas about democracy and communism, definitions of good manners, and rules for driving a car.

Certain aspects of any given culture are unique to that culture. Some striking examples of cultural diversity were shown earlier in this chapter. These differences probably emerge because of other differences that exist. Societies differ in their physical environment, in their natural resources and climate. They differ in their neighbors—how many they have and whether they are warlike or friendly. They differ in their political boundaries—some are isolated behind mountain ranges or oceans, while others are separated by no more than a line on a map. Societies differ in their history and in the values and beliefs that are important to them.

Along with diversity, however, we find similarity. Many aspects of a culture are shared with other cultures. General patterns recur frequently—a family system, the incest taboo, a system of religion. Variation in culture traits and patterns is more likely to occur in certain specific practices than in general patterns. Cultures constantly change as old traits and patterns die out and new ones are introduced through invention from within or diffusion from some other culture. Soccer is becoming popular in the United States. Many school children are playing it, a professional soccer league has been started, a soccer player won a superstar competition, and several famous international players are now playing for United States teams. Those ball-handling differences previously mentioned may disappear in a few years. Some cultures change rapidly, others slowly; but change is inevitable.

Culture and Personality

Personality and temperament vary from one culture to another. As we noted, Margaret Mead described a variety of relationships between sex and temperament in three primitive societies. Ruth Benedict, in her book *Patterns of Culture,* describes two distinct character traits she observed in her comparison of primitive societies in North America. The Zuni are described as "Apollonian" in that they are extremely self-controlled. They emphasize formality, sobriety, and inoffensiveness, they are not individualistic, and they are traditional, frowning on anything new or different. The Kwakiutl, on the other hand, are described as "Dionysian" in that they emphasize self-gratification to excess. They are wildly ceremonious and strive for ecstasy, which is achieved through complete loss of self-control. Benedict reports that dancers were sometimes tethered by four ropes so that they might not do irreparable damage to themselves in their frenzy.

David Riesman in *The Lonely Crowd* describes the effect of culture on personality in a somewhat different manner. His subject is American character, and he describes how character and personality change as other aspects within the culture change. According to Riesman, three types of social character have been dominant in American society. In earlier years the dominant type of character was *tradition-directed*. In a tradition-directed culture, behavior is carefully controlled. Routine orients and occupies the lives of everyone. Ritual, religion, and custom are dominant. New solutions are not sought, and change is very slow. Later, the *inner-directed* type of character appeared. Inner-directed people are taught early in life to have an inward focus, with emphasis on the self and its needs and gratifications. Other persons are not of crucial importance. Individuals may be internally driven toward such ideals as power and wealth; they are encouraged to set their own goals and to be on their own. Their lives are concerned with self-mastery and accomplishment. Finally and more recently, the *other-directed* type of character appeared. The chief interest for other-directed people is to be liked by other people. According to Riesman, other-directed people have built-in radar systems that search out the reactions and feelings of others so that they may adapt themselves to them. These people are more concerned with conformity, are shallower, friendlier, more unsure of themselves, and more demanding of approval from others. The peer group is all-important, as is the front that one puts up. Riesman believes that these types of character result from other changes within the culture, such as population growth or change, along with changes in economic, industrial, and agricultural techniques and urbanization. Again the major point for us is that the culture people live in plays a major part in determining who they are and how they behave, including patterns of personality and character.

Stanley Milgram designed an experiment to test cultural differences in conformity.[6] He had subjects listen to two tones and then tell him which tone was longer. Each experiment involved six subjects. Five of the subjects, however, were confederates of the experimenter. The five confederates answered first, and their decisions on the tones were heard by the real subject, who answered last. The confederates were instructed to give wrong answers on about half the trials. What does the subject (number 6) do when he hears the five others respond one way and he hears the tones another way? The subject is faced with the clear choice of being independent and giving the right answer regardless of what the others say, or conforming and going along with the group. Milgram tried his experiment on one hundred French students in Paris and one hundred Norwegian students in Oslo. He found that the Norwegians were more conforming, the French more independent. The differences weren't large, but they were consistent. Through a number of trials under varied conditions the Norwegians voted with the group more often than did the French. By way of explanation, Milgram describes Norwegian society as highly cohesive. The Norwegian tends to identify with the group and has a strong sense of social responsibility. The French, on the other hand, show much less consensus in their social and political life and more of a tradition of dissent and critical argument. Milgram's research demonstrates cultural differences in personality characteristics between what many would consider to be very similar nationality groups.

American males have one of the highest heart-disease rates in the world. By contrast, Japanese males have one of the lowest rates. There is obviously a cultural factor at work here, but which cultural factor is it? For years scientists thought the explanation to be diet. The Japanese diet of fish and rice is much lower in cholesterol than is the American diet of meat and dairy products. However, a nine-year study completed in 1975 of 4,000 Japanese-Americans living in this country found another cultural factor to be the culprit.[7] The key turned out to be *lifestyle*. The Japanese living in the United States who maintained their traditional lifestyle—downplaying individual competition and accepting their place in family and society—had low heart-attack rates *regardless* of what they ate, how much they smoked, their blood pressure, or their weight. Those Japanese who adopted the American lifestyle (or personality) and became impatient, aggressive, hard driving, competitive go-getters were five times as likely

---

[6]For a more complete report of this study see Stanley Milgram, "Nationality and Conformity," *Scientific American* 205 (December 1961), pp. 46–51.

[7]This study was done at the School of Public Health at the University of California at Berkeley and reported in newspapers and news magazines beginning in August 1975.

to have heart attacks as those who maintained Japanese ways. The Japanese culture is apparently better able to protect the individual against the effects of pressure and stress. Unhappily, then, one's culture dictates not only how one will live, but also how and why one will die.

Ethnocentrism and Cultural Relativism

Ethnocentrism describes a type of prejudice that says simply, my culture's ways are right and other cultures' ways, if they are not like mine, are wrong. Racism (a particular race is superior to others) and sexism (one sex is superior) are related to ethnocentrism but are more specific types of prejudice. Informal practices and formal policies (who gets hired, who gets paid most) may emerge to support racism, sexism, and ethnocentrism, as well as other types of prejudice. The ethnocentric person says that the familiar is good and the unfamiliar or foreign is bad. An ethnocentric person in the United States might maintain, among other things, that non-Christians are barbarians, that Eskimo tribes practicing sexual hospitality are totally lacking in moral fiber, that anybody who eats dogmeat, horsemeat, or people is not civilized, that democracy is the only way of government, and generally that we are doing other cultures a favor when we go in and Americanize them.

Being ethnocentric to some degree is difficult to avoid. Informally, in interacting with family and friends, and formally through a kind of indoctrination in the educational system, we are frequently taught that our ways are best and, at least by implication, others' ways are less good. The mass media encourage ethnocentrism by treating the foreign and unfamiliar in terms of easily recognized stereotypes. It is probably true that enthnocentrism is impossible to escape, as it is encouraged in one way or another by most of the institutions (family, church, schools, government) in any society. This is at least partly because there are positive functions to ethnocentrism. Ethnocentrism probably leads to greater group solidarity, loyalty, and patriotism, and a certain degree of ethnocentrism may be essential for the survival of a culture. The effects of ethnocentrism are complicated—as we reinforce our belief in the goodness of our own ways, we make unfair and often derogatory judgments about the beliefs of others.

Even social scientists (who should know better) sometimes run into difficulty when studying other cultures. Since most social scientists are white middle-class representatives of the dominant culture, they may have a tendency to describe phenomena that are different—Amish, Eskimos, delinquent gangs— from the viewpoint of their own value system rather than from the viewpoint of the people they are studying. As you come across descriptions of research in this book and elsewhere, see if the research seems to have been influenced by ethnocentrism. See if you can detect ethnocentrism in the choice of topic, the way the research is done, or in the interpretation of results.

Related to ethnocentrism but opposite in meaning is the concept of **cultural relativism.** Cultural relativism suggests that each culture be judged from its own viewpoint without imposing outside standards of judgment. Behaviors, values, and beliefs are relative to the culture in which they appear. The cultural relativist believes that what is right in one society may be wrong in another and that what is considered civilized in one society may be seen as barbaric in another, but that basically judgments should not be made about the "goodness" or "badness" of traits in cultures other than one's own. The point is that although cultures share many values, beliefs, and behaviors, there are also differences between cultures. When one evaluates particular traits, one should do it from the viewpoint of the society in which they appear.

Subculture and Counterculture

Most societies, especially large, complex societies like the United States, have groups that, by their traits, beliefs, or interests, are somewhat separated and distinct from the rest of society. Members of such a group may share many of the characteristics of the dominant culture, but they have some of their own specific customs or ways as well. If these groups have definite boundaries and if their differences with the rest of society have some permanence, they are called **subcultures.** Sociologists generally use the term *subculture* to refer to groups that stand out in that some of their values and customs are different from or even at odds with those of the rest of society. The sociologist asks such questions as: How do the subculture's values differ from those of the dominant culture? Is there conflict? Does the dominant culture attempt to change the subculture? What does the subculture do to maintain its separate identity?

Some religious groups, the Amish for example, seem to qualify as subcultures. A major problem for the Amish, as for many subcultures, is to maintain their identity, even their existence, in the face of a dominant culture frequently hostile to their beliefs. The opposition of the Amish to electricity (which meant no lights at night on their horse-drawn carriages) and their opposition to any formal education beyond the eighth grade brought well-publicized confrontations with the authorities in several Midwestern states. Other examples of subcultures might include terrorist organizations, college students, Hare Krishnas, Chicanos, the Hutterites, professional baseball or football players, and sociologists.

The line of distinction between culture and subculture is not always clear. Some believe that over a period of time societies go through a melting-pot experience, in which different nationality, racial, and interest groups become so mixed and merged together that their subcultural differences cease to exist. The result of the melting-pot experience would be a society representing a mix of the remnants of former subcultures.

There is an element of conflict in some subcultural behavior, and this has led to the use of the term **counterculture.** The central element in a counterculture is opposition to or conflict with certain norms and values of the dominant culture. Campus uprisings in the 1960s were attributed to a college student counterculture which was disenchanted with certain aspects of American culture and tried to encourage change through marches and sit-ins in campus buildings. Other examples of countercultures might include youth gangs, motorcycle gangs, revolutionary groups, and terrorist organizations. *Subculture* is the more general term, *counterculture* the more specific. Countercultures are subcultures, but only those subcultures that include the element of opposition to the dominant culture could be called countercultures.

SUMMARY

In the first chapter in this section on socialization and culture, we focused on how individuals develop into social beings. In this chapter, we have turned our attention from individuals and the processes of socialization and self-development to the stage or setting where these processes take place. This setting is called the social environment, and we have introduced concepts that can be used to examine the social environment in more detail. Individuals exist in specific societies and cultures. Further, individuals will occupy numerous positions, be governed by rules, and behave in a variety of ways that are sometimes appropriate, sometimes inappropriate, but seldom unusual. The basic fact in this chapter is that individuals' membership in a given society and culture, whose patterns and customs developed long before them and will probably long outlive them, affects and explains much of their behavior.

Norms are the rules of society. We operate effectively and behavior becomes predictable because of them. Norm breakdown occasionally occurs, and when it does, it may produce crises both for society and for individuals. Norms vary in strength— "shoulds" are called folkways, "musts" are called mores. There are group norms and societal norms, and sometimes these sets of norms are in conflict. When this happens, it produces problems for people who are influenced by the conflicting sets of norms. A status is a position in society, and role describes the behavior of one who occupies a status. Norms define the boundaries for role requirements, but within these boundaries there is variation in how the role is actually performed. Statuses, which may be either achieved or ascribed, are ranked in value or prestige. When a person occupies several statuses with contradictory role requirements, role conflict may occur. Role strain may result from one who tries to play a role that includes conflicting expectations.

Society is defined as a continuing number of people living in a specific area who are relatively organized, self-sufficient, and independent, and who share a common culture. Culture is made up of the learned, shared patterns of behavior and knowledge common to a society. There are material and non-material aspects to a culture. Subcultures refer to groups that share many of the traits of the dominant culture but have some unique customs and traits as well. Our cultural and subcultural affiliations are of crucial importance in determining who we are and what we do. The concept of ethnocentrism helps us to understand the familiar tendency to assume that the world everywhere is the same as it is here, and that if by some chance it's not, it should be. On the other hand, cultural relativism is an attitude that judges each culture from its own viewpoint.

The first of the readings which follow deals with norms and culture. Edward Hall shows that how people view time and space determines how they communicate, and that these norms vary more than we might think from one culture to another. In the next reading Stanley Milgram describes what happens in an experimental situation when subjects find themselves in roles that have conflicting norms: Should they follow orders and hurt someone, or should they respond to the cries of pain and disobey orders? In his classic article, "One

Hundred Percent American," Ralph Linton deals with the problem of whether new elements of the American culture are introduced from within through invention or are adapted from other cultures through the process of diffusion.

Terms for Study

achieved status (69)	role (68)
ascribed status (70)	role conflict (70)
counterculture (77)	role requirements (69)
cultural relativism (76)	role strain (70)
culture (72)	sanction (66)
ethnocentrism (76)	social structure (64)
folkways (66)	society (63)
ideal norms (67)	statistical norms (67)
material culture (73)	status (68)
mores (66)	subculture (77)
nonmaterial culture (73)	values (64)
norms (64)	

Reading 3.1

THE HIDDEN DIMENSION

EDWARD T. HALL

Norms tell us the appropriate behavior in a specific situation. Norms may vary from one situation to another, and especially from one culture to another. Behavior that is appropriate in one culture may be an insult in another. This is true even in such seemingly innocent activities as how loud we talk, the value of smells, whether to maintain eye contact in conversation, or whether to move one's chair about. In this excerpt from his book *The Hidden Dimension*, anthropologist Edward Hall shows how different cultures vary in their use of space as compared with Americans, and how this affects patterns of communication.

GERMANS

Germans and Europeans generally will schedule fewer events in the same time than Americans will. Americans structure time tightly and are sticklers for schedules. On the other hand, Americans treat space more casually, even wastefully, in the eyes of many Europeans. Private or personal space is very important to Germans. Prisoners of war built partitions, tiny dwelling units, so that each could have his own space. German houses with balconies are arranged so that there is visual privacy; yards tend to be well fenced. German doors are thick and substantial, and kept closed in contrast to American doors, which are more flimsy and likely to be open. Germans want to know where they stand and object strenuously to people who "get out of line" or who do not obey signs such as "keep out," or "authorized personnel only." The feeling that many Americans have that Germans are overly formal can be seen in the handling of chairs. Americans tend to move their chairs about to get closer or to get a better view. In Germany, however, it is a violation of the mores to change the position of your chair. Light furniture is disliked because it seems flimsy and because people move it and thereby destroy the order of things—they intrude on one's private space. In one instance, a German newspaper editor who had moved to the United States had his visitor's chair bolted to the floor "at the proper distance" because he couldn't tolerate the American habit of adjusting the chair to the situation.

ENGLISH

In the United States we use space as a way of classifying people and activities, whereas in England it is the social system that determines who you are. In the United States, your address is an important cue to status. The Englishman, however, is born and brought up in a social system—he is Lord _____ no matter where you find him. The middle-class American feels he has a right to have his own room whereas the middle- and upper-class Englishman is brought up in a nursery shared with brothers and sisters and may never have a permanent "room of his own." Consequently, the English are puzzled by the American need for a secure place in which to work, an office. Americans working in England may become annoyed if they are not provided with what they consider appropriate work space. When the American wants to be alone he goes into a room and shuts the door—he depends on architectural features for screening. For an American to refuse to talk to someone else present in the same room, to give them the "silent treatment," is the ultimate form of rejection and a sure sign of great displeasure. The English, on the other hand, lacking rooms of their own since childhood, never developed the practice of using space as a refuge from others. Public silence in their case may represent a way of finding privacy.

Americans living in England have trouble adjusting to English ideas regarding neighbors. The fact that you live next door to a family does not entitle you to visit, borrow from, or socialize with them, or your children to play with theirs. English relationships are patterned not according to space but according to social status. In England and in Europe generally, Americans are continually accused of loud talking. Americans tend to increase volume with distance, and in many situations they do not care if they are overheard. The English *do* care and they have developed skills in beaming the voice toward the person they are talking to, carefully adjusting it so that it just barely overrides the background noise and distance. For the English to be overheard is to intrude on others. Even eye behavior in conversation varies: the English look straight at you and blink to let you know they have heard whereas the gaze of the American tends to wander about.

JAPANESE

The concept of the center that can be approached from any direction is a well-developed theme in Japanese culture. Japanese name intersections rather than the streets leading to them. How one gets from point A to point B seems almost whimsical and the "correct route" is not stressed as it is with us. Taxicab drivers have to ask local directions at police booths, not just because streets are not named but because houses are numbered in the order in which they were built. To us the walls of a house are fixed. In Japan they are semifixed. The walls are movable and rooms are multipurpose. Depending on the time of day, the room can include all outdoors or it can be shrunk in stages until all that remains is a boudoir. Some Americans feel that Japanese talk around and around the point and never get to it. Some Japanese wonder why Americans have to be so logical all the time. Crowding is distasteful to Americans, while it is less likely to bother the Japanese. Japanese feel it is congenial to sleep close together on the floor. This seems to indicate a disinterest in privacy. However, a Japanese has strong feelings against sharing a wall of his house or apartment with others. He considers his house and the zone immediately surrounding it as one structure. This free area is considered to be as much a part of the house as the roof. Traditionally, it contains a garden even though tiny, which gives the householder direct contact with nature. The Japanese garden itself, in keeping with the Japanese concept of space, is designed to be enjoyed from many points of view.

ARAB WORLD

Pushing and shoving in public places is characteristic of Middle Eastern culture. While for the American this may seem "pushy" and rude, for the Arab there is no such thing as an intrusion in public. Public means public—if A is standing on a street corner and B wants his spot, B is within his rights if he does what he can to make A uncomfortable enough to move. To the Arab good smells are pleasing and a way of being involved with each other. They consistently breathe on people when they talk. To smell one's friend is not only nice but desirable, for to deny him your breath is to act ashamed. Americans, on the other hand, trained as they are not to breathe in people's faces automatically communicate shame in trying to be polite. Arabs look each other in the eye when talking with an intensity that makes most Americans highly uncomfortable. To view the other person peripherally is regarded as impolite, and to sit or stand back-to-back is considered very rude. Privacy in a public place is foreign to the Arab. Business transactions in the bazaar are participated in by everyone. In terms of personal space, Arabs don't mind being crowded by people but hate to be hemmed in by walls. Ideally, homes must meet at least three standards: much unobstructed space without walls or partitions (so the family can be together), very high ceilings, and an unobstructed view.

In summary, views of social and personal space differ cross-culturally. By examining them it is possible to reveal hidden cultural frames that determine the structure of a given people's perceptual world. Perceiving the world differ-

ently leads to different definitions of what constitutes crowded living, different interpersonal relations, and a different approach to both local and international politics.

Questions 3.1

1. ''Peoples' norms concerning space determine their patterns of communication.'' Explain.
2. Show how the terms or concepts ''ethnocentric,'' ''cultural relativism,'' and ''culture and personality'' might be used in this article.

Reading 3.2

SOME CONDITIONS OF OBEDIENCE AND DISOBEDIENCE TO AUTHORITY

STANLEY MILGRAM

Stanley Milgram is a social psychologist and professor at City University of New York. In this excerpt from one of his research papers he describes what happens when people are faced with conflicting norms. Milgram's research question is this: If a person tells a second person to hurt a third person, under what conditions will the second person refuse to obey?

The situation in which one agent commands another to hurt a third turns up time and again as a significant theme in human relations. It is powerfully expressed in the story of Abraham, who is commanded by God to kill his son. It is no accident that Kierkegaard, seeking to orient his thought to the central themes of human experience, chose Abraham's conflict as the springboard to his philosophy.

War too moves forward on the triad of an authority which commands a person to destroy the enemy, and perhaps all organized hostility may be viewed as a theme and variation of the three elements of authority, executant, and victim. We describe an experimental program, recently concluded at Yale University, in which a particular expression of this conflict is studied by experimental means.

In its most general form the problem may be defined thus: if X tells Y to hurt Z, under what conditions will Y carry out the command of X and under what conditions will he refuse. In the more limited form possible in laboratory

Adapted from *Human Relations*, February 1965, pp. 57–76. Reprinted by permission of the author. A more thoroughgoing analysis of the experiments described in this article may be found in Stanley Milgram's *Obedience to Authority*, published by Harper & Row, 1974. A 45-minute film depicting the experiments is available to educational groups. It is entitled *Obedience* and is distributed by the New York University Film Library, 41 Press Annex, Washington Square, New York, N.Y. 10003.

research, the question becomes: if an experimenter tells a subject to hurt another person, under what conditions will he refuse to obey. The laboratory
problem is not so much a dilution of the general statement as one concrete expression of the many particular forms this question may assume.

One aim of the research was to study behavior in a strong situation of
deep consequence to the participants, for the psychological forces operative in
powerful and lifelike forms of the conflict may not be brought into play under
diluted conditions.

This approach meant, first, that we had a special obligation to protect the
welfare and dignity of the persons who took part in the study; subjects were, of
necessity, placed in a difficult predicament, and steps had to be taken to ensure
their wellbeing before they were discharged from the laboratory. Toward this
end, a careful, post-experimental treatment was devised and has been carried
through for subjects in all conditions.

The subjects used in all experimental conditions were male adults, resid-
ing in the greater New Haven and Bridgeport areas, aged 20 to 50 years, and
engaged in a wide variety of occupations. Each experimental condition described in this report employed 40 fresh subjects and was carefully balanced
for age and occupational types. The occupational composition for each experiment was: workers, skilled and unskilled: 40 percent; white collar, sales, business: 40 percent; professionals: 20 percent. The occupations were intersected
with three age categories (subjects in 20s, 30s, and 40s, assigned to each condition in the proportions of 20, 40, and 40 percent respectively).

The focus of the study concerns the amount of electric shock a subject is
willing to administer to another person when ordered by an experimenter to
give the "victim" increasingly more severe punishment. The act of administer-
ing shock is set in the context of a learning experiment, ostensibly designed to
study the effect of punishment on memory. Aside from the experimenter, one
naive subject and one accomplice perform in each session. On arrival each subject is paid $4.50. After a general talk by the experimenter, telling how little
scientists know about the effect of punishment on memory, subjects are informed that one member of the pair will serve as teacher and one as learner. A
rigged drawing is held so that the naive subject is always the teacher, and the
accomplice becomes the learner. The learner is taken to an adjacent room and
strapped into an "electric chair."

The naive subject is told that it is his task to teach the learner a list of
paired associates, to test him on the list, and to administer punishment whenever the learner errs in the test. Punishment takes the form of electric shock,
delivered to the learner by means of a shock generator controlled by the naive
subject. The teacher is instructed to increase the intensity of electric shock one
step on the generator on each error. The learner, according to plan, provides
many wrong answers, so that before long the naive subject must give him the
strongest shock on the generator. Increases in shock level are met by increasingly insistent demands from the learner that the experiment be stopped
because of the growing discomfort to him. However, in clear terms the experimenter orders the teacher to continue with the procedure in disregard of the
learner's protests. Thus, the naive subject must resolve a conflict between two

*mutually incompatible demands from the social field. He may continue to fol-
low the orders of the experimenter and shock the learner with increasing severity, or he may refuse to follow the orders of the experimenter and heed the
learner's pleas. The experimenter's authority operates not in a free field, but
against evermounting countervailing pressures from the person being
punished.*

A few technical points need to be considered before the findings of the
study are described. For the purpose of delivering shock, a simulated shock
generator is used, with 30 clearly marked voltage levels that range from 15 to
450 volts (and each activated by one of 30 individual level switches set in a
horizontal line). The naive subject is given a sample shock of 45 volts to convince him of the authenticity of the instrument. The generator bears verbal des-
ignations that range from "Slight Shock" to "Danger: Severe Shock."

The responses of the victim are standardized on tape, and each protest is
coordinated to a particular voltage level on the shock generator. Starting with
75 volts the learner begins to grunt and moan. At 150 volts he demands to be let
out of the experiment. At 180 volts he cries out that he can no longer stand the
pain. At 300 volts he refuses to provide any more answers to the memory test,
insisting that he is no longer a participant in the experiment and must be freed.
In response to this last tactic, the experimenter instructs the naive subject to
treat the absence of an answer as equivalent to a wrong answer, and to follow
the usual shock procedure. The experimenter reinforces his demand with the
statement: "You have no other choice, you must go on!" (This imperative is used
whenever the naive subject tries to break off the experiment.) If the subject refuses to give the next higher level of shock, the experiment is considered at an
end. A quantitative value is assigned to the subject's performance based on the
maximum intensity shock he administered before breaking off. Thus any subject's score may range from zero (for a subject unwilling to administer the first
shock level) to 30 (for a subject who proceeds to the highest voltage level on the
board). For any particular subject and for any particular experimental condition the degree to which participants have followed the experimenter's orders
may be specified with a numerical value, corresponding to the metric on the
shock generator.

This laboratory situation gives us a framework in which to study the subject's reactions to the principal conflict of the experiment. Again, this conflict is
between the experimenter's demands that he continue to administer the electric
shock, and the learner's demands, which become increasingly more insistent,
that the experiment be stopped. The crux of the study is to vary systematically
the factors believed to alter the degree of obedience to the experimental commands, to learn under what conditions submission to authority is most proba-
ble, and under what conditions defiance is brought to the fore.

This series consisted of four experimental conditions. In each condition
the victim was brought "psychologically" closer to the subject giving him
shocks.

In the first condition (Remote Feedback) the victim was placed in another
room and could not be heard or seen by the subject, except that, at 300 volts, he
pounded on the wall in protest. After 315 volts he no longer answered or was
heard from.

The second condition *(Voice Feedback)* was identical to the first except that voice protests were introduced. As in the first condition the victim was placed in an adjacent room, but his complaints could be heard through a door left slightly ajar, and through the walls of the laboratory. It is difficult to convey on the printed page the full tenor of the victim's responses, for we have no adequate notation for vocal intensity, timing, and general qualities of delivery. Yet these features are crucial to producing the effect of an increasingly severe reaction to mounting voltage levels. In general terms, however, the victim indicates no discomfort until the 75-volt shock is administered, at which time there is a light grunt in response to the punishment. Similar reactions follow the 90- and 105-volt shocks, and at 120 volts the victim shouts to the experimenter that the shocks are becoming painful. Painful groans are heard on administration of the 135-volt shock, and at 150 volts the victim cries out, "Experimenter, get me out of here! I won't be in the experiment any more! I refuse to go on!" Cries of this type continue with generally rising intensity, so that at 180 volts the victim cries out, "I can't stand the pain," and by 270 volts his response to the shock is definitely an agonized scream. Throughout, he insists that he be let out of the experiment. At 300 volts the victim shouts in desperation that he will no longer provide answers to the memory test; and at 315 volts, after a violent scream, he reaffirms with vehemence that he is no longer a participant. From this point on, he provides no answers, but shrieks in agony whenever a shock is administered; this continues through 450 volts. Of course, many subjects will have broken off before this point.

The third experimental condition *(Proximity)* was similar to the second, except that the victim was now placed in the same room as the subject, and 1½ feet from him. Thus he was visible as well as audible, and voice cues were provided.

The fourth, and final, condition of this series *(Touch-Proximity)* was identical to the third, with this exception: the victim received a shock only when his hand rested on a shockplate. At the 150-volt level the victim again demanded to be let free and, in this condition, refused to place his hand on the shockplate. The experimenter ordered the naive subject to force the victim's hand onto the plate. Thus obedience in this condition required that the subject have physical contact with the victim in order to give him punishment beyond the 150-volt level.

Forty adult subjects were studied in each condition. The data revealed that obedience was significantly reduced as the victim was rendered more immediate to the subject.

Expressed in terms of the proportion of obedient to defiant subjects, the findings are that 34 percent of the subjects defied the experimenter in the Remote condition, 37.5 percent in Voice Feedback, 60 percent in Proximity, and 70 percent in Touch-Proximity.

If the spatial relationship of the subject and victim is relevant to the degree of obedience, would not the relationship of subject to experimenter also play a part? There are reasons to feel that, on arrival, the subject is oriented primarily to the experimenter rather than to the victim. He has come to the laboratory to fit into the structure that the experimenter—not the victim—would provide. He has come less to understand his behavior than to <u>reveal</u> that behavior to a competent scientist, and he is willing to display himself as the scientist's purposes require. Most subjects seem quite concerned about the appearance they are making before the experimenter, and one could argue that this preoccupation in a relatively new and strange setting makes the subject somewhat insensitive to the triadic nature of the social situation. In other words, the subject is so concerned about the show he is putting on for the experimenter that influences from other parts of the social field do not receive as much weight as they ordinarily would. This overdetermined orientation to the experimenter would account for the relative insensitivity of the subject to the victim, and would also lead us to believe that alterations in the relationship between subject and experimenter would have important consequences for obedience.

In a series of experiments we varied the physical closeness and degree of surveillance of the experimenter. In one condition the experimenter sat just a few feet away from the subject. In a second condition, after giving initial instructions, the experimenter left the laboratory and gave his orders by telephone; in still a third condition the experimenter was never seen, providing instructions by means of a tape recording activated when the subjects entered the laboratory.

Obedience dropped sharply as the experimenter was physically removed from the laboratory. The number of obedient subjects in the first condition (Experimenter Present) was almost three times as great as in the second, where the experimenter gave his orders by telephone. Twenty-six subjects were fully obedient in the first condition, and only 9 in the second. Subjects seemed able to take a far stronger stand against the experimenter when they did not have to encounter him face to face, and the experimenter's power over the subject was severely curtailed.

Moreover, when the experimenter was absent, subjects displayed an interesting form of behavior that had not occurred under his surveillance. Though continuing with the experiment, several subjects administered lower shocks than were required and never informed the experimenter of their deviation from the correct procedure. (Unknown to the subjects, shock levels were automatically recorded by an Esterline-Angus event recorder wired directly into the shock generator; the instrument provided us with an objective record of the subjects' performance.) Indeed, in telephone conversations some subject specifically assured the experimenter that they were raising the shock level according to instructions, whereas in fact they were repeatedly using the lowest shock on the board. This form of behavior is particularly interesting: although these subjects acted in a way that clearly undermined the avowed purposes of the experiment, they found it easier to handle the conflict in this manner than to precipitate an open break with authority.

Experiments in this series show that the physical presence of an authority is an important force contributing to the subject's obedience or defiance. Taken together with the first experimental series on the proximity of the victim, it would appear that something akin to fields of force, diminishing in effectiveness with increasing psychological distance from their source, have a controlling effect on the subject's performance. As the victim is brought closer, the *subject finds it harder to administer shocks to him. When the victim's position is held constant relative to the subject, and the authority is made more remote, the subject finds it easier to break off the experiment. This effect is substantial in both cases, but manipulation of the experimenter's position yielded the more powerful results. Obedience to destructive commands is highly dependent on the proximal relations between authority and subject.*

One general finding that merits attention is the high level of obedience manifested in the experimental situation. Subjects often expressed deep disapproval of shocking a man in the face of his objections, and others denounced it as senseless and stupid. Yet many subjects complied even while they protested. The proportion of obedient subjects greatly exceeded the expectations of the experimenter and his colleagues. At the outset, we had conjectured that subjects would not, in general, go above the level of "Strong Shock." In practice, many subjects were willing to administer the most extreme shocks available when commanded by the experimenter. For some subjects the experiment provides an occasion for aggressive release. And for others it demonstrates the extent to which obedient dispositions are deeply ingrained, and are engaged irrespective of their consequences for others. Yet this is not the whole story. Somehow, the subject becomes implicated in a situation from which he cannot disengage himself.

The departure of the experimental results from intelligent expectation, to some extent, has been formalized. The procedure was to describe the experimental situation in concrete detail to a group of competent persons, and to ask them to predict the performance of 100 hypothetical subjects. For purposes of indicating the distribution of break-off points judges were provided with a diagram of the shock generator, and recorded their predictions before being informed of the actual results. Judges typically underestimated the amount of obedience demonstrated by subjects.

What is the limit of such obedience? At many points we attempted to establish a boundary. Cries from the victim were inserted; not good enough. The victim claimed heart trouble; subjects still shocked him on command. The victim pleaded that he be let free, and his answers no longer registered on the signal box; subjects continued to shock him. At the outset we had not conceived that such drastic procedures would be needed to generate disobedience, and each step was added only as the ineffectiveness of the earlier techniques became clear. The final effort to establish a limit was the Touch-Proximity condition. But the very first subject in this condition subdued the victim on command, and proceeded to the highest shock level. A quarter of the subjects in this condition performed similarly.

The results, as seen and felt in the laboratory, are to this author disturbing. They raise the possibility that human nature, or—more specifically—the kind of character produced in American democratic society, cannot be counted on to insulate its citizens from brutality and inhumane treatment at the direction of malevolent authority. A substantial proportion of people do what they are told to do, irrespective of the content of the act and without limitations of conscience, so long as they perceive that the command comes from a legitimate authority.

Questions 3.2

1. How is role strain illustrated in this article?
2. What conflicting norms did the subjects face? How did they resolve the conflicts?
3. Under what conditions were subjects most likely to comply with the experimenter's instructions? Why?
4. A number of the principles or characteristics of scientific inquiry are outlined in Chapter 1. Show how these principles are illustrated in Milgram's research.

Reading 3.3

ONE HUNDRED PERCENT AMERICAN

RALPH LINTON

The content of a culture—skills, customs, material objects, and nonmaterial ideas—comes from several sources. Some aspects of culture appear spontaneously and are developed from within the culture through the process of invention. Much more, however, is borrowed from other cultures through the usually unconscious process of diffusion. Anthropologist Ralph Linton wrote this passage some years ago. It is often quoted and still remains a classic at demonstrating the importance of diffusion. Much of what we thought was "one hundred percent American" actually came long ago from societies we never heard of.

There can be no question about the average American's Americanism or his desire to preserve this precious heritage at all costs. Nevertheless, some insidious foreign ideas have already wormed their way into his civilization without his realizing what was going on. Thus dawn finds the unsuspecting patriot garbed in pajamas, a garment of East Indian origin; and lying in a bed built on a pattern which originated in either Persia or Asia Minor. He is muffled to the ears in un-American materials; cotton, first domesticated in India; linen, domesticated in the Near East; wool from an animal native to Asia Minor; or silk, whose uses were first discovered by the Chinese. All these substances have been transformed into cloth by a method invented in Southwestern Asia. If the weather is cold enough he may even be sleeping under an eiderdown quilt invented in Scandinavia.

On awakening he glances at the clock, a medieval European invention, uses one potent Latin word in abbreviated form, rises in haste, and goes to the bathroom. Here, if he stops to think about it, he must feel himself in the presence of a great American institution; he will have heard stories of both the quality and frequency of foreign plumbing and will know that in no other country does the average man perform his ablutions in the midst of such splendor. But the insidious foreign influence pursues him even here. Glass was invented by the ancient Egyptians, the use of glazed tiles for floors and walls in the Near East, porcelain in China, and the art of enameling on metal by Mediterranean

From *The American Mercury*, April 1937, pp. 427–429. Reprinted by permission of the publisher.

artisans of the Bronze Age. Even his bathtub and toilet are but slightly modified copies of Roman originals. The only purely American contribution to the ensemble is the steam radiator.

In this bathroom the American washes with soap invented by the ancient Gauls. Next he cleans his teeth, a subversive European practice which did not invade America until the latter part of the eighteenth century. He then shaves, a masochistic rite first developed by the heathen priests of ancient Egypt and Sumer. The process is made less of a penance by the fact that his razor is of steel, an iron-carbon alloy discovered in either India or Turkestan. Lastly, he dries himself on a Turkish towel.

Returning to the bedroom, the unconscious victim of un-American practices removes his clothes from a chair, invented in the Near East, and proceeds to dress. He puts on close-fitting tailored garments whose form derives from the skin clothing of the ancient nomads of the Asiatic steppes and fastens them with buttons whose prototypes appeared in Europe at the close of the Stone Age. This costume is appropriate enough for outdoor exercise in a cold climate, but is quite unsuited to American summers, steam-heated houses, and Pullmans. Nevertheless, foreign ideas and habits hold the unfortunate man in thrall even when common sense tells him that the authentically American costume of gee string and moccasins would be far more comfortable. He puts on his feet stiff coverings made from hide prepared by a process invented in ancient Egypt and cut to a pattern which can be traced to ancient Greece, and makes sure they are properly polished, also a Greek idea. Lastly, he ties about his neck a strip of bright-colored cloth which is a vestigial survival of the shoulder shawls worn by seventeenth-century Croats. He gives himself a final appraisal in the mirror, an old Mediterranean invention, and goes downstairs to breakfast.

Here a whole new series of foreign things confront him. His food and drink are placed before him in pottery vessels, the popular name of which—china—is sufficient evidence of their origin. His fork is a medieval Italian invention and his spoon a copy of a Roman original. He will usually begin the meal with coffee, an Abyssinian plant first discovered by the Arabs. The American is quite likely to need it to dispel the morning-after effects of overindulgence in fermented drinks, invented in the Near East; or distilled ones, invented by the alchemists of medieval Europe. Whereas the Arabs took their coffee straight, he will probably sweeten it with sugar, discovered in India, and dilute it with cream, both the domestication of cattle and the technique of milking having originated in Asia Minor.

If our patriot is old-fashioned enough to adhere to the so-called American breakfast, his coffee will be accompanied by an orange, domesticated in the Mediterranean region, a cantaloupe domesticated in Persia, or grapes, domesticated in Asia Minor. He will follow this with a bowl of cereal made from grain domesticated in the Near East and prepared by methods also invented there. From this he will go on to waffles, a Scandinavian invention, with plenty of butter, originally a Near-Eastern cosmetic. As a side dish he may have the egg of a bird domesticated in Southeastern Asia or strips of the flesh of an animal domesticated in the same region, which have been salted and smoked by a process invented in Northern Europe.

Breakfast over, he places upon his head a molded piece of felt, invented by the nomads of Eastern Asia, and, if it looks like rain, puts on outer shoes of rubber, discovered by the ancient Mexicans, and takes an umbrella, invented in India. He then sprints for his train—the train, not the sprinting, being an English invention. At the station he pauses for a moment to buy a newspaper, paying for it with coins invented in ancient Lydia. Once on board he settles back to inhale the fumes of a cigarette invented in Mexico, or a cigar invented in Brazil. Meanwhile, he reads the news of the day, imprinted in characters invented by the ancient Semites by a process invented in Germany upon a material invented in China. As he scans the latest editorial pointing out the dire results to our institutions of accepting foreign ideas, he will not fail to thank a Hebrew God in an Indo-European language that he is a one hundred percent (decimal system invented by the Greeks) American (from Americus Vespucci, Italian geographer).

Questions 3.3

1. While it is true that many material objects have come to us through diffusion, most of the nonmaterial aspects of American culture are original and the products of invention. Discuss.
2. This article was written in 1930; the same sort of statements could not be made today. Discuss. To prove the point, draw up a list of aspects of American culture developed through invention.
3. Analyze Linton's article, using the terms "ethnocentrism" and "cultural relativism."

II
SOCIAL
ORGANIZATION

In preceding chapters we have looked at basic units of analysis used by sociologists to understand, describe, and explain human behavior. In this section our view becomes more general. If we combine these basic units and move to a higher level of abstraction, we come to the concept of social organization. If, in a like manner, we were analyzing football, we could first look at the basic elements—players, a ball, a marked-off field, and maybe some spectators. But our description is helped a great deal if we move to the next level and describe a football game, because it is now necessary to look beyond the elements and deal with the combination of the setting, the rules, shared expectations, and interaction patterns of participants—in other words, the social organization present that allows twenty-two players, six officials, and 20,000 observers to mutually participate in and get something out of the same event.

As there is an extensive degree of organization to a football game, so there is to society. The basic elements of a society are a number of people and an inhabitable geographical area. But no understanding of a society is obtained until we study the patterns of interaction and organization that are characteristic of the people. We see that cities exist (why do they?), that highways link cities, that educational facilities are developed, that some individuals are more highly valued than others, that governments run the cities. These things don't just happen by accident; they are evidences that there is organization to society. People cooperate, interact, and share expectations and mutual interests, and there is a structure or system to society much as there is to a building or a machine or a football game—parts link together to form a complex whole. The **social organization** of society is frequently referred to as a *social fabric,* an integrated set of norms, roles, cultural values, and beliefs through which people interact with each other, individually and through groups. The terms *social organization* and *social structure* (which we discussed in Chapter 3) are very similar concepts and are often used interchangeably. Although *social structure* can be used to refer more to a stable network of elements through which people relate to each other and *social organization* can be used to refer more to the continually changing ordering and coordination of human activities, it is probably not worthwhile to try to make a distinction between the terms.

Studying various aspects of the social organization and social structure of society is the central task of sociology. We undertake this analysis in a variety of ways. It is as if we were looking at a subject, society in this case, through a number of windows. Each window is of a different shape, size, thickness, and color of glass. So, though we are looking at the same subject, each approach gives a somewhat different viewpoint, emphasizing certain aspects and ignoring others. The following chapters will analyze the social organization of society through several windows. Groups will be the topic of Chapter 4, and several types of groups will be discussed in detail. Chapters 5 and 6 will deal with types of social differentiation. In Chapters 7, 8, and 9 we will discuss institutions as the sociologist sees them. And Chapter 10 will cover population and ecology.

4

Groups

The group is a major unit of analysis for sociologists. A group, simply defined, is a collection of people. Not all collections of people, however, are defined as groups. Are the people on a bus a group? How about red-haired people between the ages of thirty and forty-five? Or what about the students at a large university? At the same time, collectivities that *are* defined as groups may vary tremendously in some characteristics. Your family, my sociology department, a college's football team or a sorority, and the President's Cabinet could probably be defined as groups, but they are quite different in many dimensions—size, complexity, type of interaction, division of labor. Much of the study of social organization, therefore, could center around two questions: What constitutes a group, and how is the group developed? What are the different types of groups?

WHY STUDY GROUPS?

Sociologists study groups for several reasons. The division of labor and sharing of interests and jobs that occurs in groups makes it possible to complete tasks that would be impossible for individuals alone. Far more important for the sociologist, however, is the role the group plays in the socialization and development of the individual. To a great degree, we feel that a person *is* the sum of the groups he or she belongs to. Transmission of culture and learning of values, attitudes, and ways of behaving and believing occur mainly in groups. As we have pointed out in Chapters 2 and 3, socialization and development of self and personality are interactive processes. Individuals interact with others and modify their own behavior according to their interpretations of the responses of others. These others are individuals—mother, father, teacher, a significant other person. These others are also groups. Most of the socialization process, both primary and secondary, takes place in *groups*. First the family, then the classroom group, the team or club, the social group, the professional organization, and numerous other voluntary and involuntary associations influence and shape the individual.

The group is more than just the sum of the people who belong to it. Perhaps a good example of this is to compare a family of five people with five people we pick at random on the street. Even if we set each "group" in front of the fire or TV or around the same dinner table and start them interacting, the differences between the two would be clear. We would shortly see that the real family group had developed a set of norms, roles, and relationships to each other that went far beyond the five people. Because of the presence of this network of relationships and understandings that exists in groups, the impact or power of the group in influencing the individual is extensive.

To get a better idea of the importance of groups, imagine the effects on two people of belonging to the following contrasting groups. One person is raised in a family in which competitiveness is valued—family members are constantly competing with each other and with outsiders. The other is raised in a family in which competition is discouraged. One is raised in a family that pursues artistic endeavors, and the other in a family that prefers athletics. One is a Jehovah's Witness, the other a member of a Unitarian church. One is a member of a rock group, the other is a member of a chamber music group. One is on the high school basketball team, the other is on the yearbook staff. One goes to the University of California at Berkeley, the other goes to West Point. One goes through basic training in the Marine Corps, the other joins the Peace Corps. One is raised in a modern Western family, the other in a primitive tribal family.

You're probably thinking, "Sure, the Berkeley grad is a lot different from the West Point grad, but they had some of those differences before, so one chose Berkeley and the other West Point." That's probably true, but those differences, too, can be explained by other earlier group memberships and experiences. Each set of group experiences prepares and inclines the person toward another set, then another set, and so on. Or, consider this example. Here is a forty-six-year-old doctor at the top of his field who climbs mountains, builds sailboats, races sports cars, writes books, and is a male chauvinist pig. How did this superachiever get this way? Was he born this way? Certainly not, says the sociologist. Study his socialization patterns through numerous group contexts, and you will find the answer. It may not be easy, but the basic explanations are in the complicated interaction between group and individual.

Groups are important, then, for the ways they affect and shape the individual. We can also study the way groups interact with other groups, how they affect and shape each other. Groups with mutual interests may find themselves supporting each other's activities. Likewise, groups are frequently in conflict with other groups. Since groups are often organized around common interests, and since other groups' interests are bound to be somewhat different, group conflict is almost commonplace. We can quickly think of conflict between employer and employee groups, between political groups, between consumer and business groups, and so on. The level of conflict may vary from easily tolerated disagreement at one extreme to serious, prolonged attempts to eradicate the other group at the other extreme.

GROUPS AND NONGROUPS

Sociologists say that a **group** exists when you have a number of people who (1) have shared or patterned interaction and (2) feel bound together by a "consciousness of kind" or a "we" feeling. "Consciousness of kind," a phrase coined by Franklin Giddings, refers to the individual's awareness of important similarities between himself and certain others and to the awareness that the individual and other group members have common loyalties, share at least some similar values, and see themselves as set apart from the rest of the world because of their membership in this particular group. There are tremendous varieties, sizes, and shapes of groups. A group may be as small as two people or almost infinitely large. Groups may be simple in structure or exceedingly complex; they may involve close, intimate relationships between members or more distant and infrequent personal contacts. In other words, the definition of group—patterned interaction and "we" feeling—may fit an enormous variety of situations: a family, a basketball team, a sociology class, IBM, or General Motors.

This definition of groups, imprecise as it may seem, allows us to distinguish groups from other types of collectivities of people, which we could call nongroups. One type of nongroup, which we will call an **aggregate** (or aggregation), consists of a number of people clustered together in one place. Examples of aggregates might be all the people in New York City, or the pedestrians at a busy intersection waiting for the light to change to "walk," or all the people in North America, or the passengers on a jet from New York to San Francisco. A second useful nongroup, called a **category**, consists of a number of people who have a particular characteristic in common. Examples of categories would be all females, or all red-haired people, or all pilots, or all teenagers, or all whites.

Although we have called them nongroups, aggregates and categories may be transformed into groups should they develop patterned interaction among members and consciousness of kind. For example, let's examine our aggregate of ten people waiting at the intersection for the light to change to "walk." Then suppose it *doesn't* change—for five, ten, even fifteen minutes the light refuses to budge from "wait." The pedestrians, strangers until now, begin talking to each other about the impossible situation. Should they race across through traffic against the light? Where's the cop?—you can never find one when you really need one. Some interaction takes place, and a consciousness of kind develops— a group of good people being victimized by a lousy, mechanical light. Or, take the passengers on the jet from New York to San Francisco, another aggregate. Somewhere over Pennsylvania the pilot says to himself, "I'm sick and tired of

Group members have common loyalties

flying to San Francisco all the time; I guess I'll go to the North Pole." The passengers, who did not know each other before, begin to interact, possibly in an agitated manner, and by the time they reach the Arctic Circle there would probably be highly developed interaction.

Categories may also become groups. All the red-haired people between the ages of thirty and forty-five would constitute a category, as would all carpenters of Irish ancestry. But suppose the middle-aged redheads decided to get together and put out a journal telling of their common problems and aspirations. Or suppose the Carpenters of Irish Ancestry decide it's time to start an organization (CIA?), have a convention, and elect officers. In each case we might have a category developing into a group. These sound farfetched, but the point is that sociologists study both groups and nongroups (categories and aggregates), and the lines between these collectivities are somewhat fluid and easily crossed.

The study of people and society is a large task. It is made more manageable if the whole is broken down into more basic parts. Much of our study is of various types of groups, and the rest of this chapter will be devoted to this. We can also divide a society into categories (males, upper-class blacks, teenage white females) and aggregates (a crowd, a city). This makes our analysis easier (smaller units) and more precise (the units now have some characteristics in common). In later chapters we will examine categories and aggregations.

TYPES OF GROUPS

The New York Times has described one of the most unusual clubs in the world made up of a small number of usually serious scientists stationed at the South Pole. It is called the "300 Club." Those who want to join must wait until the temperature is at least 100 degrees Fahrenheit below zero, then strip completely nude and dash 100 yards across the ice to a marker designating the South Pole and 100 yards back to the scientific hut. Anyone surviving becomes a member of this very exclusive group.

Social groups may be classified in many ways as the following categories illustrate. In some groups membership is automatic and the participant has no choice; in others the option is open and individuals may join or not as they wish. These two types are called involuntary and voluntary groups. **Involuntary groups** might include the family one is born into or the army platoon one is drafted into. **Voluntary groups** would include any of a vast number that the member may exercise some choice in joining—lodges, fraternities, bridge clubs, student governments, political organizations. **In-groups** are groups that *I* belong to, that *I* identify with, that are *my* groups, while **out-groups** are groups that I do not belong to or identify with.

Reference groups are groups that serve as models for our behavior, groups we may or may not actually belong to, but whose perspectives we assume and mold our behavior after. A reference group may be made up of people one associates with or knows personally, or it may be an abstract collectivity of individuals who represent models for our behavior. Each individual has many reference groups. As a teacher I would have certain reference groups, as a sociologist others, as a husband others, and as a handball player still others. One's **peer group** is made up of people of relatively the same age, interests, and social position with whom one has reasonably close association and contact. A peer group may consist of a class at school, a street gang, or an occupational group such as the members of a college sociology department or a group of lawyers in a law firm. Not all the members of a peer group are necessarily friends, but the peer group exercises a major role in the socialization process. During adolescence, it may be *the* major socializing agent.

Groups whose members come predominantly from one social-class level are called **horizontal groups.** Examples of horizontal groups would include almost any organization formed along occupational lines—an association of doctors, carpenters, or actors. If a group includes members from a variety of social classes, it could be called a **vertical group.** Vertical groups are more difficult to find in American society, since many divisions are made along social-class lines. A church congregation might constitute a vertical group, and in some cases an army platoon made up of draftees would include members from a variety of social classes. Groups are also categorized according to their longevity. A group brought together to perform a single, short-term task could be called a **temporary group,** whereas a longer-lasting collectivity like a family could be called a **permanent group.** Groups are defined as open or closed according to the ease of gaining membership. A white fraternity is often a **closed group** as far as a black male is concerned, but the U.S. army is probably a very **open group** for the same individual. Now, what type of group is the "300 Club"?

PRIMARY AND SECONDARY GROUPS

A family and a draftee's army platoon are involuntary groups, but they are quite different sorts of groups. A basketball team and the members of a large college class are voluntary groups, but again they are very different. Groups vary along a number of dimensions, and one of the most important of these is how primary or secondary each group is. For example, a family and a basketball team are more primary than an army platoon and a large college class. Primary groups play an important role in human development. Most of the socialization process—learning society's norms and roles, development of the self—takes place in small primary groups. The **primary group** was first described by Charles H. Cooley as referring to groups in which contacts between members are intimate, personal, and face-to-face. A great part of the individual's total life experience is bound up in the group and is known to other group members. The primary type of relationship is one involving deep and personal interaction and communication. This interaction is an end in itself—primary groups often exist because of the value of the primary relationship rather than because of other specific goals or tasks. People conform in primary groups because of strong informal norms—for example, fear of being ostracized, scorned, or ridiculed—rather than because of any formal written rules.

A **secondary group,** on the other hand, is more impersonal. Interaction is more superficial and probably based on utilitarian goals. That is, the person is less important than a particular skill he or she may offer the group. Interaction and communication are based on the value of one's particular skill rather than on interest in one's general personal qualities. It is probably most helpful to see the concepts of primary and secondary as opposite ends of a continuum. The completely primary or completely secondary group may seldom be found. Rather, groups vary in their degree of primariness or secondariness. Moving from primary to secondary along the continuum we might see these groups: a married couple, an extended family including parents and grandparents, a basketball team, a sorority, a professional organization or labor union, the employees of a large corporation.

SMALL GROUPS

The study of small groups has long been a central interest of sociology and social psychology. Small groups have become popular in a number of areas recently. Small groups are used as vehicles for treatment—group therapy has proven to be a useful mechanism for change in prisons, mental hospitals, and organizations dealing with alcoholism and drug usage. Sensitivity training groups and encounter groups have become popular on college campuses and with large organizations as techniques for improving communication, interaction, and self-understanding. The small class is believed to work better than the large class in the educational process.

Small groups, as we are describing them here, combine a primary type of interaction with a task orientation. Achievement of the task—better education, self-understanding, improved communication and management skills—is facilitated by the primary group atmosphere. Social scientists have done extensive research on small groups. In the following paragraphs we will discuss ways of studying small groups and some of the characteristics of small group behavior.

Small groups are studied in a variety of ways. Each method focuses on a different perspective of small group interaction. Robert Bales has developed a technique called **interaction process analysis (IPA)**.[1] In this technique, the interaction of group members is observed and categorized by researchers as they watch the group through one-way windows or monitor their behavior with tape recorders. A basic assumption of IPA is that groups function to solve problems. Four main problems confronting small groups are:

1. Adaptation to outside factors that influence the group (control by or cooperation with others).
2. Instrumental control over performing group tasks (assigning jobs, making decisions).
3. Expression and management of group members' feelings (expressing dissatisfaction or pleasure, dealing with interpersonal problems, relieving tension).
4. Development and maintenance of group integration (cohesion, willingness to do things, satisfaction).

Group members interact in a variety of ways (verbally, with gestures, through facial expressions) to solve the problems confronting them. The researchers studying the group break this interaction down into small parts or *acts.* An act may be verbal or nonverbal behavior and must be communicated to at least one other person in the group. An act can come from a long interaction or a short one. For example, a discussion between two people may result in only one act, whereas in another situation one sentence may involve two or three acts. Typically, a sentence or an independent clause in a sentence is considered an act.

The IPA observer then places each act into one of twelve categories. This classification of bits of interaction into predetermined categories is really IPA's major distinguishing feature. Table 4.1 outlines the twelve act categories and

TABLE 4.1   Interaction Process Analysis (IPA) Categories

Act Categories	General Areas	Typical Group Response
1. Shows solidarity 2. Shows tension release 3. Shows agreement	Positive reactions	25%
4. Gives suggestion 5. Gives opinion 6. Gives information	Answers	56
7. Asks for information 8. Asks for opinion 9. Asks for suggestion	Questions	7
10. Shows disagreement 11. Shows tension 12. Shows antagonism	Negative reactions	12

[1]Bales's major work is *Interaction Process Analysis* (Cambridge, Mass.: Addison-Wesley, 1950). Shepherd's summary of Bales's work has been especially helpful: see Clovis Shepherd, *Small Groups* (San Francisco: Chandler, 1964), pp. 27–36. Also see Michael Olmsted, *The Small Group* (New York: Random House, 1959), pp. 117–132, and *The Small Group*, 2d ed. by Michael Olmsted and Paul Hare (New York: Random House, 1978).

four general areas into which the act categories fall. It also shows a profile of the responses of a typical group, which we will discuss more in a moment.

The coach of a professional basketball team is talking to the team at half-time. They look like a small group, so let's try IPA on them. Their problem seems to be that they are behind the Boston Celtics by thirty-nine points. Little does the coach know that, in IPA language, their plight can be defined in terms of four problems. The major problem as the coach sees it is *adaptation to outside factors:* the darn Celtics, the hostile crowd, the uneven floor. *This* is the problem he must deal with. But it is also likely that the halftime discussion will involve *instrumental control over performing group tasks* (someone must stop the Celtics' center, who has already scored fifty points); *expression and management of feelings* (Fogarty, who is guarding the Celtics' center, kicks the water cooler across the locker room); and *development and maintenance of group integration* (the coach explains that the team must stand together and help Fogarty out in this difficult time). Now, observe the discussion and check off the acts as they occur. Most of the coach's remarks fall in the answers area. He *gives suggestions* and *opinions* (suggests that Blatt stop shooting at the wrong basket, tells Ragley that his broken arm seems to be hindering his dribbling, and reminds Henson that they are playing basketball, not football). The assistant coach *gives information*—shooting percentages and number of rebounds. Forgarty *asks for information* regarding how to keep the opposing center from scoring so much. Martinez provides *tension release* by telling what he did on his summer vacation. The coach *shows tension* and *antagonism* by telling Martinez to shut up or he will punch his lights out. But the team leaves the halftime talk on a positive note: They *show solidarity* by crowding together and clasping hands before stumbling back onto the court.

Although most groups are more sophisticated and their interaction more complicated than that of our hapless basketball team, the example does illustrate how group interaction might be recorded by the IPA observer. At this point, we should look again at Table 4.1. The right-hand column shows a profile of the responses of a typical group. When the interaction that occurs in a typical group is broken down into acts, roughly fifty-six percent of these acts will be answers of one sort or another. Many groups are not typical, however. For example, if satisfied and dissatisfied groups are compared it is found that satisfied groups give more suggestions and have more agreement while dissatisfied groups make more requests for information and have much more disagreement.

There appears to be an optimum pattern for most effective group performance. If the percentage of answers rises too high, the group may get the feeling of a dictated decision. If the percentage of answers drops too low, the group may be seen as a waste of time. Typically, groups have two positive reactions to each negative reaction. Too many negative reactions and the group turns into a name-calling session; too many positive reactions and it becomes a mutual admiration society.

According to Bales's observations, the life history of a group moves through several stages. In the beginning stage the group focuses on problems of orientation (facts and information). In the middle stage the group is concerned with problems of evaluation (opinions). In the final stage the group deals with problems of control and decision (suggestions).

This should give some idea of Bales's IPA. As you can see, this method involves counting and classifying each bit of interaction in an experimental problem-solving group. It differs from other approaches in that a large amount of detailed factual material is collected. Critics of this type of research on small groups are dubious about the created-in-the-laboratory nature of these experiments; they suggest that in real life small groups may behave differently from the way they behave in labs. Perhaps you should pick a group and try it out to see whether the categories and percentages that Bales suggests really fit.

J. L. Moreno developed a technique called **sociometry** that provides a quite different way of studying small groups. Here the focus is more on the *who* of interaction rather than on the *what*. Sociometry looks not at the nature or type of interaction, as Bales's IPA does, but at the direction of interaction—who interacts with whom. Members of the group being studied are asked questions like, "Who is your best friend in the group?" or "Who would you most like to work with on an important project?" The patterns and directions of interaction are then graphed as in Figure 4.1. This figure represents a sociogram of the members of a volunteer fire department. Each member of the group was asked three questions: "Who would you most prefer to have help you fight a fire?" "Who would you most prefer to have help you plan a social function?" and "Who is your best friend in the department?" The lines and arrows in the sociogram represent the resulting choices. For example, fireman 13 chose fireman 11, firemen 1 and 7 named each other, and so on. Not all the selections are shown in this sociogram in order to keep it from getting too complicated. Those near the center of the sociogram were chosen more often—fireman 11 was named twenty-eight times, fireman 9 fourteen times, fireman 4 not at all. Several typical sociometric patterns appear in this figure. Fireman 4 was not chosen and is called an *isolate*. Firemen 5, 10, and 13 were named only once each and are near-isolates or *neglectees*. Fireman 11 was chosen by nearly everybody and is termed a *star*. Rank in the department and political preference are shown in the sociogram to see whether these explain patterns of selection. One of the assistant chiefs was more popular than the chief, and the three captains are all near the center of the sociogram. Hosemen, the lowest rank, are consistently around the edge. More detail on fireman 11 indicates that aside from being a Republican and a captain, he is one of two men in the department with a college degree, he is the third oldest member, he is one of five Catholics, he has the highest social-class standing in the department, and he participates actively in departmental activities.

As a technique for the study of groups, sociometry presents both advantages and disadvantages. On the positive side, it helps uncover informal interaction and friendship patterns, and helps to identify variables associated with leadership and social isolation. On the negative side, sociometry is somewhat static and, unless repeated often, does not take into account the fluid and rapidly changing nature of group structure. It is an effective technique for mapping interaction but does not provide an in-depth analysis of that interaction.

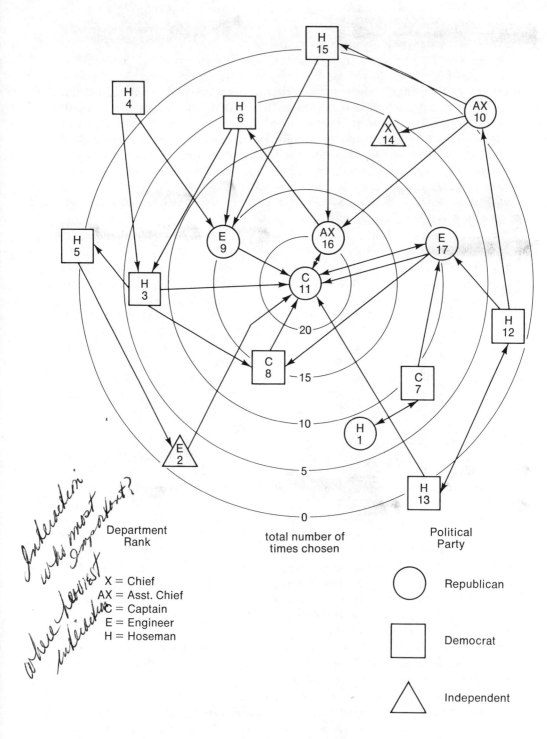

FIGURE 4.1 Sociogram of a Volunteer Fire Department.

Another way of studying small groups is by means of **participant obser-vation.** Here, the researcher joins the group being studied and becomes in-volved in its activities—one learns about the group by becoming part of it. (See the discussion of Whyte's participant observation study of Cornerville in Chap-ter 1, p. 16). We can see that participant observation is often less controlled and provides less of the sort of detail that either IPA or sociometry gives. A talented observer, however, can use participant observation to achieve an analysis of more depth, can uncover meanings of actions, and can present a dynamic pic-ture of a group's behavior. I have a feeling that if I were studying a group—the Hell's Angels, the SLA, the Pittsburgh Steelers, and the President's cabinet come to mind—I'd learn more through participant observation than I would through IPA or sociometry. Essentially, though, the method to use depends on the type of group being studied and on what it is you want to find out. In par-ticipant observation, the observer always has to be cautious in order that his or her presence in the group doesn't unduly change the group's behavior and that he or she doesn't become so much a part of the group that objectivity is lost. Both of these are crucial problems that the participant observer has to face.

Small Group Research

The following paragraphs summarize some small group research that I have found particularly interesting. Social psychologists have long been fasci-nated by conformity, and a number of studies have examined the effects of group pressure on individual judgment and behavior. (Milgram's study of con-formity in France and Norway discussed on p. 74 is an example of this.) A sta-tionary light in a dark room appears to move; this is called the *autokinetic effect.* Muzafer Sherif asked subjects to judge how far the light moved. When small groups were tested, they quickly arrived at agreement on the light's move-ment—a group norm. When the members were tested individually, they stuck to the earlier established group norm. When other subjects were tested indi-vidually *first* (no group norm available), their judgments of the light's move-ment were more variable and erratic. In other studies, Solomon Asch asked small groups of people to compare the lengths of lines. Some members of the group were stooges, or confederates of the researcher. The stooges were in-structed to make obviously wrong selections—two lines that were of different lengths were said to be the same. In studies involving eight stooges and one subject, the subject was faced with the choice of going along with the majority or making an independent judgment. Many avoided stress and simply went along with the majority.[2]

There is variation in how small groups handle deviants. Laboratory ex-periments indicate that if one person continues to disagree with or block a posi-

---

[2]Muzafer Sherif, *The Psychology of Social Norms* (New York: Harper, 1936). Solomon Asch, "Effects of Group Pressure on the Modification and Distortion of Judgment," in *Groups, Lead-ership and Men*, edited by M. H. Guetzkow (Pittsburgh: Carnegie, 1951), and S. Asch, "Studies of Independence and Conformity: A Minority of One Against a Unanimous Majority," *Psycho-logical Monographs* 70, no. 9 (1956), Whole No. 416.

tion on which the rest of the group agrees, there is a tendency to reject the deviant. In another study of Quaker work groups and army basic-training squads, however, another pattern emerged. Robert Dentler and Kai Erikson found that in some groups, deviant behavior helps maintain group equilibrium, and attempts to alienate a member whose behavior was deviant were resisted. Mentally ill (schizophrenic) members of basic-training squads were taken care of by the other recruits. Others performed the deviant's duties, they became very protective of him, and when he was finally hospitalized, other squad members became disturbed and angry at his removal.

Leadership and other roles in small groups follow certain predictable patterns. For example, two types of leaders that have been observed are the task leader and social-emotional leader. The *task leader* possesses skills or characteristics that the group values highly, but he or she is not highly approachable. The *social-emotional leader* is highly approachable; he or she is the one to whom other group members can complain, show affection, or in other ways express feelings. The social-emotional leader may have some influence on the task leader. Other group roles are described by the terms *nice guys, ignored,* and *rejected. Nice guys* are approachable—not as much as the social-emotional leader but enough that their membership and contributions are valued. Those *ignored* are members who are usually inactive; they are an unknown quantity to the rest of the group. Those *rejected* are members perceived as unapproachable because they have no skills or characteristics valued by the group or because of hostile or confusing behavior on their part.[3]

A study of deviants in small groups was concerned with finding out whether the deviant's rank in the group would affect the punishment he received. Twenty-five members of a college fraternity's pledge class were divided into four groups. Each group was told by an officer of the fraternity that another member of the fraternity had violated some rules and would have to be punished. The identity of the offender (independent variable) was changed for each group, and each group was asked to determine the appropriate punishment (dependent variable). Here are the descriptions of the four offenders:

> *Offender for Group 1.* Highest social position, fraternity officer, very well liked, task and social-emotional leader.
>
> *Offender for Group 2.* High social position, best-liked member of the sophomore class, social-emotional leader.
>
> *Offender for Group 3.* Not identified by name—just as "a member of the sophomore class."
>
> *Offender for Group 4.* Low social position, not very well liked.

The groups were told that the deviant had duplicated and sold fraternity files. They were given twenty minutes to discuss the case and were told to individually and anonymously write down the appropriate punishment. Group 1 all felt the deviant should give a formal apology. Group 2 felt the deviant should be

---

[3]The studies discussed in this and the previous paragraph are summarized by Shepherd in *Small Groups,* pp. 69 and 74–79 (see footnote 1).

given a one-month to one-semester suspension. Group 3 felt a one-semester suspension to be appropriate with one member voting for a one-year suspension. Most of the members of group 4 felt the deviant should not be allowed to eat or sleep in the house, and one member voted for expulsion from the fraternity. We see that deviants are punished not so much according to what they have done, but according to their position or status in the group. The high-ranking individuals were lightly punished; the low-ranking person's punishment bordered on ostracism—he was physically removed from group activity. As the author of the study puts it, "The higher the position of a person within a group, the more lenient will be his punishment for deviance; the reason for this being that the higher the social position of a person, the more value he has to the group and the more they would have to lose by rejecting him."[4]

Some of the effects and constraints that small groups have on behavior can be seen in the actions of people on juries. The jury usually quickly selects a person of high status (wealth and/or education) as foreman. People of high status are more active on the jury—they talk more, have more influence, and are seen as more competent. Low-status people tend to defer to the higher-status members. Men are more active on juries, but women are better jurors—they take more care in considering testimony. Jurors are very reluctant to come back without a verdict. The self-confidence of witnesses often has more effect on the jury than the logic or soundness of what they say. Juries often try the lawyer rather than the person he or she is representing. Finally, the mere fact of a person's being brought to trial makes him or her suspect in the eyes of the jury, in spite of the presumption of innocence in our court system.[5]

How do juries reach decisions? Sometimes in strange and peculiar ways. The jury of ten women and two men at the trial of the Chicago Seven (seven young men charged with inciting a riot during the 1968 Democratic convention) argued and horse-traded for four days before they could reach a verdict. At first a majority of eight favored convicting all of the defendants while three jurors insisted on complete acquittal. Agreement was finally reached late at night with each group holed up in a separate hotel room. One juror reported that "Feelings were so high, with the two groups against each other, we just didn't feel at ease in there in the jury room together." After much argument, " . . . we agreed we should not be a hung jury. We decided to compromise, and it was just a question of how to compromise." Another juror who favored convicting all and admitted that there was not one of the defendants she really liked said, "Half a chicken is better than none at all. We were all anxious to go home." The jury found five of the seven defendants guilty.

Reported in *Time*, March 2, 1970, pp. 8–11.

---

[4]Lowell W. Gerson, "Punishment and Position: The Sanctioning of Deviants in Small Groups," *Case Western Reserve Journal of Sociology*, vol. 1 (1967), pp. 54–62.

[5]For more detail on these and other studies of jury behavior, see Hans Toch, ed., *Legal and Criminal Psychology* (New York: Holt, Rinehart and Winston, 1961).

FORMAL ORGANIZATIONS

The new director of the Department of Motor Vehicles (DMV) ran head-on into a problem recently. He had DMV workers paint "no parking" in Chinese in no-parking areas around the DMV buildings. There were already signs in English and Spanish as part of a program to help people unfamiliar with English. The director was proud and the local newspaper published a picture of the new signs. But the next day they were gone, painted over. It seems that a grounds supervisor had also seen the picture in the newspaper, had checked around and couldn't find the necessary work order for having the signs painted, and had them painted over. The next day the director had the signs painted in Chinese again, but only after he had obtained the necessary work order. "It was his first real experience with bureaucracy, and he lost it to the paper pushers," reported a spokesperson.

Large-scale formal organizations are an essential part of modern society. These organizations, often called **bureaucracies,** arise as societies' activities become increasingly planned rather than spontaneous. People discovered long ago that if several people got together and planned an activity—building a car, educating a student—they often got the job done more rapidly and efficiently than if each pursued the task in his or her own way, spontaneously and haphazardly. Arthur Stinchcombe defines a formal organization as any social arrangement in which the activities of some people are systematically planned by other people in order to achieve some special purpose. Those who plan the activities automatically have authority over the others. Formal organizations seem to arise in societies with a money economy that are pursuing complex tasks requiring the coordinated efforts of a number of people. As the size of the organization increases, administrative tasks multiply, and this encourages further bureaucratization. There is an enduring quality about these organizations— people leave, but like the building they worked in, their jobs and the organization remain, seemingly forever.[6]

Some years ago, sociologist Max Weber identified the characteristics of an abstract or pure form of bureaucracy: (1) There is a precise division of labor, so that each individual in the organization is a specialist—an expert in performing a specific task. (2) There is a hierarchy of authority, a chain of command in which each individual is clearly in control of some and clearly responsible to others. (3) There is an exhaustive and consistent system of rules designed to assure uniformity in the performance of every task. (4) Social relationships between individuals in the organization, especially between superiors and their subordinates, are formal and impersonal. (5) The bureaucracy is technically highly efficient, much like a machine. (6) Employees are highly trained for their task; they are, in turn, protected from arbitrary dismissal—their job constitutes a career with possibilities for advancement according to seniority and/or achievement.

---

[6]See Arthur Stinchcombe, "Formal Organizations" in *Sociology: An Introduction*, 2d ed., edited by Neil Smelser (New York: Wiley, 1973). Also see Peter Blau and Marshall Meyer, *Bureaucracy in Modern Society*, 2d ed. (New York: Random House, 1971), and H. H. Gerth and C. W. Mills, *From Max Weber: Essays in Sociology* (New York: Oxford University Press, 1958).

Weber was talking about how bureaucracies in an abstract sense might operate. Formal organizations in fact do not necessarily resemble Weber's description on all or even most points. In any organization, much that is unplanned occurs. The chain of command is often circumvented. Shortcuts reduce bureaucratic red tape in a variety of ways. Relationships between individuals are often personal and informal. Organizations occasionally are grossly inefficient. In fact, to counteract the somewhat negative view that many people have of the huge bureaucracy, organizations often consciously attempt to look and act less formal, less bureaucratic. Nevertheless, Weber's description provides us with a useful abstraction of the general characteristics of large organizations.

The bureaucracy I'm most familiar with is a university. If Max Weber wandered through our institution, he would probably note the following. *Division of labor, specialization:* There are groundskeepers, secretaries, computer operators, librarians, janitors, and professors. The professors teach specific courses in specific areas, and these courses seldom overlap. In the sociology department I teach criminology, and another person teaches courses on Middle Eastern societies. We are both sociologists, yet he knows little about my area and I even less about his. We are all highly specialized. *Hierarchy of authority:* There is an authority ladder in each section. There is a massive organizational chart for the college (which in fact looks like a map of the Los Angeles freeway system and I'm certain is understood by no one). Hierarchy runs from students (at the bottom) to professors to department heads to associate deans to deans to associate vice presidents to vice presidents to the president. Each must answer to the one above. *System of rules:* Classes must be added or dropped by a certain day. Grades must be turned in by professors in a certain way by a certain time. Lists of rules describe how students may complain about injustices and how faculty may deal with unruly students. A faculty member wishing to leave campus to go to a professional meeting in another city must fill out a pile of forms weeks in advance of the trip. People are promoted by a mathematical model so complex that it defies comprehension. *Relationships are formal and impersonal:* All are handled alike, people in the same circumstances must be handled the same—the rules say so. We are all cogs in a large machine, and the machine works better if it does not have to concern itself with exceptions. People I know well become members of committees (budget, promotion, grievance), and suddenly they become very formal and impersonal. *The bureaucracy is highly efficient:* We have an assembly-line process with which we mass-educate thousands of students. We take flocks of uneducated high school seniors and after only four years of subjecting them to some forty sophisticated courses of instruction, we produce educated people. *Highly trained employees, protected from dismissal:* Most of the faculty have Ph.D.'s or the equivalent in their area of specialization. After being with the organization for a set number of years, tenure (protection from dismissal) is granted.

But there is another side—the nonbureaucratic side of the bureaucracies, the informal organization in the formal organization. Our institution has that as well. Specialization breaks down somewhat as instructors, because of changing enrollment patterns, move into new teaching areas. It is common knowledge

ERNEST BRADSHAW

"I work in a kind of bank, in the auditing department. I supervise about twenty people. We keep an eye on the other areas. We do a lot of paper checking to make sure nobody inside is stealing. It's kind of internal security." The company is a large one—about five thousand employees. . . .

That's the thing you get in any business. They never talk about personal feelings. They let you know that people are of no consequence. You take the job, you agree to work from eight thirty to five and no ifs, ands, or buts. Feelings are left out. I think some of the other supervisors are compassionate, as I think I am. But they take the easy way out. You take a person that's minimal, you rate him as average. He'll get a raise in six months. When you write a person as minimal, the person won't get a raise and he's subject to lose his job. Everybody takes the easy way out and just put down a person's average. This takes away all the pressures. I felt it has to be one way: be truthful about a person 'cause it's gonna come up on' em sooner or later. I look at people as people, person to person. But when you're on a job, you're supposed to lose all this.

If it's a small organization, you don't need anything like that. You don't need appraisals. Everybody knows everybody. In a larger company people become pawns. These big corporations are gonna keep on growing and the people become less and less. The human being doesn't count any more. In any large corporation it's the buck that counts. . . .

I'm usually at the desk by eight o'clock, half an hour before work starts. Getting set up for the day, writing programs, assigning different jobs to different people. When they come in we take a head count. You see who's late and who's not. You check around and make sure they start at eight thirty and not go in the washroom and powder their nose for fifteen minutes. You make sure when they go for breaks they take fifteen minutes not twenty. You check for lunch hours, making sure they take forty-five minutes and not an hour. And that they're not supposed to make personal telephone calls on the bank's phone. All you're doing is checking on people. This goes on all day.

The job is boring. It's a real repetitious thing. I don't notice the time. I could care less about the time. I don't really know if it's five o'clock until I see somebody clean up their desk. At five I leave for school. It's always the same. Nothing exciting ever happens.

It's just this constant supervision of people. It's more or less like you have a factory full of robots working the machinery. You're there checking and making sure the machinery is constantly working. If it breaks down or something goes wrong, you're there to straighten it out. You're like a foreman on the assembly line. If they break down, replace them. You're just like a man who sits and watches computers all day. Same thing.

that contrary to the hierarchy of authority, the university is really run by the secretaries. They are here every day, they work longer hours, they have more knowledge about how the place really works, and they end up making or influencing many of the decisions. Informal small primary groups arise within the organization that counteract formality and impersonality. Often these cut across the authority structure as well. Several faculty lunch groups constantly meet to pass on information and to plan strategy. A phone call to the right person (usually a secretary) quickly cuts through the system of rules and bypasses miles of red tape. The typical organization is so large that it cannot keep track of bits and pieces. Many professors do not turn in travel plans; they know that they could leave for months and never be missed. And efficiency? The car manufacturer proudly counts the number of units manufactured—3,000 cars today. What they don't tell us is that 2,500 broke down within a mile of the assembly line. Our institution graduates 2,000 people a year, but there is growing concern over the inability of many of the graduates to read and understand the diploma they receive.

I have perhaps exaggerated to make the point—bureaucracies and large organizations have typical formal characteristics that develop because of their size and functions. They also have typical informal characteristics that develop because of the needs of the people that work in the organizations.

Types of Organizations

People who study organizations often come to the conclusion that organizations can be categorized. Two typologies are shown in Table 4.2. Weber categorized organizations according to their authority and internal structure, whereas Katz and Kahn typed organizations according to the type of function they performed.

Charisma, which is a basic factor in Weber's charismatic retinue, refers to a certain superior quality an individual may have that sets him or her apart from others. This individual is viewed as superhuman and capable of exceptional acts—the sort of person you might follow to the ends of the earth if you were asked to.

Remember when you encounter typologies that the categories are seldom as clearly cut and exclusive in real life as they appear to be in a table. A given organization may cut across or be included in several categories because it may, in its various parts, show several structures or perform a variety of functions. Consider again, for example, the university. It is an adaptive organization, but it is a production and maintenance organization as well. Although it is probably basically a modern professional organization, parts show the modern bureaucracy at its extreme, some of the administration is definitely feudal, and perhaps one could even find a charismatic leader complete with followers or disciples (most likely the football coach during a winning season).

Formal Organizations—Consequences and Concerns

Parkinson's Law: The Formula of 1,000
Any enterprise with more than 1,000 employees becomes a self-perpetuating empire, creating so much internal work that it no longer needs any contact with the outside world.

TABLE 4.2 Types of Organizations

Weber—Based on Type of Authority and Structure	Characteristics	Examples
Charismatic retinue	Made up of the followers and disciples of a charismatic leader	Followers of civil rights leader Martin Luther King, Jr.; Reverend Moon's Unification Church; Jim Jones's People's Temple; followers of a great scientist or artist
Feudal administration	Separate from but responsible to a parent organization; has local autonomy to act in terms of own interests; is obligated to superiors, but there is no constant flow of orders or supervision	New-car dealerships; chain or franchised stores, agencies, or theaters
Modern bureaucracy	Close to Weber's characteristics of bureaucracy: specialization, hierarchy of authority, system of rules, formality	Governmental agencies, large public utilities, military organizations
Modern professional organization	Bureaucratic but with more individual freedom, more decentralization of responsibility once the individual's competency is certified	Universities, large hospitals

Katz and Kahn—Based on Type of Function	Characteristics	Examples
Production or economic organization	Creates wealth, manufactures goods, makes things or produces services that are consumed by society	General Motors, IBM, an advertising agency, Pacific Telephone
Maintenance organization	Socializes people for their roles in other organizations and in society	Churches, schools, health and welfare organizations, rehabilitation and reform organizations
Adaptive organization	Creates knowledge, develops theories, applies information to existing problems	Universities, research organizations, organizations dealing with the arts
Managerial or political organization	Judges, coordinates, and controls people; generates and allocates power	Federal and state government, pressure groups, labor unions, special interest groups

Arthur Stinchcombe, "Formal Organizations" (see footnote 6); Daniel Katz and Robert Kahn, *The Social Psychology of Organizations* (New York: Wiley, 1966), Chapter 5; and Richard H. Hall, *Organizations: Structure and Process* (Englewood Cliffs, N.J.: Prentice-Hall, 1972), Chapter 2.

A proliferation in society of large organizations and the bureaucratic values of efficiency and rationality will have consequences, some obvious, some less so. Large organizations allow the performance of tasks that could not otherwise be accomplished. There is undoubtedly greater efficiency in producing products. At the same time, alienation may result when workers see themselves as small cogs in a huge, impersonal machine. Stinchcombe states that in societies dominated by formal organizations, people tend to become specialists in particular activities. Educational institutions respond by encouraging students to concentrate on learning a specific technique or skill rather than attaining a broader, more general education. In societies dominated by formal organizations, a larger percentage of a person's social relationships is planned instead of spontaneous. Interaction is more superficial, and emotions play less of a part in social relationships of this type. People are judged more by what they *do* (actions) than by what they *are* (their more permanent qualities). To put it another way, interaction of all types, on the job or off, is more secondary, less primary. Some analysts of modern society have commented with concern on the decline in the number of primary groups with which one can affiliate. They argue that groups and contacts are becoming increasingly secondary in modern industrialized countries like the United States.

There have been many attempts to categorize societies, and often these attempts involve the variables of modernization and industrialization. Anthropologist Robert Redfield contrasted folk and urban societies. He used the term *folk societies* to describe isolated villages in less industrialized countries, which were small, homogeneous, relatively self-contained, and largely based on subsistence activities. *Urban societies* referred to modern Western industrialized nations. Redfield saw folk and urban as opposite ends of a continuum along which societies at various degrees of development could be placed. Sociologist Emile Durkheim used the terms *mechanical solidarity* and *organic solidarity* to describe types of social cohesion that occur in small, homogeneous, preindustrial societies and in modern industrialized societies. Mechanical solidarity is likely to exist in a small homogeneous society and describes uniformity among people and lack of differentiation or specialization. Organic solidarity is likely to exist in complex societies, which are characterized by more specialization and division of labor, and consequently, increasing individualism. Ferdinand Toennies also described two contrasting types of societies with the terms *Gemeinschaft* and *Gesellschaft*. The **Gemeinschaft** is a more primary and closely knit society in which relationships are personal and informal and there is a commitment or identification with the community. The **Gesellschaft** is a more secondary society based on contractual arrangements, bargaining, a well-developed division of labor, and rational thought rather than emotion. Relationships between people are impersonal and utilitarian.

Many who feel as Cooley did that primary group relationships are of great importance in the socialization process and the development of the self and personality are concerned that the increasing secondariness or *Gesellschaft*-like nature of modern societies will have serious effects on the developmental processes. Some would no doubt point to high rates of divorce, rising crime and delinquency, increased mental illness, and other individual and group pathologies as consequences of restricted primary group contacts. Others would argue that these conditions are merely the consequences of any modern, complex society. Moreover, the huge, complicated, multilayered bureaucracies that perform tasks for us today are highly efficient even though somewhat impersonal. To idealize the *Gemeinschaft* society, they would argue, is unrealistic and shows a lack of understanding of the positive aspects of the large organizations of today. They would conclude that there is not really more pathology (crime, marital breakup, mental illness); our efficient bureaucracies just do a better job of ferreting it out and letting us know about it.

About twenty-five years ago William H. Whyte, Jr., wrote *The Organization Man*, in which he painted a rather gloomy picture of how large organizations were affecting people's lives. Americans have long been guided by what has been called the Protestant Ethic—the idea that pursuit of individual salvation through hard work, thrift, and competitive struggle is the heart of the American achievement. According to Whyte, a new ethic has emerged as a consequence of the proliferation of large organizations. Now the young person going out into the world believes that to make a living he must do what somebody else tells him to do. The idea of individual achievement and the encouragement of personal creativity is disappearing. Instead, the guiding values of the organization man include a belief in the group as source of creativity, in belongingness and togetherness, and in the value of fitting in. These phrases are part of the organizational ethic: "Be a compromiser." "Maintain group solidarity at all costs." "Don't rock the boat." "The unorthodox can be dangerous." The organization man is conforming and "well-rounded"; he looks at his company this way:

> Be loyal to the company and the company will be loyal to you. After all, if you do a good job for the organization, it is only good sense for the organization to be good to you, because that will be best for everybody. There are a bunch of real people around here. Tell them what you think and they will respect you for it. They don't want a man to fret and stew about his work. It won't happen to me. A man who gets ulcers probably shouldn't be in business anyway.[7]

The goals of the organization and the goals of the individual are the same. People don't buck the system; they cooperate with it.

Where did the organization man come from? He was produced by a society that is now geared to the large organization. The educational system, which is increasingly influenced by business, is the first step. The university curriculum has become more practical, vocational, and job oriented, with a declining emphasis on liberal arts and the humanities. And the organization man ten years later? He lives an outgoing friendly life of inconspicuous consumption in suburbia where he joins clubs, has kids, plays golf, and where all the houses, cars, appliances, lawns, and even people tend to look alike.

---

[7]William H. Whyte, Jr., *The Organization Man* (Garden City, N.Y.: Doubleday, 1956), p. 143.

And if the individual messes up, can't hack it, gets disgusted, and drops out, whose fault is it? The organization's? Certainly not. It's the *individual's* fault—he or she doesn't fit in. Our worship of organizations bothers Whyte, and he objects to the emerging values and behaviors that result.

Is it really as bad as he says? It's hard to accurately calculate the effects of formal organizations, since they are so much a part of our lives, but remember, he wrote *The Organization Man* many years ago, and we are certainly a far more bureaucratized society now.

Can Formal Organizations Change?

In sometimes interesting ways, formal organizations modify their forms and structures and change their philosophies. For example, bureaucracies have long held a basic belief in specialization—the simpler the task, the better and more efficiently it can be performed. (See Weber's first characteristic of bureaucracy.) Break the job down into its basic parts. Make it simple, precise, and repetitive, and the worker can't possibly mess it up. Well, this sort of approach to tasks—three turns on the same nut with the same wrench 3,000 times a day—may *be* more efficient, but people don't like it. They get bored, job satisfaction goes down, and absenteeism goes up. The new fad in management is to reverse the cherished specialization ethic and *enrich* jobs, make them more interesting, more varied, not so repetitive. This view has been widely picked up by industry and by business graduate schools. The new pitch is that jobs should be meaningful, self-fulfillment is a worthwhile goal, and work groups are important for improving job satisfaction. Workers will take more pride in the product if they can follow it all the way through, performing a variety of tasks toward its completion.

They may be right, and it certainly sounds like a more enlightened approach to the work situation. But a skeptic might inquire as to management's reasons for this new approach. Companies like to feel they are progressive. And, of course, it's good for the image. Ads have portrayed the happy Swedish automobile workers who get to work on a car through the whole construction process. You just *know* that's a better car. Industry can be humanistic after all. But the clincher for the organization is the economic payoff. Improved worker morale means less absenteeism, employee turnover, and sabotage, and improved quality of product. The best of all possible worlds exists if organizations can improve their image and cut costs at the same time. Imagine the company's dilemma, however, if the new program increases worker morale, happiness, and self-fulfillment—but efficiency and output are unchanged or reduced.

Bureaucratic formal organizations are dominant today; every year more and more people work for them. But what of the future? Will the classic bureaucratic structure described by Max Weber continue to be the prevailing mode of social organization? A number of experts, including Alvin Toffler and Warren Bennis, think not. Toffler predicts that in the future we will witness not the triumph, but the breakdown of bureaucracy.[8] He calls the organization of the future the "ad-hocracy" (from the Latin, *ad hoc:* meant for a particular purpose or goal). A number of factors are leading to the demise of old-style bureaucracy. Mergers, organizational upheavals, and internal reorganizations are occurring at rapidly increasing rates, and this is disrupting once-stable bureaucratic rules and structures. Individuals' places in the organization are less stable—they are shifted from one task to another. There is a rapid increase in project or task-force management. Teams are put together to perform specific short-term tasks, and when finished the teams are disassembled and the people are reassigned, "exactly like mobile playgrounds." It is this particular characteristic that Toffler means by his term "ad-hocracy." Weber's hierarchy of authority is collapsing also, and the chain of command is altered. The rapidity of events and the need for quick actions mean that decisions are being made at all levels without waiting for higher-ups to approve.

Like Toffler, Warren Bennis believes that bureaucracies worked well in stable societies for routine tasks. But with the rapid change of today, those characteristics—routine, stability—are disappearing. The future will see adaptive, short-term, rapidly changing, temporary systems—task forces that solve specific problems. Gone will be permanence and enduring relationships between an individual and the organization. Gone will be the powerful hierarchies of authority that kept the individual in line. Loyalties will be to one's profession rather than to the organization. All of this, according to Toffler, is caused basically by the rapidity of change. To keep pace, organizations will adapt and change their structure and hence, ad-hocracy. But what's the price? Much is unforeseen, but Toffler and Bennis suggest that there wll be strains on the adaptability of people. We should anticipate substantial social strains and psy-

---

[8]The ideas of Toffler and Bennis in this and the following paragraphs are summarized from *Future Shock*, by Alvin Toffler (New York: Random House, 1970), Chapter 7.

chological tensions, and many will experience "future shock" as the future arrives too soon.

Several factors might be remembered as we consider Bennis's and Toffler's speculations about the formal organization of the future. Weber's general characteristics of bureaucracy should not blind us to the fact that individual differences in organizations (as in people) are vast. Some are more affected by change and more responsive to it than others. For example, educational institutions are probably more likely to react to demands for change than are military organizations. Bureaucracies may be responsive to change in one area but resist it in another. The auto industry changes styles yearly, but its responses to suggestions of environmentalists come more slowly. Some organizations generate member loyalty more easily than others. Compare turnover rates in several organizations with which you are familiar. Short-term task groups probably do work well in some situations, but to generalize is risky. And finally, organizations traditionally have been very slow to change. Problems inherent in industrial bureaucracies have been discussed for well over one hundred years, yet little has changed. Today we are more bureaucratized than ever—large formal organizations are the handmaidens of mass society. Under these conditions it is hard to imagine that the changes predicted by Toffler and Bennis will take place, but time will tell.

SUMMARY

The social organization or *social fabric* of a society is woven of cultural norms, values, beliefs, and patterns of behavior through which people interact with each other. The analysis and description of this social organization is a major area of study for sociologists. The analysis of the social organization of a society can be approached from a number of viewpoints. The viewpoint we have taken in this chapter introduces the concepts of group, category, and aggregation. A group exists when a number of people have shared or patterned interaction and feel bound together by a consciousness of kind. A collectivity of people lacking these traits is called a *category* (if they have a particular characteristic in common) or an *aggregate* (if they are located in a specific area).

Sociologists categorize groups in a variety of ways. Of special importance are primary groups, small groups, secondary groups, and formal organizations. Ways of studying small groups were described as well as some of the effects small groups have on their members. Characteristics of past, present, and future bureaucracies were compared. By categorizing and analyzing specific types of groups we are better able to understand and explain the variety, importance, and effect of the group affiliations that individuals have. With the number of different types of groups we have discussed here, it is probably clear that a given group will cut across types and carry several labels. I work for a large formal organization in which I am a member of a sociology department that could be described as a reference group, a peer group, an in-group, a voluntary group, a horizontal group, a permanent group, a closed group (depending on the job market and how many professors are seeking the California climate), and sometimes more a primary group, sometimes more a secondary group.

Three readings follow. The first is an excerpt from the book *Tally's Corner* by Elliot Liebow. This is a study of black streetcorner men, and the selection here describes a particular pattern of primary relationships and small group life. The second reading is an excerpt from Christopher Edwards' book *Crazy for God* in which he describes how group pressure can be used to manipulate the individual. The next reading, by Elinor Langer, describes a large, formal organization. Her article on the New York Telephone Company illustrates many of the characteristics of bureaucracy that we have discussed.

Terms For Study

aggregate (95)	open group (97)
bureaucracy (106)	organic solidarity (111)
category (95)	out-group (97)
charisma (109)	participant observation (103)
closed group (97)	peer group (97)
folk society (111)	permanent group (97)
Gemeinschaft (111)	primary group (98)
Gesellschaft (111)	reference group (97)
group (95)	secondary group (98)
horizontal group (97)	sociometry (101)
in-group (97)	temporary group (97)
interaction process analysis (99)	urban society (111)
involuntary group (97)	vertical group (97)
mechanical solidarity (111)	voluntary group (97)

Reading 4.1

FRIENDS AND NETWORKS

ELLIOT LIEBOW

Primary relationships take a variety of forms—a couple dating, a family, maybe an athletic team, or a work group in a large organization. In this excerpt from *Tally's Corner*, Elliot Liebow describes the primary relationships existing among lower-class black streetcorner men in Washington, D.C.

More than most social worlds, perhaps, the streetcorner world takes its shape and color from the structure and character of the face-to-face relationships of the people who live in it. Unlike other areas in our society, where a large portion of the individual's energies, concerns and time are invested in self-improvement, career and job development, family and community activities, religious and cultural pursuits, or even in broad, impersonal social and political issues, these resources in the streetcorner world are almost entirely given over to the construction and maintenance of personal relationships.

On the streetcorner, each man has his own network of these personal relationships and each man's network defines for him the members of his personal community. His personal community, then, is not a bounded area but rather a web-like arrangement of man-man and man-woman relationships in which he is selectively attached in a particular way to a definite number of discrete persons. In like fashion, each of these persons has his own personal network.

At the edges of this network are those persons with whom his relationship is affectively neutral, such as area residents whom he has "seen around" but does not know except to nod or say "hi" to as they pass on the street. These relationships are limited to simple recognition. Also at the edges are those men and women, including former friends and acquaintances, whom he dislikes or fears or who dislike or fear him. These relationships are frequently characterized by avoidance but the incumbents remain highly visible and relevant to one another.

In toward the center are those persons he knows and likes best, those with whom he is "up tight": his "walking buddies," "good" or "best" friends, girl friends, and sometimes real or putative kinsmen. These are the people with whom he is in more or less daily, face-to-face contact, and whom he turns to for emergency aid, comfort or support in time of need or crisis. He gives them and receives from them goods and services in the name of friendship, ostensibly keeping no reckoning. Routinely, he seeks them out and is sought out by them. They serve his need to be with others of his kind, and to be recognized as a discrete, distinctive personality, and he, in turn, serves them the same way. They are both his audience and his fellow actors.

It is with these men and women that he spends his waking, nonworking *hours, drinking, dancing, engaging in sex, playing the fool or the wise man, passing the time at the Carry-out or on the streetcorner, talking about nothing and everything, about epistemology or Cassius Clay,[9] about the nature of numbers or how he would "have it made" if he could have a steady job that paid him $60 a week with no layoffs.*

So important a part of daily life are these relationships that it seems like no life at all without them. Old Mr. Jenkins climbed out of his sickbed to take up a seat on the Coca-Cola case at the Carry-out for a couple of hours. "I can't stay home and play dead," he explained, "I got to get out and see my friends."

In general, close friendships tend to develop out of associations with those who are already in one's network of personal relationships: relatives, men and women who live in the area and spend much of their time on the street or in public places, and co-workers. The result is that the streetcorner man, perhaps more than others in our society, tends to use the same individuals over and over again: he may make a friend, neighbor and co-worker of his kinsman, or a friend, co-worker and kinsman of his neighbor. A look at some of the personal relationships can illustrate the many-stranded aspects of friendship and the bi-directional character of friendship on the one hand, and kinship, neighbor, co-worker and other relationships on the other.

When Tonk and Pearl got married and took an apartment near the Carry-out, Pearl's brother, Boley, moved in with them. Later, Pearl's nephew, J. R., came up from their hometown in North Carolina and he, too, moved in with them. J.R. joined Tonk and Boley on the streetcorner and when Earl told Tonk of some job openings where he worked, Tonk took J. R. with him. These three, then, were kinsmen, shared the same residence, hung out together on the streetcorner, and two of them—for a time at least—were co-workers.

Preston was Clarence's uncle. They lived within a block of each other and within two blocks of the Carry-out. Clarence worked on a construction job and later got Preston a job at the same place. Tally, Wee Tom and Budder also worked at the same construction site. The five men regularly walked back from the job to the streetcorner together, usually sharing a bottle along the way. On Friday afternoons, they continued drinking together for an hour or so after returning to the streetcorner. Tally referred to the other four men as his "drinking buddies."

Tally had met Wee Tom on the job. Through Tally, Wee Tom joined them on the walk home, began to hang around the Carry-out and finally moved into the neighborhood as well. Budder had been the last to join the group at the construction site. He had known Preston and Clarence all along, but not well. He first knew Tally as a neighbor. They came to be friends through Tally's visits to the girl who lived with Budder, his common-law wife, and his wife's children. When Tally took Budder onto the job with him, Budder became a co-worker and drinking buddy, too. Thus, in Tally's network, Wee Tom began as co-worker, moved up to drinking buddy, neighbor and finally close friend; Budder from neighbor and friend to co-worker. Importantly, and irrespective of the direction in which the relationships developed, the confluence of the co-worker and es-

---

[9]Cassius Clay is now known as Muhammad Ali.

pecially the neighbor relationship with friendship deepened the friend relation-ship.

One of the most striking aspects of these overlapping relationships is the use of kinship as a model for the friend relationship. Most of the men and women on the streetcorners are unrelated to one another and only a few have kinsmen in the immediate area. Nevertheless, kinship ties are frequently man-ufactured to explain, account for, or even to validate friend relationships. In this manner, one could move from friendship to kinship in either direction. One could start with kinship, say, as did Preston and Clarence or Boley and Tonk and build on this, or conversely, one could start with friendship and build a kin relationship.

The most common form of the pseudo-kin relationship between two men is known as "going for brothers." This means, simply, that two men agree to present themselves as brothers to the outside world and to deal with one an-other on the same basis. Going for brothers appears as a special case of friend-ship in which the usual claims, obligations, expectations, and loyalties of the friend relationship are publicly declared to be at their maximum.

Sea Cat and Arthur went for brothers. Sea Cat's room was Arthur's home so far as he had one anywhere. It was there that he kept his few clothes and other belongings, and it was on Sea Cat's dresser that he placed the pictures of his girl friends (sent "with love" or "love and kisses"). Sea Cat and Arthur wore one another's clothes and, whenever possible or practical, were in one another's company. Even when not together, each usually had a good idea of where the other was or had been or when he would return. Generally, they seem to prefer going with women who were themselves friends; for a period of a month or so, they went out with two sisters.

Sea Cat worked regularly; Arthur only sporadically or for long periods not at all. His own credit of little value, Arthur sometimes tried to borrow money from the men on the corner, saying that the lender could look to his "brother" for payment. And when Sea Cat found a "good thing" in Gloria, who set him up with a car and his own apartment, Arthur shared in his friend's good fortune. On the streetcorner or in Sea Cat's room, they laughed and horsed around to-gether, obviously enjoying one another's company. They cursed each other and called each other names in mock anger or battle, taking liberties that were re-served for and tolerated in close friends alone.

The social reality of the pseudo-kinship tie between those who are "going for brothers" is clearly evident in the case of Richard and Leroy. Richard and Leroy had been going for brothers for three months or so when Leroy got in a fight with a group of teenagers and young adults. Leroy suffered serious inter-nal injuries and was hospitalized for more than a month. One week after the fight, Richard and one of the teenagers who had beaten up Leroy, and with whom both he and Leroy had been on friendly terms, got into a fight over a private matter having nothing to do with Leroy, and Richard killed the teen-ager. Richard was immediately arrested and the police, acting on information from the dead boy's friends, relatives, and others in the community, charged him with first degree murder for the premeditated revenge killing of one who had beaten up "his brother." But when it was established that Leroy and Rich-

ard were not related in any way the charge was dropped to murder in the second degree. The dead boy's friends and relatives were outraged and bewildered. To them, it was clearly a premeditated and deliberate killing. Hadn't Richard and Leroy been going for brothers? And hadn't Leroy been badly beaten by this same boy just eight days earlier?

Questions 4.1

1. What is meant by "going for brothers"?
2. Why would the relationships described in this reading be referred to as primary rather than secondary?
3. Give examples of peer group, reference group, and primary group from this reading.
4. What methods did Liebow apparently use to study the relationships on Tally's corner? What other methods could have been used, and what are the advantages and disadvantages of each?

Reading 4.2

CRAZY FOR GOD

CHRISTOPHER EDWARDS

"Groups are important for the ways they affect and shape the individual." We don't generally think of the coercive power of groups or of how they indoctrinate members but that is also part of group life. Group pressure is a powerful and very effective instrument for producing individual change as can be seen in this excerpt from Christopher Edwards' book, *Crazy for God.* After his graduation from Yale, Edwards traveled to Berkeley where he met some young people who invited him to a training camp for a "fun weekend." This led to his joining the Reverend Moon's Unification Church. He spent seven months as a "Moonie" until he was kidnapped by his father and deprogrammed.

After a quick lunch on the lawn, Family members jumped to their feet, took their guests by the hands, and led them to a nearby field to play dodge ball. As I kicked at the ground, sending up clouds of dust, I savored schoolboy pleasures revisited. I looked around at the usual sea of smiling faces. But now deep in the Family members' eyes I glimpsed a chilling single-mindedness, an intent that both bewildered and fascinated me. What lay behind this supposedly innocent game?

Each group divided up into one of two teams. Each team was appointed a captain who suggested a cheer and team chant. During the entire game our team chanted loudly, "Bomb with Love," "Blast with Love," as the soft, round balls volleyed back and forth. Again I felt lost and confused, angry, remote and

From the book, *Crazy for God* by Christopher Edwards. © 1979 by Christopher Edwards. Published by Prentice-Hall, Inc., Englewood Cliffs, N.J. 07632.

helpless, for the game had started without an explanation of the rules. The guests were being moved around the field like robots on roller skates.

"Listen, Chris," Jacob called from the sidelines. "If you don't understand the rules, just chant or cheer as loudly as possible. The important thing is to do whatever a Family member tells you. Remember, unity is everything here."

I dutifully started shouting.

"Louder, louder, Chris. That's it. Just follow me." He placed me in a new position and I clapped mechanically. A few minutes later, he moved me again.

I noticed how aggressively the Family members played, how they constantly eyed their guests, coaxing them to chant out loud. As I clapped and shouted, I could feel my tension slipping away, my sense of involvement growing. In spite of myself, I felt a desire to merge into this Family, this group, this game, to become a part of this vibrant, loving circle. "Give in, Chris," urged a voice within me. "Just be a child and obey. It's fun. It's trusting. Isn't this the innocence, the purity of love, you've been searching for?"

The game ended before I had figured out the rules. . . .

Davey read the work assignments for each group. I was assigned to the trail crew, a group that was clearing a path up to the hills so that Family members could conduct spiritual hikes at sunset. After being given our picks and axes in the barn we proceeded to the trail. As we started to work, Edie shouted:

"Now, remember, first-weekers can't talk to first-weekers. Second-weekers can't talk to second-weekers. Promise you'll obey that!"

I resented this kind of regimentation, but I kept my mouth shut.

Seeing how awkwardly I was handling my pick, Scott stepped over to show me how to use it. As we were chatting, Jim suddenly appeared at our side.

"Hey, you're both first-weekers! You aren't allowed to talk to each other. If you want to know something or need help, just ask an older brother or sister. That's what we're here for. We've all been first-weekers. We know it's tough."

Annoyed at the interruption, I muttered "Okay," and picked away silently. Apparently sensing my anger, Jim suggested:

"How 'bout a song?" Did he really think he could dissipate my negative feelings that easily?

Jim distributed songbooks to the "new members," as first-weekers were called. All afternoon, we took turns singing religious and patriotic solos as everybody else busily picked and shoveled away. The hours passed quickly. My initial resentment toward Jim gradually melted away in the mass effect. . . .

The fifty people crammed in the little trailer suddenly whistled and burst into simultaneous applause. Everyone was smiling, grinning from cheek to cheek, delighted by Heavenly Father's power. Marilyn sat down, beaming. We all dug into our squash, bean, and salad dinner as Moses, at the center of the circle, called on another person to give testimony.

I could feel myself getting high, high from this smiling group, this happy Family surrounding me. Whatever my doubts might be, it seemed that this loving circle must have an element of goodness. And if there is goodness, then mustn't it be true?

"Individual Entertainment" followed. Various members of the audience volunteered to sing selections out of the songbook on an impromptu stage. What innocent joy, this entertainment was, I thought, a great way for guests to release their inhibitions and prove themselves to older members. Mary stood up and sang "Go Down, Moses." Keith, as an older member, sang a more militant song of self-righteousness, "Marching on, Heavenly Soldiers." The crowd cheered frantically. Edie, who was keeping close tabs on me as usual, elbowed me.

"What, Edie?"

"Well, aren't you going to sing? You're the only second-weeker who hasn't sung."

"I am?"

"Sure. Now, go sing."

"No thanks. I don't care to."

"Go. Go do what you're told."

"No. C'mon, Edie, I don't want to."

Phil, overhearing the conversation, collapsed in prayer behind me to ask for the salvation of my soul. I could feel my face grow hot. No one had ever prayed for me before, let alone for God to forgive me for not singing. Maybe I just had a lot to learn about the way in which God works . . .

"Don't be such a spoiled child, Chris," Edie persisted. "Now, come on, do what I tell you. It's for your own good. And remember, if you want to grow in the Family you have to follow center. Come on, are you afraid of what people will think of you? Are you really afraid?"

Me—afraid? I'd never thought of it that way. It looked like I'd have to prove to her that I wasn't and that I wanted to be part of this Family.

"What should I sing?"

"Sing something that indicates your rebirth as a heavenly child. Sing something you'd never sing in Old Life."

As she said Old Life, Edie wrinkled her nose. She paged through the songbook, paused to think, tugged my shirt. "Sing 'God Bless America.' Go on!"

No, I could never sing that song. My God, I had been so ashamed of my country, a country consumed by worship of the dollar and aggrandizement of the self. What would my leftist college friends think if they saw me now? But since that was the most difficult song to sing of all, I decided I'd have to do it to prove to myself that I could, that I could even become a heavenly child if I wished. Edie raised my hand, and Moses called on me. I stood up and walked over to the stage.

"God Bless America—Land that I love . . ." I began in a choked voice. An image flashed across my mind. I was nine years old, at a baseball game with my brother and Dad. A scratchy record was playing the National Anthem as the Yankees paused from their pregame warm-up. I felt the same lump in my throat that I was feeling now.

As I continued, singing louder, my voice cracked with emotion. My hands trembled. Everyone was staring at me, trying to establish eye contact, looking completely transfixed in typical Family fashion. My voice trembled and I began to choke again as I spilled out the faintly remembered words.

"God bless America—My home sweet home!"

The audience rose in unison, breaking into frenetic applause. Two brothers picked me up, led me around the room, and dropped me off next to an ecstatic Edie. Tears streamed down my face, tears of joy or sadness, or God knows what in this chaotic caldron of unbridled emotion.

I was a little child once again, the child who cried when Tarzan slipped from his vine or Lois Lane got captured by crooks. The Family kept jostling me, elbowing me, shaking my hand. Nobody had ever loved me so much, nobody had really cared. . . . This was where I wanted to stay, where I could be loved and accepted. This was the place where God wanted me to be. . . .

Remembering how Jacob had handled me that first weekend, I set out to do the same with Bill, to establish a good "give and take," as the lectures called it. It was essential for him to trust me, to consider me his friend, as I led him through the group rituals, deliberately creating a new reality for him, the reality of the group. One of my aims was to "love-bomb" him, to appeal to his ego in every way possible. I wanted him to feel as positive about himself as possible, for he had to feel accepted enough to want to stay before we could remold him, reshape him into the heavenly child we wanted him to be. I couldn't love him for what he was, for according to the Principle he was a product of Satan's world; I loved him for what I wanted him to become, an obedient follower of Reverend Moon, the mysterious Messiah behind this movement.

After two hour-long lectures, I took Bill aside and asked him, "What do you think of the Farm, Bill?"

"It's really amazing. The group's sincerity and dedication are fantastic. But I have so many questions about the lectures and about the social service projects in Berkeley which nobody will talk about in any detail. And I can't get accustomed to the group life in our circles here. You know, how everything comes from or goes to Edie. Is this true in all the groups?"

"Well, yes. We feel that older members have a special relationship to God, so the elder members direct the activities and mediate the conversations."

"I find that hard to accept, Chris."

"But you get used to it. You will learn that everything works better that way. And you'll find that the older members have a great deal of wisdom."

"Maybe so, but Edie can't or won't answer all my questions."

"Don't worry. They'll all be answered in time. You have to have faith, brother. Just have faith."

I patted him on the back and hugged him.

Our group walked out to the field for the usual weekend dodge ball game. Edie was the team captain for the four groups that composed our team.

"Okay, brothers and sisters. We have to think up a name for ourselves. How about the Heavenly Hustlers?"

"How 'bout the Boonville Bombers?"

"How's that, everybody?" Edie cried.

"Great!"

"Great! Just great!"

"Great!"

"Great!"

As I said "great," I could hear the emptiness in my voice; I could feel a haunting hollowness in my head. The word echoed over and over after it spilled automatically from my lips. Over the weeks I learned that this word was an instant Family turn-on, as well as a term of obedience. I had learned to say "great" whenever somebody asked me if everything was all right, when they spoke in a tone that indicated that he or she demanded acknowledgment of the God-given authority of their orders.

I had noticed older Family members use the cue phrase in answer to their central figures even in the moments of depression, hopelessness, and despair they experienced while under heavenly subjugation. Their faces looked as rigid as mine, and their cheeks must have hurt as much as mine often did, the muscular pain of constant smiling, hour after hour, day after day.

So it would be the Boonville Bombers vs. Father's Flying Forces. Edie quickly explained the rules of the game, too quickly for the newcomers to understand, leaving them dependent on their spiritual parents, as I had been the first week. I marveled at the beauty of the system.

"Just follow me. I'll help guide you," I explained to Bill. Each team formed three lines, the front line always throwing the ball and back lines moving forward as the front-liners were knocked out of the game.

I realized by now that this was a particularly violent game, one in which a person could unleash his aggressions, his frustrations, at being controlled and manipulated. The older Family members played it extremely well, and I found myself getting better at playing it each weekend, enjoying this rare moment of individual expression. As the game progressed, Bill looked toward me, helplessly, for instructions. I told him where to stand, how to clap and chant, how to dodge the ball.

Edie took me aside. "How's Bill doing?"

"Okay so far. I've been establishing common bases and we're having good give-and-take. I think that he is beginning to look up to me."

"Good! Is he with us yet?"

"Not completely, but I'll see what I can do at lunch."

"Good going. You're quite a heavenly child, Chris." She gave me a broad smile and whispered in my ear: "Your Heavenly Father loves you!" I grinned. We did a "choo-choo-choo," and I fell back into line, into the game.

Bill was obviously enjoying the game now, happy to be part of a team. I knew that teaching teamwork, teaching that mutual interdependence was the first step on the road to indoctrination. Edie had explained that you have to consider yourself to be part of the team before you can accept the ideology of the team. This is a most important point, for it means that group affiliation is a stronger force than ideology, which only justifies and reinforces the affiliation.

As the game progressed, I walked around Bill, encouraging him to clap and chant. The group got very, very high off this chanting. Angry faces, excited faces, joyous faces, all united under one common objective. The game ended when the last person was knocked out of the roped-off square. The team huddled momentarily and Edie shouted:

"What are you going to do?"

"Face the ball!" we shouted.

"What else?"

"Catch the ball!"

"What else?"

"Throw the ball!"

"What else?"

"Win the game! Yay, yay!" we all shouted as the new game began. Bill looked confused.

"Where do I stand?" he pleaded once again.

"Right here." By the hand I led the Harvard grad student to his position. He passively followed.

"Now, catch the ball, face the ball, throw the ball. Win the game! Let's have a choo-choo."

Dazed, Bill chanted with me as I grabbed his hands and shook them up and down in ritual.

"Choo-choo-choo. Choo-choo-choo. Choo-choo-choo. Yay, yay—Pow!" He giggled, and I smiled, reinforcing his childish behavior. Recently divorced, confused about the meaning of life, this lonely academic, starved for affection, was finding the simple love and acceptance he sought in this classless universe of giggling children.

Bill had the final shot in the game, smashing a fat little girl in the knee with the flexible rubber ball, winning a victory for the Boonville Bombers. Everybody crowded around him, mussing his hair, shaking his hand, patting his bottom. He was all smiles, feeling the love radiating from each member of the team—purposeful affection that older Family members could turn on and off at will. Everybody was high once again.

"How did you like the game, Bill?"

"Great, just great!" he said, parroting those around him. . . .

"I'd like to be excused to go to the bathroom" Bill announced. Edie looked startled.

"Can't you wait until the group is finished?" she asked sharply.

"No, I want to go now."

"You must obey the rules of the group, Bill. That was assumed when you came here."

"Sorry, but I have to go now."

"Okay, Chris will go with you."

We trotted off together. As Bill entered the stall, he said "Gee, I don't know why you had to come along."

"It's part of the Heavenly life, brother. We have to be so close that we'd follow each other anywhere." I didn't tell him that the real reason I had followed him was the Family's belief that Satan would attack him if he was left alone. Satan lurked everywhere, even in those stalls. Reverend Moon himself had been quoted many times as saying: "Satan is everywhere, and you are vulnerable to his attack!"

As we left the brothers' bathroom, I reached for Bill's hand. This time he instinctively pulled back. Looking him straight in the eyes, I said sternly, "You want unconditional love, don't you?"

"Why, yes, but . . ."

"No buts. If you want unconditional love, you have to obey the rules. That's all there is to it. As the principles say, Truth is Truth."

Bill reluctantly took my hand, and we returned to our circle, where Edie was leading a sensitivity game designed to get the group accustomed to taking orders from their leader, their center person.

"Now, I want everybody to lie down in the circle and put your feet in the center of the circle. Wiggle your toes. That's it. Now, wiggle your toes to say hello to the partners across from you. Good."

I admired the Family's genius, for I realized that this seemingly innocent exercise was, in fact, part of a complex and powerful mechanism for gaining control. I was to learn over the next few months that it worked as follows: You were cajoled to give up control to a person for five minutes, and that person structured your environment for that time. Then you gave up control for another twenty minutes, following the wave of group singing. Then you listened to lectures, giving up your critical control, since control in the discussion groups was contingent upon accepting the ideology of the lectures. You actually begin to listen to the lectures only to gain an awareness of what the group leaders would do to you and how they would justify it, for at that point it becomes a matter of survival.

Bill seemed to be responding well. When Edie asked for his inspiration, he replied, "I'm really impressed by the people here. I can't believe there's a community like this, smack in the center of California, a community of such loving, growing people—a real family. It's just tremendous. It's . . ."

Questions 4.2

---

1. Outline the techniques the group in this selection used to manipulate the individual. Do groups generally use these same sorts of techniques to get group members to conform? If "yes," show how; if "no," are you sure? And why don't they?
2. Why are these group pressure techniques so effective? Discuss in terms of primary group, reference group, in- and out-group, socialization, resocialization, etc.
3. What was the point of age-segregating (first-weekers and second-weekers) the prospective members?

Reading 4.3

INSIDE THE NEW YORK TELEPHONE COMPANY

ELINOR LANGER

Formal organizations are everywhere in modern industrialized societies. It has been estimated that more than ninety percent of the work force in the U.S. is employed in formal organizations. In Max Weber's typology, the New York Telephone Company is a good example of a *modern bureaucracy*. Journalist Elinor Langer worked for the phone company, and here she describes how a large bureaucratic organization works.

From October to December 1969 I worked for the New York Telephone Company as a Customer's Service Representative in the Commercial Department. My office was one of several in the Broadway–City Hall area of lower Manhattan, a flattened, blue-windowed commercial building in which the telephone company occupies three floors. The room was big and brightly lit—like the city room of a large newspaper—with perhaps one hundred desks arranged in groups of five or six around the desk of a Supervisor. The job consists of taking orders for new equipment and services and pacifying customers who complain, on the eleven exchanges (although not the more complex business accounts) in the area between the Lower East Side and 23rd Street on the North and bounded by Sixth Avenue on the West.

My Supervisor is the supervisor of five women. She reports to a Manager who manages four supervisors (about twenty women) and he reports to the District Supervisor along with two other managers. The offices of the managers are on the outer edge of the main room separated from the floor by glass partitions. The District Supervisor is down the hall in an executive suite. A job identical in rank to that of the district supervisor is held by four other men in Southern Manhattan alone. They report to the Chief of the Southern Division, himself a soldier in an army of division chiefs whose territories are the five boroughs, Long Island, Westchester, and the vast hinterlands vaguely referred to as "Upstate." The executives at _____ Street were only dozens among the thousands in New York Tel alone.

Authority in their hierarchy is parceled out in bits. A Representative, for example, may issue credit to customers up to, say, $10.00; her supervisor, $25.00; her manager, $100.00; his supervisor, $300.00; and so forth.

. . . Securing the position was not without hurdles. I was "overqualified," having confessed to college; I performed better on personnel tests than I intended to do; and I was inspected for symptoms of militance by a shrewd but friendly interviewer who noticed the several years' gap in my record of employment. "What have you been doing lately?" she asked me. "Protesting?" I said: "Oh, no, I've been married," as if that condition itself explained one's neglect of social problems. She seemed to agree that it did.

The Representative's course is "programmed." It is apparent that the phone company has spent millions of dollars for high-class management con-sultation on the best way to train new employees. The two principal criteria are easily deduced. First, the course should be made so routine that any employee can teach it. The teacher's material—the remarks she makes, the examples she uses—are all printed in a loose-leaf notebook that she follows. Anyone can start where anyone else leaves off. I felt that I could teach the course myself, simply by following the program. The second criterion is to assure the reproducibility of results, to guarantee that every part turned out by the system will be inter-changeable with every other part. The system is to bureaucracy what Taylor was to the factory: it consists of breaking down every operation into discrete parts, then making verbal the discretions that are made.

Soon acting out the right way to deal with customers became more impor-tant than self-instruction. The days were organized into Lesson Plans, a typical early one being: How to Respond to a Customer if You Haven't Already Been Trained to Answer His Question, or a slightly more bureaucratic rendering of that notion. Sally explained the idea, which is that you are supposed to refer the call to a more experienced Representative or to the Supervisor. But somehow they manage to complicate this situation to the point where it becomes confus-ing even for an intelligent person to handle it. You mustn't say: "Gosh, that's tough, I don't know anything about that, let me give the phone to someone who does," though that in effect is what you do. Instead when the phone rings, you say: "Hello. This is Miss Langer. May I help you?" (The Rule is, get immediate "control of the contact" and hold it lest anything unexpected happen, like, for instance, a human transaction between you and the customer.)

He says: "This is Mr. Smith and I'd like to have an additional wall tele-phone installed in my kitchen."

You say: "I'll be very glad to help you, Mr. Smith (Rule the Second: Always express interest in the Case and indicate willingness to help), but I'll need more information. What is your telephone number?"

He tells you, then you confess: "Well, Mr. Smith, I'm afraid I haven't been trained in new installations yet because I'm a new representative, but let me give you someone else who can help you." (Rule the Third: You must get his consent to this arrangement. That is, you must say: May I get someone else who can help you? May I put you on hold for a moment?)

The details are absurd but they are all prescribed. What you would do naturally becomes unnatural when it is codified, and the rigidity of the rules makes the Representatives in training feel they are stupid when they make mis-takes. Another lesson, for example, was: What to Do if a Customer Calls and Asks for a Specific Person, such as Miss Smith, another Representative, or the Manager. Whatever the facts, you are to say "Oh, Miss Smith is busy but I have access to your records, may I help you?" A customer is never allowed to identify his interests with any particular employee. During one lesson, however, Sally said to Angela: "Hello, I'd like immediately to speak to Mrs. Brown," and An-gela said, naturally, "Hold the line a minute, please. I'll put her on." A cardinal sin, for which she was immediately rebuked. Angela felt terrible.

Company rhetoric asserts that this rigidity does not exist, that Representa-tives are supposed to use "initiative" and "judgment," to develop their own lan-

guage. What that means is that instead of using the precise words "Of course I'll be glad to help you but I'll need more information," you are allowed to "create" some individual variant. But you must always (1) express willingness to help and (2) indicate the need for further investigation. In addition, while you are doing this, you must always write down the information taken from the customer, coded, on a yellow form called a CF-1, in such a way as to make it possible for a Representative in Florida to read and translate it. "That's the point," Sally told us. "You are doing it the same way a rep in Illinois or Alaska does it. We're one big monopoly."

The logic of training is to transform the trainees from humans into machines. The basic method is to handle any customer request by extracting "bits" of information: by translating the human problem he might have into bureaucratic language so that it can be processed by the right department. For instance, if a customer calls and says: "My wife is dying and she's coming home from the hospital today and I'd like to have a phone installed in her bedroom right away," you <u>say</u>, "Oh, I'm very sorry to hear that sir, I'm sure I can help you, would you be interested in our Princess model? It has a dial that lights up at night," meanwhile <u>writing</u> on your ever-present CF-1: "Csr wnts Prn inst bdrm immed," issuing the order, and placing it in the right-hand side of your work-file where it gets picked up every fifteen minutes by a little clerk.

The knowledge that one is under constant observation (of which more later) I think helps to ensure that contacts are handled in this uniform and wooden manner. If you varied it, and said something spontaneous, you might well be overheard; moreover, it is probably not possible to be especially human when you are concentrating so hard on extracting the bits, and when you have to deal with so many bits in one day.

Sometimes the bits can be extraordinarily complicated. A customer (that is, CSR) calls and says rapidly, "This is Mrs. Smith and I'm moving from 23rd Street to 68th Street, and I'd like to keep my green Princess phone and add two white Trimlines and get another phone in a metallic finish and my husband wants a new desk phone in his study." You are supposed to have taken that all down as she says it. Naturally you have no time to listen to how she says it, to strike up a conversation, or be friendly. You are desperate to get straight the details.

The dehumanization and the surprising degree of complication are closely related: the number of variables is large, each variable has a code which must be learned and manipulated, and each situation has one—and only one—correct answer. The kind of problem we were taught to handle, in its own language, looks like this:

> *A CSR has: IMRCV EX CV GRN BCHM IV*
> *He wants: IMRCV WHT EX CV WHT BCHM IV*

This case, very simplified, means only that the customer has regular residential phone service with a black phone, a green one, and an ivory bell chime, and that he wants new service with two white phones and a bell chime. Nonetheless, all these items are charged at differing monthly rates which the Representative must learn where to find and how to calculate; each has a separate installation charge which varies in a number of ways; and, most important, they represent only a few of the dozens of items or services a customer could possibly want (each of which, naturally, has its own rates and variables, its own codes).

He could want a long cord or a short one, a green one or a white one, a new party listed on his line, a special headset for a problem with deafness, a touch-tone phone, and on and on and on. For each of the things he could possibly want there would be one and only one correct charge to quote to him, one and only one right way to handle the situation.

Observers at the phone company. They are everywhere. I became aware of a new layer of Observation every day. The system works like this. For every five or six women there is, as I have said, a Supervisor who can at any moment listen in from the phone set on her desk to any of her Representatives' contacts with a customer. For an hour every day, the Supervisor goes to a private room off the main floor where she can listen (herself unobserved) to the conversations of any of her "girls" she chooses. The women know, naturally, <u>when</u> she is doing this but not <u>whose</u> contact she is observing.

Further off the main floor is a still more secret Observing Room staffed by women whose title and function is, specifically, Observer. These women "jack in" at random to any contact between any Representative and a customer: their job is basically to make sure that the Representatives are giving out correct information. Furthermore, these observers are themselves observed from a central telephone company location elsewhere in the city to make sure that they are not reporting as incorrect information which is actually correct. In addition the Observers make "access calls" by which they check to see that the telephone lines are open for the customers to make their connections. This entire structure of observation is, of course, apart from the formal representative-supervisor-manager-district-supervisor-division-head chain of managerial command. They are, in effect, parallel hierarchical structures.

One result of the constant observation (the technology being unbounded) is that one can never be certain where the observation stops. It is company policy to stress its finite character, but no one ever knows for sure. Officials of the Communications Workers of America have testified, for instance, that the company overindulged in the wired-Martini stage of technology, bugging the pen sets of many of its top personnel. At _____ Street there were TV cameras in the lobby and on the elevators. This system coexists with the most righteous official attitude toward wiretapping. Only supervisors and managers can deal with wiretap complaints; Federal regulations about the sanctity of communications are posted; and the overt position toward taps, in the lower managerial echelons, is that they are simply illegal and, if they exist, must be the result of private entrepreneurship (businesses bugging one another) rather than Government policy.

"If someone complains about a tap," Sally said, "I just ask them: Why would anyone be tapping your phone?" Consciousness of the Government's "internal security" net is simply blacked out. Nonetheless, the constant awareness of the company's ability to observe creates unease: Are the lounge phones wired into the Observing structure? Does the company tap the phones of new or suspicious personnel? Is union activity monitored? No one can say with confidence.

The system of Observers is linked with the telephone company's ultimate weapon, the Service Index by which Errors are charted and separate units of the company rated against each other. Throughout training—in class and in our days on the floor—hints of the monumental importance of the Index in the psychic life of the employees continually emerged. "Do you know how many Errors you're allowed?" Sally would ask us. "No Errors"—proud that the standard was so high. Or: "I can't afford an Error"—from my supervisor, Laura, on the floor, explaining why she was keeping me roped in on my first days on the job. But the system was not revealed in all its parts until the very end of training when as a pièce de résistance the manager, Y, came in to give a little talk billed as a discussion of "Service" but in fact an attempt to persuade the class of the logic of observation.

Y was a brooding, reserved man in his mid-twenties, a kind of Ivy League leftover who looked as if he'd accidentally got caught in the wrong decade. His talk was very much like Sally's. "We need some way to measure Service. If a customer doesn't like Thom McCann shoes he can go out and buy Buster Brown. Thom McCann will know something is wrong. But the phone company is a monopoly, people can't escape it, they have no other choice. How can we tell if our product, Service, is good?" He said that observation was begun in 1924 and that, although the Company had tried other methods of measuring service, none had proved satisfactory. Specifically, he said, other methods failed to provide an accurate measure of the work performance of one unit as opposed to another.

. . . The company gave every woman a Christmas present: a little wooden doll, about four inches tall, with the sick-humor look that was popular a few years ago and still appears on greeting cards. On the outside the doll says "Joy is . . ." and when you press down the springs a little stick pops up that says "Extensions in Color" (referring to the telephone extensions we were trying to sell). Under that label is another sticker, the original one, which says "Knowing I wuv you." The doll is typical of the presents the company distributes periodically: a plastic shopping bag inscribed with the motto "Colorful Extensions Lighten the Load"; a keychain with a plastic Princess telephone saying "It's Little, It's Lovely, It Lights"; plastic rain bonnets with the telephone company emblem, and so forth.

It is obvious that the gifts are all programmed, down to the last cherry-filled chocolate, in some manual of Personnel Administration that is the source of all wisdom and policy; it is clear from their frequency that a whole agency of the company is devoted to devising these gimmicks and passing them out.

Another characteristic of the telephone company is a kind of programmed "niceness" which starts from the top down but which the women internalize and mimic. For management the strategy is clear (the Hawthorne experiments, after all, were carried out at Western Electric): it is, simply, make the employees feel important. For trainees this was accomplished by a generous induction ceremony complete with flowers, films, a fancy buffet, and addresses by top division representatives, all of which stressed the theme: the company cares about you.

The paternalism, the "niceness," filters down and is real. Employees are on a first-name basis, even the women with the managers. The women are very close to one another, sharing endless gossip, going on excursions together, and continually engaging in ceremonial celebration of one another's births, engagements, promotions. The generosity even extends to difficult situations on the job. I have, for example, seen women voluntarily sharing their precious closed time when one of them was overcommitted and the other slightly more free.

The women have a strangely dissociated attitude toward company operations that aren't working well. What company policy is—that is, the way they learn things are supposed to be—gets pressed into their heads so much that they get a little confused by their simultaneous understanding that it isn't really working that way at all. I pointed that out a lot to see what would happen. For instance our lesson books say: "Customers always get Manhattan directories delivered with their regular installations." I said, in class: "Gee, that's funny, Sally, I had a telephone installed recently and I didn't get any phone books at all." Sally would make sure not to lose control and merely repeat: "Phone books are delivered with the regular installations."

Questions 4.3

1. Illustrate Weber's characteristics of bureaucracy with examples from the description of the phone company.
2. What are the disadvantages and advantages—to employees, to the general public—of the bureaucratic characteristics of the phone company?
3. Illustrate different types of groups (voluntary-involuntary, in-out, reference, etc.) with examples from the description of the phone company.
4. "Organizations consciously make attempts to look and act less formal, less bureaucratic. . . ." Does the New York Telephone Company do this? If so, how?
5. Draw a comparison between the phone company and a formal organization that you are familiar with, such as the college or university you are attending. How are they similar and how different? Would your formal organization work better or worse if it was more like the phone company?

5
Social Differentiation: Social Class

Sociologists study groups and nongroups in order to understand the social organization of society. The previous chapter dealt with groups—specifically, small primary groups and large formal organizations. In this chapter our attention turns to nongroups. Many sociologists spend much of their time specializing in the study of *categories* of people—people who have a particular characteristic in common but who do not constitute a group. Those who specialize in the study of older people, an age category, are called gerontologists. Others study race, ethnic, religious, social-class, and sex categories.

The process of defining, describing, and distinguishing between different categories of people is called *social differentiation*. People differ across a range of variables, and some of these categories we find ourselves in automatically—age, sex, race. Other categories have a greater degree of flexibility and to a certain extent one's position can be changed—social class, religion. (Recall the discussion of ascribed and achieved status in Chapter 3.)

As we pointed out in the previous chapter, members of a category may become a group if they become involved in shared or patterned interaction and feel bound together by a consciousness of kind. People belonging to categories—race, religion, age, sex—obviously share common values and interests, and the formation of smaller groups along these lines naturally follows. This chapter and the next, however, focus on categories in the larger sense, and we will examine what sociologists know about the general characteristics of social-class, race, ethnic, age, and sex categories.

SOCIAL STRATIFICATION

Semper Anglia—A dignified English solicitor-widower with a considerable income had long dreamed of playing Sandringham, one of Great Britain's most exclusive golf courses, and one day he made up his mind to chance it when he was traveling in the area.

Entering the clubhouse, he asked at the desk if he might play the course. The club secretary inquired, "Member?" "No, sir." "Guest of a member?" "No, sir." "Sorry."

As he turned to leave, the lawyer spotted a slightly familiar figure seated in the lounge, reading the London *Times*. It was Lord Parham. He approached and, bowing low, said, "I beg your pardon, your Lordship, but my name is Higginbotham of the London solicitors Higginbotham, Willingby and Barclay. I should like to crave your Lordship's indulgence. Might I play this beautiful course as your guest?"

His Lordship gave Higginbotham a long look, put down his paper and asked, "Church?" "Church of England, sir, as was my late wife." "Education?" "Eton, sir, and Oxford." "Sport?" "Rugby, sir, a spot of tennis and number 4 on the crew that beat Cambridge." "Service?" "Brigadier, sir, Coldstream Guards, Victoria Cross and Knight of the Garter." "Campaigns?" "Dunkirk, El Alamein and Normandy, sir." "Languages?" "Private tutor in French, fluent German and a bit of Greek."

His Lordship considered briefly, then nodded to the club secretary and said, "Nine holes."

The study of *social stratification* arises out of the recognition that people are ranked or evaluated at a number of levels. As the geologist finds layers when examining a cross section of the earth, so the sociologist finds layers in the social world. Societies today are stratified into many layers, but this was not always the case. Hunting and gathering societies, the oldest known, were very equalitarian. Members of these small (fifty people or less) societies spent all their time finding food—there was little if any division of labor and little social differentiation. The horticultural societies which followed were larger (from 200 to four million people). They were able to cultivate domestic plants and thereby produce a surplus which led to activities beyond pure survival. Jobs aside from food gathering emerged and accumulation of wealth began. Specialization, division of labor, and presence of a surplus produced the beginnings of social differentiation and stratification.

This trend continued in agrarian societies. Improved tools—the plow replaced the digging sticks and hoes of the horticultural societies—meant more efficient and productive use of the land and greater surpluses. This meant that a smaller proportion of the population remained involved in food production while more occupied themselves as makers of tools and weapons, as miners, merchants, traders, and soldiers. This division of labor and greater surpluses in agrarian societies brought pronounced social stratification and social class differences. Finally, industrial societies have an even greater division of labor and surplus, and stratification is marked as we would expect. Surprisingly, there seems to be *less* difference between the top- and bottom-class positions in industrial societies than there was in the earlier agrarian societies. Why? Perhaps this is because the wealth at the top is so great that it is more easily shared. Or perhaps it is because the skills of those in the middle of the class structure—of scientists and technicians—are so important in an industrial society that these workers can claim a greater share of the pie. Or perhaps it is because effective birth control techniques in industrial societies have limited the population to sizes in which wealth is more likely to be shared.[1]

We find in societies today that people are *unequal*—they are constantly evaluated and ranked by others on a number of criteria. The idea exists that we are all created equal, but what is really meant is that we all have an equal chance to become unequal. Even that is not true, though, because some people have an obvious head start and others are blocked from the time they are born. For example, imagine two boys, Billy and Tommy. *Billy* is the one-year-old son of black parents in rural Mississippi. His parents are tenant farmers, the family income is less than $3,000 a year, he has six brothers and sisters, and neither of his parents went beyond the eighth grade in school. *Tommy* is the one-year-old son of white parents in Scarsdale, New York. His father is a surgeon, his mother is an author, the family income is over $80,000 a year, he has one brother, and both his parents are college graduates. Now map out each boy's future. What are the chances of each living to the age of six? Of graduating from high school? Of going to college? Of going to an Ivy League school? Of receiving regular medical and dental care? Of living to the age of sixty-five? Of getting married while still in his teens? Of having many children? Of having an arrest record? Of going to prison? Of having his name in *Who's Who in America?* Two healthy, happy, bouncing babies, but their life chances are vastly different.

PARALLEL STRATIFICATION SYSTEMS

Most societies have more than one system of stratification. These several or parallel stratification systems are based on different factors. The system we

---

[1]The major source for this section is *The Structure of Social Inequality* by Beth E. Vanfossen (Boston: Little, Brown and Company, 1979), Chapter 3.

usually use when discussing social class is based on occupation, education, wealth, power, and prestige. We could refer to this as socioeconomic status. Another stratification system might be based on race—individuals are ranked high or low purely on the basis of racial characteristics. We see this kind of stratification in the United States and to a greater extent in South Africa. Age, sex, and religion may be the bases for other stratification systems. In some societies, older people automatically have higher status than younger people. In Northern Ireland in the late 1960s and 1970s, the battles between the Protestants and Catholics frequently made news. Northern Ireland is religiously stratified: Protestants have higher status than Catholics.

When there are a number of parallel stratification systems, an individual will be ranked in several different systems at the same time. One may be ranked in terms of race, then in terms of socioeconomic factors, then in terms of age, and so on. And though the stratification systems are parallel, they are not necessarily equal. The status of an American black who is upper-class in terms of wealth and occupation may be roughly equivalent to the status of a white who is middle-class in wealth and occupation. The discrepancy is explained by the existence of two stratification systems—one that ranks a person according to socioeconomic status, a second according to race.

Our society, then, is stratified in numerous ways. In the remainder of this chapter and in the next chapter we will examine several ways by which people are categorized and stratified. The subject of this chapter will be socioeconomic stratification. The following chapter will deal with race, ethnic, sex, and age categories.

SOCIOECONOMIC STATUS AND SOCIAL CLASS

Status symbols vary by country and by sex. A poll published in Paris in August 1975 found that the most admired symbols of status for French women were (1) a chauffeur-driven car, (2) a set of jewels, and (3) an ocean cruise. The status symbols ranked highest by French men were (1) the Legion of Honor medal, (2) a private swimming pool, and (3) a live-in maid.

The ultimate in the United States in 1982? Perhaps a Dupont pen in tortoise-shell enamel ($250), a Breguet wristwatch guaranteed for a century ($25,000), a watch by Piaget or Patek Phillippe, Gucci loafers, or a pearl necklace from Tiffany (subdued elegance at $375,000); a castle in Germany, Ireland, or Spain; certainly a car—a Porsche 928 (around $45,000) or Mercedes-Benz, a Ferrari Mondail 8 ($64,000), or for more comfort, a Rolls Royce Camargue ($156,000).

Status based on socioeconomic factors represents one of the major systems of stratification. Following the ideas of Max Weber, socioeconomic status is usually determined by wealth, power, and prestige.[2]

---

[2]H. H. Gerth and C. W. Mills, *From Max Weber: Essays in Sociology* (New York: Oxford University Press, 1958), Chapter 7.

Wealth

Generally, when comparing and evaluating people, we rank those higher who have the greater wealth and store of material possessions—type and size of house, area of residence, make and number of cars, quality of clothes, and so on. In a society that places value on wealth and material possessions, it becomes important to allow others to find out how well-off one really is, and so we have status symbols. If a person drives a Rolls Royce, Lincoln Continental, or exotic foreign car with a low-numbered license plate, lives in Beverly Hills or on Park Avenue, is mentioned in the society pages, winters in Palm Springs and summers in Switzerland, then we have a pretty good idea of where he belongs on the social-class ladder. The game gets complicated, however, when status symbols change or become generally available. Then it becomes more difficult to tell who ranks where. Only the Internal Revenue Service knows for sure.

Wealth is strongly correlated with education, income, and occupation, and when socioeconomic status is measured, these other factors are usually included. Income refers to current earning capacity, whereas wealth refers more to an accumulation of money and property over time. Some of the relationships between income and education are shown in Tables 5.1 and 5.2. Table 5.1 shows the median number of school years completed by the head of the family for different levels of family income. Table 5.2 takes a slightly different approach to

TABLE 5.1   Family Income and Education, 1979

	Family Income				
	Under $5,000	$5,000– 9,999	$15,000– 19,999	$35,000– 49,999	$50,000 and Over
Median school years completed by head of family	10.1	10.7	12.2	12.8	16.5

U.S. Bureau of the Census, *Statistical Abstract of the United States*, 1981 (102d ed.), Washington, D.C., p. 436.

TABLE 5.2   School Years Completed and Median Income, 1979

	Median Income 1979	
School Years Completed	**Males**	**Females**
Less than eight	$5,900	$2,900
Eight	7,900	3,300
High school: four years	13,300	5,100
College: four years	19,100	8,100
College: five or more years	22,800	11,900

U.S. Bureau of the Census, *Statistical Abstract of the United States*, 1981 (102d ed.), Washington, D. C., p. 145.

the same issue, showing how particular levels of education affect one's earning power. In addition, the data in Table 5.2 provide an example of parallel stratification systems in the United States. Women's income, like men's, is related to education; but stratification based on sex is clearly shown when we see that women with the same education generally earn less than half the salaries of men.

Power

People are also ranked according to the amount of power we think they have. *Power* refers to the ability of one party (either an individual or a group) to affect the behavior of another party.[3] Individuals who run things, who make the important decisions in our cities or at a national level, whether they are formally elected or informally appointed, are accorded high status by those who know of the power they exercise. Elected government officials, advisers to presidents, and consultants in high, mysterious-sounding positions are automatically given high status because we know that they are at or near the centers of power.

Power is a fascinating variable that stimulates numerous questions: Who has it? How did they get it? How is it used? How is power distributed in society? Some analysts of American society believe that power is concentrated in the hands of a few people who are not directly responsible to anyone else. Others believe that power is fairly equally spread across a number of interest groups who respond to the will of the people. These issues are hotly debated, and we will return to them in more detail in Chapter 9.

Some theorists suggest that it is basically wealth (accompanied by the related variables of education and occupation) that establishes a person's position in society, and that this wealth *leads* to power. Wealth is not shared equally in our society and it never has been. In 1972, the wealthiest one percent of the population had twenty-one percent of the personal wealth. As the data in Table 5.3 indicate, the top fifth of the population control far more than their share of national income, and the poorest fifth have only five percent of the national income. To put it another way, one-fifth of the population in the United States has nearly half of the income, and this relationship has not changed at all in nearly thirty years.

TABLE 5.3   Proportion of Income Received by Each Fifth of the Population

	1950	1979
Top fifth	43%	42%
Second fifth	23	24
Third fifth	17	18
Fourth fifth	12	12
Bottom fifth	5	5

U.S. Bureau of the Census, *Statistical Abstract of the United States, 1981* (102d ed.), Washington, D.C., p. 438.

---

[3] This definition comes from *The Structure of Social Inequality*, p. 138 (see footnote 1).

Prestige

Prestige means distinction or reputation and refers to how we subjectively evaluate others. It is usually connected to a position that one holds in society. Some positions have high prestige (doctor, Supreme Court justice), others carry lower prestige (shoe shiner, garbage collector). Prestige—distinction in the eyes of others—is less concrete than wealth and power. It is no less important, however. In fact, if they had the opportunity to choose, many would probably rather have prestige than wealth.

In 1947, North and Hatt asked a national cross section of people to evaluate a series of occupations as "excellent," "good," "average," "somewhat below average," or "poor." This resulted in an occupational prestige scale that has been widely used by sociologists.[4] The study has been repeated and updated numerous times since 1947, and the occupational prestige scores have remained amazingly consistent. Table 5.4 compares several occupations and their prestige scores from the first North-Hatt study with some scores from a study in California done in 1967. The highest prestige rating an occupation can obtain by the North-Hatt method is 100, the lowest is 20. The California study included some deviant occupations that didn't appear in the earlier study.

TABLE 5.4　Prestige Scores for Selected Occupations

Occupation	Original North-Hatt 1947	California Study 1967	
		College Students	Noncollege Adults
U.S. Supreme Court Justice	96	96	93
Doctor	93	96	96
State governor	93	91	93
College professor	89	89	90
Lawyer	86	94	90
Minister	86	79	80
Nuclear physicist	86	95	95
Public school teacher	78	78	80
Railroad engineer	77	68	75
Electrician	73	74	73
Policeman	67	68	69
Carpenter	65	66	70
Garage mechanic	62	57	64
Barber	59	59	63
Store clerk	58	55	57
Truck driver	54	54	59
Bartender	44	52	45
Gambler	—	39	30
Prostitute	—	29	23
Racketeer	—	28	23

[4]Cecil North and Paul Hatt, "Jobs and Occupations: A Popular Evaluation," *Opinion News* 9 (September 1947), pp. 3–13.

There appears to be some stability in how people view occupations—most of them show similar scores twenty years later. On the other hand, a few do change as their importance and notoriety fluctuate (lawyer, nuclear physicist, minister). In the California study the college students generally tended to rank uneducated occupations (except for bartender) lower than the noncollege adults did. The college students also were less condemning of the deviant occupations than were the noncollege adults.

Davis and Moore believe that the prestige and status accorded one's position are determined by its scarcity or importance to society and by the amount of training or talent needed to obtain the position.[5] Logically, we would expect that one holding a position high in prestige would receive greater financial rewards than would one in a position of less prestige. This is usually true, but not always. A carpenter or plumber often makes more money than a teacher, but the teacher, whose skill requires more training, has higher occupational prestige (this may make the teacher *feel* better, but won't pay the bills).

People in the situation just described—material wealth but low prestige, or vice versa—are victims of **status inconsistency.** They are status-inconsistent because the factors that determine their ranks in society are not consistent with each other. If we recall that there are many stratification systems—race, religion, age, sex, as well as socioeconomic factors—it is clear that there are many

[5]Kingsley Davis and Wilbert Moore, "Some Principles of Stratification," *American Sociological Review* 10 (April 1945), pp. 242–249.

possibilities for status inconsistency. Examples of status-inconsistent people in the United States would include a college-educated carpenter, a wealthy business executive with an eighth-grade education, a Catholic President, or a person of recent wealth but no prestige. The problem for the status-inconsistent person is that he behaves toward others in terms of his high rank (wealthy business executive) but others tend to behave toward him in terms of his low rank (eighth-grade education). Some sociologists report that status inconsistency may lead to other things: stress, political liberalism, involvement in social movements, withdrawal, or psychosomatic illness.[6]

Functional Analysis and Conflict Theory

This is perhaps an appropriate time to review the theories mentioned in Chapter 1. The concept of stratification provides a basis for examining some of the differences between two of the theories, functional analysis and conflict theory.

Functional analysis holds that societies are made up of complex and interconnected parts, each of which performs certain activities (functions) to maintain the existence of the society as a whole. Functionalists like Parsons and Davis and Moore suggest that stratification systems fit the pattern well. Their argument goes something like this: Societies that are at all complex must have an extensive division of labor to accomplish tasks and assign workers to positions—this will guarantee smooth functioning and maintain stability. But the positions are not all equally important. Some (the doctor, for example) require greater skill or responsibility than others. In order to guarantee that the most qualified people, the ones with special talents, will be encouraged to seek these jobs, greater rewards must be offered. Differential rewards result in development of different classes of people. Every society must have a system that ensures that the most important positions will be filled by the most qualified persons. Hence, stratification, a functional necessity.

Conflict theorists see it differently. While functionalists suggest that stratification ensures the smooth and efficient operation of society, conflict theorists find that stratification is caused by the domination and exploitation of one group by another. Conflict theorists believe that society is best understood as a struggle—a conflict—for scarce resources such as food, land, wealth, or power. Certain groups of people, perhaps because of inheritance or use of force, gain more of these resources and are able to acquire a privileged position. People who have gained high positions will inevitably act in terms of self-interest and continually strive to maintain and increase their influence.

The key for conflict theorists is control of scarce goods and services—those who can gain this control will hold power and prestige. Certain occupa-

---

[6]See Gerhard Lenski, "Status Crystallization: A Non-Vertical Dimension," *American Sociological Review* 19 (August 1954), pp. 405–413; Gerhard Lenski, "Status Inconsistency and the Vote: A Four Nation Test," *American Journal of Sociology* 32 (April 1967), pp. 298–302; and "Status Consistency and Right-Wing Extremism," *American Sociological Review* 32 (February 1967), pp. 86–92.

tions are rewarded more than others, not because of the importance of the task (the functionalist argument), but because of the bargaining power of the group. For example, if an occupation, by requiring apprenticeship or complicated certification, limits membership to a very few, then the services of those few will be in greater demand. Perhaps doctors are highly paid not because they have some special skill but rather because admission to medical school is artificially limited. Or a group may enhance its position by creating demand where none existed. The fashion industry, with its designer jeans and running shoes, may be an example.

The functionalists see society as a smooth-running machine with the parts fitting nicely. The conflict theorists see an exploitive adversary system involving coercion and force with dominant classes manipulating and controlling subordinate classes. It seems hard to believe that these two groups of theorists are talking about the same thing. They are presenting contrary but valid interpretations of the same set of observations.[7]

How Many Social Classes?

A variety of factors, then, produce a layered society. The question of just exactly *how many* layers or social classes has long been of interest to sociologists. Karl Marx was an economic determinist in that he felt that a person's position in the economic structure of society determined his life style, his values, his beliefs, and his behavior. In his writings in the mid-nineteenth century, Marx described societies as composed of two classes, the *bourgeoisie*, or capitalists, and the *proletariat*, or workers. The bourgeoisie controls the capital, the means of production. The proletariat owns only its own labor. Marx envisioned a continuing struggle between these two classes, leading to the overthrow of the bourgeoisie by the proletariat, and eventually the emergence of a classless society.

Studies of social class in the United States have produced varying results. Lloyd Warner studied a New England community and discovered six social classes. August Hollingshead, using a technique similar to Warner's in a Midwestern town, found five social classes. Joseph Kahl also developed a system of five social classes. According to Kahl, the upper two classes (upper and upper-middle) account for about ten percent of the population and include the "big" people, the important people. The other three classes (lower-middle, working, and lower) account for about ninety percent of the population and include the "little" or "common" people. Others have performed similar studies of a number of communities, and the results are often the same—five or six social classes. Table 5.5 outlines a typical American community in terms of six social classes and describes some of the characteristics of each social class.

Other students of stratification believe that it distorts the picture to speak in terms of specific social classes, whether two, three, five, six, nine, or whatever. It is more accurate, they feel, to speak of a stratification continuum, consisting of many rankings with small gradations between them (much like a

---

[7]This section benefits from the discussion in *The Structure of Social Inequality*, Chapter 2 (see footnote 1).

TABLE 5.5 Social-Class Portrait of a Typical American Community

Class	Proportion of Community	Characteristics
Upper-upper	1–2%	These people have wealth, power, and social repute gained through long residence in the community, a prominent family name, and an Ivy League education. One can only be born or occasionally marry into this level. Lineage is important. There is reverence for the past and graceful living.
Lower-upper	1–2	These people have wealth and power, but the tradition of upper-classness is lacking. Money is too new, and there is no prominent old family name. Several generations of breeding, right schools, careful marriages, and hope may get them into upper-upper.
Upper-middle	10–12	These are professionals and successful merchants who may belong to the country club and will have college degrees, but from the state university instead of Ivy League schools. They have less wealth and prestige than classes above, but they are still important people. They are career-oriented joiners.

⬥ Important People—"Big" People ⬥
⬥ Common People—"Little" People ⬥

Class	Proportion of Community	Characteristics
Lower-middle	33	These small businessmen, salesmen, clerks, and foremen have average income and education (high school plus) and white-collar jobs. They are active in fraternal, veterans, and religious organizations, are religious, family-centered, and moralistic, and live the Protestant Ethic: frugality, respectability, thrift, and hard work.
Upper-lower	33	These are blue-collar workers who earn less, probably didn't graduate from high school, and are more likely to be employees than employers. They belong to trade unions and aim at getting by. Their jobs are routine and uninteresting, a way to earn a living only.
Lower-lower	15–20	These are unskilled workers who dropped out of school early and are frequently unemployed. They married young and quickly had more children than the family could afford to support. They have unhappy marriages and cramped and dilapidated housing, and they see the world as a dog-eat-dog jungle. They are pessimistic, resigned, and apathetic.

Summarized from Harold M. Hodges, Jr., *Social Stratification* (Cambridge, Mass.: Schenkman Publishing Co., 1964), pp. 60–70; and from Joseph Kahl, *The American Class Structure* (New York: Holt, Rinehart and Winston, 1957), Chapter 7.

thermometer) and with no readily discernible social-class categories. Logically, this approach makes sense and may be the most accurate description of the way things really are. However, since people seem to believe in social classes, and since teachers and researchers often find it easier to make distinctions among several broad categories than among numerous slightly differing gradations, we usually view stratification in terms of specific classes. Most often this involves the Warner or Kahl categories or a similar modification.[8]

Determining Social Class

Sociologists have developed several ways of determining social-class rank. These methods include the subjective, reputational, and objective techniques. In the *subjective* method, the person is asked what social class he thinks he belongs to. This seems a rather naïve method, but many argue as Marx did that the world is divided along class lines and that a person's social-class identification is very much a part of his or her self-image—it is much of what he or she *is*. This view holds that social class is important to people, that these people therefore have a high degree of class consciousness, and that they should be able to place themselves accurately in the social-class spectrum.

The *reputational* method involves finding out what others think. People from the community are selected to act as prestige judges, and these judges in turn evaluate others in the community. Social class becomes what selected people say it is. This method is similar to the subjective technique, and again it hinges on community members' class consciousness. The *objective* method differs from other methods in that individuals are evaluated in terms of certain specific factors that sociologists assume are related to social class. For example, Warner examined four factors when he used the objective technique: the individual's occupation, his or her source of income, the type of house, and the area of the city in which he or she lives. By knowing these facts about a person, Warner felt that he could objectively place him or her in a specific social class. Other objective factors that have been used include years of education, amount of income, type of possessions, even type and quality of home furnishings.

Using any of these methods, especially the objective, may give the impression that social class is a very clear-cut phenomenon and that each person can be adequately plugged in. This, of course, is an oversimplification. The categories are not precise and are not always related one to another. For example, in what social class do we put the status-inconsistent person whose occupational prestige is low, income is high, who lives in an apartment in a slum, and is a college graduate—and when we ask her, she says she doesn't believe in social class?

Social Class and Behavior

When the *Titanic* sank in 1912, three percent of the women in First Class died, but forty-five percent of the women in Third Class perished. It was sup-

---

[8]In this section we have directly or indirectly referred to several classic works in stratification. Lloyd Warner's study of Newburyport, Massachusetts, was first described in Lloyd Warner and Paul S. Lunt, *The Social Life of a Modern Community* (New Haven, Conn.: Yale University Press, 1941). Robert S. Lynd and Helen M. Lynd described stratification in a Midwestern city in *Middletown* (New York: Harcourt, 1959) and *Middletown in Transition* (New York: Harcourt, 1963). So did August Hollingshead in *Elmtown's Youth*, first published in 1949 and now available as *Elmtown's Youth and Elmtown Revisited* (New York: Wiley, 1975). Stratification along a continuum is discussed by John Cuber and William Kenkel in *Social Stratification in the United States* (New York: Appleton-Century-Crofts, 1954).

posed to be women and children into the life boats first, but the death rate was higher for children in Third Class than for men in First Class.[9] We saw at the beginning of this chapter that the life chances of Tommy and Billy were affected drastically by their social class. It is clear that social class is related to numerous patterns of behavior. We would expect patterns of consumption to vary by social class. Who owns two cars, for example? In 1977, it was nine percent of people with incomes under $3,000, twenty-eight percent with incomes $10,000–$15,000, and forty-nine percent with incomes over $25,000.

Other less obvious differences between social classes have been studied. Lower-class people seem oriented more toward taking pleasure in the present than toward planning for future goals. Middle-class people are more prone to defer gratification. There seems to be a link between low status and prejudice. That is, lower-class people are more likely than middle-class people to be intolerant of minorities and foreigners.[10]

Studies of social class and mental illness have found that psychoses, particularly schizophrenia and manic-depressive disorders, are more prevalent among lower-class than middle-class people. Middle-class people, on the other hand, are more likely to be neurotic (or so diagnosed by psychiatrists) than are lower-class people. There are class differences in treatment as well. Middle-class people are likely to have psychotherapy, highly qualified practitioners, and more thorough treatment of mental illness. Lower-class people are more often treated by interns and less qualified practitioners and are more likely to be subjected to questionable procedures (shock treatments, lobotomies, and drugs).[11]

Voting behavior is affected by many factors, and social class is certainly one of them. Lower-class people are more likely to vote Democratic, and middle- and upper-class people are more likely to vote Republican. In addition, middle-class people are more likely to vote than are lower-class people. Turning to deviant behavior, we find that homicide is more prevalent among lower-class people than among middle-class people in the United States and throughout the world. Assault is also a lower-class phenomenon.[12]

Several sociologists have studied social-class variations in patterns of leisure and recreation. Hodges found in his survey of "Peninsula People" that upper-class people watched television an average of sixteen minutes per week night, whereas lower-lower-class people watched an average of 180 minutes a night. Thirty-three percent of the uppers said that they never watched television, while only six percent of the lower-lowers said they never watched. The results of a Gallup Poll on this same subject are shown in Table 5.6. Reading books and magazines increases as one goes up the social-class ladder. The

[9]Walter Lord, *A Night to Remember* (New York: Holt, Rinehart and Winston, 1955).

[10]The research on prejudice is summarized in Harold M. Hodges, *Social Stratification* (Cambridge, Mass.: Schenkman, 1964), pp. 210–220.

[11]A. B. Hollingshead and F. C. Redlich, *Social Class and Mental Illness: A Community Study* (New York: Wiley, 1958).

[12]Marshall Clinard and Robert Meier discuss the data on homicide in *Sociology of Deviant Behavior*, 5th ed. (New York: Holt, Rinehart and Winston, 1979), p. 199.

TABLE 5.6   Television Viewing as a Favorite Evening Pastime, 1977

Annual Income	Percentage
Under $5,000	42
$7,000 to $9,999	32
$20,000 or more	22

Excerpted from *Social Indicators III* (Washington, D.C.: U.S. Government Printing Office, 1980), p. 557.

higher one's social class, the more one is likely to be involved in sports as a participant; the lower one's class, the more likely that person is to be involved as a spectator.[13]

Interest and participation in sports and other recreational activities also varies by income. For example, a recent Gallup Poll asked people to name their favorite spectator sport. Those with annual incomes under $5,000 were much more interested in baseball and bowling, while those earning more than $25,000 were much more interested in football. Interest in other sports, such as golf and basketball, didn't vary from group to group.

In terms of the way they raise their children, middle-class parents are probably more permissive, lower-class parents more rigid. Melvin Kohn reports that middle-class mothers value self-control, dependability, and consideration, while lower-class mothers value obedience and the ability in a boy to defend himself. Vanfossen suggests that the way children are raised reflects their parents' work situation. The middle-class child is raised in an atmosphere which values independence, achievement, curiosity, autonomy, and *self* control. The lower-class child is raised in an atmosphere that emphasizes the immediate and concrete rather than the new and unfamiliar; he is taught to focus on getting by, and he learns obedience, conformity, propriety, and control by *others*.[14]

Many of the current theories attempting to explain delinquent and criminal behavior are based on social class. Walter Miller, for example, argues that lower-class juveniles who become delinquents do so because of the lower-class value system. Values and beliefs important to lower-class youth include trouble, toughness, smartness, excitement, fate, and autonomy (resistance to being bossed or controlled). Miller believes that the greater presence of these values in the lower class than in other social classes makes it inevitable that many lower-class children will run afoul of the law. He seems to be saying that we have two different cultures—middle-class and lower-class—but the *laws* in United States society emerge solely from the middle-class culture, and therefore one should expect that most *illegal* behavior will come from the lower-class culture. The rather pessimistic inference from this theory is that the only way to make it is to become middle-class.

Several other theories examine the social-class-linked motivations for delinquency in a slightly different way. Albert Cohen and Richard Cloward and

---

[13]Hodges, *Social Stratification*, p. 161 (see footnote 12).

[14]See Melvin Kohn's book, *Class and Conformity* (Homewood, Ill.: Dorsey Press, 1969), and the discussion by Vanfossen in *The Structure of Social Inequality*, pp. 272–273 (see footnote 1).

Lloyd Ohlin agree that ours is a middle-class-based society, but they do not believe that it is a lower-class value system or culture that leads one to delinquency. Rather, they feel that the basic problem arises out of the lower-class individual's attempt to move into the middle class. It is Cohen's view that most who try to make it will not. Anticipating failure, their reaction is to invert the middle-class system—to do just the opposite of what middle-class people say is correct. The result is malicious, nonutilitarian, frequently criminal behavior. Cloward and Ohlin agree with Cohen up to the point of the reaction of inverting the values of the middle class to spite them. Cloward and Ohlin believe that the lower-class individuals still want to make it and that when they see they cannot succeed legally, they decide to try it illegally. They become involved, therefore, in utilitarian property crime, which allows them to collect the good things, the symbols of status associated with middle-class culture. Regardless of whether the theorists agree on particulars, the important factor in all of these theories is that they are based on social class. The social class to which people belong apparently provides them with a characteristic view of the world that does much to determine their behavior.

The theories discussed above deal only with lower-class crime and may leave one with the impression that all crime is committed by lower-class people. This is a common error that is made if one looks only at arrest figures, which *are* higher among the lower class. Middle-class people commit different types of crimes—fraud, embezzlement, white-collar offenses—that are less easily detected and punished. Also, middle-class people have the financial resources to deal with the law, to avoid arrest to begin with, and to obtain better legal defense should arrest occur. Typically, the middle-class juvenile delinquent is informally apprehended and returned to his or her parents, whereas the lower-class delinquent is formally arrested and sent to a juvenile hall. The actual extent of hidden middle-class crime is hard to assess. It may be that if all offenses could be known, the differences between social classes would be only in types of offenses, not in their numbers of offenses.[15]

As one might expect, the likelihood of being a *victim* of crime also varies by social class. The pattern is a curious one, however, as can be seen in Table 5.7. As income increases, the chances of being a victim of theft (larceny-theft, burglary, auto theft) increase, but the chances of being a victim of violent crime (homicide, assault, rape) decrease.

---

[15]The original works referred to in this section include William C. Kvaraceus and Walter B. Miller, *Delinquent Behavior: Culture and the Individual* (Washington, D.C.: National Education Association, 1959); Walter Miller, "Lower-Class Culture as a Generating Milieu of Gang Delinquency," *Journal of Social Issues* 14 (1958), pp. 5–19; Albert K. Cohen, *Delinquent Boys: The Culture of the Gang* (New York: Free Press, 1955); and Richard Cloward and Lloyd Ohlin, *Delinquency and Opportunity* (New York: Free Press, 1960). These and other class-related theories of delinquency are summarized in Hodges, *Social Stratification*, Chapter 10 (see footnote 15), and in many textbooks on criminology—for example, Walter C. Reckless, *The Crime Problem*, 5th ed. (New York: Appleton-Century-Crofts, 1973), Chapter 2.

A recent study supports the idea of little relationship between class and criminality. See "The Myth of Social Class and Criminality: An Empirical Assessment of the Empirical Evidence" by Charles Tittle, Wayne Villemez, and Douglas Smith, *American Sociological Review* 43 (October 1978), pp. 643–656.

TABLE 5.7   Crime Victims and Income, 1974

Annual Family income	Rate per 1,000 People 12 and Over	
	Violent Crime	Crimes of Theft
Under $3,000	54	81
$10,000–14,999	28	94
$25,000 and over	25	128

Social Indicators, 1976 (Washington, D.C.: U.S. Government Printing Office, 1977), p. 248.

Social Mobility

Social mobility refers to movement within the social-class structure. This movement can be up, down, or sideways. **Horizontal social mobility** refers to movement from one occupation to another within the same social class. If an architect becomes a minister, or if the mail carrier becomes a carpenter, we would say that horizontal social mobility has occurred—occupational change but no change in social class. The term is also used by sociologists to describe geographical mobility, moving one's home from one place to another. Vertical social mobility is more relevant to our discussion here, however. **Vertical social mobility** refers to movement up or down the social-class ladder, movement from one rank to another.

Societies with unlimited possibilities for vertical social mobility are described as *open*. Those with no possibilities for mobility are called *closed*. In reality, all societies rank somewhere between the extremes of completely open and completely closed. India's system of stratification, for example, is nearly closed. Lines between levels or castes are often firmly drawn; moving from the caste into which one is born may be difficult if not impossible. Some have suggested that we have a type of caste system in the United States relative to blacks and whites. That is, there is a firm line between black and white stratification systems, and although a black may rise within the black class system, he is either blocked from the white system or is automatically assigned low rank in the white system. In societies with stratification systems that are more open, mobility from one level to another may be both possible and frequent.

Examining mobility in a given country is a complicated procedure. Americans, for example, have traditionally considered their system to be completely open. Mobility and achievement were available to anyone who worked hard and led a clean life. We *know* that the rags-to-riches, Horatio Alger story is *true* and *we* can make it too. America is not like other countries where class lines are difficult to cross. The truth is, mobility is very much the same in all modern industrialized countries. The dramatic leap from rags to riches is a rare occurrence indeed. Mobility, when it occurs, is usually in a series of small steps and possibly over several generations. Pure luck, of course, can increase one's opportunities, as can the needs of technology—the widening of the computer industry, for example. We find more mobility within classes (horizontal mobility) than between classes (vertical mobility). While there seems to be more upward vertical mobility than downward, and many are mobile, few move very far.

A study of mobility of men and women in the United States reported an interesting finding: women are more mobile, both upward and downward, through marriage than men are through occupations. Men are much more likely to inherit their fathers' statuses than are women. Because our society lacks mechanisms for women to directly inherit occupations, they are freer to marry into statuses both above and below their origins.[16]

If I have convinced you that it is difficult but you still want to become upwardly mobile without relying completely on luck, there are a few general rules to follow. Defer gratification, marry late, and have a small family if you must have one. If you live in a small town, leave. Vertical mobility is easier in middle-sized and large cities. If you are an immigrant to the United States, be Japanese, Jewish, or Scottish. These groups are more mobile than other immigrant groups, who more often than not come in at the bottom of the social-class ladder and stay there. In modern societies in which skills and knowledge are increasingly important, education is essential for upward mobility. In the United States a college degree helps. For some it is not only the degree, but the right school—Harvard, Yale, Radcliffe, Princeton—that is essential to mobility. Finally, if all else fails in your quest for upward mobility, marry someone who has followed the above rules.

But before you decide to move up, beware of the consequences. Sociologists have been studying the social-psychological effects of upward mobility. One result of uprooting oneself from the past and moving to a new level is that it becomes difficult to form satisfying relationships. One is alone, a **marginal person** between two worlds and a member of neither. Another view agrees that socially mobile people are isolates, but argues that they were isolates to begin with. They were unhappy and isolated, and this led to attempts at mobility, so they are really no worse off. A third view of the situation (and the one that is most accurate according to current research on social mobility) is that socially mobile people have few problems because they are so anxious to get to the next level that they adopt the patterns of behavior of that level long before they ever get there (anticipatory socialization). Consequently, they are accepted and much at home when they finally arrive.[17]

In a society that is upwardly oriented, downward mobility is hard to take. Studies cite relationships between downward mobility and both suicide and mental illness (especially schizophrenia). The same factors that are related to upward mobility are conversely related to downward mobility. Marrying early, having a large family, or failing to get an education may do it. Personal factors may help: business failure, sickness, or rejection of the ethic that says that climbing the social ladder is important.

---

[16]Ivan Chase, "A Comparison of Men's and Women's Intergenerational Mobility in the United States," *American Sociological Review* 40 (August 1975), pp. 483–505.

[17]See the discussion of social mobility and its effects in *Social Stratification in America* by Leonard Beeghley (Santa Monica, Calif.: Goodyear, 1978), pp. 311–318. Also see Hodges, *Social Stratification*, Chapters 12 and 13, especially p. 266.

POVERTY AND WELFARE

Earlier in this chapter we learned that wealth is an important variable in determining social class and that wealth is not equally shared in American society. The top twenty percent of the population controls forty-two percent of the national income, but the poorest twenty percent have only five percent of the national income (see Table 5.3, p. 138). This calls our attention to one of this country's major social issues: poverty. Poverty is a major social issue because of the links between it and crime, delinquency, self-esteem, mental illness, educational opportunities, physical health, life expectancy, infant mortality, and numerous other factors.

The United States government has developed a definition of poverty that is based on the amount of money needed to buy a nutritionally adequate diet (assuming that no more than one-third of the family income is used for food). The poverty line varies according to family size, location, and the value of the dollar. In 1981, for example, the poverty line for a nonfarm family of four was $9,287. In 1981, thirty-one million people (roughly fourteen percent of the population) were below the poverty line. Large as that number is, it is not nearly the whole picture of poverty in this country. The poverty line refers to a so-called survival income, and there are many people who are above the poverty line but who don't have a normal or acceptable standard of living. They may live in dwellings without electricity or running water, or in conditions in which, although they may be able to survive, they know that most of the rest of the people in the country live far better than they do. It is difficult to arrive at an accurate estimate of how many poor and near-poor there are, but the bottom twenty percent of the population is the figure often used. Roughly forty-five million people would fall into this category, and as we can see from Table 5.3, they were no better off in 1979 than they were in 1950. In each year they had only five percent of the total income although they represented twenty percent of the population.

Unemployment, inflation, and recession are part of the poverty picture. Although family income increased between 1980 and 1981, because inflating dollars bought less, families' "real" income *dropped* by three and a half percent. This forced more Americans below the poverty level—at fourteen percent, the highest rate of poverty since 1967. In late 1981, more than eight and a half million workers were unemployed—roughly eight percent of the population. Teenagers, minority teenagers, and minorities generally were especially hard hit by unemployment.

Who are the poor? Obviously poverty doesn't strike all equally. The characteristics of the poor (see Table 5.8) show them to be the young and the elderly, members of ethnic and racial minorities, women who are heads of households, the illiterate and unemployable, and the disabled and handicapped. Poverty is higher in certain parts of the country, primarily in rural areas and in the South.

How does a society that sees itself as a land of opportunity deal with the existence of poverty? In curious and interesting ways. One approach is to hide it. The poor are located in areas we don't see and consciously avoid. The sick and aged are almost by definition invisible. The subject is not popular and won't be found on prime-time television except for an occasional documentary. The

TABLE 5.8   Who the Poor Are—Persons Below Poverty Level, 1980

Group	Percent of Population
National average	13
Whites	10
Blacks	33
Spanish origin	26
Age under 18	18
Age over 65	16
Living in the South	17
Living in central cities	17
Female householder (no male present)	33
Male householder (no wife present)	11

"Money Income and Poverty Status of Families and Persons in the United States: 1980," *Current Population Reports*, Series P-60, no. 127.

poor have no economic or political clout. The poor are a large but essentially anonymous and hidden group; we try to deny their existence.

Another way of dealing with an unwelcome problem is to blame the victim. William Ryan begins his book *Blaming the Victim* with the story of actor Zero Mostel impersonating a pompous senator investigating the origins of World War II. The climax of the senator's investigation comes when he booms out with triumph and suspicion, "What was Pearl Harbor *doing* in the Pacific?" Exactly. The poor are poor because they are lazy, unintelligent and lack motivation, tend to drink and have loose morals, can't manage money, and don't want to work anyway. Blaming the victim released the nonvictims from responsibility for the victim's plight. Recent studies have found that many Americans (often, a majority of those asked) believe that (1) most people on welfare who can work don't try to find jobs, (2) many people on welfare are not honest about their need, (3) many mothers on welfare have babies to increase their welfare payments. In fact, studies of those on welfare show that all of these beliefs are *incorrect*.[18]

Why do we have these beliefs about the poor? Probably because Americans fervently believe in the work ethic. All able-bodied people should work, their income should come from work, and the more hard-working they are the better people they are. Work is good—even if it is low-paying, exhausting, and degrading temporary work. There is also a welfare ethic, which emphasizes that no one should accept money unless absolutely necessary. This leads to suspicions regarding welfare recipients, more extensive monitoring to find suspected welfare cheaters, and confirmation of the view that people who take charity were bad people to begin with.

---

[18]The major sources I am using in this section on poverty are Leonard Beeghley, *Social Stratification in America* (Santa Monica, Calif.: Goodyear, 1978), Chapter 8; Jonathan Turner and Charles Starnes, *Inequality: Privilege & Poverty in America* (Pacific Palisades, Calif.: Goodyear, 1976); Jerome Skolnick and Elliott Currie, *Crisis in American Institutions*, 5th ed. (Boston: Little, Brown, 1982); and William Ryan, *Blaming the Victim*, rev. ed. (New York: Random House, 1976). Facts on money and numbers come from *Statistical Abstract*, 1981.

The study of welfare beliefs and facts is discussed in Beeghley, pp. 135–138.

SCHIZOPHRENIA AT *THE NEW YORKER*

The New Yorker, while not the most popular magazine in America, reaches a so-phisticated, highly literate, affluent, mostly urban audience. It's a concerned audience that seems to care about pollution, nuclear fallout, poverty, and racism. In November 1981, *The New Yorker* contained a series of articles on "The Under-class," a group of people not easy to define (from two million to 18 million people) but whose members are believed to be "responsible for a disproportionate amount of the crime, welfare costs, the unemployment, and the hostility that beset many American communities." The articles examine a social experiment: the Manpower Demonstration Research Corp. (MDRC) which operates work programs to bring un-derclass members back into the world of conventional work by offering appropriate training in basic skills.

As we read about the efforts of the MDRC our eyes may occasionally drift to the adjoining advertisements. As we read about the makeup of the participants in the MDRC Program—30 percent have never worked, 75 percent have not completed high school, 90 percent are black or Hispanic—we see on the same page a Tiffany ad for a $16,000 18-karat gold wristwatch. As three undercover policemen are de-scribed going into a sleazy Manhattan hotel "pervaded by the smell of marijuana and the stench of urine," across the page we find a Fortunoff ad for a diamond-and-ruby-encrusted sapphire hanging from a gold chain. Price: $18,000. Other ads on the pages carrying the series include: a $50 bottle of 21-year-old Scotch; a $2,350 Rolex watch; a $199 fountain pen; a $1,750 diamond-gold-and-steel Ebel sports watch; an $18,490 Audi sedan; a $4,250 Crocodile attache case; a $70,000 Van Cleef & Arpels platinum-and-diamond bracelet; a $550 butane cigaret lighter; a $95 gold-plated ballpoint pen; and $125 sterling silver cuff links.

Finally the series closes by emphasizing that there are no conclusive answers to these gnawing problems, and that "in the end it has to do with values." An accom-panying ad describes Cheeca Lodge on the Florida Key of Islamorada where for the winter season beginning December 20, a couple can rent an ocean-front villa for $155 a night.

From "The Money Tree" by Milton Moskowitz, © 1981 Los Angeles Times Syndicate. Reprinted with permission.

Finally, we should recognize that poverty is *functional*. The existence of the poor and their exploitation benefits other Americans in many ways. The poor do society's dirty work—the dirty, dangerous, undignified, and menial jobs. They work for low wages, and as domestics, for example, they make life easier for the middle and upper classes. The existence of poverty creates all sorts of jobs and occupations to service the poor—social workers, police of-ficers, ministers, pawn shop operators, and the peacetime army (which recruits heavily from the poor). The poor help the economy by purchasing goods that the more affluent don't want—day-old food, second-hand clothes, and deterio-rating merchandise. In many ways, then, the existence of poverty is advan-tageous to the nonpoor segment of American society.[19]

---

[19]Herbert Gans, "The Positive Functions of Poverty," *American Journal of Sociology* 78 (September 1972), pp. 275–289; and Beeghley, *Social Stratification in America*, p. 140.

Welfare

The welfare system was devised ostensibly to assist the victims of poverty, to help them fare well in society. The idea of welfare has been around for a long time. Originally, churches were the primary agencies for charity and relief giving, but as the urban labor class grew, attempts to control the poor emerged. In 1351 under King Edward III of England, a law established maximum wages, required the unemployed to work for whoever demanded, restricted the travel of workers, and forbade charity to the able bodied. In large part, these have become the basic features of welfare in America today.[20]

Public program social welfare expenditures in 1979 were more than $427 billion. These programs included aid for families with dependent children (AFDC), Medicaid, aid for the aged, the blind, and the disabled, food stamps, veterans' aid, workmen's compensation, black lung benefits, and so on. The list of programs is long, and the amount of money spent is substantial and increasing sharply.

Critics of the welfare system, however, believe that in spite of the huge amounts of money spent, the system actually operates to *perpetuate* poverty. Those statutes that Edward III established over 600 years ago helped him *control* the poor. Piven and Cloward argue that our current system has the same intent—to regulate and exploit the poor. During periods when high unemployment leads to public unrest, welfare programs are expanded to absorb and pacify the masses. At times of political and economic stability and low unemployment, welfare rolls are narrowed, forcing people into low-paying jobs in the labor market.[21]

Turner and Starnes suggest that we really have two systems operating, a *wealthfare* system and a *welfare* system. The wealthfare system enables the middle and especially the upper class to maintain their privileged position by allowing them to avoid taxation and by giving them and the businesses they own and operate direct cash payments and subsidies. The wealthfare system is an example of the exercise of power, and it works through the intricacies of the federal tax system. A quick example: In 1968 a family with an income of less than $2,000 a year paid twenty-seven percent of its income in taxes; a family with an income of over $50,000 a year paid less than seven percent of its income in taxes. In which case was the tax bite more painful? Who does the system work for?

The welfare system exists, according to Turner and Starnes, because it appears to be a humanitarian effort to keep people from starving; it is politically necessary because the numbers of poor give them some power and they may revolt; and it is a nice balance to and keeps attention diverted from the far more expensive wealthfare system. The welfare system perpetuates poverty by keeping payments low, by forcing people to work in any available job, and by diffusing any collective power the poor may have.[22]

---

[20]Turner and Starnes, *Inequality: Privilege & Poverty in America*, p. 122.

[21]Frances Piven and Richard Cloward, "The Relief of Welfare," in Skolnick and Currie, *Crisis in American Institutions*, 3d ed. Also see Beeghley, *Social Stratification in America*, pp. 139–140.

[22]Turner and Starnes, *Inequality: Privilege & Poverty in America*, pp. 62–63, and 93.

What is the answer? Recognizing that poverty is a problem that we want to solve and trying to redistribute wealth and resources, perhaps through a guaranteed annual income—possibly in these ways inequality could be reduced. But we cannot be hopeful about the prospect. If our analysis is accurate, the middle and upper classes benefit from the system as it exists. Poverty is unpleasant, but the alternative to it—massive changes in existing education, government, and economic institutions—and the threat change suggests is more unpleasant for the affluent to consider, and power resides with privilege. Again we must consider power—who has it, how it is used, and for whose benefit.

SUMMARY

Sociologists study the social organization of society by studying groups and nongroups. The subject of the previous chapter was groups. The characteristics of groups were discussed as well as the variations in behavior in small and large groups. This chapter focuses on social differentiation. What we have done here is examine characteristics that make people *different*. People fall into a number of categories—age, sex, race, social class, religion—by which they differ. These are not groups as we discussed them earlier; they are nongroups, *categories*, very large collectivities of people.

A central point here is not only that people are separated into categories, but that these categories are *ranked*. People act as though some are better and some are worse than others. This introduces the idea of social stratification—in all societies people are ranked across a number of variables. In this chapter we have focused on the ranking relative to socioeconomic status.

The important variables in socioeconomic status are wealth, power, and prestige. Wealth, income, and education are separate variables but closely related. Several interesting debates run through the discussion of social class. Who has the power in the United States? What does the American class structure look like? It depends on whom you ask. Some see a continuum with no specific classes; others see three, four, five, six, or even more reasonably well-defined classes.

We found that social class is related to numerous aspects of behavior—voting, mental illness, recreation patterns, homicide, prejudice, child-rearing patterns, suicide, consumption patterns, and delinquency. Vertical social mobility refers to movement up or down the social-class ladder. Analysis of social mobility in the United States indicates that Horatio Alger doesn't live here anymore—few people move very far up or down the ladder.

Some forty million people are poor or nearly poor in this country. Their poverty and the ways society deals with it are a major social issue for Americans. Analysis of the welfare system suggests that although it was established to help the poor, it may actually operate to perpetuate poverty.

In the next chapter this analysis of social differentiation will continue as we direct our attention to other categories: race, ethnicity, sex, and age.

In the first of the readings which follow, William Ryan examines several conflicting models in an attempt to try to understand what we really mean by equality. Next are two interviews from Studs Terkel's book, *American Dreams: Lost and Found.*

Terms for Study

conflict theory (141–142)	social mobility (148)
functional analysis (141)	social stratification (134)
horizontal mobility (148)	status inconsistency (140)
marginal person (149)	vertical mobility (148)
power (138)	wealthfare system (153)
prestige (139)	welfare system (153)
social differentiation (133)	

Reading 5.1

THE EQUALITY DILEMMA

WILLIAM RYAN

In this excerpt from his book *Equality*, William Ryan examines two conflicting models of equality, Fair Shares and Fair Play. Ryan suggests that a dilemma we face in American society is that although the Fair Play model is favored by most Americans, this favor is based on faulty assumptions; perhaps the Fair Shares model is more appropriate and closer to what is really meant by equality. Ryan is a psychology professor at Boston College.

Thinking about equality makes people fidgety. Insert the topic into a conversation and listen: voices rise, friends interrupt each other, utter conviction mingles with absolute confusion. The word slips out of our grasp as we try to define it. How can one say who is equal to whom and in what way? Are not some persons clearly superior to others, at least in some respects? Can superiority coexist with equality, or must the one demolish the other? Most important, are the existing inequalities such that they should be redressed? If they are, what precisely should be equalized? And by whom?

We feel constrained by the very word—to deny equality is almost to blas-

pheme. Yet, at the same time, something about the idea of equality is dimly sinful, subject to some obscure judgment looming above us. It is not really adequate to be "as good as." We should be "better than." And the striving for superiority fills much of the space in our lives, even filtering into radio commercials. Listen to a chorus of little boys singing, "My dog's better than your dog; my dog's better than yours." They are selling dog food, it turns out, and apparently successfully, which must mean that a lot of people want very much to have their dogs be better than your dogs. Their dogs!

This passing example suggests how far it is possible to carry the competition about who and whose is better. The young voices sing fearlessly. There is little danger that some fanatic will leap up and denounce the idea of one dog's being superior to another or quote some sacred text that asserts the equality of all dogs. In regard to people, however, we do hesitate to claim superiority or to imply inferiority. No commercials announce, "My son's better than your son" or "My wife's better than yours" or, most directly, "I'm better than you." That we remain reticent about flaunting such sentiments and yet devote ourselves to striving for superiority signals the clash of intensely contradictory beliefs about equality and inequality.

We all know, uneasily but without doubt, that our nation rests on a foundation of documents that contain mysterious assertions like "all men are created equal," and we comprehend that such phrases have become inseparable components of our license to nationhood. Our legitimacy as a particular society is rooted in them, and bound and limit our behavior. We are thus obliged to agree that all men are created equal—whatever that might mean to us today.

But our lives are saturated with reminders about whose dog is better. In almost all our daily deeds, we silently pledge allegiance to inequality, insisting on the continual labeling of winners and losers, of Phi Beta Kappas and flunkouts, and on an order in which a few get much and the rest get little.

We re-create the ambiguity in the minds of our children as we teach them both sides of the contradiction. "No one is better than anyone else," we warn. "Don't act snotty and superior." At the same time we teach them that all are obliged to get ahead, to compete, to achieve. Everyone is equal? Yes. Everyone must try to be superior? Again, yes. The question reverberates. . . .

It should not surprise us, then, that the clause "all men are created equal" can be interpreted in quite different ways. Today, I would like to suggest, there are two major lines of interpretation: one, which I will call the "Fair Play" perspective, stresses the individual's right to pursue happiness and obtain resources; the other, which I will call the "Fair Shares" viewpoint, emphasizes the right of access to resources as a necessary condition for equal rights to life, liberty, and happiness.

Almost from the beginning, and most apparently during the past century or so, the Fair Play viewpoint has been dominant in America. This way of looking at the problem of equality stresses that each person should be equally free from all but the most minimal necessary interference with his right to "pursue happiness." It is frequently stressed that all are equally free to pursue, but have no guarantee of attaining, happiness.

The Fair Shares perspective, as compared with the Fair Play idea, con-

cerns itself much more with equality of rights and of access, particularly the implicit rights to a reasonable share of society's resources, sufficient to sustain life at a decent standard of humanity and to preserve liberty and freedom from compulsion. Rather than focusing on the individual's pursuit of his own happiness, the advocate of Fair Shares is more committed to the principle that all members of the society obtain a reasonable portion of the goods that society produces. From his vantage point, the overzealous pursuit of private goals on the part of some individuals might even have to be bridled. From this it follows, too, that the proponent of Fair Shares has a different view of what constitutes fairness and justice, namely, an appropriate distribution throughout society of sufficient means for sustaining life and preserving liberty.

So the equality dilemma is built in to everyday life and thought in America; it comes with the territory. Rights, equality of rights—or at least interpretations of them—clash. The conflict between Fair Play and Fair Shares is real, deep, and serious, and it cannot be easily resolved. Some calculus of priorities must be established. Rules must be agreed upon. It is possible to imagine an almost endless number of such rules.

- Fair Shares until everyone has enough; Fair Play for the surplus
- Fair Shares in winter; Fair Play in summer
- Fair Play until the end of a specified "round," then "divvy up" Fair Shares, and start Fair Play all over again (like a series of Monopoly games)
- Fair Shares for white men; Fair Play for blacks and women
- Fair Play all the way, except that no one may actually be allowed to starve to death.

The last rule is, I would argue, a perhaps bitter parody of the prevailing one in the United States. Equality of opportunity and the principle of meritocracy are the clearly dominant interpretation of "all men are created equal," mitigated by the principle (usually defined as charity rather than equality) that the weak, the helpless, the deficient will be more or less guaranteed a sufficient share to meet their minimal requirements for sustaining life.

The Fair Play concept is dominant in America partly because it puts forth two most compelling ideas: the time-honored principle of distributive justice and the cherished image of America as the land of opportunity. At least since Aristotle, the principle that rewards should accrue to each person in proportion of his worth or merit has seemed to many persons one that warrants intuitive acceptance. The more meritorious person—merit being some combination of ability and constructive effort—deserves a greater reward. From this perspective it is perfectly consistent to suppose that unequal shares could well be fair shares; moreover, within such a framework, it is very unlikely indeed that equal shares could be fair shares, since individuals are not equally meritorious.

The picture of America as the land of opportunity is also very appealing. The idea of a completely open society, where each person is entirely free to advance in his or her particular fashion, to become whatever he or she is inherently capable of becoming, with the sky the limit, is a universally inspiring one. This is a picture that makes most Americans proud.

But is it an accurate picture? Are these two connected ideas—unlimited *opportunity and differential rewards fairly distributed according to differences in individual merit—congruent with the facts of life? The answer, of course, is yes and no. Yes, we see some vague congruence here and there—some evidence of upward mobility, some kinds of inequalities that can appear to be justifiable. But looking at the larger picture, we must answer with an unequivocal "No!" The fairness of unequal shares and the reality of equal opportunity are wishes and dreams, resting on a mushy, floating, purely imaginary foundation.*

Income in the United States is concentrated in the hands of a few: one-fifth of the population gets close to half of all the income, and the top 5 percent of this segment get almost one-fifth of it. The bottom three-fifths of the population—that is, the majority of us—receive not much more than one-third of all income. Giving a speech at a banquet, a friend of mine, James Breeden, described the distribution of income in terms of the dinners being served. It was a striking image, which I will try to reproduce here.

Imagine one hundred people at the banquet, seated at six tables. At the far right is a table set with English china and real silver, where five people sit comfortably. Next to them is another table, nicely set but nowhere near as fancy, where fifteen people sit. At each of the four remaining tables twenty people sit—the one on the far left has a stained paper tablecloth and plastic knives and forks. This arrangement is analogous to the spread of income groups—from the richest 5 percent at the right to the poorest 20 percent at the left.

Twenty waiters and waitresses come in, carrying 100 delicious-looking dinners, just enough, one would suppose, for each of the one hundred guests. But, amazingly, four of the waiters bring 20 dinners to the five people at the fancy table on the right. There's hardly room for all the food. (If you go over and look a little closer, you will notice that two of the waiters are obsequiously fussing and trying to arrange 10 dinners in front of just one of those five.) At the next-fanciest table, with the fifteen people, five waiters bring another 25 dinners. The twenty people at the third table get 25 dinners, 15 go to the fourth table, and 10 to the fifth. To the twenty people at the last table (the one with the paper tablecloth) a rude and clumsy waiter brings only 5 dinners. At the top table there are 4 dinners for each person; at the bottom table, four persons for each dinner. That's approximately the way income is distributed in America—fewer than half the people get even one dinner apiece.

When we move from income to wealth—from what you <u>get</u> to what you <u>own</u>—the degree of concentration makes the income distribution look almost fair by comparison. About one out of every four Americans owns <u>nothing</u>. Nothing! In fact, many of them <u>owe</u> more than they have. Their "wealth" is actually negative. The persons in the next quarter own about 5 percent of all personal assets. In other words, half of us own 5 percent, the other half own 95 percent. But it gets worse as you go up the scale. Those in the top 6 percent own half of all the wealth. Those in the top 1 percent own one-fourth of all the wealth.

These dramatically <u>unequal</u> shares are—it seems to me—clearly <u>unfair</u> shares. Twenty million people are desperately poor, an additional forty million don't get enough income to meet the minimal requirements for a decent life, the great majority are just scraping by, a small minority are at least temporarily *comfortable, and a tiny handful of persons live at levels of affluence and luxury that most persons cannot even imagine.*

The central problem of inequality in America—the concentration of wealth and power in the hands of a tiny minority—cannot, then, be solved by any schemes that rest on the process of long division. We need, rather, to accustom ourselves to a different method of holding resources, namely, holding them in common, to be <u>shared</u> amongst us all—not divided up and parceled out, but shared. That is the basic principle of Fair Shares, and it is not at all foreign to our daily experience. To cite a banal example, we share the air we breathe, although some breathe in penthouses or sparsely settled suburbs and others in crowded slums. In a similar fashion, we share such resources as public parks and beaches, although, again, we cannot overlook the gross contrast between the size of vast private waterfront holdings and the tiny outlets to the oceans that are available to the public. No one in command of his senses would go to a public beach, count the number of people there, and suggest subdividing the beach into thirty-two-by-twenty-six-foot lots, one for each person. Such division would not only be unnecessary, it would ruin our enjoyment. If I were assigned to Lot No. 123, instead of enjoying the sun and going for a swim, I might sit and watch that sneaky little kid with the tin shovel to make sure he did not extend his sand castle onto my beach. So, we don't divide up the beach; we own it in common; it's <u>public</u>; and we just plain <u>share</u> it.

We use this <u>mode</u> of owning and sharing all the time and never give it a second thought. We share public schools, streets, libraries, sewers, and other public property and services, and we even think of them as being "free" (many libraries even have the word in their names). Nor do we need the "There's no such thing as a free lunch" folks reminding us that they're not really free; everyone is quite aware that taxes support them. We don't feel any need to divide up all the books in the library among all the citizens. And there's no sensible way of looking at the use of libraries in terms of "equal opportunity" as opposed to "equal results." Looking at the public library as a tiny example of what Fair Shares equality is all about, we note that it satisfies the principle of equal access if no one is <u>excluded</u> from the library on the irrelevant grounds of not owning enough or of having spent twelve years in school learning how not to read. And "equal results" is clearly quite meaningless. Some will withdraw many books; some, only a few; some will be so unwise as to never even use the facility.

The <u>idea</u> of sharing, then, which is the basic idea of equality, and the <u>practice</u> of sharing, which is the basic methodology of Fair Shares equality, are obviously quite familiar and acceptable to the American people in many areas of life. There are many institutions, activities, and services that the great majority believe should be located in the public sector, collectively owned and paid for, and equally accessible to everyone. We run into trouble when we start proposing the same system of ownership for the resources that the wealthy have corralled for themselves. It is then that the servants of the wealthy, the propagandists of Fair Play, get out their megaphones and yell at everybody that it's time to line up for the hundred-yard dash.

One can think of many similes and metaphors for life other than the footrace. Life is like a collection of craftsmen working together to construct a sturdy and beautiful building. Or, a bit more fancifully, it is like an orchestra— imagine a hundred members of a symphony orchestra racing to see who can finish first! When we experience a moving performance of the Eroica, *how do we judge who the winners are? Is it the second violins, the horns, the conductor, Beethoven, the audience? Does it not make sense to say that, in this context, there are no losers, that all may be considered winners?*

Most of the good things of life have either been provided free by God (nature, if you prefer) or have been produced by the combined efforts of many persons, sometimes of many generations. As all share in the making, so all should share in the use and the enjoyment. This may help convey a bit of what the Fair Shares idea of equality is all about.

Questions 5.1

1. Distinguish between the Fair Shares and Fair Play views of equality. What are the problems or dilemmas with each?
2. Would functional theorists and conflict theorists respond differently to this selection? If so, how? If not, why not?
3. Is William Ryan a functionalist or a conflict theorist? Explain your choice.
4. Select the definition of equality that makes most sense to you and defend it. Briefly describe a program to make it work in the United States.

Reading 5.2

AMERICAN DREAMS: RAFAEL ROSA AND LINDA CHRISTIANSON

STUDS TERKEL

In his book *American Dreams: Lost and Found*, Studs Terkel interviewed hundreds of people across the country. They talked about their past, their present, and their hopes for the future. The two people here are different in many ways, one of which is their position on the social-class ladder.

RAFAEL ROSA

He's a bellhop at a small theatrical hotel in Manhattan. He is forever smiling, eager to please, and quick to talk. He is the second youngest of ten brothers. He is nineteen.

"My parents were born in Puerto Rico. They been here a good seventeen years. My father works right here in the hotel, a houseman. My parents at home *speak Spanish. I was born here in New York City, so when I went to school, my Spanish started turnin' poor. I figured it this way: I might as well hang on to both languages. Now when a Spanish-speaking person comes up to me, I like stutter. I made it to second year at high school."*

My American Dream is to be famous. Like a big boss at a big firm, sit back, relax, and just collect. Oh, I treat my employees nice, pay 'em real good, don't overwork 'em too much, not like most bosses, they fire you right away.

I really would like to have a chauffeur-driven limousine, have a bar one side, color TV on the other. The chicks, the girls, oh yeah. Instead of coming in at eight in the morning and leavin' at eight in the afternoon. Maybe I'll invent something one of these days and wind up a millionaire. As for now, I'd really like to be chief pilot at the air force.

As I ride my bike here in New York, I see all these elegant-looking people, fancy-dressed, riding around in a limousine, just looking all normal. I figured if they can do, why can't I? Why can't I just go out there and get myself driven around for a while? I haven't hit it big yet, but I'm still working on it.

As I started growing older, I figured it's a jungle out there, you better grab a vine. So I grabbed a vine, and here I landed. (Laughs.) It's really hard out there in the city; you can't get a job any more. I would just like to be on TV, a newsman or something.

My friends are always talkin' about havin' a nice sheen. That's a nice car or van, something set up real nice on the inside with foldaway beds and wall-to-wall carpeting and paneling, fat tires, mufflers sticking out on the side, and speeding. Usually, they get together on this highway and they would race each other at the flat. It's really incredible. I don't see how these guys can do that. Drag racing.

I wanted to be a taxi driver. I figured it would be an exciting job, just riding around all day. Plus I had that driving fever. Most of the time, I dream I can fly, be all the way up there on the top. But I don't see how, unless I invent something, eh? Anti-gravity belt or something like that. It would cost a lot of loot just to make one of those. I'm a bicycle mechanic now. I ride 'em on one wheel also, but I don't think that's gonna get me far. I'd really like to be a motorcycle driver and explore the world.

Most of the time, I'm usually out in the streets, lookin' around. Scope on the nice women who pass by. I like their wardrobes and the way they walk, the way they talk. I should really be a gift to all women. I don't know how I'm gonna do it, but it's gotta be done somehow. (Laughs.)

My brother works in the post office, makin' some all-right money. My other brother works in a factory, getting some good money as long as he can put in overtime. We're all in the same business, tryin' to move up, tryin' to see if we can get this "flat fixed" place or a grocery store. With the right location, we'll move up.

I would really like to invest in something real big, like in baby food. You can never run out of baby food. And cars. We'll never run out of cars as long as we don't run out of people. I could invest in tires. Where there's tires, there's automobiles. I guess I'm gonna have to hit it big.

People today are more like keepin' it to themselves. They don't let their emotions show. They're afraid to lose respect, cool. I'm open most of the time, I kinda like to turn off and on. I'm the kind of guy that gets along with everybody. I'm Puerto Rican and I got the complexion of a Negro, so I can fall to either side. I've been chased by whites a couple of times, but nothing special happens.

What's goin' on these days with all the violence, a person's gotta think twice of walking down the street. One time I got mugged in the South Bronx. Three guys jumped me as I was walking down this dark street. One guy stops me for a cigarette, and as I go to give him one, two guys grab me from behind. They just started beatin' on me and took all my money and left me on the floor and fled. I recovered, and now I think twice about it. Before I was mugged, I walked down any street. I'd rather walk around a dark street than go through it, no matter how much time it's gonna take me to get there. If people call ya, I just keep on walking if I don't know the person. I look back and just keep walking.

I suggest: Don't walk alone at night. Walk with a stick to protect yourself. Don't get too high because it slows down your reflexes. You gotta keep your head clear. They say: Never look back. In real life, you gotta look back.

LINDA CHRISTIANSON

She reflects on life in one of the country's wealthiest communities. It is a suburb of a large northern city.

There is no industry in this town. The shopkeepers and the gas station owners don't live here. They simply maintain the services that keep the town alive. The people who live here work in the big city. The men commute. There's a very rigid schedule as to which train the men take in the morning and which train they come home on in the evening. The men insist on sitting in the very same seat in the same car every day.

Oh (laughs), Heaven forbid you've got to go to the grocery store to get some milk at, oh cripes, what is it? at five-fifteen or five twenty-one or some weird hour. Everything in town stops. It's like watching a Mack Sennett movie. The cars come from everywhere and converge on the train station from all directions. Traffic is blocked. You can't move. It lasts only about ten minutes. All these men with their brief cases come zooming out of the cars of the train, scurrying in all directions. All their wives have a certain place that they wait. The men without even looking make a beeline for the car.

This town has more Mercedes per square inch than any place in the world, I think. Before that it was always the Ford station wagon. Not Buick. It's that play at modesty. We can afford a Cadillac, but they're so gauche. Yet they can be lavish in other matters, like vacations. It was a big thing when you got back from Bangkok or Madagascar or Hong Kong, and you threw a dinner party with the food of that country and invited everyone you knew so you could brag about it.

The little wives in the waiting cars, if you lined them up, they'd look like little penguins in a row. The same topcoat, ubiquitous beige. The same style shoes, the same style skirt, almost the same color hair, a little light brown with a

little bit of gold in it. Never blond. Oh, no. Never dark brown or black either.
Just shithouse mouse brown.

I am a product of World War Two. The movies I saw as a child, the stories I
read in children's novels, were all the same thing. As a woman, I'm going to
grow up, have a little white house and a white picket fence, have a husband
who's very, very well-to-do in some sort of a profession. We're going to wear
pretty, lovely clothes. We're going to still be wearing a gingham apron when he
comes home from work and be taking chocolate-chip cookies out of the oven.
We're going to live happily ever after. It's the American Dream.

There's this unwritten statement: there's unlimited funds. The man
works, but it's somewhere off. He wears a suit, he doesn't wear working clothes.
You take vacations to lovely places all over the world. Somehow the children
are taken care of. They don't go with you. You and your husband go on this
romantic vacation somewhere. Anything is possible. You simply want it, and it
is. That's the dream I grew up with.

I lived in Europe for a year and had picked up enough languages to get a
job as translator for a manufacturing firm doing foreign business. I left that job
quickly because my boss decided to play a little game called chase me around
his desk. I got a job in a brokerage firm. I did meet and marry a man, a very,
very wealthy man.

His family is one of the richest in the city. It isn't that they're just wealthy
in money, they're wealthy in power, political power as well as having friends in
universities, where they've established chairs.

I found this family was day and night from mine. I would invite them over
for dinner. Say I would have some nice placemats at the table. Immediately my
mother-in-law would say: "How much did these cost?" It was: "I got this new
car and I paid eight thousand dollars." It wasn't: "I got this new car and I'm
thrilled and, boy, I can't wait to drive you around the block." It was just a whole
new ballgame.

I myself now have picked it up. Instead of my bragging how much this
costs, I've gone the opposite way. I'll brag about such a bargain something is. "I
have a couple of little antique things that I've found in junk shops that I think
cost two or three dollars." When a guest praises them, I'll say: "Yes, why in
1966, I picked that up for two dollars." As soon as it's out of my mouth, I go:
Oooh, don't say that. I've become what I didn't like about them.

At the brokerage house I worked for, everybody lived in this community.
The movers and shakers, who are the grandsons and great-grandsons of the
founders of the firm, the who's who. A young man was hired and doing quite
well. Bright, well-educated, you'd have thought he could easily walk through
the door. But he and his wife made one very big mistake. They didn't move from
the city to a stepping-stone community. If you want to wiggle in the back door
of this community without having had your grandfather or great-grandfather
as a founder, and without having been in the social register for centuries, there
are ways to do it, but you have to work very slowly. You have to establish yourself. The man has to have proved himself in his corporation, at least at the executive vice-president level. The wife has to establish herself in the right kind of
charity work. You do it by steps.

This man and his wife had the registered two children. He decided to build a home in this community and was excited, telling me about it. One day, my boss and another senior partner, without trying to hide their voices, complained of all these people from the city moving in. Who do they think they are? They're not part of us. After I left the firm, I ran into this man. He had overheard the conversation and never forgot the hurt. He had thought he was in. I'm talking about a white Anglo-Saxon Protestant well-mannered, well-educated man. I'm not talking about anyone from any weird or ethnic group. Yet he wasn't one of them.

Because of my husband's position, I didn't have nearly as difficult a time. Yet, talk about an ordeal! I found out there were no children living close-by where we lived. The homes are large, with lawns as big as a football field. When you talk about houses on the block, you might have to walk a block to get to another house. I had two small children and wanted them to have a place to play. I was told of a private club in town. The best thing about it was their summer camp program for children. You had to join this club in order for your kids to get in. To be accepted in this club, the directors have to approve you. If you get one blackball, you cannot join. So we'll have a cocktail party and the directors will meet you.

The cocktail party was to begin at five-twenty. What a weird time, I thought. Why not five, why not five-thirty? We got there a few minutes early. All of a sudden umpteen station wagons came zooming into the driveway. The ladies, in their little deck-shoe costumes, with their plain little cotton skirt and plain little white blouse with little Peter Pan collars, hopped out of the cars. The men, in their very, very subdued suits, with the brief cases, came hopping out. They all came tromping in.

They quickly went to the bar, each grabbed their drink, and one by one made their way over to us. Very few of them said "Hello" or "How are you?" The first question to me was: What was my sorority? Then: What school did I go to? What was my maiden name? And then they turned on their heels. The men, after doing this with my husband, turned on their heels. Within forty minutes maximum, it was over. I'd never been to a more unusual social affair. It was a tribalistic ritual. I was the meat on the altar, the lamb. Thank God I didn't drop an hors d'oeuvre.

By this time, I had been well instructed by my mother-in-law how to dress. I was wearing a two-year-old suit. I barely had any makeup on. I spoke very softly, a "well-modulated" voice. I passed because I didn't say anything controversial. I didn't have a chance to say anything. . . .

For me, it was a difficult world to exist in. My divorce was messy. In this kind of community, once a couple is divorced, the woman loses her status. She may have been accepted before, she may have been president of this society or chairman of this benefit, as I was. But she's out. Oh yes, I was written up many times at such and such a ball, wearing a blah blah blah gown. I was dropped like a hot potato. The people who were not in were nice and kind. The people who were in were distantly polite or actually rude.

I lived the American Dream. I was married to a multimillionaire. I had immediate status. I was living in a house worth a million dollars. I took trips all *over the world. I had servants. All these things without working for them. But it was so goddamn much work. For every dollar of affluence, you end up getting two dollars' worth of trouble.*

I'm getting back to the values I had before. I didn't exactly start out from sour milk, so I'm not that far away from the cream. I don't think I could ever stand being poor. I'm quick enough about my wits that I guess I never would be. I'll get enough, whatever "enough" is. I don't know.

Questions 5.2

1. Outline the characteristics of social class that are illustrated in this selection.
2. Analyze and describe each person's situation using the following topics or concepts: parallel stratification systems, determinants of social class, social class and behavior, and horizontal and vertical social mobility.
3. "The major distinguishing feature between these two people is their social class." Discuss, pro and con.
4. These selections came from a book entitled *American Dreams*. Is there a common "American dream"? If so, what is it?

6

Social Differentiation: Race, Ethnicity, Sex, Age

The previous chapter introduced the idea of social differentiation, which refers to the fact that people in society fall into categories because of such characteristics as age, sex, race, and social class. The study of these categories is very helpful because it gives us a more precise picture of society, of the characteristics that bind people together, and of how these affect their behavior.

We found that social differentiation leads to social stratification. People tend to *rank* other people according to the categories into which they fall. In Chapter 5 we discussed the stratification produced by socioeconomic factors. Socioeconomic status can be described as an achieved status because there is some flexibility in the ranking—one can perhaps move up or down the social-class ladder. In this chapter we look at categories that are more firmly established. They are automatically conferred, and there is little an individual can do to change them. We call them *ascribed* statuses.

MINORITY STATUS

Minority status is an important ascribed status and can be helpful in explaining how people interact with one another. Minority status not only names the group or category to which one belongs, but it also describes one's social position, how one is likely to be treated by others.

We will find in this chapter that groups of minority status may be considered lower in social standing than the rest of society; they may be subject to domination and may be denied certain rights and privileges.

It is important to understand that minority status is a social condition, not necessarily a statistical one. A minority could represent a majority of a society's population but hold minority status because of the way they are viewed and treated by other segments of society. For example, women in the United States are a numerical majority but have minority status because they are not treated on a level of equality with men. For years the black population in South Africa has held minority status even though it greatly outnumbers the white population, which has been dominant. In most instances minority groups do represent a smaller proportion of the population—blacks and Hispanic-Americans in the United States, for example—but it is important to recall the *social* nature of minority status.

Where do definitions of minority status come from? Who decides? A number of factors are probably at work. Some decisions about minority status arrive through custom and tradition. People who are successful are sometimes proprietary about their good fortune and look down on those who aspire to the same position. Some groups blend in more easily or appear to. If their skin color and language are the same and their cultural backgrounds are similar to those of the society they are entering, their differences will be less apparent, and they will be more likely to escape minority status. And we learned in the last chapter of the importance of wealth and power. Assume that there is a limited supply of the good things in life—it follows that those with wealth and power will want to protect their positions by denying access to them by others. By labeling and treating categories of people differently—as if of lower quality—they are effectively removed as threats to established positions of privilege. The creation and maintenance of minority status can work much the same way as the treatment of the poor that we discussed in Chapter 5.

RACE AND ETHNICITY

We have learned that people differ and are ranked by such socioeconomic factors as wealth, education, occupation, power, and prestige. People also differ and are ranked by race and ethnicity. A person's race and ethnic affiliation confer on him or her a status or position in society—and sometimes this is a minority status.

Race is a vague and ambiguous term. It is generally defined as a group of people bound together by hereditary physical features. The difficulty with the notion of race is that practically no pure races exist. Substantial biological mixing has blurred boundaries to the point that it is difficult to define uniform hereditary physical features. Scientists attempting to define race have named anywhere from three racial categories to more than thirty. Three definitions of race—biological, legal, and social—seem to emerge.[1] A biological definition is based on observable physical features such as skin color, hair texture, and eye color, or on differences in gene frequencies. A legal definition is that incorporated into the laws of states or nations. For example, the law in one state has defined a black as a person who has "one-eighth or more Negro blood," while in other states a black is a person with "any ascertainable trace of Negro blood." A social definition refers to what members of society feel to be the important distinctions about race. Brewton Berry has suggested that in the United States the social definition of a black is anyone who identifies himself as black or who has any *known* trace of black ancestry. It can be seen from this that the term *race* is not a precise term, but it is nevertheless widely used.

A sociology class is shown slides of people who identify themselves as blacks but who, because of an absence of typical racial characteristics, don't *look* like blacks. The class (which is predominantly white) is asked to identify the race or nationality of the light-skinned, straight-haired people on the slides, and the guesses range across the globe. Finally the class is told, "They are all American Negroes." The reaction is astonishment, of course, because "they don't look like blacks." This illustrates several things, among them the difficulty of defining race, the blurring of racial boundaries, and the importance of the social definition—once the class is told that the people on the slides identify as blacks (probably because of some black ancestry), the class believes it. No question about it, regardless of how they look.

When race is discussed, the question of racial differences inevitably comes up. That is, do races biologically differ in such areas as I.Q., achievement, or susceptibility to diseases? The haziness in definitions of race supplies part of the answer: If the boundaries of race are unclear, how can any statements about racial differences be made? Nevertheless, they are, as witness the controversy over inherent racial I.Q. differences. A conclusion to this discussion that is favored by most social scientists is that there are no significant differences *caused* by race. There are numerous differences among people caused by cultural, social, and geographic factors, however, and these are often thought to be racial differences. For example, certain gene frequencies and blood characteristics have developed in particular areas of the world. Population groups migrating from those areas—regardless of race—carry these characteristics to other parts of the world. Apparently, a specific blood characteristic that has survival value in areas of high malaria incidence has developed in populations in parts of Africa and the Middle East. This same blood characteristic also leads to sickle-cell anemia, a disease that has victimized blacks in the United States. Is sickle-cell anemia linked to race? No, because nonblacks who have migrated to other parts of the world from those same areas of Africa and the Middle East

---

[1]This distinction is suggested by Brewton Berry in *Race and Ethnic Relations*, 3d ed. (Boston: Houghton Mifflin, 1965), Chapter 2.

may also have it. Likewise, differences in attitude, achievement, and perception are explained by cultural differences—one culture emphasizes achievement, another tranquility, one is aggressive, another encourages passivity, and so on. In short, social scientists argue from a cultural determinist viewpoint and reject the idea of racially caused differences. Many people remain unconvinced, however, and the argument will undoubtedly continue.

Ethnicity or *ethnic group* are more useful terms than *race*, at least from a sociological viewpoint. Members of an ethnic group are bound together by cultural ties, which may have several origins. When groups migrate to a new area, their ties to a previous culture may remain strong. Religious beliefs may also provide a basis for ethnicity, as in the case of the Jews, the Amish, and the Hutterites. The term *ethnicity* is useful because it appropriately brings to focus cultural similarities, which to the social scientist are more important and have more explanatory power than racial similarities.

Prejudice and Discrimination

Prejudice has been defined as a fixed attitude—favorable or unfavorable—toward a person or thing, probably not based on actual experience. A prejudiced person ignores the individual and his particular qualities or characteristics, and groups the person with others who happen to have the same skin color (brown or yellow), or speak with the same accent (New England), or have the same type of name (Cohen, Greenberg), or come from the same part of the country (South).

Prejudice tends to be generalized. People who are prejudiced against one group will probably be prejudiced against others. Some years ago E. L. Hartley asked college students what they thought of Canadians, Turks, Jews, atheists, Irish, Negroes, Wallonians, Pireneans, Danireans, and other groups. He found that people who were prejudiced against blacks were also likely to be prejudiced against Jews, Wallonians, and Danireans. Now there are about fourteen million Jews in the world, but no Wallonians or Danireans. Hartley used these fictitious groups to see how people would react to groups they knew nothing about. He found that people tend to generalize their prejudices.[2]

Discrimination is actual behavior unfavorable to a specific individual or group. When people are denied equal treatment, they are being discriminated against. Discrimination occurs when a person is denied a desired position or right because of irrelevant factors—for example, when skin color is used to determine eligibility to vote, or when religious affiliation is used to determine where one may reside.

Prejudice and discrimination are usually associated but not always. The situation gets complicated when people think one way but behave another way. Robert Merton attempted to describe what happens by suggesting four categories of people.[3]

---

[2]E. L. Hartley, *Problems in Prejudice* (New York: Kings Crown Press, 1946).

[3]Robert K. Merton, "Discrimination and the American Creed," in *Discrimination and National Welfare*, edited by R. M. MacIver (New York: Harper & Brothers, 1949), pp. 99–126. Also see Berry's summary in *Race and Ethnic Relations*, 3d ed., pp. 300–302 (see footnote 1).

Unprejudiced nondiscriminator or all-weather liberal: confirmed and consistent liberal; not prejudiced; doesn't discriminate; believes in American creed of justice, freedom, equality of opportunity, and dignity of the individual.

Uprejudiced discriminator or fair-weather liberal: thinks in terms of expediency; not prejudiced but keeps quiet when bigots are about; will discriminate for fear that to do otherwise would "hurt business"; will make concessions to the intolerant.

Prejudiced nondiscriminator or fair-weather illiberal: timid bigot; doesn't believe in the American creed but conforms to it when slightest pressure is applied; hates minorities but hires them to obey the law.

Prejudiced discriminator or all-weather illiberal: a bigot, pure and unashamed; doesn't believe in the American creed and doesn't hesitate to tell that to others; believes it is right and proper to discriminate, so does.

The origins of prejudice are explained in various ways. Some psychologists believe that there is a certain type of personality—called an *authoritarian personality*—that is especially prone to prejudice.[4] The authoritarian personality is also ethnocentric, rigidly conformist, and worships authority and strength. According to psychologists, the authoritarian personality can most often be traced to faulty emotional development born of harsh discipline and lack of affection and love from one's parents during childhood. Most sociologists believe that prejudice, like other attitudes and behaviors, is learned in interaction with others, mainly in the family, and that personality is not as important as the social or cultural situation in which one interacts. We learn race prejudice in the same way we learn how to eat with a fork, study for a test, or drive a car. Also, certain life situations affect how this learning takes place. For example, people who are downwardly mobile—moving from middle to lower class—show more intense feelings of prejudice toward blacks and Jews; and in times of rapid social change, prejudice and discrimination may become more intense and more generalized.

Sociologists also associate stereotyping with prejudice. In **stereotyping,** we apply a common label and set of characteristics to all people in a certain category, even though none or only some of the people in that category fit the description. The stereotyped male college professor is absent-minded, smokes a pipe, is an extreme liberal, wears horn-rimmed glasses and a tweed jacket with elbow patches, and generally is not much in touch with the real world. This image is applied to everyone in the college professor category even though most do not fit the part. Professors will probably survive their stereotype without damage because the characteristics of the stereotype are not negative. Besides, a person *chooses* as an adult to become a college teacher and, therefore, to enter a stereotyped category.

Someone of minority status, on the other hand, who is stereotyped from birth as ignorant, lazy, dirty, happy-go-lucky, morally primitive, emotionally unstable, and fit only for menial work can be psychologically damaged by the effects of the lifelong stereotype. When others react to us on the basis of such stereotypes, it strongly affects our self-concepts—the way we see ourselves.

---

[4]T. W. Adorno et al., *The Authoritarian Personality* (New York: Harper & Row, 1950).

This again is the self-fulfilling prophecy, which we discussed several times earlier. Remember what happened to the "bright" rats and "dull" rats? Or what happened when teachers thought some of their students were "academic spurters"?

Several theories have been offered to explain prejudice and discrimination. One such theory explains conflict between unlike groups in terms of scapegoating. If attention can be focused on some out-group, this may strengthen the boundaries and unity of the in-group. It is suggested that the Nazis' attack on the Jews before and during World War II had this motivation. Marxist theory holds that economic competition is the best explanation for prejudice and discrimination. When access to desired goods or valued positions in society is limited, discrimination against certain categories of people helps ensure that others can more easily dominate and obtain their goals. By reducing the status of others to second-class citizens, by eliminating certain people from highly valued jobs, education, and access to wealth, we can guarantee that our own path is free of obstacles. Some have said that the conflict that arises when unlike groups meet may be best and most simply explained as resulting from a struggle for status between competing groups.

The common areas of discrimination in the United States include employment, education, housing, and, to a lesser extent, voting. In the following paragraphs we will take a brief look at some patterns of prejudice and discrimination as they affect blacks, Indians, Hispanic-Americans, and Jews.

Blacks

There were 26.5 million blacks in the United States in 1980 or roughly twelve percent of the population. Blacks have been a part of American history from its beginning; the economy of the earliest days of our settlement was based on slavery. We are still trying to overcome the effects that the culture of slavery had on blacks and whites in America. Certain dates stand out:

1619 Twenty blacks purchased from a Dutch ship

1644 First slaves imported directly from Africa

1861–1865 Civil War with emancipation as a major issue

1865 Legal abolition of slavery by the Thirteenth Amendment to the Constitution

1896 *Plessy* v. *Ferguson* decision by the Supreme Court supports "separate but equal" doctrine

1918–on Black migration from the rural South to jobs in the urban North

1954 *Brown* v. *Board of Education* decision by the Supreme Court states that "separate facilities are inherently unequal"

1956 Montgomery bus boycott led by Martin Luther King, Jr.

1960–1965 Passive resistance, sit-ins, demonstrations

1965–1970 Urban riots, beginning of black militancy, and "Black Power"

1970–1982 Prison riots, widespread disagreement over busing to achieve school desegregation, affirmative action, court suits over "reverse discrimination"

The Kerner (riot commission) Report in 1968 stated that "our nation is moving toward two societies, one black, one white—separate and unequal."

Some examples of how separate and unequal status affects other conditions of life are shown in Table 6.1.

Jobs, Income, Unemployment Median income for white families in 1980 was $21,900; for black families, it was $12,670 (see Table 6.2). The unemployment rate for blacks was double that of whites (thirteen percent compared to six percent annual average for 1980). The jobless rate for white teenagers was

TABLE 6.1 Comparison by Race on Selected Characteristics

	White	Black
Birthrate per 1,000 people, 1979	15	22*
Life expectancy, 1979		
Males	71	66*
Females	78	75*
Infant deaths per 1,000 live births, 1978	12	21*
Caloric intake per day, 1974	2,017	1,825
Percent illiterate, 1979	0.4	1.6
Divorces per 100,000 people, 1980	92	203
Homicide victims per 100,000 people, 1978		
Males	9	59
Females	3	13
Suicide victims per 100,000 people, 1978		
Males	20	11
Females	7	3
Percent unemployed, 1980	6	13*
Percent below poverty line, 1981	11	34
Mental hospital admissions per 100,000 people, 1970		
Males	299	648*
Females	184	453*
Percent of families earning under $5,000, 1980	5	17
Percent of families earning $25,000 and over, 1980	42	20
Percent completing 4 years of college, 1980	18	8

*For this category, designation is "black and other"; blacks make up about ninety percent of this group.

U.S. Bureau of the Census, *Statistical Abstract of the United States*, 1981 (102d ed.), Washington, D.C.; from Census Bureau documents; and from *Social Indicators III.*

TABLE 6.2 Median Income (in 1980 dollars) and Race

	White Families	Black and Other Families
1950	$10,388	$ 5,636
1960	14,301	7,917
1970	19,134	12,180
1980	21,900	12,670*

*Black families only

"Money Income and Poverty Status of Families and Persons in the United States: 1980." *Current Population Reports*, Series P-60, no. 127.

about sixteen percent, but the comparable figure for black and other teenagers was about thirty-six percent in 1980. Blacks represented a larger proportion of the poverty group in 1979 than in 1959 despite the fact that average income had gone up. In other words, the economic position of blacks had improved, but it had improved faster for whites. Another sign of economic difficulties is the fact that the percentage of black soldiers in the Army doubled between 1971 and 1980; twenty-one percent of the enlisted personnel in the Army in 1980 were black. Blacks continued to move into white-collar jobs in the 1970s but at a slower pace than in the 1960s. Black men in white-collar jobs rose slightly from twenty-two percent in 1970 to twenty-three percent in 1977; for black women the percentage rose from thirty-six percent in 1970 to forty-four percent in 1977.[5]

A recent study analyzed occupation, unemployment, and income in the United States and concluded that some whites, particularly in the South, continue to benefit from the subordinate position of blacks. Because of the subordinate position of blacks, these whites (in white-collar and higher-income jobs) gain higher occupational status, lower unemployment, higher family income, and reduced labor costs. The author of the study concluded that in recent American history, the supposed improvement in racial equality has been grossly exaggerated. Some whites (who appear to be of high status and income) will continue to oppose advancement of blacks due to their own self-interests.[6]

Education   Blacks receive less education than whites in the United States as Tables 6.3 and 6.4 indicate. The gap is closing but slowly. The U.S. Supreme Court outlawed segregated schools in the *Brown* v. *Board of Education* decision in 1954, but integration of schools did not proceed very rapidly; more than two-thirds of Southern black children were still attending all-black schools in 1968. However, a dramatic change did take place between 1968 and 1974. In 1974 only eight percent of Southern black children were still in schools in which all students were minorities (blacks, Asians, Spanish-Americans), whereas in the North and West fourteen percent of black students were in such schools. More black students were in mainly white schools in 1974 in the South than in the North and West. These statistics reveal that, despite a tendency to accuse Southerners of racism in America, all areas of the nation share the guilt. Segregation in housing (especially *de facto*) has certainly been increasing much more rapidly in the ghettos of northern cities than it has in the South.

In the mid-1970s the issue of busing was more heated than ever. Several controversial reports by James S. Coleman provoked much discussion. A 1966 Coleman report concluded that deprived students did better educationally

---

[5]Much of the data in this and following paragraphs comes from the comprehensive report, "The Social and Economic Status of the Black Population in the United States: An Historical View, 1790–1978," *Current Population Reports*, Series P-23, no. 80, published by the U.S. Bureau of the Census (Washington, D.C.: U.S. Government Printing Office, 1979), and from *Statistical Abstract of the United States, 1981*.

[6]George Dowdall, "White Gains from Black Subordination in 1960 and 1970," *Social Problems* 22 (December 1974), pp. 162–183.

TABLE 6.3   Median School Years Completed and Race

	White	Black
1960	10.9	8.0
1970	12.2	9.9
1980	12.5	12.0

U.S. Bureau of the Census, *Statistical Abstract of the United States, 1980* (102d ed.), Washington, D.C., p. 142.

TABLE 6.4   Level of Education for People 25 Years Old and Older, 1980

Percent of the Population with:	Whites	Blacks	Hispanic-Americans		
			Mexican-Americans	Puerto Ricans	Cubans
Less than five years of school	3%	9%	21%	15%	6%
Four years of high school or more	71	51	40	38	55

U.S. Bureau of the Census, *Statistical Absract of the United States, 1981* (102d ed.), Washington, D.C., p. 141.

when their classmates came from backgrounds emphasizing educational achievement. The idea was to improve the educational chances of blacks by busing them from their poor school districts to higher-quality white school districts. Many court decisions, many complicated school board plans, and many demonstrations later, people on both sides of the issue continue to wonder if busing works.[7] At any rate, the supposed improved education available to blacks has not significantly improved their performance, and many whites are moving to private schools in the cities or public schools in the suburbs. Far from desegregating schools, busing seems to be resegregating them. Coleman completed another report in 1975 in which he too concluded that this desegregation may be increasing segregation. He cited new research showing that desegregation has little, if any, effect on students' performance in many of the participating schools. It now seems that the importance of family background in determining educational achievement was seriously underestimated in the early studies. Moving an educationally deprived student to an educationally rich school is fine, but apparently the important factor is what goes on at home, which does not change.

The picture is brighter at colleges and universities. College enrollment increased more rapidly for blacks than for whites between 1970 and 1980. A gap remains, however. The percentage of black high school graduates enrolled (twenty-eight percent) was still below that of white high school graduates (thirty-two percent) in 1980.

---

[7]See the editorial by Norman Cousins in *Saturday Review*, 24 January 1976. The report of James S. Coleman et al. is "Equality of Educational Opportunity" (Washington, D.C.: U.S. Government Printing Office, 1966).

Housing   Finding adequate housing is difficult for blacks. First there were restrictive laws, and now tacit agreements keep blacks out of the better districts in most cities and suburbs of the North, West, and South. Because middle-class whites are leaving the cities for the suburbs, *de facto* segregation is turning the inner cities into black ghettos. Blacks isolated in these areas find their housing, their public facilities, and their schools automatically segregated and made inadequate by the lowered tax base, the backwardness (and often helplessness) of city government, and the exploitation or apathy of absentee landlords and local business people.

Voting, Elected Officials   Blacks have been denied the vote for years in the South. However, implementation of the Civil Rights Act, calling for federal voting registrars in the South, seemed to change this form of discrimination. Voter registration figures in eleven Southern states in 1960 indicated that sixty-one percent of the eligible whites were registered, as compared to twenty-nine percent of the eligible blacks. By 1980, however, seventy-nine percent of the whites and fifty-eight percent of the blacks were registered. In 1970, there were fewer than 1,500 black office holders. In July 1980, 4,890 blacks were holding office in forty-three states and the District of Columbia. However, blacks still account for fewer than one percent of all elected officials. The increase in elected officials has been most predominant in the South.

American Indians

In the middle and late nineteenth century, Americans believed in the doctrine of Manifest Destiny, which held that it was the destiny of the United States to expand its territory and enhance its political, economic, and social influence over the whole of North America. And so, the original occupants of the land, the American Indians, were killed, captured, displaced, and placed on reservations as settlers moved west. It was too bad, as one Army general who supervised the removal of the Indians put it—they were a brave and proud people but they finally realized that it was their destiny to "give way to the insatiable progress of [the white] race. . . ."[8]

In his book, *Custer Died for Your Sins*, Vine Deloria, Jr., discusses an interesting paradox in American society. Americans are told not to trust Communist countries, for they do not keep treaty commitments. We fought in Vietnam for years and thousands of people lost their lives ostensibly because the United States had to keep its commitments in Southeast Asia. The paradox is this: At the very time that we were spending $100 billion keeping commitments in Vietnam, the United States government was also breaking the oldest Indian treaty, the Pickering treaty of 1794 with the Seneca tribe of the Iroquois Nation. In fact, as far as breaking treaties is concerned, it is doubtful if anybody can beat our record. Deloria reports that "America has yet to keep one Indian treaty or

---

[8]General Carleton's views on Manifest Destiny and the Indians are quoted by Dee Brown in *Bury My Heart at Wounded Knee* (New York: Holt, Rinehart & Winston, Bantam Books, 1971), p. 31.

agreement despite the fact that the U.S. government signed over 400 such trea-
ties with Indian tribes."[9]

Desirable land has been systematically taken from Indians, who are then
relocated on reservations in less desirable areas. Indians held 138 million acres
in 1887; this had been reduced to 55 million acres by 1970 and to 53 million by
1980. If formerly undesirable land becomes desirable because of the discovery
of oil, or if it contains a river needed for power or irrigation, or if it is considered to be a prime area for development of any kind, further relocation and
manipulation of Indian rights and lands are sure to follow.

The 1970 Census reported there are approximately 800,000 American Indians. Median family income was $5,800 a year, Indian unemployment was
higher than for other groups, and the income of thirty-three percent of Indian
families was below the poverty level. Median years of schooling received by
Indians was 9.8, and thirty-three percent were high school graduates. Living
conditions on reservations have long been substandard. Life expectancy of Indians lags about seven years behind that of whites. Death statistics provide further evidence of the effects of minority status. Indians are less likely to die of
heart disease and cancer than other Americans but about three times as likely
to die of accidents. Indians have a high birth rate (about two and a half times
that of whites), but Indian deaths in infancy and early childhood are about double that of other Americans. Indian deaths from cirrhosis of the liver are more
than double the national average, by homicide more than triple, and by tuberculosis four times the national average. Indian alcoholism and suicide rates are
also very high, and suicide is especially high for Indians in their late teens and
twenties.[10] Dr. Bertram Brown, a director of the National Institute of Mental
Health, has stated that Indians suffer greatly the effects of isolation and alienation from society brought on by the general neglect of many generations. Racism and bigotry have an adverse effect on mental health, and the American
Indian has been the victim of this abuse longer than any other American.

Hispanic-Americans

Americans of Spanish origin have become this country's fastest growing
minority. Census figures put the number of Hispanics in the United States in
1980 at 14.6 million. If illegal aliens are included, the figure increases to over 20
million. Population projections suggest that the Hispanic population may outnumber that of blacks within the next decade. The major unifying factors for
Hispanic-Americans are their religion (Roman Catholicism) and their language,
but many diversities exist as well. Seven million Hispanics are of Mexican origin and have settled in the West and Southwest (probably nearly two million in
Los Angeles alone). Some 700,000 Hispanics have come from Cuba, more than
half of whom have settled in the Miami area. More than one million Hispanics
from Puerto Rico are living in the New York City area.

---

[9]Vine Deloria, Jr., *Custer Died for Your Sins* (New York: Macmillan, 1969), pp. 28–29.

[10]The information on birth and death rates and causes comes from "Natality and Mortality of
American Indians compared with U.S. Whites and Nonwhites," by Charles Hill and Mozart
Spector, *Public Health Reports*, vol. 86 (March 1971), pp. 229–246.

Most Hispanic-Americans, however, face the conditions that seem to accompany minority status. Their income is lower and their unemployment rate higher than that of whites. Twenty-six percent of persons of Spanish origin were below the poverty level in 1981 (compared to about fourteen percent of other Americans). Many Chicanos in the West are migrant farm workers laboring in the fields of California and Oregon. Farm labor is seasonal, uncertain, underpaid, and subject to difficult working conditions. Hispanic-Americans are much underrepresented in political and governmental positions. In 1978 there were no Hispanics in the Senate and five in the House of Representatives compared to sixteen blacks and twenty-two Jews in the House. Hispanics hold three percent of the jobs in federal government, whereas blacks hold sixteen percent. Hispanics are low in voter registration—less than forty percent of those eligible are registered. Perhaps the most serious problem for Hispanic-Americans is in the area of education. They have a high dropout rate as can be seen in Table 6.4. The central issue is language and the necessity for bilingual education. Look, for example, at the Southwest, where the Mexican-American is the largest culturally distinct minority group. According to a May 1972 report by the U.S. Commission on Civil Rights, schools in the Southwest exclude the Chicanos' Spanish language, exclude their Mexican heritage, and discourage their participation in school affairs. Nearly fifty percent of Mexican-American first graders do not speak English as well as the average Anglo first grader. They have to learn a new language in addition to the other material being taught. By the twelfth grade, sixty-three percent of all Chicano students read at least six months below grade level. Before the end of the twelfth grade, forty-seven percent of the Chicanos will have left school. Only seven percent of the secondary schools in the Southwest offered a course in Mexican-American history. More than four million persons in the Southwest identify Spanish as their mother tongue, but the schools (seventy-five percent of the elementary, ninety pecent of the secondary) communicate with parents (send notices, conduct meetings) only in English.

The debate over bilingual education centers around the following dilemma: Should all students be forced to speak English, with the result that many will fall behind and drop out, or should bilingual programs be established, with the result that many students will have little skill in English in a specialized technological society in which knowledge of English is essential?[11]

Jews

There are approximately fourteen million people of the Jewish faith in the world. There are six million Jews in the United States or roughly three percent of our population. Religion is the foundation, but being Jewish also involves an ethnic and cultural identity. Unfortunately, persecution has been a consistent factor in Jewish cultural history. They were forced off their land and driven into other areas as early as the sixth century B.C. Especially sharp conflict between Christians and Jews emerged after the third century A.D. Starting around

---

[11]See the article on Hispanic-Americans in *Time*, October 16, 1978, pp. 48–61. Some of the numbers came from *Statistical Abstract of the United States, 1981*.

the tenth century Jews were segregated into ghettos, at first voluntarily, then on a compulsory basis. In 1555, the Pope decreed that Jews must be segregated strictly in their own quarter of the city surrounded by a high wall with gates closed at night. Jews were forced out of certain occupations and denied citizenship. They were used as scapegoats to distract attention from other issues and to promote national unity. This was played to its most horrible extreme during World War II with the extermination of six million Jews in Germany.

The consequences of minority status for Jews in the United States do not seem to be as severe as they are for other groups that we have looked at. This is probably because Jews are less visible than most minority groups and because they have been more upwardly mobile through their emphasis on education and participation in the professions. Jews have faced certain types of prejudice and discrimination in the United States. For a time, certain jobs were not open to Jews. Colleges and universities, especially in the Eastern United States, had quotas covering the percentage of Jews they would accept. As recently as 1958, thirty-three percent of the real estate agents in a large Midwestern city reported they did not want to rent to Jews, and a study of 3,000 resorts across the country in the same year found that twenty-two percent discriminated against Jews. In the late 1960s and 1970s, such overt discrimination against Jews probably declined, although anti-Jewish prejudice remains. Of some current concern are the quotas and preferential treatment being received by some groups in education and employment which, it is argued, favor one minority to the exclusion of others.

Jews represent a powerful interest group that the government must consider in its policies toward Israel and the Middle East, and occasionally, events evoke memories of the atrocities in Germany and galvanize Jewish political action groups—most recently, the 1978 march in Skokie, Illinois, by members of the American Nazi Party.

PATTERNS OF INTERACTION

When populations that differ by race or ethnicity come together, a number of different reactions may occur, some peaceful, others not.[12] **Annihilation** is the elimination of one group by another. It may be intentional, as in the case of the Nazis' attempted extermination of a whole ethnic group—a practice called *genocide*—or it can be unintentional, as in the case of American Indians fallen prey to illnesses brought in by European settlers. **Expulsion** refers to the removal of a group from the territory in which it resides. The Japanese on the West Coast during World War II were removed from their homes and placed in detention camps, and American Indian tribes were forced from their homes onto reservations. **Segregation** refers to the setting apart of one group. It is not as extreme as expulsion, but the separation is nevertheless obvious. The segregation may be physical—to a separate area of the city—or it may be social as

---

[12]These paragraphs on patterns of interaction are drawn from Berry, *Race and Ethnic Relations*, 3d ed., Chapters 7–12 (see footnote 1).

when people living together are limited in how and with whom they may interact. Segregation (from the minority's viewpoint) may be involuntary—blacks in America—or voluntary. Avoidance (voluntary self-segregation) occurs when a culture such as the Amish in America wants to maintain its identity and uniqueness against the influence of the dominant culture and therefore voluntarily separates itself.

Assimilation and amalgamation are other patterns of interaction occurring between unlike groups. **Assimilation** refers to the mixing and merging of unlike cultures so that two groups come to have a common culture. When two cultures meet, one outcome would be that each culture adopts some of the other's traits so that the result is a true melting pot—the emergence of a new culture different from either of the old cultures. More often, however, assimilation means that the incoming or minority culture adapts to the dominant culture. **Amalgamation** refers to biological (rather than cultural) mixing. Amalgamation seems invariably to accompany the meeting of racial and ethnic groups, despite the best efforts of some to legislate against it. A **marginal person** is defined as one who lives between two antagonistic cultures, a product of each but a member of neither. Studies indicate that the consequences of marginality can be severe—personality disturbances or feelings of inferiority. Marginality is often defined as a product of amalgamation, but it may also result from cultural mixing (the Southern rural migrant to the urban North, for example).

Cultural pluralism describes a pattern of interaction in which unlike cultures maintain their own identity and yet interact with each other relatively peacefully. Switzerland is usually cited as the best example of pluralism in that peoples of several nationalities and religions and even three or four different languages are able to get along peacefully. According to Brewton Berry, few countries have been able to successfully accomplish a system of pluralism. Some minorities at some times in the United States have voiced a preference for cultural pluralism, but the dominant culture seems to look either toward integration or toward discrimination and segregation.

MINORITY GROUP REACTIONS

The patterns of interaction described above are usually dictated by the dominant group. What then of minority group reactions to domination? Gordon Allport has outlined some types of reactions in his book, *The Nature of Prejudice*.[13] The simplest response is to deny that one is a member of that minority group—members of one race pass as members of another, people change their names to get rid of their ethnic identification. Similarly, **acculturation** refers to attempts by members of minority groups to assimilate, to blend in and take on as many characteristics of the dominant culture as possible. Hiding resentment behind withdrawal and passivity—"the mask of contentment"—is another reaction. Secession refers to the formal withdrawal of a group of people from a

---

[13]See Gordon Allport, *The Nature of Prejudice* (Garden City, N.Y.: Doubleday, 1958), Chapter 9.

political, religious, or national group. The South seceded prior to the Civil War, and the citizens of Quebec have been considering secession from the rest of Canada. *Self-hatred* is another reaction, with the minority group identifying with the dominant group. Studies of Nazi concentration camps showed that after years of suffering, inmates began identifying with the guards. The prisoners wore bits of the guards' clothing, they became anti-Semitic, and in general they adopted the mentality of the oppressor. Likewise, if blacks value light skin more than dark, they may be accepting whites' evaluation of skin pigmentation. Self-hate may lead to aggression against one's own group, as when a segment of the minority that thinks of itself as being a higher class takes out its frustrations on a lower-ranked segment. Minorities sometimes show greater *prejudice* against other minorities, and in other cases the opposite reaction—greater *sympathy*.

A *strengthening of in-group ties* is another reaction by minorities to domination. **Nativism** is a type of rejection of the dominant culture in which people attempt to improve their own existence by eliminating all foreign persons, objects, and customs. This has been seen recently in the United States with slogans such as "Black Power" and "Don't buy where you can't work," and by the focus on the development of ethnic identity through emphasizing the minority's cultural and historical roots. Minorities may react to domination by using *aggression*. The aggression may be individual and reflected in crime patterns, or it can be collective and culminate in urban disturbances or riots. In milder form, the aggression may appear in the literature and humor of the minority group as it makes fun of or shows its bitterness toward the majority group. In fact, humor is a common way of expressing feelings about other groups. In the following not very representative examples, who is putting down whom?

> A black woman from Harlem wins the Irish sweepstakes and decides to buy a fur coat. She tries on a coat at Saks Fifth Avenue and it comes down to her ankles. As she looks at herself in the mirror, she turns to the saleslady and says, "Do you think this makes me look too Jewish?"

> A priest and a rabbi are each driving down a New York street. The rabbi stops at a light and the priest runs into him. An Irish cop comes up to the priest and asks, "Ah, Father, how fast might the rabbi have been going when he backed into you?"

> Dick Gregory: "I sat in at this place for three years and when they finally waited on me I found out they didn't have what I wanted."

> What do you have when you cross a WASP and a chimpanzee? A three-foot-tall, blond company president.

FEMALE AND MALE

Is a person upper-middle class or lower-middle class? Is an Amercan Indian white? Difficult to say, but the question of female and male—no problem at all. There are arguments over how many social classes exist, to say nothing of the problem of determining the social class of a particular individual. The answer depends on the variables and method of analysis that are used. The boundaries of race and ethnicity are blurred—in many cases the best answer seems to be that people are what they define themselves to be. Sex categories are more easily defined, at least biologically. This is one distinction that people have felt confident about for ages. And if occasional doubts do pop up, a scientific test can be applied. One of the more intriguing aspects of the Olympic Games is the sex test that is used to make sure that males are not masquerading as females.

The paradox in this situation is that although people confidently feel and always have felt that they have a clear grasp of the biological fact, until recently few have considered the *social* consequences of sex differences. Karl Marx wrote about the consequences of social-class differences over one hundred years ago, and he wasn't the first. The consequences of racial differences have been a central issue in the United States for decades. But the consequences of the minority status produced by sex differences have only recently—perhaps in the last ten years—become a topic drawing widespread and serious attention.

Socialization and Sex Roles

Thirty pairs of parents were questioned within twenty-four hours after the birth of their first child and were asked to "describe your baby as you would to a close relative." Hospital information on the babies showed that the fifteen boy babies and the fifteen girl babies *did not differ* on such objective data as birth length, weight, irritability, etc. But the parents said that girl babies were softer, littler, more beautiful, prettier, finer featured, cuter, and more inattentive than the boy babies. The fathers tended to label or stereotype the babies in this fashion more than the mothers. The authors of the study suggest that sex-typing, and sex-role socialization have already begun at birth.[14]

How could this be? One day after birth and already babies are showing definite sex differences in terms of physical appearance and temperament. The answer, of course, is that *it isn't so*. People assume that males and females are born with different abilities and temperaments. People assume it to be so, and then behave as if it *were* so. We tend to act toward children one way if they are male, another way if they are female. We expect them to be a certain way, and they turn out that way. The self-fulfilling prophecy rides again.

To place the assumption about so-called inherited sexual characteristics in correct perspective, recall Margaret Mead's description of sex and temperament among the Arapesh, Mundugumor, and Tchambuli (p. 71). There was great variety in the behavior of the sexes in those societies. Compared with sex roles in America, roles were modified and reversed. The explanation is not that these societies are strange and peculiar, but more simply that the sex roles learned in those societies are different from those learned here.

Like other roles, sex roles are learned through the socialization process. It is possible that in our society the teaching of sex roles starts even earlier than the teaching of other roles. As we saw above, parents immediately start acting

---

[14]Jeffrey Rubin, Frank Provenzano, and Zella Luria, "The Eye of the Beholder: Parents' Views on Sex of New Borns," *American Journal of Orthopsychiatry* 44 (July 1974), pp. 512–519.

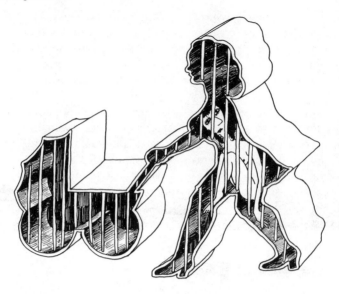

differently toward their children based on their sex. Look at their toys: Boys get tractors, trucks, tools, guns, athletic equipment; girls get dolls, cooking sets, play perfume and cosmetic kits, pretty clothes. Friends and grandparents, scandalized to hear that the mother concerned about sex typing bought her son a doll, were only partly mollified to find that at least it was a boy doll. Few families escape the typing. Our family stopped at a gas station in southern France in which the pumps were operated by a female attendant. Our four-year-old son Jeff studied the situation for a long time and finally said: "What's that lady doing working in the gas station? I don't like it—it doesn't look too good." Jeff's mother: "They can work there too. They can work anywhere." Jeff: "No, they are supposed to go to the store and stuff. . . ." And that from a child of parents who should know better.

The schools continue the pattern. Textbooks from Dick and Jane on up portray boys in active, aggressive, so-called masculine roles and girls in passive, tender, so-called feminine roles. A study of teachers in nursery schools found that they spent more time with the boys in the class than with the girls. Boys were encouraged to work harder on academic subjects. They were given more rewards and more directions in how to do things. Boys were given instructions, then encouraged to complete the task themselves. If the girls did not quickly get the idea, the teacher would often intervene and do the task for them. There was one exception: The teachers did pay more attention to the girls on feminine-sex-typed activities such as cooking. Even here girls got praise and assistance, whereas boys received detailed instructions. The boys were given more attention, and the environment was much more of a learning experience for them than it was for the girls.[15]

---

[15]Lisa Serbin and Daniel O'Leary, "How Nursery Schools Teach Girls to Shut Up," *Psychology Today* 9 (December 1975), p. 57.

Another group of researchers working in the Boston area found that sex-role differences were well developed in the majority of children by the age of five. The children knew which personality traits were "masculine" and which were "feminine." They knew which jobs were for men and which were for women. The experimenters developed a curriculum that attempted to make the children more flexible in their assumptions about the sexes. The outcome of the program was mixed. To the researchers' surprise, many of the fifth- and ninth-grade boys with whom they worked became *more* stereotyped in their views of women and more rigid and outspoken about what they thought to be women's place. The effects on the girls in the program were more positive, showing attitude change away from typical stereotypes and increased self-esteem.[16] The researchers are hopeful about the school program they tested, but it's not enough by itself. The socialization agents include family, peers, teachers, literature, entertainment, mass media, and the whole social tradition that socializes people to believe in the inherent psychological, temperamental, and attitudinal differences between the sexes. It should not surprise us at all that boys grow up to be doctors and mechanics and girls grow up to keep house, have babies, and take care of their families. They have been socialized into these roles from the very beginning.

Consequences of Sex-Role Typing

The results of sex-role typing are many and varied, and not all the benefits are for males. The male is restricted in how he may show emotion—he is strong and silent, he does not show weakness, and he keeps his feelings under careful rein, at least outwardly. The female has far greater freedom to express emotion. The male is subject to much more stress and pressure to achieve and be successful. This is probably part of the reason why males have a shorter life expectancy, more heart disease, higher rates of suicide and hospitalization for mental illness and related pathologies. (See Table 6.1, p. 172.) Women have been much less involved in crime and deviant behavior than have men, and this too is related to sex-role differences. Some men would like to change roles, to be househusbands, staying home and cooking, working in the garden, and taking care of the kids. What are their chances in a society that sets up sex roles like ours does?

The major consequence of sex-role typing, however, is that women are not able to participate fully in American society, a society in which they make up fifty-one percent of the members. People are becoming more sensitive to the unfairness of this situation, and women's frustration is increasing.

There is ample evidence of the effects of sex typing. Table 6.5 shows the years of education completed by males and females in the United States in 1980. An interesting contrast appears. More women than men graduate from high school, but more men go on to and graduate from college. A high school

---

[16]This research is summarized by Carol Tavris in "It's Tough to Nip Sexism in the Bud," *Psychology Today* 9 (December 1975), p. 58. Ms. Tavris states that the full report of this research by Marcia Guttentag is available in *Undoing Sex Stereotypes* by Marcia Guttentag and Helen Bray (New York: McGraw-Hill, 1976).

TABLE 6.5   Years of School Completed by Sex, 1980

	Males	Females
High school graduate	33%	41%
One to three years college	16	14
Four years or more college	21	14

U.S. Bureau of the Census, *Statistical Abstract of the United States, 1981* (102d ed.), Washington, D.C., p. 142.

education is seen as adequate for many women, but the ambitious male goes on to improve his career chances.

The percentage of workers with income and how much they earn is shown in Table 6.6. The proportion of men working has not changed much in thirty years, while the proportion of women working has gone up substantially. But now check their income—how fast is that gap closing?

Next, compare income level for the same occupation, as in Table 6.7. It is apparent that for the same category of job, women are paid far less than men.

Women represent more than forty percent of the work force but generally hold lower-skilled and lower-paying jobs. Women are always well represented at the sales and clerical levels, but seldom anywhere else. Even when a woman does the same work as a man, she gets paid less for it. Women represent more than fifty percent of the nation's registered voters but in 1980 held only twelve percent of the elective positions. In 1981 there were nineteen women in the House of Representatives (out of more than four hundred), two women in the U.S. Senate (out of one hundred), and the first female United States Supreme Court Justice was appointed in 1981. Women make up about thirteen percent of the nation's lawyers, judges, and doctors, and four percent of the nation's dentists. Women constitute eighty-four percent of the elementary school teachers but only about thirty-seven percent of the school administrators. Female representation in higher education follows somewhat the same pattern. In 1980 over fifty percent of high school graduates were women, but they accounted for only forty-eight percent of the bachelor's degrees, forty-nine percent of the master's degrees, and thirty percent of the doctorates.

Is Change Coming?

In 1975, instead of citing the "Man of the Year" as usual, *Time* gave its annual award to "Women of the Year" in recognition of women's accomplishments. Polls show that many support the aims and efforts of the women's movement to change women's status in society. More women are elected to public positions. Women's enrollment in business, medical, and law schools has increased substantially. Churches hve ordained women and are creating opportunities for leadership roles. Over ninety percent of the jobs in the military are now open to women, and of two million people in the military by 1980, some 170,000 (eight percent) were women. Many police departments across the country now have women in jobs equal to those of male police officers. Women's participation in organized sports is increasingly accepted. And even in crime, where men have predominated, women seem to be catching up. Arrests of

TABLE 6.6   Median Income of Employed People Over Fourteen, by Sex

	Males		Females	
	Percent with Income	Median Income	Percent with Income	Median Income
1950	90%	$ 2,570	43%	$ 953
1960	91	4,080	56	1,261
1970	92	6,670	67	2,237
1979	95	11,845	89	4,354

U.S. Bureau of the Census, *Statistical Abstract of the United States, 1981* (102d ed.), Washington, D.C., p. 444.

TABLE 6.7   Median Income by Occupation of Year-round Full-time Workers Over Fourteen in 1980, by Sex

	Males	Females
Professional and technical	$23,026	$15,285
Sales workers	19,910	9,748
Clerical	18,247	10,997
Craft workers	18,671	11,701
Laborers	12,757	9,747

"Money Income and Poverty Status of Families and Persons in the United States: 1980," *Current Population Reports*, Series P-60, no. 127.

males were up eight percent between 1971 and 1980; arrests of females for the same period were up nineteen percent.[17]

Is equality, then, just around the corner? Probably not. Look at the facts—eighty-seven percent of the nation's lawyers, judges, and doctors are males, as are ninety-six percent of the dentists, and so on. A 1982 study looked at male and female MBA's from Stanford four years after graduation: women's income was averaging $7,000 a year less than men's. A few women climb the ladder; most do not. In 1978 *Fortune* conducted a survey of the 1,300 top companies and found only one female chief executive (Katherine Graham of the Washington Post Co.) and only ten female top executives out of a total of 6,400 officers and directors. Further, the number isn't growing—in the previous survey in 1973, there were eleven women on the list.[18] Often, the achievements of the successful are widely publicized, perhaps unintentionally giving the impression of great gains. Even those women who are successful inevitably have horror stories to tell of the subtle pressure and overt discrimination used against them. A woman is still usually paid less than a man for the same work, regardless of level.

In June 1982, the Equal Rights Amendment (ERA) went down to defeat, three states short of the thirty-eight needed for ratification. There were many

[17]*Statistical Abstract of the United States, 1981* and *Uniform Crime Reports, 1980* were helpful in this section.

[18]*Fortune* 98 (July 17, 1978), p. 59, includes detailed sketches of the ten who made it.

reasons for its failure, among them a lack of support in male-dominated legislatures and differences of opinion among women themselves as to how the ERA would affect their roles. Backers of the ERA have vowed to work for the defeat of the politicians who opposed them, and to reintroduce the amendment. Given the conservative mood of the nation and of the Congress, the effort promises to provide a continuing challenge.

The greatest success of the women's movement has been in raising people's awareness of the existence of sex-role stereotypes and sex discrimination. Change is occurring, and the progress in reducing education and job discrimination is consistent if not dramatic. Changing traditional patterns of socialization for the young and resocializing adults is difficult at best. Even sociologists (who should know better) are culprits. As recently as ten years ago the subject was foreign to us—it was seldom a textbook topic or a research interest. We weren't paying any attention either.

THE ELDERLY

Hope Bagger at the age of seventy was called for jury duty but then told to go home because she was too old. Mrs. Bagger, now eighty-six, is an active member of the Gray Panthers, an organization seeking to remedy the way society treats old people. In some parts of the world old age is seen as a virtue, life in its very highest form. The elderly are revered and are well cared for by society as a whole. In this country the elderly find that they are forced to retire, have trouble getting other jobs, and are exploited if they do get work. As one member of the Gray Panthers put it, the young seem to feel that old people descended from outer space. They forget that the elderly have a past and a future.

A baby born in 1900 had a life expectancy of forty-eight years; a child born today has a life expectancy of more than seventy years. There were 25.5 million people sixty-five and older in the United States in 1980, and the number will continue to increase. Many of the elderly are poor and out of work, over fifty percent are widowed, the suicide rate of older males is high, and age often compounds the effects of other minority statuses.

Aging affects people both physically and socially. In a general sense, physical aging begins in people around the age of thirty and continues throughout the life span. Certain body functions, muscle tone and strength, and the senses all reach their peaks around thirty and decline thereafter. Although many people tend to view it as such, aging is not a disease. People are more likely to die as they get older because the body becomes more vulnerable to outside influences, less adaptable, and more affected by stress and crisis.[19]

Social aging is more treacherous, yet potentially easier to deal with than physical aging. Social aging refers to the attitudes we have about older people. We are indoctrinated with the idea that the old are different and inferior to the

---

[19]Anita Harbert and Leon Ginsberg, *Human Services for Older Adults: Concepts & Skills* (Belmont, Calif.: Wadsworth, 1979), Chapters 1 and 2.

rest of us. We stereotype the aged, and they are victims of prejudice and dis-crimination. In fact, American society treats the elderly with the same sort of stereotyping, the same institutionalized discrimination as that based on sex and race. The old are thought to be unintelligent, asexual, unemployable, mentally ill, and hard to get along with. The fact that many if not most older people are *not* this way is beside the point. We continue to make them retire before they want to, refuse to hire them, and pay them less when they do get a job. And the self-fulfilling prophecy suggests to us that if people are viewed and treated a certain way long enough, they tend to become that way.

What do the elderly want? Our stereotypes about aging again help us. A life of leisure—sit out the last twenty years on the porch swing or in front of the tube. Grow old gracefully. A time of disengagement. Relax now—the important things are done. On the contrary, to remain in good health old people need what everyone needs: work to do, money to live on, a place to live in, and other people to care for and to care for them. Society should recognize that the elderly are an important resource.[20]

As with many other victims of minority status, the elderly are becoming politically active. It probably starts with consciousness raising and moves to more militant stands on issues through collective action. Groups like the Gray Panthers, the National Retired Teachers Association, the National Council of Senior Citizens, and the American Association of Retired Persons have formed a "gray lobby" of enormous strength in Washington. They have not lost a major campaign. The gray lobby has defeated the AMA on Medicare, big businesses on forced retirement, and taxpayer groups on social security.[21]

It is important, then, that the elderly not be viewed as social obsoletes. They *do* have a past and a future. And remember that unlike many minority statuses, this is one that happens to *all* of us—if we're fortunate.

SUMMARY

This is the second of two chapters on social differentiation. Here we exam-ined the characteristics of race, ethnic, and sex categories. Social differ-entiation refers to the dividing of people into categories according to social or biological characteristics such as race, sex, social class, or religion. We found earlier that social differentiation often leads to social stratification. That is, these categories are ranked; some are seen as better than others.

One common component of these categories is that of minority status. The fact that categories are ranked and the consequences of this ranking were the central topics of this chapter. Prejudice, discrimination, and stereotyping are commonly used to reaffirm the status ranking that we believe in. They help us keep others "in their place." We examined the types of reactions that occur

---

[20]Alexander Comfort, "Age Prejudice in America," *Social Policy*, November/December 1976, pp. 3–8.

[21]David H. Fischer, "Books Considered," *The New Republic*, December 2, 1978, pp. 31–36.

when populations of different races or ethnic backgrounds meet as well as the reactions of minority groups themselves to discrimination.

We examined a number of statistical examples of differential treatment—differences in education, jobs, income, opportunities in life, crime and deviant behavior, sickness, and others. Less easily displayed statistically but more important as a human concern is the effect of continued differential treatment on *how one sees oneself.* Some concepts studied earlier—socialization, role, self-concept, self-fulfilling prophecy—help us understand the critical significance of minority status for the individual's development.

In the first of the readings which follow, a black woman describes her experiences with prejudice and discrimination in America. In the second, a former director of the U.S. Immigration and Naturalization Service talks about immigrants—why they continue to stream into the United States and the problems they face when they get here. The next reading examines sex discrimination in a work situation, the work situation being a bar near a college campus. The final reading is an excerpt from Dee Brown's *Bury My Heart at Wounded Knee*, which describes the consequences for the American Indians of the western expansion of the United States between 1860 and 1890.

Terms for Study

acculturation (179)	genocide (178)
amalgamation (179)	marginal person (179)
annihilation (178)	minority status (167)
assimilation (179)	nativism (180)
authoritarian personality (170)	prejudice (169)
cultural pluralism (179)	race (167–168)
discrimination (169)	secession (179)
ethnicity (169)	segregation (178)
expulsion (178)	stereotyping (170)

Reading 6.1

DRYLONGSO: ELLA TURNER SURRY

JOHN LANGSTON GWALTNEY

In *Drylongso*, John Gwaltney provides a self-portrait of black America, a description of the conditions of life through the voices of those who have lived it. Gwaltney is an anthropologist at Syracuse University.

If life were a matter of rich recompense for noble service, Mrs. Surry's wealth and happiness would defy estimation. But in this world as it actually is, for all her gallantry she has lost the battle against the street. She has been mugged, her possessions have been stolen and the house she strove so mightily to purchase is a crumbling, beleaguered island in a sea of urban decay. She lives in a bombed-out city and has had to take cover in her own house from the fire of her own army in her own country, but she is still clinging to sanity somehow.

Have I encountered discrimination?! I was told by my adviser in high school when I wanted to take the secretarial course, "You cannot take it. Who's going to employ you? You people don't have any businessmen who are going to employ you and the white businesses are not going to employ you. You're a nice girl, but this is not the course for you. You're not going to be able to go to college and there's just no future in it for you." I can see that little thin lady right now and I remember her name, too. She gave me the facts.

Now, I'll tell you another thing that I was just discussing with my children: when I was coming along looking for a job, if they would employ a Negro they would specify in the paper whether they wanted a light-colored one or not. I can remember an incident with another lady. I can call her name, I remember it as well as if it had happened yesterday. Mrs. Peters! She had a store on Main Street. I answered this ad because I was desperate. I wanted a summer job. She wanted a waitress and she asked me over the phone, "Are you light?" I tried to ignore the question because I wanted the job, but she asked me again, "Are you light?" It wasn't this black or white thing then, because black was a fighting word then for some people. So I said to her, "I am colored." So I went up and she gave me the job. But this is the way it was. It was put right out in the papers. I tried to tell my girls about that. No bones about it—they specified when they wanted light-colored or fair-skinned.

There was one other black girl working at this place, in the kitchen. She was dark and she was washing dishes. Now, I quit that job because of that girl. I was in the dining room and there were two white girls working there with me. I called my orders to the kitchen and this girl in the kitchen would bring them to the serving window when she wasn't busy washing dishes; then I would take them from there. Well, you see, I was very busy because I worked one half of the dining room by myself and the two white girls worked the other half to-

gether. I had a habit of never writing down my orders; I liked to try to keep them in my mind. I used to pride myself on my memory and I never used a pad or pencil. Now, this girl that was working in the kitchen was rather slow. She had been told by Mrs. Peters never to come into the dining room. Now, this was just a luncheonette on Main Street. Well, this black girl—I think her name was Tina—could see that I was really busy, so she came into the dining room to bring two orders. Well! Mrs. Peters saw her and stamped her feet and said, "You black nigger, I told you never to enter this dining room!" Tina ducked back in the kitchen, and after I came out of shock I came out of that dining room taking off my apron! Now, at the time the dining room was full. It was so busy that Mrs. Peters didn't notice me at first. But when she looked around I had on my street dress and was ready to go. She said, "Where are you going? Are you sick?" I said, "Yes, I'm sick." I said, "Because if you'll think that way of her, you'll think that way of me." She said, "Think what way of who?" By that time she had forgotten all about what she had said. So I reminded her and she said, "You can't leave like this. The dining room is full." I said, "Watch me!" I said I would come back on payday for my money, and went home. When I told my mother what had happened, she said, "You did absolutely right." Now, Mrs. Peters herself evidently had to get out there on that floor and hold those customers that lunch hour I left. She came to my house, and while she was sitting in my living room she raised my salary three times! I knew I was good at what I was doing, you see. But I wouldn't go back there. When I went there to get my salary, however, I saw that the other black girl was still working there.

I have always been conscious of a kind of pride—not this kind of pride they got in the streets now. It was that real pride from knowing who you were. My grandfather made me feel that way before I was a teenager. It had something to do with knowing where you had come from and knowing your family's history. He made me conscious of the fact that I was black and that I had a history like everybody else. That was something different than the garbage they handed out in school that kept telling us how much we owed Lincoln. Every time you heard his name mentioned you were supposed to bump your head on the floor five times. He said, "Read and see behind this Lincoln business so you will see what the whites are trying to do." He got me to read about a lot of people. He introduced me to Harriet Tubman. Now, there was a person I really admired! I've read that she was supposed to have these dizzy spells, but I believe that this was an act that this woman had to get her point across. I don't think she could really have been sick and did all the things that she got done. I think she had an act which made people do what she wanted to do. She had to play the game to get her point across. We have always been the best actors in the world because we have always had to live at least two lives and we have done that successfully.

I remember another incident. This lady was in her eighties and she had never been married and she put this ad in the paper for a girl to come in and do her little washing and cleaning. So one day I took a girl up to her apartment—I was the elevator operator. Now, this girl wasn't up there but a hot minute. When I brought her down she didn't look but so happy, so I just said to myself, "I see you didn't get the job." She was a very neat and clean, heavy-set dark girl. I had no sooner got this girl out of the building when I was called to the seventh floor again. The old lady who put the ad in the paper asked to see me. She asked me, "What was the idea of bringing that girl up there?" I said, "Well, she said that she wanted to see you." She said, "Well, don't you ever bring anybody as black as that up to see me again, because I'm not going to hire anybody that black." I said to her, "I've never seen a black person in my life!" She said, "Well, you should have taken a good look at that one!"

You ask me if I ever encountered discrimination! It was right up to your nose. I worked half of Mrs. Peters' dining room—that's right, it was sectioned off in thirds, well, supposedly in thirds, but my third was the entire back half of the room. You see, I had the biggest third. Now, these two blondes worked the front, but I had the whole back of the room and the sides, too. That's the way it was and if you wanted to work you had to accept it. We had to work.

Now, we were talking about how white people expect more of black people. I just thought of an incident that will show you what I mean: I was in the hospital and I was sharing this room with a white woman. Now, we had both had operations and we were just laying there together. Now, I had had serious surgery. I was a diabetic, 240 blood pressure. Now, I got up at night when the doctors and nurses weren't watching me and washed out my nightgown because my husband was working, all my children were small and I didn't have anybody at home to do for me. Now, this white woman, who was evidently quite well-off, she said to me, "Sweetheart, would you mind if I asked you a question?" Now, I knew when I heard that "Sweetheart" that I was going to get hit with something. Oh, I knew that! This was the approach—"Sweetheart" or "Darling." Her incision was draining very copiously and this was messing up her beautiful silk pajamas. She said, "I don't want to ask my daughter-in-law to wash these because they are so messy, but would you mind washing them out for me?" I simply told her that I was doing my own but I wasn't going to do anybody else's. I told her that I didn't think that her daughter-in-law would mind doing that for her because a little blood wouldn't hurt her any more than it would me. She turned her back to the wall and cried. She was quite upset. Said she didn't know that this would offend me. Now, she didn't want to ask her daughter-in-law, but she felt no qualms at all about asking a total stranger because I was black! I shouldn't mind this blood and drainage! Now, I was dealing with my drainage, but she didn't feel that it was necessary for her to deal with hers. Now, she hadn't had the extensive kind of surgery that I had had. You see, when they look at a black person they see someone who is supposed to be able to stand much more heat than they can. I'm supposed to be able to stand much more work than they can without getting tired. These lazy Negroes are the ones who dig ditches and build roads and lift heavy pots and things. . . .

I think black people are more reasonable than white people. I don't know, maybe the word is not "reasonable," but I think that we are much more clever than they are because we know that we have to play the game. We've always had to live two lives—you know, one for them and one for ourselves. Now, the average white person doesn't know this, but, of course, the average black per-

son does. *If you sit on any bus coming from the suburbs and hear black people laughing about the fool things they have done at work, you'll know how many of us are playing this game.*

I used to work for this Jewish lady. It was one of the first jobs I got. Now, this lady had all these old hats that looked like something from a Slabtown convention. You see, I had to get there at seven and then I would clean until twelve or twelve-thirty for fifty cents. To ease her conscience she would take a shopping bag and clean out her refrigerator and her closet. There was always one or two of these ridiculous hats and some little dabs of salmon cakes or something else which she would have thrown out. Well, I just transported her garbage to my house, where I threw it out. I wouldn't have eaten any of her food because she was a nasty cook. She just didn't wash her hands. It wasn't a racial thing, it's just that she was one of these people who would set up all day picking their corns and then go right into the kitchen without washing her hands and start cooking! With us, even if you had just gotten out of the bathtub you washed hands before you started messing with anybody's food! And when she cleaned her closet she would fill up a shopping bag with all these old hats and dresses, and say, "Give these to your mother." We'd sit around the table at home and laugh at this stuff and sometimes the kids would play with it and then my mother would say, "When you get finished with that stuff, put it in the garbage." But that lady just knew it was good enough for us. She could see my mother going to church in that junk. She always stressed the fact that it was a nice hat. You know that old saying that so-and-so's behind would make somebody a Sunday face? Well, that's how she felt. Her garbage was supposed to be something special because it was her garbage. Her garbage would be Sunday best for my mother because my mother was black and she wasn't supposed to know about any value but the value this white woman put on this old stuff. If that old hat had Rosendorf's label in it, that was supposed to be it for you in them days.

I'll tell you another incident. My grandmother sewed. She didn't just pick it up, she took domestic science in college and was very good at it. She used to make me all types of clothing, really beautiful things. I had this Southern white teacher and she asked me where did my mother work? I said, "My mother doesn't work." So when I went back to school my mother went back with me. This was one of two times that my mother ever went to school. My mother asked the teacher what she meant by asking where she worked. It turned out that the teacher really wanted to know where I had gotten the clothes that my grandmother made for me. My mother told her that she did not work and that my grandmother made the clothes. Now, this white Southerner automatically assumed that if I were a black child and dressed well that somebody—some white person my mother worked for—had to have given me these clothes. . . .

I'm not just talking about these days but when I was coming along or when any generation of black people was coming along. If you find a black doctor, you know that took blood, sweat and tears. Most black people think that they are mentally and physically better than white people, and I think that they are physically superior to white people. I think it goes back to slavery-time. I think that only the strongest of us were able to survive, so that gave us better stock to start with. In those days ninety-nine-pound weaklings just couldn't make it. Those fields separated the strong from the weak and only the strong were permitted to breed, generally, and they tried to inbreed the strong. We fought their battle while they sat on their verandas drinking their dern mint juleps! We were out there making it. Our bodies were conditioned by all that hard work and living in those huts. Only the strong could survive. We lost the weak by the wayside. So, therefore we are superior! As a race we are sturdier and made out of better material. Now, in the Depression we weren't jumping out of windows because we didn't have a steak. We simply boiled a pot of beans and kept on get'n up. If we lose a million dollars they won't be putting us away in mental hospitals. We can cope with adversity much better than they can. We've had our trial by fire, still are having it.

Questions 6.1

1. Outline situations of prejudice and discrimination illustrated in this reading.
2. Illustrate types of minority group reactions (see text) shown in this reading.
3. Write a short essay on the effects of prejudice and discrimination on the individual, using concepts like socialization, self, looking-glass self, significant and generalized other.

Reading 6.2

AMERICAN DREAMS: LEONEL CASTILLO

STUDS TERKEL

In this interview from Terkel's *American Dreams: Lost and Found*, Leonel Castillo discusses the plight of the immigrant; why they come to America, what happens to them here, and the consequences for America of their being here.

Former director of the United States Immigration and Naturalization Service (INS).

"My father's father came from Mexico to Victoria, Texas, in 1880. He paid a toston, a half-dollar. That automatically made him a U.S. citizen. In the early years of the century, he was fighting for the right to bury Mexicans in the same grounds as Anglos. There was no place to bury Mexicans. He finally got a piece of land from some German Lutherans. It was deeded to our family and the Mexican community in perpetuity. My grandfather and his friends cleared the land for the first funerals. We've kept the records since 1898. We have many, many people buried there."

New immigrants are trying all over again to integrate themselves into the system. They have the same hunger. On any given day, there are about three million throughout the world who are applying to come to the United States and share the American Dream. The same battles. I still read old newspaper clips: 1886. Housemaid wanted. We'll accept any person, any color, any nationality, any religion, except Irish. (Laughs.) Rough ads: No Irish need apply.

Most of the undocumented here without papers, without legal permission, think they're gonna go back home in six months. Relatively few go back. Some old Italians are going back to <u>pensionares</u>, and some old Eastern Europeans are going back home. But, by and large, immigrants, old and new, stay. They don't feel they know anyone in the old village. Their children don't speak Polish or Italian or Greek. Their children are used to air conditioning, McDonald's.

The Vietnamese boat people express it as well as anyone. They don't know if they're gonna land, if the boat's gonna sink. They don't know what's gonna happen to 'em, but they've a hunch they might make it to the U.S. as the "freedom place."

There is the plain hard fact of hunger. In order to eat, a person will endure tremendous hardship. Mexican people who come here usually are not the most destitute. Someone who's too poor can't afford the trip. You've got to buy <u>coyotes</u>. A <u>coyote</u> is a smuggler of people. He's also called a <u>pollero</u>. Pollo is chicken. He's the one who guides chickens through the border.

Sometimes the whole family saves up and gives the bright young man or the bright young woman the family savings. It even goes in hock for a year or two. They pin all their hopes on this one kid, put him on a bus, let him go a thousand miles. He doesn't speak a word of English. He's only seventeen, eighteen years old, but he's gonna save that family. A lot rides on that kid who's a busboy in some hotel.

We've had some as young as eleven who have come a thousand miles. You have this young kid, all his family savings, everything is on him. There are a lot of songs and stories about mother and child, the son leaving who may never return. We end up deporting him. It's heartrending.

He's the bright kid in the family. The slow one might not make it, might get killed. The one who's sickly can't make the trip. He couldn't walk through the desert. He's not gonna be too old, too young, too destitute, or too slow. He's the brightest and the best.

He's gonna be the first hook, the first pioneer coming into an alien society, the United States. He might be here in Chicago. He works as a busboy all night long. They pay him minimum or less, and work him hard. He'll never complain. He might even thank his boss. He'll say as little as possible because he doesn't want anyone to know what his status is. He will often live in his apartment, except for the time he goes to work or to church or to a dance. He will stay in and watch TV. If he makes a hundred a week, he will manage to send back twenty-five. All over the country, if you go to a Western Union office on the weekend, you'll find a lot of people there sending money orders. In a southwest office, like Dallas, Western Union will tell you seventy-five percent of their business is money orders to Mexico.

After the kid learns a bit, because he's healthy and young and energetic, he'll probably get another job as a busboy. He'll work at another place as soon as the shift is over. He'll try to work his way up to be a waiter. He'll work incredible hours. He doesn't care about union scale, he doesn't care about conditions, about humiliations. He accepts all this as his fate.

He's burning underneath with this energy and ambition. He outworks the U.S. busboys and eventually becomes the waiter. Where he can maneuver, he tries to become the owner and gives a lot of competition to the locals. Restaurant owners tell me, if they have a choice, they'll always hire foreign nationals first. They're so eager and grateful. There's a little greed here, too. (Laughs.) They pay 'em so little.

We've got horrible cases of exploitation. In San Diego and in Arizona, we discovered people who live in holes in the ground, live under trees, no sanitation, no housing, nothing. A lot of them live in chicken coops.

They suffer from coyotes, *too, who exploit them and sometimes beat 'em.* Coyotes *advertise. If the immigrant arrives in San Diego, the word is very quick: where to go and who's looking. He'll even be approached. If he's got a lot of money, the* coyote *will manage to bring him from Tijuana all the way to Chicago and guarantee him a job. He'll get all the papers: Social Security, birth certificate, driver's license. The* coyote *reads the papers and finds which U.S. citizens have died and gets copies of all their vital statistics. In effect, the immigrant carries the identity of a dead person.*

Often the employer says he doesn't know anything about it. He plays hands off. He makes his bucks hiring cheap labor. The coyote *makes his off the workers.*

Coyotes *come from the border with these pickup trucks full of people. They may put twenty in a truck. They bring 'em in all sorts of bad weather, when they're less likely to be stopped. They might be going twenty, twenty-eight hours, with one or two pit stops. They don't let the people out. There's no urinal, no bathroom. They sit or they stand there in this little cramped space for the whole trip.*

A truck broke down outside Chicago. It was a snowstorm. The driver left. People were frostbitten, lost their toes. In Laredo, the truck was in an accident. Everybody ran off because the police were coming. The truck caught fire. No one remembered the two fellows in the trunk. It was locked and no keys. Of course, they burned to death. The border patrol found thirty-three people dying in the deserts of Arizona. They were saved at the last minute and deported. I'll bet you a dollar every one of them, as soon as they are well enough, will try again.

At least a quarter of a million apprehensions were made last year. If we apprehend them at the border, we turn 'em around and ask them to depart voluntarily. They turn around and go back to Mexico. A few hours later, they try again. In El Paso, we deported one fellow six times in one day. There's a restaurant in Hollywood run by a fellow we deported thirty-seven times. We've deported some people more than a hundred times. They always want to come back. There's a job and there's desperation.

In World War Two, we recruited Mexicans to work here. As soon as the war ended and our young men came back, we deported them. In 1954, the de-

portation problem was so big that the general in charge of immigration ordered Operation Wetback. That one year, we had a million apprehensions. It was similar to what we did during the depression. We rounded everybody up, put 'em on buses, and sent them back to Mexico. Sometimes they were people who merely looked Mexican. The violations of civil liberties were terrible.

Half the people here without papers are not Mexicans. They're from all over the world. They came legally, with papers, as tourists ten years ago. They're much harder to deal with. We're discussing a program that would allow people to have permanent residence, who have been here seven years or more, have not broken any laws, have paid taxes and not been on welfare. You can't be here and become a public charge. All too often, the public gets the impression that all immigrants are on welfare. It's the exact opposite. Very few go on welfare.

A lot of people who are humanitarian, who believe they should be hospitable toward the stranger, are very restrictive when it comes to their jobs. (Laughs.) We've had protests from mariachis and soccer players. The mariachis are upset because the Mexicans were coming in and playing for less. The manager of soccer teams would rather hire the foreign nationals because often they're better players.

We get people coming in from Haiti, the poorest country in the western hemisphere. They come over by boat and land in Florida. The Floridians raised hell about this. I've even had Cuban-Americans tell me that Haitians were going to destroy their culture. There's a weird pecking order now.

We make three thousand apprehensions at the border every weekend. It's just a little fourteen-mile stretch. Our border patrol knows this little fellow comin' across is hungry. He just wants to work. They know he's no security threat. They say: "It's my job." Many of them come to have a great deal of respect for the people they're deporting. What do you think of a person you deport three, four times, who just keeps coming back? You would never want to get in the same ring with that person.

I'm torn. I saw it in the Peace Corps, when I was in the Philippines. A mother offered you her infant. You're just a twenty-one-year-old kid and she says: "Take my child, take him with you to the States." When you see this multiplied by thousands, it tears you up.

It's clear to me that the undocumented, even more than the immigrant, is a contributor to our society and to our standard of living. It's one of the few groups that has no parasites. They walk the tightrope and try not to fall off. If you're a citizen and you fall, we have a net that catches you: welfare, food stamps, unemployment, social services. If you're undocumented and fall off that tightrope, you can't go to any of the agencies because you may end up bein' deported. He can't draw welfare, he can't use public services. He's not gonna call a policeman even when he's beat up. If he's in a street fight and somebody whips him bad, assaults him, robs him, rapes her, there's no complaint. In Baltimore, an employer raped two girls. The person who complained wouldn't give us the names of the victims because she was afraid we'd deport 'em. We end up in this country with enormous abuse against four million people.

The only thing that helps me is remembering the history of this country.

We've always managed, despite our worst, unbelievably nativist actions to re-juvenate ourselves, to bring in new people. Every new group comes in believing more firmly in the American Dream than the one that came a few years before. Every new group is scared of being in the welfare line or in the unemployment office. They go to night school, they learn about America. We'd be lost without them.

The old dream is still dreamt. The old neighborhood Ma-Pa stores are still around. They are not Italian or Jewish or Eastern European any more. Ma and Pa are now Korean, Vietnamese, Iraqi, Jordanian, Latin American. They live in the store. They work seven days a week. Their kids are doing well in school. They're making it. Sound familiar?

Near our office in Los Angeles is a little café with a sign: KOSHER BURRITOS. (Laughs.) A burrito is a Mexican tortilla with meat inside. Most of the custom-ers are black. The owner is Korean. (Laughs.) The banker, I imagine, is WASP. (Laughs.) This is what's happening in the United States today. It is not a melting pot, but in one way or another, there is a melding of cultures.

I see all kinds of new immigrants starting out all over again, trying to work their way into the system. They're going through new battles, yet they're old battles. They want to share in the American Dream. The stream never ends.

Questions 6.2

1. We learned in Chapter 5 that poverty is functional. Discuss the proposition that illegal immigrants are functional—our society allows illegal immigration to continue because of the positive functions that are provided.

2. From Castillo's viewpoint, who is the victim, the immigrant or United States? Why? What do you think?

Reading 6.3

THE COCKTAIL WAITRESS

JAMES SPRADLEY AND BRENDA MANN

A part of sex-role socialization is that women and men learn a division of labor. There are certain things that men do and certain things that women do. We would like to believe that there are functional reasons for such a division of labor, but perhaps it's more likely that the separation of roles is another, often unconscious, way of "keeping people in their place."

In this excerpt from their book, *The Cocktail Waitress: Women's Work in a Man's World*, anthropologists Spradley and Mann describe a situation in which the division between women's work and men's work is very clearly established. Their research was done in a college bar located in a large midwestern city in which Mann worked as a cocktail waitress.

...*Even in the smallest society it is impossible for everyone to work at all the things that need to be done. For this reason every culture contains rules for allocating jobs, every society has a division of labor. In a Bushmen band in South Africa, for example, men track down wild animals to provide meat for the people while women dig roots and gather berries to add to the common food supply. Among the Kurelu of New Guinea, men protect the borders of the tribal territories from attack and participate in offensive warfare. The women, on the other hand, have their assigned tasks such as gathering salt by soaking banana leaves in a salt spring, drying the leaves, and then burning them to retrieve the salt. In some societies, young girls are assigned the task of caring for small children, boys take the herds of goats or cattle for pasture and water, old men stay home to protect women and children, and young men do the heavy work of house-building. Every culture, then, has a division of labor, and we were not surprised to find this a feature of bar culture. Indeed, if the fifteen or twenty people who work at Brady's Bar all came to work on the same night and tried to carry out the same activities at the same time, chaos would reign. If all the employees took orders from customers, if all crowded together behind the bar at the same time to mix drinks, and if, each evening, everyone tried to do everything, the confusion and disorder would eventually destroy the bar. Like a small tribal band, the people who work at Brady's share a set of rules for allocating jobs and dividing up necessary tasks.*

The men who work in the bar mix drinks, serve the customers seated around the long horseshoe bar, control the money, and manage business transactions with the outside world. The women, on the other hand, focus their activities on serving the customers who sit at tables.

One of our first goals was to discover the nature and meaning of these female role assignments. Our primary question was, "What does a person have to know in order to do what a cocktail waitress does?" The answer initially appeared rather simple—she has to find out what customers want to drink, tell the bartender, carry drinks back to the table, collect the payments, and later clear away empty glasses.

· · ·

It is 12:40 A.M. and Sandy knows that in twenty minutes the bar will close. She would like to tell the six guys at the corner table that the time has come to order their last drinks for the evening because it is near closing. Last call generally occurs around 12:45 and if she doesn't give last call soon, it will be impossible to get them to leave before 1:30 A.M., since they will take that long to finish their drinks. But the appointed time comes and goes. Although it would be a simple matter for her to tell the table, "Last call, would you like anything else to drink?" and in fact, she wanted to announce it fifteen minutes ago, she cannot take this simple step on her own initiative. At 12:55, Jim, the bartender working the lower section of the bar tells her "Give last call." Finally, she can make this announcement to the customers seated in her section. Because he delayed his permission, however, it will be closing time when Sandy delivers the last round of beers to the six guys from St. John's, and much later before she can retrieve the empty bottles. The cultural rules at Brady's Bar require that a male must tell the waitress when it is time for last call, and they require that a female must serve the last round to the tables. Over and over again we discovered such arbitrary rules interlocking male and female performances.

· · ·

"Could I please have a vodka tonic, Ted?" Denise asked, giving him her sweetest smile. She knew what the answer would be but it never hurt to try. Sometimes you can catch the bartender in a benevolent mood.

"Look, you know you can't have a drink. You start work in a little while and you might fall on that pretty face of yours. Do you want a Coke?"

"Okay. But how about some quarters for the juke box?" Ted handed her four quarters, she picked out her favorites and then went back to eating her sandwich and sipping her Coke. She sat there, listening to her music, and watching Ted clean up the bar—restocking the beer, and washing the dozens of dirty glasses that had accumulated during the lunch hour rush.

Two employees sitting at the bar, hanging around before work; one has the right to drink anything, the other does not. The reason for this restriction? Being a female. This particular rule may be unique to Brady's Bar, but we found this simple pattern of interaction repeated itself again and again in other situations. These specific cases merely reflect an important rule in our culture that governs much of male-female interaction, what we call <u>the handicap rule.</u> At every turn, we discovered evidence that the cultural rules at Brady's Bar place certain handicaps on all those players who were born female.

Let's go back to the social encounters between male and female workers at Brady's Bar. Here, the arbitrary handicap rules imposed on females are often hidden or at least justified as instinctual, God-given traits: "Women can't hold their liquor," "Women are too emotional." As in the wider culture, females are repeatedly required to play with an arbitrarily imposed handicap. It is as if all the players in the game made a tacit agreement that women must play by different rules than men. Even a suggestion to make these rules the same arouses male anger, and all the waitresses soon find this out as the following example makes clear. One night Denise was hanging around before work, and Ted asked her to watch the bar for a few minutes. Dave, one of the bartenders for the evening, came in and sat down. "Hey, bartender!" he called to Denise as he playfully banged his fist down on the bar. "I'll have a bourbon sour." Feeling especially powerful behind the bar, Denise replied, "Oh, I'm sorry, Dave, but you're working tonight. No drink for you. How about a nice big Coke?" The tone of her voice indicated to Dave that she was teasing, and Dave's response was also outwardly light: "Be a good bartender now and give me my drink!" And, of course, she complied. But Denise could tell she had said the wrong thing. She had unmasked the handicap rule by her actions, momentarily exposing its arbitrariness. Later that night, after the bar closed and all the employees gathered at the bar for a drink, Dave served the others, ignoring Denise's request for a gin and tonic. Denise was then forced into the position of having to beg Dave before he would serve her a drink—a kind of ritual reminder that she is not to question the implicit handicap rule.

· · ·

"Hey, Mike. Stubbs. How are you?" Mark stood up and playfully punched Mike on the shoulder and he returned the greeting. Both of the guys nodded and smiled at Denise. Mark turned to Denise and said, "Hey, Denise. Be a good girl and get behind the bar for me." The way he said it, she felt he was both giving her permission and giving her an order, but this was an opportunity that no waitress passed up. She crawled under the gate that closes at the end of the bar and turned to Mike and Stubbs for their order. "Schlitz for both of them," said Mark. Denise opened one cooler after another until she found the one containing the Schlitz, found the opener attached to the side of the cooler, opened them and placed them on the bar in front of Mike and Stubbs. She looked around for the beer glasses, and by the time she had placed a napkin with a glass on it in front of each of them, they were halfway finished with their bottles. The minutes dragged slowly by as the men talked, but Denise busied herself exploring behind the bar; opening coolers to find out where the different kinds of beer were, checking the ice supply, examining the different bottles of liquor. Another customer came and looked surprised to see her there but ordered a bourbon sour as if nothing was out of order.

"Bartender. Oh, bartender. Can I have another beer?" That was Stubbs, calling attention to this reversal of roles. Mike joined in, "Me too. Isn't that a funny looking bartender? Mark sure has changed. That's a nice dress you have on, Markie." Denise smiles and concentrates on opening two more beers. She places them in front of the two guys, "Here you are." She took one of the dollar bills from the counter and rang it up on the cash register. Same old jokes every time a girl gets behind the bar. She had seen it happen to others and knew what to expect. She always felt somewhat uncomfortable back there but it was fun, the opportunity to mix drinks. Like the other girls, she watches the bartenders make drinks all night, every night, and so she knows almost as well as they do how to make a vodka gimlet, a Tequila Sunrise, an Old Fashioned, or anything else. While it never lasted very long, it was fun to work behind the bar, a special treat. All of the girls respond eagerly when Mark or one of the other bartenders sets aside the rules governing female behavior that normally keep them out of that area.

What we have witnessed here is a kind of role change, what we call the <u>cross-over phenomenon.</u> Situations in which men and women temporarily reverse their roles are not uncommon in our society. Whenever male and female activities are linked together, opportunities for individuals to cross over present themselves. Mr. Jones, for example, normally drives when his wife is in the car, but he lets her drive this morning so he can read some papers for an early meeting at the office. On other mornings he pulls up to his office building, and she slides over to take his place behind the wheel and drive home. Mrs. Jones normally bathes their two children after dinner each night, but on Tuesdays her husband takes over and performs this task so she can attend the University. The cross-over phenomenon probably occurs in all cultures of the world. The cultural rules for crossing over and doing tasks assigned to the opposite sex could easily be <u>symmetrical.</u> That is, on occasion men do women's work and vice versa. In the process there is an open appreciation for this exchange of responsibilities that are usually divided. But the rules that regulate the cross-over phenomenon in Brady's Bar are not the same for each sex. They are asymmetrical, functioning in such a way as to put women at a disadvantage in the game of social interaction.

Although Denise and Sandy and the other waitresses get behind the bar occasionally, and they are always eager to do so, bartenders never cross over to perform some of the female tasks in the bar. If Rob and Denise were sitting at the bar and a group of customers came in and sat at a table, Denise could never turn and say, "Rob, will you take care of those customers for me?" Even if she were busy taking his place behind the bar and customers entered, no bartender would voluntarily get up to wait on the tables for the cocktail waitress. Denise would simply come from behind the bar, wait on the table, go back behind the bar and fix the drinks herself, and then serve them. This is expected of her. Furthermore, none of the waitresses would think of asking the men to clean the tables or to wait on their customers. They have learned the rules well. Both men and women seem to act as if the tasks assigned to women at Brady's might have a polluting affect on men, contaminating their ritual purity. The reverse is not true. A man loses if he does women's work and participates in the cross-over phenomenon, and so he avoids it or refuses to switch. A woman gains and is usually eager to cross over.

An interesting dimension of this cross-over phenomenon relates to the way it requires the female to express gratitude. When a man crosses over to assist a woman, she should thank him, expressing gratitude to him for his assistance. If one of the male employees ever stepped in to assist a busy waitress, it would be seen as an act of chivalry and the girl in question would openly express her gratitude. But when a woman crosses over to assist a man, engaging in some typical male activity, such as tending bar, she must still express gratitude for he has allowed her to partake of a more valuable social world. It is doubtful that a husband would thank his wife for driving the car when they are traveling to-gether. After all, in our cultural idiom he has "let her drive." His wife, on the other hand, would express gratefulness if he cooked dinner or did the dishes for her. When a waitress at Brady's is allowed to tend bar she feels that a priv-ilege has been extended to her. Not only does she operate with a handicap but she almost always sees these particular rules as legitimate.

Denise has just waited on a table and after she serves them she stops to chat with a regular customer who is sitting next to the table. While she's talk-ing, Dave calls her from across the bar so she quickly excuses herself and goes to see what he wants. "I need some stuff from the cooler. Get me some Heineken lights and a bottle of juice. Okay? That's a sweet girl." He turns back to his discussion with a friend sitting across the bar while Denise heads back through the kitchen to the cooler. "Why can't Dave get this stuff himself anyway?" she grumbles to herself. "He's always sending us back to carry this stuff. It should be his job, not the waitresses'." Denise thought about the time she had brought this up one night after work and had gotten nowhere. "Bartenders are never idle," she was told, "When they aren't mixing drinks and serving the bar, they are P.R.'ing and that is good for the bar." "So," thought Denise, "They call standing around talking to friends, P.R.'ng, but if we do it, they call it loafing." Although she may be able to visit a little later in the evening, even then, because of this handicap rule, she will have to do it so as to avoid the accusation that she is merely wasting time, loafing around.

...Waitresses feel that the division of labor is far from equal. George performs the major task of mixing drinks and ringing up the total for the order on the cash register. And Stephanie must do all she can to make this easy for George: translating the customer's order into language the bartender can immediately recognize; adding straws and fruit to the drinks; stirring the drinks as the mix is added to the alcohol; totaling the order for him; handing him the correct amount of money for the order; and finally, placing the drinks on the tray. While it would be possible for George to help Stephanie by performing some of these tasks himself, he does not. New girls often wait for the bartender to do things like place drinks on the tray or add up the prices, but they rapidly learn that it is their duty to make things as easy as they can for the bartender. "When I first started," says Joyce, "I gave the bartender the order and just stood there." But Joyce soon noticed the other girls helping by adding the nuts and straws to the drinks. A couple of times, Dave asked Joyce to do those things for him, and it wasn't long before Joyce just started doing all those things automatically.

The division of labor between bartenders and waitresses is clearly based on sex. Work is divided up in an arbitrary manner, men sometimes doing in their part of the bar what women are doing in theirs. But although arbitrary, this division is not casual nor easily changed. A female bartender or a male waiter are innovations which would be strongly opposed. The handicap rule helps keep women in their place and reinforces the centrality of males in social life. As we saw, even the suspension of the handicap rule in one or another situation, as when a benevolent bartender occasionally offers a waitress a drink before work, is a male prerogative, one that elicits expressions of appreciation from females. Again, in the cross-over phenomenon, we saw the subtle ways inequality can express itself—women seeking to do men's tasks and men avoiding female tasks, even though some of the activities are seemingly identical. The division of labor at Brady's Bar, and in society generally, has a much deeper significance than efficient service to paying customers. Routine tasks are transformed into symbols of sexual identity. The "job" becomes a "ritual" to publicly announce the significant differences our culture attaches to sexual gender. It says to everyone in the bar: "There is a woman, there is a man."

Questions 6.3

1. Using this selection, illustrate examples of discrimination based on sex. A double standard exists—show how.
2. What is the "handicap rule"? Give examples of this in other aspects of life.
3. What is the "cross-over phenomenon"? Give examples of this in other aspects of life.
4. This study involved participant observation (see Chapter 1). Illustrate potential strengths and weaknesses of this approach using this selection as example.

Reading 6.4

WOUNDED KNEE

DEE BROWN

In his book, *Bury My Heart at Wounded Knee*, Dee Brown writes about the critical period between 1860 and 1890, the thirty years during which the culture and civilization of the American Indian was destroyed. Brown tells the story in an unusual way— he uses the viewpoint and the words of the victims, the Indians. The story is a haunting and depressing one and includes descriptions of the long walk of the Navahos, the war to save the buffalo, the war for the Black Hills, the flight of the Nez Perces, and Geronimo, the last of the Apache chiefs. The following excerpt from Brown's book describes the end of it, the "battle" at Wounded Knee Creek in South Dakota in late December of 1890. The Indians' lands were gone then, their chiefs were dead or imprisoned, their own numbers decimated by thirty years of battles, by disease, by living on crowded reservations in unfamiliar places, and by heartbreak. In early December 1890 the great chief Sitting Bull was assassinated. Then . . .

As soon as Big Foot learned that Sitting Bull had been killed, he started his people toward Pine Ridge, hoping that Red Cloud could protect them from the soldiers. En route, he fell ill of pneumonia, and when hemorrhaging began, he had to travel in a wagon. On December 28, as they neared Porcupine Creek, the Minneconjous sighted four troops of cavalry approaching. Big Foot immediately ordered a white flag run up over his wagon. About two o'clock in the afternoon he raised up from his blankets to greet Major Samuel Whitside, Seventh U.S. Cavalry. Big Foot's blankets were stained with blood from his lungs, and as he talked in a hoarse whisper with Whitside, red drops fell from his nose and froze in the bitter cold.

Whitside told Big Foot that he had orders to take him to a cavalry camp on Wounded Knee Creek. The Minneconjou chief replied that he was going in that direction; he was taking his people to Pine Ridge for safety.

Turning to his half-breed scout, John Shangreau, Major Whitside ordered him to begin disarming Big Foot's band.

"Look here, Major," Shangreau replied, "if you do that there is liable to be a fight here; and if there is, you will kill all those women and children and the men will get away from you."

Whitside insisted that his orders were to capture Big Foot's Indians and disarm and dismount them.

"We better take them to camp and then take their horses from them and their guns," Shangreau declared.

"All right," Whitside agreed. "You tell Big Foot to move down to camp at Wounded Knee."

The major glanced at the ailing chief, then gave an order for his Army ambulance to be brought forward. The ambulance would be warmer and would give Big Foot an easier ride than the jolting springless wagon. After the chief was transferred to the ambulance, Whitside formed a column for the march to Wounded Knee Creek. Two troops of cavalry took the lead, the ambulance and wagons following, the Indians herded into a compact group behind them, with the other two cavalry troops and a battery of two Hotchkiss guns bringing up the rear.

Twilight was falling when the column crawled over the last rise in the land and began descending the slope toward Chankpe Opi Wakpala, the creek called Wounded Knee. The wintry dusk and the tiny crystals of ice dancing in the dying light added a supernatural quality to the somber landscape. Somewhere along this frozen stream the heart of Crazy Horse lay in a secret place, and the Ghost Dancers believed that his disembodied spirit was waiting impatiently for the new earth that would surely come with the first green grass of spring.

At the cavalry tent camp on Wounded Knee Creek, the Indians were halted and children counted. There were 120 men and 230 women and children. Because of the gathering darkness, Major Whitside decided to wait until morning before disarming his prisoners. He assigned them a camping area immediately to the south of the military camp, issued them rations, and as there was a shortage of tepee covers, he furnished them several tents. Whitside ordered a stove placed in Big Foot's tent and sent a regimental surgeon to administer to the sick chief. To make certain that none of his prisoners escaped, the major stationed two troops of cavalry as sentinels around the Sioux tepees, and then posted his two Hotchkiss guns on top of a rise overlooking the camp. The barrels of these rifled guns, which could hurl explosive charges for more than two miles, were positioned to rake the length of the Indian lodges.

Later in the darkness of that December night the remainder of the Seventh Regiment marched in from the east and quietly bivouacked north of Major Whitside's troops. Colonel James W. Forsyth, commanding Custer's former regiment, now took charge of operations. He informed Whitside that he had received orders to take Big Foot's band to the Union Pacific Railroad for shipment to a military prison in Omaha.

After placing two more Hotchkiss guns on the slope beside the others, Forsyth and his officers settled down for the evening with a keg of whiskey to celebrate the capture of Big Foot.

The chief lay in his tent, too ill to sleep, barely able to breathe. Even with their protective Ghost Shirts and their belief in the prophecies of the new Messiah, his people were fearful of the pony soldiers camped all around them. Fourteen years before, on the Little Bighorn, some of these warriors had helped defeat some of these soldier chiefs—Moylan, Varnum, Wallace, Godfrey, Edgerly—and the Indians wondered if revenge could still be in their hearts.

"The following morning there was a bugle call," said Wasumaza, one of Big Foot's warriors who years afterward was to change his name to Dewey Beard. "Then I saw the soldiers mounting their horses and surrounding us. It was announced that all men should come to the center for a talk and that after the talk they were to move on to Pine Ridge agency. Big Foot was brought out of his tepee and sat in front of his tent and the older men were gathered around him and sitting right near him in the center."

After issuing hardtack for breakfast rations, Colonel Forsyth informed the Indians that they were now to be disarmed. "They called for guns and arms," White Lance said, "so all of us gave the guns and they were stacked up in the center." The soldier chiefs were not satisfied with the number of weapons surrendered, and so they sent details of troopers to search the tepees. 'They would go right into the tents and come out with bundles and tear them open," Dog Chief said. "They brought our axes, knives, and tent stakes and piled them near the guns."

Still not satisfied, the soldier chiefs ordered the warriors to remove their blankets and submit to searches for weapons. The Indians' faces showed their anger, but only the medicine man, Yellow Bird, made any overt protest. He danced a few Ghost Dance steps, and chanted one of the holy songs, assuring the warriors that the soldiers' bullets could not penetrate their sacred garments. "The bullets will not go toward you," he chanted in Sioux. "The prairie is large and the bullets will not go toward you."

The troopers found only two rifles, one of them a new Winchester belonging to a young Minneconjou named Black Coyote. Black Coyote raised the Winchester above his head, shouting that he paid much money for the rifle and that it belonged to him. Some years afterward Dewey Beard recalled that Black Coyote was deaf. "If they had left him alone he was going to put his gun down where he should. They grabbed him and spinned him in the east direction. He was still unconcerned even then. He hadn't his gun pointed at anyone. His intention was to put that gun down. They came on and grabbed the gun that he was going to put down. Right after they spun him around there was the report of a gun, was quite loud. I couldn't say that anyone was shot, but following that was a crash."

"It sounded much like the sound of tearing canvas, that was the crash," Rough Feather said. Afraid-of-the-Enemy described it as a "lightning crash."

Turning Hawk said that Black Coyote "was a crazy man, a young man of very bad influence and in fact a nobody." He said that Black Coyote fired his gun and that "immediately the soldiers returned fire and indiscriminate killing followed."

In the first seconds of violence, the firing of carbines was deafening, filling the air with powder smoke. Among the dying who lay sprawled on the frozen ground was Big Foot. Then there was a brief lull in the rattle of arms, with small groups of Indians and soldiers grappling at close quarters, using knives, clubs, pistols. As few of the Indians had arms, they soon had to flee, and then the big Hotchkiss guns on the hill opened upon them, firing almost a shell a second, raking the Indian camp, shredding the tepees with flying shrapnel, killing men, women, and children.

"We tried to run," Louise Weasel Bear said, "but they shot us like we were buffalo. I know there are some good white people, but the soldiers must be mean to shoot children and women. Indian soldiers would not do that to white children."

"I was running away from the place and followed those who were running away," said Hakiktawin, another of the young women. "My grandfather and grandmother and brother were killed as we crossed the ravine, and then I

was shot on the right hip clear through and on my right wrist where I did not go any further as I was not able to walk, and after the soldier picked me up where a little girl came to me and crawled into the blanket."

When the madness ended, Big Foot and more than half of his people were dead or seriously wounded; 153 were known dead, but many of the wounded crawled away to die afterward. One estimate placed the final total of dead at very nearly three hundred of the original 350 men, women, and children. The soldiers lost twenty-five dead and thirty-nine wounded, most of them struck by their own bullets or shrapnel.

After the wounded cavalrymen were started for the agency at Pine Ridge, a detail of soldiers went over the Wounded Knee battlefield, gathering up Indians who were still alive and loading them into wagons. As it was apparent by the end of the day that a blizzard was approaching, the dead Indians were left lying where they had fallen. (After the blizzard, when a burial party returned to Wounded Knee, they found the bodies, including Big Foot's, frozen into grotesque shapes.)

The wagonloads of wounded Sioux (four men and forty-seven women and children) reached Pine Ridge after dark. Because all available barracks were filled with soldiers, they were left lying in the open wagons in the bitter cold while an inept Army officer searched for shelter. Finally the Episcopal mission was opened, the benches taken out, and hay scattered over the rough flooring.

It was the fourth day after Christmas in the Year of Our Lord 1890. When the first torn and bleeding bodies were carried into the candlelit church, those who were conscious could see Christmas greenery hanging from the open rafters. Across the chancel front above the pulpit was strung a crudely lettered banner: PEACE ON EARTH, GOOD WILL TO MEN.

Questions 6.4

1. Describe the treatment of the Indians in terms of the patterns of interaction described in the text. What is the pattern today?

2. Discuss the concept of Manifest Destiny: What might have caused it to appear? Were there other victims in addition to the Indians? What are the consequences of this doctrine for its adherents as well as its victims? Is this doctrine still with us?

3. Research the Indian situation in your area—what tribe lived there and what happened to them?

7

Institutions: Family

So far we have peered through several windows in order to discover the social organization of society. One view of social organization is through study of the nature and structure of groups. Analysis of the characteristics of categories and social differentiation provides another view. In this chapter, the study of social institutions will provide us with a third perspective.

One way of understanding social institutions as a concept is to describe the emergence of an institution. All societies have certain constant and important central needs or problems that must be dealt with. A society, if it wants to survive, must deal with such issues as reproduction of the species, socialization of the young, distribution of goods and services, care for the sick, and so on. Norms and roles emerge to organize and regulate behavior as society deems appropriate. And so, a system of social relationships, a pattern of organization develops. **Social institutions**, then, refer to this organized system of social relationships, common to all societies, which emerges to deal with certain basic problems.[1]

For example: Society's basic task of reproducing the species leads to the development of particular patterns of behavior. A society supports some of

---

[1]This benefits from the discussion of social institutions by S. N. Eisenstadt in the *International Encyclopedia of the Social Sciences* (New York: Crowell, Collier, and Macmillan, 1968), 14: 409–429.

these behaviors (say, heterosexual contact) and discourages others (indiscriminate mating outside of marriage). This reflects the development of norms: consistent views about the way things should and should not be done. The development of these norms and roles whereby the experimental becomes expected, the spontaneous becomes formalized, is the process of *institutionalization*. As this proceeds and the system of social relationships becomes more and more organized, an institutional area emerges—in this case the institution of the *family*.

The study of social organization makes a good deal more sense if we integrate several of the concepts we have studied. For example, merge the concepts of social institutions and groups as in Table 7.1. Certain basic problems lead to the development of corresponding institutional areas. Next, groups perform the functions that are important to the institutional area. Two important factors—

TABLE 7.1   Institutions in the United States

Basic Problem or Issue Faced by Society	Institutional Area	Institutional Organization or Large Organizations	Institutional Units or Small Groups
Reproduction of the species	Family	Planned Parenthood; an organization of marriage counselors	My family
Socialization and training of the young	Education	University of California; Boston school system	A kindergarten class; a graduate seminar
Explanation for the unknown or uncertain	Religion	Catholic church; the Council of Churches	Wednesday evening Bible study group; a Sunday school group
Distribution of goods and services	Economics	General Motors; IBM	Several assembly line workers installing brakes on Fords; the steno pool handling the Phillips account
Development of rules and regulations to govern people's behavior	Government	U.S. Senate; State Assembly	Township subcommittee on dogcatching
Use of free time; time away from work	Leisure	Professional Golfers Assoc.; NCAA; Sacramento Recreation Association	A professional basketball team; a bowling team
Care and treatment of the sick	Health care	Massachusetts General Hospital; Kaiser Health Plan	Doctors and nurses on a cardiac ward; technicians in a medical lab
Collection and organization of empirical knowledge	Science	National Science Foundation; Salk Institute	Several astronomers studying the universe; a group of biologists experimenting with virus strains

the individual's interests and the institutional norms—come together in groups. These groups are of various sizes and complexities—from large, formal organizations to small, personal, primary groups.

Let's follow an example across Table 7.1. People in most societies are concerned with life after death and seek an explanation for what is unknown or uncertain. Great power or faith may be invested in an idol, a god, a person, or an idea. At first experimentally and spontaneously, then more consistently, and finally in a formalized fashion, norms and roles emerge defining behaviors and beliefs felt to be appropriate in that society. This could be called the institutional area of religion. In America the institution of religion is organized around norms favoring Christianity. Groups perform the functions essential to the institutional area. Large organizations such as the Catholic, Presbyterian, and Baptist churches of America, and small groups such as the Wednesday evening Bible studies or Sunday school groups make up the *locus* in which individual interests and institutional norms intersect. It is in these groups that the institutional norms are played out. This same pattern is repeated in other institutional areas, as can be seen in the table.

In some institutional areas—particularly the family—smaller groups are all-important and assume the major, almost exclusive, role. In other institutional areas, especially economic and governmental, larger groups play a major role. The important fact, however, is that we can combine group and institution to understand social organization.

As you look at Table 7.1, it becomes apparent that institutional areas are not necessarily separate and isolated from each other. In fact, there is a good deal of overlap between them. Socialization of the young takes place in the family, and in educational and religious institutions as well. Groups from many institutional areas (science, health care, religion, education, leisure, government) fill economic functions—scientists, doctors, priests, teachers, professional basketball players, and lawyers are earning a living. So these institutional areas are overlapping circles, each intersecting with others in sometimes complicated ways.

Since the institutional areas are interrelated, we should expect that change in one institutional area will be related to change in another. Child labor laws, reform movements, and the organization of labor have led to shorter work days and work weeks and much greater free time, which in turn have given us the institutional area of leisure. Increased employment of women (economic) has had effects on the family. The increase of women's rights in general is having a tremendous impact as women are treated as equals in all institutional areas. An economic decline in the 1970s and early 1980s had consequences for higher education—college students became more concerned about getting jobs and moved to business administration and other so-called job-related majors and away from the liberal arts and social sciences. Politicians running for office must contend with the effect of economic factors on voting behavior. When Russia launched its first Sputnik in 1957, many people in the United States became concerned that we had "fallen behind." One response was a renewed emphasis on science in schools: change in one area (education) in order to bring change in another (science). So it is clear that, although we have introduced the institutional areas as separate entities, they are closely related and intersect at many points. As we said earlier, the social organization of society is best seen as a social fabric—a network of norms, roles, and values through which people interact individually and in groups, and this point is evident again as we examine social institutions.

Although the same institutional areas are found in many societies, they may not *look* the same in every society. The mountain-dwelling Arapesh of New Guinea and the campus-dwelling college students of America both operate within the institutional area of the family, for example, which involves elaborate procedures for courtship, marriage, and raising of children, and yet the specific practices of the two societies are vastly different. Not only will the content be different, but the same institutional area in different societies may, at least to an extent, focus on different cultural concerns and serve different functions.

Institutions change, as do all aspects of human behavior. Change in institutions probably occurs more slowly than does the change in behavior and values of smaller elements like groups and individuals. Institutional change also varies from one society to another. To make a comparison of extremes, modern industrialized countries, for the most part, change more rapidly than primitive preliterate societies. Even within one society, one institutional area may change slowly, another rapidly. We will discuss this topic of social change in more detail in Chapter 11.

In summary, social organization can be examined at several levels. We can understand people's behavior by focusing on the dynamics and characteristics of group behavior and on the particular types of groups people belong to. We can also understand behavior by focusing on the attitudes, values, norms, procedures, and symbols that are part of certain institutional areas. Finally, the analysis is improved further by combining concepts and observing that groups operate in the context of the norms, roles, and values of an institutional area. To get a better idea of how the concept of institution is applied to specific areas of human behavior, the remainder of this chapter and the next two chapters will examine several institutional areas in more detail.

FAMILY

Sociologists have always looked with great interest on the institution of the family, mainly because we tend to see the family as the most basic of all institutions, and perhaps also because there are such tremendous variations in family practices from one culture to another. These variations never cease to fascinate, and ethnocentrism plays a part in this fascination. Many people are convinced that their own way is the right and best way, and they are amazed to find other people behaving differently. This ethnocentrism is unfortunate. Perhaps these issues can be placed in better perspective if we examine cross-culturally some similarities and differences in family structure.

Structural Variabilities: How Do Family Structures Differ?

Anthropologists, who study primitive societies all over the world, find that the structure of the family is almost infinitely variable. Imagine almost anything, and there is probably a society someplace that practices it (of course, the people there would be aghast if they knew the strange things *we* were doing).

It usually begins with some form of mating ritual—a first date, or a woman may inherit a husband, or a man may buy a spouse or two, or fall in love. Or capture a mate. On the east coast of Greenland, the man goes to the woman's tent, grabs her by the hair, and drags her off to his tent.

In some cultures, parents are responsible for arranging marriages for their children. Chinese Empire law from around 1700 stated that a family elder who failed to find a husband for any young woman belonging to his household was condemning her to an unfulfilled life, and was liable to receive publicly eighty blows with the bamboo.[2] In India if a young woman's parents had been unable to find a husband for her as late as three years after she had reached puberty, then she could arrange a marriage for herself, but in doing this she would bring great disgrace on her family. Normally the marriage partner was chosen by the parents together. In China, however, it was typical for the final decision on a prospective husband to be made by the young woman's father, and for the mother to select her son's future wife. Correct order had to be observed in marrying off children—eldest children must be found mates first. This led to problems if the eldest child was unattractive or if younger children were especially attractive and precocious. This in turn forced desperate parents to trickery, switching one daughter for another at the last minute. Recall from the Bible that Jacob thought that he had married Rachel but found out the next morning that the bride that he had spent the night with was her elder sister Leah.

Beyond these prescribed, ritualistic mate selection practices, there is also "love" as the basis for choosing a partner. This works in different ways: *Exchange theory* proposes the idea of a marketplace in mate selection. A mate seeker wants to maximize his chances for a happy marriage and looks for a good deal, a bargain if possible, in which his own assets and liabilities are compared with those of the potential partner. He continues the relationship on the assumption that he will get more out of it than it will cost. Anyone different from and especially below his own level of exchange is likely to be out of luck. *Complementary needs* theory suggests that people select partners who make up for, balance, or supply needs that they themselves don't have. Thus the talker looks for a listener, the eater for a cook, or the Mercedes-Benz fancier for a millionaire.

Role and *value* theories of mate selection suggest that people who share common values and common definitions about roles are more likely to select each other. If she is a big-city sports-minded Episcopalian and he is a small-

---

[2]The discussion in this paragraph is taken in part from David and Vera Mace, *Marriage: East and West* (Garden City, N.Y.: Doubleday, 1960), pp. 141–142.

COURTSHIP AMONG THE DOBU

Marriage is set in motion by a hostile act of the mother-in-law. She blocks with her own person the door of her house within which the youth is sleeping with her daughter, and he is trapped for the public ceremony of betrothal. Before this, since the time of puberty, the boy has slept each night in the houses of unmarried girls. By custom his own house is closed to him. He avoids entanglements for several years by spreading his favours widely and leaving the house well before daylight. When he is trapped at last, it is usually because he has tired of his roaming and has settled upon a more constant companion. He ceases to be so careful about early rising. Nevertheless he is never thought of as being ready to undertake the indignities of marriage, and the event is forced upon him by the old witch in the doorway, his future mother-in-law. When the villagers, the maternal kin of the girl, see the old woman immobile in her doorway, they gather, and under the stare of the public the two descend and sit on a mat upon the ground. The villagers stare at them for half an hour and gradually disperse, nothing more; the couple are formally betrothed.

From this time forward the young man has to reckon with the village of his wife. Its first demand is upon his labour. Immediately his mother-in-law gives him a digging-stick with the command, "Now work." He must make a garden under the surveillance of his parents-in-law. When they cook and eat, he must continue work, since he cannot eat in their presence. He is bound to a double task, for when he has finished work on his father-in-law's yams he has still to cultivate his own garden on his own family land. His father-in-law gets ample satisfaction of his will to power and hugely enjoys his power over his son-in-law. For a year or more the situation continues. The boy is not the only one who is caught in this affair, for his relatives also are loaded with obligations. So heavy are the burdens upon his brothers in providing the necessary garden stuff and the valuables for the marriage gift that nowadays young men at their brother's betrothal escape from the imposition by signing up with the white recruiter for indentured labour.

From *Patterns of Culture* by Ruth Benedict, copyright renewed 1962 by Ruth Valentine, pp. 133–135. Reprinted by permission of the publisher, Houghton Mifflin Company.

town sedentary Baptist (different values) or if she wants to stay home and cook and he pushes her to study medicine (differing role expectations), they will probably look elsewhere. *Process* theory suggests that mate selection involves a number of social and psychological processes. The field of potential mates is progressively narrowed down by physical attraction, religious and racial differences, role and value similarities, psychological influences, and so on. Murstein (an exchange theorist) believes that most of us may settle for a partner rather than choose one—only people with many assets and few liabilities actually choose each other, the rest of us just settle.[3] How depressing. . .

At any rate, whom you date, buy, inherit, are forced to accept, capture, or settle for is related, in part, to whether your society practices endogamy (marriage within a certain group) or exogamy (marriage outside that certain group). In the United States, as in most societies, both are practiced. We forbid marriage within the immediate family, and it is necessary to marry an outsider:

---

[3]These two paragraphs on courtship theory benefit from the discussion by Marcia and Thomas Lasswell in *Marriage and the Family* (Lexington, Mass.: D. C. Heath, 1982), Chapter 6.

COURTSHIP AMONG THE MUNDUGUMOR

The love-affairs of the young unmarried people are sudden and highly charged, characterized by passion rather than by tenderness or romance. A few hastily whispered words, a tryst muttered as they pass on a trail, are often the only interchange between them after they have chosen each other and before that choice is expressed in intercourse. The element of time and discovery is always present, goading them towards the swiftest possible cut-and-run relationship. The words in which a slightly older man advises a boy give the tone of these encounters: "When you meet a girl in the bush and copulate with her, be careful to come back to the village quickly and with explanations to account for your disappearance. If your bow-string is snapped, say that it caught on a passing bush. If your arrows are broken, explain that you tripped and caught them against a branch. If your loin-cloth is torn, or your face scratched, or your hair disarrayed, be ready with an explanation. Say that you fell, that you caught your foot, that you were running after game. Otherwise people will laugh in your face when you return." A girl is similarly advised: "If your ear-rings are torn out of your ears, and the cord of your necklace broken, if your grass skirt is torn and bedraggled, and your face and arms scratched and bleeding, say that you were frightened, that you heard a noise in the bush and ran and fell. Otherwise people will taunt you with having met a lover." Foreplay in these quick encounters takes the form of a violent scratching and biting match, calculated to produce the maximum amount of excitement in the minimum amount of time. To break the arrows or the basket of the beloved is one standard way of demonstrating consuming passion; so also is tearing off ornaments, and smashing them if possible.

Before she marries, a girl may have a number of affairs, each characterized by the same quick violence, but it is dangerous. If the matter is discovered the whole community will know that she is no longer a virgin, and the Mundugumor value virginity in their daughters and brides. Only a virgin may be offered in exchange for a virgin, and a girl whose virginity is known to be lost can be exchanged only for one whose exchange value has been similarly damaged. However, if a man marries a girl and then discovers she is not a virgin, he says nothing about it, for his own reputation is now involved and people would mock him. Sometimes the bush meetings are varied by an accepted lover's slipping into the girl's sleeping basket at night. Fathers may, if they wish, sleep with their adolescent daughters until they marry, and mothers have a similar right to sleep with their sons. Particularly jealous fathers and particularly possessive mothers exercise this privilege. Often, however, two girls are allowed to sleep together in a basket; if one of the pair is away, the other temporarily has the basket to herself. If she receives a lover in her sleeping basket, she risks not only discovery but actual injury, for an angry father who discovers the intruder may fasten up the opening of the sleeping-bag and roll the couple down the house-ladder, which is almost perpendicular and some six or seven feet in height. The bag may receive a good kicking and even a prodding with a spear or an arrow before it is opened. As a result, this method of courtship, although very occasionally resorted to by desperate lovers in the wet seasons when the bush is flooded, is not very popular.

From *Sex and Temperament in Three Primitive Societies* by Margaret Mead. Copyright © 1935, 1950, 1963 by Margaret Mead. Reprinted by permission of William Morrow and Company, Inc.

exogamy. At the same time interracial marriages are often discouraged, and some religious groups encourage their members to marry people of the same faith: endogamy. The number of spouses you may have at one time varies depending on the culture in which you live. **Monogamy** means one spouse at a time. It is estimated that most people in the world practice monogamy. The United States is technically monogamous, but with our high rate of divorce and family instability it might be more accurate to say that we practice a type of serial or musical-chairs monogamy.

Polygamy is marriage to more than one spouse and includes three types: polygyny, polyandry, and group marriage. **Polygyny** refers to the practice of one man having several wives at a time. G. P. Murdock studied 250 societies and found that polygyny was the preferred form of marriage in seventy-seven percent of them, although, as mentioned above, most people in the world practice monogamy.[4] Even in polygynous societies, most people practice monogamy. Although both sexes favor polygyny in such societies, the wealthy are more able to afford it and are more likely to practice it. **Polyandry** refers to the very rare practice of one woman having several husbands and, when it occurs, is usually found in poor societies with a shortage of women. Occasionally such societies kill female babies to keep the population down. When the woman becomes pregnant, deciding which husband is the father is a problem. This is usually solved by some sort of ceremony—possibly by shooting arrows at a distant target and designating the owner of the nearest arrow to be the father. **Group marriage** refers to the marriage of two or more men to two or more women at the same time. The successful, long-term practice of group marriage is extremely rare and when it does occur is usually limited to closed groups or communes.

Family practices vary in many other ways in societies across the world. Where do newlyweds live after marriage? They may be expected to live with the husband's family, or with the wife's family, or to alternate between the husband's and wife's families. In some societies (such as the United States) the couple is expected to live apart from both families. How is ancestry traced? In some societies family lineage is traced through males, in others through females, and in still others through both sides equally. As to who has the formal power and legal authority in the family and makes the decisions, in **patriarchal** societies it is the male and in **matriarchal** societies, the female. It is interesting to note that many of the different practices we have mentioned arise at least partially in reaction to the incest taboo. Almost all societies forbid or at least limit sexual contact between family members, restrictions which are called incest taboos. The particular lines of the taboo vary from one society to another. To help regulate the situation, various rules—residence, descent, etc.—were developed. It should be clear by now that almost any imaginable practice exists in some society somewhere. And all of it seems to work.

A number of other terms have emerged that help describe aspects of family structure. The family one is born into is called the **family of orientation.** The family of which one is a parent is called the **family of procreation.** The **nuclear family** includes the married couple and their children. The **extended family** includes more than two generations in close association or under the same roof, and the **compound family** includes multiple spouses—several wives and/or husbands at the same time.

---

[4]George P. Murdock, *Social Structure* (New York: Macmillan, 1949), p. 28.

In summary, we could describe the peculiar American family as a nuclear, monogamous, patriarchal, exogamous structure practicing marriage by romance.

Functional Uniformities: How Are Families Alike?

The institution of the family exists in all societies in some form. Functional analysis explains it this way: A family must serve a purpose, fill basic needs, and perform essential tasks. Those who have studied family institutions have discovered a number of such functions, some obvious and important and some less obvious. An obvious function of the family is to provide for continuation of the species. Societies, to exist, need people; the institution of the family functions to control reproduction. A second function of the family is the control of sex expression. The family institution attempts to deal with powerful sexual needs and desires by defining the who, when, where, why, and how of sexual activity.

A third function of the family is to care for and socialize children. The baby cannot survive without the care that the family provides. Socialization of the young by the family transmits the culture and prepares the child for participation in the adult world. Much of the child's later life is patterned on family models. It is possible that personal pathology and individual unhappiness will follow from inadequate family models or a bad family atmosphere. It may frequently be the case that the child is the defenseless target of the parents' own frustrations, anxieties, neuroses, and maladjustments.

The family may also function to provide close affectional and emotional ties for the individual. In some societies, many groups and associations may perform this function, but in mass, industrialized, secondary societies such as the United States, the family may be one of the few remaining places where primary relationships are possible. The family also functions to provide placement or status ascription. The family we are born into provides us with a *place* in society. If a person is a Protestant, middle-class, Midwestern, American Democrat, it is more than likely to be because he or she inherited certain statuses—religion, social class, region, nationality, political preference—from his or her family of orientation.

These are some of the functions of the family, and there are probably others. These functions are not necessarily completely separate from each other—reproduction of the species and control of sex expression would seem to be related. And further, other institutions may serve some of the same functions the family institution serves. The institution of education certainly deals with socialization of the young and transmission of culture, as does the institution of religion.

THE FAMILY: CONTRAST AND CHANGE

We have made the point that while the family exists everywhere, there are many variations in the form it takes. Also, the family continually changes, in some societies more rapidly than in others, and a variety of forces produce these changes. A brief look at several family systems will help illustrate this point.

The Family in China

In his book on the family, Ross Eshleman describes several stages of change in the Chinese family.[5] China is a country with a population four or five times as large as the United States with a family system far different from ours. The traditional family was the dominant type of family in China up to 1900 or so. The clan was the central characteristic of the traditional family and was made up of all persons with a common surname who descended from a common ancestor. A clan could be as large as several thousand persons and included gentry (intellectuals, landowners, government officials) and peasants who cultivated the land. The clan performed major functions such as lending money to members, establishing schools, settling disputes, collecting taxes, and maintaining ancestral burial grounds. Ancestors were worshipped (given offerings of goods and food) even after death.

Males were dominant in the Chinese family. A wife had to obey three persons: her father before marriage, her husband after marriage, and her son after her husband died. Female infanticide was common especially among the poor. Marriages were arranged through matchmakers—many women met their husbands for the first time on their wedding day. Women's duties were to have male children and aid in the work. Men could have additional wives, but women could have one husband and were not allowed to remarry if widowed. Binding of women's feet was practiced. This reduced the foot in length to about three inches and resulted in permanent crippling. Footbinding was practiced more among the upper class than among the peasants because the latter needed freedom of movement in order to work in the fields. Suicide was seen as a socially acceptable way for women to deal with their problems.

Change began to modify the traditional Chinese family in the 1900s. These changes were influenced by what was going on in the rest of the world, especially in Russia. Karl Marx's collaborator Friedrich Engels felt that in a capitalist society the family becomes the chief source of female oppression. Private property leads to subjugation and slavery of women and elevation of the status of men. One of the consequences of the revolution in Russia was the passage there of new marriage and divorce laws, the granting of abortion on demand, and the granting of legal equality to women.

China did not follow the Russian pattern precisely but did work to reform what were seen as the evils of the traditional family. A Communist Party conference in 1922 called for equal voting rights for women and an end to the traditional maltreatment of women. The Marriage Law of 1950 represented a major attempt to restructure the traditional family. This law enacted a new democratic marriage system based on free choice of partners, monogamy, and equal rights for both sexes. It prohibited bigamy, child betrothal, and infanticide. It gave husband and wife equal status in the home, granted divorce if

---

[5]J. Ross Eshleman, *The Family: An Introduction*, 3d ed. (Boston: Allyn and Bacon, 1981), Chapter 6.

both wished to, and allowed the woman if divorced to keep property that belonged to her prior to her marriage.

So what emerges as the Chinese family of today? As we might expect, characteristics of both the traditional family and of the family changed by law. Rural and urban differences are great—the rural families keep more of the traditional practices than the urban. Generally, while women have made progress toward equality, discrimination still exists in access to jobs and pay. Most of the important jobs are held by men; and sons are valued over daughters. Parental arrangement of marriages still occurs, while premarital sex and illegitimate births are infrequent and divorce is not widespread.

In conclusion, what happened in China was that changes in the political system produced pressures for change in other institutions. Communist ideology and the economic goals of the state pushed for a changed family in which women were more equal and able to participate in production, where family or clan-held property was confiscated and clans became communes. The consequence is that the contemporary Chinese family is vastly different from the traditional, but has many remnants of the traditional, and is described as strong and stable.

The Black Family in America

When we speak of the "family in America" as we will shortly (p. 218), we should recognize that we are generalizing about families. We group together different types of families—rural and urban, western and southern, middle class and working class, Amish and Presbyterian. Although these are generally similar, they may have certain specific differences. These differences may emerge because of economic position, geographic location, or historical events. Blacks in America have experienced a series of transitions or crises which are unique and have affected the structure of the black family.[6]

1. Transition from Africa to America: Blacks came to a white society, black traditions and cultural patterns were disrupted, and blacks were placed in a condition of slavery.

2. Transition from slavery to emancipation: Most blacks remained on plantations as low-paid tenants, but some black males left to search for work and this strained family ties.

3. Transition from rural to urban areas: Movement to urban areas by males to find jobs disrupted family life.

4. Transition from South to North to West: Again, nuclear and extended family ties were disrupted by geographic separation.

5. Transition from negative to positive social status: With improving conditions in jobs, education, and income, a larger working class and middle class developed replacing the predominantly lower-class black family. This brought with it corresponding changes in family life.

---

[6]This discussion follows that by Eshleman (see footnote 5) in Chapter 7 of his book on the family. Also see the original work by the Billingsleys: Andrew Billingsley and Amy Tate Billingsley, "Illegitimacy and Patterns of Negro Family Life," in Robert W. Roberts, *The Unwed Mother* (New York: Harper, 1966), pp. 133–149; and Andrew Billingsley, *Black Families in White America* (Englewood Cliffs, N.J.: Prentice-Hall, 1968).

6. Transition from negative to positive self-image: Increasing emphasis on the uniqueness and value of being black and of the black cultural heritage leads to an improved self-image.

The transitions or crises that blacks have experienced have resulted in three distinct types of family structure. The *matriarchal family* is the least stable of the three types and has the most problems. A female is head of the family because there is either no father, a temporary or series of temporary fathers, or a father present but the mother is the dominant authority figure. Many of these families live below the poverty line. A single parent plus economic difficulties combines to place great pressure on the family unit.

The *egalitarian family* has husband and wife living together, is middle or working class, and the husband has stable employment. The majority of black families appear to fit into this category. The third type is the *patriarchal family*. In this family the father makes most of the major decisions. This type of family is found especially among upper-class blacks, although it may be found in other classes as well. Within-group marriage, inherited wealth, isolation from classes ranked lower, not politically active are characteristics of these families as of other upper-class families.

In summary, the black family takes several quite different forms. The causes for these patterns can be seen as a consequence of historical events experienced by blacks in American society.

THE FAMILY IN AMERICA

If we look at the American family over the last hundred years or so we can see a number of changes. The family is smaller than it used to be—there are fewer children and fewer adults. Birth rates have been dropping in the United States over a long period of time with the result that the 1970s had the lowest rates on record. The large-family model of the nineteenth century has given way to the smaller family of two children or less. Some of the changing feelings about appropriate family size have happened fairly recently. Table 7.2 shows attitudes of wives regarding expected births, and we can see substantial change in just an eleven- or twelve-year period. The American family is also small in that it is a nuclear rather than an extended family. The extended family of a century ago had aunts, uncles, parents, grandparents, and children all assembled under the same roof. Compare that with the nuclear family of today and think of the differences in roles, division of labor, diffusion of responsibilities, child care, expression of affection and emotion, and individual free-

TABLE 7.2 Lifetime Births Expected by Wives 18 to 34 Years Old

Year	One or Less	Two	Three or More
1967	8%	31%	61%
1978	17	49	33

U.S. Bureau of the Census, *Social Indicators III*, p. 39.

dom. The change from the extended to the nuclear family brought tremendous changes in the roles of individual family members. The family of today is segregated: Each segment of that large extended family of one hundred years ago now lives by itself as a separate family unit.

Today's family is probably more egalitarian and less patriarchal. People share authority more than they used to, and women are making many of the important decisions. The woman has developed equality in other ways relating to family structure. She is more likely to be working outside the home while married. The possibility of career has given her alternatives to early marriage or even marriage at all. If she does marry, she has a greater say in which mate to choose and in the type of role she will play as wife. Likewise, equality has brought major changes in the role of males: unusual words like "househusband" and "paternity leave" are creeping into the vocabulary.

The American family has moved from farm to city. Last century's farm family now lives in or near an urban area. And the family is much more geographically mobile than it used to be. Some twenty percent of the people in the United States move every year.

The family used to be the all-powerful institution, but gradually other institutions—religious, educational, governmental—have become involved in some of the functions that the family formerly handled exclusively. So far this has resulted not in the disappearance of the family but in increased emphasis on or importance of the remaining functions that the family fills and a jealous guarding of them: "Sex education in the schools?? Certainly not! Keep it in the home where it belongs!" As mentioned before, it may be that one of the major functions of the family in mass society is to provide for the affectional and emotional needs of people. The family is nearly the last refuge of the true primary type of relationship, and if it is accurate to call this a basic social need, then this function of the family becomes exceedingly important as other functions decrease in importance.

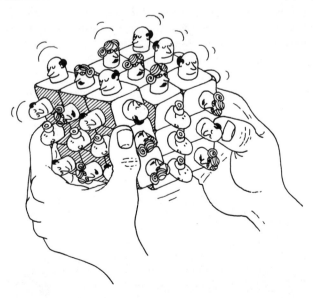

Pursuing this point a bit further, let's examine a recent study that explored some of the correlates of individual happiness. Angus Campbell conducted an interview survey of 2,000 adults that related people's happiness, satisfaction, and stress levels to their family situation.[7] Campbell and his colleagues studied nine categories of people in various stages of the life cycle. These categories included young people about to be married, married people with children, married people without children, divorced people, widows, and those who never married. The researchers found that single women were happier than single men. As Campbell puts it, the old stereotype of the carefree bachelor and anxious spinster is backward; you are more likely to find carefree spinsters and anxious bachelors. The researchers also found that married people were happier and more satisfied with their lives than single (unmarried, divorced, or widowed) people. The newly married without children showed the highest levels of satisfaction. Parenthood produces stress, however—happiness and satisfaction ratings drop when children arrive. The ratings then remain only average until the children are eighteen, and at that point the parents' happiness and satisfaction ratings again begin to rise. Many couples decide to stay childless, and these couples, especially the husbands, report high satisfaction with life and little stress. Campbell and his colleagues found that people whose marriages fail are miserable being single, and most of them remarry soon. Divorce seems to hit women harder as they are forced to work and care for children with little emotional and economic support. They feel the greatest stress and pressure of any group. The conclusion? If the findings of this study can be generalized, then it seems that marriage is an important factor in definitions of happiness and satisfaction in life for both sexes. Children put a crimp in things: Happiness levels tend to drop when they arrive, and the desire to have children is apparently decreasing. This research seems to support the idea that a major function of the family today is to provide affectional ties and emotional support to the married couple.

Several interesting changes took place in the American family between 1970 and 1980. Whether these represent basic long-term modifications or short-term soon-to-be-reversed trends remains to be seen. A 1980 Census Bureau paper tells us of the following:[8]

Later Marriage   The median age at first marriage continued to rise in 1980 for both men and women as can be seen in Table 7.3. The changes are slight from year to year, but this is the highest the median age of marriage has been since the turn of the century.

---

[7]See Angus Campbell, "The American Way of Mating: Marriage Si, Children Only Maybe," *Psychology Today*, vol. 8, no. 12 (May 1975), pp. 37–43. Also see Angus Campbell, Philip Converse and Willard Rodgers, *The Perceived Quality of Life* (New York: Russell Sage, 1975).

[8]Numerous Census Bureau documents were used for this section on marriage and divorce. Especially see "Marital Status and Living Arrangements: March 1980," *Current Population Reports*, Series P-20, no. 365 (Washington, D.C.: U.S. Government Printing Office, 1981); monthly and yearly *Vital Statistics* reports; and *Statistical Abstract of the United States*, 1980.

TABLE 7.3 Median Age at First Marriage, by Sex

	Male	Female
1890	26.1	22.0
1930	24.3	21.3
1940	24.3	21.5
1950	22.8	20.3
1956	22.5	20.1
1960	22.8	20.3
1970	23.2	20.8
1975	23.5	21.1
1980	24.6	22.1

U.S. Bureau of the Census, "Marital Status and Living Arrangements: March 1980," *Current Population Reports*, Series P-20, no. 365.

Staying Single   Later marriage means that the proportion of adults staying single is increasing. This trend started in the 1960s and continued through the 1970s. This is especially notable in age groups where most people have traditionally married as is shown in Table 7.4.

Living Alone   There were eighteen million people living alone in 1980 (as compared to eleven million in 1970) which represented nearly one quarter of all households. Most of the growth in this category came from divorced or never-married persons and persons under thirty-five years old. Sixty-two percent of those living alone were women.

Unmarried Couples   The number of households occupied by two unrelated adults of the opposite sex tripled between 1970 and 1980. The partners were generally of the same age group, and the majority involved two adults under thirty-five years of age.

Divorce   Marriage and divorce rates in the United States are shown in Table 7.5 (also see Table 7.4). Marriage rates have fluctuated over the years with

TABLE 7.4 Family Change 1970 to 1980

	1970	1980
Males still single of those aged 20 through 24	55%	69%
Females still single of those aged 20 through 24	36%	50%
Males still single of those aged 25 through 29	19%	32%
Females still single of those aged 25 through 29	11%	21%
Number of divorced males per 1,000 people	35	79
Number of divorced females per 1,000 people	60	120
Proportion of children under 18 living with two parents	85%	77%
Average size of household	3.14	2.75

U.S. Bureau of the Census, "Marital Status and Living Arrangements: March 1980," *Current Population Reports*, Series P-20, no. 365.

**TABLE 7.5 Divorce and Marriage in the
United States (Rates per 1,000 People)**

	Marriage	Divorce
1920	12.0	1.6
1930	9.2	1.6
1940	12.1	2.0
1950	11.1	2.6
1960	8.5	2.2
1970	10.6	3.5
1972	11.0	4.1
1974	10.5	4.6
1976	10.0	5.0
1978	10.5	5.2
1980	10.9	5.3

U.S. Bureau of the Census, *Statistical Abstract of the
United States*, 1980 (101st ed.), Washington, D.C., p.
61; and *Vital Statistics.*

no particular pattern apparent, but divorce rates have gone up sharply, starting
in the middle 1960s to their highest ever in 1980. One of the many consequences
of this increase is that in 1980 more than one out of every five children lived in a
one-parent family.

The American family of today, then, is many things. Young people seem to
be postponing marriage, perhaps because of unstable economic conditions, perhaps because a new variety in living arrangements enables people to enjoy primary group benefits without the necessity of a traditional marriage. A recent
study of the Common Market countries of western Europe found that the people who rated themselves happiest were those who were living together without
being married. People who do marry, marry later. Some population analysts
take this as a hopeful sign. Maybe Americans are being more careful about selecting mates. Taking more time and marrying at a later age may lead to more
stable marriages in the long run, and perhaps today's high divorce rates will
begin to decline. At any rate, if the marriage is not happy, it is likely to be dis-
solved quickly. There are more single-parent families due to both divorce and to
single people being allowed to adopt children. The nuclear family (two parents
plus children) is a major part of American family life, but it continues to shrink
in size as the birth rate drops. The retired couple in their sixties and seventies
represents another facet of the American family, one whose numbers are growing substantially as our population grows older and as the birth rate decreases.
Other agencies or groups may develop to help fill family functions. And maybe
the current popularity of sensitivity-training and encounter groups in general is
a search for the primary relationship that has been typically fulfilled by the
family.

Perhaps, then, we see two contrasting threads in the American family. One
is an experimental, postponing-or-never-marrying, alternative-life-style thread;
the other is the traditional nuclear family, progressing from young to middle-

aged parents with their children to elderly retired couples. Time has changed the nuclear family—it is a smaller unit with more equal relationships between partners. Although the two threads are contrasting, they also intersect: Many people may find themselves first being experimental and later following a more traditional path as their own needs and definitions undergo change.

FAMILY PROBLEMS

Several times in this book we have examined the contrasting viewpoints provided by the functional theorists and the conflict theorists. When the family is studied, one generally starts (as we did on p. 215) with the functions that the family provides. The family in all societies does have numerous and important functions, but the conflict theory approach deserves examination as well. Just as the family fulfills certain functions, it provides a setting for conflict. As we noted earlier, Engels felt that the capitalist family was the chief source of female oppression, and the "battle between the sexes" is probably waged more often in the family arena than anywhere else. Conflict is a sign that all is not well, and in this section we will examine the evidence of problems and instability in the American family.

Divorce is a good place to start in looking at family problems. There were 1.2 million divorces in 1980 and the divorce rate from the middle 1960s on has climbed sharply. Divorce is rising in many countries, but the United States continues to have one of the highest rates in the world. Why? Among the many explanations offered, the following seem most convincing. Divorce is becoming more and more accepted. It is not the stigma it once was, and people are much more inclined to use it today. Laws have changed—many states have enacted no-fault divorce laws, making divorces much easier to obtain. Another explanation has to do with the emphasis on individuality and happiness. Parties to a marriage that isn't working are less likely to want to stick with it today than they used to be. The view is that if you're not happy, then get out and try again, or try something else. The woman (as well as the man) knows that she has a good chance to make a meaningful life for herself in some other way than by staying in a bad marriage. And with fewer children, perhaps fewer marriages are kept together "for the sake of the children." Unmarried people living together also separate of course, and in the late 1970s courts were faced with several difficult cases that were essentially requests to have the legal benefits of divorce (community property and alimony payments) extended to people who had never married.

A recent study of husbands and wives attempted to find out what factors in the marriage were most likely to cause either party to think about divorce. Some interesting relationships were discovered. The wife's thoughts of divorce were *increased* if she had work experience, if she had a youngest child between the ages of six and eleven, and if she felt that housework should be divided equally. Her thoughts of divorce *decreased* according to her age at marriage (the older she was when she got married, the less likely she was to think of divorce), the length of the marriage, and if her husband contributed to the housework. The husband's thoughts of divorce were *increased* if his wife worked outside the home, if there were religious differences, and if his wife believed that housework should be divided equally. His thoughts of divorce were *decreased* by the presence of a child under six, by the length of the marriage, and by being older than his wife. These findings are explained in part by the fact that women's economic roles are changing faster than men's. This has increased her freedom and independence and has modified some of her attitudes about what should happen in marriage. Some husbands are having difficulty adjusting to these changes.[9]

An even more obvious example of conflict within the family is family violence. Nearly one-fifth of all murders in the United States involve a person killing a member of his or her own family. Spousal abuse and child abuse are much more widespread than was thought, and they may be the most underreported of all crimes. Some recent research reports that in sixteen percent of the families studied there was an act of violence by one partner against the other within the past year.[10] If this is projected over the life of the marriage, violent acts occurred in twenty-eight percent of the marriages. The researchers feel that this estimate is low and that the actual rate of family violence includes fifty to sixty percent of all couples. Generalizing from this study, it is estimated that 1.8 million wives are beaten by their husbands every year, and surprisingly, over two million husbands are beaten by their wives.

There are other conditions of concern in American society whose roots may be traced to the family. Nineteen percent of the arrests for violent crime and forty percent of the arrests for property crime in 1980 were of people under the age of eighteen. Suicide rates among teenagers are increasing. Drug and alcohol abuse by both young people and adults are serious problems. Illegitimate births increased by fifty percent in the last decade so that by 1981, one of every six American babies was born to an unwed mother.

The explanation for at least some of what is happening to the family is not difficult to find. Society changes and its institutions change as well. Fewer bonds tie family members together today, and the consequence is seen in divorce, and in young people leaving home earlier. Both parents are more likely to be working, meaning that children may be supervised less closely than they used to be or that outside agencies, day-care centers for example, play an increasingly important role in "family" life. Less desire for having children, along with increased freedom and independence for women, has led to increasingly diverse arrangements for satisfying affectional and emotional needs. It is likely that we will see more changes and redefinitions in the family as other aspects in society continue to change.

---

[9]See "Considering Divorce: An Expansion of Becker's Theory of Marital Instability," by Joan Huber and Glenna Spitze, *American Journal of Sociology*, vol. 86, no. 1 (July 1980), pp. 75–89.

[10]The research was done by Murray A. Straus, Richard J. Gelles, and Suzanne K. Steinmetz and is reported in their book, *Behind Closed Doors: Violence in the American Family* (Garden City, N.Y.: Doubleday, 1980), Chapter 2.

THE FAMILY OF THE FUTURE

And what of the family of the future? Jean Lipman-Blumen painted the following picture of the American family of the next two decades.[11] There will be fewer of the typical nuclear families that consist of two parents and one or more children. Instead, there will be more single-parent families. This will occur, she feels, because marriage and remarriage rates will continue to decline while divorce rates will continue to climb. More single-parent families will combine with others in the future for shelter, food, child care, and companionship. Lipman-Blumen feels that the smaller families of the future will be less segregated than those of today—they will get together for mutual support and cooperation. Shortened work weeks will have men at home more, which will mean that they will be playing a more real (and less ceremonial) role in the family. Women will be working more, meaning that household tasks will be more shared in the family of the future. In the early 1980s, a growing list of companies had established paternity leave programs, supporting the idea of increased male involvement in child rearing and increased female involvement in careers outside the family. One such program (New Jersey Bell) allowed a parent of either sex to take up to six months "newborn child" leave without pay, guaranteeing a job of the same status and salary upon return.

The Census Bureau offered an optimistic note in 1982. It predicted that marriage will make a comeback, that the divorce rate will decline, that mobility will decrease, and that family life will stabilize. The primary reason for this prediction (made by the head of the Census Bureau) is that the large numbers of people born during the "baby boom" between 1946 and 1964 are reaching an age in which they will "settle down" and experience greater marital stability.

Another look at the future is provided by Charles Zastrow.[12] He sees the family being significantly affected by technological changes, and consequently, he imagines the possibility of human embryo transplants, test-tube babies, manipulation of the genetic code to control aging and disease, and even cloning, in which an identical new organism (a biological carbon copy) is produced from the nucleus of a single cell. It is hard to believe that these things could happen, and yet scientists report that in only a few more years they could be a reality. Zastrow believes that technological changes will encourage the family of the future to experiment with new forms. There will be more childless couples. Parents will put off child-rearing until after retirement, when they have more time—test-tube babies and adoption will allow parents to be of any age. Professional parents will be trained and licensed and have the responsibility of raising the children of those who do not want to or are unable to. Marriage patterns

---

[11]This is taken from Jean Lipman-Blumen, "Changing Sex Roles: Their Implications for Family Structure" (paper presented at the Pacific Sociological Association Meeting, San Diego, California, March 1976.) Jean Lipman-Blumen is affiliated with the Women's Research Program at the National Institute of Education.

[12]Charles H. Zastrow, "Dramatic Changes Foreseen in the American Family of Tomorrow," *International Journal of Sociology of the Family*, vol. 3 (March 1973), pp. 93–101.

will also become more experimental, thinks Zastrow, and will include such variations as serial marriages (successive temporary alliances), contract marriages, trial marriages, open marriages, group or communal marriages, and homosexual marriages and adoptions. In addition, the single life may become more romanticized and idealized in the future with the result that more people will never marry.

The institution of the family changed slowly for two hundred years and now appears to be changing so rapidly that accurate predictions of the future are impossible. What are the future consequences of present changes and innovations? During 1978, the world witnessed the first human embryo transplant, in December 1981 a test-tube baby was born in the United States, and there continues to be much debate over the wisdom of manipulating the genetic code. In his book *Future Shock*, Alvin Toffler warned us that more innovations and changes are taking place now than at any time in human history. What will be the effect of these changes on the family of the future? It will be interesting to see.

SUMMARY

The major topics of the previous chapters in this section on social organization were groups, categories, and social differentiation. These concepts permit the study of a number of different types of collectivities of people. In this chapter we moved to another, somewhat more abstract level, and focused on social institutions. Sociologists define an institution as a system of social relationships, an organized way of doing things that meets certain basic needs of society. All societies have basic needs—reproduction of the species and socialization of the young, for example. Consequently, many of the same institutions—family, religion, education, government, economics—appear in all societies, although the content of a given institution may vary from one society to another. As societies develop and change, other institutions, such as science and leisure, may emerge.

Sociological research and study is more apt to be concerned with specific institutions than it is with the concept itself. The major part of this chapter has presented an analysis of the institution of the family. We examined cross-cultural variations in courtship and the family to make the point that although the institution of the family exists everywhere, it is not the *same* everywhere. Constants or uniformities were discussed, and the functions that the family seems to fulfill were outlined. Change is an inevitable part of family structure and we illustrated this by looking at the family in China and at the black family in America. Finally, we examined the family in America from several perspectives: current trends and changes, problems, and predictions about the family of the future.

Several readings follow. In the first, David and Vera Mace relate an interview with some young women in India who cast American courtship patterns in an unusual light. In the second reading, Jane Howard wonders if friends can be family and if good families have common characteristics. In the third reading, Lillian Rubin looks at marriage in the working class family and examines the contrast between the dream and the reality.

Terms for Study

complementary needs theory (211)	matriarchal family (218)
compound family (214)	matriarchal societies (214)
egalitarian family (218)	monogamy (214)
endogamy (212)	nuclear family (214)
exchange theory (211)	patriarchal family (218)
exogamy (212)	patriarchal societies (214)
extended family (214)	polyandry (214)
family of orientation (214)	polygamy (214)
family of procreation (214)	polygyny (214)
group marriage (214)	process theory (212)
incest taboo (214)	role and value theories (211)
institutionalization (208)	social institution (207)

Reading 7.1

MARRIAGE EAST AND WEST

DAVID AND VERA MACE

In this excerpt from the book *Marriage East and West*, the Indian women interviewed by David and Vera Mace suggest some potential problems with American courtship practices.

"Tell us," said Kusima, "about the young people in the West. We want to know how they get married."

Night was falling at the close of a sultry Indian day. A cool, refreshing breeze playfully caressed the glittering black tresses of the girls' hair and set their gay saris fluttering. All teen-agers, they had been invited along by our host because we had expressed a desire to know what Indian young people thought about love and marriage. The girls, ten of them, were squatting on the veranda floor in a wide circle. Being awkward Westerners who couldn't sit comfortably on folded legs, we had been provided with low stools.

We gave as good an account as we could of how our young people are free to meet each other and have dates; how a boy and girl will fall in love; and how, after a period of going steady, they become engaged and then get married. We knew that young people in the East live a very restricted life, and have their marriages arranged for them by their parents, so we felt a little relieved that they had chosen to question us about our delightful romantic traditions. We didn't want to make them too envious, but we naturally were glad to demonstrate our superiority in this matter of finding a mate.

When we had finished, there was a meditative silence. Concluding that they had been impressed, we decided to start a discussion.

"Wouldn't you like to be free to choose your own marriage partners, like the young people do in the West?"

"Oh, no!" several voices replied in chorus.

Taken aback, we searched their faces.

"Why not?"

"For one thing," said one of them, "doesn't it put the girl in a very humiliating position?"

"Humiliating? In what way?"

"Well, doesn't it mean that she has to try to look pretty, and call attention to herself, and attract a boy, to be sure she'll get married?"

"Well, perhaps so."

"And if she doesn't want to do that, or if she feels it's undignified, wouldn't that mean she mightn't get a husband?"

"Yes, that's possible."

"So a girl who is shy and doesn't push herself forward might not be able to get married. Does that happen?"

"Sometimes it does."

"Well, surely that's humiliating. It makes getting married a sort of competition in which the girls are fighting each other for the boys. And it encourages a girl to pretend she's better than she really is. She can't relax and be herself. She has to make a good impression to get a boy, and then she has to go on making a good impression to get him to marry her."

Before we could think of an answer to this unexpected line of argument, another girl broke in.

"In our system, you see," she explained, "we girls don't have to worry at all. We know we'll get married. When we are old enough, our parents will find a suitable boy, and everything will be arranged. We don't have to go into competition with each other."

"Besides," said a third girl, "how would we be able to judge the character of a boy we met and got friendly with? We are young and inexperienced. Our parents are older and wiser, and they aren't as easily deceived as we would be. I'd far rather have my parents choose for me. It's so important that the man I marry should be the right one. I could so easily make a mistake if I had to find him for myself."

Another girl had her hand stretched out eagerly.

"But does the girl really have any choice in the West?" she said. "From what I've read, it seems that the boy does all the choosing. All the girl can do is

to say yes or no. She can't go up to a boy and say 'I like you. Will you marry me?' can she?"

We admitted that this was not the done thing.

"So," she went on eagerly, "when you talk about men and women being equal in the West, it isn't true. When our parents are looking for a husband for us, they don't have to wait until some boy takes it into his head to ask for us. They just find out what families are looking for wives for their sons, and see whether one of the boys would be suitable. Then, if his family agree that it would be a good match, they arrange it together."

Questions 7.1

1. Evaluate the Indian women's critique of American practices. Where are they right, and where do they misinterpret or misunderstand? What are the advantages and disadvantages of the Indian system of marriage? How is ethnocentrism a part of the discussion?
2. This interview was conducted in the late 1950s. How would a description of courtship in America in the 1980s change the responses of the Indian women?

Reading 7.2

FAMILIES

JANE HOWARD

Do family members need to be related by blood? Not necessarily, according to Jane Howard. Relatives sometimes fail to be friends, but with luck, friends can be transformed into relatives, members of one's clan. Further, good families, whether they be related by blood or friendship, seem to have certain characteristics in common.

Jane Howard, author of several best-sellers, studied some 200 family groups. Out of this came her book *Families*, from which the following excerpt is taken.

Call it a clan, call it a network, call it a tribe, call it a family. Whatever you call it, whoever you are, you need one. You need one because you are human. You didn't come from nowhere. Before you, around you, and presumably after you, too, there are others. Some of these others must matter a lot—to you, and if you are very lucky, to one another. Their welfare must be nearly as important to you as your own. Even if you live alone, even if your solitude is elected and ebullient, you still cannot do without a clan or a tribe.

The trouble with the clans and tribes many of us were born into is not that they consist of meddlesome ogres but that they are too far away. In emergencies we rush across continents and if need be oceans to their sides, as they do to ours. Maybe we even make a habit of seeing them, once or twice a year, for the *sheer pleasure of it. But blood ties seldom dictate our addresses. Our blood kin are often too remote to ease us from our Tuesdays to our Wednesdays. For this we must rely on our families of friends. If our relatives are not, do not wish to be, or for whatever reasons cannot be our friends, then by some complex alchemy we must try to transform our friends into our relatives. If blood and roots don't do the job, then we must look to water and branches, and sort ourselves into new constellations, new families. . . .*

If some of our friends are not in effect part of our family, then they ought to be, and soon. Friendships are sacred and miraculous, but they can be even more so if they lead to the equivalent of clans. If the important people in my life discern in my friend a fraction of the worth that I do, and if those who matter to him can understand his affinity for me, then we are on our way: the dim but promising outline of a new sort of family emerges.

I have been hearing quite a bit of talk about "support systems." The term is not among my favorites, but I can understand its currency. Whatever "support systems" may be, the need for them is clearly urgent, and not just in this country. Are there not thriving "megafamilies" of as many as three hundred people in Scandinavia? Have not the Japanese for years had an honored, enduring—if perhaps by our standards rather rigid—custom of adopting non-relatives to fill gaps in their families? Should we not applaud and maybe imitate such ingenuity? And consider our own Unitarians. From Santa Barbara to Boston they have been earnestly dividing their congregation into arbitrary "extended families" whose members are bound to act like each other's relatives.

As a member in reasonable standing of six or seven tribes in addition to the one I was born to, I have been trying to figure which characteristics are important for families to have.

1) *Good families have a chief, or a heroine, or a founder—someone around whom others cluster, whose achievements and example spur others on to like feats.*
2) *Good families have a switchboard operator—someone who keeps track of what all the others are up to. This person feels driven to keep scrapbooks and photography albums up to date so that the clan can see proof of its own continuity.*
3) *Good families are much to all their members, but everything to none. They have many outside interests—parents are nearly as devoted to what they do outside as they are to each other and their children. Curiosity and passion are contagious. Everybody, where they live, is busy.*
4) *Good families are hospitable. They are generous with honorary memberships for friends, whom they urge to come early and often and to stay late. There is the sense that surrounding relatives and friends may at any time become part of the inner circle.*
5) *Good families deal squarely with direness. Pity the family that supposes it can avoid for long the woes to which all flesh is heir. Lunacy, bankruptcy, suicide, and other unthinkable fates sooner or later afflict the noblest of clans with an undertow of gloom.*
6) *Good families prize their rituals. Nothing welds a family more than these. Rituals are vital especially for clans without histories, because they evoke a past, imply a future, and hint at continuity. A clan becomes more of a clan each time it gathers to observe a fixed ritual, grieves at a funeral, and devises a new rite of its own.*
7) *Good families are affectionate.*
8) *Good families have a sense of place—if not a home, then a set of totems and*

icons that make short-term quarters feel like home. Rooms with stoves or fire-places and round tables which inspire good conversation will help.

9) *Good families, not just the blood kind, find some way to connect with posterity. It is a sadly impoverished tribe that does not allow access to, and make much of, some children. Those without children might build homes, plant trees, write books or symphonies or laws, but even so there should be children nearby.*

10) *Good families honor their elders. The wider the age range, the stronger the tribe.*

Questions 7.2

1. How do Howard's characteristics of "good families" fit with the standard functions of the family? Are certain of the functions emphasized more than others? Is Howard suggesting certain new functions?

2. According to Howard, whoever you are, you need a family. Why?

3. How should "family" in Howard's sense (a group formed by both blood and friendship ties) be defined? Develop an adequate definition.

Reading 7.3

MARRIAGE: THE DREAM AND THE REALITY— THE BEGINNING YEARS

LILLIAN BRESLOW RUBIN

This excerpt from Lillian Rubin's book, *Worlds of Pain: Life in the Working-Class Family*, examines problems facing working-class couples in the early years of marriage. One of Rubin's major concerns in this selection is the effect of social class on family structure and on the difficulties that confront young couples.

SO THE ODYSSEY STARTS—each partner not thinking much about the other, each wrapped up in his or her own dreams. For her, the realization of her womanhood—a home and family of her own. For him, the fulfillment of his manhood—a wife to care for him, sons to emulate him, and daughters to adore him. For both, an end to separateness, to loneliness.

With luck, the first few months seem to fulfill the dream. Even though she may be working, it's considered a temporary state. Her dominant emotional energy centers on the tasks of home building; his, on bringing home a pay check sufficient to the demands. Each night he comes home tired, but happy to be greeted warmly by a loving wife.

The few who are older when married—where the men already are established in trades—are spared the need to deal with economic problems at once. Similarly, those who were married before have laid aside some of their naïve expectations and are better prepared to meet the problems inherent in any new marriage. But most are married very young and with little understanding of what they're getting into. For them, the dream fades quickly before the harsh and tedious realities of everyday life.

The men, most barely out of their teens, are often intermittently employed at unstable, low-paying jobs. The few who have settled on a trade are only just beginning to find their way into it; the jobs they hold usually are unsteady, not protected by seniority. For them, being married means drastic changes in life-style and self-concept:

Was there some period of adjustment after you were married?

Was there? Wow! Before I got married, I only had to do for myself; after, there was somebody else along all the time. *I mean, before, there was my family but that was different. They weren't there all the time; and even though I had to help out at home, they weren't absolutely depending on me.*

Then, I suddenly found I had to worry about where we'd live and whether we had enough money, and all those things like that. Before, I could always get a job and make enough money to take care of me and give something to the house. Then, after we got married, I suddenly had all those responsibilities. Before, it didn't make a difference if I didn't feel like going to work sometimes. Then, all of a sudden, it made one hell of a difference because the rent might not get paid or, if it got paid, there might not be enough food money.

But since your family was poor, you already knew something about things like that, didn't you?

Yeah, but it was different. That was my father's responsibility. I even sometimes was mad at him when I was a kid because he didn't do better by us. And, I don't know, maybe I just always figured I'd be more of a man than he was. I mean, I guess I always knew that's what getting married meant, that I'd have to take on all those responsibilities. But it's different when it really happens to you.

> [Thirty-year-old refinery operative,
> father of three, married ten years.]

Exacerbating the financial problems of most of these young couples was the fact that the children were born just months after the wedding. The modal time between marriage and the birth of the first child was seven months, the average, nine months—leaving little time for the young couple to stabilize their financial position before assuming the burdens of parenthood. Unlike the professional middle-class families I met where, on the average, the first child was born three years after they were married and where most wives worked during that time, the working-class families were forced almost at once to give up the wife's earnings. The professional families thus are doubly advantaged. Their jobs pay more and offer career patterns that are more stable than those in the blue-collar world. And by deferring childbearing, young wives are able to work while the men are becoming established.

Other investigators, observing the same phenomena, have theorized that it is precisely those differences that account for professional success—that is, that putting off marriage and childbearing is a symbol of the middle-class ability to defer immediate gratifications in the interest of future rewards. Conversely, the early marriage and childbearing of the working class allegedly is symptomatic of their inability to defer gratifications and the cause of their low status in the society. If one examines the facts through a less self-righteous and self-congratulatory prism, however, we can see instead that it is those at the lower ends of our socio-economic order who are forced to delay gratifications, while those at the upper levels usually manage to have their cake and eat it. For example, among the college-educated middle class, premarital sexual behavior is not only more widely held to be legitimate but the opportunities for engaging in such behavior are more readily and comfortably available. In the last decade, even dormitories—those last bastions of parietal regulations—largely have given up the attempt to control the sexual activities of their student residents. For those young people, a bed and privacy are easily found; sex can be undertaken in leisure—a sharp contrast from the stories told by most working-class youth who still must resort to the back seat of a car or a dark corner in a park.

Similarly, for highly educated middle-class women to delay childbearing may simply be to defer one pleasurable activity in favor of another since they often do some kind of interesting and rewarding work that pays substantially more than the low-level clerical, sales, or factory work available to most high-school-educated working-class women. Most of the middle-class women I talked to, for example, worked at interesting jobs that they liked—social worker, freelance editor, writer, teacher, accountant, office manager, personnel manager, calligrapher. Those who either did not enjoy working or who had jobs they found dull and unrewarding often had their first child in considerably less than the three years cited as the average—a decision that can be made in professional families without the enormous economic costs exacted in the working class.

Indeed, children born just months after the wedding added emotional as well as economic burdens to the adjustment process. Suddenly, two young people, barely more than children themselves, found their lives irrevocably altered. Within a few months—too few to permit the integration of the behaviors required by new roles in new life stages, too few to wear comfortably even one new identity—they moved through a series of roles: from girl and boy, to wife and husband, to mother and father.

They often responded with bewilderment, filled with an uneasy and uncomprehending sense of loss for a past which, however difficult, at least was known:

I was so depressed and I felt so sad all the time. I felt like I'd fallen into a hole and that I could never climb out of it again. All I wanted was to be a little girl again, real little, so that somebody would take care of me.

... an angry and restless discontent with an uncomfortable present:

I don't know why but I was just angry all the time. Everything she did would make me angry—crazy angry.

... and an enormous well of fear about an unknown future:

All of a sudden, you couldn't tell what would happen tomorrow. I was scared out of my wits half the time; and when I wasn't scared, I was worried out of my mind.

As with all of us, however, such a welter of feelings are rarely recognized, let alone understood. At best, we are aware only that we're experiencing turmoil without knowing what it's about. One young mother expressed it well:

All I knew was that I was churning up inside all the time.

Most immediately, both wives and husbands knew that the fun and good times that had brought them together were gone—replaced by a crying, demanding infant, and the fearsome responsibilities of parenthood. No longer were they free to run around with the old crowd, to prowl the favored haunts, to go to a movie, bowling, or partying whenever the mood struck. Both wives and husbands were shaken as it quickly became clear that the freedom they had sought in marriage was a mirage, that they had exchanged one set of constraints for another perhaps more powerful one. They felt stuck—thrust abruptly into adulthood, unexpectedly facing the fear that their youth was behind them.

The struggle to adapt simultaneously to so many new situations was complicated by young husbands who were jealous of their wives' suddenly divided time and attention. Before they had a chance to adapt to a twosome in marriage, they became a threesome, with the third member of the household a noisy, demanding, helpless infant. The young wife, anxious about her capacity to be a good mother, became absorbed in the child. Between household and baby-tending chores, both days and nights were full, leaving little time and energy for companionship or lovemaking. The young husband, until then accustomed to being the center of her life, felt excluded and deprived. Each time he made a move toward her that was rebuffed, the situation worsened. He became more hurt and jealous; she became more angry and defensive. The conflict escalated—both husband and wife acting out their frustration in painful and hurtful ways. Typical of such interactions is the story told by this couple, both twenty-nine, married ten years. The husband:

Our first kid was born less than a year after we were married. By the time he came, it seemed like she'd either been pregnant or with the baby the whole time we were married.

When we were first married, I'd come home from work and she'd be kind of dressed up and fixed up, you know, looking pretty for me. Then she kept getting bigger and bigger, and she'd be tired and complaining all the time. I could hardly wait for her to finish being pregnant. And when that was over, she was too busy and too tired to pay me any mind.

I used to get mad and holler a lot. Or else I'd stay out late at night and get her worried about what I was doing. We had nothing but fights in those days because all she wanted to do was to take care of the baby, and she never had any time for me. It sounds dumb when I talk about it now—a man being jealous of a little kid, but I guess I was.

The wife:

It felt like I was going crazy. There I was with a new baby and he was all the time nagging at me for something or other. Instead of helping me out so that I wouldn't be so tired, he'd just holler, or else he'd run out and stay out all night. Then he'd come home and expect me to be friendly and loving. Why should I? What was he doing for me? I didn't like being stuck with all those dirty diapers any more than he did, but <u>somebody</u> had to do it and he sure wasn't.

We used to have the most terrible fights after my son was born; it was just awful. I couldn't understand how he could be jealous of a little, tiny baby, but he was. It made me so mad, I just didn't know what to do. But I sure didn't feel much like loving him.

Parents in professional middle-class families have a sense of their own success, of their ability to control their world, to provide for their children's future, whatever that might be. For them, the problem is not how to support the children through tomorrow, not *whether* they can go to college or professional school, but *which* of the prestigious alternatives available to them ought to be encouraged. For working-class parents, however, the future is seen as uncertain, problematic. For them, the question is most often *whether*, not *which*— and that "*whether*" more often asks *if* children will finish high school; *if* they will grow up without getting "*into trouble*"; *if*, even with maximum vigilance, they—the parents—can retain some control over their children's future.

Complicating the matter still further, the men and women of these families are not at ease with most of the public or private institutions that share responsibility for socializing young children. They can't do much about the public schools with their mandatory attendance requirements and their "too liberal" teachers, although in recent years they have been trying. But they *can* keep their children at home with them as long as possible. Thus, where nursery school attendance is a commonplace among the children of middle-class families, it is rare among those of the working class—not primarily for financial reasons, nor because working-class parents value education less, but because they look with question and concern at the values that are propagated there:

I think little kids belong at home with their mothers not in some nursery school that's run by a bunch of people who think they're experts and know all about what's good for kids and how they're supposed to act. I saw some of those kids in a nursery school once. They act like a bunch of wild Indians, and they're dressed terrible, and they're filthy all the time.

> *[Twenty-seven-year-old housewife,*
> *mother of two, married seven years.]*

So strong are these feelings that even in those families where mothers work part- or full-time, institutional childcare facilities are shunned in favor of arrangements with grandmothers or neighbors—arrangements that keep children close to home and in the care of people who share parental values. Typical are these comments from one young couple. The twenty-five-year-old wife, mother of two, married seven years, who works part-time as a file clerk, says:

I don't want my kids brought up by strangers. This way it's just right. My mother-in-law comes here and stays with them and it's family. We don't have to worry about what kind of stuff some stranger is teaching them. We know they're learning right from wrong. I'd be afraid to leave them in a school or someplace like that. I'd worry that they might get too far away from the family.

Her husband, a twenty-seven-year-old refinery worker, agrees:

I wouldn't let Ann work if we couldn't have my mother taking care of the kids. Even though it helps out for her to work, I wouldn't permit it if it meant somebody I didn't know was going to raise my kids and tell them how to act and what to think. With my mother, I know it's all okay; she teaches them the way she taught me.

Thus, both husbands and wives agree on the primacy of their parental responsibilities. But the costs to a marriage of ordering priorities thus can be heavy. For the demands of parenting often conflict with the needs of the wives and husbands who are the parents—needs for privacy, for shared adult time and leisure, for companionship, for nurturance from a husband, a wife.

Finally, these early years bring with them the inevitable in-law problems. Despite the prevalence of mother-in-law jokes that focus on the wife's mother, it is not the men but the women who complain most regularly and vociferously about mothers-in-law, especially in the beginning years of the marriage. Fully half the working-class women spoke of problems with mothers-in-law as second only to the financial ones; a few even put the in-law problems first. The primary struggle was over "who comes first"—wife or mother:

That first year was terrible. He called her every single day when he came home from work. As soon as he'd walk through the door, he'd go to the telephone to talk to his mother. And then, a few times he went to see her before he ever even came home. That really did it. I said, "Listen buster, this has to stop. I'm not going to take that anymore. Either I'm going to come first or you can go live with your mother."

[Twenty-four-year-old typist,
mother of two, married five years.]

He was so used to helping out around his mother's house that he just kept right on doing it after we were married. Can you imagine that? He'd go there and help her out with the yard work. Here our yard would need trimming, and he'd be over there helping his mother.

[Thirty-eight-year-old housewife,
mother of four, married twenty years.]

He used to stop off there on his way home from work and that used to make me furious. On top of that, they eat supper earlier than we do, so a lot of times, he'd eat with them. Then he'd come home and I'd have a nice meal fixed, and he'd say he wasn't hungry. Boy, did that make me mad. We were always having these big fights over his mother at first.

[Thirty-two-year-old housewife,
mother of three, married thirteen years.]

This is not to suggest that conflicts around in-laws do not exist in other strata of society. But no professional middle-class wife or husband talked of these problems with the heat and intensity that I heard among the working-class women. Partly, that may be because few of the middle-class couples had families who lived close by at the time of the marriage which often took place when husbands were still in professional schools far from their hometowns. This gave these young couples a chance to negotiate the initial adjustment hurdles without interference from either family. Equally important, however, even when they live in the same city now, most of these professional couples do not have the kinds of relationships with parents that keep them actively intertwined in their lives. No grandparent in a professional family, for example, baby-sits with young children while their mother works—a common arrangement among working-class families, one which makes it difficult for the young couple to insist upon their autonomy and independence, to maintain their privacy.

Adding to the in-law problems, many of the women were aggrieved be-

cause their mothers-in-law had spoiled their sons—waiting on them, tending their every need, always sacrificing self for the men and boys in the family— thus making the lives of their wives more difficult. For men like these expected similar "services" from their wives—services most modern young women of any class are not so willing to perform:

His mother was like a maid in the house, and he wanted me to do the same kinds of things and be like her. I know it's my job to keep the house up, but wouldn't you think he could hang up his own clothes? Or maybe once in a while—just once in a while— help clear the table?

> [Twenty-eight-year-old housewife,
> mother of three, married ten years.]

Again, obviously, it is not only working-class mothers who spoil their sons. Still, no middle-class wife offered this complaint—a fact that, at least in part, may be because the professional men all had lived away from home for several years before they married. Without a mother or wife to do things for them, these men had to learn to care for themselves—at least minimally—in the years between leaving the parental home and getting married. In contrast, the working-class men generally moved from parental home to marriage, often simply transferring old habits and living patterns, along with their wardrobe, to a new address.

Indeed, overriding all these reasons why more working-class than professional middle-class women had complaints about mothers-in-law may be the simple fact that most working-class men lived with their families and contributed to the support of the household before they were married. Their departure from the family, therefore, probably is felt both as an emotional and an economic loss. Mothers, already experiencing some panic over the loss of maternal functions which have provided the core of their identity for so long, suffer yet another erosion of that function—a problem women in professional middle-class families deal with when children leave for college rather than when they marry. And the family economy, relying on income from all its working members, suffers the loss of his dollar contribution:

His parents didn't accept me at all. Tim was a devoted son and his mother needed that; she couldn't bear to give him up to anyone. Then, he also helped out a lot when he was living there. They needed the money and he turned his pay check over to his mother. They made me feel like I was taking a meal ticket from them when we got married.

> [Thirty-year-old file clerk,
> mother of four, married twelve years.]

These, then, were the beginning years—the years when illusions were shed along with childhood; the years when the first disappointments were felt, the first adjustments were made; the years of struggle for stability economically and emotionally—both so closely tied together; the years during which many marriages founder and sink. Some of these couples had already had that experience once; they were determined not to let it happen again.

Questions 7.3

1. What are the adjustment problems faced by the young couples described in this article? Describe how and why these problems affect working-class and middle-class couples differently.

2. Contrast male and female roles in middle- and working-class families.

3. Outline the basic differences between the middle-class family and the working-class family (not the married couple, but the family they came from).

4. Take several concepts from earlier chapters (for example, role, role strain, role conflict, socialization, status, anomie, etc.) and show how they might relate to the material discussed in this selection.

8
Institutions: Religion

... I will give a short account of the psychology of myself when my hansom cab ran into the side of a motor omnibus, and I hope hurt it.

... In those few moments, while my cab was tearing towards the traffic of the Strand ... I did really have, in that short and shrieking period, a rapid succession of a number of fundamental points of view. I had, so to speak, about five religions in almost as many seconds. My first religion was pure Paganism, which among sincere men is more shortly described as extreme fear. Then there succeeded a state of mind which is quite real, but for which no proper name has ever been found. The ancients called it Stoicism, and I think it must be what some German lunatics mean (if they mean anything) when they talk about Pessimism. It was an empty and open acceptance of the thing that happens—as if one had got beyond the value of it. And then, curiously enough, came a very strong contrary feeling— that things mattered very much indeed, and yet that they were something more than tragic. It was a feeling, not that life was unimportant, but that life was much too important ever to be anything but life. I hope that this was Christianity. At any rate, it occurred at the moment when we went crash into the omnibus.[1]

In our discussion of institutions in Chapter 7, we suggested that all societies have certain constant and important central needs or problems that

---

[1]From "An Accident" by G. K. Chesterton in *Tremendous Trifles* (New York: Sheed and Ward, 1955), pp. 29–33.

must be addressed. Norms and roles emerge, and a pattern of organization or social institution develops. In the previous chapter we looked at the family, and in this chapter we will examine the institution of religion.

Certain eternal questions face all of us: What happens after death? What is the meaning of life? Given the misfortunes of the present, can there be hope for the future? As people struggle with these concerns, they develop a set of beliefs, norms, and roles that represent their attempts to answer the questions. We refer to this increasingly organized set of norms and roles that develops as the institution of religion.

The central concerns from which the institution of religion develops are usually abstract—much more so than those we discussed in the last chapter on the family. One consequence is that definitions of and explanations for the institution of religion are more varied than are those for some other institutions. For example, Andrew Greeley suggests that religion has at its origins the human propensity to hope; that in the face of life disappointments hope needs to be renewed; that a variety of experiences may renew hope; and that religion is a collectively created phenomenon which effectively renews hope. This approach focuses on what religion *does* (renews hope), while some other approaches focus on what religion *is* ("a set of sacred beliefs and symbols").[2]

Religion, like the family, has appeared in all societies. If one compares different societies, however, one finds tremendous variation in religious practices. To get an idea of the variation, look at Tables 8.1 and 8.2. Table 8.1 shows a breakdown of the religious population of the world. Table 8.2 shows recent membership figures in the United States. Not all of America's churches are included in Table 8.2—only those with memberships of at least 500,000 are listed. View the figures in these tables with a certain amount of care. Religious bodies count membership in different ways. For example, some churches count all baptized persons including infants, while others count only those people who have attained full membership (usually meaning that they are over thirteen

TABLE 8.1   Religious Population of the World, 1979–1980

Christian		997,000,000
Roman Catholic	580,000,000	
Eastern Orthodox	76,000,000	
Protestant	341,000,000	
Jewish		14,000,000
Muslim		589,000,000
Shinto		57,000,000
Taoist		31,000,000
Confucian		156,000,000
Buddhist		255,000,000
Hindu		478,000,000

The 1982 *World Almanac*.

---

[2]Andrew Greeley, *Religion: A Secular Theory* (New York: The Free Press, 1982), Chapter 1.

years of age). Thus, these figures should be taken as no more than general estimates.

All countries have at least one religion, although not all people are religious. Ethnocentrism relates to our discussion of religion as it does to our discussion of the family. The lack of acceptance of others' ways of doing things, the hostility to difference, is probably even more pronounced with regard to religion. Whereas people with peculiar practices (different from ours) in marriage, family, clothing, or eating are seen as different, primitive, or ignorant, people of different religious beliefs are frequently seen as evil, pagan, or guided by the devil. Great rivalries and conflicts have occurred between religious groups, for religious faith and conviction can be a powerful force. Knowing that "it's God's will" or that "God is on our side" has justified all kinds of behavior.

RELIGION: ELEMENTS, CONFLICT, FUNCTIONS

Sociologists who study religion are not concerned with the possible truth or falsity of religious beliefs. They are interested in what people believe and especially in what believing does for people. Although there is great variation among religions, a discussion of some common definitions and descriptions may help our understanding of the institution of religion. Religion may be described as a unified system of beliefs, feelings, and behaviors related to things defined as sacred. Societies define things as sacred—objects (a tree, the moon, a cross, a book), animals, ideas (science, communism, democracy), people (Buddha, Christ, saints). When things become sacred, they are endowed with a spe-

TABLE 8.2　Membership in Selected Religious Bodies in the United States, 1980

Adventist	600,000
Assemblies of God	1,200,000
Baptist	27,000,000
Christian	1,000,000
Churches of Christ	2,500,000
Disciples of Christ	1,200,000
Eastern Orthodox	4,800,000
Episcopal	2,800,000
Jehovah's Witnesses	570,000
Jewish	3,000,000
Latter-Day Saints	4,800,000
Lutheran	8,600,000
Methodist	12,900,000
Pentecostal	2,400,000
Presbyterian	3,600,000
Roman Catholic	49,600,000
United Church of Christ	1,750,000

The 1982 *World Almanac.*

cial quality or power and are treated with awe, reverence, and respect. Beliefs about the sacred things develop, and often what people choose to believe is of a supernatural quality. A set of appropriate feelings—reverence, happiness, sadness, fear, terror, ecstasy—are established. Finally, behaviors (or rituals) are developed consistent with the beliefs and feelings—confessional, rosary, communion, dietary laws, or the content of a particular worship service.[3]

Religion may be examined from several viewpoints, and two of the theories we discussed in Chapter 1 are useful here. The *conflict* perspective focuses on the role religion plays in social conflict. Contrasting religious beliefs have often been a source of conflict—take, for example, the battles between Protestants and Catholics in Northern Ireland over the past decade or so. Religious differences may also become the basis for political differences as currently in the Middle East. Karl Marx was critical of religion because of people's tendency to use it in times of uncertainty or stress. Marx described religion as the opiate of the masses because he felt that it took their minds off their real problems in favor of the other-worldly answers of Christianity. The working class's real problem in Marx's view was its manipulation and exploitation by the wealthy industrialists—the bourgeoisie—in capitalist economic systems. Religion was a needless distraction that could only slow the workers' revolt and subsequent freedom from oppression.

Religion plays an important role in social conflict according to conflict theorists because the dominant religion in society usually represents the dominant social class. The dominant religion supports the status quo, offers justifica-

---

[3]Much of our discussion in this section is drawn from Charles Glock and Rodney Stark, *Religion and Society in Tension* (Chicago: Rand McNally, 1965). This definition of religion is close to that of Glock and Stark. In their book, Glock and Stark trace the background of their definition, which includes the works of Durkheim, Yinger, Parsons, Nottingham, and Williams.

tions for existing class lines, and operates to make working-class and lower-class people satisfied with their condition. The conflict between social classes may lead to the emergence of specific religious groups that represent specific class interests. A recent example is the People's Temple of the Reverend Jim Jones, which reportedly drew much of its membership from the ranks of the disaffected and alienated in society. According to the conflict perspective, a consequence of the development of class-based religions is that often what appear to be religious differences between opposing religious groups (for example, Protestants and Catholics in Northern Ireland) actually turn out to be class differences. One religious group represents money and propertied people, and the other represents the working class. Conflict, then, is a central element in the discussion of religion according to this viewpoint.

Functional analysis is a second way of examining religion. This approach focuses on the functions that religion offers for society. First, religion provides a way for people to deal with the unknown; it supplies some measure of certainty in an uncertain world. There are a number of things we cannot explain. There are many other things that can be explained and understood but are still difficult to accept—the certainty of death, the loss of loved ones. Religion enables people to adjust to these situations by providing a sacred, supernatural being or object to explain the unknowable; religion provides a belief system to deal with situations difficult to accept—for the certainty of death, a life after death. Anthropologists have noted that sacred rituals and beliefs are usually found in situations that are hardest to control, where there is most uncertainty. Our own appeals for divine guidance and support usually come at intervals when uncertainty is present: when the jet accelerates for takeoff, or just before a particularly difficult test.

Religion also functions to provide people with a perspective, a viewpoint, a way of looking at the world. It provides value orientations as to how the world ought to be; it gives meaning to life. Max Weber held that people are motivated by ideologies or beliefs that stem in great part from religious origins, and that these are more basic than the economic values believed by Marx to be so important. In his classic work *The Protestant Ethic and the Spirit of Capitalism*, Weber's analysis of history led him to the conclusion that the beliefs surrounding Protestantism were central to the rise of capitalism. For example, Protestant values encourage the view that work is a calling: to work hard is virtuous, acquisition is supported, sobriety is encouraged. Far from being a needless distraction, religion is the source, according to Weber, of many of a society's most basic values, perspectives, and orientations to the world.

Religion may serve an integrative function in that it promotes solidarity. People with similar beliefs and viewpoints are drawn together, are more unified than those without this common experience. The presence of religion does not guarantee solidarity within a society, however, as other factors are also important. Many societies—the United States, for example—have several religions, and these may be in conflict with each other. In this case there may be a degree of solidarity among those of the same faith but an absence of solidarity in the society—religion may prove to be disintegrative for society even though it is integrative for the individual.

Religion may function as an agency of social control. We noted earlier that religion provides people with a value orientation, a perspective on life, a view of the world. From shared viewpoints, common agreements arise as to what people should and should not do. Since these norms emerge from a religious base, the church becomes involved in ensuring that they are observed. They may be informally encouraged or enforced, or they may be enacted into law. For example, many religions provide for the education of the young in schools run by the church. Some churches do not recognize marriages that take place outside the church. The clergy perform marriages and engage in marriage counseling. A little more indirectly, through pressure groups and lobbies, religions are involved in ensuring the passage or rejection of laws that they feel are crucial; laws dealing with liquor, pornography, abortion, and birth control are recent examples in the United States. In countries where there is less separation of church and state, religious organizations and their representatives are more directly involved with government in determining right and wrong.

In a variety of ways, then, organized religious groups assert moral authority and attempt to provide guidance—they act as agents of social control. Problems may arise when values and viewpoints on issues change, as they have, for example, on legalized abortion and birth control in the United States. Formal church doctrines change much more slowly than do the values and attitudes of the people. The result is that the social control function of the church is compromised when its members no longer hold its values. It is likely that if this occurs on many issues, the authority of the church will be seriously undermined. In fact, a report published in March 1976 relates how this happened recently. In 1968, Pope Paul VI ruled against the use of artificial birth control by Catholics. Earlier in the 1960s the Second Vatican Council had made church reforms that were well accepted by Catholics in the United States. However, the Pope's 1968 ruling was, according to Andrew Greeley, who studied the consequences and authored the report, "as far as the American church goes, one of the worst catastrophes in religious history." The birth control ruling did serious damage to the authority of the church and to the credibility of the Pope. Apparently as a consequence of the ruling, between 1963 and 1974 weekly attendance at Mass dropped from seventy-one to fifty percent, monthly confession dropped from thirty-eight to seventeen percent, families who favored a son becoming a priest dropped from sixty-three to fifty percent, parochial school enrollment dropped from 5.6 million to 3.5 million, and so on. The Pope's ruling was issued to restore faith in the church, but, in pushing a view no longer held by most members, it in fact badly weakened it.[4]

How is religion in America best explained in a functional sense? Greeley suggests a combination of three factors: belonging, meaning, and comfort. Belonging refers to the idea originated by Durkheim that religion is the source of social interaction; it provides the cement that holds society together in the face of internal and external threats. It provides unity. Meaning refers to Weber's

---

[4]This project was researched by the National Opinion Research Center in Chicago, directed by Andrew Greeley. See Andrew Greeley, William McCready, and Kathleen McCourt, *Catholic Schools in a Declining Church* (Mission, Kan.: Sheed & Ward, 1976).

idea that religion provides a way of looking at the world, a set of definitions and ideas which guide one's thinking. Religion gives meaning to that which is difficult to interpret. It also influences the character and direction of other institutions (economic, for example) because people have a view of the world which is shaped by their religion. Finally, religion provides comfort, serenity, and reassurance. It supports existing institutions and provides social stability. Greeley believes that it is these three factors, especially the relationship between the meaning and belonging functions, that are responsible for the vigorous religious behavior in the United States.[5]

The functions we have discussed—to explain the unknown, to provide a viewpoint (meaning), to afford solidarity (belonging), and to exercise social control—represent some of the more obvious functions of religion. These are not mutually exclusive, and there are others as well. It is interesting to note here while we are discussing functions that *magic* in primitive societies and *science* in more advanced societies serve many of the same functions as religion. In fact, it is sometimes difficult to distinguish between what is magic, science, or religion.

RELIGIOUS ORGANIZATIONS

So far we have examined the elements of religion (beliefs, feelings, and behavior related to sacred objects) and some of the functions religion may serve. Religion may also be studied from the viewpoint of the organizational structure of religious groups. What we know about bureaucracies and large organizations may be applied to churches. One way of categorizing religious bodies would be in terms of their ceremony, their pattern of public worship. Greeley suggests the breakdown shown in Table 8.3. Religious ceremony is examined in terms of how rational or emotional it is (Apollonian or Dionysian, respectively), and by the degree of formality (simple church or high church). This provides four categories, each of which describes a fairly distinct type of religious experience. Apollonian-simple church appears often in American

TABLE 8.3 Types of Religious Ceremony

	Simple Church (simple, informal, casual)	High Church (formal, complex ceremony)
Apollonian (rational, sober, unemotional)	Traditional Protestant-Presbyterian, Congregational, Methodist	Latin mass, solemn high mass of Roman Catholic Church
Dionysian (emotional, nonrational, ecstatic)	Pentecostal, holy roller, snake handlers	Coptic mass, Javanese dance

[5]This comes from Andrew Greeley's book, *The Denominational Society* (Glenview, Illinois: Scott, Foresman and Company, 1972), Chapter 2.

Protestant denominations. Services are "relatively plain and simple and at the same time sober, restrained, and dignified." Even the hymns are sedate and restrained. Dionysian-simple church ceremonies involve "direct intervention of the spirit" and a simple and matter-of-fact approach to prayer, which at the same time encourages members to freely and openly express their emotions. Apollonian-high church services are "dignified, rational, and restrained, while at the same time elaborate, artistic, and stylized." Dionysian-high church services are ecstatic, emotional, and nonrational, and at the same time elaborate, artistic, and stylized. This is a difficult combination and this category of experience is not frequently found in churches in the United States. Greeley notices several trends: Along the simple-church–high-church dimension, Catholicism in this country seems to be moving in the direction of simple church while some Protestant denominations are going the other way. Along the Apollonian-Dionysian dimension, however, the direction is clear. The revolt against scientific rationalism is leading churches to become increasingly Dionysian—nonrational, emotional, and ecstatic.[6]

Terminology has also been developed to categorize churches in terms of the size and scope of the organization. One distinction that is commonly made is between church and sect. The **church** is large and highly organized, represents and supports the *status quo*, is respectable, and membership is usually automatic—one is born into the church. The **sect**, on the other hand, is smaller and less organized, and membership is voluntary. Members of sects usually show greater depth and fervor in their religious commitment than members of churches. The sect is more closely associated with the lower classes, the church with the middle and upper classes. The sect usually arises because of protest when church members become disaffected. They may feel that the church is too compromising or religiously too conservative, or in some other way is not responding to the wishes or convictions of its membership. The disaffected, deciding they would rather switch than fight, establish a sect based on purity of belief and the individual religious needs of its membership.[7]

Yinger sees church and sect as two types on a continuum of religious organizations. He adds several other types, including denomination and cult, as is shown in Table 8.4. The **denomination** appeals to a somewhat smaller category of people than the church—a racial ethnic, or social-class grouping. Yinger defines **cult** as a small, short-lived, often local group, frequently built around a dominant leader. Cults and sects arise, it is argued, because people feel deprivation in some form—poverty, ill health, value conflict, anomie. It is this deprivation that leads to the formation of new religious movements. Once formed, the movement may later die out, or it may become larger, more established and

---

[6]The categories and quotes discussed in this paragraph and in Table 8.3 come from Andrew Greeley's book *The Denominational Society* (Glenview, Illinois: Scott, Foresman and Company, 1972), pp. 23–24.

[7]These paragraphs on types of religious organizations make use of material from Glock and Stark, *Religion and Society in Tension*, Chapter 13 (see footnote 3), and from J. Milton Yinger's book, *Religion, Society and the Individual* (New York: Macmillan, 1957), Chapter 6, especially pp. 142–155.

conservative, and move to another category of organization—from cult to sect to denomination, for example.

RELIGION IN AMERICA

To a sociologist looking at religion in the United States, certain aspects stand out. In America as in other coutries there is *differential involvement* in religious activities. If we take church attendance as a measure of religious involvement, we find that women are more active than men, Catholics more than Protestants, college-educated more than those with high school education or less, people over thirty more than those under thirty, and people in the East most and people in the West least. Middle- and upper-class people attend and participate in church activities more than those of the lower class. Lower-class people tend to show greater intensity and emotion in religious feeling. Religious groups seem to be stratified according to social class. Episcopalians, Congregationalists, and Jews tend to be of higher social class than Presbyterians and

TABLE 8.4   Religious Organizations

Church	Large; universal appeal; very respectable; members are born into it; supports the status quo and existing nonreligious (secular) institutions; formal structure	Example: Roman Catholic Church of the Middle Ages
Denomination	Less universal appeal but organized around class, racial, or regional boundaries; conventional and respectable; less emotionalism and fervor than is shown in the sect; mainly middle class; stable, organized, and at peace with secular institutions	Examples: Presbyterian Church, Lutheran Church
Sect	Smaller; arises out of protest; membership is voluntary; uncompromising on religious doctrine; more emotional; less formal organization; more withdrawn from society and at war with secular institutions; it alone "has truth"; mainly lower class	Examples: pentecostal and evangelical movements, Jehovah's Witnesses
Cult	Smallest; less organized, somewhat formless and often short term; frequently centered around a charismatic leader; concerned mainly with problems of the individual (loneliness, alienation); more exotic ritual; may focus on the religious (salvation) or on the more secular (self-improvement, self-awareness)	Examples: snake worshipers, People's Temple, urban store-front churches

COMING OUT OF THE CULTS

Many young adults, some say as many as two or three million, have become involved in cults in the 1970s. Psychologist Margaret Thaler Singer studied several hundred people who had recently left groups such as the Children of God, the Unification Church of Reverend Moon, the Divine Light Mission, and the Church of Scientology. The people were generally middle and upper-middle class, around twenty-three years old, with some college education. Many joined cults during periods of depression and confusion, when life seemed meaningless. Cults supplied ready-made friendships and decisions about life. Exclusion of family and other outside contacts, rigid moral judgments of the unconverted outside world, and restriction of sexual behavior all worked to increase followers' commitment to the goals of the group and in some cases to its powerful leader. Indoctrination by the cult gradually eliminated any conflicting ties or information.

Coming out of the cult was not easy. Cult life usually provided a twenty-four hour schedule of work and ritual; members had tasks and purpose, their life was planned. After leaving, members felt at loose ends; they became depressed over the years they had lost. Some felt guilt over being involved in deception, especially over recruitment and fund-raising. They were lonely—leaving a cult meant leaving friends and the intimacy of sharing a significant experience. Ex-cultists found it hard to make decisions for themselves, they became indecisive. Many also tended to slip back into altered trancelike states of consciousness— "spacing out" or floating. Cult-encouraged thought patterns continued: don't question, don't doubt, accept uncritically and passively. Some were fearful of the cult. They worried about retaliation for leaving and even over chance street meetings with cult friends. Ex-cultists also experienced difficulty in their relationships with family and friends. They felt that "people were staring." Difficult questions were asked or implied: How could you do it? Why didn't you leave? Further, returnees often want to talk to people about the positive effects of the cult experience, the good things that happened. Yet, they feel that outsiders refuse to hear anything but the bad.

Adapted from "Coming Out of the Cults," by Margaret Thaler Singer, *Psychology Today,* January 1979, pp. 72–82. Copyright © 1979 Ziff-Davis Publishing Co.

Methodists, who in turn tend to rank higher than Baptists and Catholics. This ranking in great part reflects ethnic or national origin and recency of migration to the United States. The religion and social-class picture is complicated by the apparent tendency of Americans to change their religious affiliation as they move up the social-class ladder.[8]

Great *religious diversity* characterizes this country. The United States has no official state-supported religion. America, unlike some countries, has attempted to maintain a separation between church and state. Broadly speaking, three religious bodies—Protestant, Catholic, and Jewish—dominate. However, there are numerous Protestant denominations, of which the largest are Baptist, Methodist, Lutheran, and Presbyterian, as well as a multitude of sects and cults. Some authorities have noted this diversity in American religious groups

---

[8]George Gallup conducts a yearly poll on church attendance. Family income and occupational status as related to denomination are provided by Galen Gockel, "Income and Religious Affiliation: A Regression Analysis," *American Journal of Sociology,* vol. 24, no. 6 (May 1969), pp. 632–647. The NORC study (again directed by Greeley) was reported in newspapers and news magazines in late October 1975.

and have argued that, on the contrary, the differences are in name only. They believe that there is a growing consensus on religious beliefs and that we are approaching a common religion in America that is eroding the traditional differences between Protestantism, Catholicism, and Judaism. Glock and Stark tested this idea by asking a number of members of Protestant and Catholic churches about their beliefs. They conclude that great diversity *does* exist, not only between Protestants and Catholics but between various Protestant denominations as well. In fact, Glock and Stark believe that the differences between various Protestant denominations are so great that it is inappropriate to speak of "Protestants"—there is no such thing as a unified Protestant religion. Some of the results of Glock and Stark's research are shown in Table 8.5. It is apparent from these data that members of different Protestant denominations have marked differences in belief. These differences are reflected in numerous areas and seem to indicate that a common American religion, at least in terms of beliefs, does not now exist.[9] On the other hand, Protestantism, Catholicism, and Judaism in the United States are probably peculiarly American. Often they differ markedly from their antecedents in other countries. The melting pot has modified traditional religions so that they all probably reflect the cultural values of the United States. In this sense, at least, there is a "common American religion," and we will return to this when we discuss the secularization of American religion.

In the late 1970s the White House was occupied by a President who was a born-again Christian, and numerous people on the national scene, from Watergate conspirators to athletic heroes, publicly became religious. This trend has continued in the 1980s. The United States appears to be going through a religious revival of sorts with renewed interest in fundamentalist, pentecostal, and evangelical types of experiences. Some traditional churches have discovered, often to their embarrassment, that many of their members found themselves attracted toward more emotional and exotic religious conduct—

TABLE 8.5 Percentage of Members of Various Religious Groups Who Held the Following Beliefs to Be "Completely True"

	Congre-gation-alists	Meth-odists	Presby-terians	Missouri Lutherans	Southern Baptists	Catholics
Belief in the existence of God	41%	60%	75%	81%	99%	81%
Belief that Jesus was born of a virgin	21	34	57	92	99	81
Belief in life after death	36	49	69	84	97	75
Belief in the existence of the Devil	6	13	31	77	92	66
Belief in original sin	2	7	21	86	43	68

Adapted from Charles Glock and Rodney Stark, *Religion and Society in Tension* (Chicago: Rand McNally, 1965), Chapter 5.

[9]For a more complete analysis of this topic, see Glock and Stark, *Religion and Society in Tension*, Chapters 4 and 5 (see footnote 3).

faith healing, speaking in tongues, mass revival meetings, and so on. Young people seem to be especially attracted to and active in evangelical movements. At the same time, an increasing interest has developed in Eastern religions and mysticism. Religion and religious organizations seem to be continually in the public eye. Members of Hare Krishna chanted in the streets . . . the government investigated Scientology . . . Reverend Moon's Unification Church held mass rallies, there were charges of brainwashing converts, and parents attempted to kidnap their children back . . . the People's Temple at Jonestown in Guyana was the site of a mass suicide. Religious behavior in general seemed to fragment and take many different forms. As we will see in a moment, overall church attendance did not increase in the late 1970s and early 1980s—it was the *form* of religious expression that was undergoing change. Great diversity continues to characterize religion in America.

Religion in America is *losing functions*. Other institutions are taking over the traditional functions that religion has served. Education and socialization of the young is handled for the most part by educational institutions rather than by the church. More dramatic is the rise in the importance of science. Today we tend to put our faith in science rather than religion when dealing with the unknown or uncertain. Scientific knowledge increasingly forces a redefining of religious beliefs. How do you describe heaven when rockets and spaceships are racing through the universe to the moon and beyond? What is the soul when hearts and possibly even brains can be transplanted from one body to another? Today it seems that we look to science for the answers rather than to religion— the scientist is more of a folk hero than is the minister. We might predict that either religion will change to adapt to a scientific world or that religion will have ever decreasing influence. Some religious organizations, in a spirit of "if you can't lick 'em, join 'em," are attempting to develop new functions to replace those they have lost. Usually this means becoming more "this-worldly" and less "other-worldly." The new church looks like a social work agency, and religious leaders frequently lead the way in speaking out on social issues. Ministers and priests put their bodies on the line in the 1960s in civil rights demonstrations in the South. Individual representatives of the church have, among other things, spoken out on the draft and the war in Southeast Asia and have been active in the farm labor movement in California and the Southwest. Churches have provided food and shelter for youth "doing their own thing." It is frequently noted that the minister in the pulpit sounds more as though his college degree were in psychology or sociology than in theology.

These trends may not be widespread or even widely accepted in the very churches in which they are taking place. Some argue that these changes are certain guarantees of the decline of religion. After all, formerly churches were offering something different, a special way of looking at the world unattainable elsewhere. Now the church is no different from other secular organizations and loses any unique appeal it might have had. Others believe, however, that in a changing world, religion too must change or run the risk of becoming irrelevant to modern people.

Finally, the *secularization of American religion* bears discussion. By secular

THE TNEVNOC CULT

The 1970s have witnessed a profusion of new religious movements, and as these groups have grown in size and wealth, there has been a parallel spread of alarm at the tactics by which they recruit and hold members. Allegations of deception, seduction, hypnosis, brainwashing, and other forms of mind control are made.

David Bromley and Anson Shupe argue that characteristics of this "cult menace" are not new but have been a persistent feature in our history. They describe the Tnevnoc cult, a once-powerful and widespread religious movement of the nineteenth century. Young women at school were openly recruited and induced to commit themselves totally to the cult. Once they had joined the Tnevnocs, they had to surrender all aspects of their former lives: All possessions were taken away; all luxuries and even basic amenities were eliminated; members had their hair cut off; they could not own or look into mirrors; they were permitted no outside visitors during the first year; they could write no more than four letters a year; they could not associate with the opposite sex; and they had to accept cult leaders in parental roles. Cult life was relentless and consuming: Members were wakened at 4:30 A.M. and spent a long day at manual labor mixed with meditation, mind-numbing chanting, and compulsory religious ceremonies. Like the Hare Krishna they carried prayer beads, which they used in their repetitive, monotonic chanting. In a bizarre ceremony involving ritualistic cannibalism, Tnevnocs consumed food that symbolically represented parts of the dead founder's body. All loyalty had to be channeled to the cult and its leaders. In one macabre nuptial ceremony, members were required to become the living brides of the dead cult leader.

The group that Bromley and Shupe are talking about is not all that obscure. It is a Roman Catholic convent (*Tnevnoc* spelled backwards). The description doesn't mention the other side of the picture—the sense of majesty, purpose, and personal fulfillment that nuns feel, or the order, stability and integration of the convent as a social organization. The methods may seem strange but socialization and resocialization take place in elite military units, communes, convents, religious groups, and social movements seeking radical social change. These groups seek the total commitment of their members, which means detachment from former lifestyles and attachment to new ones. Society's response to what it sees groups doing depends on the group's *degree of legitimacy.* The less the degree of a group's legitimacy, the more objections a society raises to its behavior. Much as the Unification Church, Hare Krishna, and Children of God are currently labeled "cults," the Catholic Church once was pejoratively lumped with groups such as the Mormons and Masons despite enormous doctrinal and organizational diversity. Bromley and Shupe suggest that groups that seek to initiate sweeping social change become the focus of hysterical reactions well out of proportion to the real threat they present and that most religious movements through American history have gradually accommodated to the larger society.

Adapted from "The Tnevnoc Cult" by David G. Bromley and Anson D. Shupe, Jr., with the permission of *Sociological Analysis* and the authors.

we mean nonspiritual, nonsacred, this-worldly. Americans seem to be religious and nonreligious at the same time. Millions of Bibles are sold yearly, and polls indicate that over ninety percent of Americans say they believe in God, and yet fifty-three percent of the people asked could not name one of the four authors of the first four books of the New Testament, less than fifty percent could name at least four of the Ten Commandments, and forty-six percent of those polled by Gallup in 1980 felt that religion was losing its influence. Americans believe in prayer, in heaven and hell, and in life after death, and yet church attendance has dropped from forty-nine percent in a given week in 1958 to forty percent in 1971, and remains at that level today. In 1957, ninety-seven percent of Americans identified with a religious denomination. Yet at about the same time a panel of outstanding Americans, when asked to rate the most significant events in history, gave first place to Columbus's discovery of America. Christ's birth or crucifixion came in fourteenth, tied with the discovery of the X ray and the Wright brothers' first flight.[10] Religion used to be of vital significance; it guided the pioneers' way of life. People read the Bible regularly at family gatherings. It was the law, and its teachings were carefully followed. As society changes in other ways, so does religious observation. Today people join churches and say they are religious, but perhaps the meaning and reasons have changed. Although many remain religious in the traditional sense, many others are religious for social and secular reasons—it looks right, it makes one respectable. Religion is used to get other desired things. Belonging to the right church will help the aspiring businessman make the right contacts, meet the right people, have the right friends. Athletic teams pray before games; even the U.S. Marine Corps holds special religious services before shooting the rifle on qualification day. We seem to feel that if we have religion—belong or go to church—other good things will happen to us. The result is an increasing secularization of American religion. As Will Herberg puts it, contemporary American religion is *man-centered*. People, not God, are the beginning and end of the spiritual system of much of present-day American religiosity. The result is a religiousness without religion, a way of sociability or belonging rather than a way of orienting one's life to God.[11]

Making categorical statements about religion in America is risky business, however. In 1980, sixty-nine percent of Americans polled were members of churches or synagogues, fifty-five percent said religion was important in their personal lives, and the public consistently says that it has more confidence in the church and organized religion than in other key institutions. Although less than half of Americans are in church on a given Sunday (forty percent in 1980), this is higher than in most other predominantly Protestant nations in the world. As we noted, there seems to be a resurgence of interest, especially among young people, in evangelical and Eastern religions. Next to the secular strain of religion is another strain emphasizing its spiritual and emotional aspects. This seems to be the keynote of religion in America: great variation in belief and practice.

---

[10]Many of the statistics in this and the following paragraph come from *Religion in America 1981*, a Gallup Opinion Index, report no. 184, January 1981. Also see Will Herberg's interesting book, *Protestant-Catholic-Jew* (Garden City, N.Y.: Doubleday, Anchor Books, 1960), Chapter 1. Also Glock and Stark, *Religion and Society in Tension*, Chapter 4 (see footnote 3).

[11]Herberg, *Protestant-Catholic-Jew*, Chapter 11, especially p. 268 (see footnote 10).

SUMMARY

Religion has been the subject of this second chapter on social institutions. We have suggested that institutions emerge because of important needs that societies have. In the case of religion, these needs involve renewing hope, giving meaning to life, explaining the unknown, and dealing with death. Religion may be involved in other functions such as socialization, social control, and the promotion of solidarity and unity. Religion also plays an important role in social conflict: Marx felt that religion distracted people from their real problems, making it less likely that these problems would ever be corrected. Religious groups may battle each other, or support one social class, ethnic, or racial group to the disadvantage of another.

After examining religion from the functionalist and conflict perspectives, we dealt with the diversity of religious groups by suggesting several ways of distinguishing between different types of religious organizations. Finally, we suggested that religion in America is characterized by differential involvement in religious activities, much religious diversity, an apparent loss of functions, and some interesting trends around the topic of secularization.

Two readings follow. The first is an excerpt from an article by John Lofland in which he outlines the techniques used by one group (the DPs) to help convert prospective members to the DP religion. In the second article, Nathan Gerrard deals with serpent-handling religions. Gerrard makes the point that there is great diversity in practices within a given institution. In addition, we see the use of several methods of analysis—in this case, social class and institution—with one concept helping to explain the characteristics of the other.

Terms for Study

church (246)	functional analysis (243)
conflict theory (242)	religious diversity (248–249)
cult (246)	sect (246)
denomination (246)	secularization (250–252)

Reading 8.1

"BECOMING A WORLD-SAVER" REVISITED

JOHN LOFLAND

A central fact for religions is that they must have members for the organization to continue. How they go about getting members is a matter of some interest. Established churches count on new members being born into the church. Other churches may hope that neighborhood convenience, common social class, racial or ethnic interests, or the comments of satisfied customers will bring new members. These low-keyed approaches contrast with more active attempts—advertising on television or sending out missionaries to convert the heathen. But how does one successfully approach a disinterested and perhaps hostile audience?

John Lofland, a sociologist at the University of California at Davis, has written a book, *Doomsday Cult*, and a number of articles about an organization he calls the DPs, who are actually the followers of Reverend Moon, commonly referred to as the "Moonies." According to Lofland, the DPs have developed an "ingenious, sophisticated, and effective conversion organization," and in this excerpt from one of his articles he describes the conversion process in terms of five phases: picking-up, hooking, encapsulating, loving, and committing.

PICKING-UP

Reports of people closely involved with the movement suggest that the multimillion dollar media blitzes and evangelical campaigns that made DPs famous and virtual household words in the seventies were not significant ways in which people began DP conversion involvement. Perhaps most commonly, it began with a casual contact in a public place, a "pickup." Indeed, DPs spent time almost daily giving hitchhikers rides and approaching young men and women in public places. Display card tables for front organizations were regularly staffed in the public areas of many campuses as a way to pick up people.

The contact commonly involved an invitation to a dinner, a lecture, or both. Religious aspects would be muted or denied. As described in Doomsday Cult, *this strategy of covert presentations was employed in the early sixties with but small success. It became enormously more successful in the early seventies due to several larger-scale shifts in American society. First, the residue of the late sixties' rebellion of youth still provided a point of instant solidarity and trust among youth, especially in places like State U City, a major locale of public place pickups. Second, even though the number of drifting and alienated youth was declining from the late sixties, there were still plenty of them. They tended to be drawn to certain West Coast college towns and urban districts. DPs concentrated their pickups in such areas, with success.*

HOOKING

1. The prospect arrived for dinner to find fifty or more smiling, talkative young people going about various chores. The place exuded friendliness and solicitude. He or she was assigned a "buddy" who was always by one's side. During the meal, as phrased in one report,

> various people stopped by my table, introduced themselves and chatted. They seemed to be circulating like sorority members during rush.

Members were instructed, indeed, to learn all they could about the prospect's background and opinions and to show personal interest. In one training document, members were told to ask: " 'What do you feel most excited about. . . .' Write down their hooks so that the whole center knows in follow up." The prospect's "buddy" and others continually complimented him: you have a happy or intelligent face; I knew I would meet someone great like you today; your shoes are nice; your sweater is beautiful; and so forth. The feeling, as one ex-member put it, was likely to be: "It certainly felt wonderful to be served, given such attention and made to feel important."

2. It is on this foundation of positive affect that they slowly began to lay out their cognitive structure. That same first evening this took the form of a general, uncontroversial, and entertaining lecture on the "principles" that bound their Family group. Key concepts include sharing, loving one another, working for the good of humankind, and community activity. Chang and his movement were never mentioned. At State U City (and several other places with the facilities), prospects were invited to a weekend workshop. This was conducted at The Farm in the State U City case I am following here, a several-hundred-acre country retreat some fifty miles north of Bay City. A slide show presented the attractions of The Farm. During the three years of most aggressive growth (1972–1974), probably several thousand people did a weekend at The Farm. Hundreds of others had kindred experiences elsewhere.

ENCAPSULATING

The weekend workshop (and longer subsequent periods) provided a solution to two former and major problems. First, by effectively encapsulating prospects, the ideology could be progressively unfolded in a controlled setting, a setting where doubts and hesitations could be surfaced and rebutted. Second, affective bonds could be elaborated without interference from outsiders.

Focusing specifically on The Farm, the encapsulation of prospects moved along five fundamentally facilitating lines.

1. Absorption of Attention. All waking moments were preplanned to absorb the participant's attention. The schedule was filled from 7:30 a.m. to 11:00 p.m. Even trips to the bathroom were escorted by one's assigned DP "buddy," the shadow who watched over his or her "spiritual child."

2. Collective Focus. A maximum of collective activities crowded the waking hours: group eating, exercises, garden work, lectures, games, chantings, cheers, dancing, prayer, singing, and so forth. In such ways attention was focused outward and toward the group as an entity.

3. Exclusive Input. Prospects were not physically restrained, but leaving was strongly discouraged, and there were no newspapers, radios, TVs, or an easily accessible telephone. The Farm itself was miles from any settlement. Half of the fifty or so workshop participants were always DPs, and they dominated selection of topics for talk and what was said about them.

4. Fatigue. *There were lectures a few hours each day, but the physical and social pace was otherwise quite intense. Gardening might be speeded up by staging contests, and games such as dodgeball were run at a frantic pitch. Saturday evening was likely to end with exhaustion, as in this report of interminable square-dancing.*

> It went on for a very long time—I remember the beat of the music and the night air and thinking I would collapse and finding out I could go on and on. The feeling of doing that was really good—thinking I'd reached my limit and then pushing past it. [At the end, the leader] sang "Climb Every Mountain" in a beautiful, heartbreaking voice. Then we all had hot chocolate and went to bed.

A mild level of sexual excitement was maintained by frequent patting and hugging across the sexes. Food was spartan and sleep periods were controlled.

5. Logical, Comprehensive Cognitions. *In this context, the DP ideology was systematically and carefully unfolded, from the basic and relatively bland principles to the numerologically complex, from the Garden of Eden to the present day, following the pattern I reported in chapter 2 of* Doomsday Cult. *Indeed, if one accepted the premises from which it began, and were not bothered by several ad hoc devices, the system could seem exquisitely logical. The comprehensiveness combined with simplicity were apparently quite impressive to reasonable numbers of people who viewed it in The Farm context. Indeed, the "inescapable" and "utterly logical" conclusion that the Messiah was at hand could hit hard: "It's so amazing, it's so* scientific *and explains* everything.*"*

The encapsulating and engrossing quality of these weekends was summed up well by one almost-convert:

> The whole weekend had the quality of a cheer—like one long rousing camp song. What guests were expected (and subtly persuaded) to do was participate . . . completely. That was stressed over and over: "give your whole self and you'll get a lot back," "the only way for this to be the most wonderful experience of your life is if you really put everything you have into it," etc.

LOVING

But the core element of this process was deeper and more profound than any of the foregoing. Everything mentioned so far only in part moved a person toward a position in which they were open to what was the crux: the feeling of being loved and the desire to "melt together" (a movement concept) into the loving, enveloping embrace of the collective. (Indeed, we learn again from looking at the DPs that love can be the most coercive and cruel power of all.)

The psychodynamic of it is so familiar as to be hackneyed: "people need to belong, to feel loved," as it is often put. People who want to "belong" and do not, or who harbor guilt over their reservations about giving themselves over to collectivities, are perhaps the most vulnerable to loving overtures toward be-longing. The pattern has been stated with freshness and insight by a young, recently-Christian woman who did a Farm weekend, not then knowing she was involved with the DPs:

> When I did hold back in some small way, and received a look of sorrowful, benevolent concern, I felt guilt and the desire to please as though it were God Himself whom I had offended. What may really have been wisdom on my part (trying to preserve my own boundaries in a dangerous and potentially overwhelming situation) was treated as symptomatic of alienation and fear; and a withholding of God's light. Those things are sometimes true of me, and I am unsure enough of my own openness in groups that I tended to believe they were right. Once, when [the workshop leader] spoke to us after a lecture, I began to cry. She'd said something about giving, and it had touched on a deep longing in me to do that, and the pain of that wall around my heart when I feel closed off in a group of people. I wanted to break through that badly enough that right then it almost didn't matter what they believed—if only I could really share myself with them. I think that moment may be exactly the point at which many people decide to join [the DPs].

The conscious strategy of these encapsulating weekend camps was to drench prospects in approval and love—to "love bomb" them, as DPs termed it. The cognitive hesitations and emotional reservations of prospects could then be drowned in calls to loving solidarity:

> Whenever I would raise a theological question, the leaders of my group would look very impressed and pleased, seem to agree with me, and then give me a large dose of love—and perhaps say something about unity and God's love being most important. I would have an odd, disjointed sort of feeling—not knowing if I'd really been heard or not, yet aware of the attentive look and the smiling approval. My intellectual objection had been undercut by means of emotional seduction.

Or sometimes the group would burst into song: "We love you, Julie; oh, yes we do; we don't love anyone as much as you." I read it this way: we could love you if you weren't so naughty. And, of course, they would love her.

This incredibly intense encapsulating and loving did not simply "happen." DPs trained specifically for it and held morale and strategy sessions among themselves during the workshops.

> On Sunday morning, when I woke really early, I walked by the building where some of the Family members had slept. They were up and apparently having a meeting. I heard a cheer: "Gonna meet all their needs." And that did seem to be what they tried to do. Whatever I wanted—except privacy or any deviation from the schedule—would be gotten for me immediately and with great concern. I was continually smiled at, hugged, patted. And I was made to feel very special and very much wanted.

COMMITTING

It is one thing to get "blissed out" on a group over a weekend, but is another thing to give one's life over to it. And the DPs did not seem immediately to ask that one give over one's life. Instead, the blissed-out prospect was invited to stay on at The Farm for a week-long workshop. And if that worked out, one stayed for an even longer period. The prospect was drawn gradually—but in an encapsulated setting—into full working, street peddling, and believing participation.

Doubts expressed as time went on were defined as "acts of Satan," and the dire consequence of then leaving the movement would be pointed out. A large portion of new converts seemed not to have had extramovement ties to worry about, but those who did—such as having concerned parents—seemed mostly to be encouraged to minimize the import of their DP involvement to such outsiders and thereby to minimize the threat it might pose to them.

A part of the process of commitment seemed to involve a felt cognitive dislocation arising from the intense encapsulating and loving. One prospect, an almost-convert who "broke off" from his "buddy" after a weekend, reported:

> "As soon as I left Suzie, . . . "I had a chance to think, to analyze what had happened and how everything was controlled. I felt free and alive again—it was like a spell was broken."

Another, on being sent out to sell flowers after three weeks at The Farm, had this experience:

> Being out in the world again was a shock; a cultural shock in which I was unable to deal with reality. My isolation by the Church had been so successful that everyday sights such as hamburger stands and TVs, even the people, looked foreign, of another world. I had been reduced to a dependent being! The Church had seen to it that my three weeks with them made me so vulnerable and so unable to cope with the real world, that I was compelled to stay with them.

This "spell," "trance," or "shock" experience is not as foreign, strange, or unique as it might, at first viewing, appear. People exiting any highly charged involvement—be it a more ordinary love affair, raft trip, two-week military camp, jail term, or whatever—are likely to experience what scientists of these matters have called "the reentry problem."

Reentry to any world after absence is in many circumstances painful, and a desire to escape from that pain increases the attractiveness of returning to the just-prior world. Especially because the DP situation involved a supercharged love and support experience, we ought to expect people to have reentry unreality, to experience enormous discontinuity and a desire to flee back.

Questions 8.1

1. The DP conversion techniques are "ingenious, sophisticated, and effective" with young people. Why do they work so well?
2. Perform a functional analysis of the DP conversion techniques. What functions do they provide for potential converts? Are these similar to or different from the functions provided by religion generally?
3. Compare the DP techniques described by Lofland with Christopher Edwards's description of what happend to him in *Crazy for God* (Reading 4.2).

Reading 8.2

THE SERPENT-HANDLING RELIGIONS OF WEST VIRGINIA

NATHAN L. GERRARD

There is great diversity in religious practices, as this article by sociologist Nathan Gerrard makes clear. Gerrard feels that a group's religious practices are at least partly explained by the social class of the members. He also outlines the functions that the serpent-handling religions seem to provide for their members.

. . . And these signs shall follow them that believe; In my name shall they cast out devils; they shall speak with new tongues; They shall take up serpents; and if they drink any deadly thing, it shall not hurt them; they shall lay hands on the sick and they shall recover. Mark 16:17–18.

In Southern Appalachia, two dozen or three dozen fundamentalist con-gregations take this passage literally and "take up serpents." They use cop-perheads, water moccasins, and rattlesnakes in their religious services.

The serpent-handling ritual was inaugurated between 1900 and 1910, probably by George Went Hensley. Hensley began evangelizing in rural Grasshopper Valley, Tenn., then traveled widely throughout the South, particu-larly in Kentucky, spreading his religion. He died in Florida at 70—of snakebite. To date, the press has reported about 20 such deaths among the serpent-han-dlers. One other death was recorded last year, in Kentucky.

For seven years, my wife and I have been studying a number of West Vir-ginia serpent-handlers, primarily in order to discover what effect that unusual form of religious practice has on their lives. Although serpent-handling is out-lawed by the state legislatures of Kentucky, Virginia, and Tennessee and by mu-nicipal ordinances in North Carolina, it is still legal in West Virginia. One center is the Scrabble Creek Church of All Nations in Fayette County, about 37 miles from Charleston. Another center is the Church of Jesus in Jolo, McDowell county, one of the most poverty-stricken areas of the state. Serpent-handling is also practiced sporadically elsewhere in West Virginia, where it is usually led by visitors from Scrabble Creek or Jolo.

The Jolo church attracts people from both Virginia and Kentucky, in addi-tion to those from West Virginia. Members of the Scrabble Creek church speak with awe of the Jolo services, where people pick up large handfuls of poisonous snakes, fling them to the ground, pick them up again, and thrust them under their shirts or blouses, dancing ecstatically. We attended one church service in Scrabble Creek where visitors from Jolo covered their heads with clusters of snakes and wore them as crowns.

Serpent-handling was introduced to Scrabble Creek in 1941 by a coal miner from Harlan, Ky. The practice really began to take hold in 1946, when the present leader of the Scrabble Creek church, then a member of the Church of

God, first took up serpents. The four or five original serpent-handlers in Fayette County met at one another's homes until given the use of an abandoned one-room school house in Big Creek. In 1959, when their number had swelled several times over, they moved to a larger church in Scrabble Creek.

SNAKEBITES, SAINTS, AND SCOFFERS

During the course of our seven-year study, about a dozen members of the church received snakebites. (My wife and I were present on two of these occasions.) Although there were no deaths, each incident was widely and unfavorably publicized in the area. For their part, the serpent-handlers say the Lord causes a snake to strike in order to refute scoffers' claims that the snakes' fangs have been pulled. They see each recovery from snakebite as a miracle wrought by the Lord—and each death as a sign that the Lord "really had to show the scoffers how dangerous it is to obey His commandments." Since adherents believe that death brings one to the throne of God, some express an eagerness to die when He decides they are ready. Those who have been bitten and who have recovered seem to receive special deference from other members of the church.

The ritual of serpent-handling takes only 15 or 20 minutes in religious sessions that are seldom shorter than four hours. The rest of the service includes singing Christian hymns, ecstatic dancing, testifying, extemporaneous and impassioned sermons, faith-healing, "speaking in tongues," and foot-washing. These latter rituals are a part of the firmly rooted Holiness movement, which encompasses thousands of churches in the Southern Appalachian region. The Holiness churches started in the 19th century as part of a perfectionist movement.

The social and psychological functions served by the Scrabble Creek church are probably very much the same as those served by the more conventional Holiness churches. Thus, the extreme danger of the Scrabble Creek rituals probably helps to validate the members' claims to holiness. After all, the claim that one is a living saint is pretentious even in a sacred society—and it is particularly difficult to maintain in a secular society. That the serpent-handler regularly risks his life for his religion is seen as evidence of his saintliness. As the serpent-handler stresses over and over, "I'm afraid of snakes like anybody else, but when God anoints me, I handle them with joy." The fact that he is usually not bitten, or if bitten usually recovers, is cited as further evidence of his claim to holiness.

After we had observed the Scrabble Creek serpent-handlers for some time, we decided to give them psychological tests. We enlisted the aid of Auke Tellegen, department of psychology, University of Minnesota, and three of his clinical associates: James Butcher, William Schofield, and Anne Wirt. They interpreted the Minnesota Multiphasic Personality Inventory that we administered to 50 serpent-handlers (46 were completed)—and also to 90 members of a conventional-denomination church 20 miles from Scrabble Creek. What we wanted to find out was how these two groups differed.

What we found were important personality differences not only between the serpent-handlers and the conventional church members, but also between

*the older and the younger generations within the conventional group. We be-
lieve that these differences are due, ultimately, to differences in social class: The
serpent-handlers come from the nonmobile working class (average annual income: $3000), whereas members of the conventional church are upwardly
mobile working-class people (average annual income: $5000) with their eyes on
the future.*

*But first, let us consider the similarities between the two groups. Most of
the people who live in the south central part of West Virginia, serpent-handlers
or not, have similar backgrounds. The area is rural, nonfarm, with only about
one-tenth of the population living in settlements of more than 2500. Until recently, the dominant industry was coal-mining, but in the last 15 years mining
operations have been drastically curtailed. The result has been widespread unemployment. Scrabble Creek is in that part of Appalachia that has been offi-
cially declared a "depressed area"—which means that current unemployment
rates there often equal those of the Depression.*

*There are few foreign-born in this part of West Virginia. Most of the resi-
dents are of Scottish-Irish or Pennsylvania Dutch descent, and their ancestors
came to the New World so long ago that there are no memories of an Old World
past.*

*Generally, public schools in the area are below national standards. Few
people over 50 have had more than six or seven years of elementary education.*

*Religion has always been important here. One or two generations ago, the
immediate ancestors of both serpent-handlers and conventional-church members lived in the same mining communities and followed roughly the same religious practices. Today there is much "backsliding," and the majority seldom
attend church regularly. But there is still a great deal of talk about religion, and
there are few professed atheists.*

HYPOCHONDRIA AND THE HOLY SPIRIT

*Though the people of both churches are native-born Protestants with fun-
damentalist religious beliefs, little education, and precarious employment, the
two groups seem to handle their common problems in very different ways. One
of the first differences we noticed was in the ways the older members of both
churches responded to illness and old age. Because the members of both
churches had been impoverished and medically neglected during childhood
and young adulthood, and because they had earned their livelihoods in hazardous and health destroying ways, they were old before their time. They suffered from a wide variety of physical ailments. Yet while the older members of
the conventional church seemed to dwell morbidly on their physical dis-
abilities, the aged serpent-handlers seemed able to cheerfully ignore their ailments.*

*The serpent-handlers, in fact, went to the opposite extreme. Far from
being pessimistic hypochondriacs like the conventional-church members, the
serpent-handlers were so intent on placing their fate in God's benevolent hands
that they usually failed to take even the normal precautions in caring for their
health. Three old serpent-handlers we knew in Scrabble Creek were suffering*

from serious cardiac conditions. But when the Holy Spirit moved them, they danced ecstatically and violently. And they did this without any apparent harm.

No matter how ill the old serpent-handlers are, unless they are actually prostrate in their beds they manage to attend and enjoy church services lasting four to six hours, two or three times a week. Some have to travel long distances over the mountains to get to church. When the long sessions are over, they appear refreshed rather than weary.

One evening an elderly woman was carried into the serpent-handling church in a wheelchair. She had had a severe stroke and was almost completely paralyzed. Wheeled to the front of the church, she watched everything throughout the long services. During one particularly frenzied singing and dancing session, the fingers of her right hand tapped lightly against the arm of the chair. This was the only movement she was able to make, but obviously she was enjoying the service. When friends leaned over and offered to take her home, she made it clear she was not ready to go. She stayed until the end, and gave the impression of smiling when she was finally wheeled out. Others in the church apparently felt pleased rather than depressed by her presence.

Both old members of the conventional denomination and old serpent-handlers undoubtedly are frequently visited by the thought of death. Both rely on religion for solace, but the serpent-handlers evidently are more successful. The old serpent-handlers are not frightened by the prospect of death. This is true not only of those members who handle poisonous snakes in religious services, but also of the minority who do not handle serpents.

One 80-year-old member of the Scrabble Creek church—who did not handle serpents—testified in our presence: "I am not afraid to meet my Maker in Heaven. I am ready. If somebody was to wave a gun in my face, I would not turn away. I am in God's hands."

Another old church member, a serpent-handler, was dying from silicosis. When we visited him in the hospital he appeared serene, although he must have known that he would not live out the week.

The assertion of some modern theologians that whatever meaning and relevance God once may have had has been lost for modern man does not apply to the old serpent-handlers. To them, God is real. In fact, they often see Him during vivid hallucinations. He watches over the faithful. Misfortune and even death do not shake their faith, for misfortune is interpreted, in accordance with God's inscrutable will, as a hidden good.

Surprisingly, the contrast between the optimistic old serpent-handlers and the pessimistic elders of the conventional church all but disappeared when we shifted to the younger members of the two groups. Both groups of young people, on the psychological tests, came out as remarkably well adjusted. They showed none of the neurotic and depressive tendencies of the older conventional-church members. And this cheerful attitude prevailed despite the fact that many of them, at least among the young serpent-handlers, had much to be depressed about.

The young members of the conventional church are much better off, socially and economically, than the young serpent-handlers. The parents of the young conventional-church members can usually provide the luxuries that most young Americans regard as necessities. Many conventional-church youths are active in extracurricular activities in high school or are attending college. The young serpent-handlers, in contrast, are shunned and stigmatized as "snakes." Most young members of the conventional denomination who are in high school intend to go on to college, and they will undoubtedly attain a higher socioeconomic status than their parents have attained. But most of the young serpent-handlers are not attending school. Many are unemployed. None attend or plan to attend college, and they often appear quite depressed about their economic prospects.

The young serpent-handlers spend a great deal of time wandering aimlessly up and down the roads of the hollows, and undoubtedly are bored when not attending church. Their conversation is sometimes marked by humor, with undertones of cynicism and bitterness. We are convinced that what prevents many of them from becoming delinquent or demoralized is their whole-hearted participation in religious practices that provide an acceptable outlet for their excess energy, and strengthen their self-esteem by giving them the opportunity to achieve "holiness."

Now, how does all this relate to the class differences between the serpent-handlers and the conventional-church group? The answer is that what allows the serpent-handlers to cope so well with their problems—what allows the older members to rise above the worries of illness and approaching death, and the younger members to remain relatively well adjusted despite their grim economic prospect—is a certain approach to life that is typical of them as members of the stationary working class. The key to this approach is hedonism.

HOPELESSNESS AND HEDONISM

The psychological tests showed that the young serpent-handlers, like their elders, were more impulsive and spontaneous than the members of the conventional church. This may account for the strong appeal of the Holiness churches to those members of the stationary working class who prefer religious hedonism to reckless hedonism, with its high incidence of drunkenness and illegitimacy. Religious hedonism is compatible with a puritan morality—and it compensates for its constraints.

The feeling that one cannot plan for the future, expressed in religious terms as "being in God's hands," fosters the widespread conviction among members of the stationary working class that opportunities for pleasure must be exploited immediately. After all, they may never occur again. This attitude is markedly different from that of the upwardly mobile working class, whose members are willing to postpone immediate pleasures for the sake of long-term goals.

Hedonism in the stationary working class is fostered in childhood by parental practices that, while demanding obedience in the home, permit the child license outside the home. Later, during adulthood, this orientation toward enjoying the present and ignoring the future is reinforced by irregular employment and other insecurities of stationary working-class life. In terms of middle-class values, hedonism is self-defeating. But from a psychiatric point of view, for those who actually have little control of their position in the social and economic structure of modern society, it may very well aid acceptance of the situation. This is particularly true when it takes a religious form of expression. Certainly, hedonism and the associated trait of spontaneity seen in the old serpent-handlers form a very appropriate attitude toward life among old people who can no longer plan for the future.

In addition to being more hedonistic than members of the conventional church, the serpent-handlers are also more exhibitionistic. This exhibitionism and the related need for self-revelation are, of course, directly related to the religious practices of the serpent-handling church. But frankness, both about others and themselves, is typical of stationary working-class people in general. To a large extent, this explains the appeal of the Holiness churches. Ordinarily, their members have little to lose from frankness, since their status pretensions are less than those of the upwardly mobile working class, who are continually trying to present favorable images of themselves.

Because the young members of the conventional denomination are upwardly mobile, they tend to regard their elders as "old fashioned," "stick-in-the-muds," and "ignorant." Naturally, this lack of respect from their children and grandchildren further depresses the sagging morale of the older conventional-church members. They respond resentfully to the tendency of the young "to think they know more than their elders." The result is a vicious circle of increasing alienation and depression among the older members of the conventional denomination.

RESPECT FOR AGE

There appears to be much less psychological incompatibility between the old and the young serpent-handlers. This is partly because the old serpent-handlers manage to retain a youthful spontaneity in their approach to life. Then, too, the young serpent-handlers do not take a superior attitude toward their elders. They admire their elders for their greater knowledge of the Bible, which both old and young accept as literally true. And they also admire their elders for their handling of serpents. The younger church members, who handle snakes much less often than the older members do, are much more likely to confess an ordinary, everyday fear of snakes—a fear that persists until overcome by strong religious emotion.

Furthermore, the young serpent-handlers do not expect to achieve higher socioeconomic status than their elders. In fact, several young men said they would be satisfied if they could accomplish as much. From the point of view of the stationary working class, many of the older serpent-handlers are quite well-off. They sometimes draw two pensions, one from Social Security and one from the United Mine Workers.

Religious serpent-handling, then—and all the other emotionalism of the Holiness churches that goes with it—serves a definite function in the lives of its adherents. It is a safety valve for many of the frustrations of life in present-day Appalachia. For the old, the serpent-handling religion helps soften the inevitability of poor health, illness, and death. For the young, with their poor educations and poor hopes of finding sound jobs, its promise of holiness is one of the few meaningful goals in a future dominated by the apparent inevitability of lifelong poverty and idleness.

Questions 8.2

1. What are the functions that the serpent-handling religions provide? Relate your discussion to the four functions covered in the text.
2. How are these functions related to the social class of the members?
3. Analyze the serpent-handlers in terms of religious organization—church, denomination, sect, etc.

9

Institutions: Political Economy

In Chapter 7 we defined social institution as the norms, roles, and patterns of organization that develop around central needs or problems that societies experience. In Chapters 7 and 8, family and religious institutions were examined. In this chapter we turn to political and economic institutions.

Institutions are interrelated, with change in one inevitably affecting another. The relationship between political and economic institutions is perhaps closer than most. Looking at their central functions may help us understand this better. Economic institutions arise out of societies' efforts to produce and distribute goods and services. Political institutions refer to the social relationships surrounding the assignment and use of power. And the connection between the two? There are limited goods and services in society, and they are unequally distributed. The distribution of goods and services is determined by those with the power to make such decisions. Who has the power to make such decisions? Probably those who benefit most from the existing distribution of goods and services. So we see that the political distribution of power and the economic distribution of goods and services are closely related. Remember Murphy's Golden Rule—Whoever Has the Gold Makes the Rules.

POWER

Power refers to the ability of one party (either an individual or a group) to affect the behavior of another party. We discussed power earlier (Chapter 5) as one of three variables, along with wealth and prestige, that determine one's socioeconomic status or rank in society. Here we find that power is the main force in political institutions. Power is probably a factor in all social situations—the doctor has power over the patient, the teacher over the student, the parent over the child, and even in dating situations, one party often has superior bargaining power. In this chapter, however, we focus on power which has a more general impact, power that influences actions and decisions at the societal level.

There are three major types of power: authority, influence, and resource control.[1] These types of power generally overlap—having one type means you'll probably have another type as well. **Authority** refers to socially approved power. It has legitimacy, it is socially acceptable. People believe that it is right and appropriate that they drive their cars on the right-hand side of the road and stop at stop lights, and they would probably do so even if no one were around. Authority is often impersonal in the sense that it is linked to position rather than the character of the occupant. Students pay attention in class not because of the instructor's fantastic personality, but because the position "teacher" holds a certain authority. We said that authority was viewed as legitimate—people are socialized to obey the rules and be law abiding. At base, however, authority rests on the threat of force and coercion. The relationship is complicated—does one go along because one wants to or because of fear of the consequences? Would you stop at the stop light if no one was looking?

Authority comes in different shapes and Max Weber has identified three specific types: traditional, legal-rational, and charismatic. *Traditional authority* means that power is granted according to custom. Leaders are selected by inheritance, and people go along because "it has always been done this way." Hereditary monarchies and tribal chieftainships are examples. The leaders appear to have much power, laws tend to be understood but unwritten, and there is a sacred quality to the whole operation. Historically this has been a common type of authority but is increasingly difficult to find today. *Legal-rational authority* is more typical of modern societies. Leaders are selected to fill positions, the boundaries of which are carefully designated by a formal set of rules and procedures. The *position* has the power rather than the person occupying it. If one goes beyond the boundaries, bad things may happen. The example of Watergate and Richard Nixon is typically used to show how the legal-rational system is supposed to work—he went beyond the legitimate boundaries and was forced to leave office. Legal-rational authority is typical not only of governments but of businesses and other types of organizations.

---

[1]The major source for this chapter is *Elites and Masses* by Martin Marger (New York: Van Nostrand, 1981). I have followed Marger's organization and viewpoint on most topics. His discussion of power and the three theoretical models comes from his Chapters 2–5.

Charismatic authority is based on the unique personality of a particular person. This person—Mao, Gandhi, Martin Luther King, Castro—has authority over others based on his or her personal appeal. Charismatic authority is very unstable—it tends to emerge out of crisis and is tied to a particular person. *Pseudocharisma* is a recent addition to Weber's idea.[2] The term refers to public figures who appear to have charisma, but in fact have a packaged and carefully created image manufactured by public relations techniques. Making politicians into TV celebrities is a clear example of the development of pseudocharisma.

Influence refers to subtle, informal, indirect power based on persuasion rather than coercion and force. Lines of influence are very widespread and less easily recognized than those of authority. Parents influence behavior directly through a look or tone of voice, or indirectly because we "know how they would feel." Admirers of rock stars and other entertainment personalities may be influenced to ingest certain restricted substances or wear wild and peculiar garments. Friends exercise influence and so does the mass media. Holding an important position like "member of the board of trustees" or "chair" naturally enhances one's influence. It follows that authority and influence often go together, but occasionally their boundaries may differ. A person may have narrow authority but much influence, or vice versa.

Power as **resource control** refers not to things people do, but to their possession or control of valued items. In this case power often represents a capacity, potential, or threat to act rather than actual decision-making behavior. If you possessed great wealth, control of a major energy source, or ownership of a string of radio and TV stations, you would influence others' behavior whether you intended to or not. Think of the amazing power shift in the direction of the oil-rich Middle East in recent years.

Distribution of Power

Power is stratified in society, it is distributed unequally. Those few at the top who have it are called elites, those without it are called the masses. But beyond this, how is power distributed? What type of people have it? What is the relationship between elites and masses? Three theories provide differing answers to these questions, and as with most competing theories, there is evidence to support and refute each of them. These three approaches are called the pluralistic model, the elite model, and the class model.

The Pluralistic Model   Pluralists believe that power is diffuse, spread across many diverse interest groups. An individual's interests are protected because everyone is potentially represented by one or more interest groups. Continuous competition and conflict for power between these interest groups leads to a balance, an equilibrium, and thus no radical or rapid social change takes place. The groups resolve differences by bargaining and compromise, and be-

---

[2]The idea of "pseudocharisma" comes from Joseph Bensman and Bernard Rosenberg in *Mass, Class, and Bureaucracy: An Introduction to Sociology* (New York: Praeger, 1976), pp. 431–433, and is discussed by Marger (see footnote 1) on pp. 20–21.

cause they are specialized, no single interest group has absolute authority. Some have political power, some have economic power, some have military or religious power. Political parties, voluntary associations such as the PTA and League of Women Voters, all levels of government, and finally even the voters—all exercise power.

This traditional pluralist approach that sees the masses producing interest groups that deal with the state has been modified in a modern version called elite-pluralism. Elite-pluralism recognizes the fact that mass political participation is impossible in modern complex societies, and that small elite groups do develop and make major decisions. It is suggested, however, that these elites have competing interests and tend to balance or neutralize each other so that no one elite gains dominance.

Does it fit the facts? Critics have some doubts. They suggest that most people are not represented by interest groups, and those who are don't have much voice unless they are part of the leadership. Interest groups that do exist tend to be dominated by business and monied interests. Finally, the balance of power suggested by the pluralists just doesn't exist, argue the critics—the power differences between different interest groups are vast.

The Elite Model   The elite model is sharply different from the pluralist model. The elite model sees relatively unrestrained power in the hands of a few who rule the masses who, in turn, are apathetic and incapable of self-rule—incapable because they are poorly trained, uninformed, and unorganized. Of the early elite theorists, Pareto viewed elites as the highest achievers in society—they govern through physical coercion (the "lions") and through cunning and intellectual persuasion (the "foxes"). Mosca felt that elites gain and keep power because they are organized (whereas the masses are not), they have particular personal attributes (strength of personality or intelligence), and they control valued resources or "social forces." Michels viewed rule by a few as an inevitable consequence of large complex organizations. Because a large number of people can't make decisions efficiently, a few are given the power to make decisions on behalf of the whole, and a leadership group develops. Once in power the elite spends more and more of its time and energy maintaining its power rather than on other organizational activities.[3] For example, think of how much of a politician's time (from the President on down) is spent on activities designed to keep himself or herself in office.

Modern elite theorists see the mass as manipulated and exploited by an elite motivated by self-interest. While the earlier theorists felt the development of an elite to be inevitable, modern theorists think that such a condition can and should be avoided. Theorists today see the elite as a cohesive group of people bolstered by their control of key resources including wealth, government authority, and communication facilities. In sociologist C. Wright Mills' view, the top layer of power in society is in the hands of "the warlords, the corporation chieftains, and the political directorate" who work together to form a power

---

[3]Pareto, Mosca, and Michels are summarized from Marger (see footnote 1), pp. 65–73.

elite in America.[4] According to Mills, decisions are made in this country by a few people, and they govern a fragmented mass of people who have no power. Between the two is a group whose power is semiorganized and stagnant. The middle is there but it neither represents the mass nor has any real effect on the elite. The elite is highly organized and made up of military leaders (admirals and generals), politicians, and business leaders. Mills suggests that a system in which so much power is held by a few who are not responsible to anyone but themselves is both immoral and irresponsible.

Does it fit the facts? Elites unquestionably exist, and the forces in large groups and organizations work much as Michels predicted. But critics raise certain questions—must elites inevitably emerge? Are elites cohesive and do they cooperate to the extent suggested by Mills and others? Are elites only self-serving or do they work in the public interest? And is the mass as totally powerless as the elite model predicts?

The Class Model   The class and elite models are similar in that they see power concentrated in the hands of a few. They differ in their description of the elite group and its origins. The class model brings us back again to the ideas of Karl Marx. Marx starts with the idea that economic institutions are the key to society—all else stems from such economic activities as finding food, shelter, and the other necessities of life. Classes emerge based on the means of production, and in industrialized societies two classes will dominate—the bourgeoisie (capitalists) who own the means of production, and the proletariat who own only their own labor. Classes become political groups when class members realize that they need to gain and use power to protect their common interests. Continual domination and exploitation of the proletariat by the bourgeoisie means continuing class conflict. Because the economic area is so important, economic domination is the key to power and control in other noneconomic elements in society.

Contemporary class theorists grant that the worker's revolution hasn't happened, and that the classes are not as polarized as Marx predicted. In fact, the classes have become increasingly complex and diverse—in many societies the growing middle class has become a dominant feature. In spite of these changes from Marx's predictions, contemporary class theorists say that the current corporate elite has the power of a ruling class. In his book *Who Rules America?*, William Domhoff describes a governing class "which owns a disproportionate amount of a country's wealth, receives a disproportionate amount of a country's yearly income, and contributes a disproportionate number of its members to the controlling institutions and key decision-making groups of the country." Excessive wealth and income are the key—having these (which other classes do not) allows the upper class to *control* other individuals and institutions. This upper-class elite has well-established ways of training and preparing new members for future service. Bright young people are processed into the upper class by means of "education at private schools, elite universities, and elite law schools; through success as a corporation executive;

[4]See C. Wright Mills, *The Power Elite* (New York: Oxford University Press, 1959).

through membership in exclusive gentlemen's clubs; and through participation in exclusive charities."[5]

It is Domhoff's thesis that the leaders of the executive branch of the federal government are either members of the upper class or former employees of institutions controlled by members of the upper class. He cites an impressive array of evidence that describes who has the wealth and how it is used to control power. Domhoff traces the occupants of various government positions and finds, for example, that members of the upper-class power elite dominate the President's Cabinet, especially in Departments of State, Treasury, Defense, Commerce, and even Labor. Of the thirteen men who were Secretary of Defense or Secretary of War between 1932 and 1964, eight have been listed in the *Social Register*, and six of the eight people who were Secretary of State in the same period were members of the upper-class power elite.[6] Through the CIA and other agencies, the upper class has manipulated intellectuals by giving money to individuals, schools, and foundations to exert influence, to start organizations, to hold conferences and publish magazines and books. As a consequence, the elite manages ideas, co-opts potential critics, and spreads its influence internationally. Do they act for themselves or do they act for the good of the country? Domhoff's view on this point is clear as he states that no matter how much they may plead otherwise, "they are primarily self-interested partisans, their horizons severely limited by the ideologies and institutions that sustain and justify their privilege, celebrity, and power."[7]

Does it fit the facts? As we mentioned above, Marx missed on several points. The worker's revolution hasn't happened, and classes have developed in ways other than Marx predicted. Critics also suggest that the class model overemphasizes class and economic factors, and ignores the fact that elites continually emerge in modern complex societies regardless of their relationship to the means of production. At the same time, there is impressive data supporting the class viewpoint.

The major aspects of the three theories of power are summarized in Table 9.1. Each theory makes important points about the nature of power and the relationship between power and other segments of society. Each model speaks to particular characteristics of society, and each is criticized, usually from the vantage point of another model. At this point perhaps we can determine which theory best fits the facts by taking a look at some of the dominant characteristics of the political economy in the United States.

THE AMERICAN POLITICAL ECONOMY

Dominant on the American economic scene are the large corporations. Their dominance can be illustrated in several ways. They employ many and

---

[5]Both quotes in this paragraph come from *Who Rules America?* by G. William Domhoff (Englewood Cliffs, N.J.: Prentice-Hall, 1967), p.5.

[6]G. William Domhoff, *Who Rules America?*, pp. 97–99 (see footnote 5).

[7]This is from Domhoff's later book, *The Higher Circles* (New York: Random House, 1970), p. 275.

TABLE 9.1   Societal Power as Seen by the Three Models

Model	Chief Source of Power	Key Power Group(s)	Role of Masses	Function of State
Class	Control of society's productive resources (wealth)	Ruling class (owners and controllers of the corporate system)	Manipulated and exploited by the ruling class	Protect capitalist class interests; reproduce class system
Elitist	Control of key institutions, primarily the corporation and the executive branch of the federal government	Relatively cohesive power elite, made up of top corporate and government leaders	Manipulated and exploited by the power elite	Protect interests of dominant elites and their institutions
Pluralist	Various political resources, including wealth, authority, and votes	Elective political officials; interest groups and their leaders	Indirectly control elites through competitive elections and interest group pressures	Referee the arena of interest groups; create political consensus

Martin Marger, *Elites and Masses* (New York: Van Nostrand, 1981), p. 112.

have great wealth. The 100 largest industrial corporations employed over nine million people in 1979, and the 500 largest employed over sixteen million people. Of more than 2.2 million corporations in 1977, about 16,000 (less than one percent of all corporations) had more than eighty-three percent of all assets. The top 225 corporations in 1979 controlled over $700 billion in assets, an average of over $3 billion apiece.

Many of the large corporations, called multinationals, go beyond national boundaries with connections throughout the world. Table 9.2 shows the twenty largest United States–based multinationals. Several things can be observed in Table 9.2. For one, the multinationals are huge—Exxon's assets, for example, are close to $57 billion. For another, most of the multinationals make a substantial part of their profit (especially when compared to assets) *outside* the United States. In fact, their wealth is often greater than that of the countries they occupy.

The behavior of the multinational corporations raises interesting issues. Multinationals encourage development in underdeveloped countries, but whether their efforts are welcome or not is much debated. They have been charged with meddling in local politics to encourage a friendly climate for their investment. They often bring their own employees rather than using native workers, which is of little help to the local employment situation. They often produce products for their own economy that may be of little use to the local society.

The concentrated power of the large corporations is strengthened by

TABLE 9.2   The Twenty Largest United States–Based Multinationals

	Total Profit (millions)	Foreign as % of Total	Total Assets (millions)	Foreign as % of Total
1. Exxon	$6,243	62	$ 56,577	53
2. Mobil	2,813	76	32,705	54
3. Texaco	2,240	63	26,430	56
4. Standard Oil Calif	2,401	52	22,140	46
5. Ford Motor	−1,543	—	24,335	56
6. General Motors	−763	90	34,455	27
7. IBM	3,562	54	26,703	51
8. Engelhard Minerals	976	65	6,301	49
9. ITT	1,788	65	28,378	41
10. Gulf Oil	1,407	47	18,638	36
11. Citicorp	499	62	107,094	63
12. Conoco	1,026	46	11,036	36
13. BankAmerica	645	45	104,150	43
14. General Electric	1,514	23	18,511	27
15. Occidental Petroleum	2,079	93	6,630	36
16. Dow Chemical	1,212	50	11,538	46
17. Chase Manhattan	354	51	76,190	53
18. Standard Oil Indiana	1,915	45	20,167	32
19. Eastman Kodak	1,896	24	8,747	35
20. Du Pont	1,340	20	9,560	24

Adapted from *Forbes*, July 6, 1981

other factors. Corporations are often linked to each other through interlocking directorates. An individual sitting on the board of one organization is more likely than not a director of several others as well. This encourages cooperation, reduces competition between groups, and smooths the path toward greater profits. Further, although large companies appear to be publicly owned by stockholders, in fact ownership is highly concentrated. Most stock is owned by a few, and these few are often banks and other corporations. The wealthiest one percent of the population in 1972 held fifty-seven percent of all corporate stock (the wealthiest one-half percent held almost fifty percent)! Since corporate leaders sit on the governing boards of universities, higher education naturally responds to the needs of business and industry. Corporations influence the mass media either by direct ownership or because they purchase advertising. In summary, the power of corporations is great and concentrated—their influence extends to all segments of society.[8]

We have seen that corporations dominate the economy, but what of gov-

---

[8]The source for these paragraphs is Marger, *Elites and Masses* (see footnote 1), especially Chapters 6, 7, 8, and 11. Factual information on corporations comes from *Statistical Abstract of the United States: 1980*.

ernment? Does the political sector of society act as restraint? The contrary seems to be the case—the two institutions seem to work together. Corporations influence political decisions through lobbying, campaign financing, and by having their leaders move freely back and forth between the two job worlds. For example, in 1971 a professor was appointed head of an insurance regulatory agency in Pennsylvania. His task, with the support of the powers of the state government, was to reform insurance company practices. He was ambitious, interested in reform, and had power, but he ran into difficulty. Nearly all the government staff and managerial people he had to work with had a background in the insurance industry. Further, the insurance industry had a large lobbying operation—lobbyists attended legislative committee meetings and helped draft legislation favorable to the industry. Finally, good jobs in insurance companies were promised to state employees who were loyal to insurance industry needs. During the professor's three years in office (he resigned seven months early to be replaced by a candidate acceptable to the insurance industry) no legislation put forth by his department passed if it was opposed by the insurance industry.[9]

Corporate leaders serve as Presidential advisors, Cabinet officials, and heads of regulatory agencies, later to move back to the corporate world. Government, in return, supports a tax structure and tax breaks which are favorable to individuals and corporations. Louis B. Mayer, founder of MGM, saved $2 million in taxes when he retired by hiring a Washington lawyer who obtained a special tax provision which applied only to him. Government is the corporation's best customer as a major consumer of goods and services; the Department of Defense, for example, is the largest single consumer in American society. And government pursues a foreign policy favorable to corporate interests: home markets are protected, foreign markets encouraged, and continued supply of necessary foreign raw materials assured. It is clear then that government and economic elites have mutual interests—as one prospers, so does the other.

Members of the government and economic elite are generally wealthy, male, college educated with advanced degrees, and "well connected." Some from lower social classes occasionally sneak in, but not often. "The outstanding fact of elite recruitment in the United States and other Western industrial societies is that leaders are chosen overwhelmingly from socially dominant groups, and have been for many generations."[10] They differ on some issues but agree on the important ones, which should be expected given their common interests, backgrounds, and needs. The masses have little authority or influence in selecting or controlling the elites. There is potential control through the political process (voting, working for candidates) but few participate significantly and those who do tend to be from the higher social classes. Social movements

---

[9]This case is described in *The Powers That Be* by G. William Domhoff (New York: Vintage, 1978), pp. 32–36. The original source is David L. Serber, "Regulating Reform: The Social Organization of Insurance Regulation," *The Insurgent Sociologist*, Spring 1975. The Mayer example in the next paragraph is also from Domhoff, p. 29.

[10]Marger, *Elites and Masses* (see footnote 1), p. 207.

(see Chapter 12) might be effective in controlling elites but they are seldom a direct challenge.

If this is an accurate picture of the power situation in America, the pluralist model doesn't seem to fit. The elite has the power and runs things, the masses watch from the sidelines. Even with less cosmic issues on the local level, my experience suggests that elites determine policy. The speeding traffic on a busy street going by our house concerned us—writing slogans on the pavement and yelling at speeders had no effect. Lacking any authority as individuals and being good pluralists, we formed a neighborhood association to represent us before the board of supervisors. (This is a legal-rational type of community—in California only the cars have charisma.) Our position was aided, we felt, by the fact that one of the supervisors was a personal friend. This anticipated influence was countered by another neighbor who happened to be wealthy, well-connected, and politically very powerful. He was quite satisfied with the traffic on our street just as long as it wasn't on *his* street. Our attempt to close our street (supported by the majority of the neighborhood) was effectively blocked. A compromise was later reached and the city sprinkled stop signs throughout the neighborhood. The stop signs don't work, the traffic is as bad as ever, and we are back to writing slogans on the street. The person with the power won, and the situation was more characteristic of the elite model than of the pluralistic model. To a certain extent the class model was instructive as well: the upper-middle-class neighborhood got token stop signs, but I doubt that a lower- or working-class neighborhood would even have gotten as far as the board of supervisors.

SUMMARY

In this third chapter on social institutions we have focused on the political economy. Power was defined, types of power were discussed, and different models explaining the distribution of power were explored. Finally, we followed Martin Marger's argument from his book *Elites and Masses* in which he suggests that the key factor in understanding modern industrialized societies is their domination by elites from the political and economic realms. These elites have common interests, come from common backgrounds, and work together to their mutual benefit. The masses are relatively powerless and only marginally involved in the political process. There is considerable debate about the power and influence of elites and one has to decide which of the various models and explanations best fits the facts of modern society.

To understand the American political economy, one needs to look at the power and influence of large corporations. The first of the readings which follow is a description of Exxon, the world's largest industrial company. Class and elite theorists believe that a powerful group of people, well known to each other, run things in this country. In the second reading William Domhoff describes Bohemian Grove, making the point that members of the elite not only work together, they play together and make important decisions in the process.

Terms for Study

authority (267)

charismatic authority (268)

class model (270)

elite model (269)

elite-pluralism (269)

influence (268)

legal-rational authority (267)

multinational (272–273)

pluralistic model (268–269)

power (267)

pseudocharisma (268)

resource control (268)

traditional authority (267)

Reading 9.1

THE NO. 1 INDUSTRIAL COMPANY

DOUGLAS MARTIN

Large corporations are different from the rest of us—Exxon spent $100 million on changing its name! In this article by *New York Times* writer Douglas Martin, we get a look at one of the large corporations which dominate the American economic scene.

Mr. Rockefeller was right.

Although we pay homage to Jeffersonian democracy, Americans have built an economy that relies on goliaths to get the job done. And the biggest of all is Exxon, the most prominent descendant of the vast empire that John D. Rockefeller, who made no bones about the end of individualism, put together piece by piece.

The Exxon Corp., the world's largest industrial company, shuffles billions of dollars like pocket change. Its decisions shape nations and shake governments.

Consider the Colony project, a $5 billion oil shale development in the Colorado high plains. Until recently, it was the centerpiece of U.S. involvement in synthetic fuel; it was also an undertaking where Exxon, paying its own way, was a kind of equal partner with Washington, to whom lesser companies looked for financial help. Exxon withdrew from the venture, 2,000 workers got their last paychecks; 1,000 more were on their way out. A new town died and, practically unnoticed, a $100 million pipeline project to ship the shale oil was shelved.

The scale of this thing called Exxon—which opened the celebration of its 100th birthday at its annual meeting 10 days ago—is boggling. It consists of more than 400 corporate entities operating in 100 countries. Each day, six million motorists stop at Exxon's 65,000 service stations worldwide. The company's oil and gas pipelines would more than circle the earth. The cost of a single offshore drilling platform, towering higher than a 50-story building, might be *four times the size of Harvard University's annual operating budget. Each week, Exxon spends $200 million on capital projects. Last year it earned $176.53 a second. So rich is Exxon that it still gives away road maps free.*

"There is no wad of cash like this anywhere on earth," said Jack Blum, a Washington energy lawyer and former Senate investigator. "This is a wad of cash to break banks, even governments."

Take the high-speed elevator to the executive dining room on the 53rd floor of Exxon's regal white skyscraper on the Avenue of the Americas, and one finds the founder's rolltop desk still prominently displayed. Two floors below, Clifton C. Garvin Jr., chairman and chief executive officer, plus the seven men who make up his executive team, walk corridors lined with chamois and brightened by original paintings and freshly cut flowers.

Twenty-seven floors lower, technicians in what outsiders like to term "the war room" direct the far-flung movements of Exxon's tankers, a fleet on a par with the Royal Navy. In office after office, globes and world maps suggest the breadth of Exxon, the company that was a multinational 80 years before the term slipped into popular usage.

Size, indeed, sometimes seems to blind the company to all but the gigantic. What other corporation would claim that $55 million illegally doled out to Italian politicians was too small a sum to notice?

Exxon has perhaps been most deft at making its way in a changing world. From the 19th century, when companies began moving out into the world to lift other nations' oil, through the 1970s, as governments wrenched back title to their resources, Exxon has proved its skill at what amounts to statecraft, an ability to endure as a power on the world scene. Perhaps most notable, its grasp of global politics and of enlightened self-interest enabled it during the 1973-74 Arab oil embargo to shuffle oil supplies around like checkers. No nation was denied oil, but the companies nevertheless honored the letter of the embargo. "Exxon had the clearest vision of balancing all the interests and the need not to push anyone to the wall," says Jerome Levinson, former staff counsel to the Senate multinational subcommittee.

One might argue—as Exxon does—that colossal, largely undemocratic enterprises such as itself are precisely what enable America to afford democracy. It quietly points out that the $3 trillion economy of the United States, which generates one of the world's highest standards of living, rests on giant foundations—General Motors, General Electric, International Business Machines.

"Things in this country are done on a large scale," Garvin said, "and yet each one of us likes to think about things in a small way. It's always been a strange thing to me."

But what is Exxon? To begin, it is a corporation, a legal entity allowing the organization to transcend the lives of men. "A corporation doesn't have a soul to damn or a butt to kick," Henry Banta, a left-leaning energy lawyer, observes.

Exxon sprouted as the Standard Oil Co. of New Jersey with the granting of a charter to Rockefeller on Aug. 5, 1882. Originally the operating arm of John D. Rockefeller's Trust, it became the vehicle for controlling the entire skein of Standard Oil companies in 1899, after New Jersey abolished its antitrust laws and otherwise encouraged companies to incorporate there.

Then, with the Supreme Court's busting of the trust in 1911, Jersey Standard became one of 34 new oil companies, a collection including some of today's biggest—Mobil, Socal, Indiana Standard, Sohio and Arco.

One obvious definition of Exxon, therefore, is that it is a child of Rockefeller. But only up to a point. Rockefeller ceased being an active manager in 1897, and his descendants are believed to own less than 1 percent of Exxon stock. Today, Exxon is owned by 804,000 shareholders, up more than 100,000 over the last year, largely because of the company's hefty 10 percent dividend.

Another definition of Exxon is people, those dauntless employees on the television commercials who seem to be searching for energy everywhere but the hall closet. Like others in the capital-intensive oil industry, Exxon is a relatively small employer, considering its clout. Some 180,000 people work for Exxon. By contrast, the Bell system has more than one million employees, and General Motors, more than 700,000.

Exxon's comparatively small army may make up in expertise what it lacks in numbers. Fully one-third are in managerial, professional or technical slots, and they seem consumed by arcane details of highly technical tasks, speaking a language of undersea production systems, satellites and laser technology.

Visits with Exxon hands over the years—the drilling supervisor in the Louisiana bayous, top executives in posh restaurants, world-weary Middle East experts—indicate that Exxon's people, almost uniformly, are nice folks.

But they are also very much Exxon: After lunch, groups will surround television sets to watch the in-house production of "This Week at Exxon"; even in New York City, participation in the Exxon Club's sweater sales and baseball expeditions is keen. A silver-haired functionary says that after decades of cocktail parties, his wife recently remarked Exxon men tend to be smart, friendly—and boring.

Exxon is also money. In addition to leading industrial companies in sales, *assets and stockholders' equity, the company last year made more than the combined profits of—to pick a smattering of giants in other fields—International Telephone and Telegraph, Dow Chemical, Procter & Gamble, Eastman Kodak, Union Carbide, Boeing, R.J. Reynolds, Goodyear and General Motors combined.*

Still, it was not the world's most profitable company. American Telephone and Telegraph, whose return is set by regulators, earned over $1 billion more than Exxon and claimed twice the assets.

And what's in a name? Jersey Standard became Exxon in 1972, after other Standard companies successfully sued to limit use of Jersey's "Esso" brandname (derived from Standard Oil's initials). Exxon came from 10,000 names dredged up by a computer—to then be studied by lawyers, linguistic experts and other specialists to make sure the new name would have no adverse connotations in any of the multitude of languages the company deals in. Total cost: more than $100 million.

If Exxon is history, owners, people, cash and a name, it is also unmistakably a bureaucracy. Decision-making is so marked by committees, hierarchies and set processes that one employee believes the only comparable organization may be the Roman Catholic Church.

Garvin is said to devote more time to judging personnel than any other topic. Last year, he sat down with his seven top advisers 39 different times to discuss the matter. Indeed, except for the newest and lowliest, everybody at Exxon is continuously rating somebody else, planning his future. The result: The company, fairly early in careers, has identified those who may someday lead it.

"Exxon ends up with 300 guys who have board potential by their late 30s or early 40s," an observer says. (And guys it is, so far. Exxon's highest-ranking woman is Carol C. Tatkon, treasurer of Exxon U.S.A.)

The "Exxon system," says John Buckley, who left Exxon to become vice president of the Northeast Petroleum Corp., results in "dog-eat-dog competition under the patina of working together."

From another viewpoint, it can also stunt entrepreneurship and personality. "The individual bureaucrat cannot squirm out of the apparatus in which he is harnessed," Max Weber wrote.

The rigid discipline of Exxon's personnel system—with its unrelenting pull toward Exxon's center—also characterizes other aspects of the company's business. In part, this reflects an international oil company's imperative, that need for control of a disorderly commodity first voiced by Rockefeller. But it also is a direct function of Exxon's size, prestige and predisposition to do things its way.

The nature of control at Exxon has shifted in recent years, oldtimers say. The reason is the opening of the board of directors to outsiders in 1966, something Exxon long resisted. Outside directors—necessarily knowing less about the energy business—now outnumber insiders, 11 to 8. This has had the perverse effect of increasing the power of Garvin, the chief executive, while decreasing the influence of other senior management.

"The CEO used to be the first among equals, who could and did outvote him," said one of the few executives who has left the company over the years. "Now the chairman dominates the board." Garvin partly accepts the point, but

notes that board meetings can be feisty affairs. In particular, the deliberations regarding the $1.2 billion purchase of Reliance Electric in 1979 were characterized by long debates and some dissenting votes by outside directors.

The acid test of the Exxon system, as with any organization, is results. And the results in recent years have principally been a matter of good luck. Thanks to the Organization of Petroleum Exporting Countries, and the fifteen-fold price increase it spurred over the last decade, seven of the top 10 industrial companies on Fortune magazine's 1982 list are now oil companies, up from three in 1955.

But what of Exxon's success on projects undertaken at its own volition, such as finding oil and natural gas or buying Reliance? Sometimes only sheer size seems to protect it: Exxon can afford to lose.

Questions 9.1

1. Show how politics and economics might be connected in the Exxon case. How and why might government help Exxon? Would it be hard for government to control Exxon? Why or why not?
2. Show how Exxon would fit, in turn, into pluralistic, elite, and class explanations of power. Which makes most sense?
3. What characteristics of bureaucracy (from Chapter 4) do you see with Exxon?
4. What types of power does Exxon have (from text), and what type of authority (Weber, from text) best describes Exxon?

Reading 9.2

POLITICS AMONG THE REDWOODS

G. WILLIAM DOMHOFF

Is there an elite running society? William Domhoff thinks so. He describes a ruling class "which owns a disproportionate amount of a country's wealth, receives a disproportionate amount of a country's yearly income, and contributes a disproportionate number of its members to the controlling institutions and key decision-making groups of the country." They work together to exert tremendous power and influence, nationally and internationally.

They also play together, as this article on Bohemian Grove illustrates. William Domhoff is a professor of psychology and sociology at the University of California, Santa Cruz.

Ronald Reagan is many things to many people—radio announcer, actor, union leader, rancher, governor, and now President-elect of the United States. But to high level members of the corporate business community he is just an-

Reprinted by permission from *The Progressive*, 409 East Main Street, Madison, Wisconsin 53703. Copyright ©1980, The Progressive, Inc.

other fellow Bohemian—a member of a unique California social club whose yearly retreat into its redwood grove is a major social event on the calendar of the nation's power elite.

Perhaps the dozens of detailed accounts of Reagan's ascent to the White House that are sure to appear in the next few years should explore this little-known affiliation, unmentioned in Reagan's biography in Who's Who in America, *for the Bohemian Grove has provided the setting for major events in the political careers of three former Republican Presidents and has played a role in making Reagan known on a first-name basis within the small circles of the social and corporate elites. Several of his Bohemian campmates are likely to be major advisers or officers in the new Administration.*

The Bohemian Grove is a 2,700-acre campground in a virgin redwood forest on the meandering Russian River, seventy-five miles north of San Francisco. Owned and operated by the Bohemian Club of San Francisco, it has been host since the 1890s to a three-weekend respite beginning in the middle of July. Members and their guests number anywhere from 1,500 to 1,900 men on the weekends, but as few as 300 or 400 are in attendance during the week—even most of the corporate rich work during the summer, a considerable change since the more leisurely pace that prevailed before World War II.

Bohemian campers are treated to plays, skits, symphonies, band concerts, lectures, and political commentaries by top entertainers, scholars, musicians, and government officials from the local to the national level. They also trap shoot, canoe, swim, drop by the Grove art gallery, and take guided nature tours into the outer fringe of the mountain forest. But mostly a stay at the Bohemian Grove is a time for relaxation and drinking in the modest tents, lodges, huts, bunk houses, and even tepees fitting unobtrusively into the landscape along two or three unpaved roadways that join the few "developed" acres within the Grove.

Bohemian Grove resembles nothing so much as a summer camp for overgrown Boy Scouts, or maybe a collection of university fraternities displaced to an outdoor setting. Herbert Hoover, who became a Bohemian in 1913 and held forth as the encampments' final speaker every year from 1935 until his death in 1964, once called it "the greatest men's party on Earth." It provides a respite from establishment wars and from conflicts with the various activist groups within the underclasses.

One member in four, approximately, is a major business executive, director, or lawyer within the big-business community that is outlined for list lovers in the annual Fortune *line-up of the largest firms. Such reasonably well-known multimillionaires as David Packard of Hewlett-Packard, Ray Kroc of Mac-Donald's, and America's current richest man, Daniel K. Ludwig, are among the business members. There are celebrity members, too—such well-known but fading entertainers as Art Linkletter, Phil Harris, and Ray Bolger, and such traditional writers as Irving Stone and Herman Wouk.*

Then there are the associate members, several hundred strong—lesser mortals on the status ladder, but talented men nonetheless who write the skits, act in the shows, sing in the chorus, design stage sets, play in the band or orchestra, and do the paintings and sculptures that are on sale in the Grove gal-

lery. It costs them much less to be members, and most of them come from the Bay Area around San Francisco.

There are no women in the Bohemian Club, and there are no female employes at the Bohemian Grove. Last October, the Club had to defend its employment discrimination at the Grove before California's Fair Employment and Housing Commission. The proceedings revealed something of the atmosphere at the encampments, giving outsiders an insight into the fabled spirit of Bohemia. Corporate lawyer Del Fuller, secretary of the Club, argued that the presence of women would destroy the "intimacy" of the occasion because women would "distract" the more "flirtatious" of the men from the concern with just plain fellowship. He explained that the men like to let their hair down and become "boisterous," and that they would be "inhibited" by the presence of women.

Besides, continued Fuller, the men who have to dress up as women for parts in Bohemian plays would be embarrassed to do so if women were present. Under questioning, Fuller added that he had played the part of a wood nymph in the Club's centennial celebration in 1972, wearing wings and a body stocking.

When President-elect Reagan visits this enchanted Grove—he has been a member since 1975 and was a frequent guest before that—he stays at Owl's Nest, one of 130 or so little camps of ten to thirty members in which most of the men gather during their stay. Other campsites have equally strange names— Zack, Stowaway, Woof, Sons of Toil, Cave Man, Mandalay, Toyland, and even Parsonage. Most camps are organized around a small building that serves as a kind of lodge or tavern, often housing a grand piano and an unusual contraption for mixing drinks, and cluttered with photos, drawings, and memorabilia from past encampments. The sleeping quarters are close to the main lodges.

Some camps are noted for special drinks, brunches, or luncheons. Jungle Camp talks up mint juleps, free for the asking. Halcyon has a three-foot-high martini-maker constructed out of chemical glassware. Poison Oak is remembered for a Bull's Balls Lunch, featuring the testicles from the castrated herds of a central California cattle baron. The specialty at Reagan's camp is a gin-fizz breakfast—about 100 Bohemians from other camps are invited one morning during each encampment for eggs Benedict, gin fizzes, and assorted trimmings.

Reagan's fellow Owls at the Nest are a group to be reckoned with in the corporate world. Only a few other camps can claim the concentration of corporate power that resides in this twenty-two-person campsite. They include the chairmen or presidents of United Airlines, United California Bank, Dart Industries, Carter-Hawley-Hale Stores, Dean Witter Reynolds & Co., and Pauley Petroleum, along with retired chieftains from Pacific Telephone, General Dynamics, and United Airlines. And, of course, several of these campmates sit on each other's boards of directors and on many other boards as well.

From a Reagan-watcher's point of view, Justin Dart of Dart Industries is the most important member of the camp, for he is probably Reagan's closest friend and political sponsor within the business establishment. No stranger to the Grove, Dart has been a Bohemian since 1951, and he has played a central role through the years in introducing Reagan to other business leaders, whether Bohemians or not.

Mandalay Camp, perched on the hillside about 100 feet above the Grove floor and housed in beautiful redwood buildings whose sleeping quarters are called *Condemned Row,* is one of the few camps that tops Owl's Nest in overall corporate connections. However, the chairmen and presidents it boasts from General Electric, Bankers Trust, Bank of America, and Utah Mining and Construction (now merged with General Electric) have retired from their offices in the past five or six years, so Mandalay is no longer the unequivocal Number One it used to be. Nonetheless, there are still Stephen D. Bechtel Jr., chairman of Bechtel Construction, Richard P. Cooley, chairman of Wells Fargo Bank, and Jack K. Horton, chairman of Southern California Edison, among others.

Two Reagan intimates also reside at Mandalay, which is known among Bohemians for its gin-and-lemon-juice drink, its Welsh Rarebit dinners, and plush furnishings well beyond what other camps have to offer. One of these friends is lawyer William French Smith of the Los Angeles firm of Gibson, Dunn & Crutcher. The other is George P. Shultz, vice chairman of Bechtel Construction Company and a secretary of both labor and treasury during the Nixon Administration.

Smith, who along with Dart is Reagan's closest social friend with wide connections throughout the entire range of the power elite, is a quintessential interlocking overlapper. He serves as a director of Pacific Lighting, Pacific Telephone, Pacific Mutual Life, and Jorgensen Steel, but also finds time to be a regent of the University of California, a member of the executive committee of the California Roundtable, and a member of the advisory board for the Center for Strategic and International Studies at Georgetown University, from which Reagan will draw several foreign policy advisers. Shultz, who became a top Reagan adviser only after the Republican convention, is somewhat more modest in his affiliations, serving as a director of Morgan Guaranty Trust, Sears Roebuck & Co., the Alfred P. Sloan Foundation, and that favorite bete noire of Reagan's ultra-right supporters, the Council on Foreign Relations, which has about thirty-five members in common with the Bohemian Club.

Another prominent Republican at Mandalay who came to be a Reagan adviser is former President Gerald R. Ford. A close friend of Leonard K. Firestone of the tire manufacturing fortune, Ford was Firestone's guest at Mandalay several times before becoming a member of the Bohemian Club in 1977.

Hill Billies is another camp with a strong core of business executives, and it is the camp of the Vice President-elect of the United States, George Bush. The corporate parallels between the Bush and Reagan camps are instructive. Reagan rubs shoulders with the chairman of United Airlines, but Bush can lay claim to being a chum of the president of Eastern Airlines. Reagan's camp has the chair of United California Bank, but the Hill Billies include among their twenty-three members the president of the Bank of America. The president of Dean Witter Reynolds may be at Owl's Nest, but the first vice president of Blyth Eastman Dillon is under the Hill Billies' tent. When it comes to overall corporate connections, however, Hill Billies seems to have the edge, for it houses executives and directors from General Motors, Southern Pacific, Westinghouse Electric, B.F. Goodrich, Morgan Guaranty Trust, Mutual Life Insurance of New York, Superior Oil, and Metromedia.

One other member of Hill Billies, aside from Bush, recently appeared in the news: Alden W. Clausen, president of the Bank of America, was nominated by Jimmy Carter to be the next head of the World Bank. According to press reports, Carter's aides approached George P. Shultz to clear Clausen's acceptability should Reagan win the forthcoming election. Reagan gave his approval, but it is not recorded whether he was chagrined to learn from a member of Mandalay that someone from Hill Billies had gained Carter's nod instead of one of his fellow Owls.

The guest list of about 400 for each year's retreat only adds to the impression that the Grove is a playground for the powerful. Among the guests at Owl's Nest in 1980, for example, was Charles F. Luce, chairman of Consolidated Edison of New York, hosted by Edward Carlson, chairman of United Airlines. Also at Owl's Nest was William E. Simon, former Secretary of the Treasury and now a Reagan adviser, invited by Justin Dart. Guests at Mandalay included Donald M. Kendall, chairman of Pepsico and a Nixon intimate; Reginald Jones, chairman of General Electric and an adviser to Carter, and Walter B. Wriston, chairman of Citicorp and an adviser to Reagan. David Rockefeller, chairman of Chase Manhattan Bank, stayed at Stowaway as a guest of William A. Hewitt, chairman of Deere & Co. Willard C. Butcher, president of the same Chase Manhattan, was at Cave Man with John E. Swearingen, chairman of Standard Oil of Indiana. Robert D. Stuart Jr., chairman of Quaker Oats, was at the Isles of Aves with Reagan adviser Caspar Weinberger, a vice president at Bechtel Corporation and a director of Quaker Oats.

Simon at Owl's Nest and Wriston at Mandalay were not the only Reagan advisers on the 1980 guest list. Campaign chairman William Casey, a Wall Street lawyer, was staying at the Parsonage, a guest of Darrell M. Trent, himself an academic adviser to Reagan. Senator Paul D. Laxalt, at one point in charge of keeping Reagan from saying anything off the cuff, dropped in at Mandalay as the guest of a retired Anheuser-Busch executive, John Flanigan. Jack Kemp, the tax-cutting member of Congress who urged Reagan to appeal to blue-collar workers in the North, was at Toyland, the guest of George Lenczowski, a political scientist of the University of California, Berkeley, who also serves as an adviser to a Reagan-oriented think tank, the American Enterprise Institute.

How much does all this matter? What difference does it make that a socially chummy corporate community likes to do some drinking and joking with lots of Republicans and a few Democrats in rustic little campsites in the California redwoods? After all, the official motto of the club is "weaving spiders come not here," and most members agree that 80 per cent of those in attendance are so overwhelmed by the fine food, strong drink, and sterling entertainment that they couldn't remember the details of a new policy or a diabolical conspiracy from one day to the next even if they had tried to plan one. The Bohemian Grove is not a place of power in the sense of attempting to formulate new policies. Corporate board rooms, charitable foundations, and such discussion groups as the Conference Board, Committee for Economic Development, Business Council, Business Roundtable, and, yes, even the Council on Foreign Relations, are the institutional settings for those kinds of activities.

But if the Bohemian Grove is not a place of power, it is nonetheless a place *where powerful people congregate, and as such it has provided the setting for new developments in Republican politics at the Presidential level ever since 1927, when Herbert Hoover was sitting by his tent in Cave Man camp just as President Calvin Coolidge made his cryptic announcement, "I do not choose to run for President in 1928." And it was then that the Hoover campaign began. "Within an hour," Hoover wrote in his memoirs, "a hundred men—publishers, editors, public officials, and others from all over the country who were at the Grove—came to my camp demanding that I announce my candidacy."*

Dwight D. Eisenhower made what is thought to be his first general pitch to the Republican establishment with a speech at the Grove in 1950, and then became an honorary member in the same year. It was a short speech, delivered without notes, and it drew applause when Ike declared he didn't see why someone who wouldn't sign a loyalty oath should have the right to teach in a state university.

Before the talk, Eisenhower had lunch at Cave Man with Herbert Hoover and his campmates, most of whom supported even more conservative candidates than Eisenhower. Among those present as a guest was Richard Nixon, who had to wait until 1953, after he was Vice President, to become a Bohemian and a Cave Man. Nixon's memoirs suggest that a serious political discussion took place at Cave Man after the Eisenhower speech:

"After Eisenhower's speech we went back to Cave Man Camp and sat around the campfire appraising it. Everyone liked Eisenhower, but the feeling was that he had a long way to go before he would have the experience, the depth, and the understanding to be President. But it struck me forcibly that Eisenhower's personality and personal mystique had deeply impressed the skeptical and critical Cave Man audience."

Nixon himself launched his first successful Presidential campaign at the 1967 encampment by means of a Lakeside talk not far from the Owl Shrine.

He called this talk "the speech that gave me the most pleasure and satisfaction of my political career"—and one that "in many important ways marked the first milestone on my road to the Presidency . . . an unparalleled opportunity to reach some of the most important and influential men, not just from California, but from across the country." The speech was important because it unveiled a "new" Nixon to the corporate establishment, a Nixon who had decided to take the high road and rise above his usual anti-communist harangues. His new tack was what he called a "sophisticated" hard line, and apparently it met with approval from the assembled Bohemians.

The Grove also was helpful to Nixon in another way in 1967, for it was there that he and Reagan made a deal calling for Nixon to go first in Republican primaries against the more moderate opposition, with Reagan jumping in only if Nixon faltered. The ubiquitous William F. Buckley Jr. is the source of this story, but Nixon acknowledges in his memoirs that he and Reagan had a "candid discussion of the political situation as we sat outdoors on a bench under one of the giant redwoods."

It seems worthwhile to keep an eye out for the Bohemian Connection in understanding both the rise of Ronald Reagan and his forthcoming Presidency, for the Bohemian Grove provides an ideal setting for informal politics, a place to take an off-the-record look at potential candidates and advisers and to gain a first-hand impresson of a person's style and personality.

And if George P. Shultz, William French Smith, Caspar Weinberger, and a few other of the many Bohemians who supported Reagan end up in his new Administration, the only question will be whether to hold the July Cabinet meetings at Mandalay, Hill Billies, or Owl's Nest.

Questions 9.2

1. How would a pluralist argue with Domhoff over the significance of Bohemian Grove?
2. Domhoff notes a "quintessential interlocking overlapper." What is it? What is its importance for the political economy?
3. "So certain people get together recreationally once in a while—what's wrong with that?" Discuss both sides.

10

Population
and Ecology

Previous chapters in this section on social organization have examined concepts dealing with groups, categories, aggregations, and institutions. In this chapter, we will show how social organization may be analyzed through the study of population and human ecology. Population refers to the number of people in a given unit, as in a state, society, world, or universe. **Human ecology** refers to the adaptation of people to their physical environment, their location in space. **Demography** is the study of human population, its distribution, composition, and change.

As an introduction to some of the important techniques and variables, suppose we try a demographic analysis of a college sociology class. What does the professor see as he looks out at the mass of eager young faces? The total population of the class selected is 130, of which eighty are females and fifty are males. There are four Afro-Americans, eleven Asian-Americans, and 115 Caucasian-Americans. The age distribution of this "society" is overwhelmingly in the nineteen to twenty-three category, with trace amounts in ages up to forty-five. Both birth and death rates for this "society" are exceedingly low. Apparently this represents a very healthy but nonfertile tribe. The life expectancy for the majority will be one semester, although for some it may be at least double that.

Migration variables are peculiar for this tribe. Temporary immigration ("in-migration") occurs on those occasions when the class is planning to discuss sex or deviant behavior. Permanent emigration ("out-migration") occurs just before tests are scheduled or papers are due.

Ecologically, this class is also interesting. After several meetings, they arrange themselves in space consistently and predictably. There are occasional shifts as dating alliances change, but generally they sit in the same seats throughout the semester. Part of the patterning may be explained by classical ecological processes. Cooperation: *X* takes great notes, so she is constantly surrounded by *A*, *B*, and *C* (at least I think that's the reason). Competition: When asked why they sit in front, several have said they pay more attention to what is being said and they feel the instructor is more likely to remember them; consequently, they will get better grades. Films of migrating apes have shown ecological processes at work: older males proceed in front, younger males at the rear, and females protected in the middle. Do these principles apply in your classroom?

POPULATION

Demographers study populations from several viewpoints. They may want to look at population growth or its general characteristics—a statistical portrait, so to speak. A number of different variables may be used. For example, if the issue is population growth, the important variables are births, deaths, and immigration. (Population growth = births − deaths + immigration.) If the concern is a general description of the population, then age, sex, race, and ethnicity profiles and perhaps patterns of internal migration may be examined. These two concerns (growth potential and general characteristics) are related—the number of young and old people in a population as well as the number of women in childbearing ages will have an effect on birth and death rates. In the following paragraphs we will look at some of the major population variables and show how they are used in the United States and in some other societies.

Fertility
Fertility refers to the number of children born. There are several ways to measure fertility. The birth rate (or crude birth rate) is the number of live births per 1,000 people in the population. These data are often used because they are easily collected but they ignore the age structure of the population. The *general fertility rate* is a better measure and is defined as the number of births per 1,000 women aged fifteen through forty-four. The *total fertility rate* is an estimate of the average number of children born to each woman based on current rates.

Fertility has both a biological and social aspect. The physical or biological ability to reproduce (also known as fecundity) is present in most of us, and yet actual fertility rates differ greatly. A nineteenth-century Russian woman gave birth to sixty-nine children; the Hutterite women (of North and South Dakota and Canada) were averaging more than twelve children each in the 1930s; cur-

TABLE 10.1   Birth, General Fertility, and Death Rates in the United States for Selected Years

	Birth	General Fertility	Death
1930	21.3	88	11.5
1940	19.4	80	10.8
1950	23.9	106	9.6
1960	23.8	118	9.5
1970	18.2	87.9	9.4
1972	15.6	73.4	9.4
1974	14.9	68.4	9.1
1976	14.8	65.8	8.9
1978	15.3	66.6	8.8
1980	15.8	67.7	8.7
1981	15.9	67.6	8.7

U.S. Bureau of the Census, *Statistical Abstract of the United States, 1980* (101st ed.), Washington, D.C.; and *Vital Statistics.*

rently American women are averaging about two children each. The social influences on fertility are the factors that vary from one society to another. For example, fertility would be affected by age at marriage, the proportion of people who never marry, frequency of sexual intercourse, whether birth control techniques are used and how effective they are. These factors are influenced by tradition, lifestyle, standard of living, and countless other social values.[1]

Birth rates and general fertility rates in the United States are shown in Table 10.1. The birth rate reached a high of twenty-six in the late 1940s, remained around twenty-four through 1960, and then dropped to a low of 14.8 in 1976. Since that time it has been increasing slowly. The general fertility rate dropped to 65.8 in 1976—its lowest level in U.S. history (or at least since such records have been kept)—and has gone up slightly since then. The total fertility rate in 1980 was 1,875 per 1,000 women, and this has also been increasing slowly from its low of 1,768 in 1976. This means that women are averaging 1.9 children each. *Replacement level* is defined as the average number of births necessary per woman over her lifetime (say seventy years) for the population eventually to reach zero growth. The 1.8 and 1.9 births per woman is well below the replacement level but population continues to increase in the United States because of large increases in the number of women of reproductive age. The Census Bureau reports that this means that even if the present low fertility rates were to persist for some time, the population of the United States would still continue to grow by natural increase until well into the twenty-first century.

Understanding why fertility rates fluctuate will help us predict social conditions of the future, but the factors are many and complicated. This is what seems to be happening: More young women are remaining single, and divorce

---

[1] The source for this paragraph is *Population* by John Weeks (Belmont, Calif.: Wadsworth, 1978), Chapter 4.

rates are rising (see the discussion in Chapter 7). Women, especially those in the prime childbearing ages of twenty through thirty-four, are either not having or are putting off having children. A 1982 Census Bureau paper reported that *first* births to women in their thirties more than doubled in the 1970s. This produced a "mini–baby boom" and may have helped account for the slight birth rate increase in the late 1970s, since birth rates of women in their teens and early twenties continued to drop. The increased freedom of women to work outside the home, the increased use of contraceptives, and changing viewpoints about family roles have contributed to the lower birth rate. Unemployment rates and a sluggish economy are probably also contributing factors.

Worldwide birth rates in 1980 were around twenty-seven to twenty-nine per 1,000 people. African countries were highest with rates in the forties, Latin American countries were in the thirties, and the birth rates in Asian countries were about average. Countries in Europe, North America, and Oceania (Australia and New Zealand), like the United States, have rates about half the world rate. (Some of these comparisons can be seen later in this chapter in Table 10.3.) High fertility rates may, if mortality rates are low, lead to rapid population growth, and later in this chapter we will examine some of the implications and consequences.

Mortality

Mortality is the number of deaths occurring in a population. It is typically represented by the death rate (or crude death rate), which is the total deaths per 1,000 people in the population. Because death rates vary by age and sex, a more precise measure is the age-sex-specific death rate, which categorizes deaths of males and females in five-year groups—for example, males fifteen through nineteen and females fifteen through nineteen. A third useful measure is *life expectancy*. This predicts one's expectation of length of life at birth based on risks of death for people born in that year.

Mortality has two major components, life span and longevity. Life span refers to the oldest age to which human beings can live. There is some uncertainty as to just what the limits are—reports of people living to 110 and even to 120 years of age are not unheard of, and medical science continues to increase these outer limits. Longevity refers to the ability to remain alive from one year to the next, that is, to resist death. Both biological as well as social factors, of course, are integral to one's longevity. Biological determinants would include inherited genetic characteristics, strength of organs, and resistance to disease. Social factors would include lifestyle and the amount of stress and conflict it produces, the way society takes care of its members—especially the elderly— and so on. The Abkhasians in Russia and the Vilcabambas in Ecuador seem to live very long lives; it has been suggested this is due to their simple, unchanging lifestyle, their avoidance of stress, and their tendency to remain physically and mentally active throughout their lives.[2]

The importance of social factors as explanations of longevity and mor-

---

[2]The major source for these paragraphs on mortality is again *Population* by Weeks (see footnote 1). See his Chapter 6, especially pp. 106–108 and 114–119.

tality can be seen in other ways. Studies have shown that as occupational prestige goes up, death rates go down. This may be due to greater work hazards in lower-class occupations. However, since the mortality levels of "nonworking" wives seem to parallel those of their husbands, lifestyle is apparently a major factor as well. Studies have also found that deaths from communicable diseases such as tuberculosis and pneumonia are higher among lower-class people, while deaths from coronaries, diabetes, and stroke increase with upward social mobility. Yet another study has found that for virtually every major cause of death, white males with at least one year of college had lower risks of death than those with less education. The existence of mortality rate differences between different racial and ethnic groups is also probably best explained in terms of income, educational, and lifestyle differences.

Death rates in the United States are also shown in Table 10.1. We see that they have declined, but over the last fifty years they haven't changed much and over the last decade, hardly at all. Sharp drops in the death rate occurred in the late nineteenth and early twentieth centuries as medical science gained control of many infectious diseases. Life expectancy has risen accordingly to its current rates of about seventy years for males and seventy-seven for females. Death rates in European countries are very similar to ours, but rates in some other countries (see Table 10.3) are double ours. This is changing rapidly, however, as health care and disease control measures spread and countries share their discoveries. So we witness a growth in population caused not by rising fertility, but by declining mortality.

Migration

Migration is defined as a permanent change of residence, with the consequent relocation of one's interests and activities. The number of dimensions—who moves, how often, where, and why—makes migration the most complex of the population processes. Internal migration generally describes migration within a country, while international migration refers to migration from one country to another. There are many reasons why people migrate, and these have been summarized into what is called the "push-pull" theory. This theory suggests that one reason people move is because they are pushed out of their original home—by a bad climate, unpleasant treatment by others, legal harassment, and so on. The other reason people move is because they are pulled by the attractions of another place. Those close to this theory suggest that motivation to improve one's lot is stronger than the desire to escape existing conditions; we could conclude that the *pull* motivation is more influential than the *push*. It does seem, as Weeks points out, that migration associated with career advancement is a common theme in society today.[3]

Americans are a very mobile group—forty-five percent of all persons five years old and over moved during the 1975–1980 period. Some types are more prone to migration than others, however. Young adults have the highest rates—seventy-seven percent of those aged twenty-five through twenty-nine moved be-

---

[3]See *Population* by John Weeks (see footnote 1), Chapter 7.

tween 1975 and 1980. Often these are young married couples with no children or very young children. College graduates are more likely to move than high school graduates, who in turn are more mobile than those with less education. All of this tends to support the idea that people are being pulled to areas that are more economically attractive for them.

Patterns of internal migration continually change. People used to migrate from farm to city, and later from city to suburb. In the middle and late 1970s, a new trend developed—the rapid growth of small communities and increasing migration to rural areas. Rural counties that had lost population in the 1960s were gaining again in the 1970s. The Census Bureau reported in 1980 that non-metropolitan areas continued to grow more rapidly than metropolitan areas. Migration flow in the United States is directed to rural and to sunbelt areas; people are leaving the Northeast and North Central states and moving to the West and South. Florida, California, and Texas gained the most people between 1970 and 1980, each showing an average gain of over 200,000 people a year. No other state gained as many as 100,000 a year. To give you some idea of who is going where, Table 10.2 shows the *percentage* population change for selected states. It is apparent that population is being redistributed, at least in part, as a result of changing recreation and leisure patterns.

International migration to the United States has gone through several stages. Prior to World War I, immigrants were admitted freely. Then, as people became concerned about "racial purity," job competition, and political "undesirables," immigration laws became very restrictive. Policies were relaxed somewhat in the middle 1960s, but admission quotas continue to be weighted in favor of professional occupations, while the overall numbers allowed in are small. In 1979, approximately 460,000 people immigrated to the United States. Figure 10.1 shows where most of them came from.

The consequences of migration are many. For the individual, uprooting oneself and trying to adapt to a new environment will involve stress, and the burden of coping will be greater in the absence of familiar support groups. The

TABLE 10.2 Population Change in the United States 1970–1980 (National Population Increased 11.4 Percent)

States Losing Population or Gaining Less Than 4%	Percent Change	States Gaining Most Population	Percent Change
New York	−3.8	Nevada	63.5
Rhode Island	−0.3	Arizona	53.1
Pennsylvania	0.6	Florida	43.4
Massachusetts	0.8	Wyoming	41.6
Ohio	1.3	Utah	37.9
Connecticut	2.5	Alaska	32.4
New Jersey	2.7	Idaho	32.4
Illinois	2.8	Colorado	30.7
Iowa	3.1	New Mexico	27.8
South Dakota	3.6	Texas	27.1

"Population Profile of the United States: 1980," *Current Population Reports*, Series P-20, no. 363.

community being left may lose a valuable segment of its population. The target community has a growing population to assimilate with the accompanying problems of housing, mass transit, health care, job opportunities, municipal services, and how to pay for it all. This has led some communities and even states to devise policies to limit migration to their areas.

Other Population Measures

Fertility, mortality, and migration are the major demographic variables, but there are some other measures that help describe certain population characteristics. One of the simplest and most direct measures is population size. The world population is over four billion, and the population of the United States in January 1982 was 230 million. That means we are smaller than Russia (about 270 million) and India (about 700 million) but larger than Canada (about twenty-five million) and France (about fifty-five million). More detailed profiles based on sex, age, race, religion, and ethnicity are also of interest. *Sex ratio* is defined as the number of males per 100 females. The sex ratio in the United States in 1980 was around ninety-five, or ninety-five males for every 100 females. Regional patterns show that large cities and the New England and Atlantic states have a low sex ratio (fewer males than females), whereas rural areas and the Mountain and Western states have a high sex ratio (more men than women). The *median age* of a population designates the midpoint of the age range. Median age data can give us some hints about longevity in a society. In 1980 the median age of whites in the United States was thirty-one, of blacks twenty-five, and of hispanics twenty-three. The U.S. median age in 1970 was

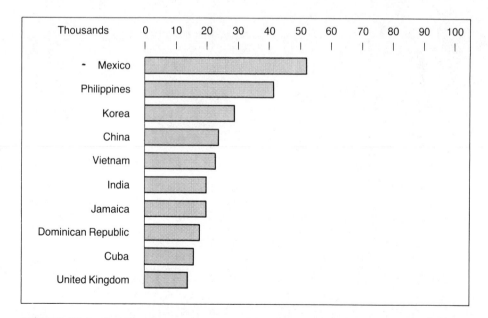

FIGURE 10.1   Immigrants, by Selected Country of Birth, 1979. From U.S. Bureau of Census, *Statistical Abstract of the United States, 1981* **(2d ed.), Washington, D.C., p. 88.**

twenty-eight, and in 1980 was thirty, which suggests that our population is getting older. An age profile of the U.S. population indicates the same thing— fewer teenagers, and more elderly people and people in their late twenties and thirties. Between 1970 and 1980, the population aged fourteen and younger decreased by almost seven million people, while the population sixty-five years old and over grew from twenty to 25.5 million, an increase of twenty-eight percent.

Several variables, such as age and sex, can be profiled together graphically in a figure called a population pyramid. Figures 10.2 to 10.5 illustrate the distinctive age and sex profiles present in different communities and countries. Figure 10.2 gives an age-sex profile for Norfolk, Virginia, a city with a large military base and, consequently, a concentration of young people, especially young males. Figure 10.3 profiles St. Petersburg, Florida, a city attracting older, retired people. Countries also produce distinctive population pictures depending on their birth and death rates. Mexico (Figure 10.4) has a high birth rate and a young population, while Sweden (Figure 10.5) has a low birth rate and a balanced population in terms of age. As you look at these profiles, imagine the types of problems and social consequences suggested by each. What types of social services would be necessary given each profile?

We have examined the major population variables—fertility, mortality, and migration—and other measures which allow demographers to predict future population changes and to provide a statistical portrait of societies. Population data, carefully collected and analyzed, are useful in social planning. Population profiles in terms of age and sex enable planners to determine the number of schools needed, the number and proportion of apartments and homes to build,

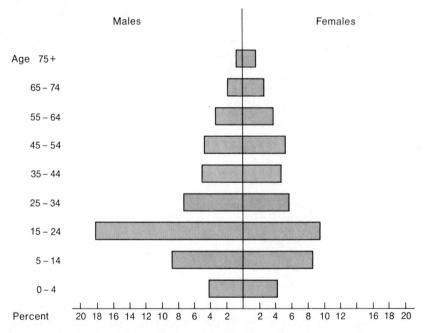

FIGURE 10.2   Population Pyramid for Norfolk, Virginia, 1970.

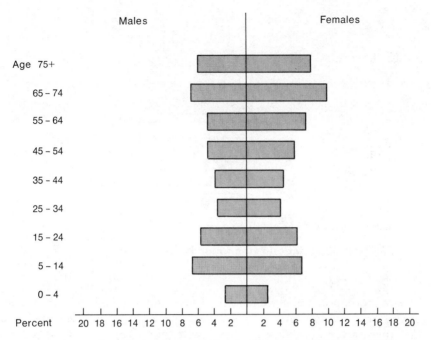

FIGURE 10.3   Population Pyramid for St. Petersburg, Florida, 1970.

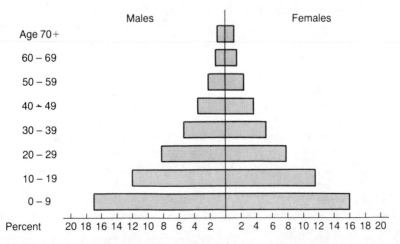

FIGURE 10.4   Population Pyramid for Mexico, 1978.

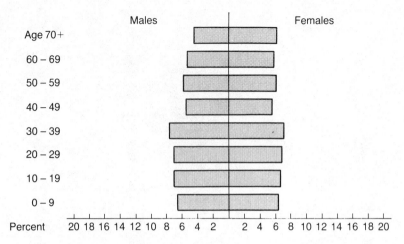

FIGURE 10.5 Population Pyramid for Sweden, 1978.

the types of recreation and child care facilities required, and so forth. When we hear that a group of city planners is developing a community with no schools (because there are no children), no tennis courts (because tennis is too strenuous), and many recreation centers and shuffleboard courts, it is safe to assume that population data evidenced a need for a planned community for the elderly.

HUMAN ECOLOGY

Biologists have for some time studied the interrelationships and interdependence of plants and animals—the balance of nature. Living organisms are dependent on other organisms and pattern themselves in space accordingly. Why don't porcupines live in the desert? It may be because they would get sand in their quills, but most certainly because their food supply—the bark of certain trees—does not grow there. Likewise, all organisms live in certain places and patterns but not in others. Social scientists noticed that people, too, locate themselves in space in specific patterns, and this gave rise to the study of human ecology.

Flying over the United States, we see that people are not equally distributed but are grouped in clusters. There are fewer clusters in the West and more in the East. Most of the clusters are on rivers, lakes, or oceans. Highways run through the clusters, and various natural resources are nearby. There are fewer clusters where the climate is severe or the terrain rugged. People pattern themselves in space in predictable ways. They group together in cities, for in cities mutual cooperation and a complex division of labor allow people to accomplish much more than they could as isolated individuals. These cities are located to take maximum advantage of natural factors—waterways for transportation, resources for technological needs.

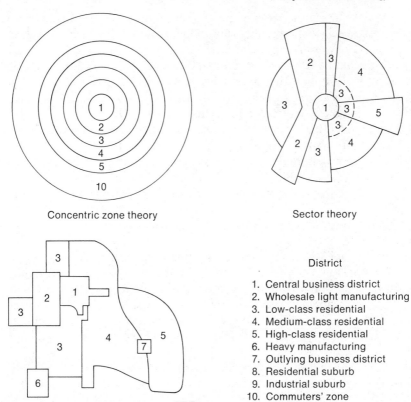

Concentric zone theory

Sector theory

District

1. Central business district
2. Wholesale light manufacturing
3. Low-class residential
4. Medium-class residential
5. High-class residential
6. Heavy manufacturing
7. Outlying business district
8. Residential suburb
9. Industrial suburb
10. Commuters' zone

Multiple nuclei theory

**FIGURE 10.6   Three Generalizations of the Internal Structure of Cities.
From C. D. Harris and Edward L. Ullman, *Annals* 242 (November 1945),
pp. 7–17.**

If we look more closely at the cities, we see that they also have consistent
patterns. One city patterning first suggested by Ernest Burgess has five concentric circles or zones (see Figure 10.6). The small inner circle is called the
central business district and contains the major stores, banks, offices, and government buildings, the downtown area of the city. The next circle is called the
zone in transition and contains rundown buildings, slums, a high proportion of
minority groups, some industry, and higher rates of unemployment. The third
ring is called the workingman's zone and contains small apartment buildings
and older single-dwelling units. The middle-class residential district is the
fourth zone and contains better private residences and high-class apartments.
Finally, the suburban or commuter's zone contains larger estates, golf courses,
and makes up the upper-class residential district. Generally speaking, as one
moves from Zone 1 (central business district) outward toward the suburbs, pop-

ulation density decreases, home ownership increases, the proportion of foreign-born decreases, social class rises, crime rate decreases, land cost decreases, and family size decreases. The pattern of the city may be affected by how fast the city develops, by the influence of cars, and by natural obstacles—hills, oceans, rivers. So a given city may not fit this design exactly, but many cities are close to this general pattern.

Other consistent city patternings have been suggested and are also described in Figure 10.6. Homer Hoyt feels that cities are more accurately described as sectors with a specific type of land use than as concentric zones. He believes that expensive high-rent areas follow patterns of city growth outward from the center like wedges of pie or spokes of a wheel. High-rent areas develop along the path of major streets, highways, or other major transportation lines. This type of growth outward could be along rivers or rapid transit systems, for example, and would often cut across the concentric circles suggested by Burgess.

Multiple nuclei describe a city in which a number of specialized centers or downtowns develop, each of which exerts dominance over its particular area. These centers may exist from the beginning of a city's development (as in London) or may develop later as the city grows and expands. Industry and residential areas grow up around each nucleus. Los Angeles, which has been called "a bunch of suburbs in search of a city," is an example of multiple-nuclei development.

More recent theories of city patterning include social area analysis and factorial ecology. These techniques focus on a city's census tracts and obtain information across many variables (median rent, median education, percentage of the population married and employed, the racial and ethnic mix, and so on). Tracts are then compared in an attempt to isolate the factors that distinguish between tracts and that explain city patterning. These techniques are usually computerized and are very precise.[4]

How are these patterns explained? People arrange themselves in space according to social and cultural values that they believe to be important. It is apparent from previous paragraphs that economic competition has much to do with spatial arrangement in cities. Land is in greatest demand and, therefore, is most expensive in the center of the city. Banks, large stores, businesses, office buildings, and government buildings can afford the cost of locating here because of their importance, business volume, and/or financial base. Structures whose economic effect is less dramatic—homes, apartment buildings, schools, country clubs—are usually located away from the center of the city where land

---

[4]Original sources referred to in this section include: Ernest Burgess, "The Growth of the City," in Robert Park and Ernest Burgess, *The City* (Chicago: University of Chicago Press, 1925), p. 51; Homer Hoyt, *The Structure and Growth of Residential Neighborhoods in American Cities*, U.S. Federal Housing Administration (Washington, D.C.: U.S. Government Printing Office, 1939), Chapter 6; and C. D. Harris and Edward L. Ullman, "The Nature of Cities," *The Annals* 242 (November 1945), pp. 7–17.

Also see the discussion and summary of these theories in Noel Gist and Sylvia Fava, *Urban Society*, 6th ed. (New York: Thomas Y. Crowell, 1974), Chapter 6; or Ralph Thomlinson, *Urban Structure* (New York: Random House, 1969), Chapter 8.

is cheaper. Other social values are also reflected. Many cities have set aside large green areas in those parts of the city where land is most expensive. Parks near the centers of London and Paris, the Boston Commons, and Central Park in New York are but a few of numerous examples illustrating that economic competition is not the sole determining factor in spatial arrangement. Racial and religious minority groups generally reside in separate areas of the city. This separation or segregation sometimes occurs by choice of the minority group, but more often it represents the wishes and values of the majority group. Social-class groupings also separate themselves into different parts of the city, and inevitably areas develop reputations that attract certain types of people and discourage others. As Otis and Beverly Duncan have pointed out, "spatial distances between occupation groups are closely related to their social distance."[5] In a variety of ways, then, we see that spatial arrangement reflects social and cultural values.

It is both important and interesting to note that spatial arrangement *affects* social interaction. People interact with those who live next door or across the street, unless it's a wide and busy street. People living toward the middle of the block have more social contacts than those living on corners. Friendships develop more on the side of the house where the driveway is located, especially if there are adjacent driveways—driveways are natural areas for gathering and talking. A family that doesn't mix or fit or is unfriendly often acts as a boundary; neighbors have difficulty interacting past this boundary as they would across a busy street. Such habits become so ingrained that when a new family moves into the house, it may inherit the previous family's reputation as a social boundary.[6]

William Michelson in his book *Man and His Urban Environment* outlines a number of factors that correlate with spatial arrangements in addition to those we have already mentioned. He finds, for example, that physical and social pathologies—crime and social and physical illness—are related to certain spatial factors. The health of women and their children living in self-contained houses was compared with the health of those living in three- and four-story apartments. The sickness rate of the apartment dwellers was fifty-seven percent greater than the sickness rate of those living in houses as measured by first-consultation rates for any ailment. The differences were attributed to the cramped space and greater isolation of women in apartments removed from the ground. This conclusion is underlined by the fact that the women in apartments who did not have young children and were therefore able to come and go from their homes more freely had excellent health. High noise levels are related to the incidence of diseases that involve tension. Studies of overcrowding (many persons per room) and high density (many persons per acre) have found generally that *density* is more related to pathology than is overcrowding. For exam-

[5]The article by Otis Dudley Duncan and Beverly Duncan, "Residential Distribution and Occupational Stratification," is quoted here from Thomlinson's book, *Urban Structure*, pp. 12–13 (see footnote 4).

[6]For a detailed description of these interaction patterns, see William H. Whyte, Jr., *The Organization Man* (New York: Simon and Schuster, 1956), Chapter 25.

ple, in one study (after controlling for other social characteristics) the researchers found in several instances that domestic internal overcrowding (that is, at home) was not related to students' achievement in school, but the number of families on the block (density) was. Michelson reminds us that although spatial arrangement may be important, its effects are modified by cultural values. Compare, for example, the way Japanese make use of internal and external space with how Americans make use of the same space.

Different types of people have different spatial preferences. Michelson reports that people who value convenience highly are likely to prefer more mixed land uses and small lot sizes; people who value individualism highly prefer larger lot sizes. People with cosmopolitan lifestyles desire more physical separation from neighbors and place less emphasis on being near facilities and services than do people whose interests are local. Research indicates that children up to about the age of seven living in high-rise apartments cling much more closely to their parents than do children in single-family homes, who become independent at an earlier age. But past that age the patterns reverse—when they become more mobile, children living in high-rise apartment buildings spend much more time away from home than do children living in single-family houses. Finally, one study reports that although apartment dwellers do suffer more from noise disturbance than people living in homes, their main complaint is the restriction they feel on making noise themselves; this affects their leisure patterns and leads them to such sedentary practices as watching television.[7]

Ecologists use the terms *centralization, decentralization, segregation, invasion,* and *succession* to describe specific types of spatial arrangements. **Centralization** describes the tendency of people to gather around some central or pivotal point in a city. Centralization allows citizens to better fulfill social and economic needs and functions and is represented in most American cities by the central business district. **Decentralization**, on the other hand, refers to the tendency to move away from the central focus. Decentralization probably occurs at least partly because of dissatisfaction with certain of the consequences of centralization—traffic, crowds, noise, concrete, and so on—and is seen in the United States in the rush to the suburbs. **Segregation** refers to the clustering together of similar people. These similarities may be along the lines of occupation, race, religion, nationality, ethnicity, or education. **Invasion** refers to the penetration of one group or function into an area dominated by another group or function. **Succession** refers to the complete displacement or removal of the established group and represents the end product of invasion. The invasion-succession process often produces tension, hostility, and sometimes overt conflict.[8]

A brief look at the ongoing drama of the local faculty dining room illustrates some of these ecological concepts. The room was originally segregated:

---

[7]See William Michelson, *Man and His Urban Environment* (Reading, Mass.: Addison-Wesley, 1970). The comments in these two paragraphs are drawn especially from pp. 98–99, 158, 161, and 193–195.

[8]This is summarized from Thomlinson, *Urban Structure*, pp. 152–153 (see footnote 4).

faculty ate there, students ate elsewhere. Segregation also existed within the room: faculty generally sat on the south side of the room, and nonteaching staff—secretaries and administrators—sat on the north side of the room. As the college population grew, students were crowded out of other eating areas and began moving into the faculty room. Invasion had begun. Students found that the room made a convenient study area, and they brought stacks of books and papers, which further crowded out the faculty. Finally, the faculty gave up and moved elsewhere as the students took over the room. Alas, succession had occurred. . . .

Ecological arrangement in the United States has undergone change. This used to be a predominantly rural country; now most Americans live in cities or very near them. The number of people living on farms (about six million in 1980) has been declining over the past forty years as can be seen in Figure 10.7. As nations undergo technological and industrial development, probably it is inevitable that they become more and more urbanized. The transformation from rural to urban and the increased problems of the urbanized society have led to comparisons between the two ways of life. Urban life is seen as secondary, tense, complicated, and anonymous, and rural life is seen as primary, simple, peaceful, and benign. This tendency to idealize rural life may partially explain the current rush to the suburbs. Nostalgia for the rural existence may be based on fact or on wishful thinking, but some rural-urban behavioral differences do exist. There seems to be greater religious and political tolerance in cities and greater religious observance (church attendance) in rural areas. There is more

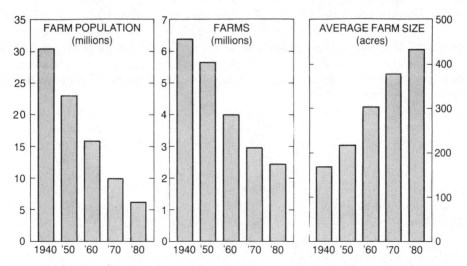

FIGURE 10.7 Changes in Farming: 1940 to 1980. From U.S. Bureau of the Census, *Statistical Abstract of the United States, 1981* (102d ed.), Washington, D.C., p. 654.

change in cities, more stability in rural areas. There is a higher level of education and a lower birth rate in cities. There is more suicide, divorce, and a lower proportion of married people in the cities. Rates of mental illness, illegitimacy, and crime may be slightly higher in cities, but because cities keep statistics better than rural areas, we cannot be sure.[9] Technological change and the spreading influence of the mass media have in a sense given all—rural and urban dwellers alike—contact with a similar culture and set of values. The result is that many former differences between rural and urban people are rapidly disappearing.

A related ecological phenomenon is the exodus from the city to the suburbs, especially by whites. The area near the center of the city (zone in transition or workingman's zone) often offers the least expensive housing in the city. As a result, lower-class and minority group members migrate into these areas, and as they move in others who can afford it leave for the suburbs. The Bureau of the Census reported in 1970 that for the first time, suburbanites outnumbered city dwellers. This exodus continued throughout the 1970s. Between 1970 and 1980, the population of central cities declined by more than thirteen million people. Of the seven metropolitan areas with a 1970 population of more than three million, four (New York, Philadelphia, Detroit, and Boston) declined in population, and one (Chicago) gained slightly between 1970 and 1980. Only two (Los Angeles and San Francisco) grew significantly. During the 1970s, central cities lost more white population than they gained black population. An interesting parallel trend developed, especially in the late 1970s: Suburbs gained black population at a faster rate than they gained white population. As blacks are able to afford it, they escape the central city and head for the suburbs as whites did before them. The heavy migration of blacks to central cities starting in the 1950s has meant that several of our largest cities have black majorities—America has become more and more racially segregated. The public school enrollments of Washington, D.C., Newark, Atlanta, San Antonio, New Orleans, Oakland, and Richmond, Virginia were all over seventy-five percent nonwhite and Hispanic in 1977. This increasing segregation is an urgent problem that American cities in particular and society in general must solve. We should note that all is not well even in white middle-class suburbia: Crime rates are going up in suburbs as fast as or faster than in city centers.

Another ecological trend occurring in the United States in the latter half of the twentieth century is the development of strip cities or megalopolises. One city and its suburbs merge and grow into an adjacent city and its suburbs. The eventual result is an unbroken series of cities for tens, and even hundreds of miles. Travelers at night over the East Coast report a constant chain of lights from north of Boston to south of Richmond, a 600-mile city. If urban or near-urban populations continue to grow, strip cities can be anticipated along the West Coast from San Francisco to San Diego, in the Midwest around the Great Lakes, in the Pacific Northwest, along both Florida coasts, and in many other places throughout the country.

---

[9]Rural-urban differences are discussed and summarized in Bernard Berelson and Gary Steiner's book, *Human Behavior* (New York: Harcourt Brace Jovanovich, 1964), pp. 606–607.

PROBLEM ASPECTS

As well as providing important information about the characteristics of societies, the study of population and human ecology calls attention to several important problems. One is what many feel will become our most serious social problem: the population explosion. For ages the human population remained fairly stable. Such things as disease, wars, and high rates of infant mortality kept births and deaths pretty much in balance. Then some 200 years ago a demographic transition occurred as death rates began to fall and population growth suddenly accelerated. A general overview of the growth of the human population over the past 10,000 years is shown in Figure 10.8.

Population increase in the last 200 years is more closely examined in Figure 10.9. The tremendous acceleration in growth since 1900 and especially since 1950 can clearly be seen.

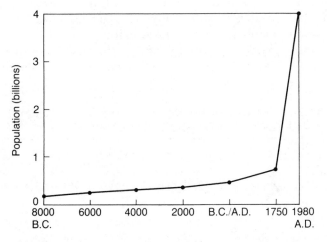

FIGURE 10.8 World Population Growth Since 8000 B.C.

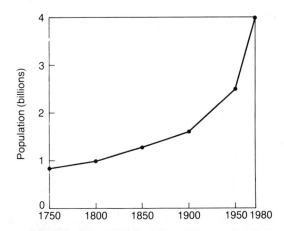

FIGURE 10.9 World Population Growth Since 1750.

Demographic transition refers to the movement of a population through three stages: (1) high birth rates and high death rates, (2) high birth rates and low death rates, and (3) low birth rates and low death rates. Western industrialized nations are in the third stage, but nations in the underdeveloped regions of the world are generally in the second stage, which means rapid population growth. Table 10.3 shows birth rates, death rates, life expectancy, and population density for several underdeveloped or Third World nations and several industrialized or developed nations. Of the underdeveloped countries, Angola, Ethiopia, Nigeria, and Zaire remain on the fringes of the first stage. Their death rates are higher and life expectancy is lower than in other countries. The remaining underdeveloped nations are clearly in stage two, just as the industrialized countries shown are clearly in stage three—low birth and death rates. It is interesting to note that population density is not as closely related to industrializaton as one might think. Some of the industrialized countries have high densities and some do not, and likewise with the nonindustrialized countries. If the nonindustrialized nations stay in stage two, however, their population densities will probably increase substantially.

With increasing control of disease and death, population is exploding in many countries of the world. We mentioned earlier, for example, that the birth

TABLE 10.3 Birth Rates and Death Rates (per 1,000 People), Life Expectancy, and Population Density in Selected Countries

Underdeveloped Nations	Birth Rate	Death Rate	Life Expectancy at Birth		Density: Population per Square Kilometer
			Men	Women	
Angola	48	25	37	40	6
Egypt	41	11	52	54	41
Ethiopia	50	25	37	40	25
Guatemala	43	13	48	50	65
India	33	15	46	45	198
Iran	38	15	58	57	22
Mexico	34	6	63	67	35
Nicaragua	40	14	51	55	20
Nigeria	50	20	37	37	81
Zaire	47	21	42	45	12
Developed Nations					
Austria	11	12	69	76	90
Canada	15	7	69	76	2
England and Wales	13	12	70	76	325
France	14	10	70	78	98
Japan	14	6	72	77	311
Spain	16	8	70	75	74
Sweden	12	11	72	78	18
United States	16	9	70	77	24

Demographic Yearbook, 1979.

rate in Mexico is more than double that of the United States; Mexico's death rate, however, has dropped to the point where it is roughly the same as ours. The result of this lowered death rate but constant high birth rate is tremendous population growth. World population is growing at a rate of well over one million people per week. At current growth rates it is reported that in 600 years or so we will have about one square foot of land per person. (*Then* maybe further reproduction will be impossible.) In many countries today, population pressure is linked to serious problems: poverty, disease, starvation, and war.

An influential essay by Thomas Malthus published in 1798 forecast trouble. Malthus stated that people have a natural urge to reproduce, and that population would increase faster than would people's ability to produce food. The situation could be helped by preventing births, but Malthus felt that postponing marriage and other types of "moral restraint" were the only acceptable means. Other methods of birth control—contraception, abortion, infanticide—were improper means. To Malthus, rational planning was the best hope for controlling the population cycle that would ultimately lead to starvation and poverty. Marx and Engels didn't go along with Malthus, primarily because Malthus felt that poverty was the fault of the poor. Marx and Engels saw poverty as the fault of a poorly organized (capitalist) society. They felt it unnecessary to limit births because advances in science and technology would enable food supplies to keep up with population growth. Modern Malthusians have thrown out the idea of moral restraint as the only acceptable means of birth control, and see far more disastrous consequences of population growth than Malthus did. Modern Marxists are more likely to recognize the presence of population growth problems.[10]

Many population experts are worried about population growth, and orga-

nizations all the way from the United Nations to your local Planned Parenthood Association are attempting to inform and enlighten people on the problem and on how to deal with overpopulation. Malthus thought postponing marriage might solve the problem. Today, birth control—the pill, abortion, sterilization— is seen as the answer. As we noted earlier in this chapter, birth rates in the United States have declined, reaching their lowest level in history in 1976. They have since increased slightly, and whether this will continue in the future is hard to guess. The rates will have to stay below the replacement level for some seventy years before population will indeed level off. Many American demographers continue to be cautious, believing that there is a population bomb latent, but not armed, in present society. A Zero Population Growth spokesman states, "The birth rate is notably fluid and capricious, strongly affected by such psychological factors as the economy or changing attitudes about the role of women." Some countries with high birth rates have encountered difficulty in introducing new population-control measures, especially when they run counter to local customs. Distrust of doctors, ignorance about biological facts or the consequences of overpopulation, desire for many sons to help farm the land, and numerous other cultural values have frustrated the efforts of people interested in population control. If the problem is ignored, or if we give up on it, it may be taken out of our hands; involuntary death control through starvation, war, or selective annihilation may be the last answer. Governmental intervention and national planning already occurring in some countries will have to become worldwide if this problem is to be effectively dealt with.

On the encouraging side, there is some evidence that perhaps the population bomb won't go off after all. Birth rates in some developing nations are beginning to decline. Some significant birth rate drops occurred for the period 1960–1970. Although many of the declines were small, seventy-eight of eighty-five nations with complete birth-registration data showed birth rate declines. This continued in the 1970s. The Census Bureau reported in December 1981 that the worldwide rate of population growth declined in the 1970s, thanks largely to China's efforts to limit births. Rate of population growth showed at least a slight drop on every continent except Africa. In mid-1978 Mexico reported a dramatic slowing in population growth, indicating that apparently the government's huge family planning program is working. A 1978 report from the United Nations states that although human numbers are growing, there are clear signs of a decline in fertility. R. M. Salas writes that in the 1970s "the world has experienced the beginning of a third wave in a series of fertility transitions. The first took place in Western Europe and North America in the 19th century; the second in Eastern Europe and Japan after World War II when population growth rates took a sharp downturn." Since the 1960s birth rates have fallen by approximately fifteen percent in three to four dozen developing nations. Why has this happened? Family planning movements may have had an effect as well as later marriage, increased literacy, and improved status of women. Whether this downward trend in fertility rates will continue long enough to have a decisive impact on world population growth remains to be seen. Even in the late 1970s, a few countries still restrict access to modern birth control methods according to the United Nations, and in some countries, possession of contraceptives is still against the law.[11]

Some people optimistically suggest that population redistribution may be a helpful way of easing pressures in certain areas, and they cite as evidence high population densities in some countries (over 300 people per square kilometer in Belgium, Holland, Japan, and England and Wales) and low population densities in other countries (two people per square kilometer in Canada and Australia, twelve per square kilometer in Russia, twenty-four in the United States). It is obvious, they suggest, that some countries are underpopulated and population redistribution would help. Paul Ehrlich disputes this and argues that overpopulation is a *world* problem, not a problem of individual countries, and redistribution of population will aggravate rather than solve the problem. More densely populated countries (such as Holland) are seldom self-sufficient and depend on the relatively underpopulated countries for resources and food. Measurements around the globe indicate that atmospheric dustiness is increasing by perhaps thirty percent per decade, and this poses a serious threat to the climatological balance. Fuels are being burned at rates that will exhaust estimated world reserves in well under a century. Pesticide residues are found everywhere, even in the fat of Antarctic penguins and in the Greenland ice cap. These facts indicate that the *world* has a population problem. Population distribution does present problems, especially in overcrowded urban areas, but the first priority in Ehrlich's opinion is not population redistribution but stopping population growth.[12]

Ecologists and urban sociologists call attention to other serious problems that are as difficult to solve as the population explosion. Specifically, they are worried about the ways we are using and destroying the environment. The automobile has taken over the American city. Most of the land area in our cities must be devoted to car-related functions—streets, highways, parking lots. With the advent of drive-in movies, drive-in restaurants, drive-in banks, drive-in stores, and now even drive-in church services, drive-in marriage ceremonies, and drive-in funeral parlors, it will soon be possible for people to go from birth to death almost without ever leaving their cars. Industries and the car are polluting our environment. Two rivers in Ohio have been declared fire hazards. Chemicals developed to control insects have turned out to be more effective than was anticipated and are now destroying other forms of wildlife. Cities are getting uglier, and urban sprawl is gutting the landscape. Cities are having increasing difficulty disposing of the huge amounts of garbage and refuse that people are producing (on the average, Americans produce more than four

---

[11]See Ben Wattenberg's article, "The Decline of the American Baby," *World*, 29 August 1972, pp. 20–23. Rafael M. Salas is executive director of the United Nations Fund for Population Activities, and the quote is from a newspaper excerpt (December 17, 1978) from the Fund's Annual Report by Atlas World Press Review.

[12]Paul Ehrlich has written a number of articles and several books on population and ecological problems. The ideas that I have summarized here come from Paul Ehrlich and John Holdren, "Why Do People Move?" which appeared in *Saturday Review*, 5 September 1970, p. 51.

pounds of pure garbage per person per day). City centers are being abandoned, and we are creating slums at fantastic rates. More and more people feel that the city is an unfit place to live—only those live there who are forced to.[13]

Perhaps we came too quickly into an urban world. It is a fact that living in cities, especially large cities, is a relatively new experience. In 1800 only about three percent of the world's population lived in cities of 5,000 or more. By 1900, the proportion living in cities had grown to fourteen percent, and by 1950, to thirty percent.[14] The United States has changed from a sparsely settled rural country to an extremely urbanized nation. Possibly our problems are to be expected due to our lack of experience with the phenomenon of urbanization.

In his book *The Human Zoo*, zoologist Desmond Morris suggests that the human being is basically a tribal or small-group animal. People are used to interacting on a localized, interpersonal basis. Relatively recently in our history we have, because of population growth and economic advantage, been forced into a supertribal or urban existence. Morris describes this new existence as "a human zoo." We have adapted well to some aspects of the supertribe—the urban environment has stimulated "man's insatiable curiosity, ... inventiveness, ... intellectual athleticism." We have adapted less well to other aspects, however, and we see suicide, war, crime, mental illness, and destruction of the environment. The simple tribesman became a citizen, but according to Morris we have not had time to evolve into a new, genetically civilized species. We have adapted somewhat to our new environment through learning and conditioning, but biologically we are still simple tribal animals. Morris concludes, "If [man] is given the chance he may yet contrive to turn his human zoo into a magnificent human game-park. If he is not, it may proliferate into a gigantic lunatic asylum, like one of the hideously cramped menageries of the last century."[15]

SUMMARY

In the previous chapters in this section on social organization we dealt with groups, categories, aggregations, and institutions. These are abstract concepts, but they are valuable for their capacity to describe and analyze the social organization of society. In this chapter, we continue to study social organization but in a somewhat different manner. The focus changes to population and human ecology, and we move from the abstract to the concrete.

Population and human ecology involve the study of numbers of people and their location in space. The major population variables are fertility, mortality, and migration. Ecological variables that we examined include study of city patterns (slums, suburbs, strip cities), ecological processes, reasons for spa-

---

[13]A detailed account of the problems facing cities is provided by Mitchell Gordon in his book *Sick Cities* (Baltimore: Penguin Books, 1965).

[14]This is summarized from Thomlinson, *Urban Structure*, pp. 46-48 (see footnote 4).

[15]Desmond Morris, *The Human Zoo* (New York: McGraw-Hill, 1969), especially Chapter 1. The quote is from page 248.

tial patterning, and consequences of spatial patterning. The study of population and human ecology supplies descriptive data about a society. These data, usually of a statistical nature, develop a picture of a society that often provides an interesting contrast to the picture supplied by the more abstract studies of groups and institutions. Finally, the study of population and ecology has today called attention to several serious problems facing us—overpopulation, urbanization, the destruction of the environment—and has encouraged development of the social planning needed to solve these problems.

Numerous books and articles have called attention to the almost insurmountable problems that the city faces. In the first of the two readings that follow, James and Carolyn Robertson describe the problems of a small California community and how the residents try to solve them. At the moment, overcrowded countries like India seem to have much more of a population problem than the United States. Wayne Davis in his article "Overpopulated America" suggests that, in fact, just the reverse is true. Given our numbers, our affluence, and our standard of living, we are in much more serious difficulty than India.

Terms for Study

centralization (300)	migration (291)
decentralization (300)	mortality (290)
demographic transition (304)	population pyramids (294–296)
demography (287)	replacement level (289)
fertility (288)	segregation (300)
general fertility rate (288)	sex ratio (293)
human ecology (287)	succession (300)
invasion (300)	total fertility rate (288)
life expectancy (290)	

Reading 10.1

THE TOWN OF LAST RESORT—MENDOCINO

JAMES AND CAROLYN ROBERTSON

The United States has changed from being a rural environment to being an environment dominated by cities. But cities have problems—pollution, crowding, traffic, inadequate services. In the 1970s many have come to the conclusions that cities don't work and that they are not particularly nice places to live. So people have headed back to small towns. Rural counties that were losing population in the 1960s were gaining population in the 1970s. In 1978, nonmetropolitan areas continued to grow more rapidly than metropolitan areas. And if the urbanites can't get away for good, maybe they can for the weekend at least—to the second home or just for a drive.

The rural small-town experience is valued today, so much so that it is getting harder and harder to find. Migration *out* of the city is placing tremendous pressures on the smaller communities as they try to maintain their identity and character. Most small communities do not have the resources to deal with invasion, but there are some successes. In *The Small Towns Book*, James and Carolyn Robertson write about the attempts of seven communities from across the country to cope with the pressures from outside. The following reading is adapted from their more detailed study of Mendocino, California.

Mendocino is a scenic day's drive from the San Francisco bay area on the rugged north coast of California. There are few places in California more attractive. It is perched on a bluff above the rocks and surf—at the very edge of the Pacific. It is a town of old houses, water towers, barns and chicken coops, plunked down in a spectacular countryside. In the little back alleys and in the empty lots are tangles of berries, flowering weeds, and nasturtiums gone wild. In spots, the old buildings lean on each other for support.

Mendocino was once a difficult-to-get-to lumber town settled by New Englanders, Finns, and Portuguese. A lumber mill, a few merchants and farmers made up the town. When the mill closed, the town went to sleep. In the late 1950s a San Francisco artist started the Mendocino Art Center and other artists soon followed. The tourists began coming—first a trickle, then a stream. Real estate offices, "prestige" homes, gift shops, a delicatessen, restaurants appeared. The town, for over a hundred years a home for children, ponies, and dogs, was invaded by outsiders.

> *This year we got tour busses for the very first time. It used to be we just got people who came here for the same reasons people came here to live. They loved the ocean, and they liked to walk in the open meadows, or in the woods around town. Or they combed the beaches. Maybe they brought paints and took a class at the Art Center—or just read a book. They were more like the rest of us. Now we're getting a different kind of tourist. I call them polyesters and double-knits. They come in motor homes. Or on Greyhound tour busses, and they don't seem to be satisfied with the town as it is. They are rewarding people who offer them a kind of entertainment or shopping that we've never had here and have no real use for. They need to be titillated. They don't take walks along the beach. They walk in my front yard. And they don't just come in the summertime anymore. They're coming all year long.*

Mendocino, like many other small communities, was discovered. Tourists, welcomed in smaller numbers, now appear to be changing the character of the town. Land developers have arrived. Property has become much more valuable and taxes are rising. Probably the most unfortunate consequence is the uncertainty and dissension among the residents themselves as they debate the town's future. Should Mendocino cash in on its sudden popularity or should it remain the private weatherbeaten small town of its past? These issues have split communities across the country as they struggle to deal with pressures from outside. Each community confronts its problems in unique ways. Mendocino's major events were the sewer, big money in town, the tax strike, and the chamber of anti-commerce.

THE SEWER

In 1972 the Environmental Protection Agency informed the town that they must stop dumping untreated sewage in the ocean—they would have to build a sewer plant. The size of the sewer plant woud determine how much the town could grow. In the debate over the town's sewer the first lines of contention between the advocates of development and the advocates of no more growth were drawn. Some residents didn't like what was happening to Mendocino but at the same time didn't want to restrict a person's freedom to do what they wanted to with their own property. Other residents who long awaited the town's revival felt the more development the better. Others saw their ideal of small town life being turned into a commercial bonanza, and they banded together to preserve Mendocino's "hometown" character.

The advocates of a bigger sewer won the first battle. The sewer would service areas not yet developed—Mendocino, it seems, would grow some more. But then things got complicated. The sewer was financed by a federal grant which required that certain conditions had to be met. For one thing, the sewer was not intended to be a stimulant to uncontrolled development of the town— there had to be a protective land-use plan for the town. In a subsequent battle over new development, the anti-development group found that certain federal requirements had not been met and they were able to obtain a state enforced moratorium on further development. Mendocino would not grow, at least not just yet.

BIG MONEY IN TOWN

In 1974 rumors began to circulate that someone was going to buy the old Mendocino Hotel on Main Street. A town landmark, the Hotel has a view of the ocean, old fashioned furniture, pretty good food, and bathrooms down the hall. The Hotel was bought by a wealthy Southern Californian who had fallen in love with Mendocino. He also bought other property in town and quickly became a major force in the community though still living in Southern California.

It's hard to tell how people feel about this. He gave a valuable piece of property to Mendocino and he remodeled the Hotel to high style California Victorian. But he doesn't live in Mendocino, his wealth comes from outside, and he is changing their town.

Other outside money began coming. Mendocino is seen as a good investment and they buy, paying high prices which drive property values up. It is the impact of this invasion of outside wealth which has had the most dramatic and potentially the most destructive effect on the little community.

THE TAX STRIKE

In California taxes are levied by the County and are based on the value of real property. Most public revenue comes from those who own real estate. Property values are determined by improvements that may have been made to the property and by what similar properties in the area are selling for. In 1975 Mendocino County re-assessed coastal properties and the property owners were notified by mail of the new value of their property.

The results were staggering. Property values had escalated by so much that taxes would increase by 4 to 10 times! Though citizens could appeal the new values, the procedure is time consuming and little understood. People were upset and many couldn't afford to pay their tax bills. They organized, held public meetings, and worked to get the word around. As the December 10th date for tax payment approached, a course of action developed. They decided on a tax strike—instead of sending tax money to the County, they sent teabags! Over a half million dollars in taxes were withheld. Nationwide attention was given to Mendocino's teabag tax protest.

THE CHAMBER OF ANTI-COMMERCE

In September 1976 a market called Corners of the Mouth was told to vacate its premises. The owner of the building wanted to remodel and install an enlarged gift and antique shop. The market had been a popular place among the locals, a social center. Many doubted the need for another gift shop and saw the eviction of the Corners of the Mouth as one more blow to the hometown and another victory for tourism. Some of the residents of Mendocino had been pushed to the limit and they fought back. They developed SCAT—Sensible Citizens Against Tourism. They parked their cars in places normally used by tourists, put posters on the cars explaining why, and passed out information to visitors. The following letter was handed out.

AN OPEN LETTER TO VISITORS

First be assured that it is not you, personally, we are questioning. Person-to-person, had we a quiet context, we would probably become friends; certainly not enemies.

Our problem is that the flood of tourists recently has passed beyond what a small town can handle and still function as a community. Noise of automobiles drowns out sounds of the ocean, even late at night. We now smell exhaust instead of salt air. Streets are littered. Townspeople cannot find places to park. Many young, creative people have had their rents increased and must now move. Taxes are rising and many oldtimers now must sell. The quiet, creative ambience of the town is dissolving, replaced by a growing number of antique stores and other tourist-oriented businesses.

We realize growth is inevitable; most of us moved here realizing Mendocino had an active tourist industry already. We accept that visitors have a legal right to come here and that property owners have a legal right to develop their land as they see fit.

But we also profoundly cherish the fact that Mendocino is a living community; this is our home; families live here. This is still a creative center where artists, poets, actors and students come to live and work and experiment.

We do not mind a reasonable number of visitors, especially visitors who will pause long enough to get to know the town, the people—will trouble themselves to feel the real Mendocino beneath the commercial veneer. We mind the inundation of the town by hordes flashing through for a few minutes or hours. We mind the rapid and sudden investment in Mendocino-as-commercial-enterprise, especially by those who live elsewhere.

So we urge you to come here infrequently, sensitive to the fact that you are entering a fragile community of real people. If you do come back, we urge you to consider staying for more than a night or two—long enough to realize that basic functions of communities are deep and personal . . . and that window dressing is not the real product. Look for the authentic work of local people. Question what you buy, whether it is locally made, or just shipped here for the tourist industry.

Please do not encourage others to come here. Present facilities—and basic services—are overloaded. We do not want more facilities to further destroy the fragile fabric of community that still exists here. Consider—and we say this respectfully—your own backyard. If you spent the time and energy there that you are spending here, wouldn't you, your family, your neighborhood, and the planet, be better off? Then, perhaps we could someday visit you and have something to gain from it.

Community in America is getting to be a lost art. Commercial, phoney tourist traps are increasingly prevalent. Help us protect, maintain, and develop the former.

—*The Mendocino SCAT Committee (Sensible Citizens Against Tourism)*

THE TOWN OF LAST RESORT

A town is only partly real estate. It is also a network of enormously complex interactions between people. This network is a live thing, the thing that makes towns live. This network is a product of the collective history of the community, and of deeply personal beliefs and convictions held by each of its residents. To ignore this network when one is at work in the machinery of public affairs is to invite chaos.

Some of the people in and around Mendocino do not agree with SCAT. They believe it is morally wrong to move to a small community and then tell others to keep away. One writes, "Don't get mean with a tourist who has come here to find some beauty. How many of us have done the same, leaving behind the sad city? All we can do is grow, deal with knowledge, using life to determine what is valuable."

Other people in Mendocino who believe they are fighting for their homes do not agree. At their backs is the Pacific Ocean. At their doors are the promoters of tourism and land speculators. To them Mendocino is a town of last resort. There isn't anywhere else to go.

A small town is a fragile affair—it is easy to unbalance. But the issues are difficult: How many gift shops are enough? Should one sell property for less than it is worth? Should anyone stand in the way of progress? The battle in Mendocino will continue, for it reflects in a smaller arena many of the basic conflicts present in American Society.

Questions 10.1

1. What are the basic conflicts in Mendocino?
2. What sort of parallels can you draw between what is happening in Mendocino and the problems big cities face?
3. What kinds of statutes would you establish to keep what happened in Mendocino from happening in your community? Or would you want to?
4. Illustrate as many of the ecological processes as you can using Mendocino as example.

Reading 10.2

OVERPOPULATED AMERICA

WAYNE H. DAVIS

Population pressure may be assessed by means of many different variables: number of people, population density, ability of the land to produce food, trends in birth rates and death rates. Wayne Davis introduces the variables of affluence and standard of living and suggests that they may be at least as important as number of people. He compares America's population problem to India's by using the concept of "Indian equivalents." Professor Davis teaches in the school of biological sciences at the University of Kentucky.

I define as most seriously overpopulated that nation whose people by virtue of their numbers and activities are most rapidly decreasing the ability of the land to support human life. With our large population, our affluence and our technological monstrosities the United States wins first place by a substantial margin.

Let's compare the United States to India, for example. We have 203 million people, whereas she has 540 million on much less land. But look at the impact of people on the land.

The average Indian eats his daily few cups of rice (or perhaps wheat, whose production on American farms contributed to our one percent per year drain in quality of our active farmland), draws his bucket of water from the communal well and sleeps in a mud hut. In his daily rounds to gather cow dung to burn to cook his rice and warm his feet, his footsteps, along with those of millions of his countrymen, help bring about a slow deterioration of the ability of the land to support people. His contribution to the destruction of the land is minimal.

An American, on the other hand, can be expected to destroy a piece of land on which he builds a home, garage and driveway. He will contribute his share to the 142 million tons of smoke and fumes, seven million junked cars, 20 million tons of paper, 48 billion cans, and 26 billion bottles the overburdened environment must absorb each year. To run his air conditioner we will strip-mine a Kentucky Hillside, push the dirt and slate down into the stream, and burn coal in a power generator, whose smokestack contributes to a plume of smoke massive enough to cause cloud seeding and premature precipitation from Gulf winds which should be irrigating the wheat farms of Minnesota.

In his lifetime he will personally pollute three million gallons of water, and industry and agriculture will use ten times this much water in his behalf. To provide these needs the U.S. Army Corps of Engineers will build dams and flood farmland. He will also use 21,000 gallons of leaded gasoline containing boron, drink 28,000 pounds of milk and eat 10,000 pounds of meat. The latter is produced and squandered in a life pattern unknown to Asians. A steer on a

Western range eats plants containing minerals necessary for plant life. Some of these are incorporated into the body of the steer which is later shipped for slaughter. After being eaten by man these nutrients are flushed down the toilet into the ocean or buried in the cemetery, the surface of which is cluttered with boulders called tombstones and has been removed from productivity. The result is a continual drain on the productivity of range land. Add to this the erosion of overgrazed lands, and the effects of the falling water table as we mine Pleistocene deposits of groundwater to irrigate to produce food for more people, and we can see why our land is dying far more rapidly than did the great civilization of the Middle East, which experienced the same cycle. The average Indian citizen, whose fecal material goes back to the land, has but a minute fraction of the destructive effect on the land that the affluent American does.

Thus I want to introduce a new term, which I suggest be used in future discussions of human population and ecology. We should speak of our numbers in "Indian equivalents." An Indian equivalent I define as the average number of Indian citizens required to have the same detrimental effect on the land's ability to support human life as would the average American. This value is difficult to determine, but let's take an extremely conservative working figure of 25. To see how conservative this is, imagine the addition of 1000 citizens to your town and 25,000 to an Indian village. Not only would the Americans destroy much more land for homes, highways and a shopping center, but they would contribute far more to environmental deterioration in hundreds of other ways as well. For example, their demand for steel for new autos might increase the daily pollution equivalent of 130,000 junk autos which Life *tells us that U.S. Steel Corp. dumps into Lake Michigan. Their demand for textiles would help the cotton industry destroy the life in the Black Warrior River in Alabama with endrin. And they would contribute to the massive industrial pollution of our oceans (we provide one-third to one-half the world's share) which has caused the precipitous downward trend in our commercial fisheries landings during the past seven years.*

The per capita gross national product of the United States is 38 times that of India. Most of our goods and services contribute to the decline in the ability of the environment to support life. Thus it is clear that a figure of 25 for an Indian equivalent is conservative. It has been suggested to me that a more realistic figure would be 500.

In Indian equivalents, therefore, the population of the United States is at least four billion. And the rate of growth is even more alarming. We are growing at one percent per year, a rate which would double our numbers in 70 years. India is growing at 2.5 percent. Using the Indian equivalent of 25, our population growth becomes 10 times as serious as that of India. According to the Rienows in their recent book Moment in the Sun, *just one year's crop of American babies can be expected to use up 25 billion pounds of beef, 200 million pounds of steel and 9.1 billion gallons of gasoline during their collective lifetime. And the demands on water and land for our growing population are expected to be far greater than the supply available in the year 2000. We are destroying our land at a rate of over a million acres a year. We now have only*

2.6 agricultural acres per person. By 1975 this will be cut to 2.3, the critical point for the maintenance of what we consider a decent diet, and by the year 2000 we might expect to have 1.2.

You might object that I am playing with statistics in using the Indian equivalent on the rate of growth. I am making the assumption that today's child will live 35 years (the average Indian life span) at today's level of affluence. If he lives an American 70 years, our rate of population growth would be 20 times as serious as India's.

But the assumption of continued affluence at today's level is unfounded. If our numbers continue to rise, our standard of living will fall so sharply that by the year 2000 any surviving Americans might consider today's average Asian to be well off. Our children's destructive effects on their environment will decline as they sink ever lower into poverty.

The United States is in serious economic trouble now. Nothing could be more misleading than today's affluence, which rests precariously on a crumbling foundation. Our productivity, which had been increasing steadily at about 3.2 percent a year since World War II, has been falling during 1969. Our export over import balance has been shrinking steadily from $7.1 billion in 1964 to $0.15 billion in the first half of 1969. Our balance of payments deficit for the second quarter was $3.7 billion, the largest in history. We are now importing iron ore, steel, oil, beef, textiles, cameras, radios and hundreds of other things.

Our economy is based upon the Keynesian concept of a continued growth in population and productivity. It worked in an underpopulated nation with excess resources. It could continue to work only if the earth and its resources were expanding at an annual rate of 4 to 5 percent. Yet neither the number of cars, the economy, the human population, nor anything else can expand indefinitely at an exponential rate in a finite world. We must face this fact now. The crisis is here. When Walter Heller says that our economy will expand by 4 percent annually through the latter 1970s he is dreaming. He is in a theoretical world totally unaware of the realities of human ecology. If the economists do not wake up and devise a new system for us now somebody else will have to do it for them.

A civilization is comparable to a living organism. Its longevity is a function of its metabolism. The higher the metabolism (affluence), the shorter the life. Keynesian economics has allowed us an affluent but shortened life span. We have now run our course.

The tragedy facing the United States is even greater and more imminent than that descending upon the hungry nations. The Paddock brothers in their book, Famine 1975!, say that India "cannot be saved" no matter how much food we ship her. But India will be here after the United States is gone. Many millions will die in the most colossal famines India has ever known, but the land will survive and she will come back as she always has before. The United States on the other hand, will be a desolate tangle of concrete and ticky-tacky, of strip-mined moonscape and silt-choked reservoirs. The land and water will be so contaminated with pesticides, herbicides, mercury fungicides, lead, boron, nickel, arsenic and hundreds of other toxic substances, which have been approaching critical levels of concentration in our environment as a result of our numbers and affluence, that they may be unable to sustain human life.

Thus as the curtain gets ready to fall on man's civilization let it come as no surprise that it shall first fall on the United States. And let no one make the mistake of thinking we can save ourselves by "cleaning up the environment." Banning DDT is the equivalent of the physician's treating syphilis by putting a bandaid over the first chancre to appear. In either case you can be sure that more serious and widespread trouble will soon appear unless the disease itself is treated. We cannot survive by planning to treat the symptoms such as air pollution, water pollution, soil erosion, etc.

What can we do to slow the rate of destruction of the United States as a land capable of supporting human life? There are two approaches. First, we must reverse the population growth. We have far more people now than we can continue to support at anything near today's level of affluence. American women average slightly over three children each. According to the Population Bulletin *if we reduced this number to 2.5 there would still be 330 million people in the nation at the end of the century. And even if we reduced this to 1.5 we would have 57 million more people in the year 2000 than we have now. With our present longevity patterns it would take more than 30 years for the population to peak even when reproducing at this rate, which would eventually give us a net decrease in numbers.*

Do not make the mistake of thinking that technology will solve our population problem by producing a better contraceptive. Our problem now is that people want too many children. Surveys show the average number of children wanted by the American family is 3.3. There is little difference between the poor and the wealthy, black and white, Catholic and Protestant. Production of children at this rate during the next 30 years would be so catastrophic in effect on our resources and the viability of the nation as to be beyond my ability to contemplate. To prevent this trend we must not only make contraceptives and abortion readily available to everyone, but we must establish a system to put severe economic pressure on those who produce children and reward those who do not. This can be done within our system of taxes and welfare.

The other thing we must do is to pare down our Indian equivalents. Individuals in American society vary tremendously in Indian equivalents. If we plot Indian equivalents versus their reciprocal, the percentage of land surviving a generation, we obtain a linear regression. We can then place individuals and occupation types on this graph. At one end would be the starving blacks of Mississippi; they would approach unity in Indian equivalents, and would have the least destructive effect on the land. At the other end of the graph would be the politicians slicing pork for the barrel, the highway contractors, the strip-mine operators, real estate developers, and public enemy number one—the U.S. Army Corps of Engineers.

We must halt land destruction. We must abandon the view of land and minerals as private property to be exploited in any way economically feasible for private financial gain. Land and minerals are resources upon which the very survival of the nation depends, and their use must be planned in the best interests of the people.

Rising expectations for the poor is a cruel joke foisted upon them by the Establishment. As our new economy of use-it-once-and-throw-it-away produces more and more products for the affluent, the share of our resources available for the poor declines. *Blessed be the starving blacks of Mississippi with their outdoor privies, for they are ecologically sound, and they shall inherit a nation. Although I hope that we will help these unfortunate people attain a decent standard of living by diverting war efforts to fertility control and job training, our most urgent task to assure this nation's survival during the next decade is to stop the affluent destroyers.*

Questions 10.2

1. What point is Davis attempting to make by introducing the concept "Indian equivalents"?
2. Davis suggests that there are two approaches to America's problem of overpopulation. What are the difficulties likely to be encountered in following these two approaches?

III

SOCIAL CHANGE AND SOCIAL DEVIATION

In Parts I and II we dealt with the individual as a member of society and the social organization of society. We saw that social organization could be studied using the following concepts: group, category and aggregation, institution, population, and human ecology. In Part III we will focus on change and deviation in society. The concepts discussed in this section will suggest that all is not as predictable and organized as previous sections may have implied. Uncertainty and instability exist in all societies and are the result of a variety of factors. *Social change* occurs and affects the way individuals and groups relate to each other. If social change is rapid and extreme, the organization of society may break down and *social disorganization* may result. In some situations, behavior occurs that is spontaneous and unstructured but not necessarily disorganized. This type of behavior is called *collective behavior.* We learned in Part I that norms and roles describe what people are expected to do in certain situations and positions. But inevitably, many individuals do *not* behave in the ways they are expected to. Societies, in turn, devise ways to encourage or even force conformity. This leads us to the final topics of *deviant behavior* and *social control.*

11

Social Change and Social Disorganization

In June, 1978, a British language expert reported that English is changing so much that in the future Americans and British people won't be able to understand each other without the help of a translator. American English is changing rapidly, and British English is retaining its more ancient character. Robert Burchfield, chief editor of the Oxford English dictionaries, states that since 1776 American English and British English have been on divergent courses and that their speakers should end up unintelligible to one another in another 200 years.

We have looked at the social organization of society for some seven chapters now. At this point society may have the appearance of a well-oiled machine clickety-clicking along—groups interacting, highly polished institutions efficiently dealing with society's central issues and conducting business as usual, populations reproducing, and people continuing to pattern themselves in space in very predictable ways. Focusing on the social organization of society is an extremely important perspective, but it unfortunately implies that conditions are constant, that all behave as they are expected to, that there are never unpredictable occurrences or failures either in people or in social conditions.

The fact of the matter is that all is *not* constant—life is not the same today as it was yesterday. The following changes come to mind. A supersonic jet makes regular flights to this country. It wasn't too long ago that it took more than twelve hours to cross the Atlantic by propeller plane; now it takes about three hours. Interest in the ozone layer, noise, and air pollution are recent concerns. The space shuttle is making fairly regular flights, test tube babies have been born and people are discussing the merits of gene manipulation. A worldwide oil crisis means that the price of gasoline continues to rise rapidly and that international power alignments are being restructured. Who could have imagined OPEC and its current importance a decade ago? The women's movement has led to new rights and new roles and resocialization for many men and women. Watergate brought a new view of presidential power and prerogative. The Supreme Court decisions on abortion and capital punishment have had far-reaching effects, and there is still much controversy about these issues.

The point is, of course, that all societies are dynamic and constantly changing. Some societies change more rapidly than others, and within a society some parts change more rapidly than other parts. Some changes may lead to improvement, to a better life for some or most of the members of society. Change may also lead to problems because, although some individuals and institutions will adjust rapidly, others will have difficulty adapting to change. We can anticipate that social change will occasionally lead to periods of social disorganization as old ways erode and collapse and new ways of behaving are developed.

Social change refers to significant alterations in social relationships and cultural ideas.[1] Social and cultural factors are combined in this definition because they are tightly interrelated. Changes in ideas and values quickly lead to changes in social relationships, and vice versa. Development of the ideas of science has led to new roles (astronauts, rocket experts) and changed social relationships. People's concerns about pollution have led to new ideas and material inventions (smaller cars with fewer harmful emissions).

Social change takes place continually and, in modern society, at ever increasing rates. Change is such a constant factor in our existence that frequently we lose sight of its extent. One way to put change in perspective is to imagine that your own life started ten years earlier than it did or to compare your life experiences with those of your parents. Technological changes probably first come to mind—high-speed travel, voyages to outer space, atomic power, transplanting organs, a computerized society. But there are other sorts of changes as well. Look at the areas in which there would be contrasts for two people with only ten years difference in their ages: the changing role of women; the size of the family one is born into; different educational philosophies and techniques; control of certain diseases and life expectancy; likelihood of getting married and if so, at what age; to demonstrate for a cause or not, and if so, what cause

---

[1]See the chapter on social change by Alvin Boskoff in Howard Becker and Alvin Boskoff, *Modern Sociological Theory* (New York: Dryden Press, 1957).

(Vietnam, legalized abortion, civil rights?); whether to go to college, and if so, what course of study to choose; the amount of leisure time available and what to do with it; and so on. And if we can find these differences across ten years, imagine the contrast over twenty or thirty years.

Change factors are related to each other in complex patterns; often the path of influence is difficult to clearly detect. Development of the contraceptive pill (new idea, invention) led to changes (more freedom) in sexual behavior. Or did concerns with increased freedom for women and with family size lead to development of contraceptive devices? Keeping in mind the complex nature of social change, perhaps we can outline some of the major factors related to change.

FACTORS RELATED TO SOCIAL CHANGE

Various attempts have been made to relate social change to other factors in the physical and social environment.[2] Some of these hypothesized relationships seem farfetched; others seem more reasonable. For example, social change has been related to the biological characteristics of a nation. Adherents of master race theories believe that societies fortunate enough to be graced by the presence of a superior race will have greater progress (and more rapid social change) than will less fortunate nations. Sociologist Robert Bierstedt points out that such theories—present at all times in all societies—are only a primitive form of ethnocentrism. A more realistic approach might hold that people who differ by race or ethnicity have different social and cultural patterns, and cer-

---

[2]This discussion is drawn in part from Robert Bierstedt, *The Social Order*, 4th ed. (New York: McGraw-Hill, 1974), Chapter 20.

tain mixtures of these in a given society could lead to greater or lesser conflict and, correspondingly, greater or lesser social change. Geographical factors may be related to change. Some countries are more favored by climate and natural resources, and this may affect their rates of technological advancement and social change. As we discussed in the previous chapter, demographic factors may lead to change. When a country faces population growth to the point of overcrowding, social relationships change, both within that society and with surrounding societies, which may be less crowded.

Social change can be observed in many different ways. Compare the lists of the twenty most-often-watched TV programs in 1961–1962 and in 1981–1982.

1961–1962	1981–1982
1. Wagon Train	1. Dallas
2. Bonanza	2. 60 Minutes
3. Gunsmoke	3. Three's Company
4. Hazel	4. Jeffersons
5. Perry Mason	5. Alice
6. Red Skelton	6. Too Close For Comfort
7. Andy Griffith	7. Dukes of Hazzard
8. Danny Thomas	8. M*A*S*H
9. Dr. Kildare	9. Monday Night Football
10. Candid Camera	10. One Day At A Time
11. My Three Sons	11. Falcon Crest
12. Garry Moore	12. Hart To Hart
13. Rawhide	13. Archie Bunker's Place
14. Real McCoys	14. Love Boat
15. Lassie	15. Trapper John, M.D.
16. Sing Along With Mitch	16. Magnum, P.I.
17. Dennis The Menace	17. Happy Days
18. Gunsmoke	18. Dynasty
19. Ben Casey	19. Laverne & Shirley
20. Ed Sullivan	20. Real People

Fewer action westerns and more situation comedies and laughs—what attitude changes are reflected here? Is it a transition from identifying with the frontier and the wild west to becoming a nation of city dwellers? Perhaps we are more desperately in need of a laugh in the 1980s?

Lists courtesy of A. C. Nielsen Company.

Social change may be a result of the influence of certain individuals. Recall how societies, and even the world, were affected and changed by Hitler, Napoleon, Einstein, Lincoln, Karl Marx, and Julius Caesar. The course of events in the United States in the mid-twentieth century was altered by men such as Franklin D. Roosevelt and Martin Luther King, Jr. It is sometimes argued that great men alone initiate significant social changes, but others maintain that such people are merely products of their society, and that if they had not appeared, someone else of the same caliber would have. The truth probably lies somewhere between these views. The cultural and societal conditions might be seen as a stage where people perform, a few in unique ways having lasting effects, many others in more commonplace and predictable ways. And, certainly, the historical aspect cannot be overlooked as a factor in change. Many great men were made by historical conditions—accidents of history. Had they appeared at another time, they would probably have passed unnoticed. Also, historical accidents or unpredictable events can lead to change: the assassination of a leader or a population-decimating catastrophe such as an earthquake or epidemic.

Ideological and technological factors are related to social change. The appearance of and commitment to ideas of socialism, democracy, Christianity, science, or progress in general have led to major social changes. The industrial revolution of the eighteenth and nineteenth centuries was a major force for change in the United States and elsewhere; its dramatic consequences are still with us today. Technological innovations and inventions that have produced tremendous social change include the wheel, the car, the birth control pill, the atom bomb, the gun, the telephone, the airplane, and the computer. It is easy to point to the dramatic inventions that affect societies, probably because their emergence seems sudden, rather than slow and evolutionary as are many changes. Sometimes the effects of inventions are less obvious. Sociologist William Ogburn recorded numerous examples of the widespread effects of technological innovations.[3] The self-starter on cars aided in the emancipation of women: It allowed women to use cars as easily as men. The invention of the elevator made possible the construction of tall apartment buildings. Living in these buildings, in turn, changed the family: Rearing of large families was more difficult, and consequently the urban birth rate declined. The invention of the cotton gin was a major factor leading to the Civil War. How? Ogburn suggests that invention of the cotton gin led to the need for more slaves to cultivate more cotton, and the greater production led to increased trade with England. This in turn led the South, which supported free trade, into conflict with the economic interests of the North, which wanted protective tariffs and restricted foreign imports, and this conflict led to war. Invention of the six-shooter, barbed wire, and the windmill made possible the settling of the Great Plains. To imply that inventions have such far-reaching effects no doubt seems as much of an oversimplification as did the "great men" theory. The lesson probably is that we cannot single out any one element or invention in a culture and attribute change to it alone.

Social change is introduced in a culture through two processes: invention and diffusion. **Invention** refers to the creation of a new object or idea. Usually, although the end product of the invention (car, airplane, telescope) is new, the parts that make it up are not. The elements have been around and are now arranged or put together in a new way. **Diffusion** refers to the spread of objects

---

[3]Ogburn's works include *Social Change* (New York: Viking Press, 1922, 1950); *The Social Effects of Aviation* (Boston: Houghton Mifflin, 1946); *Machines and Tomorrow's World*, rev. ed., Public Affairs Pamphlets, no. 25, 1946; and Ogburn and Nimkoff, *Sociology* 2d ed. (Boston: Houghton Mifflin, 1950).

or ideas from one society to another (Egypt to England) or from one group to another within the same society (upper class to lower class or black to white). Although innovation or invention attracts the most attention, most change is introduced through the process of diffusion. Remember Ralph Linton's "One Hundred Percent American" on pp. 88–90.

To sum up the many factors related to social change, we could generalize and say that social change represents the coming together of a number of events: The conditions in a particular culture at a given time in history and the change agent or catalyst (a particular person or the invention or diffusion of a new technique, object, or idea).

Rates of Change and Planned Change

Different segments of a given society frequently change at different rates. Ogburn called this condition **cultural lag.** A new element may be introduced requiring change in other areas of society, and when these other areas are slow to change, problems result. Faster cars were built in advance of highways that could handle them. Jumbo jets arrived before airports were constructed that could accommodate the increased passenger load. People's attitudes usually change far more rapidly than laws change, especially in the area of morality laws, and a cultural lag exists.

A society's receptivity to change is an important factor affecting the rate of social change. If a society has a strictly defined system of stratification or rigid institutional structure, change will be slower. If a society is isolated from others, change will be slower. Change will be more rapid in a society that emphasizes the values of individualism and self-determination than in a society that emphasizes conformity and reverence for the past and custom. William Graham Sumner believed there is a basic resistance to change in all societies in that people are basically conservative and seek stability or "strain for consistency." Resistance to change is balanced to a certain extent by people's curiosity. They continue to seek new knowledge and better ways of doing things, so change must occur.

It may be that social change is an evolutionary process beyond our control—we are at the mercy of forces that we can do nothing about. Many people believe, however, that we can do something more than just describe and accept our social environment. Rather, the environment can actually be manipulated for our benefit. One view of the process of change, as expressed by William Graham Sumner, is that social change must be slow, and change in people's attitudes must precede change in legislation. Sumner believed that laws should not move ahead of the customs of the people, or, in his words, "stateways cannot change folkways." An opposite view is that new laws can lead the way— they can change people's attitudes and behavior in necessary and beneficial ways. From 1954 on, court decisions and legislative acts have attempted to change the pattern of interaction between the races in the United States. Civil rights groups in the 1960s, feeling that change had been too slow, tried sit-ins, nonviolent demonstrations, and passive resistance to speed up the process. Both sides—those who feel change is beyond control and those who feel that change can be planned and controlled—have fuel for their arguments. The latter group can state that the conditions of minorities in America have improved. The former group, however, can call attention to unanticipated changes that have also occurred: increasing violence between the races in the 1960s, and probably a hardening of racial attitudes on the part of many people. At any rate, social scientists today feel that change within limits can be a planned phenomenon. As a result, we see the development of commissions and agencies focusing on a number of areas where it is felt that planned social change is needed.

Saudi Arabia sits atop the greatest reservoir of oil yet discovered on earth. In 1976, while working less than half her oil fields, the Saudi oil industry earned about $37.8 billion, or just over $100 million a day. This would allow the Saudis to buy (if they wanted):

all taxable real estate in Manhattan in 5 months, 27 days
General Motors in 4 months, 19 days
Bank of America in 2 weeks, 5 days
CBS in 7 days, 5 hours
all professional football teams in the U.S. in 4 days, 1 hour
Tiffany's in 5 hours, 49 minutes

In spite of this tremendous wealth, Saudi Arabia retains the characteristics of an underdeveloped country. The country lacks the schools, hospitals, roads, banks, factories, and farms that are the true bases of national wealth. One percent of the land grows food. About one person in eight can read Arabic. The life expectancy is about forty years and infant mortality is high—some Bedouin tribes still call all their sons Muhammad at birth and then, at the age of five, rename the minority who survive. The wheel was, in effect, introduced in Arabia only about fifty years ago, attached to the automobile.

Construction of roads, ports, buildings, schools, telephones, and so on, is now widespread. Improvement of social conditions will follow more slowly. *Imagine* the forces of social change focusing on this country as development of the rest of Saudi society tries to match the increasing flood of oil wealth.

From "The Arabian Ethos," by Peter A. Iseman, *Harpers* 256 (February 1978), pp. 37–56. Reprinted by permission of the Julian Bach Literary Agency, Inc. Copyright © 1978 by Peter A. Iseman. Reprinted from the February 1978 issue of Harper's Magazine.

THEORIES OF SOCIAL CHANGE

Is there any pattern to social change? Is its direction or speed predictable? These questions have fascinated people for ages, and scientists and philosophers have applied themselves energetically to the task of unraveling the mysteries of social change. Numerous theories have emerged. We will briefly examine five types of theories: cyclic, evolutionary, functional, conflict, and neoevolutionary.[4]

---

[4]The major source for this section is *Perspectives on Social Change*, 2d ed., by Robert Lauer (Boston: Allyn and Bacon, 1977), especially Chapters 2, 3, 6, 9, and 12.

Cyclic Theories   One way of understanding social change is in terms of cycles. Chinese historians gave world history neither a beginning nor an end, but saw periods of order and disorder, of prosperity and decline. A fourteenth-century Arab scholar, Ibn Khaldun, based his theory of change on the clash between nomadic and sedentary peoples. Desert nomads seek the luxuries of the city, and continually attack cities and towns. The sedentary city-dwellers are no match for the fierce nomads, and are quickly conquered. The conquerers form a new empire, but as they settle in the cities they become comfortable and sedentary like those before them and eventually are overrun by a new horde of nomads.

Arnold Toynbee saw civilizations arising out of primitive societies through a process involving challenge and response. Not all primitive societies become civilizations; those that do, do so because of their response to the challenge of adverse conditions. Toynbee mentions such adverse conditions as a difficult physical environment, land which has not been settled and tilled, sudden military defeats, and continuing external threats. Two factors are crucial: the severity of the challenge, and the development of an elite to manage the response. Most of the society is tied to the past, but led by the elite the civilization can grow by successfully responding to continuing challenges. Eventually, civilizations come apart, dividing into several groups which end up battling with each other. For Toynbee, civilization's cycle included birth, growth, stagnation, and disintegration. When he looked at the future of Western civilization, Toynbee saw several problems or challenges that he felt we had to solve: war, class conflict, population growth, and abundance of leisure time.

Pitirim Sorokin's theory of change had societies fluctuating back and forth like a pendulum through three orientations: ideational, sensate, and idealistic. The *ideational* culture emphasizes feelings and emotions—it is subjective, expressive, and religious. The *sensate* culture emphasizes the senses—it is objective, scientific, materialistic, profane, and instrumental. The *idealistic* culture is an intermediate stage emphasizing logic and rationality. Change between the three types happens because change is normal and continual in any active system. Sorokin felt that our society was in a stage of decline—we are an "overripe" sensate culture. The future looks bad for us, what with loss of freedom, growth of tyranny, deterioration of the family, and loss of creativity. But good things are ahead: "the magnificent peaks of the new Ideational or Idealistic culture."[5]

Evolutionary Theories   Many scholars have seen social change as linear—a line going in one direction, and usually that direction was progress. Auguste Comte viewed societies as moving through three stages: the theological or fictitious, the metaphysical or abstract, and the scientific or positive. Each stage represents a higher level of existence with the ultimate, the positive stage, resulting in the emergence of priest-sociologists who would lead society to a harmonious existence! Comte felt that population increase and density were especially important in influencing change. Herbert Spencer, another evolu-

---

[5]The Sorokin quotes are from Lauer, p. 47.

tionist, likened society to an organism, always growing and increasing in complexity, with its parts dependent on each other. Emile Durkheim saw societies moving from mechanical solidarity (small, primitive, homogeneous) to organic solidarity (large, complex, specialized). As all these theories differed, so did the various views of the future: Comte saw increasing progress with sociologists leading the way; Spencer saw chances for progress *or* regress; and for Durkheim, who took suicide rates as evidence of crisis in modern society, the future looked bleak.

Functional Theories   Functional analysis sees society as a system of interrelated parts and tends to emphasize social equilibrium, stability, and integration of the various pieces. Social change is difficult to accept given this basic perspective. Functional theorists like Talcott Parsons and Neil Smelser suggest that there are tremendous forces resisting change, and that these forces may perhaps be overcome slowly and adaptively because of changes outside the system, growth by differentiation, and internal innovations. Generally, however, stability and inertia triumph and change is viewed as deviant and traumatic.[6]

Conflict Theories   Conflict is universal in the world, and as a force leading to change it figures in several of the theories we have already mentioned. Current conflict theories spring from the ideas of Karl Marx, who felt the economic structure to be the foundation of society—changes or contradictions in the economic realm led to changes in other social relations. Capitalist systems were especially liable to produce conflict. The conflict would come from within as the society polarizes into two antagonistic groups: the rulers (bourgeoisie) and the ruled (proletariat). Ultimately the outcome of this struggle between classes would be a <u>revolution</u> and the emergence of a <u>classless</u> society. One of the attractions of Marxism and conflict theory as an explanation for change is that it promises people a role in determining their future. Far from being pawns manipulated by unseen forces, Marx suggests that people can recognize the conditions of their life, react to them, and change them—they can create their own destiny.

Ralf Dahrendorf, like Marx, believes that in every society some members are subject to coercion by others. This means that class conflict is inevitable, and social change which emerges out of this conflict is also inevitable. Dahrendorf believes that human development, creativity, and innovation emerge mainly from conflicts between groups and individuals. The connection between conflict and social change is well documented. Accepting the conflict approach is tempting for those frustrated with the slowness of change but lacking resources to effectively battle the "system." Over the last decade the use of violence and terrorism to produce change has become increasingly common. As Chairman Mao suggested, "Anything can grow out of the barrel of a gun. . . ."

Neoevolutionary Theories   Some theorists have begun to drift back to and rework the evolutionary ideas of yesteryear. Early evolutionary theories

---

[6]See Lauer's evaluation of functional theory, p. 89.

tended to explain or analyze change by focusing on one central factor—a uni-linear approach. This broke down when the theory didn't fit the facts of a particular culture, and when different theorists came up with different central factors. Modern, or neoevolutionary, theorists still see societies as moving through a series of evolutionary stages, but now the process is seen as multilinear. By this they mean that change is influenced by varied factors and that although there are similarities or parallels, not all cultures change in the same direction or at the same speed. The newer evolutionary theories also place more importance on cultural borrowing and diffusion than did the earlier ones.

Gerhard Lenski is a modern-day evolutionary theorist. He believes that societies move through a series of forms (hunting and gathering, horticultural, agrarian, industrial) based on their mode of subsistence. Continuity, innovation, and extinction are key elements for Lenski. *Continuity* refers to the persistence of certain elements in society and underlines the fact that even in a society that appears to be changing rapidly, most of its elements are not changing. In our society, for example, think of the alphabet, the concept of God, the calendar, or driving on the right-hand side of the road. Elements remain because they are useful, they answer society's needs, or because of the cost involved in changing them. *Innovation* results from inventions and discoveries from within as well as diffusion from other cultures. Innovation occurs at different rates in different societies because of the amount of information available, the number of people disseminating it, whether it is fundamental (the steam engine is more fundamental than the can opener), and whether society is receptive to it. *Extinction* refers to the disappearance of cultural elements or of whole societies. The consequence of these three processes is diversity and progress. Societies become more and more diverse as the processes work at different rates in different societies. Progress occurs, not necessarily in the direction of happiness or some higher state of being, but in the sense of continuing technological developments.

The process of change for Lenski is something like this: diversity among societies causes them to change at different rates, they develop increasing needs for resources, and this leads to increasing competition between societies. This in turn leads to the survival of some societies and the extinction of others. Because societies with the more advanced technologies are more likely to survive, and because technological changes are basically responsible for other changes, technology becomes the crucial factor in social change. Although the technological advances of the last 150 years have generally raised the levels of freedom, justice, and happiness for people in industrial societies, Lenski is not wildly optimistic about the future. His concern with the continuing destruction of the environment, rapid population growth, especially in Third World nations, increasing international tensions and the growing potential for nuclear war lead him to conclude that societies *must* take a more active role in planning their future. They must learn to control population and technology rather than continue to be the victims of uncontrolled growth.[7]

In looking back over these pages on social change theories, several com-

---

[7]See *Human Societies*, 4th ed., by Gerhard Lenski and Jean Lenski (New York: McGraw-Hill, 1982), especially Chapters 2–4, and 14; also see Lauer, Chapters 2 and 12.

ments come to mind. These theories were presented as though each was distinct unto itself, but in fact there is much overlap between them. Some evolutionary theories seem to incorporate cycle theory, the cycles occasionally look evolutionary, the functionalists borrow from evolutionists, while conflict seems to appear everywhere. So what provides the best explanation for social change? Does any theory fit the facts best? That, of course, depends on which set of facts you select—explanations for change in nomadic societies must be different from those attempting to explain change in post-industrial society. On the whole, I find the ideas of the conflict theorists and Lenski's neoevolutionary approach most interesting. Conflict seems to be a major element in social change, increasingly so in recent years. Antagonism between classes is commonplace in many societies and acts as a catalyst for change. Lenski's focus on the importance of technology also makes sense as I write this on a computer, read of fears of nuclear attacks and "first-strike capabilities," and watch TV reports of missiles sinking ships in the South Atlantic.

SOCIAL DISORGANIZATION

Social disorganization refers to the breakdown of norms and roles with the result that customary ways of behaving no longer operate. Suppose the star halfback in the weekend football game is given the ball to run through the opposing team's line, but instead he turns and runs fifty yards the wrong way over his own goal line. The spectators are aghast. Several plays later, a player is running with the ball (in the right direction) only to be tackled by the referee. Again, consternation, because "that's not the way the game is played." The norms are so well known that when they are flagrantly violated and seem to be breaking down, effects on participants are marked. So unusual are these events that sometimes the "norm violators" become famous. A football player had broken loose on a touchdown run in a college game some years ago. No one had a chance to get him, when suddenly an opposing player who was out of the game and sitting on the bench raced onto the field and tackled the ball carrier. The incident made the sports pages throughout the country next day, and the two players (ball carrier and tackler from the bench) appeared on a nationwide television program a few days later to describe the great event. The event was remarkable because the game just isn't played that way.

But let's get back to the spectators at our peculiar game in which on every play something strange happens: a player runs the wrong way, the wrong person is tackled, eight players come into the game as substitutes but only three leave, and the quarterback runs up into the stands to lead cheers. How long would the spectators tolerate this behavior? It is my guess that very soon they would start leaving the stands. "This is ridiculous—the rules seem to change on every play—you don't know what to expect. . . ." In like manner, extensive breakdown in a society's norms and roles may produce a condition of social disorganization. Extreme social disorganization may lead to personal disorganization in which the individual becomes upset, disaffected, demoralized, and apathetic—he may want to "leave the game."

Social disorganization is often used to describe living conditions in ghetto and slum areas, which are damaged by the effects of poverty, anonymity, overcrowding, and absence of roots or ties to the community. The person living in these conditions may, like the person watching the peculiar football game, be disgusted at the way the game is being played and decide to leave or fight back. Socially disorganized inner cities have higher rates of crime, mental illness, infant mortality, disease, and family instability. This is not meant to imply that social disorganization causes these to occur, but rather that social disorganization describes a general set of conditions under which these social problems flourish.

Anomie has also been used to describe a generalized condition of normlessness. French sociologist Emile Durkheim used the concept of anomie to describe a condition in societies in which norms and rules governing people's aspirations and moral conduct had eroded.[8] There is loss of solidarity in that old group ties tend to break down, and there is a loss of consensus in that agreement on values and norms tends to disappear. It is difficult for individuals to know what is expected of them or for them to feel a sense of close identity with the group. Anomie describes a demoralized society in which norms are rapidly changing, uncertain, or conflicting. Durkheim felt that a particular type of suicide occurs in such societies: anomic suicide, in which the individual feels lost and disaffected due to an absence of clear-cut rules and standards for behavior. Durkheim believed that abrupt economic changes—sudden inflation or depression, poverty, or wealth—might lead to anomie. This concept has received much attention recently, especially from sociologists in the areas of criminology and delinquency. Although we will return to it later, the term *anomie* is being introduced here to describe a particular type of social and personal disorganization that results when norms regulating people's aspirations and expectations begin to collapse.

Social disorganization may result from rapid social change. As social change takes place, new norms replace older ones, role behavior is modified, conflict in values occurs, and institutions assume different forms and functions. Individuals, groups, institutions, and societies must adapt to change, and for some of these it may be difficult, especially if change is rapid or if change is defined as unacceptable and is therefore resisted. In such situations we might anticipate social disorganization.

Some sociologists feel that the concept of social disorganization is not very useful. They maintain that the organization of society is constantly in flux, is always changing, and that the result is not disorganization but *reorganization*. They believe that we are really talking about another stage in the social change process rather than about social disorganization. Further, argue the critics of the concept, there is a tendency to apply the label of social disorganization to those things we dislike, to things that may contradict our own particular values or what we are used to. For example, suppose that in the United States we have high divorce and illegitimacy rates, birth control pills are freely available, and teenagers commit more crime than any other age group. Does this mean that the institution of the family in America is a victim of social disorganization, or

---

[8]Emile Durkheim, *Suicide*, translated by John A. Spaulding and George Simpson (New York: Free Press, 1951).

that it is changing to a different form of organization? Is the current situation regarding relations between blacks and whites in America symptomatic of a disorganized society or of a society undergoing change and reorganization? Youth are challenging institutions of higher education throughout the country, and in other parts of the world as well. Does this mean we have social disorganization in the institution of education, or change and reorganization?

My view is that the concept of social disorganization may be helpful in identifying a particular stage that may occur in groups or institutions as they undergo change and reorganization. To produce social disorganization, rapid social change would probably be necessary. In my view, social disorganization involves confusion, disaffection, demoralization, disorientation for individuals—in short, personal disorganization as well. At the same time, it is important to avoid using the concept of social disorganization to describe only those conditions with which we disagree.

SUMMARY

In the previous section of this book, we focused on social organization, the *social fabric* of society. There is a tendency in studying social organization to emphasize the constant, recurring, normal, stable nature of society. In fact, however, all is not as organized, predictable, and fixed as previous sections may have implied. Change and deviation are present in all societies, and this section addresses itself to those topics.

This chapter dealt with the concepts of social change and social disorganization. Social change occurs at varying rates in all societies—on this at least there is general agreement. On some other issues there is more debate: Which, if any, factors are related to change? Is change automatic and inexorable or subject to intervention and control? We have examined cyclic, evolutionary, functional, conflict, and neoevolutionary theories explaining social change. One conclusion is that social disorganization is the condition that sometimes results when norms have broken down and behavior becomes unpredictable. Although there is some disagreement over the usefulness of the concept of social disorganization, it probably is helpful in describing what may happen in periods of rapid and traumatic social change.

In the first of the readings that follow, Robert Dryfoos describes social change among Eskimos and Indians in Canada. There are numerous factors that tend to encourage change. The article by Dryfoos illustrates the point that some cultures are more effective than others at resisting change. Most often, probably, change occurs slowly without creating much disturbance in the society in which it takes place. Occasionally, however, change may be sudden and far-reaching, with dramatic effects. Lauriston Sharp describes the consequences of the introduction of steel axes into a society of Australian aboriginals. Alvin Toffler has been a major commentator on social change in modern society and the third reading examines ideas presented in his new book, *The Third Wave*. The final reading is a study of the social disorganization that occurred in the aftermath of a flood in the mining country of West Virginia.

Terms for Study

anomie (332)	invention (325)
conflict theories (329)	mechanical solidarity (329)
cultural lag (326)	neoevolutionary theories (329–330)
cyclic theories (328)	organic solidarity (329)
diffusion (325–326)	sensate culture (328)
evolutionary theories (328)	social change (322)
functional theories (329)	social disorganization (331)
idealistic culture (328)	strain for consistency (326)
ideational culture (328)	

Reading 11.1

TWO TACTICS FOR ETHNIC SURVIVAL— ESKIMO AND INDIAN

ROBERT J. DRYFOOS, JR.

Social change takes place at varying rates, even within a given geographical area. Some cultures or subcultures are more successful than others at maintaining their identity in the face of a dominant culture that tends to absorb them. Both of these situations are described in anthropologist Robert Dryfoos's article on Eskimos and Indians in Canada.

On the isolated eastern shore of Hudson Bay, about 700 miles northwest of Montreal, lies the community of Great Whale River, Quebec. It cannot be reached by road. When the ice breaks up, in mid-May, the Hudson Bay Company boat makes its way bringing stock for the store. There is an aircraft landing strip, enabling weekly service from Montreal and twice weekly service from Moosonee, Ontario. But outside visitors are usually restricted to the federal or provincial authorities, police, doctors and dentists who serve the community.

At Great Whale River, subarctic temperatures of minus 50 degrees Fahrenheit are not uncommon during the short (six-hour) days of winter. Summer brings 18-hour days, balmy temperatures (up to 85), and swarms of flies and mosquitoes. The surrounding terrain is flat and sandy rising to low, rocky hills to the east and northeast. As the village lies only 100 miles south of the timber line, the trees are small and sparse. Berries grow in season, which is short. Life is hard. The community consists of about 450 Eskimos, 225 Indians and 100 Euro-Canadians. The latter include teachers, medical personnel, Hudson Bay Company employees, representatives of both the federal Canadian government and the Quebec government, and missionaries of the Anglican and

Published by permission of Transaction, Inc., from *Transaction*, vol. 7, no. 3. Copyright © 1970 by Transaction, Inc.

Catholic churches. The Indians are trappers and hunters, trapping beaver and mink in the winter, hunting bear and smaller game year around. Although they now use rifles and shot guns, the Indians still hunt in the bush country to the east as they did in earlier times. The Eskimos are more frequently employed by the government and the Hudson Bay Company. They still hunt seal, and they too have adopted the rifle and shot gun to wound the animals initially before they are harpooned and landed. They have also continued to hunt whale and they trap in the summer, though none of this could be considered their major endeavor. The authorities recognize the difficulties of life in Great Whale River, and most of the people are eligible for and receive welfare payments and child allotments.

While both the Eskimo and the Indians have become settled residents of the village and have largely adopted the material culture of the white man, each group has maintained its own individuality and continues to speak its own language. And although very few rituals, practices or beliefs persist among members of the two native groups, considerable knowledge of the old ways still survives.

Remembrance of things past is the focus of this study; particularly the curious contrast between the remembrances of the Eskimos and the Indians of Great Whale River. The Eskimo has very largely left the past behind with his entry into the modern world; he looks back, if at all, to see a life of hardship and insecurity which he has little wish to perpetuate. Not so the Indian. His past is tenacious, and the days before the coming of the white man are mean-ingful, valued and well remembered. It is as if the bush still calls to him, and the old life holds something of the fascination of a "lost horizons" for the town-dwelling Indian.

The fact that sharp differences in recall do exist between the two native groups emerged in the course of a seven-month field study I conducted during the summers of 1964 and 1965. Why these differing perceptions should exist simultaneously is an intriguing question, especially as the history of contact with modern culture has been almost identical for each group in regard to both duration and intensity. Explanations involve the complex interplay between past and present, and among the three ethnic groups living side by side.

During my two summers in Great Whale River I interviewed approx-imately half the members of each native group, in most cases more than once. To try to insure that "no response" to questions about the past resulted from lack of traditional knowledge and not from unwillingness to answer, I at-tempted to establish a cordial relationship with each person I interviewed, and came to know some quite well. I also established good rapport with my inter-preters, some of whom I used throughout the two summers, and relied heavily on their judgement in determining the truthfulness of the replies.

Among the Eskimos, only 12 percent were able to give information about former customs and beliefs, compared to 75 percent of the Indians. Not a single Eskimo under 35 could demonstrate any recall of the traditional ways; the aver-age age for Eskimo informants was over 65. The average age for Indian infor-mants was 42, and several Indian teen-agers as well as one child of 11 were able to give information about their past.

The amount and depth of knowledge retained shows a similar pattern.

Members of both groups were asked for information about religion, rites of passage, rites of intensification, marriage and residence patterns, myths and legends, kinship, political organization and economic activities. The Indians were able to recall a total of about 85 such items, and almost invariably discussed them in considerable detail. The Eskimos recalled only 25 items, and could usually give only a skeletal version of the material they remembered.

In the traditional legends of both the Eskimos and the Indians there appears a great sea spirit which takes the form of a mermaid. Present-day experience with this mermaid is the closest to a survival of a traditional belief that I was able to discover. About 20 Indians reported that they, or someone they knew, had had some contact with the mermaid, whom they call Mentoxo—either seeing, hearing, or being affected in some way by this sea creature, in whose present existence they expressed belief. Only two Eskimos reported knowing of anyone who had encountered the Eskimo version of the mermaid, whom they call Tariup Inunga. (In most ethnographic literature this Eskimo spirit is known as Sedna, but none of the Eskimos at Great Whale River had ever heard this name, or were even able to pronounce it.) Several of the Indians who said they confronted Mentoxo dated these events within very recent years, whereas the two Eskimo reports of Tariup Inunga occurred perhaps 40 or 50 years ago.

The vitality of the past among the Indians is easily explained on one level: most Indian fathers say it is desirable for their children to learn of traditional Indian customs, and take pains to tell them about the "way things were done, and what we believed before the white man came." Practically every Eskimo, on the other hand, has dispensed with such teaching, explaining that the "old days have little value for today's children." This is true not just in the area of custom and belief, but for practical skills as well. Most Indian parents say it is valuable for the young men to be able to engage in "real" Indian activities, and teach their sons the proper techniques for hunting in the bush. Only a few Eskimo parents want their children to learn how to hunt sea mammals; most adults dismiss the idea, saying it is "too difficult for people today," or "hunting does not pay enough."

The harsh physical environment and the problems of sheer survival in traditional times may provide one clue to both what and how much of the past is recalled today. Although life was difficult for both peoples, the Eskimos faced an environment that was more continuously threatening than did the Indians. Certainly this is how it is viewed in retrospect: many more Eskimos than Indians comment that the old days were "bad," or that "there was great hunger and starvation many years ago." The Eskimos, then, may well have been more apt to recognize the advantages of Euro-Canadian culture and to welcome a way of life offering security and comfort. The Indians, with their less oppressive past, may have adopted the material culture of the white man less wholeheartedly, and this may have carried over to ideological areas as well. For example, although both groups are Christians today, the Eskimos appear to have internalized the Christian faith to a greater extent than the Indians.

Traditionally, both Indian and Eskimo culture was loosely structured, but some of the available ethnographies indicate that Indian culture was the more highly structured of the two and I would hold that this is one reason for its greater persistence. Today, Indians continue to view themselves as comprising a "tribe" or society; knowledge of the past functions as an integrating mechanism and helps to provide a sense of identity as members of an enduring, albeit fragmenting, society. The Eskimos have never considered themselves members of a cohesive group, so identification with the past would have little meaning from this point of view.

The favored position enjoyed by the Eskimos today in the eyes of the dominant white community, and the comparatively inferior status of the Indians, may well be significant in explaining their different regard for the past. I interviewed about three-fourths of the Euro-Canadian population during my study, and learned that they greatly favor the Eskimos. In general, Eskimos are regarded as more industrious and honest, practical and pragmatic, while Indians are often characterized as "dreamers." Both the Eskimos and the Indians are well aware of these attitudes; the Indians also believe they have less chance of being hired for wage labor than the Eskimos, and that they do not have equal access to government funds. Quite naturally, the Indians feel some resentment and hostility toward the white community as a result.

It is my belief that perpetuation of traditional knowledge serves the Indians as a relatively safe outlet for aggression against the whites. The passing on of stories, myths and beliefs of bygone days may also be seen as a nativistic movement, similar to the present-day mask-carving among the Onendaga, as suggested by Jean Hendry. The perpetuation of traditional knowledge may well serve to strengthen the Indians' image of themselves in the face of hostile white attitudes, especially vis-à-vis the Eskimos. Given their preferred status in relation to the Indians, the Eskimos would have no such reason to perpetuate the past, and might only alienate the dominant whites by doing so.

Shifting ecocultural patterns of the two groups may also suggest reasons for their differential recall of the past. Traditionally the Eskimos were oriented toward the sea, spending much of their time hunting seal and walrus on Hudson Bay. Today however, when an Eskimo leaves the village in the morning to hunt seal, he usually returns the same evening to a rather bustling village life. Hunting has become more and more a sideline activity, and at the urging of the white man during the last 20 to 25 years, the Eskimos have turned increasingly to various craft pursuits, especially soapstone-carving. (Soapstone-carving, formerly done only as a pleasant pastime during the long winter nights to ornament children's toys, was not a traditional economic activity of the Eskimos.) In other words, the Eskimo ecological orientation has shifted from the coast to the entirely novel one of the village; in this process, the traditional ties with the whole fabric of the past have been attenuated.

The ecocultural patterns of the Indian have not changed nearly so drastically, and he is still to some degree bush-oriented. The hunters and trappers of today must leave the village for extended periods to reach adequate game supplies—they cannot limit these activities to "off-business hours" as the Eskimos can. Indians are constantly reminded of their past by their present hunting and trapping patterns. Craft production is much less developed, though current efforts are being made to increase it. For the present, however, the Indians con-

tinue to think and talk largely in terms of their traditional bush orientation. The bush, and the old way of life that went with it, still linger as a powerfully nostalgic image to the Indians, even to those who never venture from the village now.

In summary, recollection of the past is meaningful to the Indians; it functions as a mechanism to make them "more Indian," to provide a sense of current identity. But the Eskimos have little interest in being "more Eskimo," and their past is being forgotten at an ever increasing rate.

Questions 11.1

1. Dryfoos suggests that the two groups—Indian and Eskimo—have changed at different rates. What types of evidence does he have for this conclusion?
2. What explanations are there for these different rates of change? Which of the factors related to change discussed in the text seem to fit best?
3. Which group—Eskimo or Indian—is held in higher regard by the dominant white community? Why? In your opinion, is this a typical or unusual occurrence when unlike races or ethnic groups come in contact?

Reading 11.2

STEEL AXES FOR STONE AGE AUSTRALIANS

LAURISTON SHARP

Social change occurs in all societies. Often change takes place without much disruption in the lives of people. Sometimes, however, change is extremely disturbing. This may be because the change is rapid and extensive, or because, regardless of the speed with which it takes place, people are unable to adapt to it. Social change that disrupts the order of a society may lead to social disorganization, possibly even the disintegration of the society. Anthropologist Lauriston Sharp describes what happened when missionaries gave steel axes to the Yir Yoront.

Like other Australian aboriginals, The Yir Yoront group at the mouth of the Coleman River on the west coast of tropical Cape York Peninsula originally had no knowledge of metals. Technologically their culture was of the old stone age or paleolithic type; they supported themselves by hunting and fishing, obtaining vegetable foods and needed materials from the bush by simple gathering techniques. Their only domesticated animal was the dog, and they had no domesticated plants of any kind. Unlike some other aboriginal groups, however, the Yir Yoront did have polished stone axes hafted in short handles, and these implements were most important in their economy.

Excerpted from "Steel Axes for Stone Age Australians" by Lauriston Sharp, in *Human Problems in Technological Change*, edited by Edward H. Spicer, © 1952 by the Russell Sage Foundation, Publishers, New York.

The production of a stone axe required a number of simple skills. With the idea of the axe in its various details well in mind, the adult men—and only the adult men—could set about producing it, a task not considered appropriate for women or children. First of all, a man had to know the location and properties of several natural resources found in his immediate environment: pliable wood, which could be doubled or bent over the axe head and bound tightly to form a handle; bark, which could be rolled into cord for the binding; and gum, with which the stone head could be firmly fixed in the haft. These materials had to be correctly gathered, stored, prepared, cut to size, and applied or manipulated. They were plentifully supplied by nature, and could be taken by a man from anyone's property without special permission. Postponing consideration of the stone head of the axe, we see that a simple knowledge of nature and of the technological skills involved, together with the possession of fire (for heating the gum) and a few simple cutting tools, which might be nothing more than the sharp shells of plentiful bivalves, all of which were available to everyone, were sufficient to enable any normal man to make a stone axe.

The use of the stone axe as a piece of capital equipment for the production of other goods indicates its very great importance in the subsistence economy of the aboriginal. Anyone—man, woman, or child—could use the axe; indeed, it was used more by women, for theirs was the onerous daily task of obtaining sufficient wood to keep the campfire of each family burning all day for cooking or other purposes and all night against mosquitoes and cold (in July, winter temperature might drop below forty degrees). In a normal lifetime any woman would use the axe to cut or knock down literally tons of firewood. Men and women, and sometimes children, needed the axe to make other tools, or weapons, or a variety of material equipment required by the aboriginal in his daily life. The stone axe was essential in making the wet-season domed huts, which keep out some rain and some insects; or platforms, which provide dry storage; or shelters, which give shade when days are bright and hot. In hunting and fishing and in gathering vegetable or animal food the axe was also a necessary tool; and in this tropical culture without preservatives or other means of storage, the native spends more time obtaining food than in any other occupation except sleeping.

In only two instances was the use of the stone axe strictly limited to adult men: Wild honey, the most prized food known to the Yir Yoront, was gathered only by men who usually used the axe to get it; and only men could make the secret paraphernalia for ceremonies, an activity often requiring use of the axe. From this brief listing of some of the activities in which the axe was used, it is easy to understand why there was at least one stone axe in every camp, in every hunting or fighting party, in every group out on a "walk-about" in the bush.

While the stone axe helped relate men and women and often children to nature in technological behavior, in the transformation of natural into cultural equipment, it also was prominent in that aspect of behavior which may be called conduct, primarily directed toward persons. Yir Yoront men were dependent upon interpersonal relations for their stone axe heads, since the flat, geologically recent alluvial country over which they range provides no stone from which axe heads can be made. The stone they used comes from known quarries *four hundred miles to the south. It reached the Yir Yoront through long lines of male trading partners, some of these chains terminating with the Yir Yoront men, while others extended on farther north to other groups, having utilized Yir Yoront men as links. Almost every older adult man had one or more regular trading partners, some to the north and some to the south. His partner or part-ners in the south he provided with surplus spears, and particularly fighting spears tipped with the barbed spines of sting ray, which snap into vicious frag-ments when they penetrate human flesh. For a dozen spears, some of which he may have obtained from a partner to the north, he would receive from a south-ern partner one stone axe head.*

Not only was it adult men alone who obtained axe heads and produced finished axes, but it was adult males who retained the axes, keeping them with other parts of their equipment in camp, or carrying them at the back slipped through a human hair belt when traveling. Thus, every woman or child who wanted to use an axe—and this might be frequently during the day—must get one from some man, use it promptly, and return it to the man in good condition. While a man might speak of "my axe," a woman or child could not; for them it was always "your axe," addressing a male, or "his axe."

This necessary and constant borrowing of axes from older men by women and children was done according to regular patterns of kinship behavior. A woman on good terms with her husband would expect to use his axe unless he were using it; a husband on good terms with his wives would let any one of them use his axe without question. If a woman was unmarried or her husband was absent, she would go first to her older brother or to her father for an axe. Only in extraordinary circumstances would she seek a stone axe from a mother's brother or certain other male kin with whom she had to be most cir-cumspect. A girl, a boy, or a young man would look to a father or an older brother to provide an axe for her or his use, but would never approach a mother's brother, who would be at the same time a potential father-in-law, with such a request. Older men, too, would follow similar rules if they had to borrow an axe.

It will be noted that these social relationships in which the stone axe had a place are all pair relationships and that the use of the axe helped define and maintain the character of the relationships and the roles of the two individual participants. Every active relationship among the Yir Yoront involved a definite and accepted status of superordination or subordination. A person could have no dealings with any other on exactly equal terms. Women and children were dependent on, or subordinate to, older males in every action in which the axe entered.

The stone axe was an important symbol of masculinity among the Yir Yoront (just as pants or pipes are among ourselves). By a complicated set of ideas which we would label "ownership" the axe was defined as "belonging" to males. Everyone in the society (except untrained infants) accepted these ideas. Similarly spears, spear throwers, and fire-making sticks were associated with males, were owned only by them, and were symbols of masculinity. But the masculine values represented by the stone axe were constantly being impressed on all members of society by the fact that non-males had to use the axe and had to go to males for it, whereas they never borrowed other masculine artifacts. Thus, the axe stood for an important theme and ran all through Yir Yoront culture: the superiority and rightful dominance of the male, and the greater value of his concerns and of all things associated with him. We should call this androcentrism rather than patriarchy; the man ("andros") takes precedence over feminine values, an idea backed by very strong sentiments among the Yir Yoront. Since the axe had to be borrowed also by the younger from the older, it also represented the prestige of age, another important theme running all through Yir Yoront behavior.

The introduction of the steel axe indiscriminately and in large numbers into the Yir Yoront technology was only one of many changes occurring at the same time. It is therefore impossible to factor out all the results of this single innovation alone. Nevertheless, a number of specific effects of the change from stone axes to steel axes may be noted; and the steel axe may be used as an epitome of the European goods and implements received by the aboriginals in increasing quantity and of their general influence on the native culture. The use of the steel axe to illustrate such influences would seem to be justified, for it was one of the first European artifacts to be adopted for regular use by the Yir Yoront; and the axe, whether of stone or steel, was clearly one of the most important items of cultural equipment they possessed.

The shift from stone to steel axes provided no major technological difficulties. While the aboriginals themselves could not manufacture steel axe heads, a steady supply from outside continued; and broken wooden axe handles could easily be replaced from bush timbers with aboriginal tools. Among the Yir Yoront the new axe never acquired all the use it had on mission or cattle stations (carpentry work, pounding tent pegs, use as a hammer, and so on); and, indeed, it was used for little more than the stone axe had been, so that it had no practical effect in improving the native standard of living. It did some jobs better, and could be used longer without breakage; and these factors were sufficient to make it of value to the native. But the assumption of the white man (based in part on a realization that a shift from steel to stone axe in his case would be a definite regression) that his axe was much more efficient, that its use would save time, and that it therefore represented technical "progress" toward goals which he had set for the native was hardly borne out in aboriginal practice. Any leisure time the Yir Yoront might gain by using steel axes or other western tools was invested, not in "improving the conditions of life," and certainly not in developing aesthetic activities, but in sleep, an art they had thoroughly mastered.

Having acquired an axe head through regular trading partners of whom he knew what to expect, a man wanting a stone axe was then dependent solely upon a known and an adequate nature and upon his own skills or easily acquired techniques. A man wanting a steel axe, however, was in no such self-reliant position. While he might acquire one through trade, he now had the new alternative of dispensing with technological behavior in relation with a predictable trading partner and of turning instead to conduct alone in relation with a highly erratic missionary. If he attended one of the mission festivals when steel axes were handed out as gifts, he might receive one simply by chance or if he had happened somehow to impress upon the mission that he was one of the "better" bush aboriginals (their definition of "better" being quite different from that of his bush fellows). Or he might—but again almost by pure chance—be given some brief job in connection with the mission which would enable him to earn a steel axe. In either case, for older men a preference for the steel axe helped create a situation of dependence in place of a situation of self-reliance and a behavior shift from situations in technology or conduct which were well structured or defined to situations in conduct alone which were ill defined. It was particularly the older ones among the men, whose earlier experience or knowledge of the white man's harshness in any event made them suspicious, who would avoid having any relations with the mission at all, and who thus excluded themselves from acquiring steel axes directly from that source.

The steel axe was the root of psychological stress among the Yir Yoront even more significantly in other aspects of social relations. This was the result of new factors which the missionary considered all to the good: the simple numerical increase in axes per capita as a result of mission distribution; and distribution from the mission directly to younger men, women, and even children. By winning the favor of the mission staff, a woman might be given a steel axe. This was clearly intended to be hers. The situation was quite different from that involved in borrowing an axe from a male relative, with the result that a woman called such an axe "my" steel axe, a possessive form she never used for a stone axe. Furthermore, young men or even boys might also obtain steel axes directly from the mission. A result was that older men no longer had a complete monopoly of all the axes in the bush community. Indeed, an old man might have only a stone axe, while his wives and sons had steel axes which they considered their own and which he might even desire to borrow. All this led to a revolutionary confusion of sex, age, and kinship roles, with a major gain in independence and loss of subordination on the part of those able now to acquire steel axes when they had been unable to possess stone axes before.

The trading partner relationship was also affected by the new situation. A Yir Yoront might have a trading partner in a tribe to the south whom he defined as a younger brother, and on whom as an older brother he would therefore have an edge. But if the partner were in contact with the mission or had other easier access to steel axes, his subordination to his bush colleague was obviously decreased. Indeed, under the new dispensation he might prefer to give his axe to a bush "sweetheart" in return for favors or otherwise dispose of it outside regular trade channels, since many steel axes were so distributed between natives in new ways. Among other things, this took some of the excitement away from the fiesta-like tribal gatherings centering around initiations during the dry season. These had traditionally been the climactic annual occasions for exchanges between trading partners, when a man might seek to acquire a whole year's supply of stone axe heads. Now he might find himself prostituting his wife to almost total strangers in return for steel axes or other white men's goods. With trading partnerships weakened, there was less reason to attend the fiestas, and less fun for those who did. A decline in one of the important social activities which had symbolized these great gatherings created a lessening of interest in the other social aspects of these events.

The most disturbing effects of the steel axe, operating in conjunction with other elements also being introduced from the white man's several subcultures, developed in the realm of traditional ideas, sentiments, and values. These were undermined at a rapidly mounting rate, without new conceptions being defined to replace them. The result was a mental and moral void which foreshadowed the collapse and destruction of all Yir Yoront culture, if not, indeed, the extinction of the biological group itself.

From what has been said it should be clear how changes in overt behavior, in technology and conduct, weakened the values inherent in a reliance on nature, in androcentrism or the prestige of masculinity, in age prestige, and in the various kinship relations. A scene was set in which a wife or young son, his initiation perhaps not even yet completed, need no longer bow to the husband or father, who was left confused and insecure as he asked to borrow a steel axe from them. For the woman and boy the steel axe helped establish a new degree of freedom which was accepted readily as an escape from the unconscious stress of the old patterns, but which left them also confused and insecure. Ownership became less well defined, so that stealing and trespass were introduced into technology and conduct. Some of the excitement surrounding the great ceremonies evaporated, so that the only fiestas the people had became less festive, less interesting. Indeed, life itself became less interesting, although this did not lead the Yir Yoront to invent suicide, a concept foreign to them.

The bush Yir Yoront, still trying to maintain their aboriginal definition of the situation, accepted European artifacts and behavior patterns, but fit them into their totemic system, assigning them as totems to various clans on a par with original totems. There is an attempt to have the myth-making process keep up with these cultural changes so that the idea system can continue to support the rest of the culture. But analysis of overt behavior, of dreams, and of some of the new myths indicates that this arrangement is not entirely satisfactory; that the native clings to his totemic system with intellectual loyalty, lacking any substitute ideology; but that associated sentiments and values are weakened. His attitudes toward his own and toward European culture are found to be highly ambivalent.

The steel axe, like most European goods, has no distinctive origin myth, nor are mythical ancestors associated with it. Can anyone, sitting of an afternoon in the shade of a ti tree, create a myth to resolve this confusion? No one has, and the horrid suspicion arises that perhaps the origin myths are wrong, which took into account so little of this vast new universe of the white man. The steel axe, shifting hopelessly between one clan and the other, is not only replacing the stone axe physically, but is hacking at the supports of the entire cultural system.

During a wet season stay at the mission, the anthropologist discovered that his supply of tooth paste was being depleted at an alarming rate. Investigation showed that it was being taken by old men for use in a new tooth paste cult. Old materials of magic having failed, new materials were being tried out in a malevolent magic directed toward the mission staff and some of the younger aboriginal men. Old males, largely ignored by the missionaries, were seeking to regain some of their lost power and prestige. This mild aggression proved *hardly effective, but perhaps only because confidence in any kind of magic on the mission was by this time at a low ebb.*

For the Yir Yoront still in the bush a time could be predicted when personal deprivation and frustration in a confused culture would produce an overload of anxiety. The mythical past of the totemic ancestors would disappear as a guarantee of a present of which the future was supposed to be a stable continuation. Without the past, the present would be meaningless and the future unstructured and uncertain. Insecurities would be inevitable. Reaction to this stress might be some form of symbolic aggression, or withdrawal and apathy, or some more realistic approach.

Questions 11.2

1. What changes in the Yir Yoront culture followed the introduction of the steel axe?
2. Use the terms "social disorganization," "anomie," and "reorganization" to analyze and describe the condition of the Yir Yoront.
3. Why did the Yir Yoront have such difficulty adapting to the introduction of the steel axe?
4. What elements introduced into American culture have led to dramatic social change? As you list several, discuss why they didn't have the disastrous effect that introduction of the steel axe had for the Yir Yoront.

Reading 11.3

THE THIRD WAVE—ALVIN TOFFLER

HAROLD GILLIAM

Alvin Toffler's avid interest in social change in modern societies is reflected in his books *Future Shock* and *The Third Wave*. In this selection, newspaper columnist Harold Gilliam summarizes and evaluates Toffler's latest work.

In his new book which is more positive and hopeful than his earlier Future Shock, *Alvin Toffler tells us that a Third Wave of change is thundering down on us and will drastically change the way we live and work. The First Wave of change was the Agricultural Revolution, when humans quit hunting and started to till the soil. The Second Wave was the Industrial Revolution, now approaching its terminal stages with the end of the cheap energy and cheap raw materials that made it possible. The Third Wave, about to engulf us, has no distinct name yet, but Toffler offers a field guide to its signs and symptoms and its impact on our lives.*

It will be powered not by old Second Wave fossil fuels, including uranium, but by renewable energy sources such as photovoltaics, plants like the one in the Philippines that produces electricity from coconut waste, Japan's wave-powered generator, a Soviet scheme for tethered-balloon windmills in the high atmosphere, a power-tower being built in the California desert to capture solar energy through computer-controlled mirrors, a German hydrogen-powered bus and a Lockheed plan for hydrogen powered planes.

These will be the backbone industries of the Third Wave:

•Electronics and computers, particularly home mini-computers that will run the household and even enable the house to repair itself. Electronics is giving us low-energy innovations such as the fiber-optic telephone conduit that requires one-thousandth of the energy to manufacture as old, Second-Wave copper wire.

•Space manufacturing. Orbital factories and space platforms offer the advantage of zero-gravity and zero-atmosphere environments to make things that cannot be made as cheaply or cannot be made at all on earth—crystals for lasers and fiber optics, single-crystal semiconductors, blood-clot dissolvers, hundreds of alloys. The workers, of course, will live in space for extended periods of time.

•Ocean development. Aquaculture, including fish farming and fish herding, offers "a virtually endless supply of desperately needed protein." Algae that produce oil can be grown in salt water. Manganese nodules and other deposits on the ocean floor hold promise of great quantities of minerals from copper to gold to phosphate needed for fertilizer.

•The gene industry. Genetic engineering can produce high-yielding crops that can be grown almost anywhere. It might even breed people, Toffler says, "with cowlike stomachs so they can digest grass and hay." A risky business, as Dr. Frankenstein learned. But confined to creating new food supplies, genetic engineering seems to hold great potential.

Toffler also predicts the "demassification of the media." Cable TV and video casettes will replace the mass media, including the TV networks, with hundreds of programs beamed to special tastes and needs.

Not only the mass media but mass production will be left behind as we develop technology for custom-made goods. Already the clothing industry has a computer-based laser gun that can be programmed to make a single shirt to order, faster than mass production makes standard sizes. So maybe you will some day stand in front of a video camera that sizes you up for a new suit and feeds the measurements into a computer that instructs a machine at the factory to produce exactly what you want.

Home, Toffler says, is likely to become the "electronic cottage." Millions of people will no longer commute to office buildings but will do their jobs at home, where the results will be transmitted to headquarters (or to another worker's home) by electronics. If only 12 to 14 per cent of urban commuters worked at home instead of an office, the U.S. would save enough gasoline to eliminate all oil imports. Goodby, OPEC.

Working at home might even bring the fragmented family together again. Husbands and wives and perhaps children might share jobs as well as house-

work. Mates might be selected not only for love but for potential job performance. Toffler proposes some appropriate lyrics for a future love song:

> "I love your eyes, your cherry lips,
> the love that always lingers,
> your way with words and random blips,
> your skilled computer fingers."

The "prosumer" is Toffler's neologism for the Third Wave person who is neither exclusively a producer or consumer but combines elements of both. Customer-originated manufacturing like the design-your-own clothes laser gun will be applied in other industries so that in time you might be designing your own car with a computer that would activate the factory to produce it, untouched by human hands.

More and more people will raise their own food, weave their own rugs, make their own clothing with new home technologies. Contemplating this defection from the marketplace, Toffler becomes euphoric. The energies formerly poured into building a worldwide market system are turned to higher endeavors: "New religions will be born. Works of art on a hitherto unimagined scale. Fantastic scientific advances . . . New kinds of social and political institutions," including direct democracy by two-way TV as you vote on issues of the day by home pushbutton.

There are legitimate questions: Is Toffler describing a Third Wave or an extension of the Second? He talks about the death of industrialism, but who is going to dig the iron and smelt the steel and fabricate the high-tech equipment that is going to mine the oceans and send up orbiting space factories?

We can't all work at home. The chances are there will still be grubby jobs to do, and Second-Wave basic industry is likely to be around for a long time to come. Toffler offers no solid evidence that the economies of mass production can be left behind by the use of laser guns or voice-activated computers.

"Demassification," he says, will provide freedom from time-clocks and more opportunity for individual tastes in all areas of life from setting your own work schedule to getting specialized TV programs beamed at your own needs.

OK, but in increasing the alternatives we may reach the point of diminishing returns. Too many choices can be as frustrating as too few. Computers may be capable of giving us thousands of choices and millions of pieces of information every day, but they can't give us the ability to choose wisely or to achieve some degree of composure amid all the thundering, crashing, roaring and raging around us.

Questions 11.3

1. Toffler's book appeared in 1980. How much of what he predicts for the future has already happened? Give specific examples.
2. Critique Toffler—where do his predictions seem to be off?
3. Analyze Toffler in terms of the five theoretical positions discussed in this chapter. Which category does he seem to fit into? Why? Why not the others?

Reading 11.4

EVERYTHING IN ITS PATH

KAI ERIKSON

On February 26, 1972, a makeshift mining-company dam in the hills of West Virginia gave way and a flood of water swept down Buffalo Creek. Communities along Buffalo Creek were destroyed and 125 people were killed. For the survivors, the disaster turned what had been a tightly knit community into a collection of disorganized people with no roots, no neighborhood, and little of the feeling they formerly held for each other. Sociologist Kai Erikson described the effects of the disaster in *Everything in Its Path*. In this excerpt from his book, Erikson describes the trauma of loss of communality. By communality Erikson means a state of mind shared among a particular gathering of people.

In most of the urban areas of America, each individual is seen as a separate being, with careful boundaries drawn around the space he or she occupies as a discrete personage. Everyone is presumed to have an individual name, an individual mind, an individual voice, and, above all, an individual sense of self—so much so that persons found deficient in any of those qualities are urged to take some kind of remedial action such as undergoing psychotherapy, participating in a consciousness-raising group, or reading one of a hundred different manuals on self-actualization. This way of looking at things, however, has hardly any meaning at all in most of Appalachia. There, boundaries are drawn around whole groups of people, not around separate individuals with egos to protect and potentialities to realize; and a person's mental health is measured less by his capacity to express his inner self than by his capacity to submerge that self into a larger communal whole.

I am going to propose, then, that most of the traumatic symptoms experienced by the Buffalo Creek survivors are a reaction to the loss of communality as well as a reaction to the disaster itself, that the fear and apathy and demoralization one encounters along the entire length of the hollow are derived from the shock of being ripped out of a meaningful community setting as well as the shock of meeting that cruel black water.

It is almost like a ghost town now.

It has changed from the community of paradise to Death Valley.

Some reason or other, it's not the same. Seems like it's frozen.

I have found that most of the people are depressed, unhappy, mournful, sick. When you go up Buffalo Creek the only remains you see is an occasional house here and there. The people who are living in the trailers have a depressed and worried look on their faces. You don't see children out playing and running as before. Buffalo Creek looks like a deserted, forsaken place.

What I miss most is the friendliness and closeness of the people of Buffalo Creek. The people are changed from what they were before the disaster. Practically everyone seems despondent and undecided, as if they were waiting for something and did not know what. They can't reconcile themselves to the fact that things will never be the same again.

It's kind of sad around there now. There's not much happiness. You don't have any friends around, people around, like we had before. Some of them are in the trailer camps. Some of them bought homes and moved away. Some of them just left and didn't come back. It's like teeth in an old folk's mouth down there now.

People don't know what they want or where they want to go. It is almost as though they don't care what happens anymore.

My husband and myself used to enjoy working and improving on our home, but we don't have the heart to do anything anymore. It's just a dark cloud hanging over our head. I just can't explain how we feel.

I don't know. I just got to the point where I just more or less don't care. I don't have no ambition to do the things I used to do. I used to try to keep things up, but anymore I just don't. It seems I just do enough to get by, to make it last one more day. It seems like I just lost everything at once, like the bottom just dropped out of everything.

The clinical name for this state of mind, of course, is depression, and one can hardly escape the conclusion that it is, at least in part, a reaction to the ambiguities of post-disaster life in the hollow. Most of the survivors never realized the extent to which they relied on the rest of the community to reflect back a sense of meaning to them, never understood the extent to which they depended on others to supply them with a point of reference. When survivors say they feel "adrift," "displaced," "uprooted," "lost," they mean that they do not seem to belong to anything and that there are no longer any familiar social landmarks to help them fix their position in time and space. They are depressed, yes, but it is a depression born of the feeling that they are suspended pointlessly in the middle of nowhere. "It is like being all alone in the middle of a desert," said one elderly woman who lives with her retired husband in a cluster of homes. As she talked, the voices of the new neighbors could be heard in the background; but they were not <u>her</u> neighbors, not <u>her</u> people, and the rhythms of their lives did not provide <u>her</u> with any kind of orientation.

This failure of personal morale is accompanied by a deep suspicion that moral standards are beginning to collapse all over the hollow, and in some ways, at least, it would appear that they are. As so frequently happens in human life, the forms of misbehavior people find cropping up in their midst are exactly those about which they are most sensitive. The use of alcohol, always problematic in mountain society, has evidently increased, and there are rumors spreading throughout the trailer camps that drugs have found their way into the area. The theft rate has gone up too, and this has always been viewed in Appalachia as a sure index of social disorganization. The cruelest cut of all, *however, is that once close and devoted families are having trouble staying within the pale they once observed so carefully. Adolescent boys and girls appear to be slipping away from parental control and are becoming involved in nameless delinquencies, while there are reports from several of the trailer camps that younger wives and husbands are meeting one another in circumstances that violate all the local codes. A home is a moral sphere as well as a physical dwelling, of course, and it would seem that the boundaries of moral space began to collapse as the walls of physical space were washed down the creek. The problem is a complex one. People simply do not have enough to do, especially teen-agers, and "fooling around" becomes one of the few available forms of recreation. People have old memories and old guilts to cope with, especially the seasoned adults, and drinking becomes a way to accomplish that end. And, for everyone, skirting the edges of once-forbidden territory is a way to bring new excitement and a perverse but lively kind of meaning into lives that are otherwise without it.*

A retired miner in his sixties speaking of himself:

I did acquire a very bad drinking problem after the flood which I'm doing my level best now to get away from. I was trying to drink, I guess, to forget a lot of things and get them moved out of my mind, and I just had to stop because I was leading the wrong way. I don't know what the answer is, but I know that's not it. I don't want to drink. I never was taught that. I've drunk a right smart in my life, but that's not the answer.

And a woman in her late twenties who had recently moved out of the largest of the trailer camps:

There was all kinds of mean stuff going on up there. I guess it still does, to hear the talk.·I haven't been back up there since we left. Men is going with other men's wives. And drinking parties. They'd play horseshoes right out by my trailer, and they'd play by streetlight until four or five in the morning. I'd get up in the morning and I'd pick up beer cans until I got sick. The flood done something to people, that's what it is. It's changed people. Good people has got bad. They don't care anymore. "We're going to live it up now because we might be gone tomorrow," that's the way they look at it. They call that camp "Peyton Place," did you know that? Peyton Place. I was scared to death up there. I don't even like to go by it.

Many marriages have broken up that seemed secure before the flood. My husband and I can agree on only one thing: we won't go back to Lorado. When the time comes to buy us a house, we both agree that we will face a major problem in our marriage. I hope we can agree on where to live. If not, then we may have to come to a parting of the ways after twenty-six years of marriage.

My husband and I, we was happy before the flood. We got along real good, other than just a few quarrels that never amounted to nothing. But after the flood we had fights, and it was constantly we were quarreling about something or other. We had fights. He would hit me and he would choke me and he would slap me around.

My children are changed. I sit and try to talk to them, tell them they are a family and should love each other and treat each other like brothers and sisters. But most of the time they treat each other like enemies. They're always on the firing line at each other. It's always screaming and yelling.

My grandchildren. It used to be we was the loveliest people you ever seen. We was, together. Now my grandchildren won't hardly give me a look. I don't know what's wrong. They seem like they are moody or something. My grandson there, used to be he loved me better than anything, and now he won't even look at me. He don't want to be around me. One of the granddaughters, too, is about the same. She has spells that way. I don't know. I can't understand it.

I have good new neighbors, but it's not the same. The neighbors I had before the flood shared our happiness when our babies were born, they shared our troubles and our sorrows. Here is the change. My husband has been sick going on three weeks. My old neighbors would ask about him or go see him or send him a get-well card. But he only got one card, and it was from someone away from here. The day the flood came, the people of Buffalo Creek started running, and they are still running inside their minds. They don't have time to stand and talk.

One result of all this is that the community, what remains of it, seems to have lost its most significant quality—the power it generated in people to care for one another in times of need, to console one another in times of distress, to protect one another in times of danger. Looking back, it does seem that the general community was stronger than the sum of its parts. When the people of the hollow were sheltered together in the embrace of a secure community, they were capable of extraordinary acts of generosity; but when they tried to relate to one another as individuals, separate entities, they found that they could no longer mobilize whatever resources are required for caring and nurturing.

It used to be that everyone knew everyone. When you were hitchhiking, you just put out your thumb and the first car along would pick you up. But it's not like that now. They just don't care about you now. They got problems of their own, I guess.

The changes I see are in the people. They seem to be so indifferent toward their fellow man. I guess it's because they had to watch a whole lifetime go down the drain.

I'm getting old, too, and I can't get no help. Nobody'll help you do nothing. You have to pay somebody, and they'll come and start a project for you, but then they'll walk off and leave you. It's just too much.

In general, then, the loss of communality on Buffalo Creek has meant that people are alone and without very much in the way of emotional shelter. In the first place, the community no longer surrounds people with a layer of insulation to protect them from a world of danger. There is no one to warn you if disaster strikes, no one to rescue you if you get caught up in it, no one to care for you if you are hurt, no one to mourn you if the worst comes to pass. In the second place—and this may be more important in the long run—the community can no longer enlist its members in a conspiracy to make a perilous world seem safe. Among the benefits of human communality is the fact that it allows people to camouflage what might otherwise be an overwhelming set of realities, and the question one should ask about Buffalo Creek is whether the people who live there are paralyzed by imaginary fears or paralyzed by the prospects of looking reality in the eye without the help of a communally shared filter.

Questions 11.4

1. Apply the terms "social disorganization" and "anomie" to the previous selection.
2. "It was not social disorganization but reorganization that the people of Buffalo Creek were experiencing." Analyze and comment.
3. Forecast the future of the Buffalo Creek area using the social change theories discussed in this chapter.

12
Collective Behavior

Collective behavior is group behavior that is spontaneous, unstructured, and unstable. It may be either sporadic and short term or more continuous and long-lasting.[1] Collective behavior is often hard to predict because it is not rooted in the usual cultural or social norms. Spontaneous and unstructured behavior is hard to observe or record objectively and is, therefore, difficult to study. Ethically and practically, the researcher cannot yell "Fire!" in a crowded theater, start a downtown riot, or produce a natural disaster and then observe how people behave. Although there have been some artificial or laboratory-created studies of rumor and panic, most studies of collective behavior by social scientists are after-the-fact analyses and discussions with people who happened to be involved. However, these studies have revealed that collective behavior, although spontaneous, is not as disorganized as it appears and, in fact, follows reasonably consistent patterns. Some of these patterns are examined in this chapter as we look at analyses of crowds (audiences, mobs), rumor, fads and fashions, mass hysteria, disaster behavior, publics, public opinion, and social movements.

---

[1]Treatment of concepts in this chapter in general follows the description given by Ralph Turner and Lewis Killian in their book, *Collective Behavior*, 2d ed. (Englewood Cliffs, N.J.: Prentice-Hall, 1972).

CROWDS

An outline of the major collective behavior concepts would start with the crowd. A **crowd** is a temporary collection of people in close physical contact reacting together to a common stimulus. For example, the passengers on the flight from New York to San Francisco whose pilot suddenly decides he would like to go to the North Pole might be transformed from an aggregation into a crowd (or even a mob). Crowds have certain characteristics in common. **Milling** usually occurs as a crowd is being formed. In one sense milling refers to the excited, restless, physical movement of the individuals involved. In a more important sense milling refers to a process of communication that leads to a definition of the situation and possible collective action. Not long ago, a Berkeley classroom suddenly started shaking with the first tremors of an earthquake. Almost at once the people began turning, shifting, looking at each other, at the ceiling, and at the instructor. They were seeking some explanation for the highly unusual experience and, whether spoken aloud or not, the questions on their faces were clear: "What is it?" "Did you feel it?" "What should we do?" Buzzing became louder talking, and someone shouted, "Earthquake!!!" The students began to get up and move toward the doors. Many continued to watch the ceiling. . . . Milling may involve the long buildup of a lynch mob, or the sudden reaction in a dark and crowded theater when someone shouts "Fire!!!" Milling helps ensure the development of a common mood for crowd members.

When they are part of a crowd, people tend to be *suggestible*. They are less critical and will readily do things that they would not ordinarily do alone. This is in part because, as members of a crowd, they are *anonymous*. There is a prevailing feeling that it is the crowd that is responsible, not the individual. Once one becomes a member of an active crowd, it is extremely difficult to step back,

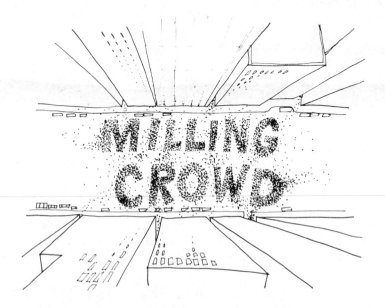

get perspective, and objectively evaluate what one is doing. Crowd members have a narrowed focus, a kind of tunnel vision. The physical presence of a crowd is a powerful force—people almost have to separate themselves from the crowd physically before they can critically examine their own behavior. There is also a *sense of urgency* about crowds. Crowds are oriented toward a specific focus or task: "We've got to do *this*, and we've got to do it *now!*" Some form of leadership usually appears in the crowd, but, as the mood of the crowd changes, the leadership may shift quickly from one individual or group to another.

There are many different types of crowds. Some are passive—those watching a building burn or those at the scene of an accident. Some are active—a race riot or a lynch mob. Some crowds have a number of loosely defined goals. Other crowds are focused on a specific goal. Turner and Killian distinguish between crowds that direct their action toward some external object—harassing a speaker until he leaves the platform or lynching a criminal—and expressive crowds that direct their focus on the crowd itself—cheering at a football game or speaking in tongues at a church service.

Controlling the behavior of a crowd is difficult because of the mass of people involved and the spontaneous nature of their behavior. Some methods of dealing with a potentially riotous crowd have been suggested, however: Remove or isolate the individuals involved in the precipitating incident. Reduce the feelings of anonymity and invincibility of the individuals—force them to focus on themselves and the consequences of their action. Interrupt patterns of communication during the milling process by breaking the crowd into small units. Remove the crowd leaders if it can be done without use of force. Finally, attempt to distract the attention of the crowd by creating a diversion or a new point of interest, especially if this can be accomplished by someone who is considered to be in sympathy with the crowd.[2]

AUDIENCES, MOBS, RIOTS

Audiences and mobs are specific types of crowds. An **audience** at a concert, football game, lecture, religious service, or burning building may usually be likened to a passive crowd. Emotional contagion is possible in such situations, and individuals are responsive in a group in ways that they would not be as individuals. Audiences at performances of rock and roll stars and in Pentecostal church services may become very expressive in a variety of possibly unpredictable ways. Comedians expect audiences to laugh at their jokes. But most comedians have "bits" that they deliver when audiences are unpredictable and don't laugh (Johnny Carson gets audience sympathy by jokingly mentioning his "war injuries"). Much of audience behavior is predictable, or at least predictably unpredictable. The football fan knows he is going to cheer at the game, the comedian's rejection bits are well prepared, and rock concerts are

---

[2]For dimensions, types, and control of crowds, see Turner and Killian, *Collective Behavior*, Chapters 5–9 (see footnote 1).

adequately staffed with police to protect the musicians, and with nurses to minister to the fans. At the same time, audiences demonstrate collective behavior characteristics in that their behavior is frequently spontaneous, and members are suggestible and anonymous.

A **mob** is a focused, acting crowd. It is emotionally aroused, intent on taking aggressive action. A lynch mob would be an example of such a crowd. A waterfight between several fraternities in Berkeley on a warm spring day spontaneously turned into a panty raid. Thousands of eager young men marched with determination through the campus community methodically stealing panties from numerous sorority houses. Afterwards, many of the participants expressed amazement that they had been involved in such behavior. Mob behavior has occurred more recently when unusual events—a severe winter storm in New Jersey and power outages in New York City—have been followed by looting and vandalism.

The lights went out in New York City at about 9:35 in the evening on July 13, 1977. The looting and property damage which followed cost businesses $135 to $150 million. Robert Curvin and Bruce Porter studied the mob behavior that occurred during the blackout and they discovered some interesting patterns. Different types of people looted at different stages of the blackout. Stage one looters started shortly after the lights went out and were generally criminal types—over eighty percent had previous arrest records. They moved in quickly and selected valuable merchandise which they could sell quickly and profitably. A typical example: a man gathered several friends and a thirty-eight-foot moving van and filled the truck twice with such goods as Pampers, baby food, color TVs, leather coats, and sneakers. Stage two looters started a little later and were primarily teenagers out looking for fun and excitement. Stage two also included unemployed, poorly educated ghetto poor under the age of thirty-five. Their looting tended to be random and unorganized. Stage three looting started several hours later and lasted into the next day. Looters at this stage were likely to be working-class people who got caught up in the street activity and felt social pressure to get involved. Better off, employed people with little if any experience in crime were common. Unfortunately for them, police were now becoming more effective and more arrests were taking place. As one participant (a salesman with a family income of $375 a week) said, "I wasn't thinking about a color TV or anything that the professional dudes were after, like cars and things. I just wanted to snatch something." A store was broken into, things were thrown out on the street, he gathered up a pile of women's clothes, a police car pulled up and he was arrested. Curvin and Porter suggest that since the looters arrested during the blackout had very high unemployment rates, the main cause of the theft and destruction was the blackout opportunity combined with the national economic decline, high unemployment, high prices for essentials, and the worsened living conditions of the poor.[3]

A **riot** describes the situation in which mob behavior has become in-

---

[3]See *Blackout Looting: New York City, July 13, 1977,* by Robert Curvin and Bruce Porter (New York: Gardner Press, 1979), and their article, "Blackout Looting," in *Society,* May/June 1979, pp. 68–76.

creasingly widespread and destructive. Riots may involve a number of mobs acting independently. Throughout our history, the United States has had riots over the issue of race: New York, 1863; Chicago, 1919; Detroit, 1943. In the 1960s, urban riots occurred with increasing frequency. The issues were social class and poverty as well as race. The Watts riot in Los Angeles in the summer of 1965 lasted six days. Nearly 4,000 people were arrested, and property damage was estimated at over $40 million. Thirty-four people were killed and over 1,000 people injured. Most of the dead and injured were blacks. In the Detroit riot in the summer of 1967 more than forty people died, and property damage was estimated at $50 million. The relatively minor incident that set off the week-long confrontation was the police closing of a "blind-pig," an after-hours tavern. A crowd collected as the police carted off the tavern's patrons, a stone was thrown, a shoe store was set on fire, and the riot was on. Campus disturbances occurred in the late 1960s at San Francisco State, Berkeley, Harvard, Columbia, Cornell, and at a number of other schools. It is likely, however, that to call these occasions riots, as the press often did, is an exaggeration of what actually happened. Riots have taken place at prisons and sporting events. A highly unusual situation occurred in 1969 when a disagreement at a soccer match led to a riot, which in turn led to a short war between Honduras and El Salvador.

England had their worst riots in a century during July 1981. Gangs of white, black, and Asian youths burned cars, stoned police, and smashed shops. In the first week, 300 policemen were injured, millions of dollars' worth of property was destroyed, and more than 1,000 people were arrested in disturbances in London, Liverpool, Manchester, and other cities. In the analysis which followed there was much disagreement over causes, but the following conditions were mentioned most often: high rates of unemployment (especially among black youth), racism, and the resentment many young people had of police and authority.

Social scientists have studied riots extensively since the activities of the 1960s. Ralph Conant has examined a number of urban conflicts, and he suggests four phases that describe the possible life history of a riot. Conant believes that not all civil disturbances go through all four stages—in fact, most do not even reach phase three but die out earlier. Typically, the temper or mood of the participants is ambivalent and unstable throughout the riot.

> *Phase One—The precipitating incident:* Some gesture, act, or event is taken by the community as concrete evidence of injustice. The incident—use of force by police, eviction of a tenant—is inflammatory because it is seen as typical of the antagonist. It is seen as ample excuse for striking back and tends to draw together a large number of people. In a community where there is much unrest, the precipitating incident may be a minor event to others, but it is very important to the members of the community.

> *Phase Two—Confrontation:* More and more people gather. Individuals suggest targets for violence and attempt to focus crowd reaction, a process called *keynoting*. Other individuals attempt to calm the crowd and encourage moderation. Police officials may appear and attempt to disrupt the keynoting by dispersing the crowd. This may have the opposite effect and raise a hostile keynoter to an

even more prominent position. Conant states that the outcome of phase two is of crucial importance. The temper of the crowd may calm, or it could escalate explosively. The response of civil authorities, of local leaders, and of news media (whether they over-report and sensationalize or show restraint) are all critical.

Phase Three—Roman holiday: Success of hostile keynoting and an explosion of activity mark the beginning of phase three. The crowd, dominated now by younger people, begins moving. Conant describes their mood as an angry, gleeful intoxication. Buildings and cars are attacked. Targets are not necessarily random but more likely selected and patterned, representing objects that rioters resent or fear. Police are taunted and attacked. Later in phase three, excitement subsides and systematic looting begins. According to Conant, behavior in the carnival-like atmosphere of the Roman holiday is explained at least in part by the amazing contradictions and ambivalences present in the urban ghetto: stores owned by hated white people and beloved contents of the stores; despised police and their admired weapons. This ambivalence extends to the riot participants, who show great changes in behavior. They can be violent one day and calm others the next day. These ambivalences toward violence and in mood make it unlikely that most riots will get to phase four.

Phase Four—Siege: Polarization of the two sides signals the end of effective communication. Curfew is declared. Warlike acts occur. Snipers attack, buildings are firebombed, and a general state of siege exists.[4]

PANIC AND MASS HYSTERIA

Panic represents a particular type of reaction in a crowd situation. Sociologically, **panic** is defined as nonadaptive or nonrational flight resulting from extreme fear and loss of self-control. Usually there is a severe threat, a limited number of ways out, a feeling of being trapped. Flight in itself does not necessarily mean panic. Some flight is rational and sensible, as when people leave in an orderly manner an area that is threatened by hurricane or flood. Panic refers specifically to flight that is nonadaptive—people stampeding through a burning building and attempting to fight their way out a door that is already hopelessly blocked. Panic differs somewhat from other forms of collective behavior in that, although it is frequently a result of the crowd situation (spontaneous and contagious), it is essentially an individualistic and competitive reaction. During a panic, each person is desperately trying to obtain an objective on his or her own, and since many others are doing the same thing, there is a good chance that some will not make it.[5]

The Iroquois Theater fire in Chicago provides an extreme example of panic and its possible consequences. During a performance on a December af-

---

[4]Ralph Conant, "Rioting, Insurrection, and Civil Disobedience," *The American Scholar* 37 (Summer 1968).

[5]This discussion of panic is drawn from Duane Schultz, *Panic Behavior* (New York: Random House, 1964), and from Turner and Killian, *Collective Behavior*, Chapters 5 and 6 (see footnote 1).

ternoon in 1903, draperies on the stage caught fire. Somebody yelled "Fire," and most of the audience panicked. Actors and musicians attempted to calm the crowd, but to no avail. There were many exit doors, but some were poorly marked and some hard to open. People were crushed against doors and on stairways; others jumped to their deaths from fire escapes. The fire was not very serious, and the fire department arrived quickly—the panic lasted only eight minutes. The death toll, however, was 602.

Mass hysteria is in some ways similar to panic and describes the situation in which a particular behavior, fear, or belief sweeps through a large number of people—a crowd, a city, or a nation. Examples of mass hysteria might include fainting at a rock concert, the fear that flying saucers are after us, or the belief that certain women are practicing witchcraft.

A SNAKE WITH BAD BREATH

A venomous snake has been haunting the people of the Pokharan desert area of Rajasthan in India. The snake, known as *peevana* or *piana*, is about twenty inches long. It steals into huts at dawn and delicately crawls onto the chest of someone asleep. It then opens its mouth wide and holds it in front of the sleeping person's nose, and the victim inhales the snake's poisonous breath. The snake appears to be sadistic as well—it lets its victims know of their fate by whipping them in the face with its tail as it slips away. Newspapers in Rajasthan recently reported that five persons fell victim to *peevana* in one village in a single day.

The *peevana* myth has endured for centuries. According to the local maharaja's gazette, the ruler once offered 1,000 rupees to anyone who could produce the reptile, dead or alive. No one has yet been able to.

RUMORS

Rumor is a type of collective behavior that may or may not be crowd-oriented. Much **rumor** is merely a form of person-to-person communication. Rumor is defined as unconfirmed, although not necessarily false, communication. It is often related to some issue of public concern. Rumors change constantly as they spread. They tend to grow shorter, more concise, and more easily told. Certain attractive details of the rumor become magnified. New details are manufactured to complete the story or to make it internally consistent. A rumor that Beatle Paul McCartney had been killed in an automobile accident swept the country in the fall of 1969. Fans of the rock music group frantically sought further proof of Paul's demise by playing Beatle records backwards and by finding clues on album covers and in photographs of the group. Even several personal appearances by the supposedly dead Beatle did little to quash the rumor. In fact, some are still suspicious today of that fellow passing himself off as Paul McCartney....

People pass rumors for many reasons. The rumor may fit with what we want to believe, with what we know to be true: "Teachers are absentminded" or "Sex education is Communist inspired." We may pass rumors on to increase our status in the eyes of others. If we were the first to get the news, we want others to know it. Or it's such a tremendous story that others are bound to think more of us when we tell it to them. Did you hear about the flying saucers over Minneapolis? About John F. Kennedy's sex life? About those giant birds perching on trees in the Southwest? About Bigfoot wandering through downtown Yakima? You *didn't?* Well, let me tell you. . . .

Rumor may have a variety of functions. It may be gossip and serve to enliven the Thursday afternoon bridge club, or it may provide a core of communication during a crowd's milling period and thus be the stimulus for crowd action.

There is a common assumption that rumors become less accurate as they are passed on. Taylor Buckner makes the point that in some situations rumors become *more* accurate. The important variables to consider are rumor set and interaction setting. Buckner suggests three rumor sets: critical, uncritical, and transmission. *Critical set* occurs when people have knowledge about the rumor's subject matter, have personal experience with it, or are habitually suspicious of rumors anyway. These people tend to eliminate inaccurate and irrelevant parts of rumors they hear and pass on only the most important parts. An *uncritical set* may exist when people have no knowledge about a situation, when passing the rumor fills a need, or during crisis situations when there is little information. People with an uncritical set may modify the rumor so it sounds better, change it to fit their own needs, devise totally new rumors to fit the situation, or in some other way contribute to the inaccuracy of the rumor. *Transmission set* means that the content of the rumor is irrelevant to the person. The person's only interest is to pass the rumor on. People who merely transmit a

LOOK — I DON'T CARE **WHAT** YOU STAND FOR.........
....I WANT SOMEONE WITH A
BIT OF **GLAMOR!**

rumor forget or reword parts but usually do not purposely distort or correct the rumor.

Group characteristics—the interaction setting—also affect a rumor's accuracy. Buckner suggests that a rumor is heard more often and evaluated more carefully in a close, more primary group (college dorm, sorority, army unit, social club, clique) than in a more diffuse or secondary group. It also follows that the more interested and involved a group is with a rumor, the more the rumor is told and evaluated. The rumor that then-Beatle Paul McCartney was dead was undoubtedly more actively discussed among rock music and Beatles fans than it was in the board room at General Motors or among people pushing rumors about flying saucers. Buckner concludes that the multiple interaction likely to occur in a close, highly involved group combined with a critical set leads to increased accuracy in the rumor. However, if the critical set is missing, greater inaccuracy results.[6]

FADS, CRAZES, AND FASHIONS

Fads, crazes, and fashions are forms of collective behavior that are usually more widespread and long-lasting than crowd behavior. **Fads** (and *crazes*) refer to the relatively short-term obsessions that members of society or members of specific groups have toward certain mannerisms, objects, clothes, or ways of speaking. Among current fads (in California at least) are roller skating, running shoes, gold chains, and video games. Past examples include pet rocks, the hula hoop, swallowing goldfish, and stuffing phone booths. Fads and crazes may interest many and burn brightly for a while, but usually they die out quickly. **Fashions** are similar but are more widespread and last longer than fads and crazes. Examples of fashions might include miniskirts, two-piece bathing suits, long hair on men, wide neckties, Mustang style in cars, ranch style in homes, and rock and folk rock in popular music.

Turner and Killian report an interesting peculiarity of fads and fashions: fashions follow the social-class structure, but fads do not necessarily follow the social-class structure. That is, fashions usually start at upper-class levels and seep downward. Fads, on the other hand, may appear anywhere in the class structure and may be adopted more quickly by members of lower social classes than by members of the upper classes. Since following fads and fashions brings prestige to people, fashion supports the *status quo* (the current prestige system), whereas fads may upset the *status quo* by granting prestige to people who otherwise have low status.[7]

---

[6]H. Taylor Buckner, "A Theory of Rumor Transmission," in *Readings in Collective Behavior*, 2d ed., edited by Robert Evans (Chicago: Rand McNally, 1975), pp. 86–102. Also see Warren A. Peterson and Noel P. Gist's article, "Rumor and Public Opinion," *American Journal of Sociology* 57 (September 1951), pp. 159–167, for a summary and analysis of some theories on rumor.

[7]Turner and Killian, *Collective Behavior*, pp. 152–153 (see footnote 1).

DISASTERS

Studies of disasters provide us with data about collective behavior. A **disaster** situation is defined as one in which there is a basic disruption of the social context within which individuals and groups function, a radical departure from the pattern of normal expectations. Such a situation almost by definition results in collective behavior.[8]

Disaster research reveals three general time periods: immediately before, during, and after the disaster. Predisaster studies have noted that making people aware of impending disaster is extremely difficult unless the group concerned has already experienced a disaster—a flood, a bombing, or an earthquake. Otherwise, people do not take the warning seriously. They look around, note that others don't seem bothered, and define the situation as normal or at least not serious. During Hurricane Camille in Mississippi in August 1969, twenty-some people were killed in an apartment house where they had decided to ride out the storm and have a "hurricane party." People tend to interpret disaster cues as normal or familiar events.

Studies of behavior *during* a disaster indicate that, contrary to popular belief, panic and loss of control are rare. Flight is a frequent response, but it usually represents an adaptive rational reaction to the situation rather than panic. Studies of behavior *after* a disaster indicate that people tend to underestimate the scope and destructiveness of the disaster. Again, people define events in terms of the familiar and normal. Often those who had clearly defined tasks in case of disaster—civil defense workers, nurses—experience severe role conflict. The conflict is between helping people in general as they are trained to do or finding and helping family and loved ones. Frequently the latter choice is made. Also, people tend to flock *to*, rather than away from, a disaster area. Within twenty-four hours after the atom bomb was dropped on Hiroshima, thousands of refugees streamed *into* the city. Airliners in trouble at major airports attract crowds of people to the scene. One such incident at New York's Kennedy Airport brought so much automobile traffic that emergency vehicles had difficulty getting through. Communication lines become clogged with calls coming *into* disaster areas. Material convergence occurs as all sorts and varieties of material are shipped into the disaster area in an effort to help the victims. Within forty-eight hours after a tornado in Arkansas, truckloads full of material began arriving. Among the mass of material that people sent were button shoes, derby hats, a tuxedo, and a carton of falsies. It took 500 workers two weeks to sort it all out. After Hurricane Camille in 1969, when supplies began pouring into Mississippi, authorities had to make television appeals to stop the shipments. The same thing happened after the February 1976 earthquake in Guatemala. Indians in an area heavily hit by the quake who usually eat corn and beans were sent canned goods they could not open and would not eat. They were also sent jars of peanut butter, boxes of cornflakes, and cans of anchovy

---

[8]This section on disaster is taken from Charles Fritz's chapter on disaster, which appears in Robert Merton and Robert Nisbet's book, *Contemporary Social Problems* (New York: Harcourt Brace Jovanovich, 1961), Chapter 14.

paste. Other useless items piling up in warehouses after the quake included canned cherries, high-heeled shoes, see-through shirts, and wigs. A Red Cross official reported that the same thing happened after the 1970 Nicaragua earthquake and the 1973 Honduras hurricane and concluded that the public simply responds, partly out of a desire to be helpful in a bad situation, partly because they just want to empty their closets. Finally, the studies report that in many cases disaster as an immediate threat produces solidarity among those experiencing it. People tend to grow closer together as a result of their attempts to fight and survive the situation.

PUBLICS AND PUBLIC OPINION

Publics and public opinion represent another aspect of collective behavior. A **public** is a number of people who have an interest in, and difference of opinion about, a common issue. A public engages in communication and discussion (more often indirect than face-to-face) and, contrary to the crowd, a public is dispersed or scattered rather than in close physical contact. **Public opinion** refers to opinions held by a public on a given issue. **Propaganda** refers to attempts to influence and change the public's viewpoint on an issue.[9]

In a complicated mass society, a great number of issues appear, and each issue has its concerned interest group or public. Membership in these publics is transitory and constantly changing. Some members of a public are vitally interested, others marginally. Members of a public may communicate by special magazines, newspapers, television, and letter writing. Professional football and baseball have their publics, the National Rifle Association is a public, the American Medical Association is a public; the issues of socialized medicine, legalization of prostitution, and elimination of the death penalty all have publics. Some publics are widespread; if the issue is the type of job the President is doing, the whole nation may become the public. Other publics may be much smaller.

Public opinion is registered in a variety of ways. It is registered when an individual running for office is defeated. It is recorded in the letters-to-the-editor column of a newspaper or magazine that prints a story with which the public agrees or disagrees. More recently, public opinion polls have become a popular way of determining what the public is thinking. Polls are avidly followed by politicians as well as by the man on the street. Polls have even been criticized because it is feared that some people look at the polls before deciding how to vote or what to think on a given issue.

There are many pitfalls in public opinion polling, and occasionally even the best pollsters go wrong. Probably the most famous miss was the *Literary Digest* poll of 1936, which predicted that Landon (Republican) would defeat Roosevelt (Democrat) for President. The *Literary Digest* obtained a biased sample by mailing ballots to people whose names, for the most part, were selected from telephone directories or from lists of automobile owners. Only forty per-

---

[9]For a comprehensive treatment of these concepts, see Turner and Killian, *Collective Behavior,* Chapters 10–12 (see footnote 1).

cent of all homes had phones in 1936 and only fifty-five percent of all families had cars, so the magazine was sampling people who were economically well-off. Another error was introduced by *mailing* ballots—people of higher income and education are more likely to return mailed questionnaires than are people with low income and education. Ballots were mailed early (September) so that last-minute changes were missed. The upshot was that *Literary Digest* asked a group of reasonably well-to-do people (who generally tend to vote Republican) who they were going to vote for. Their prediction was so grossly wrong that it is given as the reason why the magazine went out of business.[10] A number of polls picked Dewey to beat Truman in 1948, and there was a tremendous uproar in England in June 1970, when the Tories decisively won an election that all the polls predicted would be won by Labour.

Since it is usually impossible in a public opinion poll to talk to all members of the public, a sample is taken. Frequently the success of the poll hinges on the accuracy of the sampling technique. The timing of the poll is also important. Opinions change rapidly, and if the latest political poll is three or four weeks before the election, pollsters can expect to have missed many last-minute changes. A more basic fault in polling is that some people are very interested and know a lot about the issue, and others are only slightly interested and know little or nothing. Yet in most polls the responses of these two types are given the same weight. Other difficulties in sampling public opinion occur when people give pollsters answers they think the pollsters want, and when a person is a member of several conflicting publics at once, as most of us are. What if a member of the Catholic Church and mother of eleven kids is asked her opinion of government-supported artificial birth control? She may find herself a member of conflicting publics. Finally, as far as action is concerned, it is often much more important to know how a few powerful people or opinion leaders feel about an issue than it is to know what many relatively powerless people think.

In conclusion, let's examine how the public, public opinion, and propaganda might relate to a given issue, say capital punishment. Members of the public interested in this issue would include policemen, prison officials, sociologists, psychologists, social workers, and future criminals. To obtain a measure of public opinion, the pollsters might randomly select 1,000 people and ask them what they think about keeping the death penalty. The sample includes interested members of the public and disinterested bystanders, and all opinions are counted equally. (What if, for example, we find that most of those who know most about capital punishment are opposed to it, and most of those who know least about it are in favor of it? What do we do?) Suppose we find (as Gallup did in 1981) that sixty-six percent of those polled want to keep the death penalty. The public in its various forms has spoken. Since the margin is not decisive, however, the other side decides to hire a public relations firm to persuade the public a little. Propaganda begins to appear. A public-interest story in a popular magazine tells how the family of an executed man is getting along. A newspaper story appears describing a famous case in which a condemned man was

---

[10]This is summarized from Julian Simon's very complete discussion in his book *Basic Research Methods in Social Science* (New York: Random House, 1969), Chapter 8.

cleared of the crime he was supposed to have committed—but just too late. . . . An ex-warden of San Quentin is interviewed on a nationwide television news broadcast, and he relates in detail his opposition to the death penalty. A reporter, witness to an execution in the electric chair, describes it in vivid detail in a Sunday supplement. The effectiveness of the propaganda will depend on its ability to reach the audience, on the sophistication of the audience, and on the receptiveness of the audience to the new viewpoint. Let's assume that the propaganda has been cleverly conceived, and a new sampling indicates that public opinion has changed—now only forty percent want to keep the death penalty. Still, nothing happens until power is applied. A lobbyist in Washington, D.C., working for the Anti-Death Penalty League, puts pressure on legislators. Thirty thousand anti-capital-punishment letters (all remarkably similar) flood in. Finally a new law is passed, more because of the League, lobby, and letters than because of public opinion. We can see from this imaginary and oversimplified example that boundaries of what constitutes a public are obscure, polls may be misleading, public opinion may change rapidly, propaganda is frequently very useful at building or changing public opinion, and finally, public opinion must be backed by political power if meaningful action is to result.

In June 1972, the U.S. Supreme Court ruled that the death penalty was unconstitutional. Polls indicated that the public still favored capital punishment and, due to public outcry and the reverse of some of the procedures outlined above, many states reinstituted the death penalty. Finally in July 1976 the Court seemingly reversed its earlier decision and upheld many of these laws.

SOCIAL MOVEMENTS

In the chapter on social change (Chapter 11), we mentioned that many people believe that through conscious effort the environment can be manipulated and changed. One way this can happen is through a form of collective behavior called a social movement. A **social movement** is defined as a group of people acting with some continuity to promote or to resist a change in their society or group. Social movements are lasting rather than temporary, they have a distinct perspective or viewpoint, they are oriented toward a specific goal or goals, and members have a sense of solidarity or *esprit de corps*.[11] Social movements seem to be especially popular in modern mass society. In mass society there is mass confusion; that is, there are a variety of viewpoints on every issue. The United States, like other mass societies, has a multiplicity of groups from numerous backgrounds, and each group has its own values, its own way of looking at things. Individual discontent, anxiety, and frustration about the condition of the world and about one's own opportunities are all conducive to social movements.[12] Mass communication exposes us to all the confusing as-

---

[11]Ralph Turner and Lewis Killian, *Collective Behavior*, 2d ed. (Englewood Cliffs, N.J.: Prentice-Hall, 1972), p. 246.

[12]See C. Wendell King's book, *Social Movements in the United States* (New York: Random House, 1956), Chapter 1, for a discussion of social movements in mass society.

pects of the mass society and puts us immediately in touch with others who may also be frustrated and anxious and looking for a way to change things. The combination of these elements—complex societies with a variety of peoples and viewpoints, numbers of people who feel discontented or shortchanged, and a system of mass communication to tie them together—provides fertile soil for social movements.

Current examples of social movements in the United States would include pro- and antiabortion groups, the "moral majority," anti–nuclear power groups, people interested in gay rights, and groups on both sides of the gun control issue. Our recent history would also include social movements centered around civil rights, women's rights, peace, anticommunism, religion, and many other issues. Some of these movements are **revolutionary,** in that they demand a complete change in the social order. Others are **reform,** in that they seek modification in certain aspects of society.[13] Social movements of either type, however, provide an important impetus for social change.

Social movements frequently make use of public demonstrations to bring attention to the issue that they want to change. The antiwar movement of the 1960s and the gay rights movement of the 1970s are examples. Farmers descended on Washington, D.C., in several massive "tractorcades," most recently in early 1979, to bring attention to their economic problems. Sometimes, certain pressures lead groups that otherwise would not do so to use public protest as a means for change. The farmers may be one example of this, and "Anatomy of a Public Protest Action" (p. 366) describes another.

Often one social movement will develop to counter the effects of another. A current example centers upon legalization of abortion. As recently as 1966, abortion was illegal throughout the United States, although a few states would allow it if the mother's life was in danger. A social movement developed among people who, for a variety of reasons—rights of women, population control, objection to laws that discriminated against the poor—felt that abortion should be legalized. Pamphlets to citizens, letters to senators, articles in newspapers and magazines made people aware of the issue. In 1967, Colorado passed a liberalized abortion law, and soon California, New York, Hawaii, and other states followed. By early 1972, sixteen states and the District of Columbia had changed their laws. Then, in January, 1973, the U.S. Supreme Court overruled all state laws that prohibited or restricted women from obtaining abortions during the first three months of pregnancy. Seldom is social change, especially legal social change, so rapid, and seldom are the effects of a social movement so dramatic. There was an immediate outcry from those who objected to the Supreme Court's action. Groups such as "Right to Life" began forming and a social movement aiming toward restrictive abortion legislation was born. It gained momentum and reportedly was instrumental in the election and defeat of certain candidates for office in the late 1970s and early 1980s. Whether this movement will be as successful as the earlier proabortion movement is uncertain, but if intensity of feeling is any indication, it looks like the cause is here to stay.

---

[13]Turner and Killian give a brief discussion of reform and revolutionary movements in *Collective Behavior*, pp. 257–258 (see footnote 11).

ANATOMY OF A PUBLIC PROTEST ACTION

Independent truck drivers are generally viewed as middle class and politically conservative. They are not the type to get involved in challenging, confronting, mass protest actions. But on December 3, 1973, a group of owner-operator truckers blocked the entrance to the Delaware Memorial Bridge for several hours. Two days later they blockaded the Ohio Turnpike and highways in several other states. The national guard and highway patrol broke up the blockades with force. Truck windshields were broken and trucks towed off highways. Some truckers were beaten and arrested.

Charles Bisanz studied the truckers and found them to be independent and self reliant. They have a belief in success through individual accomplishment, and they view trucking as a way of life. Social networks are developed by getting together at truck stops and by communicating through citizens' band radios. In December 1973, truckers were facing a severe economic squeeze—diesel fuel had suddenly become expensive, but the increases couldn't be passed back to the consumer because hauling rates were fixed by the ICC. Truckers felt they had no clout, that Congress didn't care about them. They also felt they had no exit; trucking was all they knew, and there were no other jobs available to them except perhaps unskilled work in factories. These feelings led to the blockade in early December. Widespread publicity of the blockades led to increased interaction among truckers and further confirmation of their problems. A nationwide shutdown took place from December 13 to 15, and again from January 31 to February 9, 1974. After eight days of the second shutdown, a rate increase was granted, and the independent truckers were given recognition by the government. Bisanz concludes by suggesting that when an individual (or group) is faced with frustration and threat to a way of life, the more cut off he perceives himself to be from established channels of institutional response and the fewer exits he perceives, the more likely it is he will engage in public protest actions as a strategy for change.

Adapted from "The Anatomy of a Mass Public Protest Action: A Shutdown by Independent Truck Drivers," by Charles Bisanz, *Human Organization* 36 (Spring 1977), pp. 62–66. Reprinted with permission of *Human Organization*.

Collective behavior experts feel that social movements have a life history. One description of the lifespan of movements sees them going through four stages.[14] The *preliminary* stage involves individual excitement, discontent, and unorganized and unformulated restlessness. Mechanisms of suggestion, imitation, and propaganda are important, and an "agitator" type of leader appears. The *popular* stage involves crowd or collective excitement or unrest. The unrest is now open and widespread, and *esprit de corps* and an ideology or viewpoint become important mechanisms. The leader at this stage is a "prophet" (who puts forth a general ideology) or a "reformer" (who focuses on specific evils and develops a clearly defined program). Eric Hoffer believes that the early stages of social movements are dominated by "true believers." These are people of fanatical faith for whom mass movements have an almost irresistible appeal.

---

[14]This description of the life history of a social movement is from Rex Hopper, "The Revolutionary Process: A Frame of Reference for the Study of Revolutionary Movements," *Social Forces* 28 (March 1950), pp. 270–279.

The true believer is ready to sacrifice his or her life for a cause, any cause.[15] The third or *formal* stage of the social movement involves the formulation of issues and formation of publics. The movement becomes "respectable" in order to gain wider appeal. Issues are discussed and debated. The leaders are "statesmen." The *institutional* stage involves the legalization of the movement; the movement becomes part of the society. The leaders are of the "administrator-executive" type.

Remember that this is a generalized description. Some movements follow this pattern, some do not. The time involved in any one stage is variable. The unsuccessful social movement disappears before it can progress through all stages. The successful social movement that attains its objectives must adapt and broaden its goals, or it too will die out.

The first and most crucial task for the leaders of the Black Muslims is to keep the Movement a *movement* rather than permit it to become an institution. This does not mean that the Muslims must forsake structure and direction; on the contrary, they have one of the most effective organizational structures to be seen outside the military. But to lure the masses, they must seem to be going somewhere, not settling down. They must reflect and mobilize the masses' own dissatisfaction and urgency, building these into the corporate identity. A successful mass movement is always arriving, but never quite arrives.

From *The Black Muslims in America*, rev. ed., by C. Eric Lincoln (Boston: Beacon Press, 1973).

Finally, the *charismatic* leader figures prominently in both sociological and popular literature. As we discussed in Chapter 4 (p. 110), *charisma* refers to a certain quality an individual has that sets that person apart from other people. Charismatic leaders are treated as though they are superhuman and capable of exceptional acts. The charismatic movement follows the charismatic leader, who is a symbol for the movement and is above criticism.[16] Some movements are so closely identified with the leader that they have no goal beyond that of following the leader. Other movements, although they follow such a leader, have well-defined goals that allow the movement to continue even if the charismatic leader is lost. Examples of charismatic leaders might include Gandhi, Joan of Arc, Martin Luther King, Jr., Hitler, and Charles de Gaulle.

SUMMARY

In the previous chapter in this section on change and deviation in society we dealt with social change and social disorganization. In this chapter we ex-

---

[15]See Eric Hoffer, *The True Believer* (New York: New American Library, 1951).

[16]See Turner and Killian, *Collective Behavior*, pp. 388–392 (see footnote 11), for a more detailed discussion of the charismatic movement.

amined another form of activity that is outside the organized and ordinary—collective behavior. Collective behavior refers to spontaneous and somewhat unstructured actions by groups of people. A number of concepts and terms central to the study of collective behavior were discussed. We examined types of collectivities: crowds, audiences, and mobs. We described types of behaviors: rumor, panic, mass hysteria, fads, crazes, and fashions. Special situations involving collective behavior were noted: riots and disasters. Our discussion of collective behavior concluded with an analysis of publics, of public opinion, propaganda, and social movements.

A mob is a focused, acting crowd. A mob is hard to deal with once set in motion, but the first reading which follows relates how one of the characters in Harper Lee's novel *To Kill a Mockingbird* distracted a lynch mob. A disaster situation is defined as one in which there is a radical departure from the pattern of normal expectations. In the second reading in this section, D. L. Webber describes what happened when Darwin, Australia, was hit by a cyclone. A social movement is defined as a group of people acting with some continuity to promote or to resist a change in their society. The final reading in this chapter examines the campaign to end the nuclear arms race.

Terms for Study

audience (354)	disaster (361)
charisma (367)	fads (360)
collective behavior (352)	fashions (360)
crazes (360)	keynoting (356)
crowd (353)	mass hysteria (358)

Reading 12.1

MAYCOMB JAIL

HARPER LEE

A mob is a focused, acting crowd. It is emotionally aroused and intent on taking action. A mob is a powerful force, and it is difficult to change its direction. When the direction is changed (as it is in this fictional account), the change can be understood in collective behavior terms. Here, Scout and Jem Finch help their father, Atticus, protect a black man from a lynch mob in Harper Lee's novel *To Kill a Mockingbird*.

The Maycomb Jail was the most venerable and hideous of the county's buildings. Atticus said it was like something Cousin Joshua St. Clair might have designed. It was certainly someone's dream. Starkly out of place in a town of square-faced stores and steep-roofed houses, the Maycomb jail was a miniature Gothic joke one cell wide and two cells high, complete with tiny battlements and flying buttresses. Its fantasy was heightened by its red brick facade and the thick steel bars at its ecclesiastical windows. It stood on no lonely hill, but was wedged between Tyndal's Hardware Store and The Maycomb Tribune office. The jail was Maycomb's only conversation piece: its detractors said it looked like a Victorian privy; its supporters said it gave the town a good solid respectable look, and no stranger would ever suspect that it was full of niggers.

As we walked up the sidewalk, we saw a solitary light burning in the distance. "That's funny," said Jem, "jail doesn't have an outside light."

"Looks like it's over the door," said Dill.

A long extension cord ran between the bars of a second-floor window and down the side of the building. In the light from its bare bulb, Atticus was sitting propped against the front door. He was sitting in one of his office chairs, and he was reading, oblivious of the nightbugs dancing over his head.

I made to run, but Jem caught me. "Don't go to him," he said, "he might not like it. He's all right, let's go home. I just wanted to see where he was."

We were taking a short cut across the square when four dusty cars came in from the Meridian highway, moving slowly in a line. They went around the square, passed the bank building, and stopped in front of the jail.

Nobody got out. We saw Atticus look up from his newspaper. He closed it, folded it deliberately, dropped it in his lap, and pushed his hat to the back of his head. He seemed to be expecting them.

"Come on," whispered Jem. We streaked across the square, across the street, until we were in the shelter of the Jitney Jungle door. Jem peeked up the sidewalk. "We can get closer," he said. We ran to Tyndal's Hardware door— near enough, at the same time discreet.

In ones and twos, men got out of the cars. Shadows became substance as lights revealed solid shapes moving toward the jail door. Atticus remained where he was. The men hid him from view.

"He in there, Mr. Finch?" a man said.

"He is," we heard Atticus answer, "and he's asleep. Don't wake him up."

In obedience to my father, there followed what I later realized was a sickeningly comic aspect of an unfunny situation: the men talked in near-whispers.

"You know what we want," another man said. "Get aside from the door, Mr. Finch."

"You can turn around and go home again, Walter," Atticus said pleasantly. "Heck Tate's around somewhere."

"The hell he is," said another man. "Heck's bunch's so deep in the woods they won't get out till mornin'."

"Indeed? Why so?"

"Called 'em off on a snipe hunt," was the succinct answer. "Didn't you think a' that, Mr. Finch?"

"Thought about it, but didn't believe it. Well then," my father's voice was still the same, "that changes things, doesn't it?"

"It do," another deep voice said. Its owner was a shadow.

"Do you really think so?"

This was the second time I heard Atticus ask that question in two days, and it meant somebody's man would get jumped. This was too good to miss. I broke away from Jem and ran as fast as I could to Atticus.

Jem shrieked and tried to catch me, but I had a lead on him and Dill. I pushed my way through dark smelly bodies and burst into the circle of light.

"H-ey, Atticus!"

I thought he would have a fine surprise, but his face killed my joy. A flash of plain fear was going out of his eyes, but returned when Dill and Jem wriggled into the light.

There was a smell of stale whiskey and pigpen about, and when I glanced around I discovered that these men were strangers. They were not the people I saw last night. Hot embarrassment shot through me: I had leaped triumphantly into a ring of people I had never seen before.

Atticus got up from his chair, but he was moving slowly, like an old man. He put the newspaper down very carefully, adjusting its creases with lingering fingers. They were trembling a little.

"Go home, Jem," he said. "Take Scout and Dill home."

We were accustomed to prompt, if not always cheerful acquiescence to

Atticus's instructions, but from the way he stood Jem was not thinking of budging.

"Go home, I said."

Jem shook his head. As Atticus's fists went to his hips, so did Jem's and as they faced each other I could see little resemblance between them: Jem's soft brown hair and eyes, his oval face and snug-fitting ears were our mother's, contrasting oddly with Atticus's graying black hair and square-cut features, but they were somehow alike. Mutual defiance made them alike.

"Son, I said go home."

Jem shook his head.

"I'll send him home," a burly man said, and grabbed Jem roughly by the collar. He yanked Jem nearly off his feet.

"Don't you touch him!" I kicked the man swiftly. Barefooted, I was surprised to see him fall back in real pain. I intended to kick his shin, but aimed too high.

"That'll do, Scout." Atticus put his hand on my shoulder. "Don't kick folks. No—" he said, as I was pleading justification.

"Ain't nobody gonna do Jem that way," I said.

"All right, Mr. Finch, get 'em outa here," someone growled. "You got fifteen seconds to get 'em outa here."

In the midst of this strange assembly, Atticus stood trying to make Jem mind him. "I ain't going," was his steady answer to Atticus's threats, requests, and finally, "Please Jem, take them home."

I was getting a bit tired of that, but felt Jem had his own reasons for doing as he did, in view of his prospects once Atticus did get him home. I looked around the crowd. It was a summer's night, but the men were dressed most of them, in overalls and denim shirts buttoned up to the collars. I thought they must be cold-natured, as their sleeves were unrolled and buttoned at the cuffs. Some wore hats pulled firmly down over their ears. They were sullen-looking, sleepy-eyed men who seemed unused to late hours. I sought once more for a familiar face, and at the center of the semi-circle I found one.

"Hey, Mr. Cunningham."

The man did not hear me, it seemed.

"Hey, Mr. Cunningham. How's your entailment gettin' along?"

Mr. Walter Cunningham's legal affairs were well known to me; Atticus had once described them at length. The big man blinked and hooked his thumbs in his overall straps. He seemed uncomfortable; he cleared his throat and looked away. My friendly overture had fallen flat.

Mr. Cunningham wore no hat, and the top half of his forehead was white in contrast to his sunscorched face, which led me to believe that he wore one most days. He shifted his feet, clad in heavy work shoes.

"Don't you remember me, Mr. Cunningham? I'm Jean Louise Finch. You brought us some hickory nuts one time, remember?" I began to sense the futility one feels when unacknowledged by a chance acquaintance.

"I go to school with Walter," I began again. "He's your boy, ain't he? Ain't he, sir?"

Mr. Cunningham was moved to a faint nod. He did know me, after all.

"He's in my grade," I said, "and he does right well. He's a good boy," I added, "a real nice boy. We brought him home for dinner one time. Maybe he told you about me, I beat him up one time but he was real nice about it. Tell him hey for me, won't you?"

Atticus had said it was the polite thing to talk to people about what they were interested in, not about what you were interested in. Mr. Cunningham displayed no interest in his son, so I tackled his entailment once more in a last-ditch effort to make him feel at home.

"Entailments are bad," I was advising him, when I slowly awoke to the fact that I was addressing the entire aggregation. The men were all looking at me, some had their mouths half-open. Atticus had stopped poking at Jem: they were standing together beside Dill. Their attention amounted to fascination. Atticus's mouth, even, was half-open, an attitude he had once described as uncouth. Our eyes met and he shut it.

"Well, Atticus, I was just sayin' to Mr. Cunningham that entailments are bad an' all that, but you said not to worry, it takes a long time sometimes . . . that you all'd ride it out together. . . ." I was slowly drying up, wondering what idiocy I had committed. Entailments seemed all right enough for living-room talk.

I began to feel sweat gathering at the edges of my hair; I could stand anything but a bunch of people looking at me. They were quite still.

"What's the matter?" I asked.

Atticus said nothing. I looked around and up at Mr. Cunningham, whose face was equally impassive. Then he did a peculiar thing. He squatted down and took me by both shoulders.

"I'll tell him you said hey, little lady," he said.

Then he straightened up and waved a big paw. "Let's clear out," he called. "Let's get going, boys."

As they had come, in ones and twos the men shuffled back to their ramshackle cars. Doors slammed, engines coughed, and they were gone.

I turned to Atticus, but Atticus had gone to the jail and was leaning against it with his face to the wall. I went to him and pulled his sleeve. "Can we go home now?" He nodded, produced his handkerchief, gave his face a going-over and blew his nose violently.

"Mr. Finch?"

A soft husky voice came from the darkness above: "They gone?"

Atticus stepped back and looked up. "They've gone," he said. "Get some sleep, Tom. They won't bother you any more."

From a different direction, another voice cut crisply through the night: "You're damn tootin' they won't. Had you covered all the time, Atticus."

Mr. Underwood and a double-barreled shotgun were leaning out his window above The Maycomb Tribune office.

It was long past my bedtime and I was growing quite tired; it seemed that Atticus and Mr. Underwood would talk for the rest of the night, Mr. Underwood out the window and Atticus up at him. Finally Atticus returned, switched off the light above the jail door, and picked up his chair.

"Can I carry it for you, Mr. Finch?" asked Dill. He had not said a word the whole time.

"Why, thank you, son."

Walking toward the office, Dill and I fell into step behind Atticus and Jem. Dill was encumbered by the chair, and his pace was slower. Atticus and Jem were well ahead of us, and I assumed that Atticus was giving him hell for not going home, but I was wrong. As they passed under a streetlight, Atticus reached out and massaged Jem's hair, his one gesture of affection.

Questions 12.1

1. Outline how mob and crowd characteristics are illustrated in this selection.

2. Describe in collective behavior terminology why and/or how the lynch mob was broken up.

Reading 12.2

DARWIN CYCLONE: AN EXPLORATION OF DISASTER BEHAVIOR

D. L. WEBBER

A disaster situation is defined as one in which there is a basic disruption of the social context within which individuals and groups function, a radical departure from the pattern of normal expectations. Studies of disasters provide us with data about a particular type of collective behavior. In this paper, D. L. Webber describes what was called Australia's greatest national disaster, the Darwin cyclone of 1974.

D. L. Webber is a psychologist with the Department of Health, Darwin. He and his family were in Darwin during the cyclone and remained to help with the emergency.

On Christmas eve 1974 Darwin was being battered by the fringe winds of Cyclone Tracy. By daylight on Christmas day the cyclone had passed through Darwin wrecking the city. Cyclonic winds exceeding 217 km per hour at their peak had brought about the greatest disaster in Australian history. Forty-nine people were dead and 16 others were missing, presumed dead, on the harbour. More than 140 people were admitted to hospital, mostly on Christmas day, and over 500 people were treated at Outpatients for injuries sustained during the cyclone. Countless others were treated at suburban emergency health centres for lacerations and injuries. As the city struggled to its feet on Christmas day it was without power, water, sewerage, or any communication contacts to the suburbs. Approximately $500 million damage had been done to buildings and facilities. Massive destruction and damage to housing left much of the population

From "Darwin Cyclone: An Exploration of Disaster Behavior," by D. L. Webber, *Australian Journal of Social Issues*, February 1976. Reprinted by permission of the Australian Council of Social Service.

homeless. *Roads were blocked, debris was everywhere, and it continued to rain.*

Some weeks before 24 December 1974 there had been a cyclone alert that had ended as an anticlimax. There had in fact been no major cyclone strike in Darwin since 1937. There was no doubt about the current situation however. The Bureau of Meteorology was on full alert, regular warnings were broadcast, emergency advice given, and later people were cautioned to take cover as destructive winds would begin in a few hours. Many heeded this advice. Some even booked into hotels or moved to larger buildings.

It was Christmas eve, an earlier cyclone had passed away, and many people had no experience of cyclones. Despite the advice of authorities and the example of those who took precautions, a substantial portion of the population either went to parties or got undressed as usual and simply went to bed. For very many people there was a complete misperception of the situation.

CYCLONE STRIKE

By 11 PM Christmas eve, roofs were being lost from buildings and trees were being uprooted. By 2 AM Christmas day the power was off and radio stations had failed. People were now experiencing the nerve shattering sound of sheet iron grinding and scratching as it was hurled about by the wind. The thudding and exploding sound of beams falling, walls collapsing and heavy airborne objects smashing through houses was everywhere. Many houses simply disintegrated about the occupants. Faced with an immediate threat to life people sought shelter wherever they could find it. Some hid in baths, others lay on floors or under beds. As their houses were swept away some were able to shelter in cars parked between house piers. Most could only lie where they were, hang on and hope.

The sense of isolation during the cyclone was extreme. It was a common feeling that one was at the centre of the destruction and that other areas could not be so badly off. Only later did people realize that the destruction was almost city wide. As might be expected fear was a fairly universal and justifiable experience. Dissociation also occurred. Some people, whose houses were reasonably intact, wandered about inside in a dissociated state looking out of windows.

POST CYCLONE

With the approach of dawn the winds abated and people realized they could come out of hiding. Most were simply relieved that the ordeal was over and that they were alive. Immediately neighbours and friends were checked and given aid. Shelter had to be found for children and others. As the only major buildings in most suburbs were the schools, an exodus of people began to these buildings. Some were able to grab a few personal items, others had sense enough to bring a little food. Many just arrived in night attire or in what clothing they could quickly gather. A major social and community crisis existed.

In the meantime key personnel, maintenance crews, tradesmen and the like reported for duty as soon as they could. The hospital and police station had continued to work throughout. Water and emergency power had to be restored to such places. At dawn plant and machinery at the works depot were operating and emergency procedures that had been adopted were being implemented. Front end loaders and graders began clearing major roads; the evacuation of the sick continued.

, News of the disaster had by this stage reached the outside world. The government had been notified and the National Disaster Organization moved into action. Following a review of the situation a full scale evacuation of the city was ordered. Over the next few days more than 25,000 people were moved to southern centres by air while nearly 10,000 others left Darwin by road. The greatest natural disaster in Australia had been followed by the greatest mass movement of civilian personnel in its history. During this process, food, water, clothing, medicines and other basic needs had to be met for thousands now forced to accommodate themselves in schools and elsewhere. Behind the scenes local professionals, technicians, tradesmen and others strove to tackle these problems.

SOCIAL AND INDIVIDUAL BREAKDOWN

The trauma experienced by family units in their efforts to survive, the mass destruction of homes, the termination of jobs for many in the private sector and the breakdown of public facilities were too much for many people. After they reached safety shock set in. Hundreds milled about looking stunned and unable to act. With others panic had already taken over. They dropped all and simply drove off down the North-South Highway. By 7 AM Wednesday there was a stream of traffic heading out of the city. In their haste to leave many people left wardrobes full of clothes, personal possessions. valuables and pets. Often not even readily accessible tins of food were packed. The stream of evacuees moving down the highway was to increase over the next day. Fortunately for them relief parties were ready and waiting at towns and hamlets on the route. Free fuel, food and assistance was provided at these points.

For the thousands seeking refuge at the schools, stress, anxiety, and lack of communications began to tell. There had been no radio contact since 1:40 AM Wednesday. The ABC could not resume local broadcasting for 36 hours. No official communication existed to the suburbs and the people. Collective anxiety was expressed about where the cyclone might be or whether it would come back. Stories of destruction in other parts of town and the numbers killed were quickly passed on and exaggerated; the situation was ripe for the spread of rumours. Many common experiences were misinterpreted and became the basis of these rumours. One such rumour concerned a supposed outbreak of gastroenteritis in the population. This had its origin in the large number of people suffering gastric upset immediately after the cyclone as a result of stress.

As in all sudden emergencies an immediate and far reaching change in personal goals and the status of people occurred. New priorities were established. Skills were revalued in terms of immediate needs, and role and status changes were called for on the part of many. Suddenly plumbers, plant operators, cooks, nurses and the like became more essential than petty bureaucrats. A town that had thrived as a basically bureaucratic structure with well ordered clerical hierarchies could not make the transition to a new order. Hundreds *were disorientated, panic stricken and without any apparent social place in the city. The stage was set for mass panic and exit.*

Other signs of social breakdown began to show. Looting began in the early hours of Wednesday 25th and was to continue as a problem throughout. Scapegoats were looked for. Even the Bureau of Meteorology was being blamed for the situation. As the stress continued prejudices became heightened, fighting and violence broke out, and petty crime increased.

For those with a clearly defined role or the ability to adopt a new role the task of meeting immediate needs was immense. Such people worked with only a few hours' sleep for several days. As the emergency continued and the central disaster organization worked non-stop to deal with the situation, the effects of a breakdown in cooperative behaviour and its replacement by competitive behaviour on the part of large numbers of citizens became all too apparent.

Following the decision to evacuate by air as many people as possible from the city to southern centres, much of the competitive behaviour now became focused on this aspect as the great bulk of the population tried to escape. Women fought to get on planes, others grabbed nearby children so that they might get priority. Those women who were staying behind or helping directly in the emergency had other women approach them with a view to using their children for evacuation priority. As social dislocation continued and anxiety and panic mounted evacuation centres were sometimes mobbed and gates to planes rushed. On occasion order had to be restored by police resorting to a show of arms. The height of the disruption came with family units breaking up, men feigning injuries to get evacuated and some even dressing up as women.

Of the many who were evacuated and the few who remained, those who stayed seemed to suffer less emotional trauma and adjusted quicker to their circumstances. Those who were evacuated had the additional stress associated with the evacuation to cope with. At the airport children and adults often milled for hours awaiting aircraft seats. Confusion, crowding and stress heightened anxiety. Sleeping on wet floors or standing in rain for hours, anxious mothers or separation from families did little for most children. Under continued stress, mothers often could not attend effectively to the needs of their children.

DISCUSSION AND CONCLUSION

The basic behaviour patterns that emerged in response to Cyclone Tracy were shock, apathy, psychosomatic reactions, anxiety and panic. Sleeplessness, loss of appetite and heightened sensitivity to wind and sound also occurred. Exhaustion, depression and grief reactions were common later. Detachment and the sense of attack on personal image through home and property loss were noticeable. Loss of public communication and rumours affected the course of events for many days. The wholesale substitution of competitive behaviour for cooperative behaviour threatened the entire social fabric. The aftermath of the cyclone continues and will do so for a long time.

Recognition of these emotional factors and the implementation of programmes to cope with them have been a feature of situations elsewhere. Unfortunately no such programmes were implemented at Darwin. On the whole the crisis was approached as essentially a physical crisis by authorities and public alike, with only belated recognition that there were social overtones. A small group of personnel provided mental health resources at the local hospital. This was much too small a group to handle Australia's largest natural disaster. Although general welfare aid in the form of food, clothing and bedding, together with personnel to organize and implement relief programmes were rushed to the city, there was no infusion of mental health personnel and no opportunity for the one or two that were on hand to either influence or advise administration. Australia's greatest peace time emotional crisis had passed by without even preliminary recognition that it was indeed an emotional and social as well as physical crisis.

To the writer it appears axiomatic that where basic social units such as family structures are collapsing in response to a disaster, efforts should be directed towards re-establishing such units, and developing a sense of social cohesion. Care should be exercised not to accelerate such breakdown by unnecessarily separating families, or isolating children. Evacuation of the injured, unfit and other appropriate elements of the population was essential as a first step in dealing with the disaster. The continued freighting out of disturbed and upset people many days after the event, instead of providing local support and treatment first, is questionable.

Questions 12.2

1. In what ways does the behavior in Darwin fit with the general characteristics of disaster discussed in the text? In what ways does it differ?
2. List the collective behavior concepts involved in the study of disaster. Give examples of each from the Darwin cyclone.

Reading 12.3

A MATTER OF LIFE AND DEATH

NEWSWEEK

Social movements seem to be especially popular in mass societies where numerous viewpoints exist on every issue. Some movements have a narrow appeal with members coming from a particular stratum in society. Other movements have wider appeal collecting members from all walks of life. An example of the latter type of movement came to national attention in mid-1982. This excerpt from a *Newsweek* article describes the campaign to end the nuclear arms race.

They are homemakers and businessmen, clerks and doctors, clergymen, teachers, scientists and even military men—a cross section of Americans sud-

denly enlisted in a loosely linked, burgeoning campaign to end the nuclear arms race. Their numbers are mushrooming now like the deadly clouds they are determined to forestall, growing faster than even their own leaders ever expected. If their arguments sometimes sound simplistic or emotional, they have managed to move the crucial issue of nuclear weapons out of the rarefied domain of think-tank strategists and Pentagon planners. They differ on specific policies and tactics, but the hundreds of separate groups that make up the movement are united by a deep and urgent sense of concern that has reverberated from town meetings and county councils to the halls of Congress and the White House itself. This week they will join forces to signal a milestone of the movement: a nationwide outpouring of protest and propaganda called Ground Zero Week.

At the heart of Ground Zero Week is a dramatic reminder of just how devastating the prospect of nuclear war has become since the primitive 15-kiloton bomb that killed or wounded nearly 100,000 Japanese at Hiroshima 37 years ago. In 150 major cities and 500 smaller communities across the country, banners in prominent locations will proclaim: "In a nuclear war, if this were ground zero, every thing and every person within 2 miles of this spot would be destroyed." The schedule also includes a "March for Survival" in Austin, Texas; an ecumenical "peace witness" outside the General Electric nuclear weapons components plant near St. Petersburg, Fla., and a candlelight procession to the White House—along with seminars, films and protests at 335 colleges and a list of speakers spanning the ideological spectrum from longtime leftist activist Seymour Melman to the evangelical friend of presidents, the Rev. Billy Graham.

Many activists are already planning even larger demonstrations to coincide with a United Nations special session on disarmament this June. Others look ahead to the possibility of direct impact on this year's Congressional elections and the 1984 Presidential contest.

Many if not most of the volunteers in today's anti-nuclear campaign have never before held a banner or a vigil. Still, the seeds of their grassroots movement were carefully sown and cultivated by veteran antiwar activists. In January 1980 the Fellowship of Reconciliation held a meeting for about 30 peace groups to consider the nuclear-freeze proposal of a disarmament researcher named Randall Forsberg—a statement carefully worded to avoid any hint of unilateral disarmament. The proposal was rejected by the Democratic National Convention in August 1980, but by then it had come to the attention of James Geier, 38, a Burlington, Vt., cabinetmaker and former Army officer. After hearing a speech by anti-nuclear leader Helen Caldicott, Geier and his brother, Frank, began proposing the freeze in those last bastions of cracker-barrel democracy—Vermont's town meetings.

Some natives thought it "presumptuous" to tell the President what to do. But with skillful organizing help from the American Friends Service Committee, Forsberg's proposal swept the state like wildfire: it was approved in eighteen towns in March 1981 and 161 this year—many of them towns that had voted for Ronald Reagan. After endorsing the freeze in West Windsor, citizens rose and sang "God Bless America." Says Vermont AFSC coordinator David Mc-

Cauley: "Someone once criticized the freeze as a mom-and-apple-pie issue. That's exactly what it is."

Success in Vermont—and earlier in eight Massachusetts election districts—caught the media's attention and stimulated freeze proponents elsewhere in the country. So far, nuclear-freeze resolutions have been passed by 309 New England town meetings, 33 city councils from coast to coast, ten county councils and one or both houses in eleven state legislatures. Organizing efforts are under way in 43 states. In California this week, millionaire Harold Willens has arranged for armored trucks to pull up at county registration offices with petitions bearing 700,000 signatures—more than twice the number needed to put an initiative to the voters in November. At the recent farm and home show in Chamberlain, S.D., more than 300 ranchmen and farmers took time out to sign nuclear-freeze petitions. "This is not just attracting the Volvo-and-quiche crowd," beamed Tim Langley, director of the Peace and Justice Center in Watertown, S.D. In Washington a freeze proposal sponsored by Senators Edward Kennedy and Mark Hatfield, among others, has won the support of 24 senators and 166 House members—and prompted even greater numbers of legislators to endorse a variety of other arms-control plans.

In the view of its leaders, the movement has been fueled largely by the rhetoric and policies of the Reagan Administration on nuclear armament and U.S.-Soviet relations. It has been influenced by the example of dramatic antinuclear demonstrations in Western Europe. One of its major strengths is the widespread participation of church leaders. About 70 Roman Catholic bishops have joined the protests, basing their opposition to nuclear weapons on Catholic literature and a Vatican II condemnation of weapons that were "indiscriminate" in their destruction. Bishop Leroy T. Matthiesen of Amarillo, Texas, for example, has urged workers at the nearby Pantex plant—where all U.S. nuclear warheads are assembled—to consider whether their jobs square with morality. The Mormon Church stunned the Administration by opposing basing of the MX in Utah and deployment of nuclear arms in general. "God calls us to be the stewards of His creation, to take care of the earth and the people on it," says Erick Johnson, pastor of the Prince of Peace Lutheran Church in Dearborn, Mich. "Our technology now has developed to the point of massive destruction of the world as we know it, and that is certainly a matter of faith ... If anything, I'm not political enough."

If clergymen view nuclear policy as a moral issue, the nation's doctors have made it a pragmatic one. Groups such as Physicians for Social Responsibility emphasize the gruesome facts and figures of even a "limited" nuclear exchange in medical terms—especially the inadequacy of surviving health-care facilities and specialists to deal with the injured and dying.

Emotional Dangers: Psychotherapists also have begun to examine the emotional dangers posed by simply living with the threat of nuclear war. Yale psychiatrist Robert Jay Lifton talks of "psychic numbing," and San Francisco area therapist Chellis Glendenning sees "enormous feelings of grief and despair" among people who sign up for her group-therapy sessions ($35 for two days) on life in a nuclear age. The great majority of people may not express their nuclear concerns in everyday conversation, says Dr. John E. Mack, professor of psychiatry at Harvard. But that, Mack suggests, may be because it is not easy "to talk about the fact that you don't think your kids are going to grow up because of nuclear war."

Lending credibility to the campaign for effective arms control is the support of several nuclear experts who helped give birth to the nation's first atomic bomb. Manhattan Project veteran Marvin Goldberger, now president of the California Institute of Technology, says that today's vast stockpiles of nuclear warheads (nearly 50,000 on both sides) are "an obscenity [that] changed completely the character of warfare—and that hasn't been grasped in either the Soviet Union or the United States."

Up to now, young people—especially college students, like those who protested Vietnam—have been conspicuously absent from the anti-nuclear movement. "This is not going to be a mass movement on campus," says the Rev. Paul Dinter, leader of the Columbia University chapter of Pax Christi-USA, a Roman Catholic peace group. "Young people, for the most part, prefer not to think about it," explains southern AFSC organizer Bob Brister. But there are some signs of growing student interest. University of Michigan sophomore Liz Galst, 19, recently led 400 fellow students in a symbolic "die-in" that briefly blocked traffic on an Ann Arbor Street, and similar demonstrations are scheduled on other campuses this week. Moreover, a new group called United Campuses to Prevent Nuclear War has pledged to organize schools in every Congressional district so that candidates for House seats can be questioned on the nuclear issue.

'Dupes': Economic and geographic factors make some areas of the country more difficult than others for the anti-nuclear forces to organize. In the South and West, for example, military bases and missile sites provide many jobs and considerable local income. "We have a nuclear establishment deeply rooted in the economy," notes author Garry Wills, a professor of American culture at Northwestern University. "I don't underestimate the resistance." In Arizona, the state legislature recently passed a resolution urging Congress and the President to adopt a policy of "peace through strength," and rumors about communist support have greeted Ground Zero Week. "The people participating in this are dupes of Soviet policy, well intentioned as they may be," charges retired Army Col. Sam Sharp of Tucson. In Alabama, Rep. William Dickinson, ranking Republican on the House Armed Services Committee, has "no doubt" that the KGB's "disinformation division" is behind the nuclear freeze.

Whether the movement will become more pointedly political is a question that its leaders themselves have not agreed on. The Council for a Livable World has set up a political-action committee to help finance the right Congressional candidates. The nuclear issue is already a key element in the decision by A. Stephen Dirks, five-term Democratic mayor of Ogden, Utah, to challenge GOP freshman Rep. James Hansen, a strong supporter of a nuclear buildup.

Yet some political experts believe that the movement will be most effective if it is nonpartisan. A group of movement leaders and sympathetic congressmen has arranged to discuss that subject privately this week at the Georgetown Center for Strategic Studies. They will consider the value of nationwide hearings and local forums like those of the League of Women Voters. Rather than de-

manding support for a single anti-nuclear position, these forums would "get every candidate to think about the issue and have a position that goes beyond generalities," says direct-mail specialist Tom Mathews, who sees vast potential for fund raising among anti-nuclear activists.

Questions 12.3

1. Examine the characteristics of social movements discussed in this chapter and note those that the anti–nuclear arms movement seems to fit.
2. This has been called a "grassroots" movement. What does that mean? Is this movement revolutionary or reform? How might it become the other?
3. At what stage is this movement? Predict what will happen next.

13
Deviation
and Social Control

Experts tell us that no two people have the same fingerprints. People differ from each other in their appearance and behavior as well. Variation in behavior occurs even though we have norms and roles that specify what *should* happen and what people *should* do in almost any given situation. Social differentiation is not only tolerated but expected in social interaction. We expect people to be different from ourselves in behavior and appearance, and we would be very surprised if they were not. At a particular point, however, when differences from a group norm become great enough, social differentiation becomes social deviation.

DEFINING DEVIATION

There are a number of ways of defining deviation. Sometimes deviation and normality are defined statistically. Those around the average are considered normal, and those at the extremes are seen as deviant. If the average height of American males is 5'10", then males from 5'7" to 6'2" are probably viewed as normal, and a fellow 6'8" or 5'2" is considered deviant. Since most people have an I.Q. of between 95 and 115, that I.Q. level is "normal," and a child with an I.Q. of either 145 or 55 is deviant. Because most Americans are heterosexual and fewer are homosexual, heterosexuality is normal and homosexuality is deviant, if viewed statistically. Sociologists, however, generally do *not* look at deviation as a statistical phenomenon.

Another way of defining deviation is to liken it to a disease. The "disease" or "medical" model sees deviation as something that a person "has" that we wish he or she could get over, like a cold or the measles. People wonder, "What is *wrong* with Susan? Why does she continue to screw up? She must be crazy ..." The person behaves differently because something is wrong with the *person*. The logical next step: if we study carefully perhaps we can discover what is wrong with the person and then correct it. The medical analogy fits beautifully with this view of deviation—find the nature of the illness and prescribe a cure.

This view of deviance is a popular one—it's easily understood and it makes sense. This has meant that for years many scholars, scientists, and graduate students alike have scurried about looking for *the* cause, the explanation for the disease. As you can imagine, a number of answers have been found. Several categories of explanations come to mind.

Biological Explanations

In 1875, Cesare Lombroso stated that deviant behavior was inherited and that criminals were throwbacks (closer in the evolutionary chain) to apes. Lombroso came to this conclusion by taking a series of body measurements of institutionalized criminals and noncriminals and comparing them with those of primitive man (the criminals won—their measurements were closer to apeman than the noncriminals were). Other scientists had difficulty obtaining the same results when they repeated his work, but Lombroso's research was influential. It explained a complicated activity, crime, in a reasonably simple and straightforward way. Other studies examined criminal families (for example, the Jukes and the Kallikaks) and identical and fraternal twins to try to prove that crime was inherited. Attempts were made to relate physique and body type (fat, skinny, or muscular) to the fact of being criminal and even to the type of crime. Peculiar chromosome patterns, especially the XYY pattern, were thought to be more prevalent among prison populations and therefore a potential "disease" factor. More recently, researchers have examined brain and body chemistry and diet to see how they are related to behavior.

Psychological Explanations

The ideas of Sigmund Freud (see Chapter 2) had a great influence on those seeking the causes of deviant behavior. Researchers stressed how early childhood experiences and guilt can affect the personality. The "unconscious" became an important concept. It was seen as that part of the mind in which unpleasant, perhaps antisocial, memories are repressed or stored. Psychologists believed that these memories even though repressed would seek expression and often make their presence known in other ways—dreams, slips of the tongue, and other difficult-to-explain behaviors. Or it was surmised that an individual becomes delinquent or criminal because his superego never developed adequate strength to deal with the antisocial forces of the powerful id. A whole new vocabulary became available which focused not on biology or heredity, but on the *mind,* and it proved to be a convenient means of explaining antisocial behavior. One outgrowth of this research was the development of personality tests. These could be given to trouble-makers, potential delinquents, or people suspected of committing crime in an attempt to prove guilt or detect the problem ahead of time.

Sociological Explanations

Sociologists define deviant behavior as behavior contrary to generally accepted norms. These norms may be family, group, organizational, or social norms, often established by custom, and sometimes supported by law. Whereas the medical approach to deviant behavior infers weakness in the individual, be it biological, psychological, or whatever, sociologists believe that deviant behavior is *normal* behavior—normal in the sense that because of individual differences, diversity is to be expected in all societies. Sociologists recognize that biological and psychological factors play a part in the development of the individual as we outlined in Chapter 2, but they emphasize that deviant behavior, like nondeviant behavior, is learned, developed through the socialization process.

One problem with defining deviance this way, however, is that it is relative—what is deviant to one audience may be normal to another. For example, take the member of an urban delinquent gang—he is conforming to gang norms when he defends his turf, builds a zip gun, and saves face by fighting rather than backing down to a threat. His "deviant" behavior is learned and is as conforming in its own way as is the behavior of the middle-class college coed who conforms to the fashions, behaviors, and attitudes of those around her. There will always be differences of opinion about norms; likewise, there will be differences over what is deviant and what is normal behavior.

Again, sociologists believe that deviant behavior and crime are learned; they are consequences of social conditions. What the sociologist does, then, is try to discover the situations in society most likely to lead to crime and deviant behavior. Poverty, lack of legitimate opportunity to move up the social-class ladder, racism, sexism, and other social factors place tremendous pressures on people and may very well push some of them into delinquency and crime. Conflict between social classes which results in one class overpowering another can produce pressure leading to crime. These are *structural* conditions—they are a part of the social structure. The connection between social structure and deviant behavior is studied by people like Robert Merton, the gang theorists we mentioned in Chapter 5 (p. 146), and conflict theorists like Marx and Quinney.

Other sociological approaches address the specific ways in which crime is learned. Edwin Sutherland's theory of "differential association" says that behavior, normal and deviant alike, is learned during interaction with others. Sutherland felt that the prostitute, the professional thief, and the white-collar criminal learn to behave through association and communication with people who display deviant behavior in a favorable light. The are taught the positive rewards of that behavior—that crime does pay.

Before leaving the sociological theories of deviant behavior we should briefly look at another approach which has attracted wide interest. This approach focuses not so much on the deviant act or deviant person, but rather on the process of defining the act or person as deviant. Who make the rules? Who enforces them? On whom and why? These questions emerge from what is generally called *labeling theory*.

Labeling Theory

A 6'8'' basketball player for the University of Arkansas, sporting collar-length hair and a long drooping mustache, fouled out of three straight games. Before his next one, against Baylor, he decided to trim his hair and shave his mustache. In the Baylor game he was called for only two fouls. Two nights later, against Texas Tech, the neat, trim player played forty minutes and was still around at the end of a 93–91 double-overtime victory that knocked Tech out of the Southwest Conference lead.

The haircut? The shave?

"I think they helped," the player stated. "I hate to say it, but I guess the hairstyle did affect the refs."

Labeling theory sees deviant behavior as a product of group definitions. Becoming a deviant involves a labeling process—one is a deviant because a particular group labels him or her as such.[1] As with the basketball player, the focus changes from an examination of why the individual does peculiar things to an examination of why these things are called deviant. In 1919 lawmakers succeeded in passing the Eighteenth Amendment to the U.S. Constitution, which made the sale or manufacture of intoxicating beverages a crime. In 1933, the Twenty-First Amendment repealed the Eighteenth and decreed that drinkers were no longer criminal. Which was the majority view? Probably the latter, but the important point is that both amendments were results of the actions of rule makers who defined the same act as deviant and criminal at one time, and permissible at another time. In other words, it is labeling groups that determine who and what is deviant; *deviation is socially defined*.

Why are some acts labeled as deviant and others not? Sometimes the rule makers are motivated by moral or religious beliefs. They are strongly convinced that acts like drinking alcohol, smoking marijuana, or legalizing abortion are morally wrong and then make tremendous efforts to see their beliefs written into law. You can probably think of examples in American history, some quite recent, in which people have successfully crusaded for a cause that ultimately became law.

Perhaps rule makers are motivated by profit. If new clean air standards

---

[1]This discussion of the labeling aspect of deviation is drawn from Howard S. Becker, *Outsiders* (New York: Free Press, 1963), Chapter 1. Also see his Chapter 8 for a discussion of rule creators and rule enforcers.

The case of the hairy basketball player was described in *Sports Illustrated*, 16 February 1976.

are going to mean retooling a company's whole assembly line and spending $5 million in research and development, then you can be fairly sure that the company may spend about $3 million fighting to delay that law. Or turn it around. Imagine that I just invented an ingenious little catalytic converter that makes exhaust air *cleaner* than normal air, and I am lobbying for a law to get my invention placed on all cars. Would you believe me if I told you that I am motivated solely by concern for the environment?

Sometimes the rule makers are interested in supporting the *status quo* and protecting vested interests. Often, young politicians recently elected to Congress arrive in Washington with the idea of changing the entrenched seniority rules in the House and Senate. But the club remains. Some of the opposition to the Equal Rights Amendment probably reflects concern for vested interests and the *status quo*.

So, all sorts of motivations and justifications are used by rule makers to make rules. The result is a set of personal judgments about what is "right" and "wrong," which become justification for attempts to control people's behavior. Now rule enforcers take over. They seek out and punish those who violate the rules. Howard Becker refers to rule creators and rule enforcers, people whose profession centers around defining and regulating deviant behavior, as moral entrepreneurs. Labeling theory looks at it this way. Some people *make* rules, others *enforce* them, and out of this process certain individuals are *labeled* deviant. It is a *social* process.

To whom does the deviant label get applied? Well, not to everyone equally, of course. It depends in part on the *seriousness* of the act. On very serious behaviors (homicide, armed robbery) about which there is general agreement, the deviant label is quickly and formally applied. If the act is less serious (belching in public, dressing very strangely), the deviant label, if applied at all, will be applied less stringently. It also depends on the *vulnerability* of the person being labeled. Lower-class people and minorities are more likely to be labeled as deviant than others. It depends as well on *visibility*. If the act is obvious and occurs in full view of others, it is more likely to get a reaction.

These and other factors interact in complicated ways. Thus, in the view of the labeling theorists, calling people deviant may be an arbitrary and capricious act—telling us more about the person doing the labeling than about the person being labeled. Take the hairy basketball player once more. As you recall, he cut his hair and no more fouls were called. Tell me, which of the following was he: (1) a mild-mannered, peaceful, and orderly player victimized by referees who have a bias against grubby long-haired-hippie types; or (2) a brutal "hatchet man" whose behavior became less visible to the rule enforcers (referees) when he cut his hair? We'll never know.

A recent example of the labeling process in action has been provided by Stanford psychologist David Rosenhan. Rosenhan and seven colleagues view themselves as quite sane, but for the purposes of an experiment each went to the admissions office of a mental hospital and told the same story: They were hearing unclear voices that seemed to be saying words like *empty, hollow,* and *thud.* That was enough for the admitting psychiatrists at twelve of the hospitals; Rosenhan and his friends were diagnosed as schizophrenic and admitted. The label was applied, and it stuck. The diagnoses were not questioned by other staff members, and the pseudopatients were incarcerated for between seven and fifty-two days before being released. Although they behaved calmly and normally in the hospital, they were continually given pills (a total of nearly 2,100) to "help" them. None were released as cured—"in remission" was the final diagnosis. When a label is firmly affixed, it is very difficult to escape it. While in the hospitals, the pseudopatients took careful notes about what was happening—hospital staff either ignored this or saw it as evidence of insane compulsiveness. The pseudopatient's normal behavior was either overlooked entirely or profoundly misinterpreted. Often they would approach hospital staff with reasonable questions. In response, nurses and attendants would move hurriedly away, eyes averted. Psychiatrists also ignored the questioners. This sort of depersonalization is a predominant characteristic in labeling situations. Rosenhan is discouraged about the inability to correctly diagnose mental illness; but more to the point of our study of labeling is his comment that once a label is applied to people it sticks, a mark of inadequacy forever.[2]

PRIMARY AND SECONDARY DEVIATION

In an approach to deviation that emphasizes society's *reaction* to behavior as the labeling approach does, the distinction between primary and secondary deviation is of central importance. **Primary deviation** is not too serious and does not affect the individual's self-concept. People can rationalize primary de-

---

[2]For the complete report, see "On Being Sane in Insane Places," by D. L. Rosenhan, in *Science,* 19 January 1973, pp. 250–258. *Saturday Review* also has a good summary of the research in the 24 February 1973 issue, pp. 55–56.

"IT'S A BOY! ... I THINK ..."

For about one in every 3,000 births (about 1,000 babies a year in the U.S.) the determination of the newborn baby's sex may be difficult. These are babies who for a variety of reasons have what doctors call ambiguous genitalia. When the external sex organs do not clearly identify the infant's sex, what the doctor does next sets the course for the infant's future.

For the doctor to say, "I don't know yet," or "I'm not sure," will be very traumatic to the parents and ultimately to the baby. The father and mother should have no doubts that they have a boy or a girl. A clear-cut sex announcement is needed, because of the great importance that "the sex of rearing" plays in forming the child's own sense of sexual identity.

What does the doctor do? One obstetrician who has dealt with many such cases tells us that the size of the visible genitals is the key. "If it's small, say it's female. If in doubt, say it's female. If there is any uncertainty about the baby's eventual ability to perform sexually, it would be a serious mistake to call it a male." The doctor believes that a "male" who is incapable of functioning biologically as a male might be better off functioning as a female, even if by other standards (XY chromosomes) he might be judged male.

From *The Sacramento Bee*, February 15, 1978.

---

viant acts as being within the bounds of reasonable, acceptable, and normal behavior for people like them. It fits in with or does not seriously detract from the person's typical status and role. The doctor who splits fees, the person who drinks too much, and the eccentric college professor are all deviant to be sure, but it is primary deviation because it is not far beyond the boundaries of the conventional statuses and roles they occupy.

A process occurs whereby society reacts to continued primary deviation by expressing moral indignation, rejection, and penalties. **Secondary deviation** refers to deviation that represents a defense, attack, or adjustment to the problems created by the societal reaction to the primary deviation. The individual becomes labeled and stigmatized. The person begins to see himself as others do, the self-concept begins to change; in short, he wears the label and the self-fulfilling prophecy has done its work. It is not long before the clever lawyer who drinks a little too much becomes the drunk who occasionally practices law. As one's self-concept changes in secondary deviation, the person may become involved in a deviant subculture and gain further knowledge and skill regarding the behavior, including techniques for avoiding detection. The important factors in secondary deviation are the redefinition of self that follows society's reaction and the consequences of that redefinition for future behavior.[3]

There is a paradoxical and important outcome of this sequence: The societal reaction has the intent of stopping primary deviation, but it may force one

---

[3]The idea of primary and secondary deviation was first developed by Edwin Lemert. See his *Human Deviance, Social Problems, & Social Control* (Englewood Cliffs, N.J.: Prentice-Hall, 1967), especially pp. 17–18 and 40–64. Also see the discussion in Clinard and Meier, *Sociology of Deviant Behavior*, 5th ed. (New York: Holt, Rinehart and Winston, 1979), pp. 75–76.

into secondary deviation. This in turn often leads to an *increase* in deviant involvement and behavior. Some examples: The basketball player fouls out of a couple of games. The local paper labels him a rough and aggressive player, he begins to see himself differently, and suddenly he fouls out of *every* game. The juvenile is picked up on a minor charge such as a runaway or curfew violation. She is locked up in a detention home and treated like the other delinquents. She learns from them, starts to see herself differently, and when she is released she is ready for a full-blown delinquent career.

DEVIANT BEHAVIOR IN PERSPECTIVE

Deviant behavior is often seen as a malignant element in society to be eradicated at all costs. To say that something is deviant is to imply that something is wrong and needs to be fixed. This is an incorrect view for several reasons. First, it is important to remember that deviant behavior is basically the product of people's definitions rather than something natural or inherent. Knowing this allows us to shift our focus from the person's behavior to the question, "Why is his behavior being called deviant?" Second, Durkheim, Erikson, and others have pointed out that deviant behavior is not necessarily harmful to group life. In fact, it often plays an important part in keeping the social order intact. Deviant behavior enables groups to define boundaries—it preserves stability within the group by pointing out the contrast between what is inside the group and what is outside. Erikson suggests that without the battle between "normal" and "deviant," the community would lack a sense of identity and cohesion, a sense of what makes it a special place in the larger world.[4]

Finally, deviant behavior appears to be one of the processes involved in social change. Often, what is deviant today is accepted tomorrow and expected the next day. Maybe the people who seem to be listening to a different drummer just heard the beat before the rest of us. *Some* forms of deviant behavior represent an early adaptation to changing conditions. There are many examples of this: Deviant clothing styles of the past are the fashion of today. Yesterday's pornography is accepted literature today. Obviously there are limits—some behaviors should be considered deviant no matter what. The point is, however, that deviant behavior does not necessarily represent the evil its title implies; often it serves necessary and important functions in society, including those of defining the group's boundaries and helping to bring about social change.

CATEGORIES OF DEVIATION

It is often hard for people to reach agreement on what is deviant and what is normal. At the same time, there are some behaviors and characteristics about

---

[4]Kai Erikson deals with these ideas in detail in his *Wayward Puritans* (New York: John Wiley, 1966), Chapter 1, and in "Notes on the Sociology of Deviance," in *The Other Side*, edited by Howard S. Becker (New York: Free Press, 1964), especially pp. 9–15.

which there is more general agreement. In the following paragraphs we will briefly examine some of these categories of deviation.

Individuals who lack intelligence to the extent that they are unable to per-form the normal tasks expected of people their age are victims of *mental defi-ciency*. Current practice defines five levels of mental deficiency or retardation: *borderline* (I.Q. range of 83–68), *mild* (67–52), *moderate* (51–36), *severe* (35–20), and *profound* (below 20). The extent of mental retardation in the United States is estimated at approximately three percent of the population. More than half of the retarded receive special educational services, and a great majority of those in the 50-to-80 I.Q. levels make a satisfactory adjustment in the commu-nity at the adult level. Those with I.Q. levels between 25 and 50 are viewed as trainable in that they can learn certain skills necessary for living in the home, neighborhood, or sheltered workshop. They will, however, need some care and supervision throughout life. About five percent of all retarded fall in the pro-foundly retarded category and require complete care and supervision through-out life. Mental deficiency, especially severe retardation, may be related to genetic factors, birth trauma, or diseases of the mother prior to birth. Many instances of retardation, particularly at the higher I.Q. levels (50–80), seem to be related to factors in the social environment.[5]

Mental illnesses are commonly classified in two categories: neuroses and psychoses. Neuroses are the mildest and most common; psychoses are more severe and less common. The neurotic is anxious, nervous, compulsive, but gen-erally able to function adequately in society. The psychotic loses touch with re-ality. The psychotic may have hallucinations, incoherent speech and thought, or delusions of persecution; or he may withdraw into a dream world. Psychoses fall into two categories: organic and functional. Organic disorders are those caused by brain injury, hereditary factors, or physiological deterioration (as a result of aging or the effects of alcoholism or syphilis). Functional disorders are those without organic cause; they are based on environmental factors. Func-tional disorders represent a reaction to such things as stress or rejection, or they may possibly be a chosen alternative to an unlivable and intolerable world. Examples of functional disorders include schizophrenia and manic-depressive psychoses. Social scientists generally are more interested in the functional psy-choses because of their relationship to social factors. It is important to note that these categories (organic and functional) are not clear-cut or mutually exclu-sive. Some research has indicated, for example, that hereditary factors affect schizophrenia and that psychoses resulting from aging may be as much related to social isolation (functional) as to physiological deterioration (organic).[6]

It is difficult to estimate the exact number of neurotics in the United States. Some say we are all a little neurotic; other estimates of the number of neurotics in the population run from a high of forty percent to a low of five percent. It has been estimated that there are over two million psychotics in the

---

[5]This is summarized from *Psychology 73/74 Encyclopedia* (Guilford, Conn.: Dushkin Publishing Group, 1973), pp. 166–169.

[6]A more detailed discussion of mental illness, as well as of alcoholism, narcotics, and suicide, appears in Marshall Clinard's and Robert Meier's *Sociology of Deviant Behavior*, 5th ed. (New York: Holt, Rinehart and Winston, 1979).

TABLE 13.1   Who Drinks Alcohol?

	Highest Proportion of Drinkers	Lowest Proportion of Drinkers
Income	High income	Low income
Education	College	7th grade or less
Residence	Large city	Small city
Religion	Jews, Catholics, Lutherans	Other large Protestant denominations
Age	21–39	60 and over
Sex	Male	Female
State	Alaska, D.C., Hawaii, California, Washington	Iowa, Minnesota, Nebraska, South Dakota, North Dakota

Marshall Clinard and Robert Meier, *Sociology of Deviant Behavior*, 5th ed. (New York: Holt, Rinehart and Winston, 1979), Chapter 10; and the National Institute on Alcohol Abuse and Alcoholism.

United States. Half of all hospital beds in the country are used for the care of mental patients, and at current rates one person in ten will be hospitalized for mental illness sometime during his or her life. It is easy to see why mental illness has been called America's *major* health problem.

Drinking alcoholic beverages is relatively common in the United States, but excessive drinking, or *alcoholism,* is viewed as deviant behavior. A 1964 study reported that sixty-eight percent of Americans over eighteen drink, and a 1981 Gallup poll put it at seventy percent. Some general characteristics of drinkers are shown in Table 13.1. It should be noted that although more men than women drink, the percentage of women drinkers is increasing rapidly in the United States. Drinking and alcoholism are not identical. Some groups have relatively high alcohol consumption rates but little alcoholism. The major factors here are the group associations and cultural factors associated with drinking.

There are several types of drinkers. *Social drinkers* drink when the occasion suggests or demands it and are relatively indifferent to alcohol—they can take it or leave it. Some social drinkers drink regularly, others infrequently. *Heavy drinkers* drink more frequently and consume greater quantities when they drink. They occasionally become intoxicated. *Acute alcoholics* have much trouble controlling their use of alcohol. They may go on weekend binges or drunks. They have sober periods, but they rely more and more on alcohol. *Chronic alcoholics* drink constantly. They "live to drink, drink to live." It is difficult if not impossible for them to hold jobs, and their health will inevitably be affected. It is estimated that there are 5.5 million problem drinkers in the United States, and most of these would be termed chronic alcoholics. In a 1981 Gallup poll, twenty-two percent of all families reported having alcohol-related problems. Of an estimated 10.4 million arrests in 1980, approximately 3.3 million were for offenses directly related to alcohol (drunkenness, drunk driving, and disorderly conduct). Sociologists believe that alcoholism is a learned behavior, since drinking patterns tend to be associated with occupational groups, social classes, religious categories, and nationalities.

The use of *narcotics* is a central issue in American society. Drug use is viewed as deviant in a society dominated by the values of the Protestant ethic—hard work, self-control, and self-discipline. But use of drugs is widespread. Many youths are using marijuana, amphetamines, and LSD and other halluci-nogens. Their elders are using tranquilizers, pep pills, and sleeping pills. In the 1960s, drugs, like rock music, became a part of the culture of many youth groups. As young people became more interested in drugs, adults became more concerned about drugs, at least about those the young people were using. The result is a classic example of conflicting views about what is deviant behavior and what is not. In the middle and late 1960s, there was tremendous concern about drug usage. This resulted in passage of new drug control laws and stricter enforcement of older laws. Numerous arrests and harsh punishments followed. In the middle and late 1970s, however, things changed. There were an estimated 581,000 arrests for drug abuse in 1980, but this represented a twelve percent *decrease* from 1976. This could mean that drug usage is declining. It is far more likely that attitudes toward use of the so-called milder drugs, es-pecially marijuana, are changing, and that enforcement of existing drug laws is easing. Table 13.2 shows data from a recent survey of 17,000 high school se-niors regarding their use of drugs.[7]

Suicide is viewed as deviant behavior in the United States, as it is in most societies dominated by Christian and/or Jewish religions. Reactions vary, how-ever. Some countries have called suicide a crime and have buried suicides in special cemeteries. In some Oriental societies suicide is looked upon with less disfavor. Ceremonial self-destruction, known as *hara-kiri*, has long been a custom in Japan. Several states in the United States have classified attempted suicide as a crime, but it is unlikely that this has any deterrent effect, except possibly to ensure the success of the attempt. It is estimated that 27,000 Ameri-cans committed suicide in 1978, a rate of 12.5 per 100,000 people. Probably at least five times as many attempt suicide as actually commit it.[8]

TABLE 13.2   Percent Who Have Used Drugs in Past Month

		Class of	
	1975	1978	1981
Marijuana	27	37	32
LSD	2	2	3
Cocaine	2	4	6
Stimulants	9	9	16
Sedatives	5	4	5
Alcohol	68	72	71
Cigarettes	37	37	29

[7]This research is reported in "Student Drug Use in America: 1975–1981," published by the National Institute on Drug Abuse. Information on reported crimes and arrests comes from the *Uniform Crime Reports—1980*, which is published annually by the FBI.

[8]These figures on suicides come from *Demographic Yearbook* (a U.N. publication), and *Vital Statistics of the United States* (from the Department of Health, Education, and Welfare).

Suicide rates in selected countries are shown in Table 13.3. Patterns of deviant behavior often vary substantially from one country to another, and this is certainly true of suicide, as can be seen in Table 13.3. However, suicide statistics may be somewhat inaccurate. Countries vary in how they report suicides, and in most places it is probably underreported. In the United States, the coroner usually determines whether a death is reported as suicide. A coroner who is uncertain about the cause is more likely to label the death as due to natural causes. In addition, relatives, motivated by personal or religious beliefs, may press for a "death by natural causes" decision from the coroner.

Suicides in America are more likely to be male, white, over forty-five, single, divorced, or widowed, and Protestant. Although men commit suicide more than women do, more women than men attempt suicide. This has led some to the conclusion that at least for women, suicide may often be an attention-getting device. Men more often use guns to commit suicide; women tend to use poison. Some occupational groups are high in suicide—military officers, policemen, psychiatrists. And, interestingly, suicide is a leading cause of death for young adults.

In the late nineteenth century Emile Durkheim studied suicide in Europe and described in detail three types of suicide: egoistic, altruistic, and anomic.[9] *Egoistic* suicide occurs when interpersonal relationships are secondary, distant, and not group oriented. In such situations, the individual lacks group attachments, and when personal problems appear, the individual, in the absence of emotional support from others, resorts to suicide. The high suicide rate of single people might be an example of egoistic suicide. *Altruistic* suicide, on the other hand, is the result of strong group attachments. The individual commits suicide to benefit the group and to follow group norms. Suicides of Japanese soldiers and airmen during World War II and the self-immolation of Buddhist monks in Vietnam are described as altruistic suicides. *Anomic* suicide occurs in situations in which norms are confused or are breaking down. Economic depressions or rapid social changes that lead to disequilibrium in society and a state of normlessness may result in anomic suicides.

TABLE 13.3 Suicide Rates (per 100,000 People) in Selected Countries, 1975–1978

Hungary	43	Australia	11
Austria	25	Israel	6
Switzerland	24	Ireland	6
Denmark	23	Spain	4
West Germany	22	Costa Rica	4
Sweden	19	Greece	3
Japan	18	Mexico	2
France	17	Kuwait	0.4
Canada	14	Jordan	0.2
United States	13	Egypt	0.1

Demographic Yearbook, 1979.

---

[9]Emile Durkheim, *Suicide*, translated by John A. Spaulding and George Simpson (New York: Free Press, 1951).

DEVIANT BEHAVIOR AND CRIMINAL BEHAVIOR

A distinction should be made between deviant behavior and criminal behavior. As we have mentioned, deviant behavior, like beauty, is in the eye of the beholder. Behaviors are not naturally deviant; they are defined as deviant by groups. Similarly, reactions to deviation vary greatly. Some deviant behavior is ignored, some deviant behavior is tolerated, and some deviant behavior brings severely critical reactions by others. As behaviors fall further outside the range of what is defined as normal, societies feel that they must formally proscribe the behaviors. Rule makers decide that certain acts are a threat to the organization and structure of society and must therefore be prohibited. Laws are passed, and these forms of deviation become illegal or criminal if performed.

Conflict theorists tell us to be alert here and ask crucial questions. Who are the rule makers? Who passes the laws? The answer—middle- and upper-class representatives of the power structure. Who enforces the laws? Police, who, if they are not members of the middle class, are agents of and are working for the middle class. The theme continues for courts and prison systems. Conflict theorists suggest that we should not be surprised when arrest figures show that those without power and wealth commit most crime—the system is designed to work that way. According to this view, the whole criminal justice system from law to prison is an instrument the ruling class uses to perpetuate existing patterns of power and privilege.[10]

Law violation is called **criminal behavior,** and there are several categories of crimes. More serious acts are called *felonies* (punished by a year or more in a state prison or by death). Less serious crimes are called *misdemeanors.* The FBI has developed a list of seven major crimes: homicide, rape, aggravated assault, robbery, burglary, larceny, and auto theft. Trends in crime are studied by noting the number of crimes reported to police throughout the country. Table 13.4 shows the number of major crimes reported in the United States in 1980.

TABLE 13.4   Reported Crime in the United States, 1980

Crime	Number	Type
Murder	23,000	
Forcible rape	82,100	1,308,900 Violent (10%)
Robbery	548,800	
Aggravated assault	655,000	
Burglary	3,759,200	
Larceny-theft	7,112,700	11,986,500 Property (90%)
Motor vehicle theft	1,114,700	
Total	13,295,400	

Uniform Crime Reports, 1980.

---

[10]The conflict perspective starts, of course, with Marx. Today, the major spokesman is Richard Quinney. He has written a number of books including *Critique of Legal Order: Crime Control in Capitalist Society* (Boston: Little, Brown, 1974); and *Criminology,* 2d. ed. (Boston: Little, Brown, 1979).

Aside from the seven major crimes, a number of other acts are illegal—prostitution, gambling, fraud, embezzlement, arson, vandalism, traffic offenses, and so on. Some of the forms of deviant behavior previously discussed in this chapter may fall into criminal categories. If alcoholism means drunk driving, it becomes a crime. The sale, possession, and/or use of certain drugs becomes a crime.

One might assume that if an act is defined as criminal, there must be general agreement about it. Such a serious move by a society must mean that people are in accord with each other and that group differences and vested interests have been set aside. This, of course, is not necessarily so. One category of behaviors is called crime because it threatens the public order. There is general agreement that acts such as homicide, arson, robbery, and larceny threaten the public order. About other categories of crime, however, there may be less agreement. For example, one such category grew out of the concern, religious beliefs, and moral outrage of our Puritan ancestors, who felt that in certain areas of behavior, individuals must be protected from themselves. It is not so much that their behavior may be a threat to society as that their behavior may be a threat to themselves. Consequently, a number of acts, some of which we today call vices, were defined as crimes. These include gambling, prostitution, narcotics use, abortion, and a variety of sexual activities, including homosexuality. Opinions as to the "rightness" or "wrongness" of these acts vary from individual to individual and from group to group. In fact, however, there is a substantial demand to engage in many of these acts.

Gambling is legal in some states and is widely sought and available throughout the country even where not legal. Prostitution is legal in some areas (in all Nevada counties but two, for example). Many young people as well as some of their elders wonder at the current laws punishing marijuana use. Studies show that marijuana is widely used and is relatively easy to obtain. Laws in

TABLE 13.5   Arrests of Young People, 1980

	Percentage of Arrests for People:	
	Under 15	Under 18
Robbery	7	30
Burglary	15	45
Larceny-theft	15	38
Motor vehicle theft	11	45
Arson	25	44
Vandalism	23	49

Uniform Crime Reports, 1980.

nearly all our states outlaw sodomy, the "infamous crimes against nature," and yet Kinsey reported that many of these "crimes," which involve various types of sexual behavior, are relatively common practices. People wonder why homosexual acts between consenting adults in private are not legal if heterosexual acts under the same conditions are.

Edwin Schur has commented that since all parties involved in these actions (gambling, prostitution, abortion, etc.) are seeking them or at least consenting to them, these are "crimes without victims."[11] If there is no victim, Schur wonders whether anyone should be punished. He points out that when these activities are called crimes, they are forced underground to a certain extent and become more expensive to obtain. This leads to secondary crime—theft, for example, to obtain funds to support the primary crime, such as narcotics or abortion. So, although certain acts are defined as criminal by society, this does not mean that there is universal agreement as to their "wrongness."

Juvenile delinquency refers to young people (under twenty-one in some states, under eighteen in others) who commit criminal acts or who are wayward, disobedient, uncontrollable, truant, or runaways. Delinquency is a confusing concept. Young people *are* heavily involved in certain types of crimes, as can be seen in Table 13.5. At the same time, many young people are defined as juvenile delinquents for committing acts that are ignored if committed by adults (disobedience, running away). American law is such that we are very strict with juveniles. "Get ahold of the bad kids quick and change them so they won't grow up to worse activities." In fact, however, as we have seen in the section on primary and secodary deviation, if the juvenile is thrown into a reform school with more hardened delinquents, we almost guarantee the result we were trying to avoid. Most countries are more lenient than the United States in their treatment of juveniles.

SOCIAL CONTROL

Social control refers to the processes, planned or unplanned, by which people are made to conform to collective norms. A certain amount of confor-

---

[11]In his book, *Crimes Without Victims*, Edwin Schur discusses abortion, narcotics use, and homosexuality as victimless crimes (Englewood Cliffs, N.J.: Prentice-Hall, 1965).

mity seems to be essential in all societies. Predictability and order are necessary to the social organization of group behavior. If people could act in complete isolation, possibly they could ignore the existence of any norms. However, it is almost impossible to imagine such a situation because people do behave in groups, and, while individuality and nonconformity are very popular, we should remember that they are acceptable only when most people, most of the time, conform.

Social control may be provided in a variety of ways. We could, for example, hope that people will naturally conform; that conformity is in their nature, and it is inherent to conform. It seems, however, that people have to be *trained* to conform. Basic social control is taught through the socialization process. Shortly after the child is born, the family begins telling him or her what to do and what not to do, what is right and what is wrong. Sanctions or punishments are applied if the child misbehaves. Children who fail to conform are told, in effect, that mother and father won't love them or will beat them, depending on the family's view of proper child-rearing practices. Later, influences outside the family continue the process. Peers, teachers in the school system, the church, the mass media—all these have a profound effect on inculcating group and societal norms and encouraging conformity to group expectations. Finally, if all else fails, the society can pass laws to ensure conformity. Laws force people to conform and are a response to breakdown in other forms of social control. Again, sanctions are applied for failure. These sanctions may range from a fine to imprisonment to death.

Social control mechanisms vary depending on the type of group or society. In a primary group or small primitive society, rules are not written and social control is informal. Violators may be subjected to gossip or ridicule or possibly even ostracism; although these techniques do not have the dramatic effect of a raid by the FBI, they are surprisingly effective. In secondary groups and larger, urbanized societies, social control becomes more formal, and we have written laws, police, courts, prisons—an exceedingly complicated legal system to guarantee an acceptable degree of conformity.

Social control mechanisms also vary depending on the type of norm being violated. If the violated norm is a folkway regarded as of minor consequence to the group, informal and minor sanctions are called forth: whispering, giggling, or a little mild ridicule. If one of the mores of the group is being abused, however, more formal sanctions may be used.

Individual social control probably emerges from both internal and external sources. Internal constraints would be those aspects of the normative system that one internalizes through the socialization process. Internalized norms become the individual's conscience. External social control refers to the external mechanisms—rules and laws—applied by society. It would be fortunate if the two were in balance, but as we saw in the previous section on deviant behavior, this is frequently not the case. Take, for example, the boy whose little peers happen to be little hoods—his most important primary group is a delinquent gang. He internalizes a set of values and norms from them. He obeys the norms of the gang or he is ridiculed and ostracized. Yet in following gang social control he runs afoul of external societal social control, which in many cases makes opposing demands. To complete the dilemma, it is obvious that the social control system of the primary group, the gang, is much more important for one's behavior than is any external social control system. This type of gap occurs when the values of one segment of society are vastly different from the values of the rule makers of society.

The Reformed Mennonite Church imposed its "doctrine of avoidance" on Robert Bear of Carlisle, Pennsylvania. Commonly called shunning, this meant no one in the church including his family could speak or have anything to do with him. His wife and six children left him when the sanction was imposed. His parents died shortly after the church action and, according to Bear, "To the moment they died they looked at me with disgust. I was already burning in hell." Five years later in 1977 the punishment remained in effect.

There are about six beheadings a year in Jidda, Saudi Arabia. They take place on a public street and are well attended. A police squad car brings the victim, a Yemeni who has killed his sixteen-year-old wife. The Yemeni, chained and blindfolded, is guided to a piece of cardboard on the street, where he obediently drops to his knees. The black executioner, elegantly dressed in white with a black bandolier and sash, stands about three steps behind him with a polished, double-edged sword about three and a half feet long. A signal is given and the executioner's assistant jabs the kneeling Yemeni in the side with a sharp stick which causes his bowed neck to stiffen. The executioner is already moving and everything is soundless. He takes a few tiny ballet steps and then one long stride as the blade rises and drops through a perfect arc, severing the head in one majestic stroke. The head rolls forward, the neck spurts blood over the street, and the body topples backward. The assistant fetches the head and puts in on a stretcher, and sound returns. The crowd roars once in exclamation and disperses.

Adapted from "The Arabian Ethos," by Peter A. Iseman, *Harpers* 256 (February 1978), p. 52. Reprinted by permission of the Julian Bach Literary Agency, Inc. Copyright © 1978 by Peter A. Iseman. Reprinted from the February 1978 issue of *Harper's Magazine*.

Another type of gap or difference between internal and external social control occurs when people's attitudes, values, and norms change more rapidly than laws change. A cultural lag results. For example, there are sharp differences of opinion regarding whether to and how to enforce existing gambling and prostitution laws. Laws traditionally have been slow to change (and perhaps they should be, so as not to respond to every whim or alteration in public opinion). We might predict a pattern through which change in laws occurs: (1) attitudes change; (2) laws relating to the changed attitudes are not enforced; and (3) laws change. It is likely, however, that there is a large lapse of time between step two and step three. Consequently, when attitudes change, laws tend to be kept on the books but just not enforced as vigorously as they might be. Law enforcement agencies and individual citizens often find themselves in a difficult position because of this situation. The marijuana laws in California—first strictly enforced with heavy penalties, then less strictly enforced, now changing—are a good example of this sequence.

White-collar crime and organized crime provide examples of another type of conflict between society's laws and people's attitudes. The public favors and encourages prosecution of offenses such as burglary, assault, larceny, homicide, and sex offenses. They are indignant with the small-time thieves and quick to lock them up for their sins. On the other hand, white-collar crime is seldom punished. White-collar crime refers to the illegal acts committed by middle- and upper-class people during the course of their regular business activities, and includes such examples as the bank vice-president who embezzles funds, the physician who splits fees or performs unnecessary operations, the executive who cheats on his or her income tax, and the disk jockey who accepts payola.

Individual white-collar crime is only part of the picture. We know some corporations are engaged in unethical business practices, such as price fixing (by computer, steel, and electrical companies); false advertising (drugs, food); collusion between government regulatory agencies and the companies they are supposed to be regulating; campaign payoffs in return for favors; bribery; cost overruns on defense contracts; land fraud, computer fraud; and on and on. Take one case: General Electric, Westinghouse, and some twenty other electrical companies cooperated to fix prices of electrical equipment. Bids, supposed to be secret and competitive, were neither. The companies worked out ahead of time which company would bid lowest on a contract and what the other bids should be to make it look good. The resulting lowest bid was far higher than it should have been, and the companies made good money—in the neighborhood of $2 billion more than they should have in one seven-year period. But (surprise) they were caught. An outraged judge levied $2 million in fines (a drop in the bucket compared to the take) and sentenced seven men to thirty days in jail. See whether the average thief who steals a car or burglarizes a house gets off with thirty days. However, people were amazed at the "harshness" of the sentences in the great electrical conspiracy, for corporate criminals never go to jail, even for thirty days.

Criminologist Edwin Sutherland has maintained that more money is lost yearly through white-collar crime than through all other forms of crime combined, and that the damage to social relationships that results (no one can be trusted, everyone is on the take) is even more serious. Yet, as we said, the larceny or theft of the white-collar criminal is seldom punished, and even when it is, the penalties are slight compared with those for other crimes. Why? Well, the activity may have involved substantial skill and ingenuity and wasn't violent, so the public tends to identify with it or at least not object to it. Many times the victim (often a large organization or the public in general) is invisible or not easy to identify with. Often the culprit is a large corporation that has spent much money over the years to cultivate its image, and the public finds it difficult to believe that such an upstanding important company could be guilty of such dastardly deeds. And finally, the white-collar criminal is a "good" person—middle-class and respectable. So, the public prefers to look the other way.

Likewise, the activities of organized crime go largely unpunished, but the reasons for breakdown in social control in this case are more basic and easier to understand. Many people *want* what organized crime supplies: gambling, narcotics, tax-free cigarettes and alcohol, prostitution, and loan rackets. The conclusion is clear: The attitudes and values of society are reflected even more in punishment practices than they are in the written laws of society.

A TOMBSTONE EPITAPH—GIRARD, PENNSYLVANIA, 1870

In memory of
Ellen Shannon
Aged 26 years
Who was fatally burned
March 21st 1870
by the explosion of a lamp
filled with ''R. E. Danforth's
Non Explosive
Burning Fluid''

From *Folklore on the American Land* by Duncan Emrich (Boston: Little, Brown, 1972).

SUMMARY

The previous chapters in this section have dealt with social change, social disorganization, and collective behavior. In this chapter we returned to the topic of norms, which was first discussed in Chapter 3. A norm is defined as the accepted or required behavior in a specific situation. Most behavior is predictable because it is in accordance with generally accepted norms. However, some behavior is contrary, and this is called deviant behavior. Societies attempt to restrict the amount of deviant behavior through social control measures. This chapter addressed itself to these concepts—deviation and social control.

Individual variation and individual differences are a basic part of the human condition. When differences from group norms reach a certain point, however, social differentiation becomes social deviation. Many sociologists believe that deviation is best understood as a *labeling* process. Behaviors and/or characteristics of individuals are deviant when they are defined as such by members of society. Deviation is neither a natural nor statistical phenomenon but is a product of group viewpoints and definitions.

Criminal and delinquent behavior are also seen as products of a defining or labeling process. If society is especially concerned about certain types of behavior, it may define these behaviors as not only deviant but criminal as well. Frequently there are differences of opinion about the "rightness" or "wrongness" of particular acts. Such differences are more likely to occur in large, complex societies in which a variety of viewpoints exist about what is deviant and what is normal. These variations in definitions make it possible that within a society, a given act may be viewed as criminal and deviant, as criminal but not deviant, as deviant but not criminal, or as "normal."

We briefly examined several categories of deviation—mental illness, mental deficiency, alcoholism, drug usage, and suicide—as well as some descriptions of and explanations for criminal and delinquent behavior. Finally, we discussed social control, which refers to the processes by which people are made to conform to collective norms. Social control mechanisms are practiced by all societies and include norms internalized through the socialization process as well as laws enforced by the police and courts of a society.

The first of the readings that follow describes two people who, for quite different reasons, are labeled deviants. The article, written by one of them, relates how they react to their condition, and how society reacts to them. Society is often placed in the peculiar and hypocritical position of condemning a behavior and actively seeking and patronizing it at the same time. Gambling, prostitution, and abortion in some places are among numerous examples of this situation. Businesses and professions emerge to satisfy "deviant" needs. The second reading deals with one such profession, the professional party girl. Most forms of deviant behavior are learned behavior. Barbara Anderson in her article on wine drinking and alcoholism in France illustrates the importance of the socialization process and experiences in the cultural environment in producing a given type of behavior. The final reading is a short passage from *The Painted Bird*, which describes how a nonhuman society reacts to those who are different.

Terms for Study

altruistic suicide (393)	labeling theory (385)
anomic suicide (393)	misdemeanors (394)
criminal behavior (394)	neurosis (390)
deviant behavior (384)	organic disorder (390)
differential association (384)	primary deviation (387)
egoistic suicide (393)	psychosis (390)
felonies (394)	secondary deviation (388)
functional disorder (390)	social control (396)
juvenile delinquency (396)	

Reading 13.1

TWO DELICATE CONDITIONS

ROBIN ZEHRING

People are labeled as deviants for a variety of reasons. As this article demonstrates, you don't have to be a criminal to be deviant; being different physically is perhaps an even faster way of obtaining the deviant label. Robin Zehring is a free-lance writer living in San Francisco.

From *California Living Magazine, San Francisco Sunday Examiner & Chronicle,* 11 March 1973. Reprinted by permission of the author.

One thing about a five-foot-eight-inch-and-obtusely-pregnant woman walking down the street with a considerably shorter, cerebral-palsied male escort on crutches: They'll get noticed, all right.

Noticed like The Pox.

I, being the pregnant person and Bernard being the shorter, rarely advance more than five City yards before we are not only noticed: we are avoided with a physiological energy so overwhelming that The Natural Order of Life And Things falls shambled to the sidewalk. On account of our delicate physical conditions, I mean, one public pregnancy partnered by a crippled man and the world goes bananas.

Take, for instance, dogs. Dogs walk backwards, retreating at the mere sight of Bernard and me, misshapen beasts that we are. We've seen dogs forget they are moving and fall off the curb from just looking at us. Seen people fall off too. And trip over fire hydrants, parking meters, invisible trash or their imaginations. We've caused buses to bypass their stops, taxis to pause for red lights, cars to screech in unexpected halts at pedestrian crosswalks ("Lordy, can you imagine hitting one of those"). Children are hustled away from us ("Hey Mom whatsamatter with . . ."), adolescents cluster in giggling groups ("I wonder if they're like married or somethin'?"). No adult will meet our eyes ("For Godssake, Martha, don't stare!"). But their sidelong glances at my swollen torso and Bernard's bent legs indicate Dr. Rubin has plenty more What You Always Wanted To Knows . . . to write about.

Granted, we do walk slowly. Bernard drags his feet to reach each stretch of his stronger crutch and my feet are fluid-retentive and heavy from prenatal pressure of The Occupant (my Unborne Babe, as I call It) and likewise, they drag too. So perhaps the odds of boggled phenomena are directly related to our slow rate of speed: If you walk slowly enough, you're bound to see a dog fall off the curb eventually, or a cow jump over the moon, maybe? But Bernard, who has twenty-six years of public experience being sidetracked as a subhuman, explains to me kindly that those things are just part of it all; in fact, the slower you go, the more willing are people and buses and dogs to accept your physical handicap. Because people like you are supposed to go slowly.

"A handicapped person is one thing," cracks Bernard, "But a handicapped person in a hurry . . ."

I see what he means. Trudging (slowly) up and down the hills of Powell Street one day, Bernard and I decide to 'run' for the next cable car. Traffic at Bush Street intersection backs up three blocks, not only because we delay it a bit by crossing, but also because astonished drivers in the first few rows can't believe their eyes as down the incline I gallop, full-tilt and waving. The Occupant does cartwheels. Bernard races close behind me, his steel leg braces halfsliding on the concrete. The cable car is already sailing when the gripman sees us, rolls his eyes heavenward, and grabs the brake handle like it's the Titanic anchor, pulling back for all he's worth. The brake snags on the downhill angle. Passengers climb all over themselves (not) to see if we make it, their eyes riveted to my jouncing tummy and Bernard's steel scuttle. Both breathless, we reach the car, Bernard tossing his crutches aboard and hiking himself up. I take a deep breath, conquer the steps and we're off. Gradually, Bush Street traffic *resumes. Passengers, now timid with us at close range, study the floor. The grip-man is perspiring. The Occupant somersaults. I giggle. Bernard guffaws. "Told you so!" he chortles. "Haw, Haw, Haw!"*

I first met Bernard Maxon at The Noble Frankfurter on Powell Street when I was five months pregnant and feeling nauseous. He was at the next table, wolfing down two kosher hot dogs smothered in sauerkraut and mustard and onions, with a side order of potato salad and a hunk of Maria's Bavarian cheesecake waiting for dessert. It all looked enormously tasty and I couldn't help overhearing Bernard's vociferous manner of chewing which made it sound even tastier. I wanted to order six of everything. However, one occupa-tional dilemma of a delicate condition such as mine is relishing the idea of copi-ous food intake and then having The Occupant play soccer with it in my stomach. One learns to nibble Saltines and sip tea instead.

Bernard caught me watching him and listening to his chew. Sure, I had noticed the crutches propped against the chair next to his but I hadn't dwelled on them. I was more intrigued with his food. And yet, when Bernard noticed me noticing, I figured it was for the crutches. But he didn't. He was more interested in figuring me.

"Can't hack the hot dogs these days?" he asked, eyes twinkling behind hornrims.

I shook my head.

"Here, try one of these, I carry a spare." He rolled a pack of TUMS across my table. I blinked at them, dumbfounded. I'd never met anyone under fifty who carried spare TUMS around.

"Ulcer?" I wondered.

He began to answer with a gesture which accidentally followed through to the chair with the crutches. A clatter of aluminum banged to the floor. I started to rise.

"Hold it!" he ordered, "No bending over in your condition. It'll make you throw up." It was nice to meet a man who knew about being pregnant.

I sat as Bernard eased himself down to the floor, swept up both crutches and held them together like a canoe paddle, stiffening his body and pushing himself upwards to a standing position, much as a skier remounts with his poles. Then he sat down again and rearranged himself. The entire procedure was complete in about fifteen seconds. I was impressed.

"Pretty tricky," I said.

"That's nothing," said Bernard, "You should see me put on my socks."

I thought carefully for a moment. We had a lot in common.

"The same goes for my pantyhose."

We laughed hard together, knowing we each began the day by dressing on the floor.

In the months following, Bernard and I meet frequently for lunch. I learn to enjoy tea very much and forsake my Saltines for TUMS. We share our life stories and our hope and dream stories and our delicate condition stories which are remarkably similar and occasionally the same. Except that I, as a slightly handicapped person with a temporary condition, don't know the half of it com-pared to Bernard's life-time experience of prejudice, pain and abuse. Bernard

Maxon's got the stiffest upper lip I've ever seen. Why he hasn't drunk himself into oblivion, jumped off the Bridge, or at least clobbered someone with his crutch is beyond me until he reminds:

"Considering that from the moment I was born three months premature and motionless, what have I got to lose?"

I instinctively fold my hands across The Occupant's seven-month Mound and ponder.

What Bernard has got to lose is plenty.

Incidental losses like his balance (when Bernard sneezes hard, he falls down), his public rights to restaurant seating ("They always put me in the back so I won't upset the 'dining decorum' "), hotel reservations, rental privileges (Managers claim they're not insured), some shopping prerogatives (Antique dealers and car salesmen are rarely overjoyed when he comes clomping in; they discourage him from handling the Dresden or testing the gearshift). Also, lost privacy. A lot of people ask Bernard a lot of very personal questions. Also, lost sexual title ("Just once I'd like to be accused of rape."). And the loss of acceptance by his fellow humans as a healthy able-bodied person worthy of friendship, wisdom and strength. People constantly suggest to Bernard that he sit down—at a distance!

Some of the above also goes for being pregnant.

Major losses? Jobs. Bernard has a difficult time finding a good one, despite his six-and-a-half years of college credits, his high I.Q. ratings and physical maneuverability. He was once denied a volunteer job to help recently disabled veterans at Letterman Hospital on grounds that his presence might depress the patients.

"OK so I'd be lousy at brain surgery or fashion modeling," chides Bernard. "But jobs in management, accounting and teaching are all available to people of my qualifications. Clerical jobs: I can type forty words a minute, with my left hand. But the minute I arrive for an interview, they tell me, 'We're not hiring.' One look at me and they suggest I try elsewhere, like on the street corner selling pencils."

Working the street is not Bernard's bag. He often ends up soliciting books or real estate or vacuum cleaners by phone, dialing the numbers with his typing hand. Telephone sales jobs endure about six weeks before something happens to the Company (bankruptcy, fraud, a quick self-export by the Boss) and the phone is disconnected. So is Bernard from his income, until the next State Disability check comes through. Which doesn't go very far in paying for food and rent and medical bills and custom-altered clothing and new shoes every month and a pair of socks a day and a college education.

So there's money to lose. Ignoring the doom of a butterless future, Bernard admits a weakness for lending whatever cash he does possess. He'll even go to such lengths as borrowing from someone else and re-lending it. And seldom see it again.

"It's true, I'm flattered if people tap me for loans," he says, "It's a rebellion on my part, all related to that crippled pauper image and peddling pencils. I don't think of myself as crippled, I don't wake up in the morning and feel

it. I want to live and earn my money through normal channels, not through opportunities specifically for The Handicapped, not by dealing in money like that."

Sometimes, money like that deals him. It belongs to people who cannot dissimulate a physical handicap from the downtrodden of the world. No matter that Bernard is dressed from Bullock and Jones—*"Only place I can get to alter my pants to a twenty-eight inch waist and a 23 inch inseam without laughing"*—and his facial expression maintained with purpose and intent. He finds it necessary to avoid busy City streets around Christmas and Eastertime and on Sunday mornings when pedestrians feel particularly righteous. They press money in his hand or stuff it in his pocket before he can explain that he really doesn't want it. One time a man gave him a personal check.

Another time a lady handed him a huge tin of Almond Roca as he waited for a WALK light. *"I had to put it inside my shirt to carry it. Three more blocks, it was chocolate almond soup!"*

Once he unknowingly put his crutches down on the sidewalk, leaning forward to tie his shoelace. Got a five dollar bill doing that.

I told Bernard that so far, no one has assessed my delicate condition as pathetic or needy and handed me cash for it. Or Almond Roca either. Bernard advised me to try limping a little.

Most major of losses Bernard has got to lose is affection. Lost affection can be sad for anyone, but it's sadder when a person is excluded beforehand because of a physical handicap. Generally, people suppose that The Handicapped are probably as nice and charming and at least as deserving as anyone else—and all that—but most people don't want to get involved. And don't want their son or daughter marrying one. We are brought up to be kind on the subject. But closed.

The following advertisement that appeared in a local classified section points up reality's grim divide:

> WOMAN, slightly disabled, happy, gentle, sensitive, alive, would appreciate your friendship. Also used paperback books to read. Call or write . . .

As Bernard says, *"If you don't advertise for it, you don't get it. In the meantime, you can always read about it."*

Beginning with his premature birth Bernard has endured a holocaust of rejections by doctors, therapists, psychiatrists, faith healers, quacks, schoolmates, teachers, employers, relatives, strangers and the public at large. He doesn't talk about these times very often, apart from periodic shrugs and allusions.

But one day at lunch, Bernard cast his eyes downward at The Occupant's Full-Term Mountain and chuckled.

"Listen," he said, hand on my hand and suddenly serious. "Most people don't let me near their kids, afraid I might rub off on them or something. Do you think maybe I could hold yours once in a while?"

I told him, come time, The Occupant and I would be delighted.

Questions 13.1

1. Illustrate the terms "deviation" and "labeling" with examples from this reading.
2. Describe the reactions of people to deviants. If, instead of a cripple or pregnant woman, the object of attention were a criminal, movie star, or well-known politician, how would the reactions differ? Why or why not? Explain.
3. How did being defined as deviant affect the behavior of Robin and Bernard?
4. The reaction to deviants is the same regardless of the particular type of deviation being observed. Discuss.
5. Recall the definition of minority group and apply this concept to the people discussed in this article.

Reading 13.2

THE CORPORATION PROSTITUTE

ANONYMOUS

There are a number of different types of prostitutes: the streetwalker, the house girl, the high-class call girl. This article describes another type—the party girl, hostess, or date for the big business or corporation. She is recruited by the corporation, and her services are sought after and appreciated by the corporation's clients; and society defines her behavior as deviant and criminal although she is never punished. The author of this essay states, "This is an explanation of another field of prostitution that existed some twenty years ago, and even in this more sophisticated era, still does in all probability." The essay was written by a sociology student with a rather varied past.

"Public Relations Consultant" is to a corporation prostitute what "modeling" is to a call girl, but by whatever name, a whore is a whore. The demands are the same and whether he is a chairman of the board or straight off the street, a John is a John.

Assuming that the basic equipment is in order, there are certain refinements that determine your place in the flesh market caste system. Whether or not it is harder work to be a streetwalker is a matter of personal definition, but if a girl has a taste for a classy couch, she should apply at _____. The fringe benefits are good (they had a mandatory health plan), and sometimes you could stumble into a unique retirement plan. It may be temporary, depending upon the vagaries of the market and the Baby's own fickleness—but diamonds are ALWAYS a girl's best friend. There are drawbacks as in everything else—no tenure, you can't collect unemployment, and nobody would believe your references. However, you can tell yourself you were a highclass hooker.

More care was taken in the selection of the women than was given to that of a new vice president. There were stringent requirements and the screening was intensive. Much depended upon the sponsor, which equated to letters of reference in a more legitimate endeavor. This sponsor observed the prospective employee and assessed her qualities sometimes for a period of weeks before the initial contact was made but once the recommendation was in, the girl had her security clearance.

The major prerequisite was that the girl must be a professional prostitute, either from a good house or working her own book. Call girls (even the expensive ones) and hustlers were considered too risky, for their operation involved too many people. They were also over-exposed. It didn't seem to matter if you had started in the streets, but to have improved your situation indicated a fastidiousness and the ambition to do your own thing, which, in turn, denoted a degree of intelligence. The requirements were heavier than have-douche-bag-will-travel. The Company wanted its personal, elite stable, financed by the un-suspecting stockholders at large, covered discreetly by the Auditing Department, administered and controlled in the best tradition of American Corporate efficiency. For this they were willing to pay good money.

Under no circumstances was a freebee considered. Anyone who played for fun and games and no profit was dangerous. They had no ethical standards and the disquieting possibility of emotionalism or involvement was present. Competent detachment is an occupational hazard, or blessing, for the professional. Too often a nonprofessional falls back on outraged virtue when the demands get rough. No matter how discreetly structured or fiscally disguised, the commodity was still sex and to the businessman with a sentimental conscience, something free smacks of adultery. Besides, he could probably make it with his wife's best friend, or give his secretary a whirl, so what's the big deal.

The girl should have had legitimate experience working with the public— receptionist, hostess, entertainer—that gave her a social poise which if not real was efficiently faked. She had to be aware of the world around her and not just the world of sex, to have read a book or two that wasn't pornographic, to carry on a reasonable conversation and pretend to listen intelligently.

Appearance was important, of course. The girl had to be more than just attractive. Size, shape, personality and disposition all differed, but there was one absolute—she could not look like a prostitute. Hair styles and dress could be modified or brought into line if all the other requirements were in order, but her whole bearing must be in keeping with the carefully constructed sexual fraud—courtesans, classy broads, Princess Grace selling her ass.

Age didn't seem to be a significant factor as long as the girl was over the age of consent. You could tell the older ones, they saved their money. Years of experience was not as important as the quality of experience for some women can turn tricks most of their working lives and end up hustling still for twelve-and-two. There were, however, common characteristics and foremost among them was a taste for the good life, a tough sense of independence, and a determination to be treated as a "lady" even peripherally.

Naturally, there was one other area—sexual expertise. As a professional the talent should have been taken for granted—how many pianists audition for their concerts? If this area was checked out, it was done secretly and never mentioned, but it would have made a great work incentive plan for the recrui-

ter. In a house it was probably a "very important client" and from a book, a favor for your favorite mark.

All these qualities were essential when dealing with men who, because of their positions or their pretensions, will not tolerate a chippy. After genuflecting before the GNP, only the choicest harlots were offered by the high priests. Corporations pimp for the industrial complex and such a select clientele must be catered to, their egos stroked, their reputations protected and their fetishes fanned. Bidding for a factory site? Fly the city fathers on a party to Acapulco. Wooing a merger? Prod it with charm, grace and prowess. Pushing a political issue? Knifing a competitor? Collecting proxies? Oil leases, anyone?

The preliminaries over, the recommendation in and the surveillance completed, the subject was contacted by her sponsor, and if she was interested, an interview was arranged.

It took a really well-trained eye to find potential in me. I was still half-gamin, defiantly determined to escape the streets and refusing to recognize any handicaps I might have. I owe it all to a fighter instinct and my Uncle Harry, a Vaudeville violinist ("The Fiddlin' Coon") and when he died he left his violin up for grabs.

In my family, nothing should be a total waste. Since we were stuck with the instrument, mother managed lessons for me and I promptly fell in love with music. Another cherished family tradition is that if you have a talent you sell it, which made earning a living much easier for the girls than the boys. When I was 10 it was discovered that I could sing—so, why aren't you working? I started paying my way as a band vocalist which drew attention away from my talent as a violinist and its dubious commercial value. At 14 I was on my own, winging to support myself and the violin. Wilhelm Van Hoogstratton was conducting the Portland Symphony and accepted me as a member which gave me a glimpse of a totally new world. It was a schizophrenic existence . . . I could play Hindemith but was incapable of a grammatical conversation. A competent vocalist with poise on the stand, I didn't know there were different folks, and thought everybody slept in their slips. . . . I wore the brightest colors I could find and felt naked without a watch, bracelet, beads, earrings, AND an ankle-chain. Luckily, the Symphony wore uniforms. Having learned submission at a very early age, I also learned about this time to augment my income between music jobs.

By the time I was 20, I was in San Francisco with a child to support and a little black book I used when I needed something. I was running scared but hanging in there, reading books, learning to talk and all the nice, social graces were there, if pretentious. One night it seemed to have all paid off and without even knowing it, I was considered for the big time.

My sponsor was a prominent San Francisco Madam who never offered to hire me herself. I was singing in a Pine Street Club and she came in down the street from her house every once in a while to relax and to see if any of her girls were free-lancing. We became friendly and talked. I think what impressed her most was the way I handled a big-time pimp who wanted to take over my thing for me. Whatever her reasons she decided to be my sponsor.

I wore white gloves to my interview in an office with a view of the bay. He *sat behind a mahogany desk and lit my cigarettes with a heavy, silver lighter. When the telephone rang he apologized graciously for the interruption, treating me more like an executive secretary than an executive's whore. I was to be paid every two weeks by mail and he took my social security number for the personnel department. I would be given a wardrobe allowance and there was a prepared list of the types of clothing that should be on hand. I was to move to a "good" address (I lived on Baker Street, just over from Fillmore). Inquiry was made very solicitously as to child care arrangements for I would be traveling a great deal.*

My personal life was my own as long as it did not interfere with or threaten the Company; I was made to realize immediately that the company had a battery of lawyers and any attempts at extortion would be handled quickly and efficiently, and I was guaranteed to lose, particularly since the fact of the professionalism made me a loser to start with; he gave me the name of the doctor where I was to have a monthly examination; I would not be "on call" but would be given my assignments in a purely business-like manner and well in advance although there would be emergency calls occasionally as well as luncheon appointments. I was expected to be entertaining, listen attentively even to drunken trivia and to converse as intelligently as I could depending upon the client; however, at no time could I interject my personal affairs.

Under entertainment, the customer was always right with one exception— nothing bizarre and no S&M—if that was the kick, report it to the program director. The company would also not tolerate orgies—just lots of bread and no circuses. He told me my new company name, shook my hand, wished me good luck, courteously escorted me to the door and I never saw him again.

There was a brief training period which consisted of a dinner and some drinks with a half-hearted attempt at erudite conversation. This was to see if I could handle myself and by this time I was pretty confident of the silverware. The staff-members conducting this research were lower echelon and not at all impressed by the Courtesan Corps. They were bored and so was I. The men probably wanted to do more than go to dinner. The woman, I remember, got juiced and had to be sent home in a cab.

The first assignment was a chartered flight to Texas to entertain some board members who where conducting some high-level skullduggery. This was not a sexual scene, but it was probably felt that some women hanging around would disarm somebody. I was also thrilled over the first cruise, until I learned you weren't supposed to watch the water. The clients were politicians, military men, executives and even the young ones ran to pot-bellies. I was hostess several times for conferences and there were a lot of just dinner-dates, but other than these little bonuses it was mostly business as usual except the rhetoric was nicer. It was an organizational meat market although attractively displayed. I got a kick-back from the stores which implemented the clothing allowance, and all the head-waiters split with us but the more money I made the faster I spent it and what I didn't spend, I gave away. I became more and more resentful of the system that hired me because I was intelligent and they treated me with amused contempt because I was. Lay down or go down—it didn't matter that I knew Mozart.

There was something for everyone and our duties were many and varied ranging from the bizarre to the mundane. Sometimes, it took on all the aspects of a Grade-B movie. At informal conferences and board meetings, a few selected women would mix drinks, mingle during breaks, provide a light touch and be generally charming and genial as befits any hostess. Not all men attending these meetings were to be granted our favors and when the meeting adjourned, those of us who were to be paired off would either be among the last to leave and then go with the client, or we would have discreetly withdrawn and be waiting for them in their hotel room—never ours. As for selection, we were either told beforehand or, as would often happen, some of the men would prefer the same woman and she was held in reserve for one. Sometimes this would provide an ironic domestic touch and occasionally led to bigger and better things for the woman when he decided he didn't want her passed around any longer. The men who were not granted privileges contented themselves with flirting, squeezing, pinching and propositioning. Under no circumstances could we accept the latter. Only the men designated were to be taken to bed and you couldn't make arrangements for later with another one. I don't know how the company would know, but they did know if you started branching off for yourself.

When the company was wooing business or providing favors on a large scale, it was a different situation. Then we partied. It would be a week-end, lavishly planned—a flight, or a cruise. We would be flown to Las Vegas for instance to meet a group from the East. The women were not assigned, but were up for grabs. We spent a lot of time at Carmel and at Tahoe and once in Mexico City. The scene sometimes reminded me of a Shriner's convention on a small scale. Even this set-up could be surprising, though. Once in Carmel we spent most of the night playing bridge.

For the individual date, you went alone either meeting him at a restaurant or picking him up at his hotel. It was dinner, a show or a round of the clubs and it could be up to that point a very pleasant situation. However, afterwards it often became sticky. On a single you uncovered some strange appetites and it took a lot of handling to let him know how far he was allowed to go. If this didn't work, we reported him and he was "black-listed." However, we also knew that the customer was always right and most of his fetishes were to be catered to.

It was always strange to me that on the parties, sex was almost a secondary thing. The emphasis seemed to be on just plain swinging—drinking, dancing, and a lot of boasting. But the act itself was brief and "normal." As a matter of fact, it seemed as if they never slept and we had to go as long as they did—it was rough on us non-drinkers, believe me.

Occasionally, we acted as tour guides. Using a company car, we would drive the client (and sometimes his wife) or a group of clients around San Francisco and the environs ending up with either a lunch or a dinner at one of the more famous (to the tourist) restaurants. I got awfully sick of the Top of the Mark and Fisherman's Wharf. Once I even acted as a baby sitter for a very important executive's children and took them to the Zoo and Funland at the Beach. Quite often we would be assigned to meet a man at the airport to save him the inconvenience of the limousine and the long, boring drive to the city.

One thing I haven't mentioned was the relationship between the women. Naturally, we all knew each other for we were together quite a bit. However, no friendships ever seemed to develop. We exchanged no personal information nor, to my knowledge, did we ever contact each other away from business. Also, during working hours we did not even discuss the Johns in the powder room. We mixed together beautifully while we were working but it was a mechanical thing and all our attention was to the men and why we were there—conversations were always general and remote.

We were utilized to some extent for the relaxation of the company executives or board members. If his stay was for a number of days, you were his exclusive property during that time. If he decided he wanted a change, you were notified by the office. And his relaxation meant mostly sex. I was hired once for a week to take care of an alcoholic executive whose family was too important to allow the company to fire him.

One night on a dinner date while we were still in the lounge a nightclub hustler tried to solicit my client. I watched her with what I hoped was the proper amount of amusement and doing my best lady bit I told her to make it. She looked at me in my Original and the furs and she laughed. "Bitch," she said, "You're 'hoe-in' just like me." What's more, I knew she was right, and at that moment it seemed I had to make up my mind what I was to be and more importantly, what I wanted to be. I was talented, for my music attested to that, but I had never really failed because I had never really tried. If I put a price on my body, for whatever reason, I couldn't really complain if somebody bought the merchandise. I wasn't even too good at that for I was using the John, he wasn't using me. That particular night was just a preliminary. If I was going to be a whore, then be an honest one. If I didn't want to be a whore, the answer was simple. Don't be one. Walk away from it and keep stepping.

I never went back. I don't know how they wrote me off in Payroll, but no one came after me either. I found an agent and my son and I went on the road with a group. I discovered I was not the best vocalist in the world and the knowledge didn't shatter me for I also discovered I wasn't the worst either and better than most. In 20 years I've made a million mistakes and an equal number of wrong turns, including a very bad marriage that stretched interminably for all the same reasons. I was still whoring, but it was respectable and legitimate. However, I accept the full responsibility. It begins to look as if I might be on my way to being a really classy broad.

Questions 13.2

1. Prostitution is a crime without a victim; if there is no victim, there should be no crime and, therefore, no punishment. Discuss.
2. "Prostitution is criminal but not deviant." Do you agree or disagree? Why? Discuss.
3. Where does society focus its attempts at social control—the prostitute, the John, or the corporation? Why? Where should it? Discuss.

Reading 13.3

HOW FRENCH CHILDREN LEARN TO DRINK

BARBARA GALLATIN ANDERSON

The French consume more wine than any other people in the world. According to French government figures, thirty percent of France's men consume alcohol in amounts dangerous to their health, and fifteen percent of Frenchmen are alcoholics. Government campaigns against wine drinking have met with little success, however, because children are taught to drink wine at an early age, and their behavior is reinforced later by a number of cultural beliefs. This article by anthropologist Barbara Anderson illustrates how deviant behavior, like normal behavior, is learned through the socialization process and how conflicting definitions of behavior (deviant versus normal) may exist side by side.

Visitors to France—even those with some knowledge of life in Mediterranean cultures—are often startled by the great amount of wine-drinking they find. Frenchmen everywhere drink with unflagging dedication and a quiet passion. For two years, my husband and I lived in the Seine-et-Oise village of Wissous, an area 10 miles from Paris. As anthropologists, we were struck by the tenacity with which villagers clung to their old drinking habits, specifically wine-drinking, despite considerable pressure from the government to abandon or at least cut down on their alcohol consumption. In particular, we were interested in finding out just how these drinking practices were transmitted to the village children.

Our two daughters, Andrea and Robin, then seven and two, were with us, and our son, Scott, was born there. We participated in the village life and, where possible, penetrated behind the scenes, gathering information about village customs. Of course, the questions we asked about children's drinking habits presented problems. The questions had to be very specific, yet apparently off the cuff. Eventually we incorporated them into a rather elaborate questionnaire on child care in general.

On the questionnaire, we asked people what every member of the household had eaten or drunk in the past 24 hours—at home or away from home. When feasible, we called at the villagers' homes during meal hours. Our interest was in what they had drunk, but we tried to give our questions no particular emphasis. We were as scrupulous in our attention to the kinds and quantities of foods they ate as we were in cataloging the beverages they drank. We administered these questionnaires and conducted follow-up interviews beginning in late February and ending in late April—a period of increasing warmth, which lowered the amount of drinking slightly. (To the villagers, cold weather is often a rationale for wine-drinking.)

Now, our interest lay specifically in the village's socially accepted drinking practices. For the French, this amounts to a study of wine-drinking. Our find-

ings: Adult male villagers consumed approximately 1.58 quarts of wine per day. Women drank more than half a quart. The averages for children, however, could not be estimated—for reasons that will become clear later.

Our village was representative of France, where the total consumption of pure alcohol for the year 1955 (our study was done in 1957–59) averaged 23.78 quarts per person, or 32.1 for adults over 20. This average for adults was 16.9 quarts more than was consumed that same year by the world's second-largest wine-consuming country—Italy. The Danes drink only 3.17 quarts of pure alcohol per year. Americans drink 9.29 quarts.

According to the French government's figures, 15 percent of France's men are alcoholics, and 30 percent consume alcohol in amounts dangerous to their health. The government's National Institute of Hygiene has said that very active manual workers should not drink over one liter (1.057 quarts) of wine per day. Yet many sedentary workers, who are advised not to drink more than half a liter per day, drink a whole liter—as much as the most active workers. Alcoholism, to the average Frenchman, is identified only with reeling drunkenness.

CHILDREN ENCOURAGED TO DRINK

Now, how does this receptivity to wine-drinking take shape in the children of the village? In other words, how is wine-drinking enculturated?

First of all, in Wissous, a positive value is attached to wine. People view wine-drinking as an act of virility. Men and families cannot socialize without wine. For a host not to offer wine is at best impolite.

In addition, wine is thought to have nutritive value. One reason: Throughout the schools, the very active wine lobby distributes blotters that carry highly dubious statements. One such blotter states that a liter of wine (12 percent alcohol) has nutritive value equivalent to 850 grams of milk, 370 grams of bread, 585 grams of meat, or 5 eggs. The blotter has a drawing of a scale with a wine-bottle balancing these foods.

Wine is also believed to be necessary for working. While at work, a manual or farm worker must have wine at fairly regular intervals. The body can best endure prolonged muscular exertion, it is alleged, with the sustained, revitalizing support of wine. Strong men have a propensity for drink. It is nature's way— "C'est comme ça."

Finally, wine may not be purer than any other drink, but Frenchmen think it is. In fact, the alcohol in wine is widely believed to compensate for the unsanitary conditions under which it, and many other food products, are prepared.

These beliefs about wine are strongest among the peasants. The few upper-middle-class families of Wissous also link wine-drinking to vigor. But they are more likely to stress moderation, and they drink less wine than the peasants. The moderation of the upper-middle-class, however, does not appear to extend to apéritifs and digestifs. They drink considerably more of these than the other villagers do, at home and in cafés.

In contrast with the positive value placed on wine, the French place a negative value on Western Europe's two major nonalcoholic drinks: water and milk. The Wissous village spring water, which flows from two central fountains, is potable, but little is drunk (except in coffee), especially by the men. The local attitude is that, although a certain amount of water-drinking is inevitable, water takes second place to almost any other beverage. As one of the subway signs posted by France's powerful lobby puts it, "Water is for frogs."

In its campaign against the wine lobby, the French government has recently turned to building the image of fruit juice. Government ads show popular sportsmen drinking fruit juice with apparent gusto. But the wine lobby is still far more successful than any other lobby in France at carrying its message to the people.

As for milk, a precept firmly adhered to by all classes is summed up in a popular 1947 book on child care: "Milk should never constitute the mealtime drink." This book also states that "the quantity of milk drunk in a day should not exceed half a liter, under risk of digestive troubles such as diarrhea." In this regard, the villagers run no risks. When children stop taking the bottle, and stop eating the bouillies *(thin milk mushes) of babyhood, they rarely drink milk at all, except in* café au lait, *chocolate, or the milk-thinned vegetables called* purées.

Of course, the fact that milk is unrefrigerated, especially in the villages, does nothing to increase its appeal. And though it is pasteurized, it is not *homogenized. When poured, it goes clunk-clunk in uneven globs. And in* warm *weather, it has a strong, almost curdled flavor.*

During the time we lived in Wissous, milk was delivered to the village in huge tin urns, and poured into bottles by the grocer. Unknown to him, I once followed him to the back of his shop and saw him slosh a dirty bottle around in a tub of cold water before filling it with milk.

A book on practical child-raising, known in the village since the early twenties, differs little in its warnings about milk, but acknowledges that children cannot be "bad off" if they drink milk almost exclusively for the first two years. I quote: "One can also give at mealtime a half-glass of water lightly reddened with wine, or some beer or cider diluted with water." In general, the recent literature is more cautious. It suggests, as a more suitable time for introducing children to alcoholic beverages, four years of age rather than two.

WINE INTRODUCED AS "REDDENED WATER"

Here, then, is our major point: Wine-drinking begins while the child is still in near-infancy. And government efforts to show that wine hurts children run into a semantic trap. A child does not drink wine: *he drinks "reddened water."*

To the French, the consumption of wine in quantities of less than a fourth of a quart is equivalent to abstinence. The mother of a boy of 12 will tell you, though the boy may be sitting across from you with a glass of the diluted wine in his hand, that her son does not drink at all. By this, she means that his "reddened water" contains only a couple of soup-spoons of wine.

One day I bought refreshments for my daughter and her 11-year-old playmate at a café. The playmate ordered and drank a bottle of beer. It surprised me a little, because her mother had told me that the girl did not drink. But I am sure that, to the mother, her child's minimal and irregular intake did not constitute drinking.

If parents are drinking wine, beer, or cider, they give some—diluted with water—to their children. The younger ones sip beer or cider from a parent's glass. As they get older and more demanding, they are given small glasses of their own.

Children of lower-class homes drink more wine than children of middle-class homes, and they start drinking when they are younger. One mother even reported putting a drop or two of wine in a baby's bottle to "fortify" the milk. Generally, though, wine is first offered when the child is two or more, can hold his own glass quite safely in his hand, and can join the family at table.

In short, wine-drinking is already a habit before French children are old enough to reflect about it. If they do begin to assess their drinking practices, it is against a cultural backdrop where all the answers are value-loaded. Under the circumstances, it is hardly surprising that the campaigns in France against wine-drinking—led by teachers, social workers, and specialists in child welfare—have met with little success, and that in the past quarter-century the drinking patterns of French villagers, despite much social change and many social pressures, have hardly changed at all.

Questions 13.3

1. Make a case for each of these propositions: (a) drinking wine in France is deviant; (b) not drinking wine in France is deviant.
2. What social control techniques is the French government using to discourage wine drinking? Why aren't they working?
3. What kind of social control techniques would be most effective in this situation? Design a program that you think would work.

Reading 13.4

THE PAINTED BIRD

JERZY KOSINSKI

The point of much of the discussion in this chapter is that one way to study deviant behavior is to see it as a product of labeling some people by others. People are called deviant because of certain behaviors or characteristics they have—he is a cripple, she is pregnant, he is an ex-convict, she is a prostitute. People have a tendency, it seems, to find comfort and safety in similarity, and consequently, to seek out and call attention to the different among them. This common theme not only is behind definitions of deviant behavior but is the basis for discrimination, prejudice, stereotyping, and scapegoating as well.

This point has probably been made sufficiently well, but as a final illustration look at this amazing passage from the novel *The Painted Bird*, by Jerzy Kosinski. This book tells the story of a boy's wanderings through Poland during World War II. One of his friends is a young man named Lekh who traps birds for a living. Lekh has been having a passionate affair with a wild young woman of the forest who is called "Stupid Ludmila."

Sometimes days passed and Stupid Ludmila did not appear in the forest. Lekh would become possessed by a silent rage. He would stare solemnly at the birds in the cages, mumbling something to himself. Finally, after prolonged scrutiny, he would choose the strongest bird, tie it to his wrist, and prepare stinking paints of different colors which he mixed together from the most varied components. When the colors satisfied him, Lekh would turn the bird over and paint its wings, head, and breast in rainbow hues until it became more dappled and vivid than a bouquet of wildflowers.

Then we would go into the thick of the forest. There Lekh took out the painted bird and ordered me to hold it in my hand and squeeze it lightly. The bird would begin to twitter and attract a flock of the same species which would fly nervously over our heads. Our prisoner, hearing them, strained toward them, warbling more loudly, its little heart, locked in its freshly painted breast, beating violently.

When a sufficient number of birds gathered above our heads, Lekh would give me a sign to release the prisoner. It would soar, happy and free, a spot of rainbow against the backdrops of clouds, and then plunge into the waiting brown flock. For an instant the birds were confounded. The painted bird circled from one end of the flock to the other, vainly trying to convince its kin that it was one of them. But, dazzled by its brilliant colors, they flew around it unconvinced. The painted bird would be forced farther and farther away as it zealously tried to enter the ranks of the flock. We saw soon afterwards how one bird after another would peel off in a fierce attack. Shortly the many-hued shape lost its place in the sky and dropped to the ground. These incidents happened often. When we finally found the painted birds they were usually dead. Lekh keenly examined the number of blows which the birds had received. Blood seeped through their colored wings, diluting the paint and soiling Lekh's hands.

Stupid Ludmila did not return. Lekh, sulking and glum, removed one bird after another from the cages, painted them in still gaudier colors, and released them into the air to be killed by their kin. One day he trapped a large raven, whose wings he painted red, the breast green, and the tail blue. When a flock of ravens appeared over our hut, Lekh freed the painted bird. As soon as it joined the flock a desperate battle began. The changeling was attacked from all sides. Black, red, green, blue feathers began to drop at our feet. The ravens ran amuck in the skies, and suddenly the painted raven plummeted to the fresh-plowed soil. It was still alive, opening its beak and vainly trying to move its wings. Its eyes had been pecked out, and fresh blood streamed over its painted feathers. It made yet another attempt to flutter up from the sticky earth, but its strength was gone.

Questions 13.4

1. The painted bird is attacked by the flock because it is different. How does human society "discolor" its own members?
2. The flock pecks the painted bird to death. How do people respond to "painted birds" in their midst?
3. Pick a type of behavior and outline how it becomes deviant. Explain reactions to it by using the metaphor of the "painted bird."

14

Sociology: Another Perspective

This book has attempted to provide you with an understanding of sociology. We looked at theories, at methods, and especially at the concepts that sociologists use to gain knowledge and understanding of the human condition. At this point, we should have a reasonably good idea of what sociologists *do*.

But there is another perspective to examine. To me, an important aspect of a profession or discipline is what the occupants *think* about what they do. This is a more informal or insider's view, and gets at such issues as: How do these people see themselves? What do they feel they should be accomplishing? What are their internal conflicts and arguments? What is their level of job satisfaction and morale? Think of doctors and police officers again. They interest me partly because of what they do, but I am fascinated about what they *think* about what they do: job satisfaction, attitude toward patients or clients, morale, amount of stress and anxiety related to the job, the type of internal issues and conflicts that they argue over, and so on. The cumulative effect of these must affect one's personality and give one a particular perspective or way of looking at the world.

What this last chapter will examine, then, is the insider's view: What do sociologists think about what they do? How do sociologists see themselves, and what are some of the issues on which they disagree? How does this affect the sociologists' perspective?

A SOCIOLOGICAL PERSPECTIVE

Members of a discipline develop a particular way of looking at the world. They share these views as individuals, although the similarity of their perspectives is most readily seen when a group of people from the same discipline come together. Becoming a sociologist involves learning the meaning and use of a series of concepts and techniques and acquiring a body of knowledge. Going through this learning—a socialization process—provides one with a particular viewpoint. Members of any discipline may go through this process, and it affects the way they think, the way they talk, the way they behave.

There are a number of aspects to the sociological perspective. One is the tendency to see human behavior in the context of a group. To put it another way, sociologists understand people's behavior to be a product of their group affiliations. Consequently, in their studies, it is on these group affiliations that sociologists focus. For example, let's look at Joe Blow as some of his friends and colleagues might look at him. What stands out to his doctor is Joe's height, weight, pulse rate, blood pressure, and medical history. What his banker sees is his investment portfolio, cash reserve, and loan collateral. His minister may see him as a soul to be saved, a moral state to be improved. His professor may see him as a mind to be molded, a vessel to be filled with knowledge, or an intellect to be challenged. A sociologist looks at him and sees a white, middle-class, twenty-one-year-old man who is a member of the Democratic Party.

Sociologists typically are more interested in characteristics of categories and groups than in specific individuals, and in this sociologists differ with psychologists who are more interested in the *individual* and his or her personality, motivations, emotions, and behavior. For the sociologist, the focus in Joe's case would probably be on the characteristics of middle-class whites, of twenty-one-year-old men, or of Democrats in general rather than on Joe as an individual. The sociologist usually studies numbers of people—groups, categories, societies—and their patterns of behavior—norms, roles, and institutions.

Other aspects of the sociological perspective are discussed by Peter Berger in his book *Invitation to Sociology.* Berger feels that there is a "sociological consciousness" having several facets.[1] A *debunking* tendency of sociologists is reflected in their study of things taken for granted. Berger suggests that in analyzing the structure and institutions of societies, it is often necessary to "unmask the pretensions and the propaganda with which men cloak their actions with each other." There is a constant attempt, then, to find the underlying explanations for phenomena instead of just accepting the handy or traditional

---

[1]The discussion in the following paragraph is drawn from Berger's Chapter 2, "Sociology as a Form of Consciousness." Peter L. Berger, *Invitation to Sociology* (Garden City, N.Y.: Doubleday, 1963).

explanations that people readily give. For example, sociologists would view it as important to put common-sense explanations aside and determine what the real relationship is between narcotics legislation and drug usage, or between use of the death penalty and the homicide rate.

A part of sociology is devoted to the sudy of the *unrespectable*. Early sociologists were reformers and muckrakers. They believed that sociologists should intervene and attempt to ameliorate problem conditions to ensure social progress. This preoccupation with social problems and the unrespectable has abated somewhat today, but its influence in sociology is still strong. We see, for example, a variety of studies of underdogs, deviants, and outsiders. In addition to several studies of drug users and hippies, books have appeared dealing with such topics as shoplifting, pool playing, bar behavior, behavior of race track gamblers, prison behavior, death and dying, and mental illness, to mention a few.

This is not to imply that so-called *respectable* aspects of society are outside of the scope of sociology. On the contrary, much sociological study is of the respectable. (In fact, there has been criticism that sociology has become too interested in describing and supporting the *status quo*, and less an agent for social change.) At any rate, we could conclude that although much of sociology deals with the respectable, a prominent and growing segment of the discipline deals with the unrespectable, with problems and/or deviant aspects of society.

Berger suggests that sociologists tend to be *relativist* and *cosmopolitan* in their outlook. Sociologists are involved in studying patterns of human interaction in a variety of cultures under many different conditions. They learn that behavior, ideas, and institutions are relative, relevant to specific cultures and specific locations. In order to make judgments about or evaluate certain behaviors, sociologists must, then, apply a broader, more cosmopolitan perspective— they must take a world view, and this becomes part of their sociological consciousness.

Any similarities in outlook that are shared by sociologists emerge, to a great extent, as a result of their training. There are also many differences among them; one is evident when we examine how sociologists look at sociology.

SOCIOLOGICAL PERSPECTIVES OF SOCIOLOGY

The discipline of sociology encompasses certain themes or traditions. In combination, these traditions constitute a heritage from which all sociologists draw. A particular sociologist, however, will be influenced more strongly by one tradition or perspective than by others. Just as a doctor specializes in certain aspects of medicine and a lawyer concentrates in certain aspects of law, so the sociologist specializes in specific areas of sociology (race, social class, or deviant behavior, for example) and follows a particular theme or tradition that he or she personally feels to be most relevant.

There has always been in sociology, as in other disciplines, a debate over what we are and what we should be doing. This is a continual self-analysis, which attracts the interest and attention of many sociologists. It seems appropriate to me to describe this as "sociological perspectives on sociology." It is an interesting debate and probably reflects the growing pains of an area of study that is still trying to define itself and its place in the world of knowledge.

As we mentioned in Chapter 1, science is often divided into *pure* and *applied* categories. Into which of these categories does sociology properly fall? Sociology is seen by some as a *pure* science in that its practitioners seek knowledge for knowledge's sake alone, without regard for the possible uses the knowledge may have. In other words, sociology is a science, not a vehicle for social action. In recent years, however, a growing number of sociologists have encouraged the development of an *applied* sociology. In a variety of ways, sociologists are putting their concepts and techniques to practical use. In general, these efforts involve attempts to deal with the problems of society or of individual segments of society: industry, education, labor, government, and community. Applied sociology is often designed to encourage desired social change or to forestall undesired social change. Applied sociology has been referred to as *action sociology*, and those involved are sometimes called *social engineers*. Philip Hauser points out that with the proliferation of economic and social planning and the increase in welfare functions of government, the need for sociologists will continue to increase for the performance of both scientific and social engineering tasks.[2]

Some sociologists take a purely *scientific* perspective. For them, sociology is a social science, and they emphasize the procedures and techniques of science. Such sociologists see themselves as white-coated individuals who gain knowledge by applying scientific methods to social phenomena. They are objective, detached, free of any values or biases that might affect their work. They are, perhaps, bundles of sensory neurons moving in space, observing and recording the facts of social interaction. Sociologists today are developing sophisticated mathematical models and statistical techniques and using ever larger computers to aid them in the scientific analysis of human behavior.[3]

These are often called positivists. They adhere pretty much to the classical view of science as outlined in Chapter 1. Their role as scientist is based on the model that has worked so well for those in the physical and biological sciences, and its adoption by sociologists probably reflects the hope that our success may be as great as theirs. At the same time the positivist model in sociology is criticized by some, and for several reasons. First, there is the criticism of science in general. There is concern that blind faith in, and uncritical acceptance of, science has led people to ignore the faults of science. Questions are raised about a series of ethical considerations: Shouldn't scientists be responsible for the possible harmful uses of their discoveries? Should scientists tamper with and ma-

---

[2]Philip M. Hauser, "On Actionism in the Craft of Sociology," *Sociology Inquiry*, vol. 39, no. 2 (Spring 1969), pp. 139–147. For more on applied sociology, see Arthur Shostak, ed., *Sociology in Action* (Homewood, Ill.: Dorsey Press, 1966); and Alvin Gouldner and S. M. Miller, eds., *Applied Sociology* (New York: Free Press, 1965).

[3]A thorough and interesting discussion of several sociological perspectives, including "abstracted empiricism," is included in C. Wright Mills' excellent book, *The Sociological Imagination* (New York: Oxford University Press, 1959).

nipulate people without their knowledge, or even *with* their knowledge? Whom do the scientists represent—themselves, science in general, society, or those people (government agencies, large organizations, private concerns) who are paying their research bills? Failure to receive satisfactory answers to these questions has led many to be disillusioned with science.[4]

A second form of criticism of the positivist model is more specific to sociology. The complaint here is that the information we collect is not valid, not accurate. This is a serious criticism. Derek Phillips states in his book *Knowledge From What?* that ninety percent of the data collected by sociologists is done by means of interviews and questionnaires. What sociologists have failed to take into account, he maintains, is that the questionnaire or interview situation is a *social* situation, that statements of the people being studied are affected by the questionnaire, by their response to the interviewer and the interviewer's characteristics (sex, age, race, social class, demeanor, etc.), by the nature of the interaction between the interviewer and the interviewee, and by numerous other factors that have been left uncontrolled. The basic problem is that most sociological research is based on people's *reports* of their own behavior rather than on *actual observation* of their behavior. This is the issue of reactive versus nonreactive research, which we discussed in Chapter 1. Phillips suggests that sociologists should instead concentrate on participant observation and hidden observation techniques. Participant observation, as we mentioned earlier, involves the investigator joining or living with the subjects being studied. The researcher becomes part of the group. Studies of primitive tribes, delinquent gangs, large organizations (remember Elinor Langer's study of the telephone company, Reading 4.3), and class and ethnic structure of communities, as well as many other topics, have been made using this technique. Participant observation allows the study of some events that could not otherwise be studied, and may provide many insights that escape the more formal interview and questionnaire methods. Hidden observation refers to making use of records or traces left behind by people (checking the nose prints on the glass or the wear on the floor tile to determine the popularity of a museum exhibit) or by actually observing people without letting them know.[5] The key element in both participant and hidden observation is that we *watch* people's behavior rather than *ask them* about it. Concerns about the *accuracy* of our information, then, has led to disillusionment with some of the scientific aspects of sociology.

These problems, as well as other beliefs regarding the most appropriate path to knowledge, have led some sociologists to see the discipline not as science but as *social philosophy.* For them, sociologists are theorists, perhaps arm-

---

[4]A number of works deal with these issues. See, for example, Gideon Sjoberg, ed., *Ethics, Politics, and Social Research* (Cambridge, Mass.: Schenkman, 1967); Ralph Beals, *Politics of Social Research* (Chicago: Aldine, 1968); Irving L. Horowitz, ed., *The Rise and Fall of Project Camelot* (Cambridge, Mass.: M.I.T. Press, 1967). There is a discussion of scientific ethics in most methodology texts.

[5]Derek Phillips, *Knowledge From What?* (Chicago: Rand McNally, 1971). Also see John Lofland, *Analyzing Social Settings* (Belmont, Calif.: Wadsworth, 1971), and Eugene Webb, Donald Campbell, Richard Schwartz, and Lee Sechrest, *Unobtrusive Measures: Nonreactive Research in the Social Sciences* (Chicago: Rand McNally, 1966).

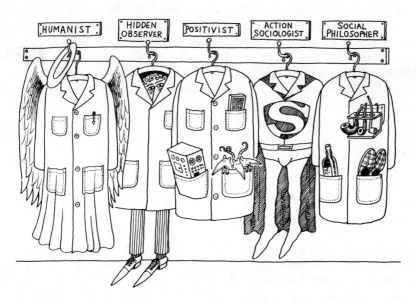

chair philosophers who sit by the fire spinning grand generalizations about the nature of the universe. They frequently have remarkable insights about human behavior. However, from the scientist's viewpoint, the social philosopher's statements are often too general and abstract to be put to empirical test. Others see sociologists-as-social-philosophers as true scholars rather than mere scientific technicians—they are widely read, masters of many disciplines, and students may gather adoringly at their feet.

Some sociologists take a *humanist* perspective. For them, the sociologist is interested in and concerned about human welfare, values, and conduct—he or she wants to improve the lot of people in general. An ultimate goal for the humanist is the self-realization and full development of the cultivated person. There may occasionally be a tendency for the humanistic and scientific perspectives to be at odds with each other. The humanist is interested in bettering the condition of people and developing the individual to the fullest. The objective of science is the gaining of empirical knowledge about the world, without regard for the possible uses of such knowledge. Don Martindale suggests that humanism is a system of values describing "what ought to be" and modes of conduct designed to secure them; science is the value-free pursuit of knowledge, of "what is," renouncing all concern with what ought to be. It has also been suggested that the scientist is more interested in the *means*—gaining knowledge; the humanist, in the *ends*—improving the lot of people. The humanist may be seen as a moralist; the scientist is seen (usually by the humanist) as amoral, sometimes as immoral.[6]

Is sociology basically concerned with gathering empirical data about people's behavior in a scientific sense or with the study of those conditions that will

---

[6]This discussion of humanistic and scientific thought follows from Don Martindale's analysis in his *Social Life and Cultural Change* (Princeton, N.J.: Van Nostrand, 1962), pp. 443–462.

enable individuals to realize their fullest potential in a humanistic sense? It is impossible to put all of sociology into one camp or the other. Most sociologists probably use a combination of scientific and humanistic viewpoints. Peter Berger expresses the view of many, however, when he argues that sociology must be used for humanity's sake. Social science, like other sciences, can be and sometimes is dehumanizing and even inhuman. It should not be. When sociologists pursue their task with insight, sensitivity, empathy, humility, and a desire to *understand* the human condition, rather than with a cold and humorless scientism, then indeed, the "sociological perspective helps illuminate man's social existence."[7]

SOCIOLOGISTS—WHAT ARE THEY AND WHAT DO THEY DO?

What makes one a sociologist? From what we have said in this chapter, a simple answer would be: one who has a sociological perspective. Also, a sociologist is a person who has earned an advanced degree in sociology. In 1980, there were about 19,000 bachelor's degrees, 1,300 master's degrees, and 600 doctor's degrees awarded in sociology in the United States. Most professional sociologists have master's degrees or doctorates, and many students who receive bachelor's degrees in sociology go into other fields, so the exact number of sociologists practicing sociology for a living is hard to determine.

Most sociologists spend most of their time teaching. Opportunities for teaching sociology are found predominantly at the college and university level, but increasing numbers of high schools are adding sociology courses to their curricula. Some sociology courses, especially at the high school level, have more of a practical, how-to-do-it focus. These courses might deal with dating, marriage and family, or personal adjustment.

Many sociologists are involved in research, either full time or in combination with their teaching. Full-time researchers may run their own research agencies, but more often they work for state or federal agencies. They may, for example, be responsible for collecting and analyzing population and census data. They may collect police arrest statistics and analyze and combine these into crime reports. Sociologists, especially at the larger universities, are about equally involved in research and teaching.

In the 1970s, job markets began changing for sociologists. Up to that time it had not been difficult to obtain a college teaching job. However, an oversupply of people with doctorates in sociology (and social science generally) developed in the 1970s. About the same time, student enrollment in sociology, which had increased rapidly in the 1960s, began leveling off in many parts of the country, and this meant fewer teaching jobs. The consequence has been that sociologists have been moving in greater numbers into applied fields. Sociologists work in a number of capacities for a variety of private, state, and federal agencies. Crimi-

---

[7]See Peter Berger's chapter, "Sociology as a Humanistic Discipline," in *Invitation to Sociology* (see footnote 1). Also see R. P. Cuzzort's discussion of Berger in Cuzzort's book, *Humanity and Modern Sociological Thought* (New York: Holt, Rinehart and Winston, 1969), Chapter 10.

nologists are hired by institutions (prisons, reformatories) and by departments of correction. Population experts are valuable in a policy-making capacity for a number of agencies. Sociologists act as consultants to cities for recreation programs, city planning, urban renewal, mass transit, and so on. The services of specialists in marriage and the family are used by schools, churches, and social agencies, and some sociologists are involved in private marriage counseling.

SOCIOLOGY AND YOU

What good has this time spent in sociology done you? For one thing, with any luck at all you are three or four units closer to that piece of paper that you came to college to collect. Maybe that is enough, but possibly something more has occurred. Admittedly it is hard to measure what might have happened. If the subject were typing and you had progressed from two words a minute to eighty, there would be tangible evidence of success. Since the subject is sociology, if you went out and solved eight social problems during summer vacation, that might prove that the course had taught you something. The problem is, however, that we are not teaching a skill or a technique but a viewpoint. And it is sometimes difficult to measure the immediate usefulness of a new viewpoint or a new way of looking at things.

After a semester of introductory sociology, you should know more about the world you live in. You certainly know more facts about that world, having stayed up until all hours sponging up facts for those tests. But principally, it seems to me that what you should have discovered from the course is a new way of looking at the world and at yourself. As C. Wright Mills suggested in *The Sociological Imagination*, the study of sociology should show you a way of evaluating yourself as more than an isolated individual in a sea of humanity. The study of sociology should help you place yourself and history in perspective, so that you can more accurately identify and evaluate the factors that affect your behavior and the behavior of others. You should be more critical, now, and more able to evaluate aspects of the world that heretofore you may have taken for granted.

"Who am I?" and "How did I get this way?" are questions that are difficult to answer to anyone's satisfaction. Perhaps a sociological viewpoint will help deal with these questions; perhaps it won't. If the sociological viewpoint only helps to make you more aware of your social environment and some of the forces at work there, the time spent has been worthwhile, for this will provide you with a greater understanding of and compassion for others.

Terms for Study

action sociology (421)	positivists (421)
applied science (421)	pure science (421)
humanistic perspective (423)	scientific perspective (421)
participant observation (422)	

Glossary

Acculturation The process of assimilating, blending in, and taking on the characteristics of another culture.

Achieved statuses Positions in society that are earned or achieved in some way.

Aggregate A number of people clustered together in one place.

Amalgamation Refers to biological (rather than cultural) mixing.

Annihilation Elimination of one group by another.

Anomie A state of normlessness; a condition in which the norms and rules governing people's aspirations and moral conduct have disintegrated.

Anticipatory socialization Occurs when a person adopts the values, behavior, or viewpoints of a group he or she would like to, but does not yet, belong to.

Applied science Concerned with the practical and utilitarian uses of knowledge, making knowledge useful to people.

Ascribed statuses Positions automatically conferred on individuals through no choice of their own; statuses one is born with.

Assimilation Mixing and merging of unlike cultures so that the two groups come to have a common culture.

Audience A collection of people at (watching, listening to) a public event; a passive crowd.

Authoritarian personality A type of personality especially prone to prejudice; tends to be ethnocentric, rigidly conformist, and to worship authority and strength.

Authority Legitimate, socially approved power.

Bureaucracy (formal organization) An organization in which the activities of some people are systematically planned by other people in order to achieve some special purpose; usually involves such characteristics as division of labor, hierarchy of authority, system of rules, impersonality, and technical efficiency.

Category A number of people who have a particular characteristic in common.

Centralization The tendency of people to gather around some central or pivotal point in a city.

Charisma A quality in an individual that sets one apart from others—the person is viewed as superhuman and capable of exceptional acts.

Charismatic authority Power stemming from the unique personality of a particular person.

Charismatic retinue A type of organization made up of followers or disciples of a charismatic leader.

Church A large and highly organized religious organization that represents and supports the *status quo*, is respectable, and in which membership is automatic; one is born into a church.

Closed group A group into which it is difficult if not impossible to gain membership.

Collective behavior Spontaneous, unstructured, and unstable group behavior.

Compound family The family resulting from polygamy; marriages involving multiple spouses—several wives and/or husbands at the same time.

426

Conflict theory A sociological theory that holds that the most appropriate way to understand society is to focus on the consequences of the conflict, competition, and discord that are common in social interaction.

Counterculture A subculture which has norms and values which are in opposition to or in conflict with norms and values of the dominant culture.

Criminal behavior Behavior prohibited by law and subject to formal punishment.

Crowd A temporary collection of people in close physical contact reacting together to a common stimulus.

Cult A religious organization that is a small, short-lived, often local group, that is frequently built around a dominant leader. The cult is smaller, less organized, and more transitory than the sect.

Cultural lag Phenomenon that occurs when related segments of society change at different rates.

Cultural pluralism A pattern of interaction in which unlike cultures maintain their own identity and yet interact with each other relatively peacefully.

Cultural relativism Opposite of ethnocentrism: suggests that each culture be judged from its own viewpoint without imposing outside standards of judgment.

Culture The complex set of learned and shared beliefs, customs, skills, habits, traditions, and knowledge common to the members of a society; the social heritage of a society.

Decentralization The tendency of people to move outward and away from the center of the city.

Definition of the situation The suggestion, first offered by W. I. Thomas, that reality is socially structured, with the result that people respond more to the meaning a situation has for them than to the objective features of that situation.

Demographic transition The movement of a population from high birth and death rates to high birth and low death rates (and rapid population growth) to low birth and death rates.

Demography The study of human population, its distribution, composition, and change.

Denomination A religious organization that has less universality than the church or the ecclesia and appeals to a smaller category of people—a racial, ethnic, or social-class grouping that is conventional and respectable.

Dependent variable The "effect"; that quantity or aspect of the study whose change the researcher wants to understand.

Deviant behavior Behavior contrary to generally accepted norms; limits are often established by custom or public opinion, sometimes by law.

Diffusion The spread of objects or ideas from one society to another or from one group to another within the same society, resulting in changes in society.

Disaster A situation in which there is a basic disruption of the social context within which individuals and groups function; a radical departure from the pattern of normal expectations.

Discrimination Actual behavior resulting in unfavorable and unequal treatment of individuals or groups.

Dysfunction An act that leads to change or destruction of a unit.

Ego In Freud's view, the acting self, the mediator between the id and superego.

Empiricism Knowledge gained through experience and sense observation.

Endogamy Marriage within a certain group.

Ethnicity Refers to people bound together by cultural ties.

Ethnocentrism   A type of prejudice that maintains that one's own culture's ways are right and other cultures' ways, if different, are wrong.

Exogamy   Marriage outside a certain group.

Experiment   Type of research in which the researcher introduces a stimulus to a subject or group and then observes the response; the researcher manipulates the independent variable (exercise, for example) and watches for change in the dependent variable (heart disease, for example).

Expulsion   Removal of a group from the territory in which it resides.

Extended family   More than two generations of the same family living together in close association or under the same roof.

Fads   The relatively short-term obsessions that members of a society or members of specific groups have toward specific behaviors or objects.

Family of orientation   The family one is born into.

Family of procreation   The family of which one is a parent.

Fashions   Temporary attachments to specific behaviors, styles, or objects; similar to fads but more widespread and of longer duration.

Fertility   Refers to the number of children born.

Feudal administration   A type of organization that is separate from but responsible to a parent organization; it has local autonomy to act in terms of its own interests.

Folk society   Robert Redfield's term used to describe isolated villages in non-industrialized countries which are small, homogeneous, relatively self-contained, and largely based on subsistence activities.

Folkways   Norms that are less obligatory than mores, the "shoulds" of society; sanctions for violation are mild.

Functional analysis   A sociological theory that focuses on the structures that emerge in society and the functions that these structures perform in the operation of society as a whole.

Gemeinschaft   Primary, closely-knit society in which relationships are personal and informal and there is a commitment to or identification with the community.

General fertility rate   The number of births per 1,000 women aged 15 through 44.

Generalized other   The sum of the viewpoints and expectations of the social group or community to which an individual belongs.

Genocide   The intentional extermination of a whole ethnic or racial group.

Gesellschaft   Secondary society based on contractual arrangements, bargaining, a well-developed division of labor, and on rational thought rather than emotion.

Group   A number of people who have shared or patterned interaction and who feel bound together by a "consciousness of kind" or a "we" feeling.

Group marriage   The marriage of two or more men to two or more women at the same time.

Horizontal groups   Groups whose members come predominantly from one social-class level, such as associations of doctors or carpenters.

Horizontal social mobility   Movement from one occupation to another within the same social class; also used to refer to spatial or geographical mobility.

Human ecology   The adaptation of people to their physical environment, their location in space.

Hypothesis   A testable statement or proposition used to guide an investigation.

Id   In Freud's view, the primitive part of the personality made up of inborn, instinctual, antisocial drives.

Ideal norms   How a person should behave in a particular situation.

Idealistic culture   Sorokin's term describing a culture midway between the sensate and ideational, which emphasizes logic and rationality.

Ideational culture   Sorokin's term describing a culture that emphasizes feelings and emotions and is subjective, expressive, and religious.

Independent variable   The "cause"; that quantity or aspect of the study that seems to produce change in another variable.

Influence   Subtle, informal, indirect power based on persuasion rather than coercion and force.

In-groups   Groups the individual identifies with and feels comfortable with.

Interaction process analysis (IPA)   A technique for group study in which interaction between group members is broken down into small parts or acts. The acts are then classified into a set of predetermined categories (shows agreement, gives information, asks for opinion, etc.).

Invasion   The penetration of one group or function into an area dominated by another group or function.

Invention   Change introduced through the creation of a new object or idea.

Involuntary groups   Groups in which membership is automatic and the participant has no choice regarding joining, such as one's family or the army platoon one is drafted into.

Keynoting   The process of focusing the behavior of an ambivalent crowd on a particular activity or issue.

Labeling   The public stamping, typing, or categorizing of a person as deviant.

Latent function   The unintended and less obvious, often unrecognized function.

Legal-rational authority   Power attached to positions rather than people; positions are defined by a formal set of rules and procedures; typical of governments and businesses in modern societies.

Life expectancy   A person's expectation of length of life at birth based on risks of death for people born in that year.

Looking-glass self   Attitudes toward self derived from one's interpretations of how others are evaluating self.

Manifest function   The intended and recognized function.

Marginal person   A person who is caught between two antagonistic cultures; a product of both but a true member of neither.

Mass hysteria   A type of collective behavior in which a particular behavior, fear, or belief sweeps through a large number of people such as a crowd, a city, or a nation.

Material culture   The real, tangible things that a society creates and uses: screwdriver, house, classroom, supersonic jet, computer.

Matriarchal society   Society in which decisions are made by females.

Mean   The sum of all the items in a series divided by the number of items; often referred to as the "average."

Mechanical solidarity   Durkheim's description of the type of social cohesion likely to exist in small, homogeneous, preindustrial societies: uniformity among people and a lack of differentiation or specialization.

Median   The middle case in a series that has been ranked or ordered by size.

Migration   A permanent change of residence, with the consequent relocation of one's interests and activities.

Milling The excited, restless, physical movement of the people in a crowd through which communication occurs leading to a definition of the situation and possible collective action.

Minority status People treated as lower in social ranking and subject to domination by other segments of the population.

Mob A focused, acting crowd, emotionally aroused, intent on taking aggressive action.

Modern bureaucracy In Weber's view, a type of large organization in which specialization, a system of rules, formality, and a hierarchy of authority are highly developed.

Modern professional organization A type of large organization in which responsibility is decentralized; less bureaucratic in Weber's sense than the modern bureaucracy.

Monogamy Marriage with one person at a time.

Mores Obligatory norms, the "musts" of society; sanctions are harsh if these are violated.

Mortality The number of deaths occurring in a population.

Multinational A large corporation whose influence goes beyond national boundaries, often with connections throughout the world.

Mysticism Information or knowledge gained by mystical means: intuition, revelation, inspiration, magic, visions, spells; tends to be private knowledge experienced only by the mystic.

Nativism The attempt to improve a people's existence by eliminating all foreign persons, objects, and customs.

Nonmaterial culture The abstract creations of a society such as customs, laws, ideas, values, beliefs.

Nonreactive research Research in which records, physical traces, and signs left by people are studied; observation of subjects without direct intrusion; subject is not aware of being studied. (Compare with *reactive research*.)

Norms The accepted or required behavior for a person in a particular situation.

Nuclear family A married couple and their children.

Open group A group that is easy to gain membership to.

Organic solidarity Durkheim's description of the type of social cohesion likely to exist in modern industrialized societies: a high degree of specialization and division of labor, and increasing individualism.

Out-groups Groups the individual does not identify with, does not feel comfortable with, and sees as different from self.

Panic Nonadaptive or nonrational flight resulting from extreme fear and loss of self-control.

Participant observation Research in which the researcher is or appears to be a participant in the activity or group that is being studied.

Patriarchal society Society in which decisions are made by males.

Peer group Consists of people of relatively the same age, interests, and social position with whom one has reasonably close association and contact.

Permanent group A group which has durability, constancy, and a long life span, such as a family.

Personality The sum total of the physical, mental, emotional, social, and behavioral characteristics of an individual.

Polyandry A form of polygamy in which one woman has several husbands at a time.

Polygamy Plural marriage; the practice of having more than one husband or wife at a time.

Polygyny   A form of polygamy in which one man has several wives at a time.

Power   The ability of one party (either an individual or group) to affect the behavior of another party.

Prejudice   Favorable or unfavorable attitudes toward a person or group, not based on actual experience.

Prestige   One's distinction in the eyes of others, one's reputation.

Primary deviation   Beginning, often minor acts of deviant behavior, which do not affect the individual's self-concept—the individual does not see himself or herself as a deviant. (Compare with *secondary deviation*.)

Primary group   A group in which contacts between members are intimate, personal, and face to face.

Primary socialization   The first socialization an individual undergoes in childhood; one must undergo this to become a member of society; it ends with the establishment of the generalized other.

Propaganda   Attempts to influence and change the public's viewpoint on an issue.

Pseudocharisma   Refers to public figures who appear to have charisma, but in fact have a packaged and carefully created image manufactured by public relations techniques.

Public   A number of people who have an interest in, and difference of opinion about, a common issue.

Public opinion   The opinions (ideas, beliefs) held by a public on a given issue.

Pure science   Attempts to discover facts and principles about the universe without regard for possible uses the knowledge may have.

Race   People related by common descent or heredity; usually identified by hereditary physical features.

Random sample   A sample of subjects in which every element in the total population being studied has an equal chance of being selected; the small sample of subjects is then theoretically representative of the larger population from which it was selected.

Rationalism   Knowledge gained through reason and logic.

Reactive research   Research in which subjects react or respond to a questionnaire or an interviewer. (Compare with *nonreactive research*.)

Reference groups   Groups that serve as models for our behavior, groups whose perspectives we assume and mold our behavior after.

Reform movement   A movement that seeks modification in certain aspects of society.

Replacement level   The average number of births necessary per woman over her lifetime for the population eventually to reach zero growth.

Resocialization   A process in which major modifications or reconstructions are made of a person's patterns of behavior, personality, and self-concept.

Revolutionary movement   A movement that seeks a complete change in the social order.

Riot   A situation in which mob behavior becomes increasingly widespread and destructive.

Role   The behavior of one who occupies a particular status or position in society.

Role conflict   Conflict that occurs when a person occupies several statuses or positions that have contradictory role requirements.

Role requirements   Norms specifying the expected behavior of persons holding a particular position in society.

Role strain   Strain that occurs when there are differing and conflicting expectations regarding one's status or position.

Rumor   Unconfirmed, although not necessarily false, person-to-person communication.

Sample   A selection of a few from a larger universe. The sample may or may not be representative of the whole depending on how it is selected.

Sanction   The punishment one receives for violation of a norm (or the reward granted for compliance with norms).

Science   The gaining of knowledge through sense observation; understanding through description by means of measurement making possible prediction and thus adjustment to or control of the environment.

Secession   The formal withdrawal of a group of people from a political, religious, or national union.

Secondary deviation   Deviant acts that represent a defense, attack, or adjustment to the problems created by reactions to primary deviation; the self-concept changes so that the individual begins to see and define self as deviant. (Compare with *primary deviation.*)

Secondary group   Group in which contacts between members are more impersonal than in a primary group; interaction is more superficial and probably based on utilitarian goals.

Secondary socialization   Takes over where primary socialization leaves off; involves internalizing knowledge of new areas and new sectors of life, of special skills and techniques.

Sect   Small religious organization that is less organized than the church, in which membership is voluntary. Members of sects usually show greater depth and fervor in their religious commitment than members of churches.

Secularization   Becoming more worldly or unspiritual as opposed to becoming more religious or spiritual.

Segregation   (1) Group conflict context: The setting apart of one group. (2) Ecological context: The clustering together of similar people.

Self   One's awareness of and ideas and attitudes about one's own personal and social identity.

Self-fulfilling prophecy   Occurs when a false definition of a situation evokes a new behavior that makes the originally false conception come true.

Sensate culture   Sorokin's term describing a culture that emphasizes the senses and is objective, scientific, materialistic, profane, and instrumental.

Sex ratio   Number of males per 100 females.

Significant others   People (mother, father, older brother, etc.) whose viewpoints and expectations the individual considers particularly important.

Social change   Significant alterations in the social relationships and cultural ideas of a society.

Social control   The processes, planned or unplanned, by which people are made to conform to collective norms.

Social differentiation   The process of defining, describing, and distinguishing between different categories of people.

Social disorganization   The condition resulting when norms and roles break down and customary ways of behaving no longer operate.

Social institutions   Organized systems of social relationships that embody some common values and procedures and meet some basic needs of society.

Social interaction   The process of being aware of others when we act, of modifying our behavior in accordance with others' responses.

Socialization   The social process whereby one learns the expectations, habits, skills, values, beliefs, and other requirements necessary for effective participation in social groups.

Social mobility   Refers to movement (up, down, or sideways) within the social class structure.

Social movement   A group of people acting with some continuity to promote or to resist a change in their society or group.

Social organization   The social fabric of society; the integrated set of norms, roles, cultural values, and beliefs through which people interact with each other, individually and in groups.

Social stratification   The division of people in society into layers or ranks. The source of the ranking may be one or a combination of factors: wealth, power, prestige, race, sex, age, religion, and so on.

Social structure   The network of norms, roles, statuses, groups, and institutions through which people relate to each other in society.

Society   A number of people living in a specific area who are relatively organized, self-sufficient and independent, and who share a common culture.

Sociobiology   The systematic study of the biological basis of social behavior in all kinds of organisms, including man.

Sociometry   A technique for group study in which group members are asked to designate the person or persons in the group whom they "like most," "would most like to work with," "would like expelled from the group," and so on. The resulting responses for all members of the group are then plotted in a figure called a sociogram, which shows the patterns and directions of interaction in the group.

Statistical norms   How a person actually behaves in a particular situation.

Status   A position in society or in a group.

Status inconsistency   The factors that determine an individual's rank in society are not consistent with each other—for example, a college-educated carpenter, or a black court justice.

Stereotyping   Using a simplified and standardized image or label to describe a group or category of people.

Subcultures   Groups or segments of society that share many of the characteristics of the dominant culture, but that have some of their own specific customs or ways that tend to separate them from the rest of society.

Succession   The complete displacement or removal of an established group; the end product of invasion.

Superego   In Freud's view, that part of the personality made up of an internalized set of rules and regulations forming the conscience.

Survey research   Research that involves the collection of information from subjects through use of questionnaires or interviews; may be descriptive or causal-explanatory.

Symbolic interaction   A sociological theory that focuses on the *process* of person-to-person interaction, on how people come to develop viewpoints about themselves and others, and on forms of interpersonal communication.

Temporary group   A group that is brought together to perform a single short-term task and that disbands at the task's conclusion.

Traditional authority   Power is granted according to custom, leaders are selected by inheritance.

Urban society   Robert Redfield's term used to describe modern Western industrialized nations; opposite of folk society.

Values   General opinions and beliefs that people have about which ways of behaving are proper and acceptable, and which ways are improper and unacceptable.

Variable   A condition or trait that changes or has different values (such as I.Q., temperature, or weight).

Vertical group   A group whose members come from a variety of social classes.

Vertical social mobility   Movement up or down the social class ladder.

Voluntary groups   Groups that have open membership; people may join or not as they wish.

Annotated
Bibliography

If you would like to delve deeper into the subjects we have discussed in this book, let me suggest the following sources, some of which have been cited in footnotes. Most are available in paperback.

1: Introduction: Knowledge, Science, and Sociology

BRONOWSKI, JACOB. *The Ascent of Man* (Boston: Little, Brown, 1973). Very readable and beautifully illustrated history of science and civilization developed from Bronowski's highly acclaimed television series.

BRONOWSKI, JACOB. *The Common Sense of Science* (New York: Random House, 1959). A short, interesting history of science.

BROWN, ROBERT. *Explanation in Social Science* (Chicago: Aldine, 1963). A detailed, systematic analysis of how social science research is done.

CHASE, STUART. *The Proper Study of Mankind* (New York: Harper & Row, 1956). An analysis of social science: what it attempts to do, its methods of inquiry, and the characteristics of individual social science disciplines.

KUHN, THOMAS. *The Structure of Scientific Revolutions*, 2d ed. (Chicago: University of Chicago Press, 1970). Kuhn describes the development of scientific knowledge in terms of revolutions between competing paradigms, or viewpoints.

MCCAIN, GARVIN, and ERWIN SEGAL. *The Game of Science*, 2d ed. (Monterey, Calif.: Brooks/Cole, 1973). A very readable description of the characteristics of science and of scientists.

RAVETZ, JEROME. *Scientific Knowledge and Its Social Problems* (New York: Oxford University Press, 1971). A thorough evaluation and critique of the scientific establishment.

SKLAIR, LESLIE. *Organized Knowledge* (Bungay, England: Chaucer Press, 1973). Sklair deals with the question of social responsibility in scientific endeavor. He demonstrates that science is the most important basis on which knowledge is organized in the modern world, and he examines the political consequences of science and technology for societies.

WATSON, J. D. *The Double Helix* (New York: Signet, 1967). A fascinating account of competition and cooperation among scientists and the process of scientific discovery.

Numerous short books dealing with social science research methodology are available. For example, see:

LABOVITZ, SANFORD, and ROBERT HAGEDORN. *Introduction to Social Research* (New York: McGraw-Hill, 1971).

LOFLAND, JOHN. *Analyzing Social Settings* (Belmont, Calif.: Wadsworth, 1971). Description of field or qualitative research with many examples.

WALLACE, WALTER. *The Logic of Science in Sociology* (Chicago: Aldine, 1971).

WEBB, EUGENE, DONALD CAMPBELL, RICHARD SCHWARTZ, and LEE SECHREST. *Unobtrusive Measures: Nonreactive Research in the Social Sciences* (Chicago: Rand McNally, 1966). *The* sourcebook for nonreactive research—provides a rationale for this type of research as well as many examples of nonreactive studies.

The following two books focus on specific sociological research efforts. A number of projects are described. We see the problems sociologists study, the methods they use, the answers they find, and the mistakes they make.

HAMMOND, PHILLIP, ed. *Sociologists at Work* (New York: Doubleday, 1967).

MADGE, JOHN. *The Origins of Scientific Sociology* (New York: Free Press, 1962).

2: Socialization and Self

ARONSON, ELLIOT. *The Social Animal*, 2d ed. (San Francisco: Freeman, 1976). This interesting and well-written book outlines the ideas and theories of the field of social psychology. Aronson defines the field and discusses such topics as conformity, self, and sensitivity-training groups.

BERGER, PETER L., and THOMAS LUCKMANN. *The Social Construction of Reality* (Garden City, N.Y.: Doubleday, 1966). This short but influential book covers primary and secondary socialization, social interaction, and society as objective and subjective reality.

BROWNFIELD, CHARLES. *The Brain Benders* (New York: Exposition Press, 1972). A study of the effects of isolation and sensory deprivation. Includes descriptions of brainwashing in China and Korea as well as in laboratory experiments.

DES PRES, TERRENCE. *The Survivor* (New York: Pocket Books, 1977). This is an anatomy of life in the death camps—an account of how people survive in the worst of all possible worlds. It deals with the problem of staying alive *and* staying human.

ELKIN, FREDERICK. *The Child and Society* (New York: Random House, 1960). Elkin defines socialization, describes its processes and agencies, and analyzes socialization in subcultural patterns and in later life.

ERIKSON, ERIK. *Childhood and Society*, 2d ed. (New York: Norton, 1963). A study of the social significance of childhood by one of the leading figures in the field of psychoanalysis and human development.

GOFFMAN, ERVING. *The Presentation of Self in Everyday Life* (Garden City, N.Y.: Doubleday, 1959). A very readable, interesting analysis of the self. Goffman uses the language of the theater to describe how we present ourselves to others and attempt to manipulate the impressions others have of us.

GOFFMAN, ERVING. *Stigma* (Englewood Cliffs, N.J.: Prentice-Hall, 1963). Goffman deals with the physically deformed, the ex-mental patient, the drug addict, the prostitute; he analyzes the stigmatized individual's feelings about himself or herself, and his or her relationship to others and management of the self-image.

Socialization and development of self can be observed in many biographical and autobiographical works. For example, see:

DAYAN, RUTH, and HELGA DUDMAN. *And Perhaps . . . The Story of Ruth Dayan* (New York: Harcourt Brace Jovanovich, 1973).

FRANK, ANNE. *Anne Frank: The Diary of a Young Girl* (New York: Pocket Books, 1967).

GIBSON, WILLIAM. *Miracle Worker* (New York: Knopf, 1957).

KELLER, HELEN. *The Story of My Life* (New York: Dell, 1961).

LINDBERGH, ANNE MORROW. *Bring Me a Unicorn* (New York: Harcourt Brace Jovanovich and New American Library, 1971).

MALCOLM X, and ALEX HALEY. *The Autobiography of Malcolm X* (New York: Grove Press, 1966).

MEAD, MARGARET. *Blackberry Winter* (New York: Morrow, 1972).

SHAINBERG, LAWRENCE. *Brain Surgeon* (New York: Lippincott, 1979).

See also descriptions of socialization into occupations. The following come to mind:

GREENWALD, HAROLD. *The Elegant Prostitute* (New York: Ballantine, 1970).

LETKEMANN, PETER. *Crime as Work* (Englewood Cliffs, N.J.: Prentice-Hall, 1973).

MILLMAN, MARCIA. *The Unkindest Cut: Life in the Backrooms of Medicine* (New York: Morrow, 1977).

NIEDERHOFFER, ARTHUR. *Behind the Shield* (Garden City, N.Y.: Doubleday, 1967).

SMITH, DENNIS. *Report from Engine Co. 82* (New York: Pocket Books, 1972).

3: Norms, Roles, Culture

There are numerous anthropological studies of exotic primitive and contemporary cultures. Old standbys:

BENEDICT, RUTH. *Patterns of Culture* (Boston: Houghton Mifflin, 1934).

MEAD, MARGARET. *Sex and Temperament* (New York: Morrow, 1935).

RIESMAN, D., N. GLAZER, and R. DENNEY. *The Lonely Crowd* (Garden City, N.Y.: Doubleday, 1953). A study of changing American character that put the terms "inner-directed," "other-directed," and "tradition-directed" into the English vocabulary.

RUESCH, HANS. *Top of the World* (New York: Pocket Books, 1951). A novel, closely based on fact, that details the fascinating and unusual culture of the Eskimo.

A number of novelists have offered us a glimpse of cultures of the future.

HEINLEIN, R. A. *Stranger in a Strange Land* (New York: Medallion, 1968).

HUXLEY, ALDOUS. *Brave New World* (New York: Harper & Row, 1969).

ORWELL, GEORGE. *1984* (New York: New American Library, 1971).

Skinner, B. F. *Walden Two* (New York: Macmillan, 1969).

4: Groups

BLAU, PETER, and MARSHALL MEYER. *Bureaucracy in Modern Society*, 2d ed. (New York: Random House, 1971). An analysis of what sociologists know about large formal organizations in theory and in practice.

CROSBIE, PAUL V. *Interaction in Small Groups* (New York: Macmillan, 1975). A series of readings that describe a number of interesting research studies dealing with various aspects of small group research.

WHYTE, WILLIAM H., JR. *The Organization Man* (Garden City, N.Y.: Doubleday, 1956). This classic work describes the new life style of Americans—life under the protection of a big organization. According to Whyte, modern Americans find jobs in large organizations that promise security and a high standard of living; in doing so, they give up the hopes and ambitions that dominated earlier generations of Americans.

There are several short texts that summarize the research and theoretical knowledge available concerning small groups:

MILLS, THEODORE.   *The Sociology of Small Groups* (Englewood Cliffs, N.J.: Prentice-Hall, 1967).
OLMSTED, MICHEL, and PAUL HARE.   *The Small Group*, 2d ed. (New York: Random House, 1978).
SHEPARD, CLOVIS.   *Small Groups* (San Francisco: Chandler, 1964).

A number of short texts summarize the research and theoretical knowledge available concerning large organizations:

DRABEK, THOMAS, and EUGENE HAAS.   *Understanding Complex Organizations* (Dubuque, Iowa: Wm. C. Brown, 1974).
ETZIONI, AMITAI.   *Modern Organizations* (Englewood Cliffs, N.J.: Prentice-Hall, 1964).
WHISLER, THOMAS.   *Information Technology and Organizational Change* (Belmont, Calif.: Wadsworth, 1970).

Several books satirize aspects of large bureaucratic organizations:

PARKINSON, C. NORTHCOTE.   *Parkinson's Law* (New York: Ballantine, 1964).
PETER, L. J., and R. HULL.   *The Peter Principle* (New York: Bantam, 1970).

5: Social Differentiation: Social Class

COLEMAN, RICHARD, and LEE RAINWATER.   *Social Standing in America: New Dimensions of Class* (New York: Basic Books, 1978). A comprehensive study of social class in America. It assesses the importance of income and education and describes a seven-class view of stratification in the United States.
LIPSET, SEYMOUR MARTIN, and REINHARD BENDIX.   *Social Mobility in Industrial Society* (Berkeley, Calif.: University of California Press, 1966). Lipset and Bendix compare rates of social mobility in the United States with rates in other industrialized countries and clearly challenge the view that the United States is the most fluid and mobile society in the world.
MAYER, KURT, and WALTER BUCKLEY.   *Class and Society*, 3d ed. (New York: Random House, 1970). A short basic text covering the central issues in social stratification.
REISSMAN, LEONARD.   *Inequality in American Society* (Glenview, Ill.: Scott, Foresman, 1973). Reissman discusses equality as a positive goal, some problems with equality, and the future of inequality. He discusses stratification produced by racial and economic differences.
SCHNORE, LEO F.   *Class and Race in Cities and Suburbs* (Chicago: Markham, 1972). A short statistical study comparing the characteristics of city and suburban populations.
SHOSTAK, ARTHUR.   *Blue-Collar Life* (New York: Random House, 1969). An exhaustive study of the blue-collar or working class in America.

There are a number of studies of the stratification in specific communities. For example, see:

BALTZELL, E. DIGBY.   *Philadelphia Gentlemen* (New York: Free Press, 1958).
HOLLINGSHEAD, AUGUST.   *Elmtown's Youth* (New York: Wiley, 1949).
HUNTER, FLOYD.   *Community Power Structure* (Chapel Hill, N.C.: University of North Carolina Press, 1953).

SEELEY, J. R., R. A. SIM, and E. W. LOOSLEY.   *Crestwood Heights* (New York: Wiley, 1963).
WARNER, W. LLOYD, and PAUL LUNT.   *The Social Life of a Modern Community* (New Haven, Conn.: Yale University Press, 1941).

For further study of poverty and the welfare system in America, see:

CAPLOVITZ, DAVID.   *The Poor Pay More* (New York: Free Press, 1963).
HARRINGTON, MICHAEL.   *The Other America* (Baltimore: Penguin, 1962).
RYAN, WILLIAM.   *Blaming the Victim*, rev. ed. (New York: Random House, 1976).
SKOLNICK, JEROME, and ELLIOTT CURRIE.   *Crisis in American Institutions, 5th ed.* (Boston, Mass.: Little, Brown, 1982).
TURNER, JONATHAN, and CHARLES STARNES.   *Inequality: Privilege & Poverty in America* (Pacific Palisades, Calif.: Goodyear, 1976).

Many novels use social class characteristics and life styles as a basic theme:

MARQUAND, JOHN P.   *Point of No Return* (New York: Little, Brown, 1949).
O'HARA, JOHN, almost any work.
SCHULBERG, BUDD.   *What Makes Sammy Run?* (New York: Modern Library, 1952).
WILSON, SLOAN.   *Man in the Grey Flannel Suit* (New York: Simon & Schuster, 1955).

6: Social Differentiation: Race, Ethnicity, Sex, Age

BARRERA, MARIO.   *Race and Class in the Southwest* (Notre Dame, Indiana: University of Notre Dame Press, 1979). Barrera builds a theory of racial inequality, especially the economic foundations of inequality, based on the historical experiences of the Chicano.
BLAU, ZENA SMITH.   *Old Age in a Changing Society* (New York: New Viewpoints, 1973). A detailed analysis of the problems facing older people in a postindustrial society.
BROWN, CLAUDE.   *Manchild in the Promised Land* (New York: Signet, 1966). An autobiography by a black who made it out of the slums of Harlem. Brown provides an insider's view of the black ghetto that is both brutal and humorous.
BROWN, DEE.   *Bury My Heart at Wounded Knee* (New York: Bantam/Holt, 1971). Describes how the American Indian was sacrificed to the doctrine of Manifest Destiny—the idea that whites are the dominant race and therefore destined to rule all of America.
DE LA GARZA, RUDOLPH, ANTHONY KRUSZEWSKI, and TOMAS ARCINIEGA.   *Chicanos and Native Americans: The Territorial Minorities* (Englewood Cliffs, N.J.: Prentice-Hall, 1973). A series of readings that examine the diverse social, educational, and governmental problems that affect Chicanos and Native Americans. The authors outline steps that can be taken to avoid continued confrontations and strife.
GANS, HERBERT J.   *The Urban Villagers* (New York: Free Press, 1962). A participant observation study of Italian-Americans in Boston's West End.
GREER, GERMAINE.   *The Female Eunuch* (New York: McGraw-Hill/Bantam, 1971). Greer's central thesis is that as wives, employees, mothers, and lovers, women are still body and soul in bondage to men and are deformed by them—made into eunuchs.
KNOWLES, LOUIS, and KENNETH PREWITT, eds. *Institutional Racism in America* (Englewood Cliffs, N.J.: Prentice-Hall, 1969). This book reveals how numerous institutions under white control deny blacks a relevant education, a voice in the political process, the right of economic self-determination, just treatment under the law, and decent health care.

Liebow, Elliot. *Tally's Corner* (Boston: Little, Brown, 1967). A participant observation study of lower-class black streetcorner men in Washington, D.C.

Millett, Kate. *Sexual Politics* (Garden City, N.Y.: Doubleday, 1970). Millett argues that the relationship between the sexes is and always has been a political one—a continuing power struggle in which women are sometimes idolized, other times patronized, always exploited.

Nava, Julian. *Viva La Raza!* (New York: Van Nostrand, 1973). An anthology designed to acquaint readers with the history and cultural past of the Mexican-American.

Rowbotham, Sheila. *Women, Resistance & Revolution* (New York: Random House, 1972). Rowbotham, a social historian, explores the relationship between feminism and social revolution and the varied historical forms that the attempt to change the position of women has taken in the West and in revolutionary countries such as China, the U.S.S.R., Cuba, Algeria, and Vietnam.

Silberman, Charles E. *Crisis in Black and White* (New York: Vintage, 1964). Highly acclaimed book that examines the situation of blacks in America. Silberman disputes the theories of some of the "authorities" and gives special attention to the problem of identification that confronts blacks.

Stoll, Clarice Stasz. *Female and Male* (Dubuque, Iowa: Wm. C. Brown, 1974). A study of sex roles, sexism in America and in social science, and the politics of gender. Discusses the process of socialization into female and male roles and the consequences.

Tavris, Carole, and Carole Offir. *The Longest War: Sex Differences in Perspective* (New York: Harcourt Brace Jovanovich, 1977). A detailed analysis of sex differences—evidence and explanations for them from a variety of theoretical perspectives.

7: Institutions: Family

Billingsley, Andrew. *Black Families in White America* (Englewood Cliffs, N.J.: Prentice-Hall, 1968). An analysis of the history, structure, aspirations, and problems of black families in a white-controlled society.

Delora, Joann S., and Jack Delora, eds. *Intimate Life Styles: Marriage and Its Alternatives* (Pacific Palisades, Calif.: Goodyear, 1972). The articles in this book analyze traditional forms of courtship and marriage in the United States along with emerging patterns of interaction involving intimacy and sex. Predictions are made regarding forms that sexual and erotic behavior will take in the future.

Goode, William J. *The Family* (Englewood Cliffs, N.J.: Prentice-Hall, 1964). A theoretical treatment of the family, dealing with mate selection, illegitimacy, family roles, and divorce.

Gordon, Michael, ed. *The Nuclear Family in Crisis: The Search for an Alternative* (New York: Harper & Row, 1972). The articles in this book deal with the family in the kibbutz, the family in socialist and welfare nations, and the current communal movement and group marriage.

Spiro, Melford E. *Children of the Kibbutz* (New York: Schocken Books, 1965). A study of child training and personality on an Israeli kibbutz, where children are raised by the community.

Two good recent texts on the family and on marriage are:

Eshleman, J. Ross. *The Family: An Introduction,* 3d ed. (Boston: Allyn and Bacon, 1981).

LAMANNA, MARY ANN, and AGNES RIEDMANN. *Marriages and Families* (Belmont, Calif.: Wadsworth, 1981).

8: Institutions: Religion

BERGER, PETER. *A Rumor of Angels* (New York: Doubleday, 1970). Sociologist Berger attempts to deal with the question of whether theological thinking is possible at all today, and, if it is, in what way.

GREELEY, ANDREW M. *Religion: A Secular Theory* (New York: Free Press, 1982). Greeley attempts to build a theory of religion organized around a number of empirical propositions.

GREELEY, ANDREW M. *The Denominational Society* (Glenview, Ill.: Scott, Foresman, 1972). A thorough study of religion in the United States with a good sprinkling of statistical data. Deals with traditional topics such as the nature, origins, and functions of religion and the characteristics of religious organizations. Also covers religion as an ethnic phenomenon, diversity within unity, the secularization myth, prejudice and conflict, and predictions for the future.

HADDEN, JEFFREY K. *The Gathering Storm in the Churches* (New York: Doubleday, 1970). Hadden describes the growing conflict between the clergy and the laity that threatens the traditional role and influence of the church in a modern secular world.

HEENAN, EDWARD, ed. *Mystery, Magic, and Miracle: Religion in a Post-Aquarian Age* (Englewood Cliffs, N.J.: Prentice-Hall, 1973). A chronicle of the varieties of religious experience in the 1970s from the "cabalistic cult of Satanism to the fusion of religion and rock music, from the Americanization of Eastern mysticism to the exuberant exhortations of the Jesus freaks." Heenan analyzes the future of this modern religious revival by means of the elements of mystery, magic, and miracle.

HERBERG, WILL. *Protestant-Catholic-Jew* (New York: Doubleday, 1960). An interesting analysis of the religions of America.

MARTIN, DAVID. *A General Theory of Secularization* (New York: Harper & Row, 1978). Martin attempts to make sense of the wide-ranging and radically different patterns of religious change covering most countries in the Christian tradition.

9: Institutions: Political Economy

MARGER, MARTIN. *Elites and Masses* (New York: Van Nostrand, 1981). A comprehensive introduction to the political economy—discusses the major theories in political sociology and the characteristics of power in advanced capitalist societies.

There are a number of interesting books that explore the nature of power and influence:

DAHL, ROBERT. *Who Governs?* (New Haven, Conn.: Yale University Press, 1961).

DOMHOFF, G. WILLIAM. *The Powers That Be* (New York: Vintage, 1978).

DOMHOFF, G. WILLIAM. *The Higher Circles* (New York: Random House, 1970).

DOMHOFF, G. WILLIAM. *Who Rules America* (Englewood Cliffs, N.J.: Prentice-Hall, 1967).

KELLER, SUZANNE. *Beyond the Ruling Class: Strategic Elites in Modern Society* (New York: Random House, 1963).

MILLS, C. WRIGHT. *The Power Elite* (New York: Oxford University Press, 1959).

ROSE, ARNOLD. *The Power Structure* (New York: Oxford University Press, 1967).

SILK, LEONARD, and MARK SILK. *The American Establishment* (New York: Basic Books, 1980).

10: Population and Ecology

BROWN, HARRISON, and EDWARD HUTCHINGS, JR., eds.   *Are Our Descendants Doomed?* (New York: Viking, 1972). This collection of papers resulted from a conference at Cal Tech and deals with the problems of rapid population growth, the distribution of human population, technological change, economic development, the environment, and the individual desires of human beings.

EHRLICH, PAUL.   *The Population Bomb* (New York: Ballantine, 1968). Biologist Ehrlich describes the crisis of overpopulation that faces us and evaluates our prospects of surviving it.

POHLMAN, EDWARD, ed.   *Population: A Clash of Prophets* (New York: Mentor, 1973). Readings—mostly from popular sources—on the population question. Includes a section on Third World reactions to population issues.

ROBERTSON, JAMES and CAROLYN.   *The Small Towns Book* (Garden City, N.Y.: Anchor Books, 1978). Describes the migration of Americans back to small towns, the resulting pressures on small towns, and how a few small towns have attempted to confront these pressures.

WARNER, SAM BASS, JR.   *The Urban Wilderness* (New York: Harper & Row, 1972). An interesting book describing the historical development of the American city.

WEBER, MAX.   *The City* (New York: Free Press, 1958). A classic sociological analysis of the development of cities in Western civilization.

WEEKS, JOHN.   *Population* (Belmont, Calif.: Wadsworth, 1978). Interesting and well-written text covering the major population processes, an overview of world population characteristics, and a discussion of major population issues.

A number of books analyze the problems of the city: urban sprawl, urban renewal, race and class conflict, municipal services, overcrowding, ugliness, mass transit, and so on. The following are among the best:

BANFIELD, EDWARD.   *The Unheavenly City* (Boston: Little, Brown, 1970).

BANFIELD, EDWARD.   *The Unheavenly City Revisited* (Boston: Little, Brown, 1974).

DOWNS, ANTHONY.   *Urban Problems and Prospects* (Chicago: Markham, 1970).

GABREE, JOHN, ed.   *Surviving the City* (New York: Ballantine, 1973).

GORDON, MITCHELL.   *Sick Cities* (Baltimore: Penguin, 1963).

HAAR, CHARLES M., ed.   *The End of Innocence: A Suburban Reader* (Glenview, Ill.: Scott, Foresman, 1972).

JACOBS, JANE.   *The Death and Life of Great American Cities* (New York: Vintage, 1961).

11: Social Change and Social Disorganization

HOFFER, ERIC.   *The Ordeal of Change* (New York: Harper & Row, 1964). An interesting if somewhat one-sided analysis of the causes and consequences of social change by the longshoreman-philosopher.

LAUER, ROBERT H.   *Perspectives on Social Change* (Boston: Allyn and Bacon, 1973). A comprehensive look at questions of youth and change, violence and change, and strategies for effecting change. Lauer discusses the various theories of social change as well as mechanisms and patterns of change.

LENSKI, GERHARD, and JEAN LENSKI.   *Human Societies*, 4th ed. (New York: McGraw-Hill, 1982). An introductory text that focuses on the evolutionary processes of change in different types of preindustrial and industrial societies.

MOORE, WILBERT E.   *Social Change* (Englewood Cliffs, N.J.: Prentice-Hall, 1963). A short but comprehensive sociological analysis of social change.

SLATER, PHILIP. *The Pursuit of Loneliness* (Boston: Beacon Press, 1970). Slater focuses on our subservience to technology and the disastrous effect this attitude is having on the quality of life in the United States. He suggests some ways that American society might be changed to avoid even further alienation and disaffection.

TOFFLER, ALVIN. *Future Shock* (New York: Random House/Bantam, 1970). Toffler discusses the social and psychological implications of the technological revolution— the problems of people and groups who are overwhelmed by change in the emerging superindustrial world.

TOFFLER, ALVIN. *The Third Wave* (New York: Bantam, 1980). In his most recent attempt to describe the future, Toffler predicts widespread changes in marriage and the family, in the work situation, in recreation and politics, in living patterns generally.

12: Collective Behavior

BERK, RICHARD A. *Collective Behavior* (Dubuque, Iowa: Wm. C. Brown, 1974). A short and concise overview of the sociology of collective behavior. Attention is given to methodological issues, outdated theories, and recent developments in theory and research.

CANTRIL, HADLEY. *The Invasion from Mars* (New York: Harper & Row, 1940). A study of the collective behavior, rumor, mass communication, and panic that resulted from Orson Welles' 1938 radio dramatization of *The War of the Worlds*.

CHAPLIN, J. P. *Rumor, Fear and the Madness of Crowds* (New York: Ballantine, 1959). Chaplin describes in detail eleven instances of mass collective behavior, including examples of mass hysteria, rumor, crowd, mob, and riot behavior. The cases range from the death of Valentino to Martians in New Jersey, from flying saucers to high treason in the State Department.

EVANS, ROBERT R., ed. *Readings in Collective Behavior*, 2d ed. (Chicago: Rand McNally, 1975). These readings describe a number of collective behavior research projects on such topics as disaster research, analyses of protests, and the testing of selected theories.

GUSFIELD, JOSEPH R., ed. *Protest, Reform, and Revolt: A Reader in Social Movements* (New York: Wiley, 1970). An excellent sourcebook on all aspects of social movements.

HERSEY, JOHN. *Hiroshima* (New York: Bantam, 1959). A journalistic account of the dropping of an atomic bomb. A fascinating and horrifying description of the process and aftermath of a disaster.

HOFFER, ERIC. *The True Believer* (New York: Harper & Row, 1951). The most famous of Hoffer's books deals with mass movements from the viewpoint of the true believer, the man compelled to join a cause, any cause.

Report of the National Advisory Commission on Civil Disorders (New York: Bantam, 1968). The report of the Kerner Commission provides a comprehensive analysis of the riots that occurred in the United States during the summer of 1967.

ROBERTS, RON, and ROBERT KLOSS. *Social Movements*, 2d ed. (St. Louis, Mo.: Mosby, 1979). A text on social movements.

SCHULTZ, DUANE. *Panic Behavior* (New York: Random House, 1964). A comprehensive analysis of panic, including a discussion of a number of theories of panic behavior in relation to actual disaster situations.

SKOLNICK, JEROME. *The Politics of Protest* (New York: Ballantine, 1969). The last chapter of this report of the National Commission on the Causes and Prevention of Violence provides an excellent short analysis of collective behavior concepts.

13: Deviation and Social Control

Becker, Howard S., ed. *The Other Side* (New York: Free Press, 1964). A series of essays by authors who, like Becker, use the labeling perspective to explain deviant behavior. The essays, which deal with a variety of types of deviant behavior, generally follow the proposition that deviance is a product of group definitions, not a product of something inherent in the act itself.

Erikson, Kai. *Wayward Puritans* (New York: Wiley, 1966). Erikson applies current theories of deviant behavior to the seventeenth-century Puritans of Massachusetts Bay. Using historical documents, he illustrates how deviant behavior served to define social boundaries and to help keep the social order intact. Crime statistics are analyzed to demonstrate that, even for the Puritans, the number of deviant offenders a community can afford to recognize is likely to remain fairly stable over time.

Reiman, Jeffrey. *The Rich Get Richer and the Poor Get Prison* (New York: Wiley, 1979). The American criminal justice system has failed according to Reiman because of the system's economic bias. Its failure will persist because the wealthy and powerful want it to. The author also examines the dangers of "noncriminal" acts, ignored by the criminal justice system.

Rubington, Earl, and Martin Weinberg. *Deviance: The Interactionist Perspective*, 3d ed. (New York: Macmillan, 1978). Readings on the interactionist or labeling perspective with sections on the social deviant, the public regulation of deviance, deviant subcultures, and deviant identity.

Silberman, Charles. *Criminal Violence, Criminal Justice* (New York: Random House, 1978). A detailed study of crime in the United States; deals with the effects of fear, poverty, race, and with the institutions—police, courts, and prisons.

The following selections present good analyses of social control agencies, such as the police and prison systems:

Niederhoffer, Arthur. *Behind the Shield* (Garden City, N.Y.: Doubleday, 1967). Niederhoffer, a former member of the New York City police, describes the profession. He calls special attention to some attitudes—authoritarianism and cynicism—that police officers develop.

Sykes, Gresham M. *The Society of Captives* (New York: Atheneum, 1958). A short but thorough analysis of an American maximum-security prison.

Wambaugh, Joseph. *The New Centurions* (Boston: Little, Brown, 1970). An interesting novel on police work during the time of the Watts riots, written by a Los Angeles police officer.

Wilson, James Q. *Varieties of Police Behavior* (New York: Atheneum, 1970). Wilson studies communities in the United States, identifies the major problems that police agencies face, and describes three styles of police behavior that seem to emerge.

There are numerous good analyses of specific types of criminal and deviant behavior:

Cressey, Donald. *Other People's Money* (Belmont, Calif.: Wadsworth, 1971).

Greenwald, Harold. *The Elegant Prostitute* (New York: Ballantine, 1970).

Ianni, Francis. *A Family Business* (New York: Mentor, 1972).

Jackson, Bruce. *Outside the Law: A Thief's Primer* (New Brunswick, N.J.: Transaction Books, 1972).

Maas, Peter. *The Valachi Papers* (New York: Bantam, 1968).

Maris, Ronald. *Social Forces in Urban Suicide* (Homewood, Ill.: Dorsey, 1969).

Sutherland, Edwin. *White Collar Crime* (New York: Holt, 1949).

TALESE, GAY. *Honor Thy Father* (Greenwich, Conn.: Fawcett-Crest, 1971).

THOMPSON, HUNTER. *Hell's Angels* (New York: Ballantine, 1966).

WALLACE, SAMUEL. *Skid Row as a Way of Life* (New York: Harper & Row, 1965).

14: Sociology: Another Perspective

BERGER, PETER L. *Invitation to Sociology* (Garden City, N.Y.: Doubleday, 1963). For Berger, sociology is a form of consciousness. This consciousness determines how sociologists behave and how they see the world. In describing what sociology is, Berger's focus is the humanistic perspective.

CUZZORT, R. P., and E. W. KING. *Humanity and Modern Social Thought,* 2d ed. (Hinsdale, Ill.: Dryden Press, 1976). An interesting discussion of the major works of fifteen social scientists who have contributed to social thought and the discipline of sociology, including Durkheim, Weber, Marx, Freud, Mills, Becker, Merton, and Goffman.

MILLS, C. WRIGHT. *The Sociological Imagination* (New York: Grove Press, 1961). Mills provides a searching critique and analysis of what sociology is and what it should be. He challenges the approaches represented by "grand theorists" and "abstracted empiricists" and describes the perspective and approach that he feels best embodies the sociological imagination.

The following two books are collections of essays that evaluate and criticize sociology from a variety of viewpoints:

DOUGLAS, JACK, ed. *The Relevance of Sociology* (New York: Appleton-Century-Crofts, 1970).

REYNOLDS, LARRY, and JANICE REYNOLDS, eds. *The Sociology of Sociology* (New York: McKay, 1970).

It is often helpful to look at the journals of a discipline to get further insight into its nature. Sociology journals include the *American Journal of Sociology,* the *American Sociological Review, Social Forces, Social Problems,* and *Sociometry.* But look especially at *The American Sociologist,* which tends to give an internal view, showing a sociology of sociology.

Index